A NEW WAY TO COOK.

SALLY SCHNEIDER

MARIA ROBLEDO PHOTOGRAPHS   DOYLE PARTNERS DESIGN   ARTISAN NEW YORK

Published by Artisan
A Division of Workman
Publishing, Inc.
708 Broadway
New York, New York
10003-9555
www.artisanbooks.com

Library of Congress
Cataloging-in-
Publication Data

Schneider, Sally.
A new way to cook /
Sally Schneider:
photographs by
Maria Robledo.
  p. cm.
Includes bibliographical
references and index.
ISBN 1-57965-249-2
1. Cookery. I. Title.
TX714 .S363 2001
641.5—dc21
2001034310

Printed in Singapore
10 9 8 7 6 5 4 3 2 1
First Paperback Edition,
2003

Book design by
Doyle Partners,
Stephen Doyle
Vivian Ghazarian

Two impromptu
Bowl and Spoon
Desserts
(pages 470-480)

For Sofia, Isabel, Luca, and Augusto, the children in my life

Contents

The purpose of this book is to introduce you to a way of cooking truly delicious food simply, easily, healthfully, and with pleasure, and to enhance the joy in sharing it. The impetus to write it—a ten-year endeavor—dates back to when I was a young chef, cooking and eating in wonderful restaurants and home kitchens in France, Italy, and the heartland of America. I adored all the rich, sumptuous food but realized I had to face the realities of weight gain, food allergies, and fluctuating blood sugar. As I grew older I became progressively more concerned about the long-term effects of a rich diet on my health and well-being.

Necessity set me on the path to find a way to cook and eat that would nurture my body as well as my soul and senses. I made myself a guinea pig for more diets and dreary "healthful" concoctions than I care to remember. I read widely on nutrition and diet, from the most iconoclastic to the most mainstream. Most of these bleak regimes addressed only the physical side of eating, ignoring the other hungers that good food satisfies: hungers for the connection it can forge to friends and nature, for its sensual beauty, its colors, aromas, flavors, and textures; for the cultural and historical meaning it expresses; and, most important, for comfort and well-being.

In order to satisfy these deeper hungers, I realized I had to devise new cooking techniques to replace the high-fat cooking methods I grew up with. I brought all my professional experience to bear on translating the recipes of memory into healthier adaptations, experimenting by radically altering classic techniques or using them in a new way. Because I believe that prohibitions against delicious fats such as butter and cream and against sugar only increase desire, I exclude nothing in my cooking and do not count fat grams. Instead, I have devised new ways to use fat's special qualities to enhance the deeper experience of eating while respecting the realities of its impact on diet and health.

I didn't start out to be a chef, and I have no formal training. In the late 1970s, I was supporting myself as a struggling photographer by working as a captain at an expensive East Side restaurant in New York City, when I awoke one morning from a dream that was to change my life. "Of course," I thought, "I'll cook." And so I did, starting in small restaurants and working my way up in professional kitchens. In 1984, a health magazine hired me to create leaner versions of the rich food of my travels. Since then, I have written about cooking and eating well for numerous publications, including *Food & Wine* and *Saveur* magazines.

The style of cooking that I have evolved is deeply influenced by the Mediterranean cooking of Italy, France, Greece, and Spain, with a good dose of American regional foods and a smattering of Asian influences. It is not simply my Greek heritage that attracts me to Mediterranean cuisines; they most closely mirror the way I like to eat and cook: simply and deliciously, in tune with the seasons. In addition, the traditional Mediterranean way of eating has proven to be profoundly wise. Without counting fat grams or calories, Mediterranean people are among the healthiest and longest-lived in the world, with low incidence of coronary heart disease and cancer. Theirs is the model for my everyday diet: largely based on plant foods such as vegetables, fruits, grains, and legumes; moderate amounts of fish, poultry, nuts, and wine; with a small amount of red meat, saturated fats, dairy products, and sugar and a minimum of prepared foods. I eat moderately day to day, and periodically I eat with abandon.

Spring
Vegetable
Ragout
(page 68)

MODERATION AND THE PLEASURE PRINCIPLE.

Food clearly has a profound emotional, even spiritual, impact on human beings. It is a primal source of pleasure, comfort, and sharing with friends, a link to culture and our roots. But the "pleasure principle" is rarely considered in the determination of well-being, where indeed it may be as critical as the obvious nutritional content of foods. When people don't feel satisfied by the food they eat, they feel deprived, cut off from well-being. They often overeat lackluster foods in an attempt to gain a feeling of satiety. Yet many of the official recommendations for healthful diet would have us strip food bare of taste if need be in order to eradicate fat, commonly viewed as the dietary cause of woes from obesity to heart disease to cancer.

In truth, the jury is still out as to exactly how fats affect our health and what a reasonable fat intake should be. After years of asserting that all fats, both saturated and unsaturated, should constitute only an austere 25 to 30 percent of our diets, many researchers now consider only saturated fats dangerous—those derived mostly from animal fats, such as those in butter, meats, poultry, and dairy products, as well as palm oil and coconut oil. Unsaturated fats, derived largely from plants, particularly the monounsaturated fats such as those in olive, peanut, and avocado oils, and the omega-3-rich fats such as those in walnut, canola, and fish oils, are now viewed as beneficial "friendly fats." It seems indisputable that throughout the world, populations with a low intake of animal fat and a high proportion of vegetable-based foods, such as grains, vegetables, fruits, and beans, which are high in fiber, antioxidants, and other phytonutrients, have lower cancer rates. In fact, olive oil seems to help reduce incidence of heart disease and cancer.

Yet even these seeming certainties have strong exceptions. One of the most compelling mysteries is what is known as the "French Paradox." In France, where people eat a high proportion of saturated fat in the form of foie gras, sausage, pâté, goose fat, cheese, cream, and butter, the incidence of fatal stroke and heart disease is astonishingly low—the second lowest of developed nations. Researchers have speculated on various factors that may contribute to this extraordinary contradiction of accepted research: a high consumption of fruits and vegetables with less of the highly processed fast, convenience, and snack foods consumed in North America; regular consumption of antioxidant-rich wine with meals and of foods such as raw milk cheeses and yogurt that provide beneficial bacteria and enzymes that help the body to digest efficiently; moderate portions of a balanced selection of foods; and the amount of exercise taken regularly. There is no question that regular physical activity is an essential part of a healthy regimen. Even moderate exercise can mitigate some of the ills associated with a high-fat or caloric diet.

Another compelling theory is that homocysteine, an amino acid formed by eating large amounts in animal protein, may be replacing cholesterol as the primary cause of vascular disease. However, when there are adequate levels of vitamins B_6, B_{12}, and folic acids in the body, elements that are not plentiful in the typical American diet high in red meat, dairy products, and highly refined processed foods, homocysteine is converted into harmless waste products or methionine, a protein. Rich sources of these nutrients are nuts, legumes, whole grains, many fruits, poultry, shellfish, eggs, dark leafy vegetables, and pork.

The French Paradox and the homocysteine theory demonstrate just how complex human metabolism is, that there are invariably clusters of factors and complex interactions to consider in formulating a sound diet. Oversimplifying nutritional research has lead to some very dangerous eating habits.

Our national vilification of fat has led many people to avoid healthful, nutrient-rich high-fat foods, including avocados, nuts, and oily fish such as salmon, which are rich in omega-3 fatty acids. The message that fats are bad and carbohydrates are good has caused many people to cut fats and protein out of their diets completely and replace them with carbohydrates such as breads, pasta, rice, and foods that are actually high in sugar. For some of these people, overeating foods that convert quickly to sugars in the body can cause a severe imbalance, leading to insulin reactions, fatigue, increased cravings, and weight gain.

A common myth is that vegetable fats such as those in margarine have fewer calories than animal fats such as those in butter and hence are more beneficial. In fact, all fats, from pork fat to olive oil, have about 40 calories per teaspoon. (Butter, at 33 calories per teaspoon, is slightly less caloric due to its milk solids and water. When these are removed, as for clarified butter, it contains 40 calories per teaspoon.) And margarine contains trans fats, artificially hydrogenated oils that are solid at room temperature, which may pose an even greater danger than saturated fat in increased risk of heart disease and cancer. Since fats contain more than twice the number of calories per gram that protein or carbohydrates have, overconsumption, even of "good fats," can lead to obesity and attendant disease; hence, the wisdom of moderation. Moderate-fat diets have been shown to be more effective than low-fat diets for weight loss and maintenance.

From a culinary point of view, fat is essential to deliciousness and a sense of satiety. It carries and harmonizes flavors and aromas and facilitates numerous effects such as caramelization and flakiness in pastry doughs. Many recipes cannot come to fruition without it; fat completes them and brings out their best. A little fat can make the difference between really enjoying eating and enduring austerity.

Salt is another commonly disparaged food that has the ability to "complete" a dish. The idea that salt, or sodium chloride, is a cause of hypertension and high blood pressure has been long debated and never conclusively proved. It is clear that moderate sodium intake, in concert with increasing fiber- and potassium-rich foods, such as vegetables and fruits, and decreasing saturated fats, can help decrease blood pressure. The National Research Council proposes that 1,100 to 3,300 milligrams (between one half and one and one half teaspoons) is a "safe and adequate range of sodium for adults," an amount easy to adhere to if you avoid eating prepared and fast foods that contain excessive amounts of salt. These foods include the predictable culprits: dried soup mixes and bouillon cubes; prepared salad dressings; ketchup; pickles; most canned soups, beans, and tuna; frozen dinners; pizzas; snack foods such as potato chips and tortilla chips; most "diet foods"; breakfast cereals; some bottled waters; and cured and smoked food.

The only absolute truth I have found regarding diet is that no one diet is good for everyone. Some people thrive on high complex carbohydrate foods such as grains and beans, while for others, protein and vegetables work well; some are salt sensitive, others are allergic to tomatoes and peppers; for some, too little "good fats" is deleterious. The only way to determine how your body reacts to certain foods is to pay attention to how you feel after eating: If you are tired, logy, or hungry soon after eating, it is possible the food disagrees with you or you are sensitive to it. Note also how you feel, generally, eating a certain diet, and experiment with the balance of foods you eat. Gradually you will learn the balance of protein, carbohydrates, vegetables, "good fats," and so on that will promote energy and a sense of well-being for you.

This book reflects a way of eating and cooking based on balance and moderation, in which every food can be eaten and enjoyed. It is mutable enough to work for a variety of dietary needs and lifestyles. I exclude no food from the ingredients I cook with except highly processed foods and foods containing trans fats. Because balanced eating depends on moderate portion sizes, I take the same approach in my recipes as the French do: Portion sizes are ample without overdoing it, and are meant to be satisfying within the context of a simple menu. Servings of red meat generally do not exceed about four ounces.

Though I use extra-virgin olive oil predominantly, I cook with all flavorful fats—including cream and butter—in the smallest amount that will produce delicious results. (I generally avoid polyunsaturated fats such as soybean, sunflower, corn, and safflower oils, because they lack flavor and provide high concentrations of less desirable omega-6 fatty acids.)

I believe salt is essential in bringing out the flavors in a dish, but none of my recipes is heavily salted, because the flavors are already concentrated and quite intense. I use small amounts of white sugar in desserts where necessary (I never use artificial sweeteners) because sugar yields the most satisfying and authentic American- and European-style desserts. And new research shows that eggs have been unnecessarily vilified and should be valued for their nutritional benefits.

Although I do not count calories or fat grams, I have included a basic nutritional analysis for each recipe (see pages 687-704) for those who wish to direct their diet in certain ways. These numbers can be useful for people who are learning to keep rough tabs on nutrients, calories, and fat. Rigid focus on numbers, though, particularly on fat grams, will strip the joy and spontaneity from eating.

HOW TO USE THIS BOOK. The layers of information in this book offer you a wealth of possibilities. You can simply pick and choose individual recipes that are delicious unto themselves, or you can use the book as a tool to learn a comprehensive array of techniques that will teach you to improvise, to cook without being bound by recipes.

Each chapter is organized in a logical progression of simple approaches or techniques, followed by recipes that illustrate them. Some techniques, labeled Guides to Improvising, are templates written in recipe form. They are intended to encourage you to cook creatively with whatever is on hand or in season.

Many recipes in each chapter can also be made as component parts to use to build dishes that are more complex. These might be as simple as a topping Rustic Garlic Toasts (page 368) with Slow-Roasted Tomatoes (page 38) to make bruschetta, or as elaborate as a Pan-Smoked Rare Tuna on garlic fried greens in a Ginger-Sake Broth and Crispy Shallots, made from four basic recipes (pages 268, 74, 582, and 48).

Enhancing dishes by use of different components is a recurring theme in *A New Way to Cook*. Easy-to-make-ahead fresh and cooked sauces, broths, flavored oils, and other flavor essences are often used to transform simple foods into something more. You'll find hundreds of ideas in the section called Flavor Catalysts (pages 536–671).

As you read through the book, you will also encounter recipes that have been highlighted as "essential." These are invaluable basic preparations that you will find yourself using over and over again. Try using them to lighten favorite high-fat recipes from other cookbooks.

Toward the back of the book, you'll find useful resources for cooking and eating in a new way. These include menus for forging entire meals out of the recipes in this book, mail-order sources for hard-to-find ingredients, and a listing of books and Web sites to help you on your own journey of exploring food and well-being. In addition, there are the nutritional analyses of all the recipes (excluding the Guides to Improvising and variations) if you wish to tailor your diet in specific ways. Use the tables that compare the saturated fat content in various cuts of meat and poultry, in cooking fats, and in dairy products to make informed choices about how to use them in your cooking.

Before you begin to cook, I urge you to read the Essential Techniques, Ingriedients, and Tools chapter (pages 1–27), which outlines the core techniques for paring down calories and fat, and enhancing flavor.

And in whatever way you choose to use this book—as you see, there are many, many ways—know that every dish is as lean and as flavorful as it can be, and every recipe is designed to be a pleasure, both to eat and to cook.

ESSENTIAL

Making Fruits
in Fragrant Syrups
(pages 466–469)

TECHNIQUES,

INGREDIENTS, AND TOOLS

T his book is about cooking intelligently to build flavor and pleasure into food in easy, healthful ways. Although techniques drive the book, and specialized ones are found in every chapter, the following are the ones I use universally: They are the foundation of *A New Way to Cook*. Becoming comfortable with them will enable you to pare down fats and calories and enhance flavor in just about any recipe or dish you wish to prepare or improvise.

CORE TECHNIQUES.

Make conscious choices in cooking and eating that are right for you. Many of the recipes in this book offer you choices, mostly having to do with the kind and quantity of fat you use: whether, for example, to serve ultra-lean buffalo steak or a richly marbled shell steak as Szechwan Pepper–Crusted Steak Smothered with Onions (page 317); whether to use extra-virgin olive oil or pancetta or unsmoked bacon in a pasta and vegetable dish; or whether or not to add a tablespoon or two of heavy cream to Saffron Fish Stew (page 260). No matter which path you take, in all the recipes the fat will be moderate, especially when compared to a classic version. I leave it to you to determine the precise degree based on what you need or desire: whether your overall diet is so rich in fruits, vegetables, and grains that it can accommodate a full-tilt steak; whether indulgence in a small amount of pancetta gives you so much pleasure it keeps you eating in a balanced way; or whether you simply prefer to cook with always delicious extra-virgin olive oil. You might even decide to add more fat to a dish to enrich it further.

You can apply this practice of conscious choosing to every aspect of your diet—in recipes you choose to cook, in menu items you choose to order when dining out. (See pages x–xiv for a discussion of fats and diet, and the tables on page 688 for a comparison of fats in meat and dairy products.)

Use high-quality ingredients. Cooking with great ingredients—those that are the least adulterated and have the most flavor—is the key to cooking simply and well. It is easier to achieve deep satisfying flavors with ingredients that are inherently delicious; for example, free-range organic chicken instead of one fed antibiotics, or a fruity extra-virgin olive oil rather than a bland one. (See Strategic Ingredients, pages 6–19, and Sources, page 711.)

Learn to construct dishes from simple elements. You don't need a complicated or labor-intensive recipe to make a complex dish. You can construct delectable dishes by combining several discrete components that offer endless possibilities for improvisation. This could be as simple as serving a grilled rosemary-rubbed chicken breast on a bed of Peperonata, a sweet pepper stew (page 63), or tossing store-bought ravioli with Sage and Garlic Oil (page 593) and some toasted walnuts.

I rely on make-ahead preparations that I call Catalysts to transform simple foods into deeply satisfying dishes. They include Flavor Essences, Dry Rubs, and Marinades, Broths, Flavored Oils, and Sauces and are grouped together starting on page 536 for easy reference. All have affinities for a wide variety of foods so you can use them in myriad ways. For example, you might use Leek Broth (page 569) as a soup base to which you add roasted vegetables and herbs, or as a sauce, enriched by a Flavored Oil or butter, for sea scallops you've crusted with Lemongrass Essence (page 546). Wild Mushroom Essence (page 544) can flavor a tomato sauce or be used as a rub for striped bass. You could make an elegant, easy Port Wine Sauce (page 637) to serve with roast filet mignon for an impromptu dinner party. This same sauce is equally good on roast chicken or game birds, with full-flavored fish such as salmon, and even grilled meaty wild mushrooms. Think of the Catalysts as resources you can use to construct dishes easily, with however much (or little) time or energy you have.

Consider flavor at every point in your cooking. Ask yourself, "What can I do to achieve the most intense, satisfying flavor as I create this dish?" What kind of fat do you want to use—olive oil for a clean flavor or bacon for a richer cured-pork flavor? Will browning the butter give a more intense butter flavor to cookies or a cake? Will a pot of beans or a chicken stew benefit from the pleasing smoky flavor of a chunk of smoked ham? Will herbs provide the flavors you want? Does a braising liquid or a broth need to be boiled down a bit to concentrate the flavors? Should you add a vanilla bean to increase the sense of sweetness in a dessert?

The most critical consideration in achieving great flavor is *seasoning*. Rather than adding more fat to make a dish satisfying, consider whether or not it is seasoned properly. A little salt or a few drops of acidity, such as lemon juice or vinegar, are often all it takes to bring out the dormant flavors in a dish, to lift flavors that seem somewhat flat. A pinch of sugar can help accentuate sweet "round" flavors that may be masked or faded in less-than-perfect tomatoes, for example, or balance sharp flavors in a vinegar-based sauce and soften rough ones from hot chile peppers or spices.

Reading through the recipes and techniques will teach you to think more specifically about flavor. But the best guide is your own senses. Learn to trust your instincts and experiment. You'll most likely make something delicious, enjoy the process, and learn a great deal.

Weigh and measure foods. Weighing and measuring ingredients accurately is the key to cooking with limited amounts of fatty or caloric foods. By measuring out teaspoons of oil for sautéing, for example, you can avoid hundreds of calories in oil you just splash in the pan. Eventually, as you become accustomed to measuring exact quantities, your eye will become trained to know just how much oil is in a teaspoon or how much steak constitutes a 4-ounce portion. You'll be able to improvise dishes without going overboard on caloric ingredients or portion sizes.

When measuring liquids, fill the measuring spoon to the top, or hold the measuring cup up at eye level to be sure you have filled it to the exact mark. For dry ingredients, overfill measuring spoons or cups, then slide a knife across the top to level them.

Many of my recipes specify weight as well as volume because it is a more accurate way of measuring something variable like a bunch of parsley. Weighing is also the best way to get a sense of portion sizes of high-fat foods such as red meats or cheeses, the volume of which can vary. For example, while the calorie count of 1 ounce of Parmigiano-Reggiano and Manchego cheese is the same, the amount by volume they yield when grated can differ by ¼ cup. Weight will always be the more exact measurement. (For more information, see Measuring Tools, page 24.)

Sauté or caramelize onions, garlic, or other aromatic vegetables using very little fat. Aromatics are vegetables such as onions, garlic, carrots, leeks, and celery that provide a base of flavors for many savory dishes. Usually the vegetables are sautéed in several tablespoons of oil to soften and caramelize them—that is, to brown their natural sugars to build deep, round flavor. However, this method also loads them up with calories and fat. My technique achieves the same effect with much less fat. You can use any fat—a vegetable oil such as olive or grapeseed oil, butter, or rendered bacon fat—depending on the flavor you want to impart.

Cook the (lightly salted) vegetables in a little fat—figure on about 1 teaspoon of fat for every 2 cups vegetables—in a covered nonstick skillet over medium-low heat for about 5 minutes, until they "sweat," releasing their juices and softening. Then take off the lid, increase the heat to medium, and sauté them, tossing frequently, until they are golden or browned, depending on the dish. The cooking times will vary according to the quantity of vegetables and the size they are cut. You can use this technique whenever you want to lighten a recipe that calls for sautéed aromatics.

Use a brush to coat foods with fat. If you brush foods with oil, butter, or another fat before roasting or grilling them, you will use far less than if you just drizzle it on. I use inexpensive natural-bristle paintbrushes for this purpose. To prevent a dry brush from soaking up the fat, first dampen it with water and squeeze it out well. If you have a lot of cut-up foods to coat, it is easier to put them in a bowl and toss and stir with the oil-dipped brush until they are completely coated.

Thinly slice boneless red meats and other high-fat foods. When a 4-ounce portion of cooked red meat—say, shell steak or pork tenderloin—is thinly sliced and fanned out on a plate, it looks like an abundant serving. I find that people accustomed to eating twice as much meat in a serving don't notice they are eating less when it is served this way. Use this technique for any food you want to serve a limited portion of, such as red meats, rare-cooked fish such as tuna and swordfish, poultry, and semi-soft cheeses.

Use a thin sharp knife such as a smoked salmon slicer to slice the food, against the grain if applicable, ⅛ to ¼ inch thick. Fan out the slices, overlapping them, on the plate. For hard cheeses such as Parmigiano-Reggiano and Manchego, use a mandoline or vegetable slicer, a vegetable peeler, or a sharp thin paring knife to make paper-thin slices.

Emulsify fats to extend them. If you want to stretch the fat you are using to dress a food, you can often do it by boiling it with some liquid, such as water, broth, reduced wine, or vinegar. Boiling causes the fat and liquid to coalesce and become creamy, as in an emulsion; in effect, the liquid becomes a vehicle for the fat, allowing it to coat foods more easily. I use this technique in various ways throughout the book: for example, to lightly coat vegetables in garlicky olive oil; to dress pasta, beans, and other starchy foods; and, especially, to make silken sauces and dressings.

Generally speaking, for every teaspoon of fat you use, figure on 2 to 3 teaspoons of liquid (for 1 tablespoon of fat, that means 2 to 3 tablespoons of liquid). Place the butter, olive oil, or rendered pancetta or bacon fat in a small heavy pan over moderate heat (you can flavor it by cooking chopped garlic, onions, or herbs in it). When the fat is hot and liquid, turn the heat to high and add the liquid. Boil for 30 seconds, or until the mixture is uniform and rather creamy, then pour it over the food.

STRATEGIC INGREDIENTS. Most of the good cooks I know are great strategists who devise ways to cook well quickly and easily no matter how busy they are. Their secret? They always have certain staples on hand that they can forge into quick meals.

If you stock a basic pantry with the essential staple ingredients described on pages 8 to 19, you can quickly cook a splendid, healthful dinner with or without the addition of fresh meats, seafood, greens, or vegetables, which can be picked up on the way home from work.

When you are in the market, keep these shopping basics in mind.

Buy organic chemical-free foods whenever possible—especially produce, meat and poultry, and dairy products. Our food supply poses dangers due to the overuse of chemicals, pesticides, antibiotics, and growth hormones. Let your supermarket management know you want organically raised fruit and vegetables, and meats, poultry, eggs, and dairy products produced without growth hormones or antibiotics. By requesting and buying organic foods, you are supporting sustainable agriculture, benefiting the environment, and ensuring that you are not buying genetically engineered foods, the safety of which is under question.

Buy pure foods made without additives. Generally speaking, the more additives something has, the less flavorful it will be—not to mention the questionable impact additives may have on the body. Additives include gums, thickeners, and preservatives in dairy products, such as heavy cream, yogurt, and cottage cheese; sweeteners and sodium in cold cereals; monosodium glutamate in canned chicken broths; and even the anticaking agents and whiteners in table salt. Low-fat foods in particular are often full of chemicals and sugars to increase shelf life, flavor, and "mouth feel."

Know your sources to make shopping easier. Take the time to locate interesting food stores in your neighborhood or area so you can work them into your routine, picking up items when you are passing by. Hard-to-find ethnic ingredients are well worth pursuing, and many can make life easier; prepared Thai green chile sauce, for example, adds the splendid flavors of lemongrass, chile, and cilantro in an instant.

Buy high-quality ingredients. There is a simple economy in money, time, and calories in buying the best, even if it is more expensive. The more flavor something has, the less you need to use, and the less you will have to work or embellish it to make it taste good. A small amount of a fruity extra-virgin olive oil will have more of an impact on taste than a greater quantity of bland olive oil. A free-range organically fed chicken will have more flavor than an ordinary supermarket chicken.

Buy locally grown foods in season. Fruits and vegetables have more flavor when they are harvested ripe and eaten quickly thereafter, so it makes sense to rely on seasonal local fruits and vegetables from produce stands, farmers' markets, and health food stores. In winter, augment your supply with imported produce that has been picked ripe in its own growing season, such as Italian blood oranges or kale. Fruit must pass an essential test: It must be fragrant, smelling wonderfully like itself, for if it has no perfume, it will have no flavor.

These staples keep for a long time so you don't have to think about them. Just take an occasional inventory and replenish your supply accordingly.

OILS

The less processed and adulterated the oil, the more healthful and better tasting it will be. Commercially processed vegetable oils are often extracted with chemical solvents and treated with additives of questionable safety. Always buy oils that are cold-pressed. Since they are quite volatile, nut and seed oils should be stored in the refrigerator.

Extra-virgin olive oil is essential in the contemporary kitchen: It is an excellent healthful cooking medium—rich in monounsaturated fats—whose flavor complements any number of foods.

Extra-virgin olive oil, which is extracted from premium-quality olives by pressure rather than with solvents, has less than 1 percent acidity. It can vary in flavor from buttery to fruity to nutty and in color from golden yellow to deep green, depending on where the olives were grown and the method of production. As with wine, it is only by tasting oils that you will discover your preferences. Their cost can vary widely, and high cost does not always indicate great oil. When I can't find an olive oil I like, I infuse decent supermarket olive oil with olives to give it truer flavor (see page 588). Because extra-virgin olive oils don't tolerate very high heat—they smoke and their flavors dissipate—reserve them for flavoring and moderate-temperature cooking. Use **pure olive oil** for panfrying and pan-searing.

Use a flavorless **vegetable oil** such as **grapeseed** or **canola** when you don't want an assertive oil flavor. Both grapeseed and peanut oils have a very high smoke point and are good for high-temperature cooking, for example, searing meats in a hot skillet.

Use **nut oils** for flavoring rather than for cooking, since they break down easily under intense heat. Look for amber-colored oils that are pressed from roasted nuts and seeds, which have a sweeter, more intense flavor than those from unroasted nuts (see Sources, page 711). They are so fragrant that a little goes a long way in salad dressings, sauces, and baking, where they can boost the flavor of nut desserts. Fine nut oils are available at gourmet stores. If you find you have bought a less intensely flavored nut oil, you can boost its flavor (see Roasted Nut Oils, page 597).

Roasted sesame oil, commonly used in Asian cooking, is pressed from toasted sesame seeds and lends a sesame flavor to salad dressings, sauces, flavored oils, and marinades. Since it is very potent, it must be used sparingly. The best brands are Japanese, such as Kadoya.

VINEGARS

Sadly, vinegar is a condiment many people overlook because they are unaware of its vast range of flavors. A well-made vinegar can impart great nuance to a dish, clarify and intensify flavors in place of salt, and allow you to greatly reduce the proportion of oil in a vinaigrette; it can even be used as a base for a sauce. With few calories and no fat, vinegar is an essential tool in healthy cooking.

Well-made vinegars, naturally fermented from good wines or fruit juices, do not have the characteristic harsh bite of most common commercial vinegars. The less processed they are, the better they tend to be: mellow and smooth, with the pure flavor of whatever they are fermented from. It is worth investing in a variety of interesting vinegars—at the least, **balsamic, Champagne, aged sherry, cider, unseasoned Japanese rice wine,** and **red wine.**

I occasionally like to treat myself to an interesting new vinegar to shake up my cooking a bit. My favorite find is a Banyuls wine vinegar from the Southwest of France. It tastes like a cross between a delicate sherry vinegar and fine Champagne vinegar, with slightly nutty floral nuances. I often use it in place of sherry vinegar.

A good balsamic vinegar is my choice for an all-purpose vinegar. True balsamic vinegars come from the provinces of Reggio and Modena in Emilia-Romagna in Italy. Each balsamic vinegar bottled in Italy must bear a code indicating its place or origin. Look for API MO, indicating Modena, or API RE, indicating Reggio. Reliable brands are Fini, Giuseppe Giusti, Elena Monari Federzoni, Cavalli, and Cattani. These fine commercial balsamic vinegars cost about $15 a bottle and are generally available in gourmet and specialty stores. (For a discussion of the fiercely expensive, artisan-made balsamics, see page 640.)

The lesser-quality balsamics that one finds in the supermarket cost about $5 a bottle. Most are poor imitations of the real thing, with rough and unbalanced flavors. To mellow and concentrate the flavor of inferior commercial balsamic vinegar, stir a little brown sugar into the vinegar. Alternatively, you can boil the vinegar down to a delicious concentrated sauce; see Balsamic Syrup, page 636.

SALT

Salt is essential to good cooking, for it brings out the flavors of foods. Various salts have strikingly different flavors. For general purposes and throughout this book, I use **kosher salt,** a refined salt that is more coarsely ground than table salt. Unlike table salt, it does not contain additives, so it has a fresher flavor. Its texture is essential for certain cooking processes, especially for curing and in dry rubs. Common **table salt** is mined from rock salt deposits of ancient sea beds and is highly processed with additives such as anticaking agents, whiteners, and iodine. It has a stale, flat, somewhat chemical flavor. Because it is so finely ground, it is about one third saltier than kosher salt. **Sea salt,** made from evaporating seawater in protected bays, has the purest, freshest flavor and can be almost twice as intense as kosher salt, so you must use it sparingly. Fine or flaked sea salt is the easiest to use; coarse sea salt often requires a salt mill to grind it. Use sea salt for salting foods after cooking and at the table. My favorite everyday sea salt is from Maldon, England, although France and Japan also produce delicious sea salts. Fleur de sel, from Brittany, is considered the caviar of sea salts. It has a complex, deeply salty taste and, some say, a faint aroma of violets. (See page 679 for ways to reduce salt in cooking.)

VANILLA

Vanilla beans, the homely brown pods from a tropical orchid, are a prime mover in dessert making. Vanilla beans have a haunting perfume that seems to release the sweetness and natural aromas of fruit, chocolate, and spices, making it possible to use less sugar in a recipe (see page 676 for how to use it). **Pure vanilla extract** is the next best thing. It has a milder, less resonant flavor than the bean, of course.

DRIED SPICES AND HERBS

In addition to seasoning and lending character to a multitude of foods both sweet and savory, dried spices and herbs can be used to crust meats, fish, and poultry before pan-searing, grilling, or broiling. Dried spices and herbs lose their potency over time and should be replaced about every 6 months. (For high-quality spices and herbs, see Sources, page 711.)

Essential spices

allspice

cayenne pepper

chili powder

Chinese five-spice powder

cinnamon, sticks and ground

cloves

coriander seeds

cumin, seeds and ground

curry powder

fennel seeds

ginger

mustard

nutmeg

paprika

peppercorns: black, white, and Szechwan

red pepper flakes or peperoncini (small dried hot Italian chile peppers)

saffron

Essential dried herbs

bay leaves, preferably imported

oregano

rosemary

sage

savory

thyme

OTHER PANTRY STAPLES

These basic staples, except flour and nuts, keep almost indefinitely. To keep nuts longer than 1 month or flour longer than 3 months, store in plastic bags in the refrigerator or freezer.

Baking soda

Baking powder, preferably nonaluminum

Wildflower honey
Granulated sugar
Dark brown sugar

Unbleached all-purpose flour

Semi- or bittersweet chocolate
Dutch-process cocoa powder

Low-sodium soy sauce

Dried fruit, such as currants, apricots, cherries

Nuts, such as pine nuts and walnuts

CANNED PLUM TOMATOES

Good-quality canned tomatoes can be turned into sauces for pasta, polenta, fish, and poultry and added to braises, chilis, and stews. Canned tomatoes should be unbroken, deep red, and sweet, rather than acidic. The best nationally available brands are Redpack, Muir Glen Organic, and Pomi.

GRAINS, BEANS, AND DRIED PASTAS

Grains, beans, and dried pastas make marvelous healthful main courses, side dishes, or embellishments, many ready in under a half hour. These include **stone-ground cornmeal** for polenta (great as both a main course and breakfast cereal); **rice** for risotto, such as Carnaroli and Vialone Nano; **grains** such as **farro, wild rice, barley,** and **brown basmati-style rices** for side dishes and pilafs; **beans and legumes,** from classic **baby white limas** and **black beans** to quick-cooking ones like **flageolets** and **lentils,** including the firm, toothsome French **lentilles du Puy** and **red lentils,** which cook into fragrant Indian-style purees; and, of course, a variety of **dried pastas,** including **orzo, linguine,** and **penne,** and a good **egg tagliatelle** or **fettuccine.**

WINES AND SPIRITS

Wines and spirits are indispensable in cooking; when subjected to intense heat, they lose most of their alcohol content and calories, leaving only flavor behind.

I always have good inexpensive **red** and **white wines** on hand. Never cook with a wine that you wouldn't be happy drinking. **Unfortified dessert wines** are useful for making fruit desserts and certain savory preparations. Although the more famous wines, such as Sauternes, Barsac, and Muscat de Beaumes-de-Venise, tend to be somewhat pricey, lesser-known and less expensive sweet wines, such as Monbazillac, Coteaux du Layon, and sweet Vouvray, can be excellent.

Fortified wines, such as Rainwater (soft) or Sercial (dry) Madeiras, dry sherry, such as fino or amontillado, and ruby port are invaluable for making quick pan sauces for meats and poultry. **Brandies, whiskies,** and **eaux-de-vie,** such as cognac, bourbon, Calvados, kirsch (cherry), and poire (pear), come in handy for flavoring desserts, especially those made with chocolate and fruit. A drizzle of grappa, a powerful alcohol distilled from the grape skins and seeds left over from winemaking, will make beef taste aged. All of these wines last for months, even years once opened (or can be bought in half bottles or sample-size "nips" if space is a problem).

By all means, keep a few bottles of more serious wines around for drinking with dinner, and have a bottle of Champagne in the refrigerator at all times, just in case.

CHICKEN BROTH

Chicken broth is extremely useful as a base for soups, stews, and sauces. Although **homemade** broths are the best, many people do not have the time to make their own, or do so only occasionally.

The **best commercial** broths available are also the most expensive ones. They are sold in specialty markets, frozen in plastic containers; they are made like homemade broths, with no added enhancers or salt. Because they are frozen, they are easy to keep on hand.

Next in quality are **low-sodium** and **salt-free** broths in cans and aseptic packaging. Because the manufacturer cannot use much salt or mono-sodium glutamate to hide a thin flavor, they tend to have a much greater proportion of real chicken broth and hence a truer flavor. When possible, buy organic broths. Swanson and Hain are reliable brands.

Avoid **regular canned** chicken broth, which is full of monosodium glutamate and salt. If you must use it, dilute it with water to lessen the saltiness (about 2 parts broth to 1 part water) and, if possible, simmer it with some meat or poultry to fortify it, as in the Shortcut Poultry, Meat, or Game Broth on page 576.

FRUITS AND VEGETABLES

Keep **lemons, limes,** and **oranges** on hand in the refrigerator for their juice and flavorful zest. **Onions** and **garlic** are essential as base flavorings for any number of dishes. Store in the driest area of the refrigerator (usually the vegetable bin) or in a cool, dark place. **Carrots, leeks,** and **potatoes** allow you to have fresh vegetables anytime. Store in the vegetable bin in ventilated plastic bags. Potatoes can also be stored in a cool, dark place.

FRESH HERBS

Fresh herbs can lift and focus the taste of a dish. **Fibrous or woody fresh herbs** such as thyme, rosemary, and sage will keep for several weeks if wrapped in damp paper towels and stored in a plastic bag. **Tender-leafed herbs** such as basil, dill, cilantro, tarragon, chives, mint, and chervil will last from 4 to 7 days stored this way.

Stock up on **exotic flavorings** when you find them in specialty and Asian markets to use in Asian and Southeast Asian dishes. These include knobs of fresh ginger; fresh lemongrass, the bulb of which gives lovely lemony-herbal flavor to soups and stews; and kaffir lime leaves, also known as citrus leaves, tough, shiny green, roundish leaves that have a haunting citrusy flavor of lime, pepper, and flowers.

BUTTER

I love butter and use it wherever its flavor is essential, as in flaky pastry for pies or beurre blanc–style sauces. While butter is a saturated fat, I feel that used judiciously, it poses no threat in the context of an overall healthy diet. It is a pure, natural product that contributes greatly to the pleasure of eating and to satiety, which are as essential to health as vitamins.

Butter is always preferable to **margarine,** which has been proven to pose serious health risks without any of the pleasurable benefits of butter. (If you want a compromise for butter with less saturated fat, see Homemade "Margarine," page 682.)

Whenever possible, I buy unsalted locally made butter made from organic milk, available at gourmet and health food stores and farmers' markets. It has a richer, fresher flavor than commercial butters do and is a good but less expensive alternative to my real preference—unsalted butters from France, which are creamier and have less water and more flavor than domestic butters.

HEAVY CREAM OR CRÈME FRAÎCHE

Sometimes nothing but heavy cream will do. It lends an inimitable silky richness to recipes. Heavy cream has 50 calories per tablespoon, of which about 36 percent is fat. Often all that is needed is a small amount—a tablespoon or two—to bring a dish to fruition. For this reason, I keep heavy cream on hand or, even better, crème fraîche, which is a cultured heavy cream that has a complex nutty flavor and thicker consistency. It also lasts several weeks longer than heavy cream.

SOUR CREAM

Regular sour cream has about half the calories and fat of heavy cream and a creamy, slightly sour flavor that is perfect in cold sauces and for last-minute enrichments of foods that won't be cooked long (it will curdle if heated too long). **Reduced-fat sour cream,** also a natural product, is a little lighter and less rich, with about 30 percent less fat and 4 fewer calories per tablespoon than regular sour cream. I find that **light sour creams**—those with 50 percent less fat than regular—can range widely in quality, depending on the formula of thickeners and flavor enhancers used to make up for the loss of fat, so I don't call for them. If you find one that is exceptional, by all means use it. Avoid **nonfat sour cream,** which has a muddy flavor and gluey texture. Another excellent substitute for sour cream is **quark,** a soft unripened cheese of German and Austrian origins that has a similar texture and flavor with fewer calories. It can, however, be difficult to find. (For a comparison of the fat and calories per tablespoon in various cream products, see page 688.)

BUTTERMILK

Buttermilk is a cultured low-fat milk with a tangy flavor and thick creamy consistency. It is immensely useful in cooking, both as a base for cold creamy sauces and as an ingredient in cakes and quick breads, where in place of fat it helps achieve a tender crumb. It lasts up to 2 months refrigerated and so is easy to keep on hand (transfer it from the carton to a clean glass bottle). You can also use **powdered instant buttermilk,** which you mix up like powdered milk. Available at health food stores, it will last indefinitely on your pantry shelf.

EGGS

Buy eggs from organically fed, free-range chickens, which have a fresher flavor and less health risk than regular eggs have. Large eggs are used in these recipes.

Egg safety. Over a decade ago, government studies began to show a high incidence of salmonella, a bacteria that causes food poisoning, in commercially produced eggs, due in large measure to the crowded and unsanitary conditions in which the chickens that lay them are raised. Salmonella can make people very ill, particularly those with compromised immune systems, the very young, and the elderly. For this reason, most food writers have taken an extremely conservative stance when it comes to eggs, advising that all eggs be cooked to an internal temperature of 160°F (or be held at 140°F for 3 minutes). At this point, the salmonella bacteria is killed—and the eggs are completely firm and rubbery. This extreme, all-or-nothing approach ignores the desire to enjoy eggs with runny yolks or the possibility that the provenance of the egg has much to do with its potential threat.

My solution has been to use eggs only from free-range organically fed chickens, which are raised in much healthier conditions than ordinary chickens. They are available at many supermarkets and all health food stores. In over a decade of enjoying several soft-cooked eggs per week, I have never become sick from eating them. In recipes that call for meringues or other raw egg preparations, I use organic eggs but include an option for making a cooked meringue. It seems to be a reasonable approach.

If you have access only to ordinary commercial eggs, or are fearful of salmonella, use them only in recipes in which they will be cooked.

Aged hard cheeses, which include cow's milk cheeses such as Parmigiano-Reggiano, aged Gouda, and Dry Jack; sheep's milk cheeses such as pecorino Romano, Fiore Sardo, pecorino Toscano, and Spanish Manchego; and aged goat cheeses such as Coach Farm grating stick or Crottin de Chavignol, are especially useful in cooking. Grated or shaved, they enhance pasta, risotto, soups, polenta, and roasted, steamed, or braised vegetables, often adding the final seasoning that brings all the flavors into harmony, like some kind of esoteric salt. They are so strong that a little goes a long way, adding only a modest number of calories and fat. I particularly love sheep's milk cheeses—the aged ones mentioned above and creamier Brin d'Amour and slightly smoky Idiazabel—for both cooking and eating.

Properly stored, these and other cheeses will keep for weeks in the refrigerator. Store cheeses you wish to continue aging in a plastic container (see page 680). Frequently used cheese, such as Parmigiano-Reggiano, is fine wrapped in wax or parchment paper and then in foil, which allows the cheese to breathe while preventing it from drying out too quickly. Tightly wrapping cheeses in plastic wrap causes them to suffocate and mold quickly.

Cheeses are also marvelous eaten at the end of a meal instead of or before dessert, in servings of no more than an ounce or two, as is done in France and Italy, where cheese is an integral part of the diet. Enjoyed at these times, cheeses, especially those made with unpasteurized milk, can act as an aid to digestion and may actually help the body deal with saturated fats. There is a world of flavors and textures to experience.

Most cheeses average about 110 calories per ounce (give or take 10 calories), with about 70 percent of their calories from fat. Mozzarella and feta have about 80 calories per ounce. How a cheese is sliced can greatly affect the perception of abundance (and the calorie count). Shaving or slicing cheese thinly on a mandoline or vegetable slicer or with a vegetable peeler can make a little seem like a great deal more, and can add great visual appeal as well.

Bacon and pancetta, the Italian-style unsmoked bacon, are usually considered taboo in healthful cooking because they are full of saturated fat. But because even a small amount can add so much flavor to a dish, I use them frequently. I freeze them in well-wrapped packages of 1 or 2 slices to draw upon as needed; they will keep for up to 3 months. If you cannot find pancetta, you can use prosciutto or serrano ham, unsmoked cured hams with a similar, though slightly less piquant, flavor. When purchasing prosciutto or serrano ham, have it sliced as you would pancetta, and ask for some of the ham fat (shopkeepers usually discard it, and will give it to you at no charge). You will need 50 percent lean meat and 50 percent fat to duplicate pancetta. Whenever possible, buy bacon, pancetta, and prosciutto cured *without* undesirable nitrites; they are available at better supermarkets and health food stores.

You can also store the delicious fat that comes from cooking pancetta, bacon, goose, ham, or duck in small jars in the refrigerator (see Rendered Bacon, Pancetta, Ham, Duck, or Goose Fat, page 681) to use at a moment's notice to add their inimitable flavor to a dish.

Olives are a staple in my kitchen. I use them often, in stews, roasts, and sauces, as an instant hors d'oeuvre, or as embellishments for pasta and pizzas. Their saltiness seasons, while their flesh yields a rich hit of flavor.

The best olives are unpasteurized, which means they have been cured either in brine or oil and not preserved by heating. Green olives are noticeably crisper, black olives meatier. When they are pasteurized, as is the case with all canned olives and most bottled, the high temperatures at which they are processed to give them long shelf life renders their flavors muted and one-dimensional.

Exposure to air causes olives to deteriorate quickly, so, when buying in bulk, look for olives that are sold in their brine, which will preserve them indefinitely. Look for plump olives, with few bruises or wrinkles (except for oil-cured olives, which are naturally wrinkled). The color of green olives should be bright and clear. Inferior olives are often aggressively flavored with hot pepper, herbs, or spices.

Many supermarkets now offer loose olives. Try different ones to see what you like. Among my favorites are Lucques, Cassées des Baux, Thassos, Nyons, Arbequina, and Gordal. Kalamatas, plump brine-cured olives from Greece, are excellent olives for cooking.

BASIC TOOLS AND EQUIPMENT.

Like most people, I don't have room for extraneous equipment. The cooking equipment I choose must be well made, long-lasting, and visually appealing, and it often can be used for multiple purposes (a stainless steel bowl set over a pan of boiling water becomes a double boiler, a strainer doubles as a flour sifter). Some of my favorite tools cost almost nothing, scavenged in flea markets and secondhand stores here and in Europe.

The following sections cover tools and equipment I consider essential. In addition, every well-equipped kitchen should include these basics:

large wooden or plastic cutting board

nesting stainless steel bowls, from 6 to 13 inches in diameter

flexible metal spatula

wooden spoons

tongs

slotted spoon

colander

fine-mesh strainer, about 8 inches in diameter

whisks: a fat balloon whisk for aerating and whipping and a narrower whisk for blending

heavy-duty kitchen shears

swivel-bladed vegetable peeler

metal box grater/shredder with several textures, from fine to coarse

ruler-shaped all-purpose plane grater

pepper mill

timer

instant-read thermometer

electric hand mixer

parchment paper

It never pays to buy cheap pots and pans. Thin, badly made pots, pans, casseroles, and baking sheets cook foods unevenly, scorch easily, and wear out quickly. Well-made pots and pans will last a lifetime. A few well-chosen items will cover most cooking needs. I find I rely on four saucepan sizes—1 quart, 1¾ to 2 quarts, 3 quarts, and 6 quarts—and a 1½-quart and 2-quart oval or round shallow casserole or gratin dish.

Saucepans and **pots** made of a heavy-gauge metal that conducts heat well and evenly are essential when cooking with less fat because they prevent scorching and encourage even browning, which builds flavor. Because different metals have different virtues and flaws, manufacturers now routinely layer several metals, such as copper and/or aluminum, both of which are excellent heat conductors but highly reactive, sandwiched between stainless steel, which conducts heat unevenly but is impervious to food reactions. All-Clad makes some of the best of these combinations. Though expensive, they come with a lifetime warranty. Although anodized aluminium is popular because of its moderate price, I find that its dark gray color makes it difficult to see the true color and consistency of liquids, particularly sauces.

Enameled cast-iron cookware, such as Le Creuset casseroles and gratin dishes, is lovely to look at and are useful for baking, long, slow braising, and steam-roasting and for making stews and soups. However, the enameled surface results in hot spots that prevent meats and vegetables from caramelizing properly without a lot of fat, so they are not effective for sautéing or browning.

I adore cooking with copper pots, casseroles, and gratin dishes because of their extraordinary conductivity and because they are aesthetically pleasing. They are so beautiful they can go from stove to table. Their drawback is that unless you have pots lined with stainless steel, the traditional tin lining can wear away over time and must be replaced (actually a simple matter of sending them by mail to a retinner; see Sources, page 711). Because they are expensive, over the years I've bought many of my copper pots at flea markets and secondhand stores at a fraction of the retail cost, polishing and retinning them if necessary to bring them back to life.

Heavy-duty nonstick skillets such as All-Clad are key tools in moderate-fat cooking to brown and caramelize foods. The new professional-grade nonstick pans are extremely durable, though they do scratch and dull after years of use. A recent innovation, the Scanpan from Denmark, is made with an extraordinarily hard ceramic-titanium surface that cannot come off. I recommend investing in 8-inch, 10-inch, and 12-inch nonstick skillets. Nonstick saucepans are unnecessary.

A **grill pan** is a heavy skillet with raised metal ridges across the bottom, used to simulate on a stove top some of the effects of grilling. The pan is heated until very hot so that when the food is added, it sears the outside quickly, as grilling does. The raised ridges allow any fat to drain off under the food as it cooks. A grill pan will not lend the smoky flavor of a true barbecue grill, but it is an excellent and simple means of quick-cooking meats, poultry, and fish. The best grill pans are made of cast iron or anodized aluminum, which can withstand extremely high heat. Stay away from nonstick grill pans or pans made of light metals, which will warp and/or cook unevenly.

An old-fashioned **cast-iron skillet** is essential for high-temperature cooking methods such as stove-top smoking, which could damage a copper or enamel-coated pot. Cast iron is practically indestructible. You can also use well-seasoned cast-iron skillets in place of nonstick cookware, for making pancakes, browning potatoes, and for searing meat and poultry in small amounts of fat without sticking (see How to Season Cast-Iron Pans, page 680). I recommend purchasing a 10- or 12-inch pan.

Baking sheets are shallow, rimmed rectangular pans used for baking and roasting. Invest in heavy-duty professional-gauge aluminum pans, also called sheet pans, and buy the largest size that will fit easily in your oven. They heat evenly, don't warp or burn, are easier to clean than flimsy baking sheets, and last for years. Nonstick pans are not necessary. Buy at least two, three, or four if possible.

The way you cut food affects not only its visual appeal but also the way it cooks and tastes. Artful cutting can make a small portion seem abundant, even indulgent.

A good basic set of **knives**, made of high-carbon stainless steel, which sharpens well and won't rust or stain, is essential. Good knives are an investment that will last a lifetime. In addition to a classic **chef's knife** for chopping, you should have a midsize **boning knife** and a **paring knife** for general use. A long thin **salmon slicer** is indispensable for slicing foods, particularly red meats and rare-cooked fish, thinly.

A **steel** is a rough steel rod with a handle used to sharpen knives. Although it is easy to learn to use, some people are daunted by them. An **electric knife sharpener** is another option that will allow you to easily sharpen your knives at home.

A **mandoline,** or **vegetable slicer,** is so useful, it's too bad more people don't know about it. It is nothing more than a rectangular plane made of wood, plastic, or steel that houses an adjustable razor-sharp blade for cutting vegetables, fruit, cheese, and other semi-firm foods quickly into consistent slices, julienne, shavings, or shreds with a minimum of effort.

Although you could pay more than $100 for a classic French mandoline, even better is the small plastic Japanese model called a Benriner cutter, for about $40. Its virtue is that you can replace the blade when it gets dull. The larger model cuts slices up to ¼ inch thick and can handle large vegetables such as rutabagas and celery root. The smaller model can cut foods up to 2½ inches wide into slices only up to ⅛ inch thick, and it has additional blades for making fine and thick julienne. Both are available at Asian grocery stores, some gourmet stores, and by mail order (see Sources, page 711).

MEASURING TOOLS

A good set of measuring tools is essential for healthful cooking and in baking. Although I dislike measuring every little thing, it is important to do so when you are learning to cook (and eat) more healthfully so you can keep close tabs on how much of high-fat or caloric ingredients you are actually using. And you will gradually train your eye so that you can make accurate estimates of quantities without measuring, both when cooking and eating out.

Graduated measuring spoons are a must in any kitchen. (There are 3 teaspoons in 1 tablespoon and 16 tablespoons in 1 cup.)

Dry measures, ranging from ¼ cup to 1 cup, for flour, sugar, and grains are graduated metal or plastic cups that are meant to be filled to the top and leveled off with a knife. **Liquid measures** for wet ingredients such as milk or eggs come in 1- to 4-cup sizes, or even larger, with measures marked on the side and space at the top to ensure against spilling. Make sure the liquid measure is at eye level when you read it. The ounce measure marked on these cups is for liquids only. To weigh ingredients, use a scale.

Many of my recipes specify weight as well as volume because it is an accurate way of measuring something variable such as a bunch of parsley or a portion of meat. I use a battery-operated **electronic scale,** because it is accurate to ⅛ ounce. If you buy a **spring scale,** test to see that it can measure small amounts—down to ¼ ounce—accurately. Either kind should have a measuring tray or bowl that can hold a quantity of food and should weigh ingredients up to at least 4 pounds. It should also allow you to reset the scale to zero after placing an empty tray or bowl on it, so you measure only what's added to the tray or bowl.

A **mortar** is a heavy bowl in which foods are pounded to a puree or coarse meal with a **pestle**, a heavy club-shaped implement. A mortar and pestle are ancient tools that you might think have no place in a modern kitchen. I use them almost daily, to pound garlic to a puree, crush spices for rubs, mash herbs with olive oil for quick, flavored oils, and so on. And certain sauces such as pesto or aïoli have a much mellower flavor when made in a mortar rather than a food processor, which renders the garlic taste in these sauces too sharp.

The best mortars are made of a somewhat rough, heavy material, such as unpolished marble or stone. The weight keeps them from sliding around on the work surface and the rough interior creates friction that helps to break down the food quickly. Pestles can be of just about any unbreakable material as long as they are the right shape: oblong with a somewhat flattened pounding end that presses and grinds food firmly against the mortar.

Over the years, I have improvised many alternatives to mortars and pestles when I haven't had access to them, such as a flat stone to pound garlic on a wooden board or a gently rounded wooden doorknob to pound foods in a heavy wooden bowl.

The **food processor** completes in minutes chores it used to take many times longer to accomplish by hand and is essential in the modern kitchen. However, the processor does have its weaknesses. Foods that have been sliced or julienned in a processor will be rougher and lack the visual appeal and precision of foods cut by hand. More important, food processors distort the flavor of certain key ingredients. Onions become acrid and watery when chopped in a food processor; they should be chopped by hand. When pureed, garlic becomes sharp and bitter; it is preferable to mash it in a mortar with a pestle (see above) and add it to your sauce.

Although the food processor has largely supplanted the **blender** in chopping and pureeing, there are certain jobs that a blender can do better than a food processor. For pureeing very liquid soups and many sauces, a blender will achieve the smoothest consistency. You can also use it to grind whole spices to a fine powder if you don't have a spice or coffee grinder.

A **food mill** looks like a saucepan with a perforated bottom. A hand-cranked blade forces food through the holes, pureeing it and removing seeds, skin, and fiber. Use a food mill when you want to avoid fibrous bits in vegetable purees and applesauce, creamy soups, and sauces. It makes peeling apples or tomatoes for sauce unnecessary.

OTHER ESSENTIALS

Paintbrushes have long been used by pastry chefs to brush the tops of pastries with glazes and egg washes. I use them routinely to brush savory foods with oil or butter, particularly vegetables and fruits that are to be roasted. Rather than pouring on too much oil, I can brush on the exact amount I need to coat the surface (see page 5).

Because these recipes employ the smallest possible amounts of fattening ingredients, use **rubber spatulas** constantly to scrape every last bit from mixing bowls and measuring cups.

Drying just-washed greens and herbs in a **salad spinner** prevents them from getting soggy and diluting the dressing in a salad, or from becoming watery when cooked. I also dry thin potato slices I've soaked to remove their starch, and greens that I have blanched; it eliminates the need to squeeze them dry. Many salad spinners are badly designed and flimsily made, with hand cranks that break easily. I recommend a Zyliss, which uses a strong pull cord wound around a center post, like a yo-yo. The removable basket can be used as a colander. I've had mine for more than ten years.

There are a few tools that, while you won't use them every day, are well worth having for the excellent results they achieve.

Nonstick bakeware liners keep foods from sticking without using oils or butter. The best and most durable are Silpat sheets, until recently available only to professional chefs. These are thin sheets of silicone plus glass fiber that withstand high heat. Teflon bakeware liners are paper-thin sheets of Teflon. While less durable than Silpats, they can be cut to fit cake pans and molds. They are available in specialty cookware shops or by mail order (see Sources, page 711).

Baking stones are flat, inch-thick sheets of high-fired brick, in circles, squares, or rectangles. Heated in the oven for half an hour before being used for breaking bread or doughs, they mimic some of the effects of a brick oven, yielding breads with excellent crusts. They are essential in pizza and focaccia making.

Many professional chefs consider an **electric vegetable juicer** essential. Without it, they could not make their sublime sauces from fresh vegetable juices. I bought an inexpensive juicer for less than $50, strong enough for this occasional use.

A trio of Thanksgiving side dishes. From top to bottom: Chestnut Puree with Fennel Seed (page 83), Roasted Winter Squash Puree (page 36), and Celery Root and Apple Puree (page 81)

VEGETABLES

In the Oven

Vegetables are not only the key to a healthy diet, they are also immensely satisfying to eat, offering an extraordinary range of flavors, textures, and pleasures. As a group, they contain most of the vitamins and minerals our bodies need. They have no cholesterol, little or no fat, and few calories, and they are packed with nutrients and fiber. They are essential in preventing disease and can help mitigate the damaging effects of gastronomic indulgence. For people (like me) who gain weight easily, they are essential to maintaining, or losing, weight because they are delicious and filling, yet low in calories.

You can use vegetables to extend other foods that for one reason or another you don't want to eat a lot of, such as pasta and red meat. An ample serving of Buttermilk Mashed Potatoes (page 77) makes a 4-ounce serving of steak seem like an old-fashioned steak-and-potatoes plate. Vegetarian Wild Mushroom Ragù (page 159) has such a meaty texture and robust flavor that people swear it contains meat. Vegetables baked into rich, lusty pasta casseroles seem like the most indulgent of creations. In sauces and soups, vegetables add a rich creamy texture that fat usually provides.

Vegetables are the mainstay of my daily diet. The techniques I have devised for cooking them healthfully are very easy to do, even when I am tired from a long day of work. Preparation time is minimal, the results deeply satisfying.

I take two main tacks in vegetable cooking. I use the oven when I want deep, concentrated, old-fashioned flavors, the stove top when I prefer to maintain bright fresh flavors of quickly cooked vegetables, like leafy greens and sugar snap peas.

Steam-roasted
leeks and fennel
(pages 56-58)

IN THE OVEN: ROASTING. The oven is my favorite tool for cooking vegetables. Roasting vegetables uncovered in the dry heat of the oven is not only a way to produce delicious easy dishes, but is an essential step in many of these recipes. By slowly evaporating the vegetables' juices and caramelizing, or browning, their natural sugars, roasting concentrates and amplifies their flavors with little effort and a minimum of fat.

I serve roasted asparagus and beets as an hors' d'oeuvre and roasted baby vegetables or onions as a side dish to accompany roasted meat or poultry, make soups of roasted winter squash, pasta sauces of roasted tomatoes, and stuff ravioli with roasted pumpkin and garlic.

Roasted Vegetables

A GUIDE TO IMPROVISING

MAKES ABOUT
4 CUPS;
SERVES 4

With this all-purpose method, you can roast a variety of vegetables either singly or in combination. Different vegetables require different cooking times depending on their thickness, density, and water content. The trick when you are roasting several vegetables is to group those of similar density together and to make sure, whether they are cut up or left whole, that they are a uniform size so that they cook in roughly the same time. Brush them with just enough fat to ensure caramelization and keep them from drying out.

> **3½ pounds vegetables,** trimmed and peeled if appropriate
>
> **1 tablespoon flavorful fat,** such as extra-virgin olive oil, Flavored Oil (pages 588–597), melted unsalted butter, or rendered bacon, pancetta, or goose fat (see page 681)
>
> **Kosher salt and freshly ground black pepper**

COOKING TIMES

For dense hard vegetables
like potatoes, root vegetables, yams, and winter squashes, sliced 1 to 1½ inches thick:
30 MINUTES TO 1 HOUR, 400°F

For medium-soft vegetables
like peppers, onions, fennel, eggplant, radicchio, zucchini, and summer squash, sliced ¼ to ½ inch thick:
30 TO 45 MINUTES, 400°F

For thin vegetables
like asparagus, green beans, scallions, sugar snap peas, and okra, left whole:
12 TO 20 MINUTES, 500°F

1. Preheat the oven to 400°F (or to 500°F for thin vegetables, such as those listed at left, which are best cooked quickly at a very high heat). If the vegetables are more than 1 inch thick, cut them into pieces roughly the same size: quarters, halves, or rounds. If they are less than 1 inch thick, leave them whole. (You can prepare many vegetables for roasting several hours ahead and store them in plastic bags in the refrigerator; the exceptions are vegetables that turn brown when cut, such as potatoes and turnips, and members of the onion family, which can become acrid.)

2. Using a lightly dampened brush, brush a baking sheet or roasting pan lightly with some of the fat. Arrange the vegetables on the pan. (If you are cooking vegetables with very different cooking times, say, winter squash and fennel, keep them separate, or use two pans, so you can start cooking the longer-cooking vegetables first.) Brush the vegetables lightly with the remaining fat or, if the vegetables are cut into small pieces, place them in a bowl and, using a brush dipped in the fat, toss them until they are completely coated. Sprinkle with salt and pepper.

3. Roast the vegetables, rearranging them every 15 minutes or so with a spatula, until they are tender and golden brown. Test for doneness by piercing them with a knife.

Although roasted vegetables are delicious seasoned with just salt and pepper, there are endless combinations of herbs and spices you can use.

Roast lightly oiled carrots with handfuls of fresh thyme sprigs, which will smoke slightly in the oven, perfuming them. Sprinkle ancho chile powder on onion and pepper slices before roasting.

Use warm spices such as cinnamon and allspice on winter squashes.

Toast equal parts cumin and coriander seeds until fragrant in a small skillet, then crush in a mortar and sprinkle over vegetables before roasting for appealing flavor and slightly crunchy texture.

Similarly, the fat you use also imparts flavor. Bacon fat gives a slight flavor of smoke, goose or duck fat an unparalleled richness, and Asian sesame oil a nutty flavor. Brown butter lends a nutty butter flavor. Olive oil is the best all-purpose fat, as well as the most healthful.

Roasted Winter Squash Slices

improvisation 1

When roasted, the flesh of winter squashes such as butternut, acorn, and kabocha becomes creamy and dense and caramelizes on the cut surfaces. Although the squash is delicious seasoned with only salt and pepper, I like to rub the slices with this Tunisian-inspired spice mix.

Preheat the oven to 400°F. In a small bowl, combine 1 teaspoon *each* ground coriander and sweet paprika, ½ teaspoon ground cumin, ¼ teaspoon caraway seeds, ¾ teaspoon salt, ½ teaspoon sugar, and a pinch of cayenne pepper. Cut off the ends of a 2½-pound winter squash, such as kabocha; cut in half and scoop out the seeds; cut each half into 6 slices about 2 inches thick. Using a lightly dampened brush, brush the flesh with 2 teaspoons extra-virgin olive oil and sprinkle with 4 teaspoons of the spice mix (or simply with salt and pepper). Arrange cut side down on a heavy baking sheet. Bake, turning once, for 30 minutes, or until the squash is tender and golden. (Serves 4.)

Roasted Winter Squash Puree

Roasted winter squashes also make wonderful purees, an unexpected alternative to mashed potatoes; they have such a fine texture and rich flavor that no additional fat is necessary. You can flavor the puree with the Tunisian spice mix above, or any other sweet spices, like nutmeg, cinnamon, or cloves.

Preheat the oven to 400°F. Cut a 2½-pound winter squash in half and scoop out the seeds. Using a slightly dampened brush, brush lightly with olive oil and place cut side down on a heavy baking sheet. Sprinkle 1 tablespoon water onto the pan. Bake for 30 minutes, then turn the squash over and bake for 15 minutes longer, or until the flesh is tender. With a spoon, scoop the flesh into the bowl of a food processor. Process to a smooth puree, about 1 minute. Stir in half the spice mix, then taste, adding more spice if desired and 1 to 2 teaspoons fresh lemon juice. (Makes about 2½ cups; serves 4.)

ROASTING VEGETABLES WHOLE

Because of their appealing shapes, smaller whole roasted vegetables make particularly charming side dishes (and cook more evenly than larger ones). These vegetables include baby carrots, parsnips, turnips, zucchini, sweet potatoes, and fennel; new potatoes and Jerusalem artichokes; miniature bell peppers; okra and asparagus. Just follow the Guide on page 34.

Served right in their skin, whole onions, such as small yellow onions, shallots, and cipolline make a lovely rustic accompaniment to roasts of beef, lamb, or chicken. Trim the stem and roots ends of the onions and, using a slightly dampened brush, brush lightly with oil. Roast in a 300°F oven until very tender, 30 minutes to 1 hour.

Roasted plantains, the cooking banana sold in Hispanic markets, are puree-tender and as satisfying as roasted sweet potatoes with a banana flavor. For savory dishes, choose plantains that are just beginning to turn from yellow to brown. For a dessert, choose ones that are black and soft. Place unpeeled plantains on a baking sheet and split the skin lengthwise across the top with a sharp knife. Bake at 400°F until tender, about 30 minutes.

Roasted Garlic

When you wrap whole heads of garlic in foil and roast them, they lose their ferocity and become a delicious mellow version of themselves, the flesh soft and puree-like. Serve one or two whole heads roasted garlic per person, letting your guests pull the cloves apart and squeeze the flesh out of its papery casing onto slices of grilled bread, or directly into their mouths.

Removed from its skin, roasted garlic can be used as a flavoring for soups, sauces, and stews; on pizzas; as a base for sauces; and most deliciously in mashed potatoes and polenta.

You can roast as many heads of garlic at once as you wish. Simply double or triple the recipe, wrapping no more than 4 large or 8 small heads in each package.

> **4 large or 8 small heads garlic** (about 14 ounces)
> **2 teaspoons extra-virgin olive oil**
> **4 sprigs fresh thyme** or ¼ teaspoon dried thyme
> **2 tablespoons water**

Preheat the oven to 400°F.

Gently peel off the papery white skin from each head of garlic to reveal the cloves, without separating them. Place the garlic on a sheet of aluminum foil. Using a slightly dampened brush, brush with the olive oil, and nestle the thyme sprigs among them. Dribble the water onto the foil. Pull the edges of the foil up and crimp tightly together to form a package. Place on a baking sheet.

Bake the garlic until the flesh is soft, about 35 to 45 minutes. To eat the garlic, pull off 1 clove at a time and squeeze the soft flesh out of the skin.

Roasted Garlic is best eaten or used when still warm. The garlic puree variation that follows, however, will keep for up to 2 weeks refrigerated, or frozen for up to 2 months. Pack into a clean, dry container, pour a film of extra-virgin olive oil on top, and cover tightly.

Roasted Garlic Puree. Allow the roasted garlic to cool. Pull the cloves apart, squeeze the soft puree out of each clove into a bowl, and mash with a fork to make a coarse puree; or puree in a food processor to make a smoother one. Alternatively, pull the cloves apart and puree them through a food mill. An average head of garlic yields 3 to 4 tablespoons puree. Season with salt and pepper to taste. (Make about 1 cup.)

WHEN COOKING WITH GARLIC

Use garlic that is firm and unsprouted. Old, sprouting garlic—cloves with green shoots growing in their center—can be sharp and bitter. Heads should be hard with no give when pressed and with no trace of mold or sprouting. Local farmers' markets, where organic and heirloom varieties are often available, are one good source. For an excellent mail-order source, see Sources (page 711).

essential recipe
Slow-Roasted Tomatoes

**MAKES ABOUT
2½ CUPS;
SERVES 8 AS AN
HORS D'OEUVRE**

When roasted slowly for a long period at a very low temperature, fresh tomatoes gradually lose moisture and their natural sugars and flavor become very concentrated. They hold an appealing shape but their texture becomes almost melting. This method works miracles with dead-of-winter, flavorless supermarket tomatoes.

I often serve these tomatoes as an hors d'oeuvre, to be eaten with fingers or on a slice of French bread. They are so versatile you can roast batches at a time to keep on hand to add a concentrated hit of bright tomato flavor to recipes for soups, stews, braises, salads, and sandwiches. See the variation that follows for making a sauce of them.

4 pounds ripe tomatoes (about 30 plum tomatoes or 12 to 16 regular tomatoes)

1½ tablespoons extra-virgin olive oil, plus extra for brushing

1 teaspoon sugar

½ teaspoon kosher salt

Freshly ground black pepper

Preheat the oven to 325°F.

Slice plum tomatoes lengthwise in half or quarter round tomatoes through the stem. In a medium bowl, toss the tomatoes with the olive oil to coat. Arrange the tomatoes cut side up on a large baking sheet. Sprinkle with the sugar, salt, and pepper to taste.

Roast for 2½ to 3 hours, until the tomatoes have lost most of their liquid and are just beginning to brown. They should look like dried apricots and hold their shape when moved. (If some tomatoes are done before others, remove them with a spatula.) Let cool to room temperature. Using a slightly dampened brush, brush with a little olive oil before serving.

IN ADVANCE If refrigerated, the tomatoes will soften and lose their chewy exterior, but their flavor will be just as good. Store them, well covered, in the refrigerator for up to 1 week or in the freezer for up to 2 months.

variation
Rustic Slow-Roasted Tomato Sauce. This sauce has a deep roasted flavor and a creamier texture than regular tomato sauces. It is excellent with all kinds of pastas and polenta, as a pizza sauce, or a topping for bruschetta, as well as on grilled chicken and heartier fish like salmon and swordfish. I sometimes like to spoon some into the center of a risotto. Spiked with a little balsamic vinegar, it makes a fine alternative to ketchup on hamburgers.

Chop the roasted tomatoes coarsely or finely, depending on the texture you want. Heat the tomatoes in a small heavy saucepan over moderate heat. Thin to the desired consistency with a little unsalted homemade (page 574) or canned low-sodium chicken broth, pasta cooking water, or meat or poultry juices, depending on what you are serving the sauce with. Just before serving, stir in ¼ cup minced fresh herbs, such as basil, cilantro, chervil, and/or chives. You can enrich the sauce with 1 tablespoon heavy cream or crème fraîche or 1 teaspoon extra-virgin olive oil. (Makes 2½ cups.)

Roasted Wild Mushrooms

Mushrooms pose a real dilemma in healthy cooking. Because they are so porous, they soak up fat like a sponge when sautéed in the traditional manner. This technique, roasting mushrooms with a little bit of oil and wine until they become tender with a slightly browned exterior, duplicates the delicious effects of sautéing with a minimum of fat and effort. These can be used in all recipes that call for sautéed mushrooms. Or, to serve them as is, toss with minced garlic and parsley à la Provençal (see the variation).

1½ pounds wild mushrooms, such as chanterelle, morel, shiitake, oyster, hedgehog, and/or portobello

1 medium onion, finely chopped

2 garlic cloves, smashed

2 juniper berries, crushed

2 sprigs fresh thyme or ¼ teaspoon dried thyme

2 tablespoons dry white wine or sherry

1 tablespoon extra-virgin olive oil

1 teaspoon grappa or cognac (optional)

½ teaspoon kosher salt

Freshly ground black pepper

Preheat the oven to 375°F.

Brush any dirt from the mushrooms with a soft brush or damp paper towel. Trim off the ends of the stems and discard. Cut the mushrooms lengthwise into halves, quarters, or eighths to make bite-sized pieces that will still retain some of the shape of the mushroom.

In a shallow casserole, combine the mushrooms, onion, garlic, juniper berries, and thyme. In a small bowl, combine the white wine with 2 teaspoons of the oil and the grappa, if using, and pour it over the mushrooms as you toss to coat them. Sprinkle with the salt and toss again.

Cover the mushrooms with foil and roast for 35 to 40 minutes, until they are tender and the juices are just beginning to caramelize in the bottom of the pan. (If there is still some liquid in the pan, uncover and roast the mushrooms until the liquid has evaporated. Continue to roast until they are beginning to brown, about 10 minutes longer.) When the mushrooms are tender, toss them with the remaining teaspoon of oil and the pepper to taste. Use as is in a recipe, or finish as directed below.

You can roast the mushrooms several hours ahead and reheat them before serving in a small nonstick skillet with a little water. IN ADVANCE

Provençal-Style Mushrooms. Mince 2 garlic cloves with ¼ tea- variation spoon salt. Sprinkle ½ cup chopped fresh flat-leaf parsley on top and mince the garlic and parsley together. Toss the hot mushrooms with the garlic-parsley mixture and serve at once.

BEYOND BUTTON MUSHROOMS

Make a mix of whatever "wild" mushrooms you find available. Try a variety beyond the ubiquitous white button mushrooms, such as cremini, oyster, shiitake, and/or portobello. Specialty markets carry seasonal wild mushrooms such as morels, cèpes (also known as porcini or boletes), chanterelles, black trumpets, lobster, hen of the woods, hedgehogs, and matsutakes, among others. As you cook with them, you will become familiar with their very different textures and flavors. Buy mushrooms without bruises or black spots and avoid those that are wrinkled or dried out. Store mushrooms for up to 3 days in a paper bag in the refrigerator. Rinse quickly or use a soft brush or a damp towel to remove any dirt and trim off the tough stem ends.

"Fried" Eggplant

essential recipe

SERVES 4

Generally speaking, the older and larger the eggplant, the tougher and more bitter the seeds will be. So, when buying standard globe eggplants, choose small or medium eggplants that are firm but not hard to the touch and have no brown spots.

Eggplants, like mushrooms, have extremely absorbent flesh that soaks up great quantities of fat when they are panfried, rendering them highly caloric. I prefer to roast them to achieve a similar effect, using only a light brushing of oil.

Use these roasted eggplant slices in recipes that call for fried eggplant, such as eggplant parmigiana or moussaka, or as a side dish or hors d'oeuvre. Or, for another layer of flavor, try brushing them with any flavored oil such as Rosemary Oil, Herb Provençal Oil, or Garlic Oil (pages 588–597).

2 medium eggplants (about 2 pounds)
2 teaspoons extra-virgin olive oil
¾ teaspoon kosher salt

Preheat the oven to 450°F.

Peel the eggplants. Slice crosswise on a slight diagonal into ½-inch slices and discard the ends. Using a lightly dampened brush, brush each slice lightly on both sides with the oil and arrange on a large baking sheet. Sprinkle with the salt and roast until the slices are tender and brown, 20 to 25 minutes.

IN ADVANCE As a warm hors d'oeuvre, the eggplant is best eaten soon after it comes out of the oven. If using it in other dishes, however, you can bake it several days ahead and set aside at room temperature to cool, then refrigerate.

Peppers Roasted with Garlic and Anchovies

SERVES 4 The food I remember long after my return home from traveling is invariably the simple, elemental dishes made with a few ingredients. These roasted peppers are one such dish. I had them in a restaurant in the ancient village of Cherasco, near Alba in the Piedmont region of Italy. The chef's method of roasting peppers with nothing more than a little anchovy, garlic, and olive oil revived my love of the bell pepper, which has suffered from overexposure in recent years. The anchovy brings out the flavors of the pepper without dominating it. This is one of the best and simplest hors d'oeuvres I know. It is also lovely as a side dish.

If you have any leftover peppers, coarsely chop them and toss them with pasta, olive oil, and Parmigiano-Reggiano cheese for a delicious supper.

4 large red or yellow bell peppers (2 pounds)

1½ tablespoons extra-virgin olive oil

8 oil-packed anchovies, drained

2 garlic cloves, thinly sliced

⅛ teaspoon kosher salt

Freshly ground black pepper

2 tablespoons chopped fresh basil or flat-leaf parsley (optional)

Preheat the oven to 450°F.

Halve each pepper lengthwise, then cut each half lengthwise in half, leaving the stem intact. Remove the seeds and, with a sharp paring knife, cut out the white membranes. Using a lightly dampened brush, brush each pepper section with some of the olive oil, and arrange cut side up on a baking sheet.

Slice the anchovies crosswise in half. Place 1 anchovy half and 2 slices of garlic in the cavity of each pepper quarter. Brush these with the remaining oil. Sprinkle lightly with salt and generously with pepper. Roast for about 30 minutes, until the peppers are collapsed, tender, and slightly browned on the edges. Serve hot or at room temperature. Sprinkle the herbs over the peppers just before serving, if desired.

You can roast the peppers up to 4 hours ahead. When they are cool, cover with plastic and leave at room temperature.   IN ADVANCE

Simple Herb- or Spice-Roasted Peppers. For an even quicker play on this dish, omit the anchovy, garlic, and basil and sprinkle the roasted peppers with chopped fresh herbs, such as thyme or savory, or spices, such as crushed cumin or fennel seeds. My favorite is a spare sprinkling of Sweet, Hot, Smoky Pepper (page 547) or smoked paprika (see Sources, page 711).   variation

Roasted Root Vegetable Hash

SERVES 4 This mélange of sliced winter root vegetables roasts into a chewy hash that makes a delicious side dish, as well as an addition to many recipes. Use it in Composed Soups (pages 396–400), in stews, and in salads based on beans or grains, or serve it as a comforting meal in itself, accompanied by a few slices of aged goat cheese.

> **3 to 3½ pounds root vegetables,** such as parsnips, carrots, celery root, parsley root, turnips, and/or potatoes, in any combination
>
> **2 medium onions,** peeled
>
> **1 tablespoon plus 2 teaspoons extra-virgin olive oil, rendered bacon or pancetta fat** (see page 681), **or brown butter** (see page 681)
>
> **¾ teaspoon kosher salt**
>
> **Freshly ground black pepper**

Preheat the oven to 400°F.

Peel the root vegetables. Cut celery root into 1-inch-thick slices, then cut each slice into ¼- to ⅓-inch-thick strips; cut crosswise to make ¼- to ⅓-inch dice. If any of the other vegetables are thicker than 1½ inches in diameter, cut them lengthwise in half, then cut crosswise into ¼- to ⅓-inch-thick slices. Cut the onions into eighths through the root ends, leaving the wedges intact. (You should have about 8 cups of vegetables.)

Using a lightly dampened brush, brush a heavy baking sheet with some of the oil. Lay the onion wedges cut side down in one corner of the pan. Scatter the root vegetables over the rest of the pan. Using the brush dipped in the remaining oil, toss and brush the root vegetables until they are completely coated with oil, then brush the tops of the onions. Sprinkle all the vegetables with the salt and pepper.

Roast, turning the vegetables every 15 minutes or so with a spatula, until they are tender and golden, about 45 minutes.

IN ADVANCE Up to 4 hours ahead, prepare all the vegetables except the onions (which will become acrid), brush them with the oil on the baking sheet, and cover tightly with plastic wrap. Set aside at room temperature. Just before roasting, arrange the onion wedges in one corner of the pan. The cooked hash can be stored, covered, in the refrigerator for up to 3 days. Warm in a nonstick skillet over moderate heat.

Roasted Asparagus with Brown Butter and Pecorino

SERVES 4

Roasting asparagus spears rather than steaming them is an easy way to achieve an appealingly rustic effect—and a more concentrated flavor. With pecorino Romano or Parmigiano-Reggiano cheese shaved over them, they make an effortless, instant hors d'oeuvre or first course. The asparagus is especially good if brushed with brown butter, whose roasted nut flavor plays off the sharp cheese, but you can also use a fruity extra-virgin olive oil.

1 tablespoon plus 1 teaspoon unsalted butter or 1 tablespoon extra-virgin olive oil

2 pounds medium-thick asparagus

½ teaspoon kosher salt

1¼ ounces pecorino Romano or Parmigiano-Reggiano cheese

Freshly ground black pepper

Preheat the oven to 450°F.

To make brown butter, in a small saucepan, cook the butter over moderately low heat until the solids that fall to the bottom are medium brown and the butter smells like roasted nuts. Remove from the heat. With a teaspoon, skim the foam off the top and discard.

Break the tough ends off the asparagus and discard. If you wish, peel the bottom third of each spear with a vegetable peeler. (This gives them a nice look but is not necessary.) Using a lightly dampened brush, brush a baking sheet large enough to hold the spears in one layer with a little of the brown butter, taking care not to include any brown solids. Spread the asparagus on the sheet and paint with the remaining butter. Sprinkle lightly with the salt.

Roast until the asparagus is tender, 20 to 25 minutes. Shave or grate the cheese over, sprinkle with pepper, and serve warm.

IN ADVANCE

Up to 6 hours ahead, trim the asparagus and make the brown butter. Brush the sheet with butter, arrange the asparagus on the baking sheet, and brush with the remaining butter. Cover with plastic wrap and refrigerate until ready to roast.

Parsnip Fries

SERVES 6 Ann Disrude, a friend and a spectacular natural cook with a fondness for crispy fried foods, serves these sublime parsnip fries with drinks before dinner. Cut into sticks, tossed with a little oil, and roasted to a supremely crisp-chewy treat, they could not be healthier or simpler to make, as is the potato variation that follows. I love them as a side dish for roasts and grilled steak.

3 pounds small or medium parsnips, peeled and cut into 4-by-⅓-inch sticks
2 tablespoons extra-virgin olive oil
1 teaspoon fine sea salt

Preheat the oven to 375°F.

Place the parsnip sticks in a bowl. Using a lightly dampened brush, toss them with the oil, making sure each one is coated. Spread them in a single layer on one large or two smaller baking sheets, making sure they aren't touching.

Roast the parsnips, tossing once or twice, until tender and browned in spots, 45 minutes to 1 hour. Sprinkle with the salt, transfer to a platter, and serve at once.

IN ADVANCE Up to 4 hours ahead, toss the parsnips. with the oil, spread them on the baking sheet(s), and cover with plastic wrap. Set aside at room temperature until ready to roast.

variation **Crisp Twice-Roasted Potatoes.** Preheat the oven to 375°F. Pierce 1½ pounds small Yukon Gold potatoes with a knife in several places, spread them on a baking sheet, and roast until very tender, about 1 hour. Halve the potatoes and smash them lightly on the baking sheet with the bottom of a glass. Using a lightly dampened brush, toss them with 1½ tablespoons extra-virgin olive oil (goose fat would be sublime) and roast, flipping occasionally, until browned and crisp, about 45 minutes. Sprinkle with 1 teaspoon fine sea salt and serve at once.

Potato Chips

These chips are better than any potato chip on the market, with a clear flavor of Idaho potatoes and butter. Rinsing thin potato slices in several changes of water removes their starch, which would inhibit crisping. They are dried, coated lightly with clarified butter, and baked on a cookie sheet until golden and crisp.

A 1-ounce serving of these chips contains more than twice as many chips but half the fat of an ounce of commercial chips. This is because most of the weight and calories in commercially fried chips comes from the fat that they have absorbed.

No one needs any instruction on eating or serving potato chips, but my friend Becky Lewis had the inspired idea one New Year's Eve of eating these chips with little dollops of sour cream and caviar.

> **1 tablespoon plus 2 teaspoons unsalted butter**
> **1 pound medium Idaho potatoes**
> **½ teaspoon fine sea salt**

Preheat the oven to 425°F.

To clarify the butter, melt the butter in a small saucepan over low heat, then heat until it stops foaming and becomes clear, with some solids floating on the top. Skim off the solids and discard. Set aside.

Peel the potatoes and slice them into 1/16-inch-thick rounds with a mandoline or vegetable slicer, placing them immediately in a bowl of cold water. Rinse in several changes of cold water, drain well, and spin dry in a salad spinner. Do not leave the potatoes in the water for more than 5 minutes, or after you have dried them, or they will curl up and won't cook evenly. Pat the potatoes dry with paper towels and place in a medium bowl.

With a teaspoon, spoon the clear clarified butter onto the potatoes, leaving the milky residue in the bottom of the pot. Using a lightly dampened brush, toss the potatoes with the butter, making sure each slice is coated. Arrange the slices in a single layer on a large heavy baking sheet, making sure they don't touch one another.

Bake on the middle rack of the oven for about 7 minutes, then check them. With a spatula, transfer the potatoes that have become golden brown and crisp to a platter lined with paper towels. Continue baking the remaining potato slices up to 3 minutes longer, checking them frequently and removing the finished ones as they are done. Do not allow the potatoes to get very brown, or they will be bitter. Sprinkle with the salt.

IN ADVANCE The chips are best eaten within a couple of days. Store in an airtight tin.

variation **Root Vegetable Chips.** Use the basic method to make delectable root vegetable chips with celery root, parsnips, and sweet potatoes. However, in order for them to brown evenly, you must blanch them first. Peel and slice the vegetables 1/16 inch thick. Bring 3 quarts water to a boil and salt liberally. Add the slices, bring the water back to a boil, and cook for 45 seconds. Drain and cool down under cold running water. Drain well again and spin dry in a salad spinner. Preheat the oven to 300°F and proceed as directed above, baking the chips until crisp and golden, 40 to 45 minutes.

variation

MAKES 1½ CUPS;
SERVES 4

If you wish to
serve more
(or fewer) people,
figure on 1 shallot,
¼ teaspoon extra-
virgin olive oil,
and a pinch of salt
per serving. **Crispy Shallots.** This recipe emulates the delicious deep-fried shallot rings chefs often use to garnish dishes. They are best if served within 1 hour.

Preheat the oven to 325°F. Slice 4 medium shallots into paper-thin rounds, less than 1/16 inch thick if possible. (This is easiest to do with a mandoline or vegetable slicer.) Blot them dry with paper towels, drizzle with 1½ teaspoons olive oil, and toss them with a lightly dampened brush to coat them completely. Scatter the shallots over a heavy baking sheet or into a large ovenproof skillet. Bake for about 18 minutes, tossing and rearranging the shallots every 5 to 6 minutes to keep them from burning and to ensure even cooking. I use a bamboo skewer to do this, and to transfer the rings to a baking sheet lined with paper towels as they become brown and crisp. (The rings do not need to be absolutely uniform; some pale patches are fine.) Sprinkle with 1/8 teaspoon salt while still hot. Leave the rings on the paper towels until ready to use.

Greek-Style Potatoes with Lemon and Thyme

I created this recipe from my memory of the lemony herbal roasted potatoes my Greek grandmother used to make. They go especially well with lamb and roasted fish. For a simple supper, top the glazed and melting potatoes with thin shavings of aged goat cheese.

SERVES 4

2 pounds thin-skinned potatoes, preferably small new potatoes, such as Yellow Finns, Yukon Gold, Bintjes, or red-skinned potatoes, peeled and rinsed well (if you can only find larger potatoes, quarter them lengthwise)

¾ **cup water**

¼ **cup fresh lemon juice**

¼ **cup finely chopped shallots** (3 medium)

1 **tablespoon fresh thyme leaves**

¾ **teaspoon kosher salt**

1 **tablespoon plus 2 teaspoons fruity extra-virgin olive oil**

1 **imported bay leaf**

Freshly ground black pepper

Preheat the oven to 375°F.

Place the potatoes in a shallow flameproof casserole large enough to hold them in one layer. In a measuring cup, combine the water, lemon juice, shallots, thyme, salt, and 1 tablespoon of the olive oil. Pour over the potatoes, and nestle in the bay leaf. Bake, rearranging the potatoes occasionally, until they have absorbed all the liquid and are very tender, about 1 hour. If there is still liquid in the pan when the potatoes are tender, place on a burner over moderate heat and simmer until no liquid remains.

Toss the potatoes with the remaining 2 teaspoons olive oil and return to the oven. Bake for 10 minutes longer, or until glazed and golden. Discard the bay leaf. Pepper generously and serve at once.

Up to 4 hours ahead, peel the potatoes; store in a bowl of cold water at room temperature. Chop the shallots, toss with the oil, cover, and refrigerate. Squeeze the lemon juice and refrigerate.

IN ADVANCE

Potatoes Roasted with Lemon and Saffron.
Follow the recipe above, using ¾ cup hot, not tepid, water. Place 1 large pinch saffron threads in a measuring cup and crush to a powder with a spoon; pour the hot water over and set aside to steep for 10 minutes. Add the lemon juice, shallots, salt, and olive oil; omit the thyme. Proceed as directed.

variation

IN THE OVEN: GRATINS. With their melting interiors and crusty tops, gratins are immensely satisfying old-fashioned dishes. I can think of no better accompaniments to roast meats or poultry. Traditionally, gratins are made with lots of butter, cheese, and cream and are often just too rich. Used judiciously and in innovative ways, these same rich ingredients yield a lighter version with the essential pleasures intact.

The Best Part of a Potato Gratin

SERVES 6

Closer to a traditional potatoes boulangère, this delicious gratin uses white wine and broth rather than cream as the liquid, so the flavor of the potatoes really comes through. As I consider the crispy top the best part of a gratin, I like to bake it in a shallow baking sheet rather than the usual casserole. A sprinkling of a flavorful aged cheese such as Parmigiano-Reggiano or Manchego melts into an abundant crisp crust. If you prefer a more traditional casserole-style gratin, see the variations that follow.

2 teaspoons unsalted butter

1½ cups rich hearty broth, such as Classic Rich Poultry Meat, or Game Broth, Shortcut Poultry, Meat, or Game Broth, Faux Veal Broth, or Hearty Porcini-Miso Broth (pages 572–576), or canned low-sodium chicken broth

¾ cup dry white wine

2 imported bay leaves or 2 sprigs fresh rosemary or thyme

1 garlic clove, smashed

1½ teaspoons kosher salt

1 teaspoon freshly ground black pepper

About ¼ teaspoon grated nutmeg

2 pounds baking or Yellow Finn potatoes, peeled

1½ ounces full-flavored aged hard cheese, such as Parmigiano-Reggiano, Manchego, aged Gouda, or pecorino Toscano, grated (about ⅔ cup)

Preheat the oven to 350°F. Grease a 10-by-15-inch rimmed baking sheet with 1 teaspoon of the butter.

Combine the broth, wine, bay leaves, garlic, salt, pepper, and nutmeg in a large heavy saucepan over medium heat. Bring to a boil, reduce the heat, and simmer until the liquid is reduced to 2 cups, about 10 minutes.

Meanwhile, using a mandoline or a vegetable slicer, slice the potatoes ⅛ inch thick.

Add the potatoes to the broth and simmer for 5 minutes, or until the mixture thickens slightly. Remove and discard the bay leaves and garlic. Pour the potatoes and liquid onto the baking sheet and gently smooth them out into an even layer. Dot with the remaining 1 teaspoon butter. Scatter the grated cheese over the top.

Bake for 50 minutes, or until golden and crusty. Let the gratin rest for 5 minutes before serving.

IN ADVANCE The gratin can be assembled up to 1 hour ahead. Cover and let sit at room temperature. As the hot potatoes will cook a bit as they stand, check the gratin after it has baked for 40 minutes.

variation **Classic Potato Gratin.** Use a 1½-quart gratin dish. Follow the recipe above, but do not sprinkle the gratin with the cheese before baking. Instead, bake it for 40 minutes, basting or brushing the potatoes once or twice with the liquid in the dish. Then sprinkle the cheese on top and bake for 20 to 25 minutes longer, until golden and crusty.

You can bake a thin layer of something delicious right in the center of a Classic Potato Gratin, such as Warm Olivada (Warm Crushed Olives; page 655), Onion Marmalade with Sherry Vinegar (page 667), Roasted Garlic Puree (page 38), or Roasted Wild Mushrooms (page 40). A few slices of fresh black truffle are astonishing. Follow the variation above. Pour only half the potato mixture into the gratin dish and smooth the top. Gently spoon over a thin layer (up to ¼ inch thick) of whatever filling you wish. Top with the remaining potatoes and liquid and proceed as directed.

variation **Creamy Potato Gratin.** Although it is possible to make a decent gratin with only whole milk, it just doesn't have the creaminess I want. A small proportion of heavy cream adds richness with significantly fewer calories than a traditional gratin. Replace the broth and wine with 1¾ cups whole milk and ¼ cup heavy cream.

Sweet Onion and Tomato Gratin

Make this gratin in late summer or early fall, when ripe tomatoes are still abundant. (The gratin will be as good as the tomatoes you use.) It is easy to make and excellent as a side dish, or as a bed for roasted or grilled fish fillets.

Because the vegetables are arranged in a thin layer, you need quite a large gratin dish. If you want to serve 8 people, double the recipe and assemble the gratin on a large rimmed baking sheet. The gratin should be baked as soon as it is assembled.

> **1 tablespoon plus 1 teaspoon extra-virgin olive oil**
>
> **2 garlic cloves,** halved lengthwise
>
> **2 medium Vidalia onions** (11 to 12 ounces), peeled and sliced lengthwise into ⅛-inch slices
>
> **1 teaspoon sugar**
>
> **½ teaspoon kosher salt**
>
> **Freshly ground black pepper**
>
> **1½ pounds ripe tomatoes**
>
> **⅓ cup dried bread crumbs**
>
> **⅓ cup freshly grated Parmigiano-Reggiano cheese**
>
> **1½ tablespoons fresh rosemary leaves** or 1½ teaspoons dried rosemary

Preheat the oven to 450°F. Brush a 2½-quart gratin dish or a large shallow ovenproof casserole (about 13 by 9 inches) with ½ teaspoon of the oil.

Rub the inside of the gratin dish well with the cut sides of the garlic, then mince the garlic. Scatter the onion slices and garlic into the dish. Drizzle the remaining 3½ teaspoons olive oil over them and sprinkle with ¼ teaspoon of the sugar, ⅛ teaspoon of the salt, and several grinds of black pepper. Toss to coat. Spread out evenly. Bake for 10 minutes.

Meanwhile, slice the tomatoes crosswise in half and squeeze gently to remove the seeds and juices. Slice the tomato halves into ¼-inch-thick wedges. In a small bowl, combine the bread crumbs, Parmigiano-Reggiano cheese, and rosemary.

Toss the tomatoes gently with the onion slices. Spread out evenly. Sprinkle with the remaining ¾ teaspoon sugar, ⅜ teaspoon salt, and a few grinds of pepper, then sprinkle with the bread crumbs and cheese. Bake for 25 minutes longer, or until the gratin is bubbling and the top is deep brown. Let cool slightly before serving.

Odds-and-Ends Gratins

You can transform leftover vegetables—whether pureed, sautéed, or braised—into delicious crisp-topped gratins using this simple method. I've "gratinéed" everything from braised root vegetables to Roasted Garlic Mashed Potatoes (page 78) to steam-sautéed broccoli or cauliflower (see page 71).

Preheat the oven to 350°F. Choose a gratin dish that will hold the vegetables in a layer no higher than 2 inches. Rub the dish with a cut clove of garlic. Let the dish dry, then rub it lightly with butter or olive oil. For every 4 cups cooked vegetables, combine 1 cup shredded Gruyère, Comté, Dry (aged) Jack, or Manchego cheese, 2 tablespoons freshly grated Parmigiano-Reggiano, and $1/3$ cup semi-dry bread crumbs. Spread the vegetables in the dish. Sprinkle the vegetables evenly with the cheese mixture. Bake until the vegetables are heated through and the top is golden brown, about 25 minutes. (Serves 4.)

Mashed Potato Cake

SERVES 4

Use this technique of coating a non-stick pan with butter and grated aged cheese whenever you want to achieve a chewy crust on a savory skillet cake made with risotto, pasta, or a stiff vegetable puree.

Serve wedges of this crusty savory cake, known as a *galette* in France, as a side dish with any number of meat, poultry, or seafood preparations. To make a crust without using a great deal of butter, I sprinkle a hot, lightly buttered nonstick pan with a little grated aged cheese, such as Parmigiano-Reggiano, which melts and forms a crust on the outside of the potato cake. Though used sparingly, the cheese contributes a mild flavor that enhances the potato without being a strong presence.

> **2 teaspoons unsalted butter**
>
> **1 garlic clove,** halved
>
> **3 cups stiff leftover mashed potatoes** (such as Buttermilk Mashed Potatoes, page 77)
>
> **3 tablespoons all-purpose flour**
>
> **A few gratings of fresh nutmeg**
>
> **Kosher salt and freshly ground black pepper**
>
> **¼ cup plus 2 tablespoons finely grated aged cheese,** such as Parmigiano-Reggiano, Manchego, Dry (aged) Jack, or aged Gouda (about 1¼ ounces)

Preheat the oven to 425°F.

In an ovenproof nonstick 10-inch skillet, melt 1 teaspoon of the butter over low heat. Add the garlic, cover, and cook gently until the garlic is translucent, about 3 minutes. Remove the pan from the heat and set aside to cool. Discard the garlic.

Put the potatoes in a medium bowl and beat in the nutmeg, flour, and salt and pepper to taste.

Sprinkle 3 tablespoons of the cheese into the skillet. Gently spoon the potato mixture into the pan, taking care not to dislodge the cheese, and press down with the back of a spoon to form a flat cake. Sprinkle the top of the cake evenly with the remaining 3 tablespoons cheese and a few grinds of pepper. Dot with the remaining 1 teaspoon butter.

Place the pan over moderate heat for a couple of minutes, until the skillet is very hot and you can hear the cake sizzle. Transfer the pan to the oven and bake for about 30 minutes, until the top is golden.

Slide a blunt knife carefully between the potato cake and the sides of the pan and lift the cake slightly to see if the bottom is brown and crisp. If not, place the skillet on a burner over moderate heat and cook for 2 to 3 minutes. Serve the cake directly from the pan, or turn it out onto a platter: Place a plate over the pan and, holding the two together, invert them so that the cake falls out onto the plate.

Up to 4 hours ahead, press the mashed potatoes into the prepared skillet, top with the cheese, and dot with butter. Cover and refrigerate until ready to bake. Bake for about 40 minutes, until the top is golden.   IN ADVANCE

IN THE OVEN: STEAM-ROASTING. Vegetables roasted in a tightly sealed foil or parchment package (*en papillote* in French) with a light brushing of a flavorful fat have a mellow, concentrated flavor. In effect, they cook in their own juices, absorbing any seasonings you wish, such as fresh herbs, spices, orange or lemon zest, crushed black olives, anchovies, and so on. The results are a cross between regular roasting and braising, slightly caramelized but moist vegetables with rich juices.

Steam-Roasted Vegetables (Papillote Cooking)

A GUIDE TO IMPROVISING

SERVES 4

You can use any number of flavorings and fats to season vegetables for steam-roasting. Some of my favorite combinations are sliced fingerling potatoes with crushed black olives and lemon zest; fresh artichoke hearts with garlic and sage leaves; carrots and parsnips with thyme; and thinly sliced red bell peppers with sliced new potatoes, smoky bacon, and shallots. The simplest—extra-virgin olive oil, salt, and pepper—yields pure vegetable flavor.

Vegetables cooked this way are delicious as is, as a side dish or a first course, with perhaps a few shavings of Parmigiano-Reggiano. I frequently toss them with pasta for an instant meal; their syrupy juices moisten it.

> **1 tablespoon plus 1 teaspoon flavorful fat,** such as extra-virgin olive oil, melted unsalted butter, or rendered bacon or pancetta fat (see page 681)
>
> **About 4 cups vegetables,** such as new potatoes, leeks, parsnips, carrots, Jerusalem artichokes, or artichoke hearts—peeled and sliced if necessary; whether whole or cut up, vegetables should be of uniform thickness and no more than 1 inch thick

Flavorings, singly or in combination, such as

> **2 or 3 garlic cloves,** thinly sliced
>
> **3 to 4 sprigs fresh herbs** or ¼ teaspoon dried herbs, such as thyme, rosemary, sage, or summer savory
>
> **10 Kalamata olives,** pitted (see page 683) and coarsely chopped
>
> **A sprinkling of Flavor Essence,** such as Sandy's Curry Powder (page 548) or Smoky Tea Essence (page 545)
>
> **1 strip lemon or orange zest** (removed with a vegetable peeler), cut into slivers (1 teaspoon)
>
> **3 to 4 oil-packed anchovies,** drained and coarsely chopped
>
> **2 tablespoons finely chopped shallots**

¼ to ½ teaspoon kosher salt

Freshly ground black pepper

1. Preheat the oven to 450°F.

2. Using a lightly dampened brush, brush an 18-by-26-inch piece of heavy-duty aluminum foil or parchment paper with a little of the fat, to within 2 inches of the edges. Brush the vegetables lightly with the remaining fat and place them on one half of the foil (it will be folded crosswise). Nestle the flavorings among the vegetables. Sprinkle with the salt and pepper to taste.

3. Fold the foil over the vegetables and seal the edges to form an airtight package: Beginning at one corner, fold a short length of the edges (about 1¼ inch) together. Holding this section in place, fold over the next 1½-inch section, slightly overlapping it so that it seals the first. Continue folding and crimping as you work your way to the opposite corner. Place the package on a baking sheet.

4. Roast for 12 minutes. Flip the package over and continue roasting for 10 to 15 minutes longer. Remove from the oven and let stand for 5 minutes. (If you are unsure that the vegetables are done, wrap your forefinger in a towel and press it against the packet. The vegetables should give slightly; if they are still hard, return the package to the oven and cook for 5 minutes longer.) Cut through the foil and peel it back, taking care to avoid the hot steam.

Steam-Roasting: Alternate Method. The vegetables can also be cooked in a tightly covered heavy vessel, such as an earthenware, copper, or enameled cast-iron casserole with a lid. The results will be slightly less juicy than with papillote cooking but will have the same concentrated flavor and richness. It is essential that the vegetables fit snugly in the cooking vessel, with little air space once the lid is in place.

Using a slightly dampened brush, brush the bottom of the pot with some of the fat. Add the vegetables and brush them with the remaining fat. Clamp the lid down to form a tight seal (if the lid does not fit tightly, place a sheet of foil or parchment between it and the pot and/or place a weight, such as a cast-iron skillet, on top of it). Roast as directed, adding 10 minutes to the cooking time.

an improvisation

Steam-Roasted Leeks Vinaigrette

Steam-roasted leeks are delicious dressed with a vinaigrette. Follow the Guide above, using 8 medium leeks (about 2¼ pounds). Trim off the tough leaves, leaving 1 inch of the green part. With a thin sharp knife, beginning about halfway up the leeks, split each leek lengthwise, leaving the root half intact. Rinse the leeks under cool running water, separating the leaves with your fingers to expose and rinse away any grit. Shake off the water and pat the leeks dry. In Step 2, brush each leek lightly with the fat and arrange them on the foil. Tuck 4 sprigs fresh thyme among the leeks. Sprinkle with the salt and pepper. In Step 4, roast for 11 minutes. Flip the package over and continue roasting for 11 minutes longer. Remove from the oven and let stand for 5 minutes. Serve warm, dressed with Everyday Vinaigrette (page 606) and garnished with ¼ cup chopped fresh flat-leaf parsley.

Steam-Roasted Fennel with Pancetta and Juniper

SERVES 4

Cooking fennel in foil renders the flavor milder and subtler and makes its normally fibrous texture almost creamy. Pancetta, the peppery unsmoked Italian bacon, combined with juniper berries and lemon zest, adds complexity to this simple treatment.

I particularly like to serve this as a side dish for preparations that are mildly flavored with fennel seeds, such as Rabbit Roasted with Fennel and Juniper (page 300) and Fennel-Roasted Fish (page 219). It is also wonderful tossed with pasta.

1 ounce lean pancetta or thick-sliced bacon, cut into ¼-inch dice (about ⅓ cup), or 1 tablespoon extra-virgin olive oil

2 large fennel bulbs (about 3 pounds)

3 garlic cloves, thinly sliced

4 juniper berries, crushed

½ teaspoon fennel seeds

Four 2-by-½-inch strips lemon zest (removed with a vegetable peeler), cut into thin slivers

½ teaspoon kosher salt

Freshly ground black pepper

1 to 2 teaspoons fresh lemon juice

Preheat the oven to 450°F.

In a small skillet, cook the pancetta, covered, over moderately low heat until the pancetta is crisp and has rendered its fat, about 6 minutes. Set aside.

Trim the fennel stalks to within 1 inch of the bulbs, reserving the feathery fronds. If the outsides of the bulbs are bruised or look tough, peel them with a vegetable peeler. Slice the bulbs lengthwise into ¼-inch-thick slices.

Using a lightly dampened brush, brush an 18-by-26-inch sheet of heavy-duty aluminum foil or parchment with a little of the pancetta fat. Brush the fennel slices lightly on both sides with the pancetta fat and arrange in 3 or 4 rows on one half of the foil. Scatter the garlic, juniper berries, fennel seeds, lemon zest, and the crisp pancetta over the fennel. Sprinkle with the salt and pepper to taste. Fold the foil over the fennel and seal the edges to form an airtight package: Beginning at one corner, fold a short length of the edges (about 1¼ inches) together. Holding this section in place, fold over the next 1½-inch section, slightly overlapping it so that it seals the first. Continue folding and crimping as you work your way to the opposite corner. Place the package on a baking sheet.

Roast for 15 minutes. Flip the package over and continue roasting for another 10 minutes. Remove from the oven and let stand for 5 minutes. With scissors, cut the package open and peel back the foil, taking care to avoid the hot steam. Transfer the vegetables to a serving dish and sprinkle the lemon juice over them. Serve hot or at room temperature.

You can assemble the packages up to 5 hours ahead; refrigerate.

Pancetta can be used with just about any steam-roasted vegetable, because it enhances flavor without being too forceful. You need only a small amount —about ¼ ounce per serving—a negligible amount of saturated fat and calories for such a wonderful effect.

IN ADVANCE

variation **Jerusalem Artichokes with Smoky Bacon.** Using bacon rather than pancetta infuses Jerusalem artichokes with a smoky flavor that makes them taste as though they were cooked over a wood fire. New potatoes or fingerlings and parsnips are also delicious cooked this way. Follow the Guide on pages 58 to 59, substituting 1 pound small Jerusalem artichokes, well scrubbed and cut into ¼-inch rounds (or in half if they are very small), for the fennel. Use bacon, not pancetta, and omit the garlic, juniper, fennel seeds, lemon zest, and lemon juice. Roast the package for 13 minutes on each side. Garnish with ⅓ cup chopped fresh flat-leaf parsley.

Mushrooms with Sake and Lemon

SERVES 4 Wild mushrooms take well to papillote cooking, releasing their abundant juices into a delicious broth. In this Japanese-inspired dish, the mushrooms are cooked in individual packages with sake, tamari, and lemon. A delicately aromatic steam bursts forth when the packages are opened at the table. This makes a lovely first course before a main course of Pan-Smoked Salmon (page 268) or grilled fish.

Traditionally, this dish is flavored with *yuzu*, a hauntingly fragrant Japanese citrus fruit that tastes like a cross between lemon, lime, and tangerine. If you can find real yuzu juice, available in many Japanese grocery stores, use it instead of the lemon juice and omit the tangerine zest.

> ½ **cup sake**
>
> 1½ **tablespoons tamari,** preferably reduced-sodium
>
> 1½ **tablespoons fresh lemon juice**
>
> 2 **teaspoons rice wine vinegar**
>
> 1½ **teaspoons sugar**
>
> ¼ **teaspoon grated fresh ginger**
>
> 1½ **pounds wild mushrooms,** such as shiitake, morel, oyster, or chanterelle, tough stem ends trimmed, halved or quartered to make bite-sized pieces
>
> 2 **teaspoons unsalted butter,** cut into small pieces
>
> 4 **thin lemon slices**
>
> **One 2-by-1-inch strip tangerine zest** (removed with a vegetable peeler) (optional)

Preheat the oven to 400°F.

In a small bowl, combine the sake, tamari, lemon juice, rice wine vinegar, sugar, and ginger. Stir until the sugar is dissolved. Set aside.

Place four 18-inch squares of heavy-duty aluminum foil or parchment on your work space. Turn up the edges of the foil to contain the liquid you will pour over the mushrooms. Arrange one quarter of the mushrooms on one half of each piece of the foil. Drizzle about 3 tablespoons of the sake mixture over each portion of mushrooms. Dot each with ½ teaspoon of the butter and top with a lemon slice and tangerine zest, if desired.

Fold the foil or parchment over the mushrooms and seal the edges to form an airtight package: Beginning at one corner, fold a short length of the edges (about 1¼ inches) together. Holding this section in place, fold over the next 1½-inch section, slightly overlapping it so that it seals the first. Continue folding and crimping as you work your way to the opposite corner. Repeat with the remaining foil. Place the packages on a baking sheet.

Bake for 20 minutes. Remove from the oven and let stand for 3 minutes.

Place each package on a serving plate. At the table, with scissors, cut around the edge of each package and peel back the foil, taking care to avoid the hot steam. Alternatively, let each guest open his or her package with a knife.

Mushrooms with Madeira and Shallots. Using classic French variation flavorings instead of Japanese brings out the earthiness of the mushrooms. Substitute ½ cup Madeira for the sake-tamari-ginger mixture. Use 2 tablespoons Madeira for each package, and add 1½ teaspoons minced shallots and a sprinkle of salt and pepper to each.

ON THE STOVE TOP: BRAISE- AND STEAM-SAUTÉING.

In most traditional stove-top methods of cooking vegetables, quite a bit of fat is used to make the vegetables taste good, whether to jazz up steamed vegetables or to ensure that sautéed vegetables are both tender and brown. I use techniques I call braise-sautéing and steam-sautéing—simple two-step processes done in a single non-stick pan—that make the most of vegetables' singular textures and flavors and produce leaner versions of stove-top classics. First, I braise or steam the vegetables in a small amount of liquid—either their own juices or some water or broth—which evaporates by the time they are tender. Then I sauté the softened vegetables in a little flavorful fat. A nonstick skillet is essential, for it allows you to use just enough fat to cook the vegetables without worrying about their sticking to the pan.

essential recipe

"Fried" Onions

MAKES ABOUT
2 CUPS;
SERVES 4

Panfried onions, tender and caramelized, are a greasy-spoon and steak-house favorite. To enjoy fried onions prepared with much less fat, cook the onions in a small amount of butter in a covered nonstick skillet, a process called sweating, so they release some of their juices and soften. Then remove the lid to let all that moisture evaporate, caramelizing them. Since sautéed or fried onions are called for in many recipes—in soups, stews, pasta, or as a pizza topping—this is an essential technique.

> **1½ pounds Vidalia or Bermuda onions,** peeled
> **2 teaspoons unsalted butter**
> **¾ teaspoon kosher salt**
> **½ teaspoon sugar**
> **Freshly ground black pepper**

Slice the onions in half through the stem. With a mandoline or vegetable slicer, or a thin sharp knife, cut lengthwise into ⅛-inch slices. (You should have about 6 cups.)

In a large nonstick skillet, melt the butter over moderately low heat. Add the onions, sprinkle with ½ teaspoon of the salt, and toss to coat. Cover and cook until the onions have released some liquid, about 13 minutes.

Uncover the pan, increase the heat to moderate, and cook, stirring occasionally, until the liquid has evaporated, about 10 minutes. Sprinkle the onions with the sugar and continue cooking, stirring frequently, until they are golden brown and caramelized, about 10 minutes longer. Add the remaining ¼ teaspoon salt and season generously with pepper. Serve warm.

IN ADVANCE Up to 4 hours ahead, cook the onions for the first 23 minutes, or until the liquid has evaporated. Set aside at room temperature. Ten to 15 minutes before serving, caramelize the onions. The cooked onions can be refrigerated, covered, for up to 4 days.

Peperonata

MAKES ABOUT 2 CUPS; SERVES 4 When juicy vegetables like sweet peppers and onions are cooked in a covered pan with a small amount of fat, they release their juices. In this recipe, the vegetables continue to cook slowly in the rich emulsion formed by simmering their juices with a little olive oil until they melt into a thick, creamy stew. With the flavor but far fewer calories than the classic oil-rich Italian peperonata, this is an eminently practical dish because it has so many applications. It can be served cold or hot, as a condiment, a sauce, or a stew in its own right. Spoon it onto garlic-rubbed toasted peasant bread for an hors d'oeuvre; use it as a sauce for pasta or an accompaniment for grilled seafood or chicken; serve it warm with goat cheese for a light lunch or with grilled sweet Italian sausages for a hearty dinner; fill an omelet with it; or use it as a topping on hero sandwiches or pizzas. With the addition of chicken broth, it becomes a soup.

1 tablespoon plus 1 teaspoon extra-virgin olive oil

1 large sweet onion, such as Bermuda or Vidalia (8 to 10 ounces), sliced ¼ inch thick

4 garlic cloves, thinly sliced

4 red and/or yellow bell peppers, quartered, core and white ribs removed, and sliced into ¼-inch strips

¼ **teaspoon kosher salt,** or more to taste

1 tablespoon tomato paste

3 to 4 tablespoons water

¼ **cup finely chopped fresh basil and/or flat-leaf parsley**

2 tablespoons toasted pine nuts or sliced, pitted (see page 683) **meaty black olives,** such as Kalamata

Freshly ground black pepper

Heat the oil in a large heavy skillet over moderate heat until hot but not smoking. Add the onions and garlic and sauté, stirring frequently, until the onions are just beginning to color, about 5 minutes. Stir in the peppers and salt and sauté for 1 minute longer.

Cover, reduce the heat to moderately low, and cook for 5 minutes, stirring occasionally, until the peppers have begun to soften. Uncover and cook, stirring occasionally, until the peppers are very soft, about 20 minutes. Stir in the tomato paste and water and cook for 10 minutes longer, or until the peppers are meltingly tender and most of the liquid has evaporated. (At this point, the mixture will have the consistency of a thick stew. If you continue cooking it over low heat, it will concentrate further, becoming more jam-like.) Stir in the basil, if using, pine nuts, and pepper. Serve warm or at room temperature.

IN ADVANCE The peperonata will keep for about 1 week, covered, in the refrigerator.

Braise-Sautéing Dense, Starchy Vegetables

A GUIDE TO IMPROVISING

SERVES 4

Use braise-sautéing for mixtures of root vegetables and other cut-up dense, starchy vegetables, including Jerusalem artichokes, carrots, sweet potatoes, rutabagas, burdock, parsley root, salsify, even fennel and celery.

Cooking dense, starchy vegetables like parsnips, celery root, and artichoke hearts in a mixture of fat and water deepens and mellows their flavor. Once the water has evaporated, the residual fat coats the vegetables, making it seem as if they are imbued with fat. Unlike with ordinary braises, for this you use just enough liquid so that it will evaporate by the time the vegetables are tender, leaving only the flavorful fat. Because there is no cooking liquid that must be poured off, all of the vitamins and nutrients remain in the vegetables.

I call this method braise-sautéing, because you can then take the method one step further and sauté the vegetables in the fat, caramelizing their surface to create a pleasing texture.

1 tablespoon flavorful fat, such as extra-virgin olive oil, Flavored Oil (pages 588–597), brown butter (see page 681) or rendered pancetta, bacon, goose, or duck fat (see page 681)

1 medium onion, chopped

4 cups peeled and diced (½-inch) **root vegetables,** such as parsnips, celery root, rutabagas, turnips, and artichoke hearts, in any combination

½ cup water

½ teaspoon kosher salt

Freshly ground black pepper

1. In a large nonstick skillet over moderate heat, heat 2 teaspoons of the fat. Add the onions to the skillet and cook, stirring frequently, until tender and golden brown, about 4 minutes. Add the root vegetables and toss to mix with the onions. Add the water and salt, cover, and cook until the vegetables are tender and the water has evaporated, about 12 minutes. (If the pan seems dry before the vegetables are cooked, add a couple of tablespoons of water.)

2. Add the reserved 1 teaspoon fat and cook the vegetables, uncovered, over moderately high heat, tossing frequently, until glossy and golden, about 5 minutes. If you wish, continue sautéing the vegetables, tossing them and shaking the pan frequently, until they become brown and crusty, about 5 minutes longer. Season with pepper and serve hot or at room temperature.

"Fried" Artichokes with Crispy Garlic and Sage

This is one of my favorite dishes. You start by making a simple garlic-and-sage-flavored olive oil. Then you braise sliced artichokes in the oil and water to tenderize them and imbue them with the oil. Once all the liquid has evaporated, you sauté the artichokes until a caramelized crust builds up, giving them the flavor of fried artichokes. The crispy garlic and sage—by-products from making the oil—make a delicious garnish.

Don't be daunted by the instructions for preparing the artichokes. It is really very easy. Once you get the hang of it, the whole dish takes less than 20 minutes to prepare (and it uses only a single pan).

I like to serve these artichokes as an hors d'oeuvre with drinks before dinner, sometimes with shavings of Parmigiano-Reggiano or pecorino cheese. They are delicious stirred into Classic Saffron Risotto (page 186) and they make a delicious and unexpected topping for pizza (see page 359). Or use them in composed salads and pasta dishes.

1 lemon, halved

4 medium-large artichokes

Sage and Garlic Oil

> **1 tablespoon plus 1 teaspoon fruity extra-virgin olive oil**
>
> **10 garlic cloves,** thinly sliced
>
> **15 fresh sage leaves**

½ cup water

½ teaspoon kosher salt

Freshly ground black pepper

To prepare the artichokes: Squeeze the lemon juice into a medium bowl and fill it with cold water. As you prepare the artichokes, add the wedges to the lemon water to keep them from turning brown. Trim all but 1 inch off the stem of each artichoke and pull off the green outer leaves from the base until only the pale yellow ones are left. (Discard the green leaves, or steam them to eat with a vinaigrette.) With a paring knife, pare away the tough green skin and leaf bumps off the bases of the artichokes. Halve the artichokes through the circumference, cutting off the cone of leaves. Cut the artichoke bottoms into eighths through the stem. Cut out the furry chokes and discard (cut along the line between the chokes and the hearts.

To make the sage oil, in a large nonstick skillet, combine the oil and garlic, cover, and cook over low heat, stirring frequently, until the garlic is barely golden, about 5 minutes. Uncover and cook until the garlic is crisp, about 1 minute. With a slotted spoon, transfer the garlic to a small bowl.

Add the sage leaves to the skillet and cook, turning once, until the leaves are darkened, fragrant, and crisp, 2 to 3 minutes. Add the sage leaves to the garlic. Spoon 1 teaspoon of the sage oil into a small bowl and reserve.

Drain the artichokes well and add them to the skillet, along with the water and salt; toss to coat. Cover the pan and cook over moderately high heat until most of the water has evaporated and the artichokes are tender but not mushy, about 12 minutes. (If the water evaporates too quickly, add 2 or 3 more tablespoons to the pan.)

Uncover, increase the heat to high and cook to evaporate any liquid remaining in the pan. Add the reserved teaspoon of sage oil and sauté the artichokes, tossing frequently, until slightly caramelized and browned, about 5 minutes. Add fresh pepper to taste and serve hot or at room temperature, scattering the garlic and sage over the top as a garnish.

IN ADVANCE

Up to 5 hours ahead, braise the artichokes until they are tender and all the liquid has evaporated (do not sauté). About 5 minutes before serving, sauté the artichokes. The cooked artichokes can be refrigerated, covered, for up to 3 days.

variation

Pasta with "Fried" Artichokes and Crispy Sage. For a stunning dinner party dish, follow the recipe above, using 2 tablespoons extra-virgin olive oil. Cook the artichokes as directed, but do not add the crispy garlic and sage to them. Remove the pan from the heat.

Bring a large pot of water to a boil and salt liberally. Add 8 ounces ziti, gemelli, or linguine and cook until al dente (tender but still slightly firm to the bite). Using a measuring cup, scoop out ½ cup of the cooking water. Drain the pasta.

Add the pasta water to the artichokes and bring to a boil. Boil vigorously for 30 seconds, or until the water and oil have emulsified.

Transfer the pasta to a large heated serving bowl. Spoon the artichokes over the pasta and toss to coat. Season with salt and pepper and scatter the reserved garlic and sage leaves over the top. Serve at once, passing ¼ cup grated Parmigiano-Reggiano cheese at the table.

Spring Vegetable Ragout

SERVES 4 On a glorious trip to Venice over a decade ago, I discovered the extraordinary affinity spring vegetables like baby artichokes, feathery wild asparagus, peas, leeks, and tiny onions have for each other, how their flavors can link and complement. Home again, this Venetian lesson in spring led me to devise a simple approach—half sauté, half stew—that would accommodate whatever combination of vegetables I happened to find in the farmers' market or my own inclination of the moment. Sometimes I replace the artichokes with new potatoes, or use sliced sugar snap peas if I can't find regular peas. If I am feeling lazy, I pare it down to just asparagus, leeks, and pea shoots, the tender leafy tendrils of the pea plant. Once the vegetables are prepared, the stew takes very little time to cook.

This dish is delicious as is for a first course or as a light lunch, or it can be enjoyed as a side dish; it is also wonderful tossed into pasta.

1 lemon, halved

2 medium artichokes

1 tablespoon plus 1 teaspoon extra-virgin olive oil

1 medium leek, white and tender green parts only, thinly sliced

4 garlic cloves, thinly sliced

½ teaspoon kosher salt

½ teaspoon sugar

1 cup water

1 pound pencil-thin asparagus, tough ends broken off, sliced on a diagonal into 2-inch lengths

2 ounces fresh morel mushrooms, stems trimmed, quartered or halved if large (optional)

1 cup shelled fresh peas (1 pound in the pod),
pea shoots, sugar snap peas (cut on a diagonal into thirds),
or shelled and peeled fava beans (see page 677)

⅓ cup finely chopped mixed herbs, such as chervil, flat-leaf parsley, chives, and/or (no more than 2 tablespoons) tarragon, in any combination

½ to ¾ teaspoon lemon zest (removed with a vegetable peeler), cut into fine slivers

Freshly ground black pepper

To prepare the artichokes: Squeeze the lemon juice into a medium bowl and fill the bowl with cold water. As you prepare the artichokes, add the wedges to the lemon water to keep them from turning brown. Trim all but 1 inch off the stem of each artichoke and pull off the green outer leaves from the base until you reach the pale yellow leaves. (Discard the green leaves, or steam them to eat with a vinaigrette.) With a paring knife, pare away the tough green skin and leaf bumps off the bases of the artichokes. Halve the artichokes through the circumference, cutting off the cone of leaves. Quarter the artichoke bottoms through the stem. Cut out the furry chokes and discard (cut along the line between the chokes and the hearts). Slice each quarter lengthwise into ¼-inch-thick slices.

In a large nonstick skillet set over moderately low heat, combine the olive oil, leek, and garlic. Cover and cook until the leek is softened, about 4 minutes. Add the drained artichoke hearts, ¼ teaspoon of the salt, the sugar, and ¾ cup of the water. Cover, increase the heat to high, and cook, tossing occasionally, until the artichoke hearts are crisp-tender, 8 to 10 minutes.

Add the asparagus and the remaining ¼ cup water, cover, and cook for 2 minutes, tossing the vegetables occasionally. (If the water evaporates too quickly, add a few more tablespoons.)

Add the morels, if using, and peas and cook for 2 minutes longer or until they are just tender and the water has completely evaporated. Stir in the minced herbs, lemon zest, plenty of pepper, and the remaining salt if necessary. Serve hot.

IN ADVANCE Prepare the artichokes up to 4 hours ahead and keep them in the acidulated water. If using fava beans, shell and peel them up to a day ahead and refrigerate. Prepare the remaining vegetables up to 5 hours ahead and store in plastic bags or covered containers in the refrigerator.

The ragout is also delicious at room temperature or warm, but its flavor and color will remain fresh for only 24 hours in the refrigerator. To reheat, toss in a medium nonstick skillet over moderate heat with a tablespoon or two of water.

Cabbage Braised with Smoky Ham and Riesling

SERVES 4

This recipe is a takeoff on the traditional French approach, in which cabbage is braised with quantities of smoked bacon, butter, and wine. Here, ham provides rich smoky flavor with far less fat than the traditional bacon. When simmered in tandem with slightly sweet wine, it makes a perfect liquid for braising cabbage, mellowing into a delicious cold-weather side dish. (Unlike the other recipes in this chapter, for this one the liquid is not evaporated.) The cabbage goes particularly well with rich meats like pork, game birds, and confit and makes an excellent base for choucroute.

If you happen to have some rendered duck or goose fat, a small amount will do wonders.

> **1 tablespoon extra-virgin olive oil or rendered duck or goose fat** (see page 681)
>
> **2 medium onions,** chopped medium-fine
>
> **2 cups Riesling, Gewürztraminer, or other mildly sweet, spicy white wine**
>
> **6 ounces lean smoked ham,** cut into 1½-inch chunks
>
> **1½ teaspoons fresh thyme leaves** or ½ teaspoon dried thyme
>
> **Pinch of red pepper flakes**
>
> **1 medium white cabbage** (about 2 pounds), preferably Savoy, halved, cored, and cut into thin strips or coarsely shredded
>
> **1 teaspoon kosher salt**
>
> **Freshly ground black pepper**
>
> **1 to 2 teaspoons vinegar:** Champagne, white wine, or cider (optional)

In a large flameproof casserole set over moderately low heat, combine the oil and onions. Cover and cook, stirring occasionally, until the onions are very soft, about 10 minutes. Add the wine, ham, thyme, and pepper flakes and bring to a simmer; cook for 5 minutes. Stir in the cabbage, salt, and black pepper to taste. Cover and simmer for 10 minutes.

Rearrange the cabbage and cook until it is tender but not mushy, about 30 minutes. Remove the ham and discard. Stir in the vinegar, if desired.

IN ADVANCE

Up to 1 day ahead, shred the cabbage; seal it in a plastic bag and refrigerate. The finished dish will keep for up to 1 week in the refrigerator.

Steam-Sautéing Green Vegetables

A GUIDE TO IMPROVISING

This recipe outlines a simple way to cook green vegetables such as green beans, broad beans, asparagus, broccoli florets, broccoli rabe, and snap peas, which benefit from a slightly different treatment from braise-sautéing. I call it steam-sautéing because the vegetables are first steamed in a small amount of water in a covered nonstick skillet to tenderize them. Then, once the liquid has totally evaporated, you tilt the pan and add a little fat, such as olive oil or butter, and whatever flavorings you want—minced garlic and chopped herbs, for example—so that they quickly fry in the pool of hot fat. To finish, you toss the vegetables in this flavorful fat, adding a little water to emulsify with the fat and gloss the vegetables.

SERVES 4

Green vegetables, such as

> **1½ pounds green beans or wax beans,** stemmed, **broad beans,** cut into 1-inch lengths, **or broccoli rabe or broccoli florets**

> **2 pounds asparagus,** tough stem ends broken off and cut on a diagonal into 2-inch pieces, **or sugar snap peas,** stemmed and stringed

½ teaspoon kosher salt

⅓ cup water

2 teaspoons flavorful fat, such as extra-virgin olive oil, Flavored Oil (pages 588–597), Asian sesame oil, roasted hazelnut or walnut oil, unsalted butter, or rendered pancetta or bacon fat (see page 681)

1 teaspoon minced fresh garlic or shallot (optional)

Fresh herbs (optional), such as

> **1 teaspoon minced savory, thyme, or rosemary**

> **2 to 4 tablespoons coarsely chopped mint, basil, chervil, or flat-leaf parsley**

Freshly ground black pepper

1. In a large nonstick skillet set over high heat, combine the vegetables, salt, and water. Cover and steam the vegetables, rearranging them occasionally, until they are crisp-tender and the water has evaporated, 5 to 8 minutes. (Check the vegetables periodically; if the water is evaporating too quickly, add a few more tablespoons.) If there is still too much water by the time the vegetables are tender, pour it off, holding the vegetables in the pan with the lid.

2. Push the vegetables to one side of the pan. Pour the fat into the empty side, sprinkle the garlic and/or herbs, if desired, into the fat, and let frizzle for a few seconds. Push the vegetables back into the fat and toss them well to coat. Continue tossing the vegetables until any water that is left on them has completely evaporated and they are glossed with a thin slick of fat; if they seem too dry, add a tablespoon or two of water to bind with the fat and coat the vegetables. Season with pepper, add salt if necessary, and serve at once.

SEASONING STEAM-SAUTÉED GREEN VEGETABLES

Although steam-sautéed vegetables are delicious unadorned, fresh herbs greatly enhance their flavor and are an easy way to improvise. Strong aromatic herbs such as rosemary, thyme, and savory have a particular affinity for fresh beans. Mint is wonderful with snap or shelled peas. Basil, flat-leaf parsley, chervil, and chives go with just about everything. Cilantro adds a more exotic Asian note when paired with roasted sesame oil.

The fat you choose also alters the character of the dish. The range is broad, from butter and extra-virgin olive oil to rendered pancetta and bacon fats to flavored oils or nut oils. One of my favorite ways to dress asparagus, for example, is with a good roasted hazelnut oil. And I keep Chinese Five-Flavor Oil (page 594) on hand in the frigerator to make instant Chinese-style vegetables.

Dark leafy greens like spinach, kale, and collards are astonishingly sat-isfying and healthful. They are a great source of beta carotene, vitamin C, iron, calcium, and dietary fiber and are extremely low in calories. Many cooks, however, use a lot more fat to cook greens than is really neces-sary—either to smooth out the strong flavor of bitter greens or to com-pensate for their being a bit watery—thus outweighing their healthy, low-calorie benefits. The following techniques for preparing tender young greens and mature greens will show you how to cook delectable healthful greens.

There is an endless array of greens you can sauté: spinach, mizuna, kale, turnip, chard, mustard, beet, collard, tatsoi, and chicory, with new greens appearing daily in the market. I often surprise my guests by serving arugula or watercress—usually thought of as salad greens—that I have sautéed in garlicky olive oil or pancetta. Their peppery flavors take well to cooking. You can also sauté combinations of greens; the key is to choose those that require the same amount of cooking time. Tender and mature greens cook differently and shouldn't be mixed.

How to Tell If Greens Are Tender or Mature. Mature greens tend to have large tough leaves. If you break off a piece and chew it, it will be leathery; it clearly needs to be cooked. Some mature greens, like dandelion and mustard, will be unpleasantly bitter even if they are not especially tough. Mature greens should be steamed or boiled briefly in water before cook-ing them (see page 75).

Tender greens tend to be smaller and more delicate and supple. If you break off a piece of a leaf and chew it, you will find you could eat the greens raw. Tender greens cook quickly and need no blanching.

To Clean Greens. To clean greens, pull off the stems, breaking them off at the leaf. Rinse the greens in several changes of water to remove all grit and spin dry in a salad spinner. To store, wrap them in damp paper towels, seal in a plastic bag, and refrigerate for up to 4 days.

A 1-pound bunch of greens will yield ½ to ⅔ pound cleaned greens.

Tender Greens Sautéed with Garlic and Olive Oil

MAKES 4 CUPS; SERVES 4

You can also use this method for mature greens that you have steamed, cooled down, and dried (page 75). Add them to the flavored oil, cover, and cook until tender, 3 to 5 minutes; then sauté.

This method works well for tender greens such as spinach, chard, arugula, watercress, mizuna, baby beet, and young dandelion or kale leaves, which wilt so quickly in the pan that they require no preliminary cooking. Once they are wilted, I toss-sauté them with olive oil that has been flavored with garlic and hot pepper flakes, a play on a classic Italian treatment for greens.

Greens cooked this way make an excellent side dish and are also great cold, with a squeeze of lemon. I sometimes use them as a bed for Warm Goat Cheese (page 451) or toss them with pasta with a few pine nuts and some shaved Parmigiano-Reggiano for an instant meal. They also make a wonderful topping for bruschetta, alone or with a thin slice of ricotta salata.

Caramelized Garlic Oil

1 tablespoon plus 2 teaspoons extra-virgin olive oil

6 garlic cloves, thinly sliced

Pinch of red pepper flakes

2 pounds tender greens, tough stems discarded, rinsed and dried in a salad spinner

Kosher salt and freshly ground black pepper

Lemon wedges for serving

To make the garlic oil, heat the oil in a large nonstick skillet or heavy flameproof casserole over moderately low heat. Add the garlic and pepper flakes, cover, and cook until the garlic is soft, translucent, and just beginning to brown. Remove the garlic with a slotted spoon and reserve.

Increase the heat to high, add the greens and a pinch of salt, and sauté, tossing with two wooden spoons, until the greens are wilted. If the greens don't wilt almost immediately, add 1 tablespoon water and cover the pan to steam them briefly until they are wilted; uncover and increase the heat to evaporate any water, then sauté. Season to taste with salt and pepper, scatter the reserved garlic over the greens, and serve at once, with lemon wedges on the side.

Sautéed Greens with Currants and Pine Nuts. Sautéed variation spinach and Swiss chard are mixed with pine nuts and raisins all along the Mediterranean coast, reflecting the Arab cultures that came there. Here is an embellishment of the recipe on page 74, using currants instead of the traditional raisins because they are smaller and give more "hits" of flavor. Pour ¼ cup boiling water over ¼ cup currants in a small bowl and set them aside to plump for 15 minutes. Drain well. Roast the pine nuts to bring out their flavor (see page 676) or leave them unroasted if pressed for time; set aside to cool.

Reduce the garlic in oil to 3 cloves. Sauté the greens as directed above. When all the moisture has evaporated, stir in ¼ cup pine nuts, the currants, and garlic. Season and serve with the lemon wedges.

Greens Sautéed with Chinese Five-Flavor Oil. When I am variation feeling lazy, I use Chinese Five-Flavor Oil (page 594), which I keep on hand in my fridge as an instant seasoning. Replace the garlic oil with an equal amount of the five-flavor oil.

Mature Greens with Bacon and Balsamic Vinegar

I use this method with mature greens such as dandelion, kale, turnip, mustard, SERVES 4 and collards that need special handling to tenderize them and to sweeten and soften their often overly bitter or peppery flavor. First, steam them, drain and cool them, and dry them in a salad spinner. Then braise the greens in a small amount of bacon or pancetta fat (along with the crisp bits of bacon or pancetta) to enhance and mellow their flavor. (Greens have an affinity with all manner of pork products.) A splash of sweet balsamic vinegar at the very end adds a sweet/sour counterpoint to the greens.

The greens are equally good hot or at room temperature. When cooked in pancetta fat, they are delicious on pasta.

> **2 pounds mature greens,** tough stems discarded, rinsed and drained
> **1 ounce lean thick-sliced bacon or pancetta,** cut into ¼-inch pieces (scant ¼ cup)
> **Kosher salt and freshly ground black pepper**
> **¼ cup balsamic vinegar**

To steam and dry the greens: Arrange a steamer rack in the bottom of a large pot and add 1½ inches of water. Bring to a boil over high heat. Add the greens, cover tightly, and steam, rearranging once or twice, until they are wilted, 1 to 2 minutes. Test a leaf to see if it is fairly tender. If not, continue cooking for 1 to 2 minutes longer. Alternatively, you can cook the greens in a large pot of salted water, then drain them well. Using tongs, transfer the greens to a bowl and rinse under cold running water until they are cool. Drain well and spin dry in a salad spinner. If you don't have a salad spinner, gather the greens into a ball and squeeze out as much water as you can. Blot dry with paper towels, then unfurl the greens with your fingers.

In a large heavy flameproof casserole or nonstick skillet, cook the bacon, covered, over moderately low heat, stirring occasionally, until it has rendered its fat and is crisp, about 8 minutes. Increase the heat to high and add the greens and a pinch of salt. Cover and cook until the greens are tender, 3 to 5 minutes. Remove the lid, reduce the heat to moderate, and cook until any liquid has evaporated, about 2 minutes. Reduce the heat to low and cook for 1 minute longer to mellow the flavor. Generously pepper, adjust the salt as necessary, and transfer the greens to a warm platter.

Add the balsamic vinegar to the pan and boil down to about 1 tablespoon. Drizzle over the greens and serve.

ON THE STOVE TOP: MASHES AND PUREES. Mashed potatoes and other vegetable purees are among the most beloved of side dishes and among the easiest to make. Although they seem quite innocent, more often than not they are a vehicle for butter and cream; it is easy to keep adding more of these fattening enrichments as you mash, for they just seem to disappear in the starchy puree. However, I use other simple techniques that accentuate the naturally creamy properties of vegetables, adding butter or other delicious fats only at the end.

Buttermilk Mashed Potatoes

essential recipe

SERVES 4

For charmingly lumpy potatoes with their skins, boil scrubbed new potatoes or finger-lings in their skins and use a fork or hand masher to mash them coarsely.

This is my favorite mashed potato recipe, which I use as a base for the more sophisticated embellishments that follow. These mashed potatoes taste as if they contain a great deal more fat than they do. I use buttermilk to mash the potatoes because it has a natural creaminess yet is far lower in fat than milk or cream, and I add a small amount of butter at the end, only after the potatoes have absorbed the liquid. The butter stays on the surface of the potatoes, its flavor readily discernible, imparting a truly rich finish.

Be sure to use fine-textured, thin-skinned potatoes like Yellow Finns or Yukon Golds, which become extremely creamy when mashed. If made with baking potatoes, the result will be grainy and watery.

> 1¼ **pounds thin-skinned potatoes,** such as Yellow Finns or Yukon Golds, peeled and cut into 2-inch chunks if large
>
> 1½ **teaspoons kosher salt**
>
> ¾ **cup buttermilk,** warmed (not hot)
>
> 1 **tablespoon unsalted butter**
>
> **Freshly ground black pepper**

Place the potatoes and 1 teaspoon of the salt in a medium saucepan, add enough water to cover, and bring to a boil over high heat. Reduce the heat to moderate and simmer until the potatoes are tender when pierced with a fork, about 45 minutes. Drain, reserving ¼ cup of the cooking water.

Return the potatoes to the pan and set over low heat, uncovered, for about 5 minutes, stirring occasionally, to let the potatoes dry out a little (too much moisture will dilute their flavor). For the smoothest potatoes, pass them through a food mill. For a slightly coarser puree, mash them with a potato masher or fork or use a hand mixer. Beat the buttermilk into the potatoes with a wooden spoon until thoroughly incorporated. If you prefer even creamier potatoes, add a little of the reserved cooking liquid. Beat in the butter, the remaining ½ teaspoon salt, and plenty of pepper. Serve at once, or keep the potatoes warm, covered, in a double boiler over hot water for up to 1 hour.

IN ADVANCE   You can make the potatoes up to 3 hours ahead. About 20 minutes before serving, warm them in a double boiler, stirring frequently, until hot.

improvisation 1   ## Mashed Potatoes Seasoned with Fragrant Oil

You can use other fats instead of butter to flavor the potatoes. Fruity extra-virgin olive oil or Flavored Oil (pages 588–597), such as Rosemary or White Truffle Oil, would be delicious. In the Southwest of France, fine roasted walnut oil is often stirred into mashed potatoes at the very last minute for a surprising effect. Use 4 teaspoons oil, blending half into the potatoes and drizzling the rest on top.

improvisation 2   ## Basil Mashed Potatoes

These fragrant, delicately flavored pale green potatoes go especially well with seafood, poultry, and lamb and veal. In a mortar, pound 30 medium fresh basil leaves with ¼ teaspoon kosher salt to a fine paste, adding 1 tablespoon extra-virgin olive oil. Alternatively, you can make the puree in a blender to give it a finer texture. Omit the butter and stir the puree into the finished mashed potatoes.

improvisation 3   ## Roasted Garlic Mashed Potatoes

These are profoundly earthy potatoes. Stir ¼ to ½ cup Roasted Garlic Puree (page 38), made from 1 to 2 heads of garlic, into the potatoes with the buttermilk. For an unusual flavor, add about 1 teaspoon ground coriander, toasted in a dry skillet until fragrant.

improvisation 4   ## Smashed Potatoes with Crushed Black Olives

Mash the potatoes coarsely with a fork so that they are still very lumpy. Substitute 1 tablespoon fruity extra-virgin olive oil for the butter. Stir in ½ cup coarsely chopped or crushed pitted black olives, such as Niçoise, Kalamata, or Gaeta.

Horseradish Mashed Potatoes

improvisation 5

Mashed potatoes are sensational prepared with fresh horseradish, which is pungent and hot. The ugly gnarled root, available at greengrocers and some supermarkets, has a distinct slightly turnipy flavor that goes particularly well with roast beef, steaks, and roast chicken. Prepared horseradish, which is preserved in vinegar, produces an unpleasantly insipid version that is not worth the effort.

Peel a 2-inch chunk of fresh horseradish. Grate it as finely as possible. Stir 2 tablespoons, or more, into the finished potatoes.

Wasabi Mashed Potatoes

improvisation 6

Wasabi, often called Japanese horseradish, is a greenish powder that is made into a paste to accompany sushi. Wasabi has a biting, somewhat herbal flavor and a surprising heat that creeps up slowly but can hit your nose in the same sinus-clearing way as does regular horseradish. Potatoes flavored with wasabi are wonderful with any Japanese-style preparation, such as Pan-Smoked Rare Tuna (page 268), Miso-Sake–Glazed Fish Fillets and Steaks (page 236), or teriyaki.

In a small bowl, combine about 1½ tablespoons wasabi powder with 1½ tablespoons hot water (or reserved potato cooking water). Stir to make a paste. Add 1 tablespoon to the potatoes, taste, and add more, if desired.

Sorrel Mashed Potatoes

improvisation 7

Sorrel is a leafy herb available most often in the spring and summer that has a tart, lemony "green" flavor. These potatoes are especially good with fish and poultry dishes.

Cut the stems off 12 ounces sorrel leaves and wash in several changes of water; spin dry in a salad spinner. Coarsely chop. In a medium heavy saucepan, melt the butter over moderate heat. Add the sorrel, cover, and cook, stirring frequently, until wilted. Uncover, reduce the heat to low, and cook, stirring, until most of the watery juices have evaporated and the sorrel has "melted" into a thick puree. Stir in salt to taste. Remove from the heat and allow to cool slightly. Stir the puree, to taste, into the finished potatoes.

Mashed Potatoes Flavored with Aged Cheese

improvisation 8

Any pungent, hard aged cheese is delicious in mashed potatoes: Its flavor is so concentrated that a little goes a long way. Grate about ⅓ cup of any of the following: aged Gouda or Dry Jack cheese, Manchego, Parmigiano-Reggiano, pecorino Romano, or goat cheese, such as Crottin de Chavignol. Beat the cheese into the potatoes with the buttermilk.

Mashed Potatoes and Root Vegetables

improvisation 9

I often substitute root vegetables like parsnips, celery roots, rutabagas, or parsley roots, either singly or in combination, for up to half the potatoes. Peel the root vegetables and cut both the potatoes and root vegetables into 1-inch chunks. Cook as directed in the Guide above, until tender, about 50 minutes; reserve ¾ cup of the cooking liquid. Substitute the reserved cooking liquid for the buttermilk and increase the butter by 1½ teaspoons.

Milkless, Creamless, Butterless Mashed Potatoes

improvisation 10

These potatoes are for those souls who cannot have any dairy products; they are delicious. Omit the buttermilk and butter. While the potatoes are cooking, combine 2 tablespoons fruity extra-virgin olive oil, 1 small garlic clove, thinly sliced, and 2 teaspoons minced fresh rosemary or sage in a small skillet, cover, and cook over low heat until the garlic is translucent and just turning golden and the herbs are very fragrant. Remove from the heat and set aside.

Drain the potatoes, reserving 1 cup of the cooking liquid, and mash them with a potato masher or fork until fairly smooth, or pass them through a food mill. Beat in enough of the cooking water to make a creamy puree, then beat in 1 tablespoon of the herb oil and salt and pepper to taste. Drizzle the rest of the oil over the top.

Celery Root and Apple Puree

Cooking watery or fibrous root vegetables like celery roots, turnips, carrots, rutabagas, and beets with a little white rice ensures that they will be exceptionally creamy and have a very pure flavor. The apples enhance and sweeten the vegetables. This puree tastes as if it has a lot of cream or butter. The technique comes from chef Michel Guérard.

SERVES 4

This recipe can be doubled or tripled. Do not double or triple the amount of milk, though—use just enough to cover the celery root by 1½ inches.

1 pound celery root, peeled and cut into 1-inch chunks

3 cups low-fat (2%) **milk** (2 cups will be left over for another use)

¾ teaspoon kosher salt

Freshly ground black pepper

2½ tablespoons white rice

2 small McIntosh apples (about 8 ounces total), peeled, cored, and quartered, or 1 small pear, peeled, quartered, and cored

2 teaspoons unsalted butter

Place the celery root in a medium saucepan, add the milk, ½ teaspoon of the salt, and a grinding or two of pepper, and bring to a boil over moderate heat. Stir in the rice, lower the heat, partially cover, and simmer for 10 minutes. Add the apples and simmer for 10 minutes longer, or until the celery root is very tender. (The milk will curdle, but the curds will be incorporated when the celery root is pureed.) Drain the mixture in a colander set over a bowl; save the cooking liquid.

In a food processor, puree the celery root mixture for 1 to 2 minutes, until perfectly smooth, adding a tablespoon or two of cooking liquid if necessary. (Save the remaining flavorful liquid for soup; it can be frozen.) Process for several minutes more, scraping down the sides several times, until you have a fine puree. Season with the remaining ¼ teaspoon salt and pepper to taste. Add the butter and process to blend.

You can make the puree several hours ahead and reheat it (or keep it warm), stirring frequently, in a covered double boiler.

IN ADVANCE

variation **Mashed Turnips with Crispy Shallots.** You can use the same method to make a delightful puree of turnips or rutabagas. Substitute white turnips or rutabagas for the celery root and use only 1 apple, cut into ½-inch dice. Season the puree with a few gratings of nutmeg and just before serving, sprinkle with Crispy Shallots (page 48).

Fresh Corn "Polenta"

SERVES 4 This simple, surprising side dish has the texture of an ethereal polenta and the pure taste of fresh corn. Instead of the surfeit of butter—3 tablespoons per serving—this polenta is usually made with, I use a couple of tablespoons of heavy cream and some grated Parmigiano-Reggiano to bind with the natural creaminess of the grated corn. This is best made with tender summer corn, whose kernels have not developed as much fibrous starch as stored corn does.

> 6 large ears corn
> ¼ cup water
> 2 tablespoons heavy cream
> ⅓ cup freshly grated Parmigiano-Reggiano cheese
> Kosher salt and freshly ground black pepper

Pull the husks off the corn and remove any silk that still clings. Place a box grater on a large baking sheet or in a large bowl. Using the side with the largest holes, grate the corn kernels until you reach the cob. You should have about 2½ cups.

Heat a large nonstick skillet over moderate heat. Add the grated corn and water. Simmer until all the liquid is absorbed and the mixture has become very thick, about 6 minutes. Stir in the heavy cream, cheese, and salt and pepper to taste. Serve at once or keep warm in a double boiler until ready to serve.

IN ADVANCE You may prepare the polenta, without the cheese and seasoning, up to a day ahead and store it, covered, in the refrigerator. Before serving, heat over low heat in a heavy saucepan or double boiler; stir in the cheese and salt and pepper.

Chestnut Puree with Fennel Seed

Chestnuts make an extraordinarily rich puree due to their very finely textured starch. Despite the "nut" in the name, they contain very little fat. Although I adore this puree, peeling fresh chestnuts is such a time-consuming job, I probably wouldn't make it as often as I do if I couldn't use prepared chestnuts. I use bottled vacuum-packed chestnuts (available in gourmet shops and some supermarkets) or frozen peeled chestnuts, when they are available. Scented with fennel and bay leaf, this puree makes a wonderful accompaniment to game, chicken, and pork dishes.

To use fresh chestnuts for this puree, follow the method on page 684 for roasting and peeling chestnuts, then proceed as directed.

> 1 teaspoon extra-virgin olive oil
>
> 2 large shallots, finely chopped (½ cup)
>
> ½ teaspoon fennel seeds
>
> 1 pound peeled chestnuts
>
> A ½-ounce chunk lean dry-cured ham or prosciutto
>
> 1 small imported bay leaf
>
> 2 cups unsalted homemade (page 574) or canned low-sodium chicken broth
>
> 1 tablespoon heavy cream or crème fraîche (optional)
>
> Kosher salt and freshly ground black pepper

In a medium saucepan over low heat, combine the olive oil and shallots. Cover and cook, stirring occasionally, until they are softened, about 5 minutes. Uncover, and cook slowly until the shallots are golden, 5 minutes longer. Stir in the fennel seeds and cook for 1 minute more. Add the chestnuts, ham, bay leaf, and chicken broth. Cover and simmer until the chestnuts are falling apart, 30 to 45 minutes. Discard the ham and bay leaf.

Process the mixture in a food processor until perfectly smooth, at least 1½ minutes. Stir in the heavy cream, if desired. Season with salt and pepper to taste.

IN ADVANCE The puree will keep, covered, in the refrigerator for up to 3 days. Before serving, heat in a medium saucepan over low heat, adding a little chicken broth or water to return it to the correct consistency.

Simply cooked "gigantes," giant lima beans (page 92), served with Greek Garlic Sauce (page 623) and roasted beets (page 683)

BEANS

AND OTHER LEGUMES

Like many American kids, I knew of legumes only through baked beans New England–style—sweet as molasses and rich with salt pork—and the dreary three-bean salads served at school. It wasn't until I started to travel, first to Latin America and then to France, Italy, and Spain, that I began to understand the profound role beans and other legumes like peas and lentils play in the cooking of other cultures. I tasted beans in elaborate casseroles layered with sausages and cured meats, stewed in rich mole sauces, in thick earthy soups, and in their simplest and most dazzling form, the season's first shell beans drizzled with fine olive oil.

These delicious creations owe their being to the eminent practicality of beans: They are an easy-to-grow, inexpensive source of protein and fiber, high in complex carbohydrates and B vitamins. A dense concentration of nutritious calories, they provided excellent fuel for hard-working people. Since they are rather bland and starchy by nature, they were traditionally dressed with quite a bit of fat, a sustaining fuel for what was then an agricultural way of life.

The abundance of calories in bean dishes is, for the most part, no longer viable for the way we live now. The question becomes how to cut down the usual amounts of fat without sacrificing the deliciousness of those traditional, healthful dishes. The answer is to start by choosing recently dried, quality beans, peas, and lentils that you can count on having good flavor and a creamy texture. Then build more flavor into the beans while enhancing their natural creaminess so that you will need only a small amount of fat. The recipes in this chapter run the gamut from Mediterranean to Mexican to Moroccan to Indian. View them all as models in which you can substitute many kinds of beans, peas, or lentils to get to know the world of flavors they offer.

BEANS, PEAS, LENTILS: THE BASICS. The following is a very brief guide to the most readily available types of dried legumes and general ways to approach cooking them. But I urge you to experiment with the multitude of less familiar legumes— from Catalunya's firm yet utterly creamy and alluring *monjetas* to the mottled beige-and-brown sweet and meaty cousin of the Italian borlotti called Tongues of Fire; the rich, winy, brown-speckled hybrid called rattlesnake, whose pods twist like a snake; or the pearly White Aztec, said to have been cultivated by both Aztecs and Anasazi of the southwestern high plains, with its subtle, herbaceous flavor.

Search out a source for *fresh* dried beans, peas, and lentils that were harvested and dried a few months ago, rather than years, as is sometimes the case with many supermarket varieties. This is, in fact, easy to do. There are interesting just-harvested varieties at local farmers' markets in the fall with evocative names like China yellow, European soldier, Calypso, scarlet emperor, Appaloosa, Jacob's cattle. Each has its own character, as you can discover by cooking them simply and tasting them. You can search out beans when you travel, for each country seems to have local favorites. (It is permissible to bring dried legumes into the United States from abroad.) Beans are so beloved in Spain there are whole stands devoted to them in local markets, each kind labeled with its place of origin.

Generally speaking, reddish beans that turn brown when cooked, such as kidney, red, scarlet runner, pinto, cranberry, and pink beans, have a rather earthy flavor and a mealy texture and are best suited for long, slow baking or stews like chili, rather than soups.

White beans, such as Great Northern, baby lima, navy (or pea), and cannellini beans, have a creamier, softer texture and milder flavor that takes well to a greater variety of flavorings and treatments. Because of their pale color, they contrast with most other ingredients, so they make a more striking presentation.

Chickpeas (garbanzo beans) have a unique nut-like flavor and somewhat crunchy texture that is particularly well suited to assertive flavorings and complex spicings, such as those of the Middle East and Morocco.

Flageolets are a pale green bean much loved in France, where they are often served as an accompaniment to roast lamb. Their flavor is a cross between white beans and fresh fava beans.

There are several varieties of lentils. Most Americans are familiar with the homely disk-shaped brown lentil. Tiny dark green lentilles du Puy from France are perhaps the most prized lentils. They hold their shape when cooked and have a less grainy texture than brown lentils, and their flavor is superb. Tiny split red lentils are used in Indian cooking. They fall apart upon cooking into a thick puree and have a delicate sweet flavor. Unlike most other legumes, lentils cook very quickly, so they can be used at a moment's notice.

Black-eyed peas are one of the most delicious dried beans, with an earthy pea-like flavor that takes well to hearty embellishments, especially smoky pork products and greens. Unlike split peas, they hold their shape when cooked. At certain times of the year, you can buy frozen black-eyed peas. If you've never tasted them before they have been dried, try them. They are much less starchy, with a sweet, fresh flavor.

Split fava beans, large flat beans with their problematic tough skins removed, are a staple of Middle Eastern cooking. They are delicious—with a flavor reminiscent of fresh peas—and quick-cooking.

See Sources, page 711, for sources of specialty beans.

1 pound dried beans (2 cups) = about 6 cups cooked, eight ¾-cup servings

1 pound dried beans, cooked = three 14½-ounce cans beans, drained

One 14½-ounce can beans = about 2 cups

Dried Beans Versus Canned. Home-cooked beans are always preferable to canned beans. Home-cooked beans retain subtle nuances of flavor that are lost in canned beans. They also have a firmer texture—and much less salt. Another advantage of cooking beans from scratch is that you can add any flavorings you want while they cook.

Canned beans do work well if the flavorings you add are assertive enough to mask the slightly overboiled taste that comes from the canning process. Be aware, however, that some brands of beans are so overprocessed they are too soft to withstand further cooking without falling apart. In my experience, Goya canned beans have the best texture and flavor. Be sure to rinse canned beans well under cold water to remove the salty cooking liquid.

Soaking and Salting Beans, Peas, and Lentils. There is an ongoing dispute about the best way to cook beans (whether or not to soak them before cooking, whether adding salt to the beans too early in the cooking toughens the skin, etc.). In cooking, there are few absolutes. When I conducted my own bean-cooking tests, I found that soaking before cooking did yield a slightly creamier bean with a more tender skin. This is especially helpful in cooking beans whose age you don't know, for older beans tend to be tougher. Soaking beans for at least 5 hours will cut the cooking time by about one third. Flageolets and tiny beans such as rice beans and green and brown lentils cook very quickly and need no soaking. If you are not able to soak your beans for 5 hours, use the quick-soak method: Bring the beans, and water to cover generously, to a boil, turn off the heat, and let them sit, covered, for an hour or two. Or simply cook them longer.

Adding salt early seemed to toughen some beans and not others. So I stay with salting them halfway through the cooking time.

As to whether soaking the beans and pouring off the soaking water reduces flatulence, there is no evidence at all that this is true. The problem of flatulence has to do with having the intestinal flora to handle them, not with how they are cooked. So cook the beans in their soaking water, which has a lot of bean flavor, or drain them if you wish.

Finally, the key to the proper cooking of legumes is not to boil them, which would burst their skin, but to cook them slowly at a bare simmer.

Cutting Down the Salt. Because beans are so starchy, they usually require quite a bit of salt to bring out their flavor. To cut down the amount of salt, add a fresh chile pepper or red pepper flakes to the cooking liquid. This adds a piquancy that sharpens the flavors without obvious hotness.

COMBINING BEANS, PEAS, AND LENTILS WITH GRAINS TO MAKE A COMPLETE PROTEIN

Although legumes are an excellent source of protein, that protein is usually incomplete; that is, it lacks one or more of the eight essential amino acids the body needs to utilize protein completely. Pairing legumes with grains or a small amount of poultry, meat, eggs, or dairy products like yogurt or cheese, which provide the missing amino acids, is a simple way to complete their protein and boost their nutritional value. This can be as simple as serving a bean dish with bread or rice.

Simple ways to turn bean recipes into complete-protein meals:

Red Lentil Stew with Caramelized Onions (page 104), served on **Foolproof Basmati Rice** (page 178) and topped with a dollop of yogurt

White Beans and Mellowed Garlic with Rosemary Oil (page 102), mashed and served on **Rustic Garlic Toasts** (page 368) to make bruschetta

Hummus (page 101), served with warm pita breads or lavash crackers

Tuscan Beans with Sage and Garlic (page 96), topped with shavings of Parmigiano-Reggiano cheese and served with **Rustic Garlic Toasts** (page 368) or slices of **Panfried Polenta** (page 201)

Chickpea Stew with Saffron and Winter Squash (page 99), served with steamed couscous or with chunks of grilled or roasted chicken

EMBELLISHED COOKED BEANS, PEAS, AND LENTILS.
Once cooked, beans, peas, and lentils can be quickly embellished any number of ways, from simply adding extra-virgin olive oil or sautéing with garlic, fresh herbs, and tomatoes to rustic gratins and quick stews. (For bean salads, see pages 441–444.)

Basic Cooked Beans, Peas, and Lentils

essential recipe

MAKES ABOUT 3 CUPS; SERVES 4

As a rule of thumb, dried beans triple in volume when cooked; 8 ounces (1 cup) dried beans will yield 3 cups cooked.

This is a basic method for cooking legumes in water with classic aromatics—onion, garlic, bay leaf, and thyme—which enhance the beans' own natural flavor. Use it to cook any dried beans that you will dress or further flavor once cooked; for example, for salads, quick sautés, braises, or gratins. The only variable will be cooking time.

Letting the beans cool in their cooking liquid saturates them with flavor, not fat. Then, when you add a little fat to the drained beans, it will gloss the outside of the beans, and its flavor will remain apparent.

This recipe can be doubled.

> **8 ounces** (1 cup) **dried beans, peas, or lentils**
>
> **1 small onion or 1 large shallot,** peeled and stuck with 2 whole cloves
>
> **2 garlic cloves,** unpeeled, lightly smashed
>
> **½ serrano or jalapeño chile,** seeded and deribbed, or ⅛ teaspoon red pepper flakes
>
> **3 to 4 fresh thyme sprigs** or ½ teaspoon dried
>
> **1 imported bay leaf**
>
> **½ teaspoon kosher salt,** or to taste

Place the beans in a large saucepan, add enough cool water to cover by 1½ inches, and soak overnight at room temperature. (Peas and lentils do not need to be soaked.)

Discard any beans that are broken, off-colored, or floating. (Or, if using peas or lentils, pick over, rinse, and place in a large scaucepan with water to cover by 1½ inches.) Add the onion, garlic, chile, thyme, and bay leaf. Bring to a boil over moderate heat, then reduce the heat to low. Cook the beans (or peas or lentils) at a bare simmer until they are just tender but not mushy—they should hold their shape; do not allow them to boil, or they will become tough. (See below for General Cooking Times for Dried Beans, Peas, and Legumes.) If necessary, replenish the water, so that it stays 1 inch above the top of the beans. Halfway through the cooking time, stir in the salt.

Remove from the heat. If you are using them right away, drain the beans, reserving the cooking liquid. Remove and discard the onion, garlic, chile, thyme sprigs, and bay leaf. If you are not using them immediately, allow the beans to cool in their cooking liquid before draining. (Keep the cooking liquid to reheat the beans or to use in many of the recipes that follow.) You can keep beans, covered and refrigerated, for up to 3 days.

GENERAL COOKING TIMES FOR DRIED BEANS, PEAS, AND LEGUMES

Dried beans come from shell beans, which are usually harvested in early fall. The beans are slipped from their pods and then laid out to dry. Beans that are within a few months of being dried cook quickly (some in as little as 30 minutes) and will have more tender skins, a creamier texture, and a discernably fresher flavor than older ones. As beans age, they lose moisture and their skins get tougher and more brittle. If they are more than two years old, they may take as long as 4 hours to cook, their tough skins never truly softening or bursting before they are tender.

The average cooking times for most beans range from 45 minutes to 1½ hours, depending on their age and size. After 30 minutes' cooking, bite into a few beans to gauge how quickly they are cooking.

If your beans are not tender by the end of the cooking time given in the recipe, just keep cooking them (at a simmer and covered), adding more water or broth as necessary to keep them covered. Unless they are extremely old, they will eventually become tender.

Creamy Versus Firm Beans. Whether or not you cover the beans while cooking will determine their texture. Beans cooked uncovered will have a firmer texture and keep their shape better, which is necessary for bean salads. Beans cooked with a lid on but slightly ajar will break down a bit and be creamier, good for thick bean soups and stews, as well as purees.

Smoky Southern-Style Beans. Southern cooks traditionally cook beans with fatty chunks of smoked pork to give them a delicious smoky, spicy flavor. However, lean smoky pork products such as country ham and tasso, the highly spiced Cajun ham from Louisiana, work just as well as fattier cuts. Add about ⅓ pound country ham or tasso, with the fat trimmed off, cut into several chunks, to the beans along with the other seasonings. Periodically skim off any foam that rises to the surface. The ham will probably have lost most of its flavor by the time the beans are cooked and should be discarded.

Ham hocks, a staple in Southern cooking, work wonderfully when cooking larger amounts of beans. (Use 1 hock per 1 to 2 pounds beans, to serve 8 to 16 people.) They have so much flavor they make a powerful cooking liquid, and the bones and collagen impart an unctuous texture to the beans. One ham hock will throw off only about 1 tablespoon of fat during the cooking. If you keep the level of the cooking liquid at least 1½ inches above the beans, and at a simmer, you can skim the fat off as it rises to the surface. If you do happen to leave the fat in, it will add at most ⅓ teaspoon, or about 11 calories, per serving (for 8 servings). Once it cools, you can pull the meat off the hock, trim off the fat, shred the meat, and mix it into the beans.

Dressing Warm Beans, Peas, or Lentils with a Flavorful Oil

A GUIDE TO IMPROVISING

SERVES 4

Beans, peas, and lentils make marvelous side dishes or beds for roasted poultry, meats, and fish. They are excellent simply tossed with extra-virgin olive oil or a flavored oil, salt, and pepper. But, because legumes are so starchy, they absorb oil like a sponge, making it necessary to add a lot of oil for its flavor to register. Tossing the drained cooked beans in an emulsion made by boiling a small amount of the oil with broth or some of the bean cooking liquid provides the same flavor with much less oil.

> **1½ to 2 tablespoons flavorful oil,** such as a fruity extra-virgin olive oil, or herb flavored oil, Saffron Oil, Roasted Garlic Oil, or Lemon Olive Oil (pages 588–593)
>
> **¼ cup liquid,** such as unsalted homemade (page 574) or low-sodium canned chicken broth, bean cooking liquid, or water
>
> **3 cups cooked beans, peas, or lentils** (page 92), drained (bean cooking liquid reserved, if possible), or canned beans, rinsed and drained well
>
> **Kosher salt and freshly ground black pepper**
>
> **¼ to ½ cup chopped fresh herbs** (optional), such as flat-leaf parsley, basil, or cilantro

In a large nonstick skillet set over low heat, combine the oil and liquid and bring to a boil. Add the drained cooked beans and toss until they are heated through and the liquid has reduced to about half, about 2 minutes. The beans will drink up the liquid and become saturated and coated with the fat. Season with salt and pepper and toss with the herbs, if using.

Tuscan Beans with Sage and Garlic

SERVES 4 In the classic Tuscan recipe *fagioli al fiasco*, beans are cooked with sage and garlic and lots of extra-virgin olive oil in a wine flask set in smoldering embers. As they absorb the oil, the beans become melting and delicious—and extremely caloric.

This adaptation employs two basic techniques for dressing starchy foods without using a lot of fat. First, frizzle sage and garlic in a small amount of olive oil to infuse the oil with intense flavor, so less is necessary. (The crisp sage and garlic make a delicious garnish.) Next, warm the beans in an emulsion of the sage-flavored oil and water, which makes a sauce that coats the beans with the oil—at only about 1½ teaspoons per serving.

Sage and Garlic Oil

2 tablespoons fruity extra-virgin olive oil

8 garlic cloves, sliced

8 large fresh sage leaves, cut on the bias into ¼-inch slices, or about 35 to 40 very small leaves left whole

¼ cup unsalted homemade (page 574) **or canned low-sodium chicken broth, bean cooking liquid, or water**

3 cups cooked white beans (page 92), drained, or canned beans, rinsed well and drained

Kosher salt and freshly ground black pepper

For the oil, in a large nonstick skillet set over low heat, combine the oil and garlic, cover, and cook until the garlic is tender and golden, about 5 minutes. With a slotted spoon, transfer the garlic to a small dish and reserve.

Add the sage leaves to the oil, increase the heat slightly, and cook until little bubbles dance around the leaves. Frizzle this way until the oil is fragrant and the sage has darkened somewhat and crisped. With the slotted spoon, transfer the leaves to the dish of garlic.

Add the chicken broth to the pan and bring to a boil. Add the beans and toss until they are heated through. Add salt and pepper to taste. Serve, scattering the reserved sage leaves and garlic over the beans.

IN ADVANCE You can prepare the dish up to 3 days ahead; cover and refrigerate. The crispy garlic and sage can be prepared and reserved for up to 8 hours; after that, stir them into the beans (they will soften and add flavor). Reheat the dish over low heat, adding a few tablespoons of water if it becomes too thick.

Beans with Pancetta and Sherry

SERVES 4

Throughout the Mediterranean region, beans are commonly cooked with a rich pork product such as cured ham or spicy sausage. In Spain, cooks often add a little dry sherry. This recipe creates an amalgam of these flavors by braising cooked beans in a quickly made broth flavored with crisp pancetta, onion, and sherry. The beans soak up flavors and once the broth evaporates, taste as if they are swathed in the pancetta fat.

You can also make this dish with dry-cured serrano ham from Spain or Italian prosciutto. Have your purveyor give you some extra fat and use 2 tablespoons each of it and the diced ham instead of the pancetta.

If you like, shave or grate ½ ounce Manchego or Parmigiano-Reggiano cheese over each serving.

> **1⅓ ounces lean pancetta or thick-sliced bacon,** cut into ¼-inch dice (about ¼ cup)
>
> **1 medium onion,** cut into ¼-inch dice
>
> **¼ cup dry sherry**
>
> **3 cups cooked beans,** such as cannellini, baby limas, or black-eyed peas (not chickpeas or lentils) (page 92), drained
>
> **½ cup water or reserved bean cooking liquid**
>
> **Kosher salt and freshly ground black pepper**
>
> **3 tablespoons chopped fresh flat-leaf parsley**
>
> **Two 2-inch strips lemon zest** (removed with a vegetable peeler), cut into slivers (optional)

In a large nonstick skillet, cook the pancetta, covered, over moderately low heat until it has rendered its fat and is crisp, about 8 minutes. Add the onions, cover, increase the heat slightly, and cook until the onions have softened and released some of their liquid, about 4 minutes. Uncover and cook, stirring frequently, until the onions turn golden brown, 5 minutes.

Add the sherry, increase the heat to moderate, and boil until almost all of it has evaporated. Add the beans and the water, cover, and cook until the water has evaporated but the beans are not dried out, about 7 minutes. (If the beans are too dry, add a tablespoon or two more water.) Season, adding lots of pepper, stir in the parsley and lemon zest, if using, and serve.

IN ADVANCE

You can prepare the dish up to 3 days ahead; cover and refrigerate. Reheat over low heat, adding a few tablespoons of water if it becomes too thick.

Flageolets with Tomatoes and Herbes de Provence

SERVES 4 Flageolets are small pale green beans prized in France for their exceptionally fine flavor, reminiscent of fresh shell beans. Like fresh green beans and favas, they have an affinity for scraggly herbs like thyme, rosemary, and savory. Scented with these herbs, tomatoes, and white wine, they make a delicate, typically Provençal stew that goes especially well with lamb. You can also make this recipe with white beans, such as navy or cannellini.

> **1 tablespoon plus 1 teaspoon extra-virgin olive oil**
>
> **1 medium onion,** finely chopped
>
> **3 garlic cloves,** finely chopped
>
> **1½ teaspoons fresh thyme leaves** or ½ teaspoon dried thyme
>
> **1½ teaspoons minced fresh savory** or ½ teaspoon dried savory
>
> **1 teaspoon minced fresh rosemary** or scant ½ teaspoon dried rosemary
>
> **½ cup dry white wine**
>
> **4 small ripe tomatoes,** seeded and chopped (drained if canned)
>
> **3 cups cooked flageolets** (page 92), drained
>
> **Kosher salt and freshly ground black pepper to taste**
>
> **1 to 2 teaspoons Champagne vinegar** (optional)
>
> **¼ cup chopped fresh flat-leaf parsley** (optional)

In a large nonstick skillet, heat 2 teaspoons of the oil over low heat. Add the onions and garlic, cover, and cook, stirring occasionally, until the onions are soft, about 4 minutes. Uncover, increase the heat slightly, and cook until the onions are golden, about 5 minutes. Stir in the thyme, savory, and rosemary and cook for 1 minute. Add the wine and simmer until it is reduced by half, about 2 minutes. Stir in the tomatoes and simmer until the juices have thickened, about 10 minutes.

Add the drained beans and simmer for 10 minutes. (If the beans become too dry, stir in a few tablespoons of the cooking liquid or water.) Season with salt and pepper to taste and stir in the vinegar, if using. Just before serving, drizzle over the remaining 2 teaspoons olive oil and garnish with the parsley, if desired.

IN ADVANCE You can prepare the dish, without the parsley, up to 3 days ahead; cover and refrigerate. Reheat over low heat, adding a few tablespoons of water if it becomes too thick.

Chickpea Stew with Saffron and Winter Squash

This hearty combination of butternut squash and chickpeas was inspired by my friend Elena Prentice, who has lived in Morocco for many years. It is good hot or at room temperature. Serve it with steamed couscous or an interesting bread to make a complete protein with the chickpeas, so no meat, poultry, or dairy is necessary.

SERVES 4

1 tablespoon olive oil

1 pound mild onions (1 large or 2 medium), cut into ⅓-inch dice (3 cups)

3 ¼ pounds butternut squash, peeled, seeded, and cut into ½-inch dice (4 cups)

¾ cup apple cider or water

3 cups cooked chickpeas (page 92), drained, **or canned chickpeas (garbanzos),** rinsed well and drained

¼ cup raisins

One 2-inch piece fresh ginger, peeled

One 1½-inch cinnamon stick

Large pinch of saffron threads (about 1 teaspoon), crumbled

½ teaspoon kosher salt

½ cup (or more) **chopped fresh cilantro**

In a large nonstick skillet, combine the oil and onions, cover, and cook over low heat, stirring occasionally, until the onions are translucent, about 20 minutes.

Add the squash, cider, chickpeas, raisins, ginger, cinnamon stick, saffron, and salt. Cover, increase the heat to moderate, and cook for 5 minutes, stirring once. Uncover and cook until the squash is very tender and the liquid has reduced enough to make a thick stew, about 10 minutes longer. Discard the ginger. Just before serving, stir in the cilantro.

IN ADVANCE

You can prepare the dish, without the cilantro, up to 3 days ahead; cover and refrigerate. Reheat over low heat, adding a few tablespoons of water if it becomes too thick.

Gratin of Beans

SERVES 8 Just about any cooked dried bean can be used to make a gratin, a shallow casserole of beans baked until they form a crust. It is a perfect way to use leftover beans, and will even work fine with drained, rinsed canned beans. My preferences are cannellini, flageolet, baby limas, and the tiny white rice beans. The beans are moistened with a rich broth, which they absorb as they cook and "melt" slightly. A sprinkling of grated Parmesan cheese becomes a crisp crust.

The gratin makes an excellent accompaniment to roasted poultry or game. Or it can be a simple supper, along with a green salad, bread, and cheese.

> **1½ cups rich meaty broth,** such as Classic Rich Poultry, Meat, or Game Broth, Shortcut Poultry, Meat, or Game Broth, Faux Veal Broth, or Hearty Porcini-Miso Broth (pages 572–576)
>
> **1 garlic clove,** cut lengthwise in half
>
> **1 teaspoon unsalted butter,** softened, or extra-virgin olive oil
>
> **6 cups cooked beans,** such as cannellini, flageolet, or baby limas (page 92), drained, **or canned beans,** rinsed well and drained
>
> **Freshly ground black pepper**
>
> **½ cup freshly grated Parmigiano-Reggiano cheese**

Preheat the oven to 400°F.

In a small heavy saucepan over high heat, bring the broth to a boil and cook until it has reduced to about 1⅓ cups, about 5 minutes.

Meanwhile, rub the inside of a 1½- to 2-quart gratin dish with the cut sides of the garlic. Allow to dry for several minutes, then rub the butter over the inside of the dish.

Add the beans to the dish, pour the broth over them, and dust liberally with pepper. Bake until the beans are very creamy and have absorbed about two thirds of the liquid, about 40 minutes.

Sprinkle the beans evenly with the cheese. Bake until the cheese is melted and golden brown, 20 to 25 minutes longer. Serve at once.

IN ADVANCE You can assemble the gratin up to 6 hours ahead; cover and refrigerate. Bring to room temperature 1 hour before baking.

Hummus (Chickpea Puree)

This revisionist hummus is lighter and fluffier than traditional versions, and each flavor is distinct. Adding toasted crushed cumin, coriander, and sesame seeds accentuates the sesame flavor of tahini and provides crackle. Serve with warm pita or another flatbread, crusty peasant bread, or with roasted beets, peppers, and eggplant.

MAKES 2½ CUPS;
SERVES 8

When flavoring beans with extra-virgin olive oil, drizzle some over the beans just before serving so that its flavor hits the palate with each bite.

1 teaspoon cumin seeds

½ teaspoon coriander seeds

1 tablespoon sesame seeds

3 cups cooked chickpeas (page 92), drained, or 2½ cups canned chickpeas (garbanzos), rinsed well and drained

3 tablespoons tahini

3 to 4 tablespoons fresh lemon juice

1 garlic clove, minced

2 teaspoons kosher salt

Pinch of cayenne pepper

About ½ cup reserved bean cooking liquid or water

2 teaspoons extra-virgin olive oil

½ cup chopped fresh cilantro

½ teaspoon slivered lemon zest

In a small skillet, toast the cumin and coriander seeds over low heat until fragrant. Crush coarsely in a mortar with a pestle or spice grinder. Add the sesame seeds to the skillet and toast, shaking the pan frequently so they don't burn. When they are golden, crush them in the mortar or coarsely grind them in the spice grinder. Set aside.

Transfer the drained chickpeas to a food processor. In a small bowl, whisk together the tahini, lemon juice, garlic, 1½ teaspoons of the salt, the cayenne, the reserved spice mixture, and 2 tablespoons of the reserved cooking liquid. Add the tahini mixture a tablespoon at a time to the chickpeas, processing until you have a medium-coarse puree. (For a coarser texture, pulse to a coarse mash, or pound in a large mortar.) Stir in enough of the reserved cooking liquid to make a soft, fluffy mixture with the consistency of mashed potatoes. Add the remaining ½ teaspoon salt, adjust the seasoning, and transfer the hummus to a serving bowl. Drizzle with the olive oil, sprinkle with the chopped cilantro and lemon zest, and serve.

You can make the hummus up to 3 days ahead; cover and refrigerate.

IN ADVANCE

SLOW-COOKED BEAN STEWS AND CASSEROLES.

Many slow-cooked bean stews and casseroles, like the French cassoulet, have their origins in farm or peasant cooking, where the fat-enriched beans were meant to sustain against hard work and cold. Nowadays, we enjoy these bean dishes for their deep, comforting flavors, but we no longer need the surfeit of fat. The challenge is how to achieve the rich, melting textures of these classic dishes in leaner ways. (For bean soups, see pages 403–405.)

White Beans and Mellowed Garlic with Rosemary Oil

SERVES 6 AS A SIDE DISH, 4 AS A MAIN COURSE

In this recipe, dried white beans are cooked with lots of whole garlic cloves until they make a thick stew that can be put to many delicious uses. They are an excellent accompaniment to roast lamb, game birds, or poultry, or make a simple meal on their own with some shaved Parmigiano-Reggiano cheese. You can also puree the beans and use them as a spread for Rustic Garlic Toasts (page 368) to make a classic bruschetta to serve with drinks.

Whatever the permutation, I drizzle a rosemary-infused oil—the only fat in the recipe—over the beans just before serving; this way, it is not totally absorbed by the beans, and its flavor remains apparent.

8 ounces (1 cup) **dried navy or cannellini beans**
soaked overnight (see page 90)

2 whole cloves

1 medium shallot

1 small dried chile or ¼ teaspoon red pepper flakes

1 sprig fresh thyme or ½ teaspoon dried thyme

1½ garlic heads (about 17 cloves), separated into cloves and peeled

½ teaspoon kosher salt

Freshly ground black pepper

Rosemary Oil

    1 tablespoon plus 1 teaspoon extra-virgin olive oil

    2 garlic cloves, thinly sliced

    2 teaspoons minced fresh rosemary

    ¼ cup chopped fresh flat-leaf parsley

Discard any beans that are broken, off-colored, or floating.

Add more water to the beans to cover by 1 inch. Stick the cloves into the shallot and add to the beans, along with the chile and thyme. Bring to a boil over moderately high heat. Reduce the heat to low, partially cover the pot, and simmer the beans for 30 minutes.

Add the garlic cloves and salt and continue cooking until the beans and garlic are very tender, about 15 minutes longer. Pepper generously and adjust the seasoning. You can serve the beans this way, like a stew, or drain them and puree in a food processor with a little of the cooking liquid.

Meanwhile, make the rosemary oil. Heat the olive oil in a small skillet over low heat. Add the garlic and rosemary, cover, and cook until the garlic is soft and golden, about 5 minutes. Set aside until ready to serve.

Just before serving, drizzle the rosemary oil over the beans. Garnish with the parsley.

IN ADVANCE You can cook the beans up to 3 days ahead; cover and refrigerate. Reheat over low heat, adding a few tablespoons of water if they have become too thick.

Red Lentil Stew with Caramelized Onions

SERVES 6 This recipe illustrates the technique of cooking legumes in a highly flavored liquid, in this case, broth with onion, cinnamon, ginger, and lemon.

Red lentils have a milder flavor and much softer texture than green or brown lentils and are traditionally used in Indian cooking to make thick stew-like purees called dals.

Dals usually contain a great deal of oil, which seems largely unnecessary given the pungent flavorings of the stew and the natural creaminess of the lentils. This recipe uses far less, and each serving is topped with caramelized onions to provide added richness.

This stew is so substantial you can eat it as a meal in itself. To make a complete protein, serve it with a dollop of yogurt or a grain dish such as Rice (or Mild Grains) with Ginger and Curry (page 178). It is also an excellent side dish for roast chicken or seafood.

1 tablespoon vegetable oil

1 medium onion, quartered lengthwise and thinly sliced crosswise

2 imported bay leaves

One 2-inch piece cinnamon stick

1½ teaspoons finely chopped fresh ginger

1 garlic clove, finely chopped

¼ teaspoon cayenne pepper

2 cups (about 1 pound) **small red lentils (masoor dal),** picked over and rinsed

3 cups unsalted homemade (page 574) **or canned low-sodium chicken broth**

2 to 3 cups boiling water

1 lemon, halved

1 teaspoon kosher salt

Caramelized Onions

>   **1 teaspoon unsalted butter**

>   **1 teaspoon vegetable oil**

>   **2 medium onions,** halved through the root end and thinly sliced lengthwise

>   **¼ teaspoon kosher salt**

>   **Freshly ground black pepper**

> **Coarsely chopped fresh cilantro** for garnish

> **Plain yogurt** for serving

In a large heavy saucepan, combine the oil, onion, bay leaves, and cinnamon stick over moderately low heat, cover, and cook, stirring occasionally, until the onion softens, 4 to 5 minutes. Uncover, increase the heat to moderately high, and add the ginger, garlic, and cayenne. Cook, stirring, until the garlic and ginger are soft, about 3 minutes.

Add the lentils and cook, stirring, until they are coated with the oil, about 3 minutes. Add 2 cups of the broth and 2 cups of the boiling water and bring to a boil. Reduce the heat and simmer for 5 minutes.

Squeeze the juice of the lemon through a strainer into the lentils. Add the lemon halves, salt, and the remaining 1 cup broth. Cover and cook over moderately low heat, stirring occasionally, until the lentils have broken down into a thick puree, 40 minutes. They should be soupy; if they get too thick, add more boiling water as necessary, ¼ cup at a time.

About 20 minutes before serving, prepare the caramelized onions: In a large nonstick skillet, combine the butter, oil, and onions. Cover and cook over moderately low heat until the onions are softened, about 5 minutes. Uncover, increase the heat to moderate, and sauté, stirring and tossing frequently, until the onions are browned, about 12 minutes. Season with the salt and pepper to taste.

Discard the lemon halves and cinnamon from the lentils and season with the salt and pepper to taste. Serve the lentils in bowls, topped with the caramelized onions, cilantro, and yogurt.

IN ADVANCE You can cook the lentil stew up to 2 days ahead; cover and refrigerate. Reheat, stirring, over moderately low heat, adding a little water or chicken broth to loosen the stew to a soupy consistency.

Fat Beans with Mole

SERVES 6

My friend Felipe Quevedo introduced me to this dish, which his mother made with the huge purple beans you see in Mexican markets. These beans, a far cry from ubiquitous refried beans we know in America, offer a perfect balance of texture, flavor, and color.

Señora Quevedo simmers the beans in water until they are almost tender, then stews them in a rich mole poblano, a chile-and-chocolate-laced sauce she makes from a prepared paste she buys in the market. Though the beans are delicious as is, it is the way she garnishes them that makes the dish unusual: spooned over crisp romaine lettuce leaves, then scattered with thinly sliced radishes and onions.

In duplicating the dish in America, I came up against two harsh facts of culinary life here: Great moles poblanos are not generally available at the local market, and a homemade one takes about thirty ingredients and several hours of work to make, too much effort in a busy life. Instead of a true mole, I use a simplified Ancho Chile Sauce that works wonderfully in the dish. (If you have access to a good rich mole poblano, simply whisk 1 cup of the paste into 3½ cups chicken broth, or to taste, and simmer for 10 minutes. Add the drained cooked beans and proceed as directed.)

The beans traditionally used for this dish are huge dark purple beans called *ayocotes* that are exceptionally flavorful and meaty. The closest beans available here are scarlet runner and sweet, black runner beans the size of limas, but smaller brown or red beans also work well.

> **1 pound dried runner beans,** soaked overnight, drained, picked over, and rinsed
>
> **1 teaspoon kosher salt**
>
> **Revisionist Mole (Ancho Chile Sauce)** (page 656) or prepared mole poblano (see Headnote)
>
> **18 tender inner romaine leaves**
>
> **9 radishes,** thinly sliced
>
> **2 medium onions,** thinly sliced, rinsed under cold water, and drained
>
> **Warm corn tortillas** for serving

Place the beans in a large saucepan and add enough cold water to cover them by 2 inches; remove any beans that float. Bring to a boil, reduce the heat to a simmer, and cook until the beans are tender but not falling apart, 2½ to 3 hours, stirring them occasionally and adding more water as necessary to keep them covered by 1 inch. Halfway through the cooking time, stir in the salt.

Drain the beans, reserving some of the cooking liquid, and return them to the pan. Stir in the mole and bring to a simmer over moderate heat. Simmer for 20 to 25 minutes, stirring occasionally, until the beans have absorbed most of the sauce. The beans should be thick and stew-like. If the sauce gets too thick, add a little bean cooking liquid (or chicken broth) to thin it out.

To serve, arrange 3 romaine leaves on each of six dinner plates. Spoon the beans over the leaves, scatter the radishes and onions over the top, and serve at once, accompanied by hot corn tortillas. Or serve the garnishes on a big platter, and allow guests to serve themselves.

IN ADVANCE You can cook the beans in the sauce up to 3 days ahead; cover and refrigerate. Reheat, stirring, over moderately low heat, adding a little water or chicken broth to loosen them to a soupy consistency. You can also freeze the beans for up to 2 months.

Rustic Cassoulet Beans

SERVES 10 AS A SIDE DISH, 6 AS A MAIN COURSE

This is an ingenious shortcut for making beans that taste like the rich melting beans of a classic cassoulet, but which happen to be low in fat. Instead of making a rich broth for cooking the beans, add the makings of the broth—aromatics, herbs, and the browned bones and trimmings from poultry or meat—directly to the beans. They release their flavor into the cooking liquid, which in turn is absorbed by the beans. The collagen from the bones and trimmings gives the beans that unctuousness usually achieved with fat.

These beans are delicious with a grating of Parmigiano-Reggiano or an aged sheep's milk cheese such as Fiore Sardo and a green salad. I often serve them as an accompaniment to grilled or roasted lamb, pork, chicken, duck, or sausage. See page 110 for a recipe using them in a simplified cassoulet.

You can use practically any dried bean in this recipe. The kind you use will determine the character of the dish. Red beans, such as cranberry beans, scarlet runners, or Appaloosas, will produce an earthier, more rustic dish, with a grainier consistency than classic white beans. Dried baby limas are currently my favorite for this dish because they are creamy yet hold their shape. Small green flageolets make a more delicate cassoulet particularly suited to lamb.

Get into the habit of stockpiling meat and poultry trimmings and bones from chicken, rabbit, duck, game birds, lamb, and pork in the freezer to fortify broths and other liquids. Carcasses from roasted chickens are especially useful. If you have no trimmings or bones, use cheap cuts of meat, such as chicken legs or pork shoulder, trimmed of all skin and fat.

1 pound dried beans, such as Great Northern, navy, cannellini, flageolet, or baby limas, soaked overnight, drained and picked over

4 whole cloves

1 medium onion, halved, or 2 large shallots, peeled

4 garlic cloves, peeled, lightly smashed

¼ teaspoon red pepper flakes

2 imported bay leaves

6 sprigs fresh thyme or ½ teaspoon dried thyme

6 to 7 cups unsalted homemade (page 574) **or canned low-sodium chicken broth**

2 pounds skinned duck or chicken legs or lean trimmings and bones from pork, lamb, or duck, with as much fat as possible removed

1 tablespoon plus 1 teaspoon olive or grapeseed oil

1 cup dry white wine

A 1-ounce chunk of smoky ham, such as Black Forest (optional)

1¼ teaspoons kosher salt

1 medium onion, chopped

1 medium carrot, chopped

2 garlic cloves, chopped

2 to 3 teaspoons fresh lemon juice

Freshly ground black pepper

Place the beans in a large saucepan. Stick the cloves into the onion or shallots. Add to the beans, along with the garlic cloves, red pepper flakes, bay leaves, and thyme. Add enough chicken broth to cover the beans by 1 inch (about 5 cups). Bring to a boil, lower the heat, and simmer for 1 hour. (Do not allow the liquid to boil, as it will toughen the beans.) Add more chicken broth as necessary to keep the liquid level ½ inch above the top of the beans.

Meanwhile, brown the meat, trimmings, and/or bones: Pat them dry with paper towels. Heat a large heavy shallow pan over moderately high heat. Add 2 teaspoons of the oil and swirl to coat the bottom of the pan. Add the meat and cook, stirring and rearranging the pieces occasionally, until they are well browned and there is a deep brown coating on the bottom of the pan, 20 to 30 minutes. Drain off any fat and discard. Add ½ cup of the wine and stir with a wooden spoon to loosen the browned bits on the bottom of the pan.

Add the meat and/or bones and liquid to the beans, along with the ham, if using, and 1 teaspoon of the salt. Simmer the beans, skimming off any fat that surfaces, until they are tender but still hold their shape, about 45 minutes longer. Drain the beans in a colander set over a bowl to catch the cooking liquid. When the beans are cool enough, pick through them and discard the meat and/or bones, bay leaves, and thyme sprigs.

In a heavy medium flameproof casserole, combine the remaining 2 teaspoons oil, the onion, carrots, and garlic over moderately low heat, cover, and cook, stirring frequently, until the vegetables are soft but not browned, about 10 minutes. Uncover, increase the heat slightly, and sauté, stirring frequently, until the vegetables are browned and caramelized, about 10 minutes longer. Stir in the remaining ½ cup wine and boil for 2 minutes. Stir in the reserved bean cooking liquid and cook at a low boil until it has reduced to 2 cups.

Add the beans and continue cooking until the beans are meltingly tender and infused with the sauce, about 20 minutes longer. If the beans become too dry, stir in chicken broth until they are the desired consistency. Stir in the lemon juice, the remaining ¼ teaspoon salt, and pepper to taste.

You can prepare the dish up to 3 days ahead; cover and refrigerate. Reheat over low heat, adding a few tablespoons of water if the beans have become too thick.   IN ADVANCE

Revisionist Cassoulet

A good cassoulet is a deeply satisfying dish, but it requires long and pain-staking preparation, difficult in these busy times.

Here is a leaner free-form version using beans that have soaked up a rich gelatinous broth, rather than fat, as a base. Creamy, comforting, and filling, it has a third of the calories and fat of a traditional cassoulet. And it is much easier to make. I bake the beans with bread crumbs and Parmigiano-Reggiano to form the traditional crust, then cook some meat, game, or poultry separately, to serve with them: grilled lean sausages, a roasted bird, or pork roast (see suggestions below). Duck, whether long-cooked melting confit legs or thinly sliced rare, pan-seared breasts, is especially good. If you wish, you can bury the meat right in the beans as in a traditional cassoulet before you bake it (be sure to remove skin and fat).

> **1 garlic clove,** cut lengthwise in half
>
> **Rustic Cassoulet Beans** (page 107)
>
> **⅓ cup soft fresh bread crumbs**
>
> **1 tablespoon plus 1 teaspoon freshly grated Parmigiano-Reggiano cheese**
>
> **Freshly ground black pepper**
>
> **6 smallish servings meat, poultry, or pork,** such as
>
> > **Revisionist Confit of Duck Legs** (page 311)
> >
> > **Spice-Rubbed Duck Steaks** (page 326), without the port wine sauce
> >
> > **Foolproof Roast Chicken with Its Own Pan Sauce** (page 291)
> >
> > **Honey-Cured Pork Loin with Peppery Juniper and Fennel Seed Rub** (page 294)
> >
> > **Homemade Duck Sausages** (page 347) or other grilled lean sausage

Preheat the oven to 400°F.

Rub the cut garlic clove over the inside of a large casserole, preferably earthenware. Allow to dry for several minutes. Spoon the beans into the casserole. In a small bowl, combine the bread crumbs, cheese, and pepper to taste. Sprinkle the beans evenly with the mixture. Bake until the beans are bubbly and the top is golden and tinged with brown, about 30 minutes.

Serve the meat alongside the beans.

You can prepare the beans without the topping up to 3 days ahead; cover and refrigerate. Let come to room temperature before assembling and baking as directed.

Bourbon Baked Beans

These beans have the melting texture and deep flavor of long-cooked baked beans without the overbearing sweetness and with a great deal less fat and calories than the Boston-style baked beans of my childhood. Replacing the traditional salt pork with pork skin adds a rich natural gelatin that makes the beans only seem as if they have soaked up delicious fat. Smoked ham lends rich pork flavor and a slight smokiness. Bourbon adds depth of flavor to the beans without making them at all alcoholic. The beans need 5 hours to cook, so plan accordingly.

Pork skin is available in the meat case of many supermarkets or from the butcher. If you can't find it, buy fresh fatback and cut the skin off with a sharp thin knife, or substitute a smoked ham hock but omit the ham.

Serve the beans with a glazed country ham or Honey-Cured Pork Loin with Peppery Juniper and Fennel Seed Rub (page 294) and Classic Coleslaw (page 423).

2 ounces pork skin

1 pound small white beans, such as navy, Great Northern, or cannellini, **or meaty speckled beans,** such as Jacob's cattle, soaked overnight

2 ounces lean smoked ham, cut into 3 or 4 chunks

1 cup chopped, peeled, and seeded tomatoes (3 to 4 fresh or canned tomatoes)

3½ tablespoons maple syrup

3½ tablespoons molasses

3 tablespoons cider vinegar

4 garlic cloves, minced

2 tablespoons dry mustard

1½ teaspoons freshly ground black pepper

½ teaspoon kosher salt

½ teaspoon ground ginger

¼ teaspoon red pepper flakes

2 imported bay leaves

1 tablespoon plus 1 teaspoon bourbon

Preheat the oven to 250°F.

Using a sharp knife, shave off any white fat left on the pork skin and discard. Place the skin in a medium saucepan with enough cold water to cover and bring to a boil over moderately high heat. Reduce the heat to moderate and simmer until softened, about 4 minutes. Drain and rinse under cold running water.

Drain the soaked beans, reserving 1 quart of the soaking liquid; pick over the beans. Transfer them to a 2-quart earthenware casserole or bean pot with a lid. Nestle the pork skin in the beans.

In a large saucepan, bring the reserved soaking water to a boil. Add the ham, tomatoes, maple syrup, molasses, vinegar, garlic, dry mustard, black pepper, salt, ginger, pepper flakes, and bay leaves. Reduce the heat and simmer for 1 minute.

Stir the tomato mixture into the beans. Cover and bake for 2½ hours. Check the beans as they cook to make sure the liquid is just covering them. If not, add a little water to raise the level.

Stir in the bourbon. Cover and continue cooking the beans for 2 to 2½ hours longer, checking them occasionally, until they are very tender.

Remove the cover and cook for 45 minutes longer. The beans should be meltingly tender and the liquid cooked down to a thick sauce. Discard the pork skin, ham, and bay leaves and adjust the seasoning before serving.

IN ADVANCE You can prepare the baked beans up to 4 days ahead; cover and refrigerate. You can also freeze them in a plastic container for up to 2 months.

BEANS IN OTHER GUISES. There are dishes that, if you didn't know they were made from beans, you would probably never guess. For example, chickpea flour is made into the delectable pancakes served in the South of France and soybeans are fashioned into mild and endlessly mutable cakes. They are among the easiest and most delicious dishes to make.

Rustic Chickpea-Flour Pancake

SERVES 4

One of the best snacks in the world can be found at Chez Maria's stand in the market in Nice. It is *socca*, a huge, thin chickpea-flour pancake that is served hot. You eat this sublime creation with your fingers, pulling off the chewy edges and then the soft crepe-like interior. It is really nothing more than a thin batter of chickpea flour, olive oil, and water that is spread into a hot oiled pan and cooked over a wood fire, but it's one great way to eat legumes.

Yearning for those flavors, I devised a way of making socca in a skillet on top of the stove. Using a nonstick skillet, I was able to cut down the amount of olive oil, most of which I brush on the top for flavor before eating. The only thing missing is the flavor of wood smoke (I sometimes add a pinch of Smoky Tea Essence, page 545, to the batter to achieve this.) Socca is very easy to make. The batter, which has no egg or leavening, will keep for several days covered in the refrigerator, so you can make it often as a snack or as a marvelous hors d'oeuvre. Put the skillet with the warm socca right on the table, and let guests help themselves.

Chickpea flour is available at gourmet stores and Italian, Spanish, and Mediterranean markets. Store it in the freezer, where it will keep for up to 3 months.

> ¾ cup chickpea flour
> ⅜ teaspoon kosher salt
> Freshly ground black pepper
> 1 cup plus 2 tablespoons water
> 2 tablespoons extra-virgin olive oil

In a medium bowl, stir together the chickpea flour, salt, and pepper to taste. Slowly whisk in the water, adding more by the teaspoonfuls if necessary to make a batter with the consistency of heavy cream. Whisk in 1 tablespoon of the olive oil. Cover and place in the refrigerator to rest for at least 30 minutes.

To cook the socca, heat a large heavy nonstick skillet over moderate heat. Brush lightly with some of the remaining olive oil. Pour about ¼ cup of the batter into the pan and tilt the pan to coat the bottom evenly with the batter, making a layer no more than ⅛ inch thick. Cook until the bottom is browned, about 1 minute. Flip the crepe over and cook for another minute, or until the second side is golden. Slide the socca onto a platter, brush with a little more olive oil, and serve hot. Repeat with the remaining batter.

You can also make individual socca in a 7-inch nonstick skillet or well-seasoned crepe pan, using 2 tablespoons of the batter per pancake.

IN ADVANCE You can make the socca batter up to 2 days ahead; cover and refrigerate.

Fresh Soybeans with Extra-Virgin Olive Oil and Shaved Cheese

SERVES 2 Fresh green soybeans are increasingly available frozen, in health food and gourmet stores and, still on the vine, at some farmers' markets in the summer. You can boil them in salted water and eat them right out of the pods. For a lovely quick supper, I like to treat them as a fresh shell bean, dressing them with olive oil and shaved aged cheese such as Parmigiano-Reggiano, or pecorino Toscano. They are available at health food stores and well-stocked supermarkets.

> **3 cups frozen fresh shelled soybeans (edamame)**
>
> **1 garlic clove,** halved lengthwise
>
> **1 teaspoon fruity extra-virgin olive oil**
>
> **Kosher salt and freshly ground black pepper**
>
> **1½ ounces aged cheese,** such as Manchego, pecorino Toscano, or Parmigiano-Reggiano

Bring a large pot of water to a boil over high heat and salt liberally. Stir in the soybeans and cook until tender but not mushy, about 3 minutes (or according to package directions).

While the beans are cooking, rub two shallow soup bowls with the cut sides of the garlic.

Drain the beans well and divide between the bowls. Toss each serving with ½ teaspoon of the olive oil and season with salt and pepper. Shave the cheese over the top and serve at once.

Of the fermented soy products, tofu is my favorite because it is not trying to be anything other than itself, unlike seitan and tempeh, which are often touted as meat substitutes. Tofu is made from soybeans that have been soaked, pureed, cooked, and formed into cakes. High in protein, it contains all the essential amino acids, has no cholesterol, and is very low in calories. It comes in a variety of textures, from very firm to custard-soft.

The problem, and virtue, of tofu is that it is extremely bland. To be eaten on its own, it must be fresh, like a good fresh cheese. Then it is a delight, with a clean, mellow, subtle flavor that is surprisingly delicious. You can buy fresh tofu at Asian markets and health food stores, where it is sold in big tubs of water; it is well worth searching it out. When I find exceptional handmade tofu in Chinatown, I buy it to eat in a simple broth, such as Ginger-Sake Broth (page 582), garnished with sesame seeds, or as a salad, chilled and garnished with grated ginger, scallion, and soy sauce or Roasted Sesame Seed Dressing (page 611).

Commercial tofu, sealed in plastic tubs and sold in supermarkets, is packed in a liquid that gives it a somewhat flat, musty flavor. It is best used in recipes that will mask this off flavor, such as soups or stews.

To refresh packaged tofu, place it in a bowl and let cool tap water run over it for several minutes. Then fill the bowl with water and refrigerate; change the water several times in the course of the day. Blot the tofu dry on paper towels before using.

Tofu can also be a good way to replace some dairy products in certain recipes, if used carefully. When pureed with good extra-virgin olive oil, it makes a creditable substitute for mayonnaise (see page 624). You can use it to replace some of the eggs in egg salad. Soy milk, made from boiling soybeans and extracting the milky liquid, can be an excellent substitute for milk on cereals, in puddings, and in shakes. In baked goods, however, it yields a dry texture and slightly flat flavor.

Lasagna Noodles
with Pesto and
Summer Vegetables
(page 128)

PASTA

N

ext to bread, pasta is the food I turn to when I need some serious comfort in a hurry. A simple bowl of linguine with broccoli rabe and olive oil holds an evocative power for me, of Italy and a way of life I yearn for.

Pasta first gained extraordinary popularity in America some years ago when nutritionists began to tout the virtues of fat-free complex carbohydrates, of which pasta is largely composed, over protein. It proved to be a deceptive notion. Like the greens in a salad, pasta's fat and calorie content is determined largely by how it is dressed; calories increase dramatically with heavy-handed embellishment. Doused in garlicky olive oil or a cream sauce, a 4-ounce portion of pasta (in itself 420 calories) can take on hundreds of additional calories, far upwards of 600 calories. For carbohydrate-sensitive people like me, traditional pasta dishes provide a triple whammy of carbohydrates, calories, and fat that my body simply turns into pounds. In order to eat the pasta I love, I had to find ways to lighten it up a bit, so that the joy it provides comes with no unwanted consequences. (When I am in Italy, all these considerations fly out the window. The artful way it is handled, the way of eating, of being, is so radically different in Italy, it changes everything—I never gain weight there. But that is another discussion, about context and balance in eating. See pages x–xiv.)

The first thing I did was to scrutinize the amount of pasta that made up a serving. I discovered that 1 cup of cooked pasta (2 ounces uncooked dried pasta or 3 ounces fresh)—at 210 calories—is completely satisfying when it is mixed with some wonderfully filling sauce based largely on vegetables, or with a bit of

Baked Penne with
Wild Mushroom
Ragù and Ricotta
Salata (page 150)

braised meat or poultry. If you find you like more pasta, or have a metabolism that can tolerate it, you can always increase the amount you cook. Each additional ounce of dried pasta will yield ½ cup when cooked and add 105 calories to the recipe.

The second thing I did was to figure out how to lighten the traditional embellishments for pasta—like garlic and oil, creamy gratins, and rich ragùs. What follows is the result.

In restaurants, cooks can't wait 12 to 18 minutes for dry pasta to cook for each order. Instead, they rely on a simple trick that is great to use at home when you have company coming.

Cook the pasta ahead of time until it is slightly underdone, drain (reserving a little of the pasta water), cool it under cold running water, drain it again, and toss it with a little olive oil to keep it from sticking together. Store it, well covered, in the refrigerator until needed. When ready to assemble the dish, heat the pasta briefly in a pot of boiling water, or directly in the sauce, with a little of the pasta water to keep it moist.

If you cook pasta in too little water, it will become gummy. For 8 ounces of pasta (4 servings) you need 4 quarts of rapidly boiling water. Be sure to salt the water heavily, so that the bland pasta absorbs enough salt to bring out its flavor. Figure about 1½ tablespoons per 4 quarts of water (the pasta will absorb only a fraction of it).

FRESH VERSUS DRIED PASTA

It used to be that we assumed fresh pasta was superior to dried, I suppose because we assume fresh anything is better. In fact, each type of pasta has its own qualities and virtues. Your concern should be in using the very best pasta you can find.

If you wish to use fresh pasta, make it yourself (page 159) or know the source you are buying it from. Most fresh pasta made in America is mass-produced and lacks the fine, light, supple quality of handmade fresh pasta. Figure on 3 ounces of fresh pasta per serving.

Fine dried pasta has a resilient, almost springy texture and a lively wheaty taste when cooked; it should not be chewy or bland. When buying dried pasta, look for artisanal Italian pastas like Rustichella d'Abruzzo, Benedetto Cavalieri, and Latini, or the more readily available good commercial brands like Barilla and Delverde.

Try a side-by-side pasta tasting to get a real sense of what's available to you. A great pasta can elevate a dish from merely good to extraordinary.

PASTA SAUCED WITH FLAVORFUL FATS. Among the simplest and most satisfying pasta dishes are those sauced with butter or oil, from simple buttered egg noodles to the classic linguine with extra-virgin olive oil and garlic. These recipes normally call for several tablespoons of fat per serving; at 120 calories per tablespoon, they can be extremely caloric. To use less of these delicious fats without sacrificing flavor, extend them by boiling them with some of the pasta cooking water (which has the viscosity and flavor of a mild chicken broth), creating an emulsified sauce that coats the pasta with flavor.

Saucing Pasta with Flavorful Fats

A GUIDE TO IMPROVISING

Using this technique, you need only about 1½ teaspoons fat to sauce a serving of pasta. Boiling the fat with some of the pasta cooking water creates an emulsified sauce that coats the pasta with flavor. If you take this method one step further and add a handful of grated cheese with the cooking water, it melts into a creamy sauce. Try the classic combination of fresh fettuccine with Caciocavallo cheese, unsalted butter, and lots of freshly ground black pepper.

SERVES 4

This method gives proportions for 4 servings. If you wish to serve fewer or more people, figure on 1½ teaspoons fat and about 1 to 2 tablespoons of pasta cooking water per 1-cup serving of cooked pasta (2 ounces uncooked).

8 ounces dried pasta (any shape)

2 tablespoons flavorful fat, such as extra-virgin olive oil, Flavored Oil (pages 588–597), unsalted butter, or brown butter (see page 681)

Pinch of sugar

½ cup freshly grated or shaved aged cheese (optional), such as Parmigiano-Reggiano, Fiore Sardo, pecorino Romano, Caciocavallo, or Manchego

Freshly ground black pepper

3 to 4 tablespoons minced fresh herbs (optional), such as basil, flat-leaf parsley, chervil, or chives

1. Bring a large pot of water to a boil. Salt it liberally, then stir in the pasta. Cook until al dente (tender but still slightly firm to the bite).

2. Using a measuring cup, scoop out ½ cup of the cooking water. Drain the pasta. Return ¼ cup of the cooking water to the pot, along with the fat and sugar. Bring to a boil over high heat. Boil vigorously for 30 seconds to create an emulsion. Return the pasta to the pot and toss to coat with the sauce, adding a tablespoon or two more water if the pasta seems dry.

3. To make a creamy sauce, add ¼ cup of the grated cheese and the remaining pasta water; stir over low heat until the pasta is creamy.

4. Pepper generously and toss with the herbs. Serve at once, passing the remaining grated cheese on the side.

an improvisation

Spaghetti with Spicy Anchovies and Parsley

SERVES 2

Anchovies packed in spicy olive oil form the base for this marvelous quick pasta. This sauce is also wonderful on steamed vegetables, mashed potatoes, and shell beans. Before following the Guide above, first make a flavored oil: Drain and finely chop 8 imported anchovies in hot chile oil and put them in a small skillet, along with 1½ teaspoons of the spicy oil, 1½ teaspoons extra-virgin olive oil, and 1 small garlic clove, thinly sliced. Warm over very low heat, stirring and mashing the anchovies, until they have fallen apart and just begin to sizzle.

In Step 1, cook 4 ounces spaghetti until al dente. In step 2, scoop out 2 tablespoons of the pasta water directly into the anchovy mixture. Drain the pasta and return to the pot. Add the anchovy sauce, ½ cup coarsely chopped fresh flat-leaf parsley, and 2 ounces fresh mozzarella, diced (optional). Toss well to coat and serve at once. (Serves 2.)

Ravioli with Garlic, Olive Oil, and Crispy Sage

SERVES 4

This dish is the traditional and much-beloved pasta *aglio e olio e peperoncino* —olive oil and garlic with a bit of hot chile pepper—taken a step further. I cook fresh sage leaves with the garlic to create a deeply flavored oil. The garlic and sage leaves become crisp in the process, making a wonderful garnish for the dish. Boiling the fragrant oil with a little of the pasta cooking water makes a delicious sauce, which I especially love on cheese ravioli, pumpkin pansotti (or ravioli), gemelli, or linguine.

Garlic and Sage Oil

2 tablespoons extra-virgin olive oil

10 garlic cloves, thinly sliced

Pinch of red pepper flakes

10 large sage leaves, cut crosswise on a diagonal into ¼-inch strips, or 24 very small sage leaves

1 pound cheese ravioli

¼ teaspoon kosher salt

Freshly ground black pepper

¼ cup freshly grated Parmigiano-Reggiano cheese

To make the oil, in a small heavy saucepan, combine the oil, garlic, and red pepper flakes, cover, and cook over low heat until the garlic has become very soft, begins to "frizzle" (tiny bubbles dance around it), and turns golden but not brown, about 5 minutes. With a slotted spoon, scoop the garlic out of the oil and place on a plate. Add the sage leaves to the pan and "frizzle" until the sage is fragrant, has darkened somewhat, and is crisp, about 3 minutes. Turn off the heat and transfer the sage leaves to the plate with the garlic; reserve.

Bring a large pot of water to a boil. Salt well and add the pasta; cook until al dente (tender but still slightly firm to the bite). Using a measuring cup, scoop out ½ cup of the cooking water and set aside. Drain the pasta.

Add ¼ cup of the pasta water to the saucepan with the garlic and sage oil and bring to a boil. Boil vigorously for 30 seconds, or until emulsified.

Return the pasta to the pot and toss to coat with the sauce, adding a tablespoon or two more water if the pasta seems dry. Stir in the reserved garlic, sage, and the salt and pepper to taste. Serve at once, passing the Parmigiano-Reggiano separately.

You can make the sage and garlic oil up to 6 hours ahead. Set aside at room temperature.

IN ADVANCE

Pasta with Garlic, Olive Oil, and Hot Pepper. To make a simple pasta *aglio e olio e peperoncino*, simply omit the sage.

variation

Brown Butter Orzo "Risotto"

Orzo, whose name means "barley" in Italian, is a delicate rice-shaped pasta that is usually served as a side dish in place of a grain. When cooked with a little more liquid than customary, it gains a creamy quality similar to risotto, in a fraction of the time. Toasting the orzo in a small amount of brown butter before boiling it gives it a buttery, slightly nutty flavor. Serve this orzo risotto as a side dish for saucy dishes and ragùs like Chicken with Sherry Vinegar Sauce (page 338) or Scaloppine Marsala (page 331).

> **1 tablespoon unsalted butter**
>
> **8 ounces** (1⅓ cups) **orzo**
>
> **3½ cups water**
>
> **1 teaspoon kosher salt**
>
> **Freshly ground black pepper**

In a large nonstick skillet or a medium heavy saucepan, cook the butter over moderately low heat until the solids that sink to the bottom are golden brown and the butter smells like roasting nuts. Add the orzo, increase the heat to moderate, and sauté, stirring constantly, until the orzo is golden and about one third of the grains are dark brown. Stir in the water and salt and bring to a boil. Cook at a low boil until the orzo is tender and most of the water has evaporated, about 11 minutes. There should be a light creamy "sauce" binding the orzo and making it slightly soupy. Add pepper to taste and serve at once.

variation

Orzo "Risotto" with Saffron and Parmesan. To make an orzo risotto with the flavors of a classic risotto milanese, do not brown the butter or orzo. Simply melt the butter and sauté the orzo lightly to coat it with butter. Substitute unsalted homemade (page 574) or canned low-sodium chicken broth for the water and add a large pinch of saffron threads. Cook for 11 minutes, or until tender and creamy. Stir in ¼ cup freshly grated Parmigiano-Reggiano and 1 tablespoon regular or reduced-fat sour cream and season with pepper.

Cold Spicy Sesame Noodles

SERVES 4

The cold spicy sesame noodles served as an appetizer in Chinese restaurants used to be like a refuge to me: I would dive into them with abandon for the pure delicious comfort they provided. Rich with oil and sesame paste, they are so fearfully caloric that my comfort was not long-lived. These days, I retreat to my homemade version.

The noodles are seasoned with a five-flavor sesame oil so aromatic that you need only a little. Once it's made, you can use this oil to season or sauté many other foods as well.

The noodles make an excellent accompaniment to Lacquered Baby Back Ribs (page 304), Honey-Cured Pork Loin with Peppery Juniper and Fennel Seed Rub (page 294), or Sesame-Crusted Swordfish (without the Cilantro and Coconut Chutney; page 243). To make a main-course salad, garnish the noodles with 3 ounces cooked shrimp or 2 ounces slivered country ham or cold roast chicken (for an additional 100 calories per serving).

> **8 ounces fresh Chinese noodles** (1/16 to 1/8 inch thick) **or commercial or homemade** (page 159) **egg linguine**
>
> **1 tablespoon Chinese Five-Flavor Oil** (page 594)
>
> **1 tablespoon plus 2 teaspoons low-sodium soy sauce or tamari**
>
> **1 tablespoon plus 2 teaspoons balsamic vinegar**
>
> **1/2 teaspoon sugar**
>
> **1/2 teaspoon kosher salt**
>
> **2/3 cup thinly sliced scallions**
>
> **1/2 cup chopped fresh cilantro**
>
> **2 tablespoons chopped roasted peanuts or cashews** or 1 tablespoon toasted sesame seeds

Bring a large pot of water to boil. Salt well and add the noodles; stir to keep them separate until the water returns to the boil. Cook the noodles until al dente, tender but still firm to the bite, about 3 minutes. Drain and run cold water over them until completely cool. Drain well.

In a medium bowl, combine the oil, soy sauce, balsamic vinegar, sugar, and salt. Add the noodles, scallions, and cilantro and toss until well combined. Cover and refrigerate for at least 1 hour before serving to let the flavors meld.

Sprinkle the noodles with the peanuts just before serving.

You can make the noodles up to 2 days ahead. Cover and refrigerate.

IN ADVANCE

Pasta with Pesto or Olive Paste

Figure on about 2 tablespoons pesto and 1 teaspoon to 2 tablespoons of the pasta cooking water per 1 cup serving of cooked pasta (2 ounces dry).

Pesto, which comes from the verb meaning "to pound" in Italian, describes a family of sauces—thick pastes really—made of various savory ingredients crushed in a mortar. Although the version made with pine nuts, basil, and Parmesan is the most famous, there are pestos made with sun-dried tomatoes, walnuts, arugula, and other herbs. Olive paste is in essence a pesto, and it makes a delicious sauce for side dish pastas like orzo. Because they invariably contain a good deal of olive oil, pestos are generally quite caloric, so when using them on pasta, dilute them slightly with pasta cooking water to make a creamy sauce that coats the pasta. Because the thickness of pestos varies, the trick is to add just enough cooking water to coat the pasta without it tasting watery.

Bring a large pot of water to a boil and salt well. Add 8 ounces pasta and cook until al dente (tender but still slightly firm to the bite). Using a measuring cup, scoop out about ¾ cup of the pasta cooking water. Drain the pasta, return to the pot, and set over high heat. Add about ½ cup pesto (page 622) or olive paste (page 683) and then add enough of the reserved cooking water, 1 tablespoon at a time as you toss the pasta, until it is coated with the pesto. Season generously with pepper, add salt if necessary, and toss with ¼ cup minced fresh herbs—flat-leaf parsley, chives, or basil—if desired. Pass ¼ cup freshly grated Parmigiano-Reggiano cheese at the table. (Serves 4.)

Lasagna Noodles with Pesto and Summer Vegetables

This is a play on two classic Ligurian pasta dishes—layered pesto lasagna and trenette with pesto, green beans, and potatoes. I use commercially made fresh pasta sheets and cut them myself, but the dish works as well with fresh fettuccine or trenette. Any number of tender green vegetables can be used; my favorite is fava beans.

SERVES 4

Scant 2 cups green vegetables, such as

Shelled and peeled fava beans (3 pounds in the pod; see page 677)

¾ pound asparagus or green beans, trimmed and cut into 1-inch pieces

¾ pound sugar snap peas, strings removed, sliced into thirds on a diagonal

12 ounces fresh pasta sheets, cut lengthwise into 2-inch-wide strips, **or commercial or homemade** (page 159) **fresh pappardelle, fettuccine, or trenette**

½ cup Mortar-Made Pesto Sauce (page 622)

Salt and freshly ground black pepper

Bring a large pot of water to a boil and salt well. Place the vegetables (except fava beans, which will already have been blanched) in a large strainer, immerse them in the water, and cook until tender, 2 to 5 minutes. Remove from the water and let drain in a bowl.

Stir the pasta into the water and cook until al dente (tender but still firm to the bite). Using a measuring cup, scoop out about ⅓ cup of the cooking water. Drain the pasta. Return the pasta to the pot or transfer to a warm serving bowl and add the vegetables. Spoon over the pesto and 1 tablespoon of the cooking water and toss the pasta until it is well coated with pesto, adding a tablespoon or two more of the cooking water if necessary to loosen it. Add salt and pepper to taste. Serve warm or at room temperature.

You can prepare the vegetables, cut the pasta (if necessary), and make the pesto up to 6 hours ahead. Wrap well or cover, and refrigerate. IN ADVANCE

PASTA SAUCED WITH BROTHS OR VEGETABLE JUICES.
Sauces made from vegetable juices and broths have a lightness and clarity of flavor that make for ethereal pasta dishes. There are endless possible combinations of broths or juices, pastas, and vegetables or herbs: They run the gamut from tortelloni sauced with vividly flavored red pepper juice to classic linguine with steamed shellfish to exquisite Japanese-style chilled noodles with a brothy dipping sauce.

Saucing Pasta with Broths and Vegetable Juices

A GUIDE TO IMPROVISING

SERVES 4

Figure on ¼ to ½ cup broth or reduced vegetable juice and 1¼ teaspoons oil to sauce a 1-cup serving of cooked pasta (2 ounces uncooked).

When you boil a rich broth or a vegetable juice with a flavorful fat, it thickens slightly into a lovely, light sauce for pasta. You can use just about any of the broths on pages 567 to 583; to improvise pasta sauces, add a few simple elements like herbs, roasted peppers, or olives, and so on. My favorite quick meal is store-bought goat cheese ravioli in Parmesan Broth (page 580) with extra-virgin olive oil and crushed olives.

If you have a vegetable juicer, the possibilities for making quick, intensely flavored sauces expand: The juices from red or yellow peppers, garden peas (frozen ones work great, too), tomatoes, and corn all make marvelous brothy sauces for pasta. The trick is to boil the raw juice down until the flavor is pleasingly concentrated. (See Tortelloni with Red Pepper–Juice Sauce, Olives, and Ricotta Salata, page 132.) If you don't have a juicer, you can usually buy fresh juices at juice bars and health food stores.

> **1½ cups broth** (pages 567–583) or 3 cups fresh vegetable juice, such as bell pepper, pea, corn, or tomato
>
> **Pasta,** such as
>
> > **8 ounces any shape dried pasta**
> >
> > **12 ounces commercial or homemade** (page 159) **fresh egg or saffron pasta or buckwheat noodles**
> >
> > **1 pound filled pasta,** such as ravioli or tortellini

Possible additions (optional), singly or in any combination, such as

> **½ cup cooked vegetables,** such as blanched julienned or diced carrots or leeks, roasted bell peppers, or roasted tomatoes

> **1 cup tender raw greens,** such as arugula, spinach, or watercress (stems removed)

> **⅓ cup pitted** (see page 683) **and coarsely chopped olives**

> **4 ounces mozzarella or ricotta salata cheese,** cubed or thinly sliced

> **4 to 8 ounces cooked chicken,** shredded, **or cooked shrimp,** sliced

1½ tablespoons flavorful fat, such as extra-virgin olive oil, Flavored Oil (pages 588–597), unsalted butter, or Asian sesame oil

Pinch of sugar

Kosher salt and freshly ground black pepper

¼ to ½ cup coarsely chopped fresh herbs (optional), such as flat-leaf parsley, basil, chives, chervil, or cilantro

¼ cup grated aged hard cheese, such as Parmigiano-Reggiano, Manchego, pecorino Romano, or pecorino Toscano

1. If you are using a broth, pour it into a small saucepan and bring to a boil. Reduce the heat to very low. If you are using a vegetable juice, pour it into a medium saucepan and boil over moderate heat until it has a nice concentrated flavor and has reduced to about 1½ cups. Keep hot while you cook the pasta.

2. Bring a large pot of water to a boil over high heat and salt well. Add the pasta and cook until al dente (tender but still slightly firm to the bite). Drain the pasta and return to the pot, along with any optional additions you wish.

3. Meanwhile, increase the heat under the broth or juice, add the fat, and boil vigorously for 30 seconds.

4. Pour the sauce over the pasta and toss to coat over moderate heat; season with the sugar and salt and pepper to taste. Stir in the herbs, if using. Divide among four heated shallow soup bowls and serve at once, passing the cheese separately.

Saffron Fettuccine in Curry and Fennel Seed Broth. an improvisation

Follow the Guide above, using Curry and Fennel Seed Broth (page 581). In Step 2, wilt fresh spinach leaves in the hot broth. In Step 3, use unsalted butter. Arrange 2 ounces grilled shrimp on top of each serving.

Tortelloni with Red Pepper–Juice Sauce, Olives, and Ricotta Salata

SERVES 4   Denver chef Kevin Taylor's pepper-juice sauce is like pure essence of red pepper. I like to pair it with meaty Kalamata olives, basil, and mild ricotta salata cheese, which melts over the hot pasta. You will need an electric vegetable juicer to juice the peppers. If you don't have one, the fresh juice bar at your local health food store may juice peppers for you. You will need about 4 cups juice.

> **Red Pepper–Juice Sauce**
>> **8 red or yellow bell peppers**
>>
>> **1 cup dry white wine**
>>
>> **2 tablespoons fruity extra-virgin olive oil,** or more to taste
>>
>> **1½ tablespoons fresh lemon juice**
>>
>> **Kosher salt**
>
> **1 pound cheese tortelloni, ravioli, or pansotti**
>
> **12 black olives,** such as Kalamata, pitted (see page 683) and sliced
>
> **½ to ¾ cup chopped fresh herbs,** such as basil, cilantro, flat-leaf parsley, or chives
>
> **Freshly ground black pepper**
>
> **4 ounces ricotta salata cheese,** shaved, **fresh or smoked mozzarella,** cut into ¼-inch dice, **or firm mild goat cheese,** thinly sliced
>
> **¼ cup freshly grated Parmigiano-Reggiano cheese**

To prepare the sauce, cut the peppers in half and remove the stems, seeds, and ribs. Slice into 2-inch pieces. Juice the peppers in an electric vegetable juicer. You should have a scant 4 cups.

In a small saucepan, combine the pepper juice and wine. Bring to a boil over high heat, reduce the heat to moderate, and simmer until reduced to 2 cups, about 35 minutes. Whisk in the olive oil, lemon juice, and salt to taste. Keep warm over low heat.

Meanwhile, bring a large pot of water to a boil and salt well. Add the pasta and cook until al dente (tender but still slightly firm to the bite). Drain the pasta and return to the pot.

Increase the heat under the sauce, add the olives, and boil vigorously for 30 seconds. Pour the sauce over the pasta and toss to coat. Toss in the herbs and pepper to taste. Divide among four heated shallow soup bowls and scatter the ricotta salata over the pasta. Serve at once, passing the Parmigiano separately.

You can juice the peppers, reduce the sauce, and add the olive oil, lemon juice, and salt up to 2 days ahead. Cover and refrigerate. When you are ready to serve, reheat the sauce, add the olives, and proceed.

Pasta with Shellfish Sauce

A GUIDE TO IMPROVISING

One of the simplest and best ways to serve pasta with shellfish is to steam the shellfish open in a flavorful base of wine and aromatics such as shallots, garlic, and herbs or spices. They release their briny juices into the wine to make a delicious brothy sauce. Then all you need to do is toss just-cooked pasta with the shellfish stew at the last minute and serve it in big warm bowls. If you use clams to make the Classic Moules Marinière (page 256) and toss it with linguine, you'll have a fine linguine with white clam sauce. Or toss rice noodles with Mussels with Lemongrass, Ginger, and Chiles (page 257) for a Thai-inspired pasta dish.

The secret is in the timing. Make the base for the shellfish steam, without the shellfish, before you put the pasta on to boil. Steam open the shellfish when the pasta is almost cooked, then combine in individual bowls.

Any Shellfish Steam recipe (pages 254–257)

12 ounces dried pasta, such as linguine or spaghetti

1. Prepare the liquid base of any of the shellfish steam recipes, without adding the shellfish and any final garnishes such as cream or herbs.

2. Bring a large pot of water to a boil. Salt well and stir in the pasta. Cook until al dente (tender but still slightly firm to the bite); drain thoroughly.

3. Meanwhile, about 2 minutes before the pasta is ready, add the shellfish to the simmering broth: Increase the heat to high, add the shellfish, cover, and cook, shaking the pan frequently to rearrange the shellfish, until all the shells have opened, about 3 to 4 minutes.

4. To serve, mound the pasta into six large warmed soup bowls. Using a slotted spoon, remove the shellfish from the broth and arrange on top of the pasta. Stir the herbs and cream into the broth, if using, and ladle over each bowl.

Gyo's Chilled Noodles with Dipping Sauce and Embellishments

SERVES 6 Gyo Fujikawa was an elegant, refined Japanese woman who grew up in America and became a famous illustrator of children's books. She was my parents' friend when I was a child and she became my friend when I grew up. She served me these delightful noodles at lunch one hot summer day, and in doing so showed me a side of herself I had never seen before: the exquisite Japanese cook.

She set a plate of the chilled noodles before me, along with myriad individual small bowls of garnishes and dipping sauce. She instructed me to place whichever garnishes I wished on the noodles, in whatever order or combination, and to use chopsticks to dip each mouthful in the cool, slightly sweet sauce.

This recipe can be made with as many or as few garnishes as you wish, to serve any number of people. Figure on about 2 ounces protein, such as chicken, pork, ham, or shrimp, and ½ to ¾ cup vegetables per person. You can prepare all of the garnishes well in advance, and the sauce must be prepared ahead so it has time to chill.

The dipping sauce is based on the Japanese broth called dashi, made from kombu—dried kelp seaweed—and dried bonito shavings. All the Japanese ingredients can be purchased at Asian grocery stores and will keep indefinitely. Alternatively, you can use instant dashi to make the broth, flavoring it as directed with mirin and tamari; you will need 2½ cups dashi.

Dipping Sauce

- ½ ounce kombu (kelp seaweed)
- 2½ cups water
- ½ ounce dried bonito shavings
- ½ cup mirin (sweet cooking wine)
- ½ cup tamari, preferably reduced-sodium
- 12 ounces dried buckwheat or green tea noodles

Suggested Garnishes

12 ounces cooked chicken, smoked ham, or roast pork, cut into julienne strips, **and/or cooked peeled small shrimp,** sliced lengthwise in half, in any combination

1 cup thin strips peeled and seeded cucumber

1 cup thin strips peeled daikon

½ cup grated peeled carrot

2 to 3 ounces enoki mushrooms, tough stems trimmed (optional)

A 1-inch knob fresh ginger, grated

2 scallions, thinly sliced on a diagonal

¼ cup slivered shiso leaves or fresh basil leaves (optional)

2 tablespoons toasted sesame seeds

To make the dipping sauce, place the kombu and water in a medium saucepan and bring slowly to a simmer over moderately low heat. Remove the kombu with tongs and discard. Remove the pan from the heat and add the bonito shavings; do not stir. When the bonito has sunk to the bottom, after a minute or two, strain the broth through a fine strainer. Press on the bonito with a spoon to extract all the liquid and then discard.

In a small saucepan, bring the mirin to a boil. Add the kombu broth and tamari and simmer for 4 minutes. Remove from the heat and allow to cool, then refrigerate until chilled.

About 15 minutes before serving, bring a large pot of water to a boil and salt well. Add the noodles and cook, stirring occasionally, until they are al dente (tender but still slightly firm to the bite). Drain and plunge into a bowl of cold water to stop the cooking. Rinse them well under cold running water to remove excess starch. Drain well.

Meanwhile, place each garnish in a small bowl.

Place a portion of noodles on each of six chilled luncheon plates. Pour the chilled dipping sauce into six small bowls. Set one at each place, along with a pair of chopsticks. Arrange the garnishes in the center of the table for guests to help themselves.

You can prepare the dipping sauce and garnishes up to 6 hours ahead; **IN ADVANCE** cover and refrigerate.

PASTA WITH VEGETABLES. In classic pasta and vegetable dishes, such as ziti with broccoli rabe and garlic, or pasta alla Norma, made with fried eggplant, the vegetables are cooked in a lot of olive oil. The oil gives the vegetables a silky richness while acting as a sauce to moisten the pasta. Unfortunately, the healthful vegetables are, as a result, laden with fat and calories.

You can achieve the same effect by other means, following the basic techniques and recipes in this section. You can use this approach with just about any vegetable, from beets and their greens to zucchini, as the recipes that follow illustrate.

Pasta with Quickly Cooked Green Vegetables in Garlicky Olive Oil

A GUIDE TO IMPROVISING

SERVES 4

Traditional pasta and green vegetable dishes like the classic ziti with broccoli rabe and garlic have a delightfully rich, melting quality due to an abundance of fat. To achieve the same effect with far fewer calories, braise the vegetables with a little water and a small amount of intensely garlicky oil instead. As the liquid evaporates, the vegetables become imbued with the fat. Tossed with a little pasta cooking water, the residual fat makes a light sauce to coat the pasta. A dividend from this method is the crispy garlic left over from making the oil, which you can use as a garnish.

Garlicky Olive Oil

8 to 9 garlic cloves, thinly sliced

2 tablespoons plus 2 teaspoons extra-virgin olive oil or 1 tablespoon plus 1 teaspoon each oil and unsalted butter

⅛ to ¼ teaspoon crushed dried Italian red pepper (peperoncino) or red pepper flakes

1 ¼ pounds vegetables, such as broccoli rabe, broccoli, fennel, or asparagus, peeled or trimmed and cut into bite-sized pieces, **or greens,** such as escarole, dandelion, or spinach, stems removed, washed and spun dry

Kosher salt

⅓ to ½ cup water

8 ounces dried pasta, such as penne, linguine, or orecchiette

Freshly ground black pepper

¼ cup chopped fresh flat-leaf parsley (optional)

⅓ cup (1½ ounces) **toasted pine nuts or walnuts,** coarsely chopped (optional)

¼ cup freshly grated Parmigiano-Reggiano or pecorino Toscano cheese

1. Put a large pot of water on to boil.

2. To make the oil, in a large nonstick skillet set over low heat, cook the garlic in the olive oil, covered, until the garlic is soft, about 5 minutes. Uncover, add the red pepper, and cook for a few minutes longer, until the garlic is golden. Using a slotted spoon, transfer the garlic to a small bowl; add 1 tablespoon of the oil and reserve.

3. Add the vegetables to the skillet, along with ½ teaspoon salt. For more fibrous vegetables, such as broccoli or broccoli rabe, add about ⅓ cup water to the pan. For greens, the residual water left on the leaves from washing should be enough to keep them moist while they cook, unless they are very tough. If they do not begin to wilt within a minute of cooking, or if they are sticking to the bottom of the pan, add a little water, 1 tablespoon at a time. Cover and cook over moderately high heat, tossing frequently, until the vegetables are tender and the water has completely evaporated. If all the water evaporates before the vegetables are cooked, add a tablespoon or two more; or, if there is water left in the pan once the vegetables are cooked through, uncover, increase the heat to high, and boil it off.

4. Meanwhile, salt the boiling water well. Add the pasta and cook until al dente (tender but still slightly firm to the bite). Using a measuring cup, scoop out about ¼ cup of the cooking water and reserve. Drain the pasta well.

5. Pour the reserved cooking water back into the pasta pot. Add the reserved garlic and oil, bring to a boil, and boil for 30 seconds. Add the drained pasta and the cooked vegetables (scrape the pan with a rubber scraper to get every bit) and toss to coat, seasoning with salt and plenty of pepper. Toss with parsley and nuts.

6. Divide the pasta among four warm shallow soup bowls, spooning some of the vegetables over each. Serve at once, passing the cheese on the side.

Penne with Broccoli Rabe, Garlic, and Peperoncino

Sautéed in garlicky olive oil, broccoli rabe, which combines the best virtues of bitter greens and broccoli, makes one of the great simple pasta dishes. (Of course, you can also use regular broccoli.)

Proceed as directed in the Guide on pages 136 to 137, using 1½ pounds broccoli rabe. Cut off the tough stem ends and discard. Separate the heads into florets. Peel the stems if they are more than ½ inch thick, and cut them into bite-sized pieces. In Step 3, to cook the broccoli rabe, add the stems to the pan first, along with ⅓ cup water, and cook, covered, for 2 to 3 minutes, until they are just beginning to soften. Then add the florets and proceed as directed.

Pasta with Beets and Their Greens

Beet greens, with a flavor similar to Swiss chard, are delicious yet too rarely served. I wilt the greens, then toss them with pasta, walnuts, garlicky olive oil, and the beets, which are cooked separately.

Follow the Guide on pages 136 to 137, using 3 pounds (3 bunches) beets, with their greens. Cut off the greens and reserve. Scrub the beets well and roast them according to the method on page 683; cool. When they are cool enough to handle, slip off the skins and cut the beets into ½-inch wedges; reserve. Remove the stems from the greens and discard. Wash the greens in several changes of water and spin dry. In Step 3, add the greens to the pan, increase the heat to high, and cover, tossing occasionally, until the greens are wilted. Uncover and toss until all the water has evaporated. Add the beets and ½ teaspoon balsamic vinegar, then proceed as directed.

Beet dishes become all the more appealing if you make them with unusual varieties of beets, like candy-striped Chioggia or deep golden yellow ones, often available in summer farmers' markets.

Tubetti with Asparagus, Morels, and Fava Beans

Like most foods that are harvested in the same season, asparagus, morel mushrooms, and various members of the pea family—fava beans, green peas, and sugar snap peas and their pea shoots—have an affinity for one another. This recipe elaborates on a favorite spring pasta dish, in which tender green vegetables are braised in garlicky pancetta fat and a little water and tossed with small tubetti pasta and fresh herbs. When I'm pressed for time, I follow the basic approach using only one or two of the vegetables.

1½ pounds fava beans, ½ pound sugar snap peas, or 1½ pounds fresh peas

1½ ounces pancetta or thick-sliced bacon, cut into ⅛-inch dice (about ⅓ cup), or 1½ tablespoons extra-virgin olive oil

2 shallots, finely chopped

3 garlic cloves, finely chopped

½ pound tubetti or small shell pasta

1 pound thin asparagus, tough bottom stems broken off and discarded, sliced on a diagonal into 1½-inch pieces

3 tablespoons water

4 ounces fresh morels

4 ounces fresh pea shoots (optional)

¼ cup minced fresh chives, flat-leaf parsley, and chervil, in any combination

Kosher salt and freshly ground black pepper

½ cup freshly grated Parmigiano-Reggiano cheese

If using fava beans, use your thumb to break open the pods along the seam and dislodge the beans inside. The beans have a thin membrane that can easily be removed if you first loosen the skins by blanching the beans. Cook the beans in rapidly boiling water for 1 to 2 minutes, depending on the size. Drain and plunge them into ice-cold water to stop the cooking. Drain again and use your thumbnail to break open the skin at one end of each bean and peel it back. Press the bean gently and it will pop right out. Set aside.

If using sugar snap peas, remove the stem ends, then slice them on an extreme diagonal into ¼-inch-wide slices. Set aside.

If using fresh peas, shell them. Set aside.

In a medium nonstick skillet, cook the pancetta, covered, over low heat, stirring occasionally, until it has rendered out its fat and is crisp, about 8 minutes. Remove with a slotted spoon and drain on paper towels. Add the shallots and garlic to the pan, cover, and cook, stirring occasionally, until translucent, about 5 minutes. Remove from the heat.

Bring a large pot of water to a boil and salt well. Stir in the pasta and cook until al dente (tender but still slightly firm to the bite). Drain well.

While the pasta is cooking, set the garlic-shallot mixture over moderate heat. Add the asparagus and the water, cover, and cook, stirring occasionally, until the asparagus are tender with a slight crispness, about 5 minutes. Stir in the morels, pancetta, and sugar snaps, if using them. Cover and cook for 2 minutes, or until the morels are tender. (If necessary, remove from the heat until the pasta has finished cooking.)

Increase the heat to moderately high heat and stir in the fava beans or fresh peas, if using, and the pea shoots, if using. Cook, stirring and tossing, until the favas are heated through and the pea shoots are just wilted. Stir in the herbs and season with salt and pepper to taste.

Toss the pasta with the vegetables and serve at once, passing the Parmigiano-Reggiano on the side.

IN ADVANCE You can prepare the vegetables up to 6 hours ahead; store, well wrapped, in the refrigerator. You can render the pancetta and cook the shallots and garlic up to 3 hours ahead. Set aside at room temperature.

Pasta with Leeks, Pepper, and Aged Goat Cheese

SERVES 4 In this recipe, leeks are cut into thin graceful rounds and cooked in pancetta, the marvelous Italian unsmoked bacon, until they are silky. When they are tossed with an aged goat cheese and some of the pasta cooking water, the cheese becomes a creamy sauce.

Using a mandoline or vegetable slicer makes slicing the leeks easy. By hand, it is a slightly more time-consuming task, though not at all hard to do.

2 pounds leeks (6 to 8 leeks)

1½ ounces lean pancetta or thick-sliced bacon, cut into ¼-inch dice (⅓ cup), or 1½ tablespoons extra-virgin olive oil

⅓ cup water

¼ teaspoon kosher salt

8 ounces pasta, such as orecchiette, campanile, or commercial or homemade (page 159) egg tagliatelle

Freshly ground black pepper

½ cup grated aged goat or sheep's milk cheese (1½ ounces), such as a Coach Farm grating stick, pecorino Toscano, or Fiore Sardo

¼ cup chopped fresh flat-leaf parsley

Trim the roots and tough green tops from the leeks, leaving about 1 inch of pale green. Slice the leeks into thin rounds. Rinse the leeks in several changes of cold water to remove any grit; drain well. You should have about 4 cups packed leeks.

In a medium nonstick skillet set over low heat, cook the pancetta, covered, stirring occasionally, until it has rendered its fat and is crisp, about 8 minutes. With a slotted spoon, remove the crisp bits to a small bowl.

Add the leeks and water to the pan, sprinkle with the salt, and toss to coat. Cover the pan, increase the heat to moderate, and cook, stirring occasionally, until the leeks are tender, about 8 minutes. Uncover and continue cooking until any remaining liquid has evaporated. Keep warm.

Meanwhile, bring a large pot of water to a boil and salt well. Add the pasta and cook until al dente (tender but still slightly firm to the bite). Using a measuring cup, scoop out ¾ cup of the cooking water and set aside. Drain the pasta and return the pasta to the pot.

Add the leeks, the reserved pancetta, ½ cup of the reserved cooking water, and set over high heat. Add the cheese and toss until the cheese is melted and creamy. If necessary, stir in a few more tablespoons of the pasta water so that the pasta is lightly glossed with the sauce. Adjust the seasoning, peppering liberally. Serve at once, garnishing with the chopped parsley.

You may cook the leeks up to 4 hours ahead; cover and set aside at room temperature.   IN ADVANCE

Orecchiette with Pancetta and Fennel. Use orecchiette and substitute Parmigiano-Reggiano for the goat cheese. Replace the leeks with 1½ pounds fennel. Cut off and discard the tough stalks. With a vegetable peeler, shave off any brown spots. Cut out the core and slice the fennel lengthwise into ¼-inch slices, then cut the slices crosswise into ¼-inch dice.

Cook the pancetta as directed on page 141 and reserve. Add 1 medium onion, peeled and finely chopped, to the fat; cover and cook, stirring occasionally, until translucent, about 5 minutes. Add about three quarters of the diced fennel, ½ teaspoon fennel seeds, and ¾ cup water. Bring to a boil, reduce the heat, cover, and simmer until the vegetables are tender and most of the liquid has evaporated, about 20 minutes.

Stir in the reserved raw fennel and the pancetta. Season with salt and pepper to taste. Remove from the heat, cover, and keep warm.

Cook the pasta and proceed as directed.

Fresh Pasta with Cauliflower, Currants, and Pine Nuts

SERVES 4 I have never found cauliflower very compelling, despite its known nutritional virtues. So I have taken my inspiration from Italy, where cooks have devised many ways of making the lowly vegetable into something delectable.

This recipe is a play on a classic southern Italian dish that marries cauliflower with anchovies, pine nuts, and currants. First I flavor a small amount of fruity olive oil with garlic and anchovies, then I boil it with some of the pasta cooking water to make a light sauce that harmonizes the seemingly disparate flavors into a splendid, healthful whole.

This dish can also be made with broccoli or some of the more unusual cruciferous hybrids that have recently been appearing in markets, such as broccoflower.

⅓ cup dry white wine
⅓ cup currants or raisins
1 head cauliflower

Garlic-Anchovy Oil

> **2 tablespoons extra-virgin olive oil**
>
> **3 garlic cloves,** minced
>
> **⅛ teaspoon red pepper flakes**
>
> **One 2-ounce can oil-packed anchovies** (about 10), drained, patted dry, and coarsely chopped

8 ounces dried egg linguine, saffron fettuccine, orecchiette, or gemelli

½ cup freshly grated Parmigiano-Reggiano cheese

¾ cup finely chopped fresh flat-leaf parsley

Kosher salt and freshly ground black pepper

1 ounce (¼ cup) **roasted pine nuts,** chopped medium-fine

In a small saucepan, bring the wine to a simmer over moderate heat and add the currants. Cover and set aside to plump for 10 minutes.

Cut the cauliflower into bite-sized florets, core and discard the stems. Steam the cauliflower in a steamer basket over boiling water for 5 to 7 minutes until tender but not mushy. Transfer the cauliflower to a bowl of cold water set in the sink and run cold tap water over the cauliflower until it is completely cool. Drain it well and set aside, or refrigerate, covered, until ready to use.

To make the garlic-anchovy oil, in a large nonstick skillet, combine the oil, garlic, and red pepper flakes. Cook, covered, over low heat until the garlic is very soft but not browned, about 3 minutes. Stir in the anchovies and turn off the heat.

Bring a large pot of water to a boil. Salt well, add the pasta, and cook until al dente (tender but still slightly firm to the bite). About 4 minutes before it is done, bring the garlic-anchovy oil to a simmer. Add the cauliflower and sauté, tossing for 2 minutes. Stir in the currants and their liquid and cook until the liquid has evaporated, about 3 minutes.

Using a measuring cup, scoop out about ½ cup of the cooking water. Drain the pasta. Add ¼ cup of the cooking water and the cauliflower mixture to the pasta pot and bring to a boil. Return the pasta to the pot along with ¼ cup of the cheese and toss to coat with the oil mixture. Stir in the parsley, salt and pepper to taste, and the pine nuts, and serve at once, passing the remaining ¼ cup cheese separately.

You can blanch the cauliflower and prepare the Garlic-Anchovy Oil up to 6 hours ahead; cover and refrigerate. **IN ADVANCE**

Pasta with Roasted Vegetables

Figure on 1¼ to 2 cups coarsely chopped roasted vegetables for 4 servings.

Roasting concentrates the flavor of vegetables while rendering them tender, using very little fat. When you toss roasted chopped vegetables with a little pasta cooking water or broth, they make a light sauce to coat the pasta. All that these soft, melting roasted vegetables, such as Slow-Roasted Tomatoes (page 38), zucchini, winter squash, garlic, or "Fried" Eggplant (page 42), need to make a satisfying pasta sauce is a handful of torn fresh basil leaves or flat-leaf parsley and some freshly grated Parmigiano-Reggiano. Or try chopped Peppers Roasted with Garlic and Anchovies (page 42) tossed with linguine, thin shavings of aged goat cheese, and freshly ground black pepper.

Pasta with Rosemary-Roasted Eggplant and Ricotta Salata

SERVES 4

This recipe is my adaptation of pasta alla Norma from Catania, Italy, birthplace of Bellini, the composer of the opera *Norma*, after which it is named. In that dish, spaghetti is tossed with fried eggplant, grated ricotta salata cheese, and, sometimes, tomatoes. Because eggplant absorbs oil like a sponge, the traditional recipe is extremely caloric. For this leaner version, the eggplant slices are brushed with a rosemary-and-garlic-infused oil and roasted until they are creamy on the inside and caramelized on the outside. Then they are diced and tossed with a light sauce of the rosemary oil and some of the pasta cooking water, and ricotta salata or manouri, a Greek cheese with a similar flavor. No further embellishment is necessary.

Garlic-Rosemary Oil

2 tablespoons plus 2 teaspoons fruity extra-virgin olive oil

2 garlic cloves, thinly sliced

2 sprigs fresh rosemary, spiky leaves pulled off and coarsely chopped (2 heaping tablespoons)

2½ pounds small or medium white or purple eggplants

1 teaspoon kosher salt

8 ounces dried ziti, penne, or spaghetti

⅓ cup chopped fresh flat-leaf parsley

Freshly ground black pepper

4 ounces ricotta salata or manouri cheese (or aged dry goat or sheep's milk cheese), cut into thin shavings with a vegetable peeler

½ cup freshly grated Parmigiano-Reggiano cheese

Preheat the oven to 400°F.

To make the garlic-rosemary oil, combine the olive oil, garlic, and rosemary in a small saucepan set over low heat. Cover and cook until the garlic is soft, about 5 minutes. Set aside.

Peel the eggplants and cut them into ½-inch-thick slices. Using a slightly dampened brush, brush 2 baking sheets lightly with some of the rosemary oil, then brush each side of the eggplant slices with oil, using about half of it in all, and arrange on the baking sheets. Sprinkle with the salt. Roast the eggplant until it is tender when pierced with a fork, about 25 minutes. Set aside to cool slightly.

Bring a large pot of water to a boil and salt well. Add the pasta and cook until al dente (tender but still slightly firm to the bite).

While the pasta is cooking, transfer the eggplant to a cutting board and cut into coarse dice.

Using a measuring cup, scoop out about ½ cup of the cooking water and set aside. Drain the pasta. Pour ¼ cup of the cooking water into the pasta pot, add the remaining rosemary oil, and bring to a boil. Add the eggplant and its juices, the pasta, parsley, and pepper to taste. Toss to coat the pasta and adjust the seasoning, adding a tablespoon or two of the remaining cooking water if necessary to moisten the sauce.

Divide among four heated serving bowls and top with the shavings of ricotta salata. Pass the Parmigiano-Reggiano on the side.

IN ADVANCE You can make the Garlic-Rosemary Oil and roast the eggplant up to 6 hours ahead. Cover and set aside at room temperature.

HEARTY PASTAS AND BAKED CASSEROLES. Ragùs are perhaps the most comforting of sauced pasta dishes, along with those that are layered with cheese and baked. Some, such as papardelle noodles sauced with a classic game ragù, are distinctly Italian. Others bear the stamp of other countries: saffron pasta gratin from France, or macaroni and cheese from America. These dishes are great for gatherings of family and friends.

Pasta with Hearty Sauces

A GUIDE TO IMPROVISING

SERVES 4

About ¾ to 1 cup ragù is usually plenty to dress a 1-cup serving of cooked pasta (2 ounces uncooked).

The word *ragù* means "stew" in Italian and usually indicates small pieces of meat, game, or poultry slowly cooked with vegetables and wine until practically falling apart into a thick rustic sauce. A ragù is designed to make the most of a small amount of meat, maximizing its flavors and extending it with other ingredients. Often ragùs are rich sauces for pasta.

The pasta is never overwhelmed by a ragù; it is mixed with just enough to give it pleasing flavor and body. Because in America, pasta is usually served as a main course, and the amounts of pasta in these recipes are moderate, I dress it with a bit more sauce than is common in Italy. Toss the cooked pasta with grated aged cheese and a little pasta cooking water to form a creamy coating, then spoon the ragù on top. The sharp cheese acts as a catalyst between the rich sauce and the pasta, heightening and balancing all the flavors. You can use this approach with many ragùs and other hearty sauces, as well as stew-like mixtures based on beans or vegetables.

8 ounces dried pasta, such as pappardelle, fettuccine, medium shells, or orecchiette, or 12 ounces commercial or homemade (page 159) fresh egg pasta

3 to 4 cups ragù or other hearty stew-like dish, such as

 Tomato Sauce, or any variations (page 652)

 Spring Vegetable Ragout (page 68)

 Peperonata (page 63)

 Wild Mushroom Ragù (page 151)

 Beans with Pancetta and Sherry (page 97)

 Tuscan Beans with Sage and Garlic (page 96)

 White Beans and Mellowed Garlic with Rosemary Oil (page 102)

½ cup freshly grated aged cheese, such as Parmigiano-Reggiano, pecorino Toscano, Manchego, Fiore Sardo, or grana padano

Kosher salt and freshly ground black pepper

1. Bring a large pot of water to a boil and salt well. Add the pasta and cook.

2. In a medium saucepan, bring the ragù to a simmer over moderate heat; cover and keep warm.

3. Cook the pasta until al dente (tender but still slightly firm to the bite). Using a measuring cup, scoop out about ¾ cup of cooking water and set aside. Drain the pasta.

4. Return the pasta to the pot and set over high heat. Pour ¼ cup of the reserved cooking water over the pasta. Sprinkle with ¼ cup of the grated cheese and toss (adding more water by the tablespoon as necessary) until the cheese has melted into a creamy sauce and the pasta is thoroughly coated. If the ragù is very thick, thin it slightly with a few tablespoons of the remaining pasta cooking water. Add salt and pepper to taste.

5. Divide the pasta among four heated shallow bowls and spoon the ragù on top. Pass the remaining ¼ cup cheese separately.

Pappardelle with Classic Game Ragù

You can use many kinds of mild game (or even chicken legs and thighs) in this classic Italian ragù. After long, slow cooking with wine, tomatoes, wild mushrooms, and rosemary, the meat is meltingly tender, literally falling off the bone. Using naturally lean game meats, removing the skin, and adding a small amount of pancetta for flavoring results in a sauce with very little fat. It is delicious on pasta such as pappardelle and orecchiette, and on polenta, whether soft or panfried. Or you can spoon a dollop of the ragù into the center of a risotto. This recipe makes about 5 cups ragù.

Game Ragù

½ **cup** (about ½ ounce) **dried mushrooms,** preferably porcini

2 cups boiling water

About 3 pounds rabbit or other mild game meat, such as pheasant or guinea hen, cut into 8 serving pieces, liver(s) reserved, or 3 pounds chicken legs and thighs, skinned

1 ounce lean pancetta or thick-sliced bacon, cut into ¼-inch dice (scant ¼ cup)

½ **teaspoon kosher salt**

Freshly ground black pepper

2 medium onions, cut into ¼-inch dice

2 carrots, cut into ¼-inch dice

2 garlic cloves, finely chopped

1 cup peeled, seeded, and coarsely chopped plum tomatoes

One 3-inch sprig fresh rosemary, spiky leaves stripped off and chopped (about 1 tablespoon)

4 whole cloves

⅛ **teaspoon ground cinnamon**

2 imported bay leaves

1 ½ **cups dry white wine**

3 cups unsalted homemade (page 574) **or canned low-sodium chicken broth**

1 teaspoon balsamic vinegar

1 teaspoon grappa or cognac (optional)

8 ounces dried pappardelle or fettuccine or 12 ounces commercial or homemade (page 159) fresh pasta

½ **cup freshly grated Parmigiano-Reggiano, Fiore Sardo, or Manchego cheese**

To make the ragù, put the dried mushrooms in a medium bowl and pour the boiling water over them. Cover and set aside to soak for 30 minutes.

Rinse the game and pat dry. Mince the liver(s).

In a large nonstick skillet, cook the pancetta, covered, over low heat until it has rendered most of its fat and is crisp and golden, about 8 minutes. Transfer the crisp pancetta and half the fat to a small bowl and reserve.

Return the skillet to moderate heat. Sprinkle the game pieces lightly with the salt and pepper. Working in batches, add the meat to the pan and brown on both sides, turning once, about 7 minutes on each side. Transfer the browned pieces to a large heavy casserole. When you have browned all the meat, discard the fat in the pan.

Strain the remaining pancetta fat into the pan, reserving the crisp pancetta. Add the onions and carrots, reduce the heat to low, cover, and cook until the vegetables begin to release their liquid, about 5 minutes. Uncover and cook, stirring occasionally, until they are golden, about 7 minutes longer. Stir in the garlic and cook for 1 minute. Mince the reserved liver, if any, and add to the pan.

Scoop the soaked mushrooms into a strainer and rinse to remove any grit; reserve the soaking liquid. Finely chop the mushrooms and add to the pan, along with the tomatoes, rosemary, cloves, cinnamon, bay leaves, and reserved pancetta. Sauté for 2 minutes. Add the wine and cook, stirring and scraping up the browned bits from the bottom of the pan, until reduced by half. Transfer this mixture to the casserole with the rabbit. Carefully pour the reserved mushroom liquid into the casserole, taking care to leave any gritty sediment behind, stir in the chicken broth, and bring to a simmer. Reduce the heat to low, cover and cook until the meat is very tender, about 1¾ hours.

Transfer the cooked game to a bowl and set aside to cool. Pour the cooking liquid into a tall container and refrigerate until the fat has risen to the surface, about 30 minutes. Skim the fat off the braising liquid and discard. Pour the cooking liquid into a 1½-quart saucepan and bring to a boil. Lower the heat and simmer until reduced to about 3¼ cups, about 20 minutes; it should taste rich and full-bodied.

Meanwhile, when the meat is cool enough to handle, pull it off the bones and shred it slightly. Add the meat to the reduced sauce and heat through. Adjust the seasoning and add the balsamic vinegar and grappa, if using. Keep warm.

Bring a large pot of water to a boil. Salt well, add the pasta, and cook until al dente (tender but still slightly firm to the bite). Using a measuring cup, scoop out about ¾ cup of the cooking water and set aside. Drain the pasta.

Return the pasta to the pot and set it over high heat. Pour ¼ cup of the reserved cooking water over the pasta, sprinkle with ¼ cup of the cheese, and toss (adding more water by tablespoons as necessary) until the cheese has melted into a creamy sauce and the pasta is thoroughly coated. If the ragù is very thick, thin it slightly with a few tablespoons of the remaining pasta cooking water.

Divide the pasta among four heated shallow bowls and spoon the ragù on top. Pass the remaining ¼ cup cheese separately.

IN ADVANCE You can prepare the game ragù, cover, and refrigerate for up to 3 days, or freeze for up to 2 months. Bring the ragù to a simmer over moderate heat while you cook the pasta.

Baked Penne with Wild Mushroom Ragù and Ricotta Salata

SERVES 6 A play on the endless baked pasta dishes made throughout Italy, this splendid casserole is what a friend's ancient Italian grandmother calls "the Big Macaroni."

This ragù, which has the earthy rusticity of a rich veal stew, illustrates the extraordinary meatiness—both in flavor and texture—of wild mushrooms. It is so versatile, I make up double or triple batches and freeze it. Then, when I am feeling lazy, I just toss it with some perciatelle or ravioli or spoon it over polenta for an instant supper. It is also a wonderful element in Open Ravioli (page 156).

Figure on 1 cup Wild Mushroom Ragù per serving for tossed pastas and polenta, ¾ cup per serving for baked and layered pastas. The recipe makes about 4 cups of ragù.

The casserole is an excellent dish to serve for a dinner party because you can assemble it up to a day ahead.

Wild Mushroom Ragù

1 cup boiling water

½ cup (½ ounce) **dried wild mushrooms,** preferably porcini or morel

2 dry-packed sun-dried tomato halves (if you can find only sun-dried tomatoes packed in oil, rinse them in hot water rather than soaking them)

1 pound fresh wild mushrooms, such as shiitake, cremini, oyster porcini, morel, or portobello, in any combination

1½ teaspoons olive oil

2 medium onions, chopped

3 garlic cloves, minced

½ cup dry red wine

2 sprigs fresh thyme or ¼ teaspoon dried thyme

One 28-ounce can Italian peeled tomatoes, chopped, with their juices

1 teaspoon sugar

½ teaspoon kosher salt

Freshly ground black pepper

½ teaspoon olive oil or unsalted butter

1 pound tubular pasta, such as penne, ziti, or macaroni

¾ cup freshly grated Parmigiano-Reggiano cheese

Freshly ground black pepper

5 ounces ricotta salata cheese, thinly sliced or shaved

To make the ragù, pour the boiling water over the dried mushrooms and tomatoes in a small bowl, cover, and set aside to soak until softened, at least 15 minutes.

Wipe the fresh mushrooms clean with a damp paper towel. Trim off the tough stems and discard. If you are using portobellos, cut out the black gills and discard. Cut larger mushrooms into ¼-inch-thick slices through the stem; leave smaller ones (under 1 inch) whole.

In a medium saucepan, combine the olive oil, onions, and garlic, cover, and cook over moderate heat until the onions begin to wilt, about 5 minutes. Uncover and sauté until they are just beginning to brown, about 2 minutes.

Meanwhile, scoop the dried mushrooms and tomatoes into a strainer, reserving the soaking liquid. Rinse them under cool water to remove any grit and press them with the back of a spoon to squeeze out the water. Coarsely chop them and set aside.

Carefully spoon about ¾ cup of the soaking liquid into the saucepan with the onions, leaving behind any grit. Add the red wine and thyme and boil for 1 minute. Add the fresh mushrooms and cook, stirring, for 1 minute. Stir in the canned tomatoes and their juices, the chopped dried mushrooms and tomatoes, the sugar, and salt. Partially cover and simmer, stirring occasionally, until the mushrooms are tender and the ragù is thick, about 15 minutes. Pepper generously.

To assemble and bake the casserole, preheat the oven to 375°F. Grease a shallow 2-quart casserole with the oil and set aside.

Bring a large pot of water to a boil. Salt well and stir in the pasta. Cook the pasta until slightly underdone (a little firmer than al dente; the pasta will continue cooking in the oven). Drain the pasta and plunge it into a large bowl of cold water to stop the cooking; run cold tap water over it until it is completely cool. Drain well again, dry the bowl, and return the pasta to it.

Add the ragù to the pasta and toss until they are thoroughly mixed and the pasta is coated. Sprinkle with ½ cup of the Parmesan and pepper to taste and toss again. Pour half the mixture into the prepared casserole. Arrange the ricotta salata shavings over the top, cover with the remaining pasta, and sprinkle evenly with the remaining ¼ cup Parmesan cheese.

Bake the pasta until heated through and the top is lightly browned and crisp, about 25 minutes. Serve at once.

IN ADVANCE You can prepare the ragù up to 3 days ahead; cover and refrigerate. Or freeze for up to 2 months. You can assemble the casserole up to a day ahead; cover and refrigerate. Allow to come to room temperature (about 1 hour) before baking.

variation **Rustic Layered Pasta Casserole.** This recipe can accommodate endless variations in the sauce, pasta, and cheese. For example, you can use Peperonata (page 63) or any of the tomato sauce variations on page 653 in place of the ragù and mozzarella cheese instead of the ricotta salata.

Gratin of Pasta with Leftover Meat Juices

The thick juices from a stew, or the concentrated brown juices from roast chicken, beef, or lamb, are delicious tossed with pasta and baked into a gratin. Get into the habit of freezing these meat juices in small containers until you have enough.

Preheat the oven to 500°F. Rub the bottom of a shallow 1½-quart baking dish (about 10 inches) repeatedly with 2 halved garlic cloves; discard the garlic. Dry for 2 minutes, then rub with 1 teaspoon olive oil.

Cook 8 ounces tubular pasta in plenty of salted boiling water until firm to the bite. Drain well and return to the pot. (If you don't want to assemble the gratin right away, plunge the pasta into a bowl of cold water to stop the cooking, then drain well. Toss with a little olive oil to keep it from sticking together, cover, and refrigerate.) Pour over ½ to ¾ cup rich meat or poultry juices and toss to coat. Scatter 3 tablespoons freshly grated pecorino Toscano cheese over the pasta and toss again, adding salt and freshly ground black pepper to taste. Spread the pasta evenly in the baking dish and sprinkle the top with an additional 3 tablespoons cheese. Bake for 15 minutes, or until the top is browned and crisp. (Serves 4.)

Macaroni and Cheese

Macaroni and cheese can be ordinary when made with processed cheese, or truly sublime made with a more interesting cheese, like a fine Cheddar or Dry (aged) Jack. It is, classically, horrifically fattening: I calculated one standard recipe at almost 800 calories per serving. But it is so beloved and essential a dish to so many people, I set my mind to creating a leaner version—it tied for first place in an informal macaroni and cheese cookoff. None of the judges knew it was a heretical lightened version.

In this adaptation, the caloric, high-fat elements are replaced by two flavorful cheeses and milk thickened with rice flour, which gives it a satisfying, creamy, buttery flavor.

This recipe can be doubled or tripled to make a large batch. Rice flour is available at health food stores and Asian markets. It can be frozen in a tightly sealed plastic container for up to six months.

SERVES 4

To create more of the appealing crisp top on dishes like macaroni and cheese and gratins, before baking, spread them out into a larger-than-usual shallow baking pan and sprinkle on a little additional grated cheese.

½ teaspoon unsalted butter, softened, **or vegetable oil**

Rice Cream

    2 tablespoons white rice flour

    2½ cups whole milk

    ¼ teaspoon salt

    1 small shallot, peeled and stuck with 1 whole clove

    1 small imported bay leaf

    Freshly ground white pepper

8 ounces elbow macaroni

3 ounces sharp Vermont Cheddar cheese or Monterey Jack, shredded (about 1 cup)

1 teaspoon Ancho Chile Essence (page 543) **or sweet Hungarian paprika**

3¼ ounces Dry (aged) Jack, aged Gouda, or Parmigiano-Reggiano cheese, grated (about ¾ cup)

Kosher salt and freshly ground black pepper

Preheat the oven to 450°F. Lightly grease a 2-quart ovenproof casserole with the butter. Set aside.

To make the rice cream, rinse a small saucepan with cold water. (This will make cleanup easy.) Add the rice flour. With a whisk, gradually beat in enough milk to make a thick paste. Then continue whisking in the remaining milk until well blended. Add the salt, shallot, bay leaf, and white pepper to taste, and bring to a boil over very low heat, whisking frequently. Simmer for 10 minutes, or until the mixture has the consistency of thick cream. Strain through a fine sieve into a bowl and set aside.

Bring a large pot of water to a boil and salt well. Add the macaroni and cook until it is almost tender but still quite firm to the bite (it will continue cooking in the oven). Drain well and return to the pot. Stir in the rice cream, Cheddar cheese, chile essence, and all but 2 tablespoons of the Dry Jack cheese. Add salt and pepper to taste.

Pour the macaroni into the casserole. Sprinkle the top with the remaining 2 tablespoons Dry Jack. Bake for 15 minutes, or until the top is golden brown. Serve at once.

IN ADVANCE You can make the Rice Cream up to 2 days ahead; cover and refrigerate. You can assemble the casserole up to 2 hours ahead; cover and leave at room temperature.

Pasta Gratin. This formula of adding one creamy and one aged cheese variation to the rice cream base to make a pasta gratin is versatile. Another good combination is a flavorful creamy goat cheese such as Bucheron and an aged grating cheese, such as Parmigiano-Reggiano or pecorino Toscano. You can also use any shape pasta you wish. Dried egg fettuccine is particularly good.

Crispy Saffron Noodle Gratin

The favorite staff lunch at a French restaurant where I worked many years SERVES 6 ago was a crispy noodle gratin, scented with saffron and served alongside a simple roasted chicken. This version of that very satisfying dish is made with a great deal less butter. A thin layer of Parmesan cheese browns on top into a marvelous crisp chewy crust. If you use a nonstick skillet, you can turn the gratin out onto a platter to serve as a noodle cake.

- **1 large pinch of saffron threads**
- **2 teaspoons hot water**
- **2 tablespoons unsalted butter**
- **1 garlic clove,** halved
- **⅓ cup freshly grated Parmigiano-Reggiano cheese**
- **8 ounces dried egg pasta** (about ⅛ inch wide), such as linguine or tagliarini, or 12 ounces commercial or homemade (page 159) fresh pasta
- **Kosher salt and freshly ground black pepper**
- **12 coriander seeds,** coarsely crushed (optional)

Preheat the oven to 475°F.

Place the saffron in a small bowl and crush to a powder with a teaspoon. Pour the hot water over it and set aside to steep for 10 minutes.

In a small saucepan, melt the butter over very low heat. Add the saffron and its liquid; when the butter starts to bubble, remove from the heat. Let sit for 10 minutes.

Rub an ovenproof 10-inch nonstick skillet or 1½-quart gratin dish with the garlic; discard. Let dry for 2 minutes. Using a slightly dampened brush, brush the pan with a little of the saffron butter. If you are using a nonstick skillet, sprinkle 2 tablespoons of the cheese evenly over the bottom.

Bring a large pot of water to a boil over high heat. Salt well, stir in the pasta, and cook until al dente (tender but still slightly firm to the bite). Drain and cool under cold running water. Drain well.

Return the pasta to the pot and toss with the saffron butter; season with salt and pepper and the crushed coriander, if using. Transfer the pasta to the prepared pan and arrange it in an even layer (taking care not to disturb the cheese). Press the noodles down lightly and sprinkle the remaining cheese over the top.

Bake the gratin until the top is brown and crusty, 30 to 35 minutes. Let sit for a few minutes. If you used a nonstick skillet, place a plate over the pan and invert the cake onto it. Then invert the cake onto a platter. Cut the gratin into wedges and serve at once.

IN ADVANCE   You can make the saffron-butter mixture and assemble the gratin up to 2 hours ahead. Cover and set aside at room temperature until ready to bake.

Open Ravioli

A GUIDE TO IMPROVISING

SERVES 4   An "open" ravioli is kind of like a sandwich: A savory filling is layered in between two squares of cooked pasta. Unlike classic crimped ravioli, the sides are left open. Then a sauce is added to complement the flavors and tie it all together. It's an easy and unexpected play on a traditional filled pasta. You can assemble the ravioli up to 1 hour ahead and set them aside, covered, at room temperature. Heat them when ready to serve.

The pasta can be cut into any size or shape: rectangles, circles, even hearts or triangles. Four-and-one-half-inch squares and 6-by-3-inch rectangles make convenient single servings. The ravioli can be filled, sauced, heated through, and served in individual shallow ovenproof soup bowls. If you don't have ovenproof bowls, assemble and bake the pasta on a baking sheet, then transfer to warmed shallow bowls and serve.

The fun part is devising delicious combinations of fillings and sauces. My favorites are the simplest: fillings of sautéed or braised vegetables and brothy sauces. The list that follows shows some particularly delicious combinations.

Filling	Sauce or Broth
Celery Root and Apple Puree (page 81)	Red Wine Essence (page 639) or Faux Veal Broth (page 572)
"Fried" Eggplant prepared with a Flavored Oil (page 42), chopped	Red Pepper–Juice Sauce (page 649) or Tomato Sauce (page 652)
Roasted Winter Squash Puree (page 36) and Roasted Garlic Puree (page 38) (both coarsely mashed)	Brown Butter and Balsamic Sauce (page 638)
Peperonata (page 63)	Parmesan Broth (page 580)
Spring Vegetable Ragout (page 68)	Garlic Broth (page 580)
Wild Mushroom Ragù (page 151) or Roasted Wild Mushrooms (page 40)	Star Anise Broth (page 581)
Simple Herb-Roasted Peppers (page 43)	Warm Anchovy and Olive Oil Sauce (page 614)

I make these ravioli with either homemade or good-quality store-bought pasta. You can cut down prepared fresh pasta sheets to the size you want. Or you can buy the dried "instant" lasagna (not the curly ones) that comes in 3-by-6-inch sheets: Boil them like ordinary pasta.

Allow 1 to 2 ounces pasta per serving, depending on the thickness of the sheets.

2 cups filling of your choice (see suggestions above)

1½ cups broth or sauce of your choice (see suggestions above)

Pasta sheets for lasagna, such as

> **12 ounces fresh egg pasta sheets,** commercial or homemade (page 159), cut into 8 sheets (approximately 4½ inches square)

> **8 sheets quick-cooking dried lasagna** (approximately 3 by 6 inches)

1½ teaspoons extra-virgin olive oil

6 tablespoons freshly grated Parmigiano-Reggiano cheese

Mild cheese (optional), such as

> **2 ounces regular or smoked mozzarella or ricotta salata,** thinly sliced

> **½ cup fresh ricotta cheese**

⅓ cup chopped fresh herbs (optional), such as flat-leaf parsley, chervil, basil, or chives

1. About 30 minutes before you wish to serve the pasta, preheat the oven to 450°F.

2. In separate saucepans, bring the filling and sauce to a simmer over moderate heat; reduce the heat and keep warm.

3. Meanwhile, bring a large pot of water to a boil. Salt well and add the pasta sheets, stirring them gently with the handle of a wooden spoon to keep them from sticking together. Cook the pasta until it is al dente (tender but still firm in the center); fresh pasta will take only a few minutes to cook, so watch carefully. Drain the pasta sheets, cool them by running cold water over them; drain again and gently toss to coat with the olive oil.

4. To assemble the open ravioli: Place 1 pasta sheet in the bottom of each of four shallow ovenproof soup bowls. Spoon ½ cup of the filling mixture over each. Sprinkle 1 tablespoon grated Parmigiano-Reggiano cheese over each, top with a layer of mozzarella or ricotta, and place the remaining pasta sheets on top. Sprinkle with the remaining Parmigiano-Reggiano cheese.

5. Cover loosely with foil and bake until heated through and the cheese is melted, 5 to 8 minutes. Transfer each serving to a warm shallow bowl. Ladle a generous ⅓ cup of the hot broth or sauce around each. Garnish with the herbs, if desired.

HOMEMADE PASTA. In many parts of Italy, pasta is still made daily, rolled out by hand with a wooden pin until it is thin enough to read through. Handmade pasta can be a revelation, with a freshness of flavor and suppleness that is at once light and rich tasting. Although commercial "fresh" pastas are widely available, they rarely measure up to the fresh pasta of my memory. When I am craving it, I make fresh pasta at home. It is easy to roll the dough using a hand-cranked pasta machine. While the result is not as fine as hand-rolled pastas, it is a creditable substitute, for much less time and effort.

Egg Pasta

Although you can use fresh pasta in just about any pasta recipe, I reserve it for those in which dried pasta just wouldn't be as good. I love fresh pasta sauced with ragùs, such as Classic Game Ragù (page 148) or Spring Vegetable Ragout (page 68), or dressed with a great butter and shavings of fresh white truffles for that penultimate pasta dish. It is a perfect accompaniment to such dishes as Chicken with Sherry Vinegar Sauce (page 338) or Celebration Guinea Hen Cooked with Black Truffles (page 309), tossed with the rich sauce. Cut into squares or rectangles, it's ideal for Open Ravioli (page 156).

MAKES ABOUT 12 OUNCES; SERVES 4 AS A MAIN COURSE

> 1¼ **cups unbleached all-purpose flour,** or more as needed
>
> 2 **large eggs,** at room temperature
>
> ½ **teaspoon extra-virgin olive oil**
>
> ⅛ **teaspoon kosher salt**

To make the dough: Mound 1 cup of the flour on a work surface. Make a well in the center of the flour; the sides should be about 1½ inches high. Add the eggs, olive oil, and salt to the well. With a fork, lightly beat the eggs, gradually incorporating flour from the inner rim, a little at a time, until the mixture forms a wet paste. With a pastry scraper, scrape up the flour from the work surface and work it into the dough.

Adding a teaspoon of flour at a time as necessary to keep the dough from sticking, knead the dough until it is smooth and elastic, about 8 minutes. The dough should feel ever so slightly sticky; if it still feels moist and sticky when pressed with a finger, knead in a little more flour. Divide the dough into 4 pieces and form each one into a ½-inch-thick disk. Wrap each disk in plastic wrap and set aside to rest 30 minutes.

To roll and cut the dough: Set the rollers of the pasta machine to the widest setting. Flatten one ball of dough into a disk and flour it lightly. Feed the dough through the machine, guiding the dough with the palm of your hand as it comes out the other side. Fold the dough into thirds and lightly flour it. Pass it through the machine three more times on the same setting, folding it each time and flouring it as necessary. Set the rollers to the next setting and pass the dough through the rollers; the pasta will form a long, narrow ribbon. Repeat without folding from here on, moving the rollers closer each time, until the pasta is very thin (the next-to-the-last or the last setting). Lay out the ribbon of dough on tea towels to dry for about 5 minutes. Repeat with the remaining dough.

(The pasta is ready to cut when it is still pliant but not so wet that it will stick to itself. If the pasta sheets appear to be drying too quickly, cover them with plastic wrap.)

For long thin noodles such as fettuccine, pass the sheets of pasta through the appropriate cutter on the pasta machine to make ⅛- to ¼-inch-wide strips.

For free-form shapes and pappardelle, lay each sheet of dough out flat on a lightly floured work surface. Using a long chef's knife or a pizza cutter, cut into desired shapes: 4½-inch squares or 6-by-3-inch rectangles for Open Ravioli (page 156), triangles, and so on; lay out on tea towels. To make pappardelle, cut each sheet into long ¾-inch- to 1-inch-wide strips. Separate the cut noodles and lay out on kitchen towels.

You can cook the cut pasta immediately or let it dry overnight to cook at another time. To dry fettuccine, lay about 10 strands at a time parallel to one another and roll them into nests. Pasta that is thoroughly dried does not need to be refrigerated.

Cook the pasta in plenty of boiling, well salted water. Fresh pasta takes only seconds to cook, so watch it carefully. Dried fresh pasta takes a little longer.

IN ADVANCE You can prepare fresh pasta up to 2 days ahead. Dust lightly with cornmeal and store in a tightly sealed plastic bag in the refrigerator. You can store dried fresh pasta in a sealed plastic bag, unrefrigerated, for up to 2 months.

Saffron Pasta. Adding saffron to the dough gives it a haunting flavor, variation a deep yellow color, and the look of handmade paper flecked with specks of crimson threads. Place 1 or 2 large pinches of saffron in a small bowl and crush them with the bowl of a spoon, making ¼ to ½ teaspoon (this will give a powerful saffron flavor). Add the saffron to the eggs when you are about to make the dough.

Herb-Patterned Pasta. One of the most beautiful homemade pastas variation is sheets of dough between which leaves of fresh chervil or flat-leaf parsley have been sandwiched; it looks as if the leaves have been captured in a veil of translucent pasta. Although it may seem difficult to do, it is really very easy, and when cut into 2-inch squares and served simply in clear broth, it is lovely.

Roll out the pasta dough as directed above until about ⅛ inch thick (about the fourth setting). Lay out the sheet on the floured work surface and place perfectly dry whole fresh flat-leaf parsley or chervil leaves over half the length of the sheet. Fold the other half of the sheet carefully over the pasta and leaves and gently smooth to remove air pockets. Then press a little more firmly to seal the layers. Continue to roll the pasta until it has been rolled through the second-to-the-last setting. Cut as desired.

Four varieties
of round-grain
"risotto" rice
(page 183)

GRAINS

Like many cooks, for much of my life, I didn't venture much beyond the staple grains of the American diet: rice, corn, and wheat. It was the increasingly strong correlation between grains and good health that sent me wandering into the mysterious world of grains. Although grains were—and still are—poorly represented in most American cookbooks, the wealth of ethnic cookbooks, restaurants, and markets in New York City became my guides into this exciting realm.

There are literally thousands of grains, over a thousand varieties of rice alone. Every day new grains become available, from exotic rices like the delicate gobindavog from India, with kernels half the size of a normal grain, and mushroomy-smelling black Japonica rice to the rustic, chewy Italian grain farro to grains with ancient origins and extraordinarily high nutritional content, like quinoa and kamut. My approach to cooking grains, at least as far as flavorings and combinations go, is largely Mediterranean influenced, with a measure of Southeast Asia thrown in.

Grains pose the same problems as any other bland starchy foods, such as potatoes or beans. When warm, they soak up any fats with which they come in contact, their natural starchiness then obscuring the fats' flavor. The techniques in this chapter demonstrate delicious ways to cook grains using as little fat as possible.

This chapter is divided into the two main categories of grains—kernel grains and milled grains—because each requires a different cooking method. Once you know the basic approaches for cooking each category, you can apply them to many kinds of grains.

Kernel grains include whole grains, such as brown rice and whole oats, whose outer husk and bran have been left intact, and refined grains, such as white rice, whose outer husks have been removed, making them quicker-cooking, more tender, and delicately flavored.

Milled grains, such as polenta, grits, semolina, and oatmeal, are those that have been ground into meals or flakes, which cook into a thick mush. Many can then be formed into cakes.

GRAINS AND NUTRITION

Grains have sustained mankind for thousands of years. They are a rich source of complex carbohydrates as well as fiber. Whole grains have significant amounts of vitamin E, B vitamins, iron, selenium, zinc, and calcium. Grains contain protein, too, although it is incomplete—it lacks some amino acids. For this reason, grains are traditionally served with foods that add complementary protein, such as beans or small amounts of meat, dairy products, poultry, or fish.

There is a school of nutrition that believes grains should form the basis of our diets because their complex carbohydrates provide sustained energy. But grains can actually be difficult for some people's systems to handle. If, like me, you are sensitive to carbohydrates, eating too many grains, or grains not balanced with some protein, will create a drop in blood sugar and energy as well as a weight gain. Wanting grains' essential nutrients and flavor, I have learned to enjoy grains in moderate amounts. The message, as always, is listen to how your body responds and plan your diet accordingly.

Because grains can become rancid easily, buy them from a purveyor with a quick turnover and then store them in the refrigerator or freezer. Fresh grains have only a faint, sweet aroma. If grains have a noticeably musty or harsh aroma, they are rancid and should not be used.

WHOLE VERSUS REFINED GRAINS

When grains are refined, varying amounts of bran, the outer covering of the kernel, are removed to make them easier to cook and digest. Along with the bran, beneficial fiber and trace nutrients are lost. Although most refined grains are fortified to return the lost nutrients, whole grains always contain more nutrients and fiber. However, some people cannot digest whole grains properly, or find that they trigger allergic reactions.

KERNEL GRAINS FROM PILAF TO RISOTTO. Every day there are new grains to discover at the market: black barley—described by one food writer as tasting like barley, wheat kernels, beans, lemon rind, and autumn leaves; Job's tears, a chewy grain with a mild flavor reminiscent of corn and barley; triticale, exceptionally rich in protein and amino acids, and tasting like a mild wild rice; Bhutanese red rice, short pink grains that taste sweet, nutty, and mildly spicy; Japonica rice, with the color of red wine and an earthy mushroomy aroma. Try them for yourself and see what their different textures and flavors inspire.

Unlike milled grains, which cook into a creamy porridge-like consistency, kernel grains retain their texture. Their uses range from elegant main-course risottos and pilafs to side dishes, salad (see pages 441–446), and "beds" for fish, meat, and poultry. Grains such as farro and barley make marvelous additions to soups, casseroles, and stews because they hold their shape in liquid. See the chart on pages 170 to 173 for fuller descriptions of the many varieties.

The time a grain takes to cook depends on its size, density, and the degree to which it has been processed. Generally speaking, the more refined the grain, the shorter the cooking time. Whole grains, which still have their tough outer husk, take two to two and a half times as long to cook, with more liquid, as refined grains. Soaking whole grains overnight in water cuts the cooking time in half and makes them more digestible.

With the exception of wild rice and rye kernels, toasting grains in a hot dry skillet or sautéing them in a little oil or butter before cooking brings out the nutty, earthy flavors and keeps them from getting sticky. To toast grains, add to a large skillet over moderate heat and toast, stirring, until fragrant and their color has deepened, about 5 minutes.

During the first part of cooking, the boiling liquid swells the starch and permeates the grains, rendering them tender enough to eat. The amount of time the grain is cooked after that is a matter of taste and desired texture:

For pilafs, grains should be tender but still distinct and fluffy.

For salads or side dishes, the grains should be slightly al dente—tender but still slightly firm in the center—so that they can be dressed without falling apart or losing their character.

For porridges, grains must be cooked at least one and a third times longer than usual (add boiling liquid as needed), until they are on the verge of falling apart and their starches have formed a creamy binding.

Cooking Different Grains Together. Combining several grains in a single recipe creates a dish with interesting textures and flavor. Take care, however, to allow for the grains' different cooking times. Add the longest-cooking grain first, followed by the next, and so on. Consult the chart on pages 170 to 173 and subtract the shorter cooking times from the longer one; the difference is the time to wait before adding the quicker-cooking grains. If you are not sure how much liquid to add, start with the smaller amount, then add more in ¼-cup increments as necessary.

This chart gives proportions for **1 cup dry grains.** Use a 2-quart saucepan with a tight-fitting lid. Once you add the grains to the boiling liquid, cover the pan and reduce to a simmer. Add ½ teaspoon salt halfway through the cooking. Check the grains for doneness toward the end of the cooking time. If necessary, add a few tablespoons more liquid, and continue cooking until done. If any liquid remains in the pan when the grain is cooked, pour it off. Let all grains stand for 5 minutes before serving.

GRAIN/DESCRIPTION	AMOUNT LIQUID (cups)	COOKING TIME (minutes)	YIELD (cups)
TENDER, PLUMP GRAINS THESE EXTREMELY VERSATILE GRAINS ARE GREAT IN PILAFS, IN SALADS AND SOUPS, AND AS SIDE DISHES. THEY CAN BE COOKED LONGER TO MAKE INTERESTING RISOTTOS.			
Farro, popular in Italy, has a mild, sweet barley-hazelnut flavor that makes it one of the most delightful and useful of grains. While in the past, farro was used to denote several ancient forms of wheat, these days it most often refers to emmer, and sometimes spelt. It is often served sauced like pasta, or in tandem with beans. Served at room temperature with ricotta, honey, and cinnamon, it makes a wonderful breakfast. Whether or not to soak and cooking times depend on its origin; check package instructions.	to cover by 3 inches; replenish as necessary	35 to 40	3
Pearl barley is hull-less, bran-less barley that has been steamed and polished, rendering it more tender than hulled barley; it is the most common form of barley. It is pleasingly chewy, with a mild, faintly herbal flavor.	3 to 3½	30 to 35	3½
Job's tears is an ancient tropical grain that cooks into large, plump, chewy grains with a sweet corn-barley flavor. Soak overnight.	3	30 to 40	2½
TOOTHSOME, CHEWY WHOLE GRAINS, GROATS, AND BERRIES ALTHOUGH MOST WHOLE GRAINS HAVE FAIRLY MILD FLAVORS, THEIR PRONOUNCED CHEWY TEXTURE CAN BE AN ACQUIRED TASTE. ALL BENEFIT FROM BEING SOAKED FOR AT LEAST 6 HOURS OR OVERNIGHT. THEY WORK BEST AS PILAFS OR SIDE DISHES, AND IN SALADS AND SOUPS, BUT WON'T COOK UP TENDER OR CREAMY ENOUGH FOR A RISOTTO. IF COOKED PAST TENDER WITH ADDITIONAL WATER, THEY CAN MAKE INTERESTING AND NUTRITIOUS BREAKFAST CEREALS.	for all these grains (except black barley) to cover by 3 inches; replenish as necessary	60 to 90	about 4 (kamut yields 2¾)
Rye berries are mildly sweet with a strong, grassy flavor.			
Oat groats are hulled whole oats that are several degrees earthier and more deeply flavored than oatmeal.			
Wheat berries, chewy, mild, and wheaty-tasting, include several different strains: **Kamut** is an ancient strain of wheat that has exceptionally large grains and a somewhat bland, nutty flavor. **Triticale,** a nutritious wheat-rye hybrid, has a mild flavor reminiscent of wild rice.			

GRAIN/DESCRIPTION	AMOUNT LIQUID (cups)	COOKING TIME (minutes)	YIELD (cups)
Hulled barley has only the outer husk removed. It has a sweet, mildly herbal flavor.			
Black barley's deep purple grains become mahogany and shiny when cooked. Their flavor suggests beans, grass, lemon zest, and nuts.	3	40	3
RICES SLENDER (LONG-GRAIN) WHITE RICES HAVE THE HUSK, BRAN, AND GERM REMOVED, SO THEY ARE MORE DELICATE AND TENDER THAN BROWN RICES. BROWN RICES, IN WHICH ONLY THE INEDIBLE OUTER HUSK IS REMOVED, RETAIN THE BRAN AND GERM, SO THAT THEY ARE MORE NUTRITIOUS AND CHEWIER, WITH AN EARTHIER FLAVOR THAN WHITE RICES. LONG-GRAIN RICES HAVE THIN ELONGATED GRAINS THAT BECOME FLUFFY AND DISTINCT WHEN COOKED.			
Carolina and other plain long-grain white rices are the most common rice eaten in the United States. Fluffy, bland, and comforting, they are good all-purpose rices. Converted rice, processed to prevent overcooking, does not have as fine a flavor or texture.	1¾ to 2	15 to 20	3
Basmati is a traditional Indian rice with a nutty, floral flavor and a fine grain. There are several varieties of basmati rice. All except Texmati should be washed before cooking. Swirl in a bowl of cold water, drain, and repeat until the water runs clear; drain again.	1¾	15 to 20	2½
Gobindavog (kalijira) is also known as baby basmati because its grains are as small as sesame seeds. It has an extremely delicate texture and basmati flavor.	1¾	15 to 20	2½
Texmati, grown in Texas, has a milder flavor than that of regular basmati.	1¾ to 2	15 to 20	2½
Brown basmati is among the more delicate brown rices.	2½	40 to 50	2½
Jasmine white rice, used widely in Thai and Southeast Asian cooking, is similar to basmati but more delicately flavored. Rinse before cooking.	2	15	4
Popcorn rice, grown in Louisiana, smells like popcorn. Do not rinse.	2	15	4
Wild pecan retains some of the bran and has a taste evocative of pecans. Do not rinse.	1¾ to 2	20	3

GRAIN/DESCRIPTION	AMOUNT LIQUID (cups)	COOKING TIME (minutes)	YIELD (cups)
ROUND (SHORT- AND MEDIUM-GRAIN) WHITE RICES ARE GENERALLY USED FOR RISOTTO AND RICE PUDDING BECAUSE THEY RELEASE STARCH WHEN COOKED TO FORM A CREAMY BINDING WHILE RETAINING A DISTINCT, YET TENDER GRAIN. THERE ARE SEVERAL VARIETIES (SEE PAGE 183 FOR AN IN-DEPTH DISCUSSION OF RISOTTO AND RECIPES).			
Carnaroli makes an exceptionally creamy risotto, so it is ideal for lower-fat risottos.	3¾ to 4	25 to 30	3½
Vialone Nano is also very creamy, with noticeably firm grains that do not easily overcook. Use it when you want to hold partially cooked risotto to finish later.	5 to 5½	25 to 30	3½
Arborio is the most common risotto rice. Because its kernels soften easily, Arborio is better for rice pudding than it is for risotto.	3¾ to 4	25 to 30	3½
Baldo, a recently developed hybrid that cooks faster than most risotto rices, is also good for rice pudding.	3¾ to 4	25 to 30	3½
Granza is a medium-grain rice from Valencia, Spain, where it is used for paella. Because it is starchy and plump, it is also excellent for risotto.	3¾ to 4	25 to 30	3½
DARK, UNUSUALLY FLAVORED RICES MAKE INTERESTING SIDE DISHES.			
Wehani is a reddish brown California basmati–brown rice hybrid with a hearty, nutty, slightly musky potato-skin flavor. Salt after cooking.	2½	40	2⅔
Red rice (Christmas rice) is a brown short-grain rice from an Asian strain. It has a somewhat musky flavor reminiscent of wild mushrooms. Rinse well before cooking. It is a bit stickier than most brown rices.	2½	45	3
Bhutanese red rice is partly milled so it cooks faster than red rice cooks. It has a mild, sweet, nutty flavor. Rinse well before cooking.	2¼	30	3
Black rice (Japonica) is a dark purple rice from California that becomes quite sticky and shiny when cooked. It has a sweet, somewhat grassy, spicy, mushroomy flavor. Salt after cooking.	1½	25	2

GRAIN/DESCRIPTION	AMOUNT LIQUID (cups)	COOKING TIME (minutes)	YIELD (cups)
OTHER GRAINS THESE ALL HAVE SOME UNUSUAL QUALITY THAT SETS THEM APART FROM MOST KERNEL GRAINS. IN SOME CASES, THEY MUST BE HANDLED A LITTLE DIFFERENTLY TO ACHIEVE THE BEST EFFECT.			
Wild rice is not really a grain, but a grass that grows in rivers and lakes, and is harvested by hand. It has more protein and B vitamins and fewer calories than most grains. Its inimitable flavor is at once grassy, herbal, and nutty.	3	50 to 60	3½ to 4
Quinoa is not a true cereal grain but is, in fact, related to the green known as lamb's quarters. This small golden grain is slightly crunchy due to the wispy germ that separates from the seed when it is cooked. Its rather grassy flavor, reminiscent of millet, peanuts, and wheat, can be an acquired taste. Rinse quinoa well in a strainer and shake dry. Or toast, stirring, for several minutes in a dry skillet.	2 to 2½	15	3
Black quinoa from Colorado, a natural hybrid of golden millet and lamb's quarters, is particularly delicious. Cook as you would regular quinoa.			
Millet is a small, birdseed-like grain with a mild, nutty corn flavor. Rinse well in a strainer and shake dry. Toast before boiling.	2½ to 3	25 to 30	3
Kasha is the common name for roasted buckwheat groats. It has a soft texture and an earthy, nutty flavor. Because the grains can become mushy, it is essential to sauté them with egg before boiling them to keep them distinct. Beat 1 egg or 2 whites, add the kasha, and stir to coat. Cook, stirring, until dry and separate. Add the liquid and cook until tender but not mushy.	2	7 to 12	3

Basic Cooked Kernel Grains

This lightened pilaf method is my favorite way to cook grains for maximum flavor with a minimum of fat. First, sauté the grains in a small amount of fat, which helps them retain their distinct texture and, more important, lends a buttery finish to the cooked grains, eliminating the need for adding fat at the end. Then, add a precise amount of liquid, which will evaporate by the time the grains are cooked, leaving all the nutrients in the pan and the kernels perfectly cooked. This method is best for grains that will stand on their own in main courses or side dishes. Simply boiling grains without sautéing them first is the right way when you want firm grains that will be embellished or cooked further, for a salad or to add to soups and stews, or when you are making porridge or cereal.

With either method, the grains can be boiled in plain water or in a flavorful liquid, such as a broth (or even herb- or spice-infused water). Simply add the flavorings directly to the cooking liquid: sautéed onions or garlic, herbs, ginger, lemongrass, kaffir lime leaves, spices, and so on. A chunk of smoky ham will impart a subtle smoky flavor to earthier grains.

If you wish to cook grains without any fat whatsoever, follow the pilaf method above, but toast the grains in a dry pan over low heat without fat until they are fragrant and have colored slightly. This will bring up their nutty flavor, although without the buttery finish that the fat achieves. For ways to embellish cooked grains, see pages 176 to 177.

1 tablespoon extra-virgin olive oil or 1½ teaspoons unsalted butter plus 1½ teaspoons extra-virgin olive oil.

½ to ¾ cup finely chopped onions or leeks or ¼ cup finely chopped shallots (optional)

1 cup kernel grain, such as rice, farro, or barley

Flavorings (optional), singly or in combination, such as

½ to 1 teaspoon spices, such as fennel, cardamom, or cumin seeds, **or Flavor Essence** (pages 541–548), such as Sandy's Curry Powder

Large pinch of saffron threads

4 to 5 sprigs fresh herbs, such as rosemary, savory, or thyme

2 imported bay leaves

1½ tablespoons grated or chopped fresh ginger

1 stalk lemongrass, trimmed and minced

2 kaffir lime leaves

2 ounces lean smoky ham, cut into 2 or 3 pieces

1 ½ to 4 cups water or broth, such as unsalted homemade (page 574) or canned low-sodium chicken broth, or Hearty Porcini-Miso Broth (page 573), or Leek Broth (page 569); refer to the chart on pages 170 to 173 for amounts

¼ to ½ teaspoon kosher salt

In a heavy medium saucepan, heat the oil over moderately low heat. Stir in the onions, cover, and cook, stirring occasionally, until soft, about 5 minutes. Add the grain and optional flavorings and stir for 1 minute to coat the grain completely with oil.

Add the water and salt and bring to a boil. Reduce the heat to low, cover, and simmer for the cooking time indicated in the chart on pages 170 to 173.

Turn off the heat and let the grain sit undisturbed for 5 minutes before serving.

USING LEFTOVER GRAINS

Most kernel grains, with the exception of risotto rices, can be reheated with little loss in flavor or texture. To reheat, place the leftover grains in a heavy saucepan over moderate heat with a tablespoon or two of water, cover, and cook, stirring frequently, until just heated through.

Leftover grains make excellent stuffings for chicken or birds. Season them with herbs, sautéed onions, nuts, and/or dried fruit.

Add leftover large, firm kernel grains such as farro and barley to soup at the last minute so they don't get mushy.

If leftover grains are still distinct and fluffy, you can make them into delicious salads. Add chopped vegetables, nuts, and herbs and dress with a vinaigrette. See page 441 for examples.

Leftover boiled grains make delicious, sustaining breakfast porridges (this won't work for grains cooked by the pilaf method with onion). Place the grains in a medium saucepan and add enough water to barely cover the grains. Cook until they have begun to fall apart into a thick porridge. You can add dried fruit while the grain is cooking if you like. Serve with milk and honey or brown sugar. Or simmer 2 cups leftover grain in 2 cups low-fat milk with ¼ cup dried fruit until hot. Wild rice is marvelous this way.

Dressing Grains with Nuts, Seeds, and Dried Fruit. Nuts, seeds, and dried fruits make wonderful instant embellishments for grains. Since they are very caloric (nuts average 175 calories per ounce), use them sparingly, adding just enough to accentuate the grain, about 1 tablespoon per serving. Roast nuts and seeds to bring out their flavor. Coarsely chop and add to the grains just before serving so that they won't get soggy.

Peanuts, almonds, cashews, pistachios, and pine nuts go especially well with milder grains and fragrant rices, and those cooked in an Indian or Southeast Asian style.

Pecans, walnuts, pine nuts, hazelnuts, and pumpkin seeds and boiled or roasted chestnuts go well with more robust grains, such as brown and wild rice, farro, and barley. (Chestnuts, the one low-fat nut, have only 60 calories an ounce.)

Small, slightly tart dried fruits such as cherries, cranberries, golden raisins, currants, and (chopped) dried apricots provide the best balance in grain dishes without being too sweet. Add dried fruit to the grain during the last 5 minutes of cooking so it has a chance to plump and soften a bit.

Dressing Grains with Cheese. Cheeses, especially those that come from the same region as the grain you are using, can add great character to a grain dish. Grits take on a distinctly Southwestern flavor when mixed with Dry (aged) Jack. Polenta soars when topped with Italian Gorgonzola, Parmigiano-Reggiano, or Fontina. That is not to say that you shouldn't mix things up as you feel like it. A risotto can be marvelous made with Spanish Manchego. Manchego is also delicious stirred into corny-tasting grains, like grits, polenta, and millet. Generally speaking, milder, less flavorful grains, such as rices, millet, polenta, grits, and farro, have the greatest affinity for cheese. The unique flavors of more robust grains like wild rice tend to fight with cheese.

Because cheese is so caloric and high in fat, always choose the most flavorful so you can use less. Generally, the harder and more pungent the cheese, the less you will need to use. So, for example, you would need 1 ounce of milder Fontina to flavor a serving of polenta, but only ½ ounce of Parmigiano-Reggiano. For one serving of kernel grains, figure on 1 tablespoon sharp grating cheese or up to 3 tablespoons of a milder cheese.

Cheeses average about 110 calories per ounce, with the exceptions of mozzarella and feta, which have about 80 calories per ounce.

Bear in mind that grains embellished with cheese should be eaten as soon as they are ready. Cheese congeals on cooling and will turn your grain dish into a solid mass.

Dressing Grains with Brown Butter, Nut or Flavored Oils, or Bacon Fat. The most delicious dressing for plain boiled grains is, without a doubt, fat. By using the lightened pilaf method to cook grains (see page 174), you will already have imbued the grains with the fat you used for sautéing, so they won't need any more. If you prefer to dress the hot grains after cooking, here are two tricks to use only ½ teaspoon of fat per serving.

Use the most flavorful fat possible: brown butter (see page 681) rather than regular butter, a good roasted nut oil (page 597 or see Sources, page 711), rendered bacon or pancetta fat (see page 681), or Flavored Oil (pages 588–597).

Extend the fat by emulsifying it with a liquid, such as water, broth (chicken, ham, or leek), orange juice, meat or poultry juices (if you are serving a roast at the same time), or the soaking liquid from dried mushrooms. This will form a dressing that will coat the grains and moisten them, making them taste as if they contain a great deal more fat than they do.

To dress 4 servings (3 cups) hot cooked grain, heat 2 teaspoons flavorful fat in a small skillet or heavy saucepan over moderate heat. Add 2 tablespoons liquid, increase the heat to high, and boil for 30 seconds, until emulsified. Pour over the hot cooked grain and toss to coat, adding salt and pepper to taste.

An ounce of hard cheese, including Parmigiano-Reggiano, pecorino Romano, Dry (aged) Jack, aged Gouda, and aged sheep's milk cheeses, yields about 5 tablespoons grated cheese.

An ounce of medium-hard cheese, including Cheddar, young Manchego, Gouda, and Fontina, yields about ¼ cup grated cheese.

An ounce of soft creamy cheese, including Gorgonzola, fresh goat cheese, and Camembert, equals 2 tablespoons.

Foolproof Rice

MAKES ABOUT
2½ CUPS COOKED;
SERVES 4

Rice is the secret bane of several excellent cooks I know, who can't seem to cook it so the grains are separate and firm yet tender. It's invariably under- or overcooked. This method employs the first steps of a pilaf: the gentle sautéing of the rice in a small amount of oil mixed with butter, which develops its flavor and, in coating the grains, ensures that they will stay separate and fluffy. Then water is added and the rice is baked. It never fails. The initial sauté has the added benefit of making the rice taste very buttery, eliminating the need to add more butter at the end. Because no flavorings are added and water rather than broth is used, the pure flavor of the grain comes through. This method works well for any long-grain rice, including fragrant basmati and wild pecan rice, as well as other whole grains, such as farro, wild rice, and pearl barley (refer to the chart on pages 170 to 173 for the quantity of liquid and the cooking time).

> 1½ teaspoons olive or vegetable oil, or unsalted butter
> 1 cup long-grain white rice
> 2 cups boiling water
> ½ teaspoon kosher salt

Preheat the oven to 400°F.

In a heavy ovenproof 1½- to 2-quart saucepan, heat the oil over moderate heat until hot. Add the rice and cook, stirring constantly, until the rice is fragrant and coated with the oil, about 2 minutes. Stir in the boiling water and salt. Cover the pan, transfer to the oven, and bake for 20 minutes, or until the rice is tender and the liquid has evaporated.

Rice (or Mild Grains) with Ginger and Curry

SERVES 4

Fragrant curry spices like cardamom, coriander, saffron, clove, ginger, cinnamon, and fennel seed are perfection with grains. Although I most commonly use basmati or jasmine rice for this recipe, other mild-flavored grains, such as quinoa, millet, brown rice, and barley, work well. This rice complements any Indian-spiced dish, but also dresses up simple roasted chicken or fish.

2 teaspoons unsalted butter

1 teaspoon vegetable oil

1 medium onion, chopped (¾ cup)

4 garlic cloves, finely chopped

1 cup basmati or jasmine rice

1¼ teaspoons Sandy's Curry Powder (page 548)
or commercial curry powder

1½ tablespoons grated fresh ginger

¼ teaspoon saffron threads, crushed and soaked in
1 tablespoon warm water for 10 minutes (optional)

1½ to 2 cups unsalted homemade (page 574)
or canned low-sodium chicken broth

¼ teaspoon kosher salt

¼ cup chopped fresh cilantro (optional)

In a heavy medium saucepan, combine the butter, oil, and onions, cover, and cook over low heat, stirring frequently, until the onions are soft, about 5 minutes. Uncover, increase the heat slightly, stir in the garlic, and cook, stirring, until the onions are golden, about 3 minutes longer. Add the rice and curry powder and cook, stirring, for 2 minutes to coat the rice with the spices and oil. Stir in the ginger and saffron with its liquid, if using, and cook for 30 seconds.

Add the chicken broth and salt, and bring to a boil. Reduce the heat to low, cover, and simmer for 17 minutes or until the rice is tender but still firm. Turn off the heat and let the rice sit undisturbed for 5 minutes. Garnish with the cilantro, if desired, and serve.

Rice (or Mild Grains) with Fennel Seeds, Bay Leaves, and Cloves. variation Grains cooked this way make a lovely salad, dressed with red onion, lime juice, and olive oil and the cilantro.

Omit the garlic, curry powder, ginger, and optional saffron. When you add the rice, stir in 10 whole cloves, ½ teaspoon fennel seeds, 2 bay leaves, and 1 cardamom pod, crushed. Remove the bay leaves before serving.

Rustic Pilaf with Madeira

Madeira, red wine, and dried wild mushrooms added to the cooking liquid make a robustly flavored pilaf with hearty whole grains such as brown rice, farro, pearl barley, Job's tears, or Japonica rice. You can combine two grains that have the same cooking time, such as farro and barley. Although this makes an excellent side dish or bed for roasted or stewed poultry, lamb, and pork, I like it best as a simple supper, with a grating of aged cheese such as Parmigiano-Reggiano or pecorino Toscano.

> **2 to 3½ cups unsalted homemade** (page 574)
> **or canned low-sodium chicken broth** (see chart, pages 170 to 173, for quantity for the grain you are cooking)
>
> **⅓ ounce dried wild mushrooms,** preferably porcini, rinsed
>
> **2 teaspoons unsalted butter**
>
> **1 teaspoon olive oil**
>
> **1 small onion,** finely chopped
>
> **1 cup grain,** such as farro, brown rice, pearl barley, triticale, or Job's tears
>
> **¼ cup dry Madeira or Marsala**
>
> **¼ cup dry red wine**
>
> **1 tablespoon balsamic vinegar**
>
> **Kosher salt and freshly ground black pepper**

Preheat the oven to 350°F.

In a medium saucepan, bring the broth to a simmer over moderate heat. Add the dried mushrooms, partially cover, and keep at a simmer.

In a heavy medium ovenproof saucepan, combine the butter, oil, and onions, cover, and cook over low heat, stirring frequently, until the onions have released their liquid, about 7 minutes. Uncover, increase the heat slightly, and cook, stirring, until the onions are soft and translucent, about 5 minutes longer. Stir in the grain and cook, stirring frequently, for 3 minutes, or until coated with oil and lightly toasted. Stir in the Madeira and wine and simmer until almost all of it has evaporated, about 3 minutes.

Strain the broth into a measuring cup. If necessary, add water to make the amount of liquid called for, depending on the grain. Pour the broth over the grain.

Cover the grain and bake for 40 minutes. Remove from the oven and let stand for 5 minutes. If there is still liquid left, place the pan over a moderate flame and boil, stirring constantly, until it has evaporated: cover, remove from the heat, and let sit for another 5 minutes before serving. Stir in the balsamic vinegar and salt and pepper to taste.

Whole-Grain Risotto. Increase the broth by 1 cup. Pour all but 1 cup variation of the broth over the grain as directed, and reserve the remaining 1 cup. Just before the grain is cooked, bring the reserved broth to a simmer. Place the pan of cooked grain over moderate heat. Add the broth, ¼ cup at a time, stirring until the grain is very creamy, like risotto. (You may not need all the broth.) Stir in 1½ tablespoons sour cream and ¼ cup freshly grated Parmigiano-Reggiano.

Mozzarella Rice

In this wonderfully simple recipe that I learned from reading Marcella Hazan, hot boiled risotto rice is mixed with fresh mozzarella cheese and fresh basil. The heat of the rice melts the mozzarella into thin strands, making an utterly satisfying quick main course. Although I usually make this dish with a round-grain risotto rice such as Arborio or Carnaroli, you can use just about any large-kernel grain you like, such as brown rice or farro. The only caveat is that this dish must be eaten at once, while it is hot, or it will cool into a rubbery mass.

SERVES 4

Mozzarella has the virtue of being lower in calories and fat than most cheeses, at only 80 calories per ounce. It is worth seeking out authentic fresh mozzarella for its sweet, milky flavor and its ability to melt in such a wonderfully satisfying way. Packaged low-moisture mozzarella is both rubbery and flavorless.

> 1⅓ **cups risotto rice,** such as Arborio or Carnaroli
>
> 1 **tablespoon unsalted butter**
>
> ¼ **cup chopped fresh basil**
>
> **Kosher salt and freshly ground black pepper**
>
> 7 **ounces salted fresh mozzarella cheese,** coarsely shredded (1¾ cups)
>
> ½ **cup freshly grated Parmigiano-Reggiano cheese**

Bring a medium heavy saucepan of water to a boil; salt liberally. Stir in the rice, reduce to a simmer, and cook until the rice is tender but still slightly firm, about 20 minutes. Drain the rice well and return it to the hot pan, or transfer it to a warm serving dish.

Toss with the butter, basil, and salt and pepper to taste. Add the mozzarella, stirring until it is stringy and melted. Serve at once, passing the Parmigiano-Reggiano on the side.

Wild Rice with Leeks and Wild Mushrooms

SERVES 4 Wild rice is delicious tossed with sautés of vegetables such as leeks and wild mushrooms and seasoned with a splash of dry sherry and lemon zest. It makes an excellent side dish for meats, poultry, and game birds, especially roast duck, or a stuffing for chickens and poussin. I often serve it with braise-sautéed artichoke hearts. You can also make this with other firm distinct kernel grains such as farro.

1 tablespoon plus 1 teaspoon unsalted butter

8 leeks, sliced into ¼-inch-thick circles, separated, rinsed, and drained (4 cups)

3 tablespoons water

½ teaspoon kosher salt

½ pound wild mushrooms, such as morel, chanterelle, bluefoot, or shiitake, stems trimmed, left whole if small, otherwise sliced (about 2 cups)

¼ cup medium-dry sherry, such as amontillado

2 cups cooked wild rice (see page 173) **or farro** (see page 170)

2 teaspoons slivered lemon zest

Freshly ground black pepper

In a medium nonstick skillet, cook the butter over moderately low heat until it is amber and smells like roasted nuts. Spoon 2 teaspoons into a small bowl and reserve.

Add the sliced leeks, water, and salt to the skillet. Cover and cook, stirring frequently, until the leeks are soft and most of the liquid has evaporated, 4 to 5 minutes. Uncover and sauté until dry.

Add the mushrooms, cover, and cook until they are wilted and soft, about 4 minutes. Toss a few times and add the sherry and cook until it has evaporated, about 2 minutes. Add the reserved brown butter and the cooked wild rice and sauté until the rice is hot; add a few tablespoons water if the mixture is dry. Stir in the slivered lemon zest and pepper to taste. Serve at once.

RISOTTO.

Risotto, the creamy Italian rice dish, has become the quintessential modern grain dish because it fits so beautifully into our pressured lives. It is easy to make, healthful, open to endless improvisation, and immensely satisfying.

THE RIGHT RICE FOR RISOTTO

Risotto is all about the rice; the flavorings and other ingredients that are added to it are secondary to the texture and flavor of the unique round grained rice—called **superfino**—used to make it. It was not until I met an Italian rice grower that I really understood the culinary possibilities in superfino rice, which goes far beyond Arborio, once the gold standard in America.

Contessa Rosetta Clara Cavalli d'Olivola produces four such rices on her twelfth-century estate in Piemonte, Italy. **Vialone Nano, Carnaroli, Baldo,** and **Arborio** all are high in starch, which binds with the cooking liquid to produce risotto's essential creamy texture. When I tasted these rices side by side, however, their unique qualities became immediately apparent, as did the dishes to which they are best suited.

Both Vialone Nano and Carnaroli make exceptionally creamy risottos, without additional butter or cream. The main difference lies in the texture of their grains. I prefer Carnaroli for risotto because it has a lovely balance of tenderness and firmness and a truly luxurious creaminess. Vialone Nano, the rice favored by Venetians, has chewier and more distinct grains, producing a heartier risotto (it absorbs about one third more liquid than the other rices). I use it in recipes where I want to hold the cooked rice before finishing the dish—either cooking a risotto halfway, then finishing it at the last minute, as chefs often do, or molding the cooked risotto into a savory cake—because there is no danger of the grains becoming mushy. In comparison to these toothsome rices, Baldo, a quicker-cooking hybrid, and the ubiquitous Arborio seem too tender for risotto. I found them to be wonderful in rice pudding (page 522), yielding a thick custardy sauce without eggs or cream and just enough texture to be interesting.

What was remarkable about all these rices was how delicious and fragrant they were. They truly tasted like rice rather than a bland vehicle for other flavorings, due in large measure to their freshness. After the harvest in October, the rice is carefully sorted to ensure plump, unbroken, uniform grains that cook evenly, the first test of really great rice. Such rice is worth seeking out. (See Sources, page 711.)

Simple Risotto

A GUIDE TO IMPROVISING

SERVES 4 AS A
MAIN COURSE, 6 AS
A FIRST COURSE

This is my lightened version of a basic risotto—flavored simply with broth and wine. It is delicious as is, or it can be embellished with cooked meats, poultry, or vegetables. It serves as a departure point for any kind of risotto you might want to make; there are literally hundreds of possibilities for varying the broth, wine, cheese, and other embellishments, as the recipes that follow illustrate. For example, you can transform this simple risotto into an herb risotto by adding ½ cup or more chopped fresh flat-leaf parsley, basil, chives, and chervil, in any combination, during the last few minutes of cooking. If you wish to embellish the risotto with cooked meats, poultry, or vegetables, figure on 1 to 2 cups, shredded, for 4 servings. You can either stir it into the finished risotto or, as in the case of a stew or ragù, spoon it right onto the center of each serving.

Classic risotto calls for quite a lot of butter, generally about 1 to 2 tablespoons per serving. I use the minimum amount necessary to sauté the rice properly—a process that develops the flavor of the rice and ensures that the grains remain distinct, yet become creamy. Then I finish the risotto with a little sour cream, which adds creaminess with very few calories.

Next to the rice, the broth is the most serious consideration in a risotto. Choose a broth that will complement the flavors you will add to the risotto; more mild-flavored broths are usually best (see Broths, pages 567–582). Risottos most often call for chicken broth. If you wish to use canned chicken broth, use unsalted or very low-sodium broths that have a truer flavor than high-sodium brands. You can always simmer the broth with chicken trimmings, bay leaves, or a chunk of Parmigiano-Reggiano rind to freshen the flavor.

5 to 6 cups rich broth, such as unsalted homemade (page 574)
or canned low-sodium chicken broth, Shortcut Poultry Broth (page 576),
or Leek Broth (page 569)

2 teaspoons unsalted butter

1 teaspoon extra-virgin olive oil

¼ cup finely chopped shallots or onions

1½ cups (10 ounces) **Italian rice for risotto,** such as Carnaroli,
Vialone Nano, or Arborio

½ cup dry white wine

1½ tablespoons regular or reduced-fat sour cream

½ cup freshly grated aged cheese, such as Parmigiano-Reggiano,
pecorino Toscano, or Manchego

Kosher salt and freshly ground black pepper

Embellishments (optional), such as

> **About ½ cup chopped fresh herbs,** such as flat-leaf parsley, basil,
> chives, and chervil, in any combination

> **1½ to 2 cups of one of the following** (if necessary, cut into
> bite-sized pieces):

>> **Roasted Wild Mushrooms** (page 40)

>> **Steam-Roasted Leeks** (page 58), without the vinaigrette

>> **Steam-Roasted Fennel with Pancetta and Juniper** (page 58)

>> **Braise-sautéed root vegetables with bacon or pancetta** (page 64)

>> **Spring Vegetable Ragout** (page 68)

>> **Roasted Winter Squash Slices** (page 35)

>> **Wild Mushroom Ragù** (page 151)

>> **Classic Game Ragù** (page 148)

1. In a medium saucepan, bring the broth to a boil over high heat; lower the heat to maintain at a simmer.

2. In a large heavy saucepan, melt the butter with the olive oil over low heat. Add the shallots, cover, and cook, stirring occasionally, until translucent, about 4 minutes. Uncover, increase the heat to moderate, and cook, stirring, until the shallots are golden. Add the rice and cook, stirring constantly, until the grains look chalky with a white dot in the center of each, about 5 minutes. (Do not allow the rice to brown.)

3. Add the wine and cook, stirring, until it has been absorbed by the rice. Stir in ½ cup of the broth. Cook at a very low boil, stirring frequently, until almost all of the liquid is absorbed, 3 to 5 minutes. Continue adding the broth in this fashion, ½ cup at a time, cooking and stirring until the grains of rice are tender yet still firm in the center and the risotto is creamy but not soupy, about 25 minutes.

4. Remove the saucepan from the heat and stir in the sour cream and ¼ cup of the cheese, and season with salt and pepper. If you wish to add herbs, stir them into the risotto. You can stir any other embellishments into the risotto or spoon some—ragùs, for example—right into the center of each serving. Serve at once, passing the remaining ¼ cup cheese on the side.

improvisation 1 ## Classic Saffron Risotto (Risotto Milanese)

Risotto milanese is probably the best-known and most versatile risotto. The saffron—added originally to give the risotto the color of gold for a special wedding feast—gives it a unique flavor that goes with many foods. Beef marrow is traditional in classic versions, but it is hard to find and adds a surfeit of calories.

Follow the Guide above, using rich unsalted homemade chicken broth (page 574) or Shortcut Poultry Broth (page 576). Before beginning the recipe, crumble a large pinch of saffron into ¼ cup warm water in a small bowl; set aside to soak for 15 minutes. After the rice has absorbed the wine in Step 3, add the saffron and its liquid along with the first ½ cup of the broth.

improvisation 2 ## Risotto with Fino Sherry

Years ago I read about a risotto that was flavored with solleone wine, a pale, dry fortified wine from Italy. I've still never tasted solleone, but I have made this delicious derivative risotto many times with dry sherry.

Follow the Guide above, using rich unsalted homemade chicken broth (page 574) or Shortcut Poultry Broth (page 576). Substitute ½ cup fino sherry for the wine and use grated aged Manchego cheese. In Step 3, after you have sautéed the rice, add only ⅓ cup of the sherry; reserve the rest to stir into the risotto just before serving with the sour cream.

Risotto with Bitter or Peppery Greens and Aged Sheep's Milk Cheese

For centuries, wild greens have been lovingly collected and cooked, prized for their refreshing, slightly bitter flavors and health-giving properties. Added to a risotto, these greens become mellowed by cooking with the creamy rice, making an earthy dish that is wonderful accompanied by shavings of hard aged sheep's milk cheese.

You will need 1¼ pounds young dandelion greens or Swiss chard, spinach, and arugula in any combination. Remove the stems, wash the greens in several changes of cold water, and spin them dry. Cut crosswise into ½-inch strips. Reduce the Parmigiano-Reggiano to ¼ cup.

Follow the Guide on pages 184 to 186. In Step 3, after the rice has absorbed 2 cups of the broth, place the greens on top of the rice and add 1 cup broth; do not stir. Cover the pot, reduce the heat to low, and cook for 3 to 4 minutes, until the greens are wilted. Remove the lid and stir the greens into the rice. Increase the heat to moderate and proceed as directed, adding as much as you need of the remaining broth ¼ cup at a time.

In Step 4, remove the saucepan from the heat and stir in the sour cream, Parmigiano-Reggiano, and salt and pepper. Scatter 2 ounces hard sheep's or goat's milk cheese, such as Fiore Sardo or pecorino Toscano, or an aged Crottin de Chavignol or a Coach Farm grating stick, thinly shaved, over each serving. Serve at once.

Risotto Made with Barley and Other Whole Grains

You can use other grains for delicious unorthodox "risotto." Brown rice and pearl barley make a hearty, slightly chewy risotto. Farro also makes a delightful earthy risotto with a sweet, nutty flavor.

Follow the Guide on pages 184 to 186, replacing the rice with whichever whole grain you wish, and be sure to sauté the grains until they are fragrant. You will need to use about 1 cup or so more broth than specified, as tougher grains need more liquid to break down enough to become creamy.

Risotto with Red Wine, Rosemary, and Champagne Grapes

SERVES 4 AS A
MAIN COURSE, 6 AS
A FIRST COURSE

Although red wine risottos are common in the regions of Emilia-Romagna and Piemonte, Alan Tardi, chef and owner of Follonico in New York City, has taken the idea further by adding a handful of tiny champagne grapes, which add a surprising tart counterpoint to the rich risotto.

This risotto is lovely both on its own and as a side dish for roasted game meats. Without the grapes, it makes a fine base for shredded leftover meats and poultry, braised wild mushrooms, or roasted onions or root vegetables.

Many full-bodied dry red wines work well in this risotto, especially Italian Barbera. It is a good way to use up leftover wine of good quality. But it is even better to open a good bottle to make the risotto and drink it while you cook.

4 ½ cups unsalted homemade chicken broth (page 574) **or Shortcut Poultry Broth** (page 576), **or canned low-sodium chicken broth**

2 teaspoons unsalted butter

1 teaspoon extra-virgin olive oil

2 medium shallots or 1 small onion, finely chopped

One 2-inch sprig fresh rosemary or 1 teaspoon dried rosemary

1 imported bay leaf

1 ½ cups Carnaroli, Vialone Nano, or Arborio rice

1 ½ cups full-bodied dry red wine, such as Barolo or Barbera

1 ½ tablespoons regular or reduced-fat sour cream

½ cup freshly grated Parmigiano-Reggiano cheese

Freshly ground black pepper

Pinch of kosher salt and/or sugar if necessary

Scant ½ cup stemmed champagne grapes

In a medium saucepan, bring the broth to a boil over high heat; lower the heat to keep at a simmer.

In a large heavy saucepan, melt the butter with the olive oil over low heat. Add the shallots, rosemary, and bay leaf, cover, and cook, stirring occasionally, until the shallots are translucent, about 4 minutes. Uncover, increase the heat to moderate, and cook, stirring, until the shallots are golden. Add the rice and cook, stirring constantly, until the grains look chalky with a white dot in the center of each, about 5 minutes. (Do not allow the rice to brown.)

Add 1 cup of the red wine and cook, stirring, until it has been absorbed by the rice. Add the remaining ½ cup wine and boil, stirring frequently, until it has been absorbed. Stir in ½ cup of the chicken broth. Simmer, stirring frequently, until almost all of the liquid is absorbed, 3 to 5 minutes. Continue adding the broth in this fashion, ½ cup at a time, until the grains are tender yet still firm in the center and the risotto is creamy but not soupy, 20 to 25 minutes.

Stir in the sour cream, half the grated cheese, and pepper to taste. Remove the bay leaf, add the salt and/or sugar if necessary, and stir in the grapes. Pass the remaining cheese on the side.

You can sauté the onion and rice up to 2 hours ahead. Set aside at room temperature.

IN ADVANCE

Risotto Cake

SERVES 4 AS A MAIN COURSE, 6 AS A SIDE DISH

Since risotto demands almost constant stirring, it is sometimes just too distracting to make when you have company. But you can cook it ahead of time and bake it in a mold at the last minute to make a dramatic crusty cake.

Risotto cakes are wonderfully versatile. Served with a salad, they make an appealing lunch or light supper. Cut into wedges, they make a delicious hors d'oeuvre to serve with drinks, and they are a fine side dish with any number of meat, poultry, or seafood preparations.

To make the crust, I sprinkle a lightly buttered nonstick pan with a little Parmigiano-Reggiano cheese, which melts into a crust. The cake is bound by the rice's creamy starch and the Parmigiano-Reggiano cheese, so it remains moist in the center. The trick is to use a rather simple risotto, one without pieces of vegetables, meats, or seafood, which could make the cake fall apart.

This is also a great way to use up leftover risotto. This recipe uses 4½ to 5 cups risotto. For 2 cups of leftover risotto, use only half the ingredients below and bake in a 7-inch nonstick skillet, to make a delectable small cake for two.

1 garlic clove, halved lengthwise

2 teaspoons unsalted butter, softened

¼ cup plus 2 tablespoons (about 1½ ounces) **finely grated Parmigiano-Reggiano, Manchego, Dry (aged) Jack, or aged Gouda**

Classic Saffron Risotto (page 186) **or Risotto with Fino Sherry** (page 186), made with ¼ cup freshly grated Parmigiano-Reggiano cheese, spread on a baking sheet and cooled completely

Freshly ground black pepper

Preheat the oven to 475°F. Rub the inside of a 10-inch ovenproof nonstick skillet with the cut sides of the garlic clove; discard. Allow the pan to dry for 1 minute, then coat it with 1 teaspoon of the butter.

Sprinkle 3 tablespoons of the cheese evenly over the bottom of the pan. Gently spoon the risotto mixture into the pan, taking care not to disturb the cheese. Press with the back of a spoon to form a flat cake. Sprinkle the top of the cake with the remaining 3 tablespoons cheese and a few grindings of pepper. Dot with the remaining 1 teaspoon butter.

Place the pan over moderate heat for a couple of minutes, until the skillet is very hot and you can hear the cake sizzle. Transfer to the oven and bake for 30 to 35 minutes, until the top is golden brown. Carefully slide a knife down the side of the risotto cake and lift slightly to see if the bottom is brown and crisp. If not, place the skillet on a burner over moderate heat and cook for about 2 to 3 minutes, until browned. Let the cake cool in the pan on a rack for 5 minutes before unmolding.

Place a round platter on top of the skillet. Using pot holders, hold the two together and quickly invert the cake onto the plate. If any of the crust sticks to the pan, carefully pry it off and fit back onto the cake. (Note: If you let the risotto cake cool too much, it may stick to the bottom of the pan. Simply place the skillet over medium heat for a couple of minutes to release the crust.) Cut into wedges and serve.

IN ADVANCE   You can prepare the risotto up to 2 days ahead; cover tightly with plastic wrap once cooled, and refrigerate. You can assemble the risotto cake up to 4 hours ahead; cover and refrigerate until ready to bake.

variation   **Risotto Cakes in Different Sizes.** You can also use this method to make "cakes" of various sizes using tart molds with removable bottoms or springform pans. One recipe risotto (4½ to 5 cups) will make one 10-inch cake, two 7-inch cakes, or six 4½-inch cakes. (Or, for one big cake to serve 12 people, double all the quantities and bake in a 12-inch nonstick skillet or a tart tin with a removable bottom or springform pan.)

Follow the method above, dividing the ingredients evenly between the pans, but if the pans are not nonstick, do not sprinkle any cheese into the pans or the cakes will stick. Instead, sprinkle all the cheese on top of the cake. Bake for 20 to 25 minutes.

Do not invert the cakes. With a knife, gently pry each cake away from the sides of the pan. Release the base, lift it away from the sides, run a thin knife or thin metal spatula under the cake, and slide onto a platter or plate.

Spring Risotto with Asparagus and Peas

Asparagus and peas appear at the same time in spring and, like all things of the same season, they bring out the best in each other. The raw vegetables are added to the cooking rice so their juices flavor the risotto.

You can use almost any kind of vegetable, from butternut squash to parsnips, in the same way. The only trick is to calculate when to add the vegetables to the rice. Longer-cooking vegetables such as winter squash should be added sooner; quicker-cooking vegetables such as leafy greens, later. The vegetables should melt into the rice without being mushy. Al dente vegetables are not appropriate in risotto.

For 4 servings, you need 2 to 2½ cups raw vegetables.

SERVES 4 AS A MAIN COURSE, 6 AS A FIRST COURSE

When making a vegetable risotto, I use the vegetable trimmings, such as tough asparagus ends and pea pods, to infuse the broth with their flavor.

8 ounces asparagus

1 pound peas in the pod or 4 ounces sugar snap or snow peas

3½ to 4 cups unsalted homemade chicken broth (page 574) **or Shortcut Poultry Broth** (page 576), **or canned low-sodium chicken broth**

2 teaspoons unsalted butter

1 teaspoon extra-virgin olive oil

2 medium shallots, finely chopped, or 1 leek, white part only, finely chopped

1 cup Carnaroli, Vialone Nano, or Arborio rice

⅓ cup dry white wine

1½ tablespoons regular or reduced-fat sour cream

½ cup freshly grated Parmigiano-Reggiano cheese

Freshly ground black pepper

Pinch of kosher salt and/or sugar if necessary

2 to 3 teaspoons fresh lemon juice (optional)

¼ cup chopped fresh chervil or flat-leaf parsley

Break the tough ends off the asparagus (when you bend a stalk with both hands, it will break at the point where it is becoming tough and dry). Coarsely chop the stems and put them in a medium saucepan. If using peas in the pod, shell them and add the pods to the saucepan. If using sugar snap peas or snow peas, pull off the stem ends to remove the tough string that runs along the "spines" and add to the pan. Add the broth and bring to a boil over high heat. Reduce to a simmer and cook for 15 minutes; keep at a simmer.

Meanwhile, slice the asparagus stalks on a diagonal into ½-inch pieces. Slice the sugar snaps or snow peas, if using, on a diagonal into ¼-inch slices. Set aside.

In a large heavy saucepan, melt the butter with the olive oil over low heat. Add the shallots, cover, and cook, stirring occasionally, until translucent, about 4 minutes. Uncover, increase the heat to moderate, and cook, stirring, until the shallots are golden. Add the rice and cook, stirring constantly, until the grains look chalky with a white dot in the center of each, about 5 minutes. (Do not allow the rice to brown.)

Add the wine and simmer, stirring, until it has been absorbed by the rice. With a skimmer, scoop the vegetable trimmings out of the simmering broth and discard. Stir in ½ cup of the broth and simmer, stirring frequently, until almost all the liquid is absorbed, 3 minutes. Add another ½ cup broth and simmer, stirring, until it has been absorbed. Stir the asparagus into the rice and add 1 cup of the broth. Cook, stirring frequently, for 3 minutes. Stir in the peas. Continue adding the broth in the same fashion, ½ cup at a time, until the rice grains are tender but still firm in the center and the risotto is creamy but not soupy. Remove from the heat.

Stir in the sour cream, about half of the Parmigiano-Reggiano cheese, and pepper to taste. Add the salt and/or sugar and the lemon juice if necessary to pick up the flavors. Garnish each serving with the herbs, and pass the remaining cheese on the side.

IN ADVANCE You can sauté the shallots and rice up to 2 hours ahead. Set aside at room temperature.

Risotto with Wild Mushrooms

This is one of my favorite risottos, at once rustic and elegant. The wild mushrooms give the risotto a heartiness that you can usually only achieve with a veal broth or rich meat ragù. On the rare occasion when I buy a white truffle, I'll shave it over this risotto.

SERVES 4 AS A MAIN COURSE, 6 AS A FIRST COURSE

This risotto is also excellent when made with other sweet, pearl-like grains, such as barley or farro. Sauté them for 5 minutes, to toast slightly, and proceed as directed, cooking the grains longer and adding more broth to achieve the creamy consistency of a true risotto.

½ **ounce dried mushrooms,** preferably porcini

1 cup boiling water

3 cups unsalted homemade chicken broth (page 574), **or Shortcut Poultry Broth** (page 576), **or Faux Veal Broth** (page 572), **or canned low-sodium chicken broth**

2 teaspoons unsalted butter

1 teaspoon extra-virgin olive oil

2 large shallots, finely chopped

1 garlic clove, minced

2 fresh sage leaves, chopped, or ¼ teaspoon rubbed dried sage

1 cup Carnaroli, Vialone Nano, or Arborio rice

½ **cup dry white wine**

½ **pound fresh wild mushrooms,** such as shiitake, chanterelle, morel, and/or porcini, in any combination, trimmed and sliced

1½ tablespoons regular or reduced-fat sour cream

½ **cup freshly grated Parmigiano-Reggiano cheese**

Freshly ground black pepper

1½ to 2 ounces fresh white truffle, or more (optional)

In a small bowl, soak the dried mushrooms in the boiling water for 30 minutes.

Remove the mushrooms with a slotted spoon, reserving the liquid, rinse, and drain well. Coarsely chop the mushrooms. Set aside.

In a saucepan, bring the broth to a boil over high heat; lower the heat and keep at a simmer.

In a large heavy saucepan, melt the butter with the olive oil over low heat. Add the shallots, garlic, and sage, cover, and cook, stirring occasionally, until the shallots are translucent, about 4 minutes. Uncover, increase the heat to moderate, and cook, stirring, until the shallots are golden. Add the rice and cook, stirring constantly, until the grains look chalky with a white dot in the center of each, about 5 minutes. (Do not allow the rice to brown.)

Add the wine and cook, stirring constantly, until the wine is absorbed by the rice, about 3 minutes. Stir in the fresh mushrooms, the reserved chopped dried mushrooms, and ½ cup of the simmering broth. Pour in the reserved mushroom soaking liquid, taking care to leave any sediment behind. Cook at a gentle simmer, stirring frequently, until almost all the liquid is absorbed, 3 to 5 minutes. Continue adding the broth in this fashion, ½ cup at a time, until the rice is tender yet still firm in the center and the risotto is creamy but not soupy.

Remove the saucepan from the heat and stir in the sour cream, ¼ cup of the Parmigiano-Reggiano, and pepper to taste. Serve immediately. Shave the white truffle, if using, directly onto the risotto at the table.

IN ADVANCE You can sauté the shallots and rice up to 2 hours ahead. Set aside at room temperature.

MILLED GRAINS FROM PORRIDGE TO POLENTA.

Of grains that have been milled into fine meals and flakes, such as oatmeal, bulgur, and cracked wheat, polenta, made of finely ground dried corn, is one of the most appealing and versatile. Simply boiled in water, it makes a thick, creamy porridge with an earthy, sweet corn taste that has an affinity for many savory Mediterranean flavors, from tomatoes and wild mushrooms to herbs and cheese. At once sustaining and delicious, it is a staple of the Italian table.

Grits, milled from white hominy and cooked the same way, might be thought of as American polenta. They have an affinity for Southwestern flavors like cilantro, cumin, chile peppers, and bacon.

Most other milled grains are usually enjoyed as hot breakfast cereals. Paired with milk, dried fruit, and honey or maple syrup, they provide complex carbohydrates and protein, a perfect, long-lasting fuel to start your day. But you can also embellish any milled grain with salt and pepper, cheese, or flavorful fats such as brown butter or a roasted nut oil and serve it as a savory side dish (see Embellishments for Cooked Grains, pages 176–177). Couscous and bulgur have a more nubbly texture that makes them excellent in salads as well. And couscous is, of course, central to the North African dish of that name. See the chart on pages 196 to 197 for descriptions of various milled grains.

Stone-ground grains have a noticeably richer flavor than mechanically milled or quick-cooking grains. They are worth seeking out.

Because milled grains often get lumpy when stirred into boiling water, always stir them into cold liquid and bring the water slowly to a boil, stirring constantly. This allows the grains to swell slowly as the water heats, ensuring lump-free porridge.

Most milled grains are cooked by simply boiling them in enough liquid to make a thick porridge. Use a heavy saucepan with a tight-fitting lid (for 1 cup grain, use a 2-quart pan). Cook until thick and creamy, adding ½ teaspoon salt per 1 cup grains halfway through the cooking.

Although grains are usually boiled in water, you can use broth, milk, or a juice such as apple or pear. You can also add flavorings to the cooking liquid: sweet spices such as cinnamon and vanilla bean or fruit peel for desserts and breakfast grains, herbs such as bay leaves and rosemary for savory dishes.

Store any leftover cooked grains, covered, in the refrigerator. To reheat, place in a saucepan over low heat and add a few tablespoons of water or milk. Stir until creamy and hot.

This chart gives proportions for 1 cup of uncooked grains.

GRAIN/DESCRIPTION	AMOUNT LIQUID (cups)	COOKING TIME (minutes)	YIELD (cups)
Cornmeal is ground from dried white, yellow, or blue corn. It can be fine, medium, or coarsely ground. Stone-ground cornmeal has a more intense corn flavor than commercial meals.	4	35	4
Grits are ground from hominy, dried corn kernels that have been treated with alkali to remove their hulls. They have a sweeter, less overtly corn flavor than regular cornmeal.	5	25 to 30	3
Polenta is the Italian yellow cornmeal used for dishes of the same name (see pages 198–205). In its place, use medium or coarse domestic stone-ground cornmeal.	4	35	4
Old-fashioned rolled oats are oats that have been steamed and flattened to cook into a creamy mild cereal. They can be used in baking for cookies. To bring out a nutty flavor, toast in a small skillet until they are a shade darker and smell nutty. Quick-cooking rolled oats and instant oats are so highly processed they have lost a great deal of flavor.	2	5 to 10	2
Steel-cut oats are oat groats that are cut into small pieces. They make a chewy, creamy porridge with a fuller flavor than one from rolled oats.	4	20 to 25	2

GRAIN/DESCRIPTION	AMOUNT LIQUID (cups)	COOKING TIME (minutes)	YIELD (cups)
Barley flakes, processed like rolled oats, make a chewy porridge with sweet, mildly herbal flavor. Toast the flakes in a dry skillet before cooking.	2	5 to 10	2½
Rolled, flaked spelt is similar to barley flakes but with a wheaty flavor. Do not boil. Instead, to make a porridge, pour boiling water over, cover, and let stand until the liquid is absorbed.	2	(standing time) 10	2½
Cracked wheat is cracked wheat berries that have not been precooked (unlike bulgur). It is chewy with a mildly nutty, toasted flavor; it is used as a cereal and in salads. Toast cracked wheat in a dry skillet before boiling.	2½	15	2½
Bulgur is wheat that has been specially processed, steamed, cracked, and sifted into 3 granulations: fine, medium, and coarse. It has a nutty, toasty flavor and is most often used in salads such as tabbouleh. Place the bulgur in a strainer, rinse, and drain. Then place in a bowl. Pour boiling water over, cover, and let stand until the liquid is absorbed, anywhere from 10 minutes for fine to 60 minutes for coarse.	2½	(standing time) fine: 10 medium: 15 coarse: 60	3
Couscous is a granular semolina (coarsely ground wheat) with a delicate, buttery flavor that takes to flavors well. It comes in fine, medium, and coarse textures. It is commonly used in traditional North African dishes, where it is steamed over an aromatic liquid. For other uses such as salads and side dishes, this modified pilaf method is easier: Sauté the grains in 2 teaspoons oil or butter for about 2 minutes. Add 2 cups boiling water or broth plus ½ teaspoon salt. Cover; set aside for 8 minutes. Fluff, add 1 more cup boiling water, cover, and let stand for 5 minutes, or until the water has been absorbed; fluff with a fork.	3	15	4

POLENTA

There are two basic types of Italian polenta: One is fine-ground, the other coarse. I recommend using the coarsely milled cornmeal, available in Italian specialty stores and gourmet markets, since it has a more interesting texture and more robust flavor.

Basic Polenta (and Other Milled Grains)

essential recipe

SERVES 4

Although polenta may look thick and creamy after 20 minutes of cooking, it takes at least 35 minutes to develop its deep, mellow flavor. In order to keep it from sticking, you have to stir it most of that time. So you have three choices: You can stir it, or enlist someone else to do it, while you chat and sip wine in the kitchen. You can cook the polenta in a double boiler for 1½ to 2 hours, a method that requires only occasional stirring—easily manageable while you prepare the rest of the meal. (This method has the added virtue of allowing you to keep the finished polenta hot and ready to serve for up to an hour.) Or you can bake it virtually unattended in the oven; it takes only 50 minutes.

Use the stove-top method for cooking other milled grains as well, by varying the amount of liquid and the cooking time (polenta and grits are among the few milled grains that take more than 15 minutes to cook). Consult the chart on pages 196 to 197.

Serve the polenta warm in any of the ways suggested below, or see page 201 for Panfried, Roasted, or Grilled Polenta.

> **1 cup polenta or yellow cornmeal,** preferably coarsely ground
> **1 teaspoon kosher salt**
> **4 cups cold water**

To cook polenta over direct heat: In a medium heavy saucepan, combine the cornmeal, salt, and water. Bring to a boil over high heat, stirring constantly with a wooden spoon. Reduce the heat to moderate and cook, stirring constantly to prevent scorching, until the polenta has no trace of bitterness, is thick and smooth, and pulls away from the bottom of the pan, about 35 minutes. If the polenta gets too thick, stir in a few tablespoons more water. Remove from the heat.

To cook polenta in a double boiler: In the top of a double boiler, combine the polenta, salt, and water (or use a stainless steel bowl set over a saucepan of simmering water). Set over, not touching, simmering water, cover with a lid (or foil), and stir the polenta frequently during the first 20 minutes. After that, stir the polenta every 20 to 30 minutes for a total of 1½ to 2 hours until the polenta is thick and has no trace of bitterness. (Replenish the simmering water as necessary.)

To cook polenta in the oven: This is another good method for when you have no time to stand and stir polenta or grits for 35 minutes, especially useful when you have company. Unlike the double-boiler method, it takes only 50 minutes. This is also an easy way to serve polenta with roasted chicken or meat: You can bake both at the same time.

To double the recipe, bring to a boil on top of the stove, then bake 1 hour 20 minutes.

Preheat the oven to 350°F. In a medium heavy ovenproof saucepan, combine the cornmeal, salt, and 3¾ cups cold water. Bring to a boil. Place uncovered on the top rack of the oven and bake for 40 minutes. Stir the polenta, then bake for 10 minutes more.

Serve the polenta warm, spooned into heated shallow soup bowls. Or, for Panfried, Roasted, or Grilled Polenta, see page 201.

THREE WAYS WITH POLENTA (AND OTHER MILLED GRAINS)

Polenta with Olive Oil or Butter and Cheese. The simplest way of serving just-cooked polenta is with a drizzle of good fruity olive oil, freshly grated Parmigiano-Reggiano (or an aged sheep's milk cheese), and plenty of freshly ground black pepper. Oil flavored with garlic and herbs (see pages 591–593) is another quick sauce. Other fats are equally delicious on polenta, such as brown butter (see page 681) or rendered pancetta fat, along with its crisp bits of pancetta (see page 681).

Grits and couscous also take well to savory treatments.

Polenta with Rustic Stews or Sauces. You can also embellish polenta with a stew or sauce. Spoon it right over soft polenta and top with a few tablespoons of freshly grated Parmigiano-Reggiano cheese. This is also a great way to serve Panfried, Roasted, or Grilled Polenta (page 201).

> **Wild Mushroom Ragù** (page 151)
> **Garlic-Scented Salt Cod Puree** (page 272)
> **Peperonata** (page 63)
> **Classic Game Ragù** (page 148)
> **Tomato Sauce** (page 652) or any variation

Breakfast Polenta and Porridges. Just-cooked polenta and other milled grains also make a delicious, sustaining breakfast porridge. Serve with hot milk, dried blueberries, currants, or nuts, and maple syrup. Or top each serving with 3 tablespoons ricotta cheese and a drizzle of honey.

Polenta with Fragrant Herb Oil and Caramelized Garlic

SERVES 4 This is one of my favorite "instant" supper dishes. Unbelievably easy, unbelievably delicious, quintessentially Italian.

Herb-Garlic Oil

2 tablespoons extra-virgin olive oil

10 garlic cloves, thinly sliced

Pinch of red pepper flakes

3 sprigs fresh rosemary, sage, or savory

Basic Polenta (and Other Milled Grains) (page 198), just made

½ cup freshly grated Parmigiano-Reggiano cheese

Freshly ground black pepper

To make the oil, in a small heavy saucepan, combine the oil, garlic, and red pepper flakes. Cook over low heat until the garlic is very soft and begins to "frizzle" (tiny bubbles dance around it) and turns golden, but not brown, about 5 minutes.

Meanwhile, strip the leaves off the herb sprigs; you should have about 2½ tablespoons leaves.

With a slotted spoon, scoop the garlic out of the oil and place on a plate. Reduce the heat to very low and add the herbs. Simmer for 3 minutes, or until the leaves have faded in color and are beginning to crisp.

Divide the hot polenta among four warm shallow soup bowls. Drizzle each serving with 1½ teaspoons oil and sprinkle with 2 tablespoons Parmigiano-Reggiano cheese and fresh pepper. Scatter the garlic and herbs on top.

IN ADVANCE You can make the oil up to 3 hours ahead. Set aside at room temperature.

Panfried, Roasted, or Grilled Polenta

SERVES 4

Because it firms when cooled, polenta can be molded into a variety of shapes. Though there are many possible molds, the easiest is simply to spread it into a loaf pan or onto a baking sheet. Once it is chilled, you can slice it and fry it in a nonstick pan, roast it, or even grill it, until it is crisp with a creamy center. (Replacing 1 teaspoon of the oil with 1 teaspoon melted unsalted butter will make it even crisper.) Serve the slices as a side dish for roasted meats and poultry or as a main course paired with any of the rustic stews and sauces listed on page 199.

> **Basic Polenta (and Other Milled Grains)** (page 198), just made
>
> **2 teaspoons extra-virgin olive oil and/or melted unsalted butter**
>
> **2 garlic cloves,** split, if roasting the polenta
>
> **Kosher salt,** if roasting

While the polenta is still hot, pour it into a 9-by-5-inch loaf pan and pat down evenly. Refrigerate until firm, at least 30 minutes. Unmold the polenta and cut into 12 slices.

To panfry the polenta: In a large nonstick or seasoned cast-iron skillet, heat half the oil over moderately high heat until hot but not smoking. Add half the polenta and fry, turning once, until golden on both sides, about 2 minutes total. Keep warm. Repeat with the remaining oil and polenta.

To roast the polenta: Preheat the oven to 500°F.

In a small bowl, combine the oil and garlic cloves. Set aside to infuse for 15 minutes.

Lightly brush the polenta slices on both sides with the garlic oil. Arrange on a heavy baking sheet or in 2 heavy ovenproof skillets (the heavier the pan, the better the bottom will crisp). Season lightly with salt. Roast in the top of the oven for 20 minutes or until golden.

To grill the polenta: Lightly brush the polenta slices on both sides with the oil. Arrange on a grill over white-hot, ash-covered coals (not open flame) and cook until the underside is golden, about 5 minutes. Flip the polenta and grill on the other side until golden, about 5 minutes longer.

IN ADVANCE

The polenta can be made up to 3 days ahead, covered and refrigerated. Bring to room temperature before proceeding.

Polenta Cake with Olive Paste and Mozzarella

SERVES 4 I first learned of the affinity of cornmeal and olives from John Thorne's newsletter *Simple Cooking*, in which he described slathering some hot corn bread with olive paste. So I decided to try it with polenta and top it with fresh mozzarella cheese. Baked in the oven, it makes the ultimate "grilled cheese."

> **Basic Polenta (and Other Milled Grains)** (page 198), just made
>
> **1 teaspoon extra-virgin olive oil**
>
> **1 garlic clove,** cut lengthwise in half
>
> **⅓ cup Olivada** (page 655) or homemade (see page 683) or commercial olive paste
>
> **8 ounces lightly salted fresh mozzarella cheese,** shredded

While the polenta is still hot, pour it onto a 12-inch pizza pan or divide it among four 5- to 6-inch ramekins or tart pans. With a metal spatula or knife dipped in cold water, spread the polenta evenly in the pan(s). Let cool for about 30 minutes, until firm.

Preheat the oven to 475°F. Brush a heavy baking sheet with the olive oil. Rub it with the garlic clove.

Gently unmold the polenta onto the baking sheet. Rub the top of the polenta gently with the cut sides of the garlic clove. Spread the olive paste evenly over the top of the polenta, leaving a ½-inch border uncovered. Scatter the mozzarella cheese evenly over the top, leaving ½-inch border all around. Bake for 5 to 6 minutes, until the cheese has melted and is beginning to brown. Serve hot.

IN ADVANCE You can mold the polenta cake(s) up to 2 days ahead, cover, and refrigerate. Bring to room temperature before baking.

variation **Polenta Cake with Fontina.** Fontina, from Italy's Val d'Aosta, is often served with white truffles, also from the region. Polenta with Fontina is sensational drizzled with white truffle oil.

Replace the mozzarella with 1 cup (4 ounces) Fontina cheese, shredded, and 1 tablespoon freshly grated Parmigiano-Reggiano. Bake as directed, pepper generously, and drizzle 1 teaspoon white truffle oil over the top of the large cake, less over each smaller one.

Polenta "Gnocchi" Gratin

I am crazy for traditional Italian casseroles that layer polenta with lots of SERVES 4 butter and cheese, so I devised a leaner version that achieves the same effect: golden and crisp on the outside, soft and tender underneath. I arrange disks of "gnocchetti" in overlapping fashion, like roof tiles or fish scales, in a baking dish and brush them with an infused butter so flavorful that only 1½ teaspoons per serving is necessary.

This is an excellent party dish as it can be prepared several hours ahead and refrigerated, covered with plastic wrap. Let stand at room temperature for an hour before baking.

> **Basic Polenta (and Other Milled Grains)** (page 198), just made
> **Sage Butter**
> > About 20 fresh sage leaves
> > 1 tablespoon plus 2 teaspoons unsalted butter
> > 1 teaspoon extra-virgin olive oil
> > 2 garlic cloves, thinly sliced
> **Freshly ground black pepper**
> ⅓ cup freshly grated Parmigiano-Reggiano cheese

While the polenta is still hot, pour it onto a flat cookie sheet or a clean cutting board. With a metal spatula or knife dipped in cold water, spread the polenta to an even layer about ⅜ inch thick, about 14 by 10 inches. Let cool for about 30 minutes, until firm.

Preheat the oven to 450°F.

To make the sage butter, stack 7 of the sage leaves and cut crosswise into the thinnest possible strips, to make a chiffonade. In a small saucepan, combine the butter, olive oil, garlic, and sliced sage, cover, and cook over low heat until the garlic is soft, about 6 minutes. Strain the flavored butter into a small bowl; reserve it along with the solids.

Brush an oval 13-by-9-inch baking dish lightly with the sage butter. Sprinkle with 1 tablespoon of the Parmigiano-Reggiano.

Moisten a 1½-inch biscuit cutter or a small glass with cold water and cut the polenta into disks. Carefully lift up the sections of excess polenta from between the gnocchetti and lay them in the bottom of the dish. Brush them lightly with sage butter and scatter the reserved cooked sage and garlic over the top. Sprinkle with 2 tablespoons of the Parmigiano-Reggiano and a few grinds of pepper. Beginning at one end of the dish, arrange the polenta disks on top of this layer, overlapping them like roof tiles. Tuck the remaining whole sage leaves under some of the disks, so that only about half of each leaf is showing. Brush the top with the remaining sage butter and sprinkle with the remaining 2 tablespoons cheese and a few grinds of pepper.

Bake on the top rack of the oven for 30 to 35 minutes, until the top is golden and crusty. Serve hot.

IN ADVANCE You can mold the polenta up to 3 days ahead; wrap well and refrigerate. You can assemble the casserole up to 3 hours ahead; cover and let sit at room temperature.

Polenta Marbled with Beans

SERVES 8 I learned this unusual polenta dish from chef Piero Ferrini at La Cucina al Focolare, a cooking school in Tuscany. Piero folded local borlotti beans into warm polenta and molded it into a loaf that he sliced and fried to make crisp, marbelized slabs.

> ⅓ **cup** (2½ ounces) **borlotti or cranberry beans,** picked over and rinsed
>
> **6 garlic cloves,** lightly smashed, tissuey skin removed
>
> **5 large sage leaves**
>
> **2 teaspoons kosher salt,** or more to taste
>
> **1½ cups coarse polenta**
>
> **4½ cups cold water**
>
> ⅓ **cup** (1 ounce) **finely grated aged pecorino Toscano, Fiore Sardo, or Parmigiano-Reggiano cheese**
>
> **Freshly ground black pepper**
>
> **1 tablespoon plus 1 teaspoon extra-virgin olive oil**

Soak the beans overnight in a medium heavy saucepan with enough water to cover by 3 inches. Drain and add fresh water to cover by 3 inches, along with the garlic and sage. Simmer until the beans are just tender but not falling apart, about 1 hour; season with ½ teaspoon of the salt after 30 minutes. Replenish the water as necessary so that the beans have plenty of water to cook in. Drain the beans and discard the garlic and sage.

In a large heavy saucepan, combine the polenta, water, and the remaining 1½ teaspoons salt. Bring to a boil over high heat, stirring constantly. Reduce the heat to medium and cook, stirring frequently, until very thick and it pulls away from the sides and bottom of the pan, about 25 minutes. Stir in the cheese and pepper to taste. Adjust the seasonings, then gently fold in the beans with a spatula, being careful not to break the beans.

Spoon the mixture into a 4-by-8½-inch loaf pan or two 3½-by-5½-inch mini-loaf pans, pressing down with the back of a spoon to remove any air pockets. Cool to room temperature, cover, and refrigerate until completely firm, about 1 hour. Unmold the polenta and cut into ½-inch-thick slices.

Heat 2 large nonstick skillets over medium heat. Add half the oil to each and swirl to coat. Arrange the slices in the pans. Fry them for 2 to 3 minutes on each side until golden and crisp, adding more oil as necessary. (Alternatively, you can brush the slices with the oil and grill them over hot coals.) Serve hot.

IN ADVANCE You can prepare the beans up to 2 days ahead and store, covered, in the refrigerator. You can assemble the loaf up to 2 days ahead and store, covered, in the refrigerator.

Mussels in Curry
Broth (page 256)

FISH & SHELLFISH

In the Oven

On the Stove Top

It seems that we have had it wrong all these years, assuming that early man was a Fred Flintstonesque carnivore and that our desire to eat meat is justified by thousands of years of history. It is likely that humanoids evolved next to bodies of water, lakes, rivers, and oceans, where they consumed fish and marine algae that contained the essential building blocks—omega-3 fatty acids—for human development. We humans still need marine foods to thrive.

Many researchers now believe that the reduced consumption of fish and marine products over the last century has virtually starved Western people of essential omega-3 fatty acids. The evidence of the benefits provided by omega-3 fatty acids is compelling, from reducing triglycerides while increasing HDL to supporting proper brain function to protecting against certain kinds of heart disease. Fish also provides high-quality protein that is rich in vitamins and minerals such as selenium, phosphorous, copper, and zinc, without the saturated fat of red meats. All this sound nutrition, coupled with the deliciousness and variety of seafood, makes it an essential component of a healthful diet.

Cooking fish remains daunting to many people. Beyond broiled fillets, shrimp, and the occasional boiled lobster, fish simply hasn't been in our culinary vocabulary until recently. Because its flesh is more delicate than that of meats or poultry and can overcook easily, fish can seem tricky to cook. This chapter will show you basic fish-cooking techniques that produce the best results with the least effort, and without relying on butter or cream to make fish moist

Fennel-Grilled Fish
(page 221), served
with Citrus and
Olive Oil Sauce for
Roasted or Grilled
Fish (page 219)
and Herb Salad
(page 415)

and flavorful. The first section covers oven methods, from roasting to papillote cooking. The second section deals with stove-top cooking, from searing and panfrying to making fragrant soups and "shellfish steams." For quick, delicious fish dishes, cook fish or shellfish using any of the simple methods described in this chapter, then pair it with a sauce or a side-dish "bed," as suggested on pages 214 to 215.

Buying Fish. The surest test of a fish's freshness is its smell. Fresh fish hardly smell, at the most like the sea, sometimes not at all. If a fish smells "fishy," it is no longer fresh. Similarly, if a fish counter or market smells strong and fishy, the quality of its product will be dubious.

The flesh of a fish should be firm, springing back when touched. It should glisten as though it had just come out of the water. As a fish begins to deteriorate, its flesh becomes increasingly dull and slimy looking, as though coated with a dirty film; gills, initially bright and cherry colored, will begin to turn brown and muddy looking; and the eyes, initially clear, will gradually begin to cloud and sink into the head. The flesh of fillets should have a bright sheen and slight translucence; the grain should be uniform, without visible gaps. Fillets that normally have some coloration, for example, swordfish and tuna, should be red-pink, not brown.

Buying Shellfish. Mollusks such as clams, mussels, and oysters should always be bought live, their shells tightly closed. If their shells gape open, they should close immediately when rapped on the counter, which indicates they are still alive; if they don't, discard them. Bad shellfish smell putrified and should be thrown out. The old admonition to eat shellfish only in the months with "R" in them has a lot of merit. These months tend to be winter months, when the water is cold and the levels of bacteria mollusks might consume are diminished. Also, the flesh tends to be sweeter and firmer, since the mollusks are not spawning.

Lobsters should always be bought live, since there is no way to tell how long a lobster has been dead once it is killed. Deteriorating shrimp will smell like ammonia and will be slimy.

It is important to buy shellfish at reputable fishmongers where they are selling either farmed shellfish or shellfish grown in monitored waters. Farm-raised mussels from New Zealand, Maine, and Washington State are among the best available nowadays, and have the added virtue of having little or no grit, sand, or beards to remove. Along with the traditional little-neck clams, delicious sweet Manila clams are widely available, as are cockles, which are smaller than either but have a lovely briny flavor.

Like any other food, fish should be consumed in moderation, because many of the world's waterways are polluted to some degree. Since fish and shellfish filter great quantities of water through their systems, these toxins and residues can build up in the flesh. It is advisable to vary the kinds and origin of seafood you eat, to avoid the ingestion of any one contaminant in quantity.

About Frozen Fish and Shellfish. Because the flesh of fish and shellfish is very delicate, any but the most high-tech methods of flash freezing can wreak havoc on it, particularly fillets and steaks. Deterioration is especially noticeable once the fish is cooked, when it loses liquid and becomes mushy, with diminished taste. The process is less damaging for frozen whole (gutted) fish; the bones and skin provide both structure and flavor. Shrimp are a notable exception and hold up well to freezing (most of the shrimp we eat has been frozen), although the flavor and texture of fresh shrimp are unparalleled.

SEARCHING OUT A FISH MARKET

Generally speaking, it is best to buy fish and shellfish from a quality fish market where you can cultivate a relationship with the purveyor and take a good look at the fish. The difficulty with buying fish in supermarkets is that there is no way to know the history of the fish, how long it has been out of the water, and so on. However, if you have no other recourse, it is possible to hedge your bets with the Supermarket Survival guidelines at right.

A TRICK FOR FISH AND SHRIMP THAT AREN'T PERFECT

Occasionally you will buy fish that is less than perfectly fresh though still quite edible. To freshen its flavor, sprinkle a couple of teaspoons of sake over it about 30 minutes before cooking. The sake will take away any off odors and sweeten the flesh.

To freshen the flavor of shrimp that have been frozen, soak them in a brine for 10 to 15 minutes. The brine: For 1 to 1½ pounds shrimp in their shells, dissolve ⅓ cup kosher salt (or 3 tablespoons sea salt, which has a fresher flavor) in 1 cup boiling water in a large bowl; stir in 3 cups cold water to cool it down. Let the shrimp soak, then drain, rinse, and pat dry.

SUPERMARKET SURVIVAL

1. Buy fish with an expiration date at least 3 days ahead, preferably longer. Fish with a date closer than that has been sitting around too long to be acceptably fresh.

2. Scrutinize the fish through the package. The qualities outlined on page 212 should apply.

3. Sniff the package. If you can smell the fish through the packaging, it is not fresh enough.

CONSTRUCTING A DISH FROM SIMPLE ELEMENTS

If you were to analyze a complex fish dish from a great contemporary chef, you would most likely find that it was composed of several distinct, separately prepared elements: A simple seared salmon fillet, for example, might be nestled on a bed of mashed potatoes and served with a rich red wine sauce. This basic approach works wonderfully at home, too: Make a quick, delicious fish dish by cooking fish or shellfish using any of the simple methods described in this chapter, then pair it with a Flavored Oil (see pages 588–597) or Sauce (see pages 605–671) or a side-dish "bed," as suggested below.

SAUCES FOR SIMPLY COOKED FISH AND SHELLFISH

Cool Sauces
FOR ROASTED, GRILLED, BROILED, OR PAN-SEARED FISH AND SHELLFISH.

Roasted Garlic Aïoli

Rouille

Romesco

Yogurt Sauce with Toasted Spices, Lime Zest, and Basil

Apple, Cucumber, or Green Mango Raita

Uncooked Fresh Tomato Sauce

Salsa made with fresh tomatoes or mangoes

Roasted Tomatillo Salsa

Charred Onion Salsa

Cilantro and Coconut Chutney

Warm Sauces
FOR ROASTED, GRILLED, BROILED, OR PAN-SEARED FISH AND SHELLFISH.

Basic Vinaigrette (warmed)

Rustic Olive Vinaigrette (warmed)

Infused Oil and Balsamic Vinaigrette

Warm Sesame, Ginger, and Scallion Vinaigrette with Salted Black Beans

Warm Anchovy and Olive Oil Sauce

Warm Curry Vinaigrette

Fruit Juice Vinaigrettes

Leek and Saffron Cream

Brown Butter and Balsamic Sauce

Shallot-and-Vinegar Butter Sauce

Vanilla Butter Sauce
(for lobster, shrimp, and crayfish)

Sorrel Butter Sauce

Herb Butter Sauce

Port Wine Butter Sauce

Spicy Carrot Juice Sauce

Red Pepper–Juice Sauce

Warm Beet Juice Vinaigrette

Roasted Tomato Sauce

Pumpkin Seed Sauce

Special Sauces

FOR OILY, RICH-TASTING, OR PARTICULARLY
MEATY FISH.

Port Wine Butter Sauce

Red Wine Essence

Balsamic Syrup

Flavored Oils

FOR ROASTED OR GRILLED FISH AND SHELLFISH,
AND TO DRIZZLE INTO STEWS AND STEAMS.

Chive Oil

White Truffle Oil

Basil (or Cilantro) Oil

Roasted Garlic Oil

Provençal Herb Oil

Saffron Oil

ACCOMPANIMENTS AND "BEDS" FOR PAN-SEARED, ROASTED, OR GRILLED FISH

Another way to serve simply cooked fish is on a bed of vegetables or grains, such as Greek-Style Potatoes with Lemon and Thyme for Fennel-Roasted Fish, or Sorrel Mashed Potatoes for Slow-Roasted Salmon. Often the bed itself is juicy enough to act as a sauce, or you can add a separately made sauce. Using any of the following recipes, make a bed on each plate, then place a portion of the fish right on top.

Spring Vegetable Ragout (page 68)

Peperonata (page 63)

Buttermilk Mashed Potatoes (page 77)

Wasabi Mashed Potatoes (page 79)

Sorrel Mashed Potatoes (page 79)

Fresh Corn "Polenta" (page 82)

Greek-Style Potatoes with Lemon and Thyme (page 49)

Sweet Onion and Tomato Gratin (page 52)

Slow-Roasted Tomatoes (page 38)

Steam-Roasted Fennel with Pancetta and Juniper (page 58)

Classic Saffron Risotto (page 186)

Risotto with Fino Sherry (page 186)

Quinoa Salad with Lemongrass, Cilantro, and Mint (page 446)

Rice (or Mild Grains) with Ginger and Curry (page 178)

Herb Salad (page 415)

The old test, to cook fish until it flakes, really indicates that the fish is overdone. Fish is cooked when the flesh has become opaque with a slight translucence and is firm, yet tender and moist. The following tests for doneness are far more accurate.

For Whole Fish: Slide a sharp paring knife into the flesh along the spine and gently lift up: The flesh should still be ever so slightly translucent near the bone but just pull away from it.

For Fillets and Steaks: Push a two-pronged kitchen fork straight down into the flesh. If you feel no resistance, the fish is cooked. If it feels as if the fork is pushing through a membrane, cook the fish for another minute or two.

Always let fish rest for a few minutes before serving.

IN THE OVEN: ROASTING. For the novice or fearful fish cook, roasting in the dry heat of the oven is the way to go. You can cook whole fish at high heat for a crisp skin and moist flesh, sear thick fillets without smoking up your kitchen, or slow-roast whole sides of salmon—all with dazzling results for little work.

Roasted or Grilled Whole Fish

A GUIDE TO IMPROVISING

I learned this simple method from my mother, who cooks fish in the traditional Greek way. She makes several shallow slashes in the sides of the fish to permit even cooking and allow some flavorings to penetrate the flesh. Then she marinates it in olive oil and lemon juice and roasts or grills it. I like to take it one step further and stuff the cavity with fresh herbs—rosemary, thyme, and bay leaves—whose flavor delicately scents the fish. You can also add spices or fresh or dried herbs to the marinade. Serve the fish with just a drizzle of fine extra-virgin olive oil or Citrus and Olive Oil Sauce.

You can roast the fish in a hot oven or grill it over a wood or charcoal fire; either way, the skin will be crisp and the flesh succulent. This method works well for both oily and white-fleshed fish. Even the homely and much maligned mackerel is delicious this way.

You can use this method for fish from 1 to 3 pounds. The only fixed proportion is the marinade. The amount and kinds of herbs you use is up to you. For a 1-pound fish, use 1 small bunch each of rosemary and thyme and 2 bay leaves.

You can use this formula for any whole fish up to 3 pounds, gutted and scaled.

To feed 1 person:
one 1- to 1¼-pound fish

To feed 2 people:
1½- to 1¾-pound fish

To feed 4 people:
one 3-pound fish
or two 1½- to
1¾-pound fish

> **Marinade** (per pound of fish)
>> **2 teaspoons extra-virgin olive oil**
>>
>> **1 tablespoon fresh lemon juice**
>>
>> **About 1 teaspoon kosher salt**
>
> **1 small bunch fresh herbs** (per pound of fish), such as rosemary, thyme, fennel fronds, oregano, and/or 4 imported bay leaves, in any combination
>
> **Sauce** (optional)
>> **Extra-virgin olive oil** (1 teaspoon per serving for drizzling)
>>
>> **Citrus and Olive Oil Sauce for Roasted or Grilled Fish** (page 219)

1. Rinse the fish inside and out with cold water; pat dry. Lay the fish on a flat platter. With a thin sharp knife, cut three ¼-inch-deep slashes in each side.

2. In a small bowl, combine the olive oil and lemon juice and rub all over the fish. Sprinkle the salt in the cavity and all over the skin of the fish. Stuff the cavity with half the herbs. Let the fish marinate for 15 to 30 minutes at room temperature.

3. Preheat the oven to 500°F. Place a rack in a shallow roasting pan.

4. Pull the leaves off several of the remaining herb sprigs and push the leaves into the slashes on top of the fish. Make a bed of the remaining herb sprigs on top of the rack and place the fish on it.

5. Roast the fish on the middle rack of the oven, figuring on slightly less than 10 minutes per inch of thickness (a 1½-pound fish will take about 14 minutes, a 3-pound fish about 25 minutes). To test for doneness, slide a sharp paring knife into the flesh along the spine and gently lift up: The flesh should still be ever so slightly translucent near the bone but just pull away from it. Transfer the fish to a warm platter.

6. **To fillet the fish:** Using a cake server or a thin pointed spatula, cut through the skin along the back of the fish. Gently slide the spatula between the spine and the top fillet; lift up the fillet and transfer to a platter or dinner plate. (If 1 fillet is meant to serve 2 people, divide it.) Slide the spatula under the spine and lift it off the bottom fillet; discard. Gently transfer the bottom fillet to the platter or second dinner plate; divide if necessary. Spoon any juices over the fish and serve at once. Pass the olive oil or sauce on the side, if serving.

Citrus and Olive Oil Sauce for Roasted or Grilled Fish

With its fresh vibrant flavor, this simple citrus and olive oil sauce is a favorite all-purpose sauce for fish, learned from chef Roger Vergé of Moulins des Mougins in the South of France.

MAKES 1½ CUPS;
SERVES 6

3 navel oranges or 4 blood oranges

1 large or 2 small lemons

⅛ teaspoon kosher salt, or to taste

Freshly ground white pepper

2 tablespoons plus 2 teaspoons fruity extra-virgin olive oil

With a thin sharp knife, cut the tops and bottoms crosswise off the oranges and lemons to expose the flesh. Stand an orange on the work surface and, working from top to bottom, carefully cut off the peel and white pith in wide strips, leaving the orange flesh intact. Then, holding the orange over a bowl to catch the juice, cut between the membranes to release the orange sections. Drop the sections into the bowl of juice. Squeeze the membranes to extract the juice and discard the membranes. Repeat with the remaining oranges and lemons.

Season the juice lightly with salt and white pepper. Add the olive oil and toss gently. Set aside until ready to serve.

You can make the sauce up to 2 hours ahead.

IN ADVANCE

Fennel-Roasted Fish

SERVES 4

In the South of France, whole meaty white-fleshed fish like *loup de mer* (bass) and *daurade royale* (bream) are commonly grilled over dried stalks of wild fennel, whose sweet smoke subtly perfumes the flesh. To achieve some of those delicious flavors at home, first rub the fish with a fennel seed–infused olive oil mixed with Pernod, the anise-flavored French aperitif, to intensify the fennel flavor. Then roast (or grill) it over fennel stalks and fronds. Their smoldering smoke will flavor its flesh. Serve it with Citrus and Olive Oil Sauce. You can prepare this recipe with either whole fish or fillets.

Look for wild fennel in specialty produce markets and at farmers' markets. It has smaller bulbs than cultivated fennel, with long feathery branches. Its sweeter flavor makes it well worth seeking out.

Fennel Seed Oil

> **1½ tablespoons fennel seeds**
>
> **1 tablespoon plus 2 teaspoons extra-virgin olive oil**
>
> **1 garlic clove,** thinly sliced
>
> **2 teaspoons Pernod or other anise-flavored aperitif**

2 large fennel bulbs (2½ pounds), with at least 5 inches of stalks and feathery fronds

One 3½-pound fish or two 1½-pound fish, such as red snapper, striped bass, or sea bass, cleaned, or four 6-ounce striped bass or sea bass fillets, with skin

2½ teaspoons kosher salt

Scant ¼ teaspoon cayenne pepper

2 tablespoons fresh lemon juice

6 to 8 thin lemon slices

½ teaspoon olive or grapeseed oil (only if cooking fillets)

Citrus and Olive Oil Sauce for Roasted or Grilled Fish (page 219)

To make the fennel seed oil, in a mortar or spice grinder, coarsely grind the fennel seeds. Add them to a small skillet, along with the olive oil and garlic, cover, and cook over low heat until the garlic is soft and the oil is fragrant (little bubbles will begin to dance around the fennel seeds), about 6 minutes. Add the Pernod and set aside to cool.

Cut the stalks off the fennel bulbs; save the bulbs for another use. Snip off the feathery fronds and coarsely chop them. You will need about 1 cup fronds. Cut the stalks lengthwise into quarters. Reserve.

If preparing whole fish: Rinse the fish inside and out with cold water. Pat dry and lay on a flat platter. With a thin sharp knife, make three ¼-inch-deep slashes across the flesh on each side. Rub the fish with the fennel oil, pushing the ground seeds into the slashes. Sprinkle the salt and cayenne into the cavity and all over the skin of the fish, then drizzle the lemon juice into the cavity and over both sides of the fish. Stuff the cavity with all but ¼ cup of the reserved fennel fronds and the lemon slices. Spread about 2 tablespoons more of the fronds over each side of each fish, pushing them into the slits.

If preparing fillets: Simply rub the fennel oil and lemon juice over them, then sprinkle with 1 teaspoon of the salt and the cayenne. Press the fennel fronds into both sides of each.

Cover the fish and refrigerate for at least 30 minutes and up to 4 hours.

Preheat the oven to 500°F.

To roast a whole fish: Make a bed of the fennel stalks on a baking sheet or in a shallow casserole. Place the fish on top of it. Roast the fish on the middle rack of the oven, figuring on slightly less than 10 minutes per inch of thickness (a 1½-pound fish will take about 14 minutes, a 3½-pound fish about 27 minutes). To test for doneness, slide a sharp paring knife into the flesh along the spine and gently lift: The flesh should still be ever so slightly translucent near the bone but just pull away from it.

To roast fillets: Score the skin to keep it from curling (see page 222). Place a heavy nonstick ovenproof skillet or a baking pan (large enough to hold the fillets in one layer without touching) in the oven to heat for 5 minutes. Pour the oil into the pan and swirl to coat completely. Add the fish skin side down and roast for 5 to 6 minutes, until the skin is nicely browned. Carefully turn the fish over and roast for 4 to 5 minutes longer. To tell if the fish is done, push a two-pronged kitchen fork straight down into the flesh. If you feel no resistance, the fish is cooked; if it feels as though the fork is pushing through a membrane, return the fish to the oven for another minute or two.

To fillet the fish: Using a cake server or a thin pointed spatula, cut through the skin along the back of the fish. Gently slide the spatula between the spine and the top fillet; lift up the fillet and transfer to a platter or dinner plate. (If 1 fillet is meant to serve 2 people, divide it.) Slide the spatula under the spine and lift it off the bottom fillet; discard. Gently transfer the bottom fillet to the platter or second dinner plate; divide if necessary.

Spoon some of the cooking juices over each fillet and serve at once, with the sauce.

IN ADVANCE

You can marinate the fish up to 4 hours ahead.

variation

Fennel-Grilled Fish. If you want to grill the fish, use a hinged fish grill to sandwich the fish and fennel branches, making it easy to turn without breaking or tearing the fish. Turn every 5 minutes, and brush the top with the marinade. Smaller fish and fillets will take about 12 to 15 minutes, larger fish 25 to 30 minutes.

Oven-Seared Thick Fish Fillets

SERVES 4

This simple method guarantees fish fillets that are browned and crisp on the outside with succulent flesh—without smoking up your kitchen. The fillets are roasted in a hot oven in a preheated metal pan so that both sides of the fish get brown and crusty, eliminating the need for preliminary stove-top searing. The fillets must be at least 1¼ inches thick; if they are too thin, they will overcook before they sear properly.

Serve the fillets with a sauce or other accompaniment (see pages 214–215).

Four 6-ounce thick fish fillets, such as striped bass, black bass, Chilean sea bass, halibut, or cod, with skin, scored

2 teaspoons kosher salt

Cayenne pepper

1 teaspoon grapeseed, peanut, or olive oil

1. Preheat the oven to 500°F. Place a heavy nonstick ovenproof skillet or baking pan in the oven to heat for 5 minutes.

2. Pat the fillets dry with paper towels. Sprinkle each fillet lightly with the salt and a pinch of cayenne.

3. Pour the oil into the hot pan and swirl to coat completely. Add the fish skin side down and roast until the skin is nicely browned, about 5 minutes, depending on the thickness of the fish. Carefully turn the fish over and roast for 4 to 5 minutes longer. To tell if the fish is done, push a two-pronged kitchen fork straight down into the flesh. If you feel no resistance, the fish is cooked; if it feels as though the fork is pushing through a membrane, return the fish to the oven for another minute or two. Remove from the oven and let rest for 2 minutes before serving.

SCORING THE SKIN TO PREVENT CURLING

In order to keep the skin on fish fillets from curling when it hits the hot pan, you need to score it first. Place the fillets skin side up on the work surface. With a thin sharp knife or a razor blade, make several shallow parallel slashes in the skin about 1 inch apart. Turn the fillets 90 degrees and make several more slashes to form a crisscross pattern.

Salt-Roasted Shrimp

SERVES 4

Roasting shrimp in their shells on a bed of coarse salt leaves them moist with a pure concentrated sea flavor—with no added calories (and very little work). They are meant to be eaten with one's fingers; cutting the shells open down the back beforehand makes them easy to peel. Serve each guest a little bowl of sauce in which to dip the shrimp, such as Shallot-and-Vinegar Butter Sauce (page 643), Roasted Garlic Aïoli (page 618), Rouille (page 619), Romesco Sauce (page 620), Cilantro and Coconut Chutney (page 665), Warm Sesame, Ginger, and Scallion Vinaigrette with Salted Black Beans (page 613), or Warm Curry Vinaigrette (page 615).

1½ pounds medium shrimp in their shells, rinsed and patted dry

About 1½ pounds kosher salt

Preheat the oven to 400°F.

With scissors, cut down the back of each shrimp, through the shell, and remove the vein. Gently loosen the shell from the flesh, but keep it attached. Rinse the shrimp well and pat dry with paper towels.

Pour the salt into a large baking dish or divide it evenly between two 10-inch skillets or among four 5-inch individual shallow baking dishes. Place in the oven to heat for 7 minutes.

Arrange the shrimp on the salt, nestling them into it slightly but leaving the top surface exposed. Bake the shrimp for 5 to 6 minutes, until they are opaque and slightly undercooked; they will keep cooking on the salt. Serve at once.

IN ADVANCE

You can clean the shrimp up to 6 hours ahead. Cover and refrigerate. Bring to room temperature 30 minutes before cooking and pat dry with paper towels.

Slow-Roasted Fish

A GUIDE TO IMPROVISING

SERVES 4 When you roast fish fillets, particularly fatty ones, very slowly at a low temperature, the flesh becomes succulent and velvety. This works well for salmon, red snapper, striped bass, and cod. It is also a good way to cook tuna and swordfish if you prefer them well-done rather than rare, since it keeps the fish from drying out and toughening. And it's a great way to cook sea scallops, too.

Slow-roasted fish has such a purity of flavor that only the simplest embellishments are necessary, although it can easily stand up to more elaborate sauces as well. A simple flavored oil, such as Chive (page 590) or Basil (page 592), is lovely, or you could serve the fish with one of the vegetable preparations or sauces suggested on pages 214 to 215. Risotto can also make a wonderful and surprising bed for the succulent fish.

> **1 teaspoon extra-virgin olive oil**
>
> **1½ pounds thick fish fillet** (1 large fillet or four 6-ounce fillets), such as salmon, striped bass, or red snapper, with skin
>
> **Kosher salt**
>
> **A small bunch of fresh thyme sprigs** (optional)

1. Preheat the oven to 275°F. Brush a baking dish lightly with half the olive oil.

2. Arrange the fish fillet(s) skin side down in the pan. Rub the top with the remaining olive oil. Sprinkle lightly with salt. Tuck half of the thyme sprigs under the fish and place the remainder on top.

3. Roast for 15 to 35 minutes, until a two-pronged kitchen fork inserted in the thickest part of the fish meets with no resistance and the flesh separates easily from the skin. An instant-read thermometer should read 120°F. (Don't worry if the top of the fish still has a slightly translucent, raw look; this is the result of the low roasting temperature. It will be cooked inside.)

an improvisation ## Slow-Roasted Salmon to Serve Cold

I like to slow-roast whole sides of salmon rather than poach them for cold salmon dishes because there is less danger of overcooking the fish. One whole 1¼-inch-thick fillet will take 25 to 30 minutes to cook. Serve with a cool, creamy sauce such as Chive Cream (page 627), Cucumber Raita (page 629), or Yogurt Sauce with Toasted Spices, Lime Zest, and Basil (page 630).

The exact cooking time will depend on the thickness of the fillets. Figure about 15 to 20 minutes for fillets less than ¾ inch thick, such as striped bass and red snapper; 25 to 30 minutes for 1¼-inch-thick salmon fillet. If you are unsure, test the fish early, then continue cooking until done.

Slow-Roasted Striped Bass with Olive Paste and Thyme

The salty-sweet flavors of olive paste, thyme, and white wine perfectly complement striped bass without overpowering it. Cooking it at a very low temperature makes it incredibly tender. Since the combination of black olive and thyme has a rather Provençal ring to it, I often serve a Sweet Onion and Tomato Gratin (page 52) as an accompaniment.

SERVES 4

Imported olive paste is available at specialty markets.

> ½ **teaspoon olive oil**
>
> 1 **garlic clove,** halved lengthwise
>
> **Four 6-ounce striped bass or red snapper fillets,** with skin
>
> **Scant 3½ tablespoons olive paste**
>
> 1½ **tablespoons dry white wine**
>
> 4 **sprigs fresh thyme**

Preheat the oven to 225°F.

Using a slightly dampened brush, lightly brush a baking dish large enough to hold the fillets in a single layer with the olive oil. Rub the bottom of the dish with the cut sides of the garlic clove, then slice the garlic into slivers and scatter them in the dish. Arrange the fish fillets skin side down in the dish. Spread each fillet with 2½ teaspoons of the olive paste. Drizzle the white wine over the fillets. Tuck the thyme sprigs under and around the fish.

Bake the fish 15 to 20 minutes, until a two-pronged kitchen fork inserted in the thickest part of the fish meets with no resistance and the flesh separates easily from the skin. Serve immediately.

IN THE OVEN: BRAISING AND STEAMING. Roasting fish with a savory liquid such as wine, hard cider, or fish broth with interesting seasonings is a simpler way to produce effects usually accomplished on top of the stove. The classic French method of braising fish, lightly covered, in a shallow casserole yields its own pan sauce, which can be enriched with a little cream or butter. Cooking fish enclosed in a foil or parchment package (en papillote) achieves the fresh, clear flavors of steamed fish without having to rig a steamer.

Braised Fish Fillets with Their Own Pan Sauce

A GUIDE TO IMPROVISING

SERVES 4

If you wish to use a nonflameproof casserole made of ceramic or glass, use a flame tamer—a metal disk placed on the open flame—to keep the casserole from cracking.

This classic French method of braising fillets with shallots, wine, vermouth, and a small amount of butter cooks the fish gently and yields delicious juices, which you can transform easily into a satisfying sauce with a clear, concentrated flavor. This approach is endlessly mutable: You can add other flavorings, such as leeks, fennel, tomato, herbs, saffron, or other seasonings, to the basic braise. You can use different wines, such as Gewürztraminer or Riesling or even dry hard cider. You can also finish the pan juices in many different ways: Highly reduce them, then mellow them with crème fraîche and herbs, or finish the sauce with more exotic flavorings, such as curry paste and coconut milk.

This method works best for fillets or steaks from lean white-fleshed fish. To use this method for whole fish, use the proportions of liquid, vegetables, and seasonings given below per each 1½ pounds of fish, multiplying them as necessary.

> **1 to 1½ teaspoons unsalted butter**
>
> **2 tablespoons minced shallots**
>
> **Flavorings** (optional), singly or in combination, such as
>
> > ½ cup finely chopped fennel or celery
> >
> > ½ cup julienned leeks or carrots
> >
> > ½ cup chopped plum tomatoes
> >
> > ½ cup thinly sliced mushrooms
> >
> > **2 to 3 teaspoons minced fresh herbs,** such as tarragon, chives, or basil
> >
> > **Pinch of saffron,** steeped in 1 tablespoon warm water for 10 minutes

1½ pounds fish fillets or steaks, such as sole, flounder, baby halibut, orange roughy, tilapia, black bass, red snapper, skate, perch, mahi mahi, striped bass, or Chilean sea bass, with skin

Wine or hard cider, such as

    ¾ cup Chardonnay, Gewürztraminer, or Riesling

    ½ cup dry white wine mixed with 3 tablespoons white vermouth

    ¾ cup very dry hard cider (11% to 13% alcohol; mix sweeter, less alcoholic ciders half and half with dry white wine)

Kosher salt and freshly ground black pepper

3 tablespoons heavy cream (optional)

¼ to ½ cup chopped fresh herbs, such as flat-leaf parsley, chives, chervil, or basil

1. Preheat the oven to 400°F. Rub a flameproof baking dish just large enough to accommodate the fish in one layer with ½ teaspoon of the butter.

2. Scatter the shallots and any other flavorings over the bottom of the baking dish. (If the flavorings you wish to use are fibrous, such as fennel, celery, or leeks, cook them first: Place the dish over low heat and add ½ teaspoon more butter. Add the vegetables and cook, stirring occasionally, until soft and translucent. Remove from the heat and allow to cool for 5 minutes.)

3. Arrange the fish skin side down in the dish and drizzle with the wine. Sprinkle with salt and pepper. Place the dish over medium heat until the liquid just begins to simmer.

4. Rub the remaining ½ teaspoon butter over a piece of foil or parchment cut to fit over the casserole. Place the foil butter side down over the fish. Bake until the fillets are firm to the touch and opaque, figuring on about 10 minutes per inch of thickness. Fillets 1 inch or more thick may remain slightly translucent on top even though they are done. To test fillets for doneness, insert a two-pronged kitchen fork straight down into the thickest part of the flesh. The fish is done if the fork meets with no resistance. Because the fish keeps cooking after it has been taken out of the oven, it's best to slightly undercook it; it will finish cooking while it rests under the foil. Transfer the fish to a warm serving dish or four individual dinner plates and cover with foil to keep warm.

5. Place the baking dish over moderately high heat and boil to reduce the cooking liquids until they are slightly concentrated and any raw wine taste has cooked away. Stir in the cream, if using, and the herbs and correct the seasoning. Spoon some of the sauce over each portion of fish.

Sea Bass in Hard Cider with Shallots and Cream

You can use the Guide on pages 226 to 227 to make a lightened version of the Normandy classic, sole braised in hard cider. Use a meaty white fish, such as Chilean sea bass or halibut, and a very dry hard cider (11% to 13% alcohol). Or mix a cider with a lower alcohol content with an equal amount of wine.

In Step 1, add ½ cup finely chopped peeled tart green apple and 2 teaspoons minced fresh tarragon along with the shallots. Increase the cider to 1 cup. After you have reduced the sauce in Step 4, stir in ¼ cup crème fraîche or heavy cream and 2 tablespoons minced fresh flat-leaf parsley.

Striped Bass with Tomatoes and Olives

Striped bass is a meaty, full-flavored fish that can stand up to olives, tomatoes, and capers in this version of the traditional Italian *pesce livornese*.

Follow the Guide on pages 226 to 227 through Step 3. In Step 4, once you have reduced the wine by half, stir in ¾ cup pitted (see page 683) and sliced black brine-cured olives, such as Kalamata, Gaeta, or Niçoise, and 1 teaspoon small capers and boil for 1 minute. Then stir in 1 cup peeled, seeded, and diced plum tomatoes, 4 teaspoons extra-virgin olive oil, and 1 teaspoon sugar. Boil for 1 minute, and stir in ¼ cup chopped fresh flat-leaf parsley.

Fillets in Green Curry Sauce

Even professional chefs rely on the occasional commercial product to make quick, delicious recipes in a pinch. Jim Peterson, a great chef and cookbook writer, taught me his favorite: a basic braised fish whose pan juices are finished with prepared Thai green curry paste and unsweetened coconut milk. The curry paste, made from green chiles, cilantro, garlic, and spices, imparts a distinctly Thai flavor, pungent, spicy, and herbal, to dishes. The coconut milk transforms it into a creamy sauce. Because commercial curry pastes can vary greatly in spiciness, it is best to start with a small amount and add more according to your taste. You can also make your own Thai Green Curry Paste using the recipe on page 561.

¾ teaspoon unsalted butter

2 tablespoons minced shallots

1½ pounds white-fleshed fish fillets, such as red snapper, striped bass, or sea bass, with skin

¾ cup dry white wine (up to 3 tablespoons can be white vermouth)

Kosher salt

2 teaspoons to 2 tablespoons prepared green curry paste or Thai Green Curry Paste (page 561)

1½ to 2 tablespoons Thai or Vietnamese fish sauce (nam pla or nuoc mam)

⅔ cup unsweetened coconut milk

3 to 4 tablespoons chopped fresh basil and cilantro, in any combination

Preheat the oven to 400°F.

Rub a flameproof baking dish just large enough to accommodate the fish in one layer with ½ teaspoon of the butter. Scatter the shallots over the bottom of the dish. Arrange the fish skin side down in the dish and drizzle with the wine. Sprinkle with salt. Place the dish over medium heat (use a Flame Tamer if the dish is not flameproof) until the liquid just begins to simmer.

Rub the remaining ¼ teaspoon of the butter over a piece of foil or parchment cut to fit the casserole and place it butter side down over the fish. Bake until the fillets are firm to the touch and opaque, about 10 minutes per inch of thickness. To test fillets for doneness, insert a two-pronged fork straight down into the thickest part of the flesh. The fish is done if the fork meets with no resistance. Because the fish keeps cooking after it has been taken out of the oven, it's best to slightly undercook it; it will finish cooking while it rests under the foil. Transfer the fish to a warm serving dish or individual dinner plates and cover with foil.

Place the baking dish over moderately high heat and boil to reduce the cooking liquid until it is slightly concentrated and any raw wine taste has cooked away. Stir in the curry paste to taste, then the fish sauce. Stir in the coconut milk and correct the seasoning. Add the herbs. Spoon some of the sauce over each portion of fish and serve.

Oven-Steaming Whole Fish (Papillote Cooking)

A GUIDE TO IMPROVISING

SERVES 2

To serve 4, double the recipe, using 2 fish and making 2 separate packages. For just 1 person, use a 1-pound fish and halve the other ingredients; cook the fish for 5 minutes less.

The age-old method of cooking fish en papillote—in a parchment paper or foil package—is in effect a way of steaming in the oven. It is much easier to do than stove-top steaming—no racks or steamers are involved—and it produces dramatic results. A whole fish, aromatics, and a small amount of a flavorful liquid, such as wine, are sealed in the package and baked. (Whole fish on the bone have a lot more flavor than fillets and are harder to overcook.) The air-tight case locks in all the flavorings and yields an abundance of flavorful juices to spoon over each serving. Very little added fat is necessary.

There are any number of possible combinations for flavorings, from classic white wine with herbs and julienne carrots and leeks to sake and sweet butter to pancetta, dry sherry, and muscat grapes.

One 1½-pound firm white-fleshed fish, such as sea bass, striped bass, or red snapper, cleaned

¼ teaspoon kosher salt

Scant ¼ teaspoon cayenne pepper

1½ teaspoons fat, such as extra-virgin olive oil, Asian sesame oil, or unsalted butter, or the fat from 2 tablespoons finely diced pancetta or bacon cooked, covered, over low heat until crisp (pancetta or bacon reserved)

1 cup vegetable or fruit garnish, such as julienned leeks, carrots, or celery, sliced mushrooms, or peeled muscat grapes

Flavorings (optional), singly or in combination, such as

> **1 to 2 garlic cloves or shallots,** minced or sliced
>
> **One ½-inch piece fresh ginger,** peeled and slivered or sliced
>
> **2 to 3 sprigs fresh herbs,** such as thyme, rosemary, basil, or tarragon
>
> **¼ to ½ teaspoon fennel seeds**
>
> **¼ to ½ teaspoon Sandy's Curry Powder** (page 548) **or commercial curry powder**
>
> **1 stalk lemongrass,** white bulb only, smashed and thinly sliced
>
> **1 to 2 strips orange or lemon zest** (removed with a vegetable peeler), cut into slivers
>
> **1 to 2 kaffir lime leaves**

¼ cup wine, such as white wine, sake, dry sherry, tawny port, or dry hard cider

1. Preheat the oven to 400°F.

2. Rinse the fish with cold water and pat dry. With a thin sharp knife, make three diagonal cuts about ¼ inch deep and about 1 inch apart on each side of the fish. Season the cavity with the salt and cayenne.

3. Place an 18-by-26-inch sheet of heavy-duty foil or parchment paper on a work surface and brush with ¾ teaspoon of the fat, leaving a 2-inch border all around. Turn up the edges of the foil slightly so that the liquid you add will be contained.

4. Place half the garnishes on one half of the foil. Place the fish on top. Place half the flavorings in the cavity of the fish. Scatter half of the remaining flavoring mixture under the fish and the rest over the top. Then scatter the remaining garnishes over the top. Drizzle the fish with the wine and the remaining ¾ teaspoon fat (and the crisp bits of pancetta or bacon, if using). Fold the foil over the fish and seal the edges: Starting at one corner, fold the edges of the foil over in a neat pleat, making sure to fold each successive pleat so it slightly overlaps the previous one to make a tight seal. Continue folding all around in this manner until the package is sealed. Slide the package onto a baking sheet.

5. Bake the fish for 25 minutes. Remove from the oven and let sit for 3 minutes.

6. Slide the papillote onto a serving platter. With scissors, carefully cut the foil around the pleats, taking care to avoid the escaping steam. Fold back the flap to expose the fish. You can serve the fish directly from the papillote or, using two large spatulas, transfer the fish to another platter. Tilt the papillote so the juices run out of one corner and over the fish.

7. To fillet the fish: Using a cake server or a thin pointed spatula, cut through the skin along the back of the fish. Gently slide the spatula between the spine and the top fillet; lift up the fillet and transfer to a platter or dinner plate. Slide the spatula under the spine and lift it off the bottom fillet; discard. Gently transfer the bottom fillet to the platter or a second dinner plate.

Spoon any flavorful juices over the fish and serve at once.

Oven-Steamed Whole Fish with Chinese Flavors

SERVES 2 This recipe translates a classic Chinese-style fish steamed with ginger, scallions, and sherry into the easier papillote method. The optional preserved black beans add an earthy flavor. They are sold at Asian grocery stores and in many supermarkets. (Because they are salted, they keep indefinitely.)

One 1½-pound sea bass, striped bass, or red snapper, cleaned

⅛ teaspoon kosher salt

1½ teaspoons preserved black beans (optional)

One ½-inch piece fresh ginger, peeled

2 scallions, thinly sliced on the diagonal

2 small garlic cloves, thinly sliced

Pinch of red pepper flakes

1½ teaspoons Asian sesame oil

3 tablespoons dry sherry

1½ teaspoons low-sodium soy sauce

¼ teaspoon sugar

4 small shiitake mushrooms, stems discarded, caps thinly sliced (optional)

¼ cup fresh cilantro leaves

Preheat the oven to 400°F.

Rinse the fish inside and out with cold water and pat dry. With a thin sharp knife, make three diagonal cuts about ¼ inch deep and 1 inch apart on each side of the fish. Sprinkle the salt in the cavity of the fish.

Place the black beans, if using, in a strainer and rinse under cold running water for 1 minute. Drain well, then finely chop. Slice the ginger into paper-thin slices, then stack the slices and cut them into fine julienne strips. You should have about 1 teaspoon.

In a small bowl, combine the beans, if using, ginger, scallions, garlic, and pepper flakes. In another small bowl, mix ¾ teaspoon of the sesame oil with the sherry, soy sauce, and sugar.

Place an 18-by-26-inch sheet of heavy-duty foil or parchment paper on a work surface. Brush with the remaining ¾ teaspoon sesame oil, leaving a 2-inch border all around. Turn up the edges of the foil slightly so that the liquid you will be adding will be contained.

Place the fish on top. Place about 2 teaspoons of the ginger mixture in the cavity of the fish. Scatter half of the remaining mixture under the fish and the rest over the top. Drizzle the fish with the sherry mixture. Scatter the mushrooms, if using, over it.

Fold the foil over the fish and seal the edges: Starting at one corner, fold the edges of the foil over in neat pleats, making sure to fold each successive pleat so it slightly overlaps the previous one to make a tight seal. Continue folding all around in this manner until the package is sealed. Slide the package onto a baking sheet.

Bake the fish for 25 minutes. Remove from the oven and let sit for 3 minutes.

With scissors, carefully cut the foil along the pleats, taking care to avoid the escaping steam. Fold back the flap to expose the fish. With two large spatulas, transfer the fish to a serving platter. Tilt the papillote so the juices run out of one corner and over the fish.

To fillet the fish: Using a cake server or a thin pointed spatula, cut through the skin along the back of the fish. Gently slide the spatula between the spine and the top fillet; lift up the fillet and transfer to a platter or dinner plate. Slide the spatula under the spine and lift it off the bottom fillet; discard. Gently transfer the bottom fillet to the platter or a second dinner plate.

Spoon any juices over the fish, sprinkle with the cilantro, and serve at once.

You can assemble the papillote up to 1 hour ahead; refrigerate. Allow to come to room temperature for 15 minutes before cooking. IN ADVANCE

Oven-Steamed Red Snapper with Fennel and Curry

SERVES 2   In this recipe, just a small amount of curry powder marries with the leeks and fennel to give a delicate perfume to the fish.

> **One 1½-pound red snapper or sea bass,** cleaned
>
> **Kosher salt**
>
> **Scant ¼ teaspoon cayenne pepper**
>
> **1 medium fennel bulb,** trimmed and very thinly sliced, 4 of the fennel fronds reserved and coarsely chopped
>
> **¼ teaspoon fennel seeds**
>
> **¼ teaspoon Sandy's Curry Powder** (page 548) **or commercial curry powder**
>
> **1½ teaspoons unsalted butter,** softened
>
> **1 small leek,** white part only, very thinly sliced or julienned
>
> **2 tablespoons dry white wine**

Preheat the oven to 400°F.

Rinse the fish inside and out with cold water and pat dry. With a thin sharp knife, make three diagonal cuts about ¼ inch deep and about 1 inch apart on each side of the fish. Season the fish inside and out with salt and the cayenne pepper and fill the cavity with the chopped fennel fronds.

Using a chef's knife, chop the fennel seeds. Mix the fennel seeds, curry powder, and 1 teaspoon of the softened butter. Set aside.

Place an 18-by-26-inch sheet of heavy-duty foil or parchment paper on a work surface. Rub the remaining ½ teaspoon butter over the foil, leaving a 2-inch border all around. Turn up the edges of the papillote slightly to hold the liquid you will be adding.

Spread half the leek and fennel slices on the foil to make a bed for the fish and dot with about half of the seasoned butter. Set the fish on top and scatter the remaining vegetables over it. Dot with the remaining seasoned butter, and drizzle with the wine.

Seal the papillote by folding the foil in half over the fish. Starting at one folded corner, fold the edges of the foil over in neat pleats; be sure to fold each successive pleat so it slightly overlaps the previous one to make a tight seal. Continue until you have reached the other corner and the edges are tightly sealed. Slide the package onto a baking sheet.

Bake the fish for 25 minutes. Remove from the oven and let sit for 3 minutes.

With scissors, carefully cut the foil along the pleats, taking care to avoid the escaping steam. Fold back the flap to expose the fish. With two large spatulas, transfer the fish to a serving platter. Tilt the papillote so the juices run out of one corner and over the fish.

To fillet the fish: Using a cake server or a thin pointed spatula, cut through the skin along the back of the fish. Gently slide the spatula between the spine and the top fillet; lift up the fillet and transfer to a platter or dinner plate. Slide the spatula under the spine and lift it off the bottom fillet; discard. Gently transfer the bottom fillet to the platter or a second dinner plate.

Spoon some of the cooking juices over each portion and serve.

IN ADVANCE You can assemble the papillote up to 1 hour ahead and refrigerate. Allow to come to room temperature for 15 minutes before cooking.

GRILLING AND BROILING. Grilling fish over charcoal or wood coals yields delicious results with minimal preparation and fat. The smoky flavor that grilling adds is all the flavoring you need. When paired with an interesting salsa or vinaigrette, grilled fish is a complete dish.

Although in theory you can broil any food you can grill, many home broilers simply do not reach the searingly hot temperature necessary to cook fish quickly, nor can they impart that inimitable smoky flavor. Fish that is simply brushed with oil and seasoned with salt and pepper—delicious when cooked on a grill—will be rather boring when cooked under a broiler. It needs added flavors to work well under a home broiler. The following recipes are the best recipes I know for cooking fish in an ordinary broiler. They are superb when cooked on a grill. (For other grilled fish recipes, see pages 217 and 221.)

Miso-Sake–Glazed Fish Fillets and Steaks

SERVES 4   Many years ago, I tasted a spectacular grilled ling cod that had been marinated in sake kasu, the dregs left from the fermentation of sake, the Japanese rice wine. The marinade both cured the flesh slightly and permeated it with a faintly sweet flavor. Grilling caramelized and glazed the surface. Kasu is very difficult to find but, happily, a combination of sake, mirin, and white miso produces a similar effect.

This marinade is spectacular with fatty or oily fish such as salmon, black cod, and bluefish as well as Chilean sea bass. White miso, a paste made of fermented soybeans, is golden in color and has a sweet, mellow flavor. Mirin is sweet Japanese rice wine. Both are available at health food stores and Asian markets.

You need to marinate the fish for at least 12 hours, so plan ahead.

Miso-Sake Glaze

> 1 cup sweet white miso paste
>
> 3 to 4 tablespoons dark brown sugar
>
> ¼ cup sake
>
> ¼ cup mirin (Japanese rice wine) or medium-dry sherry
>
> **Four 6-ounce fish steaks or fillets,** such as salmon, sea bass, yellowtail, Chilean sea bass, black cod, or very fresh bluefish
>
> 1 teaspoon olive oil

To make the glaze, combine all the ingredients in a medium saucepan and bring to a simmer over moderate heat. Reduce the heat to low and cook for 5 minutes. Set aside to cool.

Spread one third of the glaze over the bottom of a glass baking dish. Arrange the fish in the dish and spread the remaining glaze over the fillets or steaks to coat them completely. Cover with plastic wrap and refrigerate for at least 12 hours, but no longer than 24 hours. Bring the fish to room temperature 30 minutes before cooking.

To cook the fish, prepare a fire in a grill or preheat the broiler.

Scrape the glaze from the fish and discard. Pat the fish dry with paper towels and brush lightly with the olive oil. Grill or broil 3 inches from the heat for 3 to 4 minutes. Turn and cook for 2 to 3 minutes longer, or until you feel no resistance when you insert a kitchen fork into the fish. Serve immediately.

IN ADVANCE You can prepare the glaze up to 2 months ahead and refrigerate it. The fish must be marinated for at least 12 hours, or for as long as 24 hours.

The Best Way to Grill Shrimp

SERVES 4

I prefer to leave the shells on when I grill shrimp because the shells, like the bones in meat, poultry, and fish, add flavor to the flesh and protect it from drying out. To make shrimp easy to peel, cut the raw shrimp down the back. If you loosen the shells slightly, you can push a paste or marinade under the shells, which char on the grill and lock in flavor. The succulent shrimp are easily extracted with fingers or a knife and fork.

When you grill small items such as shrimp, or fragile fish, use a hinged grill basket. It holds the food tightly between two metal racks, making it easier to turn.

> 1½ pounds jumbo shrimp
>
> ¼ cup marinade or flavoring paste, such as Thai Green Curry Paste (page 561), Sesame-Ginger Marinade with Five-Spice Powder (page 557), Tandoori Marinade (page 558), or Hoisin Barbecue Sauce (page 562)

With scissors, cut down the back of each shrimp, through the shell, and remove the vein. With your fingers, gently loosen the shell from the flesh, keeping it attached. Gently pull open the shell of each shrimp and push some of the marinade over the back of the shrimp under the shell. Close the shells around the shrimp. Cover and let marinate for up to 5 hours in the refrigerator. (Remove from the refrigerator 15 minutes before cooking.)

Prepare a fire in a grill or preheat the broiler (or heat a grill pan).

Remove the shrimp from the marinade and shake off the excess, or scrape it off with your fingers. Grill or broil the shrimp about 3 inches from the heat source (or cook in the grill pan) until the shells are charred on one side, about 3 minutes. Turn and cook for another 2 minutes, or just until the shrimp are opaque throughout; do not overcook. Serve hot.

IN ADVANCE You can marinate the shrimp up to 5 hours ahead; refrigerate.

Grilled Whole Fish Wrapped in Pancetta and Herbs

SERVES 4 Because whole fish have a tendency to dry out when grilled, I like to wrap them in pancetta, the peppery unsmoked Italian bacon. I stuff the cavity with fresh thyme, rosemary, and bay leaves. As the fish grills, the exposed herb sprigs char slightly and perfume the fish, and the pancetta bastes the fish, keeping it moist and succulent, with a crisp skin. You can use a variety of white-fleshed fish, such as red snapper, striped or black bass, or porgy.

> **One 3-pound red snapper, striped bass, or porgy**
> or two 1½-pound fish, cleaned
>
> **½ teaspoon olive oil**
>
> **¾ teaspoon kosher salt**
>
> **8 imported bay leaves**
>
> **4 sprigs fresh rosemary**
>
> **4 sprigs fresh thyme**
>
> **2 ounces lean pancetta** (4 thin slices)

Prepare a fire in a grill or preheat the broiler.

Rinse the fish inside and out with cold water and pat dry.

Rub the fish all over with the olive oil and season inside and out with the salt. Stuff 4 of the bay leaves and the rosemary and thyme sprigs into the cavity of the large fish, or 2 bay leaves and 2 rosemary sprigs each into the smaller fish.

Lay the fish on a work surface. Place 2 bay leaves end to end along the length of the large fish, or 1 on each smaller fish. Lay 2 overlapping slices of the pancetta, or 1 slice for each small fish, on top of the bay leaves, across the thickest part of the fish, leaving the tail and head exposed. Holding the pancetta with one hand, turn the fish over. Repeat with the remaining bay leaves and pancetta slices. Tie several lengths of kitchen string snugly around the fish to secure the bay leaves and pancetta.

Place the fish on a lightly oiled grill rack (or in an oiled grilling basket), or broiler pan 5 to 6 inches from the heat source, depending on the intensity of the heat. Grill or broil for 12 to 15 minutes per side for large fish, 8 to 10 minutes per side for smaller fish. The pancetta and the exposed fish skin should be crisp and browned but not charred. (If either the pancetta or fish skin begins to burn, move the rack farther from the heat source.) To test for doneness, slide a sharp paring knife into the flesh along the spine and gently lift: The flesh should still be ever so slightly translucent near the bone but just pull away from it.

Remove and discard the string. Discard the bay leaves.

To fillet the fish: Using a cake server or a thin pointed spatula, cut through the skin along the back of the fish. Gently slide the spatula between the spine and the top fillet; lift up the fillet and transfer to a platter or dinner plate. (If 1 fillet is meant to serve 2 people, divide it.) Slide the spatula under the spine and lift it off the bottom fillet; discard. Gently transfer the bottom fillet to the platter or a second dinner plate; divide if necessary.

Spoon any juices over the fish and serve at once.

IN ADVANCE You can stuff and wrap the fish up to 4 hours ahead; cover and refrigerate. Allow to come to room temperature for 15 minutes before cooking.

ON THE STOVE TOP: SEARING, CRUSTING, AND PANFRYING.

Searing fish fillets and steaks in a hot pan creates a golden crust that acts as a textural counterpoint to the moist, tender, cooked flesh. Using a nonstick skillet makes this technique virtually foolproof and requires only a fraction of the fat usually necessary to keep delicate flesh from sticking.

This technique is ideal for fillets up to ½ inch thick and thicker steaks that are to be cooked rare, as both of these cook quickly. Thicker fillets are best roasted (see page 222), as the fat might burn with a longer cooking time.

SEARING, CRUSTING, AND PANFRYING: THE BASICS

Although fish can be seared after seasoning it with little more than a sprinkling of salt and cayenne, dusting the fish with a dry rub or powder—finely ground spices and herbs, from crushed coriander seeds to juniper berries—will help to form a flavorful crust. These have the added virtue of not absorbing oil the way starch-based crusts made from bread crumbs, cornmeal, or flour can.

Use fats that have a high enough smoking point that they won't burn, such as grapeseed or peanut oil. Pure olive oil is better for frying than extra-virgin olive oil; there is no point wasting money using expensive and delicate oils for frying. Butter gives a marvelous flavor but burns easily. Mix it with vegetable oil or use clarified butter (see page 681).

Leaving the skin on fillets ensures that the fish will hold together, making it easier to handle and serve. When crisped, it forms a delicious and attractive textural counterpoint to the soft flesh. Before cooking, lightly score the skin at 1-inch intervals in a crisscross fashion with a thin sharp knife or a razor blade. This will keep it from curling up as it cooks.

Pan-Seared Crusted Fillets, Steaks, and Shellfish

A GUIDE TO IMPROVISING

SERVES 4

The combinations of ground dried herbs and spices and dry rubs that complement fish and shellfish are endless. You can make them yourself using the recipes on pages 541 to 552, or buy prepared ones like garam masala and Chinese five-spice powder. My favorites include Sandy's Curry Powder (page 548), Lemongrass Essence (page 546), Szechwan Pepper Rub and Dipping Salt (page 550), and Wild Mushroom Essence (page 544).

If you want to simply sear fish without crusting it, make sure to pat it dry before you add it to the pan, or it won't brown.

> **4 to 5 tablespoons ground dried herbs or spices, Flavor Essence** (pages 542–548), **or Dry Rub** (pages 549–552)
>
> **1½ pounds cleaned fish or shellfish:** four 6-ounce fish fillets or steaks, 1½ pounds sea scallops, or 1¾ pounds shrimp, peeled and deveined
>
> **1 teaspoon kosher salt** (omit if you are using a Dry Rub)
>
> **Scant ¼ teaspoon cayenne pepper** (omit if you are using a Dry Rub)
>
> **1½ to 2 tablespoons fat,** such as grapeseed, peanut, or olive oil, or half oil and half unsalted butter or clarified butter (see page 681)

1. Spread the herbs or spices, Flavor Essence, or Dry Rub on a plate. Pat the fish dry with paper towels. Sprinkle with the salt and cayenne. Nestle the fish into the powder, pushing it around the plate so that it adheres, then turn over and repeat so that it is completely coated.

2. Heat a large nonstick skillet over moderate heat. Add half the fat and swirl it around to coat the pan. When it is hot, tap the fish lightly to knock off any loose coating and place the fish in the pan. Cook until the bottom side is crusty and golden (see Approximate Cooking Times for Pan-Seared Crusted Fillets, Steaks, and Shellfish, page 242). Turn, adding the remaining oil as you do, and sear until crusty and golden on the second side.

3. Remove from the pan and blot dry with paper towels. Let rest for a minute or two before serving.

Thin Fillets (up to ½ inch thick), such as sole, red snapper, and striped bass, Shrimp, or Sea Scallops: 1½ to 2 minutes on each side.

Rare to Medium-Rare Thick Steaks (1 inch thick), such as swordfish and tuna: 1 minute on each side for rare, 1½ minutes for medium-rare.

Well-Cooked Thick Steaks (1 inch thick), such as salmon and Chilean sea bass: Because well-cooked thick steaks need longer cooking times, the fat in which they are cooked has a tendency to smoke. If you have an exhaust fan, you can cook these on top of the stove for about 3 minutes on each side. Otherwise, pan-sear them for about 1½ minutes on each side, then finish cooking in a 275°F oven for about 10 minutes or, if you are in a hurry, a 400°F oven for 4 to 5 minutes (though the lower oven temperature is better).

Curry-Crusted Shrimp

SERVES 4

These shrimp with a curry powder crust are so delicious that they need little embellishment: Fresh lime and cilantro will do, though a quickly made fresh Warm Mango Chutney (page 664) is a perfect sweet-spicy complement.

The secret to this simple recipe is to use a fine mellow curry powder, either commercial or homemade. You can also make the recipe with fish fillets and steaks (such as striped bass, red snapper, or tuna) and sea scallops. Serve the shrimp with Basmati Rice with Ginger and Curry (page 178) or another flavored rice.

1½ pounds large shrimp, peeled up to the tail and deveined

1 teaspoon sugar

⅛ teaspoon kosher salt

⅓ cup Sandy's Curry Powder (page 548) **or commercial curry powder**

2 tablespoons olive, grapeseed, or peanut oil or 1 tablespoon each oil and unsalted butter

About 2 cups tender sprigs fresh cilantro

2 limes, cut into wedges

Sprinkle the shrimp evenly with the sugar and salt. Dust with the curry powder to form a light coating and shake off the excess.

Heat a large nonstick skillet over moderate heat. Add 1 tablespoon of the oil (or 1½ teaspoons each of the oil and butter) and heat for 30 seconds. Add just enough shrimp to cover the pan in a single layer. Cook until they are browned and crisp, about 2 minutes on each side. Transfer to a warm plate and repeat with the remaining shrimp and oil.

Arrange the shrimp on a bed of the cilantro sprigs and garnish with the lime wedges.

Sesame-Crusted Swordfish with Cilantro and Coconut Chutney

Instead of spices or herbs, you can crust meaty swordfish steaks with sesame seeds, which are small enough to adhere to the flesh without any batter. They form a crisp golden coating when the fish is panfried in aromatic sesame oil. Cilantro and Coconut Chutney is a perfect complement.

SERVES 4

> ¼ cup plus 2 tablespoons sesame seeds
>
> Four 6-ounce swordfish or tuna steaks
>
> 1 teaspoon kosher salt
>
> Scant ¼ teaspoon cayenne pepper
>
> 1 tablespoon Chinese Five-Flavor Oil (page 594)
> or 1 tablespoon Asian sesame oil plus 3 thin slices fresh ginger
>
> Cilantro and Coconut Chutney (page 665)

Sprinkle the sesame seeds into a pie plate or onto a dinner plate. Season the steaks on both sides with the salt and cayenne. Then press the steaks into the sesame seeds, turning them once and pressing the seeds into the flesh until the steaks are completely coated. Gently shake off the excess.

Heat the oil (and ginger, if using Asian sesame oil) in a large nonstick skillet set over moderate heat until hot. Place the fillets in the pan and cook until the crust is golden, about 1½ minutes on each side for medium rare, 2½ minutes on each side for well done. Transfer the fish to a cutting board.

Slice the fish into ½-inch-thick slices and fan them out on dinner plates. Serve at once with the chutney.

You can prepare the Chinese Five-Flavor Oil several weeks ahead, and the Cilantro and Coconut Chutney up to 3 days ahead.

IN ADVANCE

Crispy Salmon with Warm Lentils and Balsamic Essence

SERVES 4 This recipe illustrates the way several simple components can be combined to make a complex dish. Salmon fillets are seared skin side down in a hot pan to make the skin deliciously crispy, then served on a bed of tiny French lentils that have been cooked separately (they take only twenty minutes)— a classic combination. A sauce of reduced balsamic vinegar mellowed with a little butter ties the two together.

If your fillets are less than ½ inch thick, you can cook them entirely on top of the stove without the danger of the fat smoking before the salmon is cooked. If the fillets are thicker, finish cooking them in the oven after you have crisped the skin (although if you have a good exhaust fan, you can cook them on top of the stove without worry). The portions of salmon are slightly smaller here than in other recipes because the lentils also provide protein— and are very filling.

A Bed of Lentils

6 ounces lentils (¾ cup), preferably French lentilles du Puy

2 ounces smoky ham or prosciutto, trimmed of fat and cut into 3 pieces

4 garlic cloves, lightly crushed

1 small serrano or jalapeño chile, cut lengthwise in half and seeded (optional)

1 shallot

1 imported bay leaf

¾ teaspoon salt, or more to taste

Buttery Balsamic Essence

1 cup balsamic vinegar

1 tablespoon unsalted butter or extra-virgin olive oil

Four 5-ounce salmon fillets, with skin

Scant ¼ teaspoon cayenne pepper

Freshly ground black pepper

¼ cup chopped fresh flat-leaf parsley or chervil

To make the lentils, combine the lentils, ham, garlic, chile pepper, shallot, and bay leaf in a medium saucepan with water to cover by 1 inch. Bring to a simmer over moderate heat, then reduce the heat to low. Cook the lentils at a bare simmer for 10 minutes. (Do not allow the lentils to boil, or they will become tough.) Add the salt and continue cooking until they are just tender but still hold their shape, about 10 minutes longer. (They will continue to cook as they cool.) Let the lentils cool for about 15 minutes in their cooking water.

To make the balsamic essence, bring the balsamic vinegar to a boil in a small nonreactive saucepan over moderate heat. Reduce the heat slightly and cook until reduced to ¼ cup and thick and syrupy. Remove from the heat and set aside.

If the salmon fillets are more than ½ inch thick, preheat the oven to 400°F.

Place the salmon skin side up on a work surface. With a thin sharp knife or a razor blade, make several shallow parallel slashes in the skin of each fillet about 1 inch apart. Turn the fillets 90 degrees and make several more slashes to form a crisscross pattern. (This will keep the skin from curling when it hits the hot pan.) Sprinkle lightly with salt and the cayenne.

Heat a large heavy nonstick (ovenproof if using fillets more than ½ inch thick) skillet over moderate heat until very hot. Slide the salmon skin side down into the pan and cook until the skin is crisp and brown, 4 to 5 minutes. Turn the salmon fillets over. If they are less than ½ inch thick, cook for 1 to 2 minutes longer, until the fish is opaque and a two-pronged kitchen fork inserted straight down meets with no resistance. If the fillets are more than ½ inch thick, place the skillet in the oven and roast until the salmon is opaque, 5 to 6 minutes.

Meanwhile, drain the lentils, reserving 1 tablespoon of the cooking liquid. Remove and discard the ham, garlic, chile pepper, shallot, and bay leaf. Return the lentils to the saucepan and stir in the reserved cooking liquid and salt and pepper to taste. Heat the lentils over moderate heat, stirring frequently until hot. Toss in the parsley, cover, and keep warm.

Let the salmon rest for a minute or two.

Return the balsamic sauce to moderate heat and bring to a simmer. Add the butter and stir until blended.

Mound the lentils in the center of four dinner plates. Place 1 salmon fillet crispy skin side up on top of each mound, then spoon about a tablespoon of the sauce around the lentils. Serve at once.

You can prepare the lentils up to 3 days ahead; cover and refrigerate. Warm **IN ADVANCE** gently in a covered medium skillet, adding a few tablespoons of water if necessary. Add the parsley just before serving. The balsamic vinegar can be reduced several hours ahead, and left in the pan at room temperature. Add the butter at the last minute.

Mushroom-Crusted Bass with Port Wine Butter Sauce

SERVES 4 A dusting of powdered dried wild mushroom forms a subtly flavored crust that goes well with many kinds of seafood, especially meaty striped bass fillets. In this recipe it echoes the subtle mushroom flavor of the Port Wine Butter Sauce. You can prepare the sauce ahead so that the only last-minute preparation is searing the fish fillets.

> **Four 6-ounce striped bass fillets,** with skin
>
> **1 teaspoon kosher salt**
>
> **Scant ¼ teaspoon cayenne pepper**
>
> **1½ tablespoons Wild Mushroom Essence** (page 544)
> **or commercial wild mushroom powder** (see Sources, page 711)
>
> **Port Wine Butter Sauce** (page 644)
>
> **1 tablespoon plus 1 teaspoon peanut, grapeseed, or olive oil**

Pat the fillets dry with paper towels and place them skin side up on a work surface. With a thin sharp knife, lightly score the skin in a crisscross pattern (this will prevent the skin from contracting when it hits the pan). Turn the fillets skin side down. Sprinkle lightly with the salt and cayenne, then sprinkle liberally with the wild mushroom essence, patting gently to make it adhere. Shake off the excess.

Pour the port wine butter sauce into the top of a double boiler set over simmering water and reheat if necessary. Keep warm.

Heat a large nonstick skillet over moderate heat. Add 2 teaspoons of the oil and swirl to coat the pan. Place the fillets in the pan skin side down and cook for 2½ to 3 minutes, until the skin is crispy and brown. If the fillets begin to curl, place a flat plate or lid on them to weight them down. Turn the fillets, add the remaining 2 teaspoons oil to the pan, and continue cooking for another 2 minutes, or until the underside is crusty and brown.

Transfer the fillets to warm dinner plates. Spoon about 2 tablespoons of the sauce alongside each.

IN ADVANCE You can prepare the Port Wine Butter Sauce up to 4 hours ahead.

Five-Spice–Crusted Bass with Port Wine Butter Sauce an improvisation

Gilbert Le Coze, the late chef of Le Bernardin in New York City, crusted striped bass with Chinese five-spice powder (a mixture of fennel, ginger, cinnamon, cloves, and star anise). It's unusual and delicious. Simply substitute commercial five-spice powder for the Wild Mushroom Essence.

Crusting Fish Fillets with Starchy Coatings

A GUIDE TO IMPROVISING

The difficulty with using starchy coatings, rather than spices or herbs, to crust **SERVES 2** fish is that they are so absorbent they soak up a lot of fat. Dipping the fillets in a light egg wash first ensures a crisp, delicate coating when the fillets are fried in a small amount of fat—a happy alternative to deep-fried foods.

Innovative chefs are constantly coming up with unexpected crusts—from instant mashed potato buds, which produce an extremely delicate crust, to flour made from finely ground Arborio rice. Rice flour from the health food store works wonderfully and is even more delicate than white flour. You could also use fine-ground bulgur wheat.

The fat you choose, from olive oil to nutty brown butter, will also determine the flavor. Coarser coatings such as cornmeal will require a little more fat for frying than delicate ones. Even so, 2 teaspoons per serving is the maximum you will need.

To serve 4, double the recipe and cook the fish in batches or in two skillets.

¼ to ⅓ cup starchy coating, such as cornmeal, instant mashed potato buds, or rice flour

½ teaspoon kosher salt

½ teaspoon freshly ground black pepper (if using cornmeal)

Pinch of cayenne pepper

1 large egg

1 tablespoon water

Two 6-ounce cleaned fillets: snapper, striped bass, catfish, or flounder

3 to 4 teaspoons flavorful fat, such as olive oil, Asian sesame oil, half oil and half unsalted butter, or rendered bacon or pancetta fat (see page 681)

1. Sprinkle the coating into a pie plate or on a dinner plate and mix with the salt, black pepper, if using cornmeal, and cayenne.

2. In a wide shallow bowl, beat the egg and water with a fork. Dip 1 of the fillets in the egg wash, letting any excess drip back into the bowl, then press the fillet into the coating mixture, turning it once and patting the mixture over the fish until it is completely coated. Gently shake off the excess. Repeat with the remaining fillet.

3. Heat a large nonstick skillet over moderately high heat. Add 2 teaspoons of the fat and swirl to coat the pan. Place the fillets in the pan and cook for about 1 minute, until the bottom crust is golden. Turn the fillets over, adding the remaining 1 to 2 teaspoons fat, and cook for 1 minute longer, or until golden. Transfer the fish to hot dinner plates.

an improvisation ### Cornmeal-Crusted Fillets Fried in Bacon Fat

As every Southerner knows, there is nothing like fish that is dredged in cornmeal and fried in bacon fat. You can follow the Guide on page 247 to make this delectable dish, using a medium-coarse cornmeal and double-smoked bacon to achieve a rich smoky flavor with less fat than the traditional recipes. Serve with a creamy, cooling salad or sauce such as Cucumbers with Chive Cream (page 425) or Classic Coleslaw (page 423).

Panfried Skate with Brown Butter and Capers

SERVES 4 In the French classic skate *Grenobloise,* the beautiful fan-like wings of skate are panfried and served with a brown butter sauce—butter cooked until it gains a rich nutty flavor—finished with capers and parsley.

For this lighter rendition, I boil the brown-butter-and-vinegar sauce with a small amount of broth. The vinegar you choose will determine the character of the sauce. A combination of balsamic and aged sherry vinegars produces a rich complex flavored sauce that has a good balance of acid and sweet. Some vinegars, such as Banyuls or Cava (see Sources, page 711), give a more delicate effect but need ½ teaspoon sugar to balance their acidity.

Boned, skinned skate wings are available at better fish markets. You can also use meaty white-fleshed fish fillets, such as striped bass or red snapper.

Flour for dredging

Four 6-ounce skinned skate wing fillets

Kosher salt

Scant ¼ teaspoon cayenne pepper

3 tablespoons unsalted butter

2 tablespoons good-quality balsamic vinegar

1 tablespoon aged sherry vinegar

2 tablespoons bottled clam juice, fish broth, or canned low-sodium chicken broth

2 tablespoons capers, preferably small ones, drained, rinsed, and drained again

Pinch of sugar

¼ cup finely chopped fresh flat-leaf parsley

Sprinkle the flour into a pie plate. Pat the skate wings dry with paper towels and season each side with salt and the cayenne. Dredge the skate wings in the flour until completely coated; shake off the excess.

Heat two large nonstick skillets over moderate heat. Add 1½ teaspoons of the butter to each pan and swirl to coat the pan. When the butter has stopped bubbling, add 2 wings to each pan and cook until the underside is golden, about 3 minutes. Carefully lift 1 skate wing with a metal spatula, drop ¼ teaspoon butter into the pan, and flip the wing over onto the butter. Repeat with the remaining skate wings. Cook until they are golden on the second side and completely opaque, about 3 minutes longer. Transfer the wings to a warm serving dish or four warm individual dinner plates and cover loosely with foil to keep warm.

In a small saucepan, combine the balsamic and sherry vinegars and boil until reduced by half, about 2 minutes. Meanwhile, in another small saucepan, cook the remaining 2 tablespoons butter over moderate heat until it is golden brown and smells like roasted hazelnuts.

Pour the reduced vinegar into the butter. When the sputtering has died down, add the broth and capers. Boil until the sauce looks slightly creamy and thickened, about 30 seconds. Add the sugar, salt to taste, and parsley. Spoon the sauce over the skate wings and serve at once.

Shellfish Cooked in an Iron Skillet

SERVES 4 Mussels and clams, still in their shells, are marvelous cooked directly on a searing-hot iron griddle or skillet. So are scallops, though they are hard to find in the shells. No fat is necessary. The intense heat of the griddle causes the shells to open and heats the briny juices in the bottom shells to gently cook the flesh, yielding the purest of flavors. In Spain, it is called *a la plancha*. In France, this same method is used for *moules brûle doigts*, "burn your fingers mussels." They are particularly wonderful served right from the skillet as an hors d'oeuvre with cocktails, chilled white wine, or beer.

Cooked this way, the shellfish need only the simplest embellishment such as melted butter or Chive Oil, lightly brushed or drizzled into each shell. I also like to serve them with a warm blood orange and olive oil vinaigrette. Or you can mix and match other sauces (see the lists on pages 214–215).

Use only the freshest shellfish. I usually allow 8 pieces per serving as an appetizer. You can multiply this recipe endlessly and cook the shellfish in batches. About 32 mussels or littleneck clams will fit comfortably in a 12-inch iron skillet.

> **32 fresh mussels, littleneck clams, or singing scallops,** in the shell, scrubbed
>
> **Fruit Juice Vinaigrette** (page 617) **made with blood orange juice and extra-virgin olive oil,** 2 tablespoons melted unsalted butter, or Chive Oil (page 590)
>
> **Flaked sea salt,** such as Maldon or fleur de sel

Heat one or two large cast-iron skillets or a cast-iron griddle over high heat for 5 to 7 minutes. When the skillet is so hot that a drop of water skitters across the surface, add as many shellfish as will comfortably fit in one layer. Cook, shaking the pan occasionally, until the shellfish have opened, about 2 minutes for mussels, longer for clams and scallops.

You can serve the shellfish directly from the skillet, making sure to place it on a heavy board, or transfer them to a platter lined with about ½ inch of kosher salt. Pass the sauce separately, instructing your guests to brush or spoon a few drops of the sauce onto each mussel and sprinkle with a pinch of sea salt.

Alternatively, the shellfish can be cooked in a 450°F oven in a skillet lined with salt until they open about ¾ inch, about 10 minutes.

Simply Cooked Fish Sauced with Broth

Fish and crustaceans, such as shrimp and lobster, that have been simply cooked—by pan-searing, grilling, roasting, or smoking—can be sauced with a broth of a complementary flavor for a light, very elegant treatment. There are endless possible combinations: slices of pan-smoked tuna with ginger- sake broth garnished with a drizzle of Asian sesame oil and cilantro leaves (the oil separates into lovely beads of color in the broth) or Curry-Crusted Shrimp (page 242) with Fennel Broth (page 568). You can add a mild-flavored, soft-textured, vegetable or starch bed for the fish, such as wilted spinach or fresh pasta.

SERVES 4

2 to 3 cups broth, such as Leek Broth, Fennel Broth, White Wine Fish Broth, Star-Anise Broth, Curry and Fennel Seed Broth, or Ginger-Sake Broth (pages 568–582)

2 cups cooked vegetables, pasta, or grains (optional), such as

   Buttermilk Mashed Potatoes (page 77)

   Sorrel Mashed Potatoes (page 79)

   Celery Root and Apple Puree (page 81)

   Fine egg, green tea, buckwheat, or saffron noodles

   Roasted Wild Mushrooms (page 40)

   Steam-Roasted Leeks (page 58) without the vinaigrette

   Finely julienned leeks or carrots

   Peeled fava beans, raw pea shoots, or baby spinach

4 servings pan-seared, grilled, roasted, or smoked fish or shellfish (1½ pounds uncooked), such as

   Oven-Seared Thick Fish Fillets (page 222)

   Salt-Roasted Shrimp (page 223)

   Slow-Roasted Fish (page 224)

   Pan-Seared Crusted Fillets, Steaks, and Shellfish (page 241)

   Pan-Smoked Salmon (page 268) or **Rare Tuna** (page 268)

Garnishes (optional), such as

   ¼ to ½ cup fresh herbs (either chopped or tiny whole leaves), such as basil, chives, chervil, tarragon, flat-leaf parsley, or cilantro

   A drizzle of flavorful oil, such as extra-virgin olive oil, Flavored Oil (pages 588–597), or roasted nut oil (½ teaspoon per serving)

1. Bring the broth to a simmer in a medium saucepan and keep warm. Gently heat the vegetables, pasta, or grains, if serving, and keep warm over very low heat.

2. Cook the fish, scallops, or shrimp.

3. Make a bed of the vegetables, pasta or grains, if you have them, in each of four warm shallow bowls. Arrange the fish or shellfish on top (or simply place in the bowls).

4. Pour the broth gently around the fish. Garnish with the optional herbs and/or drizzle with oil.

Coriander-Crusted Scallops in Fennel Broth

SERVES 4   Fennel broth, enriched with a little crème fraîche, acts as a mellow sauce for seared coriander-crusted scallops. It works equally well with shrimp or flavorful fish fillets, such as swordfish, tuna, or striped bass. You can arrange the scallops on any number of beds, such as wilted fresh spinach, basmati or jasmine rice, or roasted potatoes and parsnips. My favorite is saffron noodles, available at specialty markets.

4 ounces saffron noodles or tagliatelle or linguine, commercial or homemade (page 159) (optional)

1½ to 2 tablespoons olive or peanut oil

2 cups Fennel Broth (page 568)

⅓ cup coriander seeds

1¼ pounds sea scallops, rinsed and patted dry

½ teaspoon kosher salt

Scant ¼ teaspoon cayenne pepper

¼ teaspoon sugar

1 tablespoon plus 1 teaspoon crème fraîche

¼ cup coarsely chopped fresh herbs, such as cilantro, basil, chervil, and/or flat-leaf parsley or fennel fronds

If using the noodles, bring a large pot of water to a boil. Salt well, add the noodles, and boil until al dente (tender but still firm to the bite). Drain and cool under cold running water. Drain well. Toss them lightly with ½ teaspoon of the oil to keep them from sticking together.

In a small saucepan, bring the broth to a boil over moderate heat and boil until the flavor is very concentrated and the broth is reduced to about 1½ cups, about 7 minutes. Cover and keep warm over very low heat.

In a small skillet, toast the coriander seeds over low heat until fragrant. Crush in a mortar, spice mill, or blender to a medium-fine powder. Spread on a plate.

Sprinkle the scallops lightly on each side with the salt, cayenne, and sugar. Nestle the scallops in the coriander seeds, pushing them around so that the spice adheres. Turn them over and repeat so that they are lightly coated with the coriander on both sides. Shake off the excess.

Heat a large nonstick skillet over moderate heat until hot. Add 2 teaspoons of the oil, swirl to coat the pan, and heat for 30 seconds. Add only enough scallops to cover the pan in a single layer and cook, turning once, until they are browned and crisp, about 2 minutes on each side. Transfer to a warm plate (leave uncovered) and repeat with the remaining scallops, adding as much of the remaining oil as necessary.

Stir the crème fraîche into the broth. Add the noodles, if using, and simmer just to heat them through. Arrange about ½ cup noodles in the bottom of each of four warm soup bowls. Arrange the scallops on top of the noodles or nestle them in the bowls. Ladle the broth over and garnish with the herbs.

IN ADVANCE You can prepare the Fennel Broth up to 5 days ahead. Boil, cool, and oil the noodles up to 4 hours ahead. Cover and refrigerate.

ON THE STOVE TOP: SHELLFISH STEAMS, STEWS, AND SOUPS. Because shellfish release their delicious briny juices and almost calorie-less broths within a few minutes of being steamed, shellfish steams, like the classic Moules Marinière or the exotically flavored Clams with Lemongrass, Ginger, and Chiles, are the quickest and easiest to make. Fish soups and stews, like those typical of southern France, tend to be more elaborate preparations, carefully layering flavors, texture, and different kinds of fish and shellfish for more sophisticated results.

Shellfish Steams

A GUIDE TO IMPROVISING

SERVES 4
AS A MAIN
COURSE,
8 AS A FIRST
COURSE

Shellfish steams
are wonderful com-
bined with pasta,
such as linguine or
spaghetti. Their
abundant broth acts
as a delectable
sauce. See Pasta
with Shellfish Sauce
(page 133)
for the method.

When you steam shellfish such as mussels and small clams in a flavorful liquid, they release their briny juices to create a rich broth that you can easily transform into a delectable sauce that is extremely low in calories and fat.

Traditional shellfish steams are made with liberal amounts of butter or cream, with wine as the only cooking liquid. Rather than rely on fats to mellow the winy broth, I like to add some bottled clam juice to the steaming liquid; when the shellfish open and release their juices into the wine-clam broth mixture, the resulting sauce is rich, flavorful, and abundant (about ½ cup per serving). Bottled clam juice is usually sold right at the shellfish counter. If you don't have any, you can make the recipe without it. It will yield less sauce (about ¼ cup sauce per serving) and will need the optional cream or coconut milk to mellow the wine.

You can improvise endlessly on this basic formula, using different wines or flavorings to lean the dish in many ethnic directions. For an Asian feel, pair a somewhat sweet, fruity wine like Riesling with curry, ginger, and chile pepper, finishing the sauce with a little coconut milk. Or add about 3 table-spoons Pernod or ouzo to white wine, along with 1 or 2 star anise, to make an anise-flavored broth that goes well with shellfish.

2 teaspoons flavorful fat, such as extra-virgin olive oil, unsalted butter, or the fat from 2 tablespoons finely diced pancetta or bacon, cooked slowly in a covered skillet until crisp (pancetta or bacon reserved)

¼ to ½ cup minced shallots

2 to 3 garlic cloves, minced (optional)

Flavorings (optional) singly or in combination, such as

  1 or 2 imported bay leaves

  2 to 3 sprigs fresh thyme or rosemary

  3 to 4 teaspoons minced fresh ginger

  1 small chile, seeded and minced

  3 tablespoons minced lemongrass

  2 kaffir lime leaves

  1 to 2 star anise (replace 3 tablespoons of the wine with Pernod or ouzo)

  1 tablespoon Sandy's Curry Powder (page 548) **or commercial curry powder**

2 cups wine, such as

  Dry white wine, such as Chardonnay

  Mildly sweet, fruity white wine, such as Riesling

  Spicy white wine, such as Gewürztraminer

  Young, fruity red wine, such as Beaujolais

2 cups bottled clam juice (for a tomato-based broth, substitute 1 cup chopped peeled and seeded plum tomatoes)

3½ pounds shellfish, such as mussels (debearded if necessary; see page 678), littleneck or Manila clams, or cockles, scrubbed

Creamy enrichment (optional), such as

  Up to ¼ cup heavy cream

  Up to ¾ cup unsweetened coconut milk (for Asian-flavored broths)

  1½ tablespoons unsalted butter

Kosher salt (if needed) **and freshly ground black pepper**

About ½ cup chopped fresh herbs, such as flat-leaf parsley, basil, cilantro, chervil, or chives

1. In a large heavy saucepan, heat the fat. Add the shallots, garlic, if using, and any optional flavorings. Cover and cook over low heat, stirring frequently, until the shallots are soft, about 7 minutes.

2. Increase the heat to high, add the wine and clam juice, and bring to a boil. Boil until reduced to 2 cups, about 5 minutes.

3. Add the shellfish, cover, and cook, shaking the pan frequently to rearrange the shellfish, until all the shells have opened, 5 to 7 minutes. Scoop the shellfish into large bowls.

4. Stir the optional enrichment into the winy broth and salt and pepper to taste. Spoon (or strain) the broth over the shellfish and sprinkle with the fresh herbs. Serve at once.

improvisation 1

Classic Moules Marinière

Follow the Guide on pages 254 to 255, using ½ cup shallots, the garlic, a dry white wine and mussels; omit the clam juice. Just before serving, stir in 1½ tablespoons unsalted butter as the enrichment and chopped fresh parsley as the herb.

improvisation 2

Mussels in Curry Broth

Curry and ginger make a sweet, pungent aromatic broth.

Follow the Guide on pages 254 to 255, using ½ cup shallots, the ginger, and the chile pepper, and cook as directed. Omit the garlic. When the shallots are soft, add 1 tablespoon Sandy's Curry Powder (page 548) or commercial curry powder and cook, stirring, for 30 seconds. In Step 2, use a dry white wine and the clam juice, and add a 2-inch strip of lime zest. In Step 4, scoop the shellfish into large bowls and add ¾ cup coconut milk and ½ teaspoon sugar to the broth. Use cilantro as the herb. Spoon the sauce over the shellfish and garnish with lime wedges.

Clams Steamed in Sake

SERVES 2

I often make this dish when I want an utterly quick and delicious meal. Sake, the Japanese rice wine, enriched with a little butter makes a sweeter, mellower sauce than white wine makes. It goes very well over egg pasta.

> 1½ cups sake
>
> 2 pounds small clams, such as littlenecks or Manila, scrubbed, or mussels, scrubbed and debearded (if necessary; see page 678)
>
> 1 tablespoon cold unsalted butter
>
> 1 teaspoon minced shallots
>
> Pinch of kosher salt
>
> 2 tablespoons chopped fresh cilantro, basil, or flat-leaf parsley

In a medium nonreactive saucepan, simmer the sake over moderate heat until reduced by half, 8 to 10 minutes. Add the clams, cover, and cook until they have opened, 3 to 4 minutes. Using a slotted spoon, transfer the clams to two warm shallow soup bowls.

Swirl the butter, shallots, and salt into the sake broth, bring to a boil over high heat, and boil for 30 seconds. Ladle the sauce over the clams and garnish with the herbs. Serve at once.

Mussels or Clams with Lemongrass, Ginger, and Chiles

Traditional Thai flavorings—lemongrass, ginger, and chile pepper—added to white wine and the mussel or clam juices make a heady, fragrant broth. The coconut milk mellows the flavors and adds a luxurious creaminess.

SERVES 4
AS A MAIN COURSE,
8 AS A FIRST
COURSE

2 stalks lemongrass or 1 tablespoon plus 1 teaspoon dried lemongrass, soaked in 3 tablespoons boiling water for 10 minutes

¼ cup chopped scallions

1 tablespoon plus 1 teaspoon minced fresh ginger

1 small serrano or jalapeño chile, seeded and minced

2 kaffir lime leaves (optional) or 1 strip lime zest (removed with a vegetable peeler)

2 cups dry white wine

2 cups bottled clam juice

3½ pounds shellfish, such as mussels, scrubbed and debearded (if necessary; see page 678), or littleneck clams, Manila clams, or cockles, scrubbed

⅔ cup unsweetened coconut milk

¼ to ⅓ cup chopped fresh cilantro

1 lime, cut into wedges

If using fresh lemongrass, peel away any dried outer leaves. With a thin sharp knife, trim the stalks to 2½ inches and slice each bulb crosswise as fine as possible. (You should have about 3½ tablespoons.)

In a large heavy saucepan set over moderate heat, combine the scallions, lemongrass (and its soaking liquid, if dried), ginger, chile pepper, kaffir lime leaves, wine, and clam juice. Bring to a boil and cook until the liquid is reduced to 2 cups, about 5 minutes.

Increase the heat to high, add the mussels, cover, and cook, shaking the pan frequently to rearrange the shellfish, until all the shells have opened, 2 to 3 minutes. Scoop the shellfish into large bowls.

Stir the coconut milk into the broth. Strain the broth over the mussels, taking care to leave any sand in the bottom of the pan. Toss the cilantro over the mussels and serve at once, passing lime wedges on the side so guests can squeeze them into the broth.

Fish and Shellfish Stews and Soups

A GUIDE TO IMPROVISING

SERVES 4

In this two-step method, you make the rich brothy base, then, just before serving, you gently poach the fish or shellfish in it. You need only add some fresh herbs and a drizzle of extra-virgin olive oil or heavy cream to finish the dish; embellishments such as cooked noodles or spinach build complexity. Because you can make the base ahead, this is great for dinner parties. Use any number of combinations of white-fleshed fish, broths, and garnishes, from homey to highly sophisticated, such as Chilean sea bass in Ginger-Sake Broth (page 582) with julienned leeks; sea scallops on a bed of saffron noodles in Curry and Fennel Seed Broth (page 581); or manila clams in Garlic Broth (page 580) with new potatoes, spinach, and crisp bacon.

1 quart broth, such as White Wine Fish Broth, Shortcut Fish Broth, Leek Broth, Fennel Broth, Curry and Fennel Seed Broth, Garlic Broth, or Ginger-Sake Broth (pages 568–582)

Fish and/or shellfish, singly or in combination, such as

> **Four 6-ounce fish fillets,** such as striped bass, red snapper, sea bass, or cod

> **1¾ pounds shrimp,** peeled and deveined

> **1½ pounds sea or bay scallops**

> **or the following combination of shellfish:**

>> **12 medium shrimp** in the shell

>> **8 large or 12 medium mussels,** scrubbed and debearded (if necessary)

>> **20 littleneck or Manila clams,** scrubbed

>> **8 ounces sea or bay scallops** or 16 singing scallops in the shell

Possible additions (optional), singly or in combination, such as

> **½ cup diced fresh tomatoes**

> **¼ cup sliced pitted** (see page 683) **black olives**

> **¾ cup julienned or thinly sliced fennel, leeks, or carrots,** blanched

> **1 cup steamed thinly sliced new potatoes or cooked pasta,** such as small shells

Kosher salt and freshly ground black pepper

¼ cup chopped fresh herbs, such as flat-leaf parsley, basil, chervil, cilantro, chives, or tarragon

Enrichment, such as

> **1 tablespoon plus 1 teaspoon fruity extra-virgin olive oil or Flavored Oil** (pages 588–597)

> **2 tablespoons heavy cream or crème fraîche**

1. Pour the broth into a 10- or 11-inch shallow saucepan and bring to a simmer.

2. Arrange the fish and/or shellfish in the pan, cover, and cook at a bare simmer (do not allow to boil!). Shellfish will cook first; check them after 3 minutes to see if they have opened (shrimp should be pink, the flesh opaque). Using a slotted spoon, transfer them to warm shallow bowls and continue cooking the fish for about 6 minutes longer (a two-pronged kitchen fork inserted in the thickest part will meet with no resistance). Transfer the fish to the warm bowls.

3. Add any optional additions to the broth and simmer until heated through. Season with salt and pepper and stir in the herbs and olive oil (or cream). Spoon the sauce over the fish and/or shellfish and serve at once.

A TRICK FOR COOKING FISH FILLETS IN STEWS AND SOUPS

Fish fillets are so delicate it is easy to overcook them or toughen them by cooking them at anything other than the barest simmer. To ensure perfectly tender fillets, use this trick: place a 7- to 9-inch round metal rack in a shallow 10- to 12-inch saucepan or deep skillet and pour in the broth. The rack should sit about ½ inch above the broth. If it doesn't, place it on something heatproof that will elevate it slightly, such as small ceramic ramekins; or make tight balls out of aluminum foil to act as legs. Bring the broth to a simmer over moderate heat. Arrange the fish fillets on the rack, cover the pan, and steam the fish for about 9 minutes, until cooked through. Transfer the fillets to warm shallow soup bowls. Remove the rack from the pan and finish seasoning the broth; pour over the fish.

USING A WHOLE FISH FOR SEAFOOD STEWS AND SOUPS

When I am making a seafood stew that requires both a fish broth and fish fillets, I buy a whole fish and have the fishmonger fillet it and cut up the carcass for the broth. That way, I am assured of having perfectly fresh fillets and the carcass contributes flavor and body to the sauce.

Generally speaking, a whole fish will yield a little under half its weight—about 40 to 45 percent—in fillets and about 40 to 45 percent as bones, including the head.

A variety of fish will work well in a seafood stew. Freshness should determine your choice. But choose a white-fleshed fish such as striped or sea bass or red snapper; oilier fish such as salmon or mackerel are too strong for the broth.

Saffron Fish Stew

SERVES 4 Throughout the South of France, fish and shellfish are often cooked in white wine that has been flavored with garlic, shallots, herbs, saffron, fennel, and tomato to make a rich and satisfying stew. Very little fat is necessary; the seafood juices mellow the wine and add a lovely "sea" flavor. You can make the liquid base, without the seafood, ahead. Then you simply simmer whatever fish or shellfish you wish in the broth. You can cook either fillets or shellfish or a combination, depending on what is best in the market.

Although this soup is delicious as is, I sometimes like to add a teaspoon or two of heavy cream per serving—at 16 added calories per teaspoon—to enrich the broth and harmonize the complex flavors.

Echoing the traditional accompaniments to bouillabaisse in France, toasted thin slices of baguette—4 to 5 slices per person spread with 2 tablespoons Rouille (page 619)—the saffron and hot pepper sauce—would add further dimension and body to the stew, at an additional 122 calories per serving.

Saffron-Tomato Base

½ teaspoon saffron threads (2 large pinches)

2 tablespoons hot water

1 tablespoon extra-virgin olive oil

¼ cup minced shallots

1 tablespoon minced garlic

½ teaspoon minced small serrano or jalapeño chile or ¼ teaspoon red pepper flakes

3 sprigs fresh thyme or ½ teaspoon dried thyme

½ teaspoon fennel seeds

2 imported bay leaves

2 medium leeks, white part only, finely chopped or julienned

2 tablespoons water

3 cups dry white wine

One 4-by-1-inch strip orange zest (removed with a vegetable peeler)

4 cups bottled clam juice or Shortcut Seafood Broth (page 578)

1 cup peeled, seeded, and diced tomatoes or one 14-ounce can diced tomatoes, drained

1 teaspoon sugar

Fish and/or shellfish, singly or in combination, such as

> **Four 6-ounce fish fillets,** such as striped bass, red snapper, sea bass, or cod
>
> **1¾ pounds shrimp,** peeled and deveined
>
> **1½ pounds sea or bay scallops**
>
> **or the following combination of shellfish:**
>
> > **12 medium shrimp** in the shell
> >
> > **8 large or 12 medium mussels,** scrubbed and debearded (if necessary; see page 678)
> >
> > **20 littleneck or Manila clams,** scrubbed
> >
> > **8 ounces sea or bay scallops** or 16 singing scallops in the shell, scrubbed

Pinch of kosher salt

Freshly ground black pepper

½ cup chopped fresh flat-leaf parsley

2 tablespoons heavy cream or crème fraîche (optional)

To make the saffron-tomato base, combine the saffron with the hot water in a small bowl. Set aside to steep.

In a large heavy saucepan, combine the olive oil, shallots, garlic, chile, thyme, fennel seeds, and bay leaves. Cover and cook over low heat, stirring occasionally, until the shallots are translucent, about 10 minutes. Stir in the leeks and water, cover, and cook, stirring occasionally, until the leeks are wilted, about 4 minutes. Add the white wine, orange zest, and the saffron and its soaking liquid, increase the heat to moderate, and bring to a boil. Boil for 4 minutes. Add the clam juice, tomatoes, and sugar, and cook for 20 to 25 minutes longer, until the broth has reduced to about 5 cups and the flavor is rich and mellow.

Pour the broth into a 10- to 11-inch shallow saucepan. Arrange the fish fillets or shellfish in the pan, or deep skillet, cover, and cook at a bare simmer (do not allow to boil!). The shellfish and shrimp will cook first. Check after 3 minutes to see if they have opened; shrimp shells should be pink, the flesh opaque. Transfer to warm shallow bowls with a slotted spoon and continue cooking the fish, about 6 minutes longer (a two-pronged kitchen fork inserted in the thickest part will meet with no resistance). Transfer the fish to the bowls.

To finish the sauce, stir in the salt, pepper to taste, the parsley, and cream, if desired. Spoon the sauce over the fish and/or shellfish.

IN ADVANCE You can prepare the Saffron-Tomato Broth up to 4 days ahead; cover and refrigerate. Or freeze it for up to 2 months.

Creamy Garlic Fish Soup
After a Bourride

Bourride is a voluptuous fish soup of the South of France that is usually made with only one kind of fish, rather than a multitude as in a bouillabaisse, which is poached in a rich broth that is then thickened with aïoli, the region's garlicky mayonnaise. The perfume of the garlic that is released when the aïoli is stirred into the hot broth is intoxicating.

I would never advise you to turn down a real bourride should you find yourself in Provence or in the company of a great cook. However, since the egg yolks and olive oil alone contribute upward of 400 calories per serving, I have created a fish soup with a bourride's spirit and rich taste but with a "leaner" body.

Cook several heads of garlic and rice in a good fish broth, along with traditional flavorings: orange peel, fennel seed, and saffron. When pureed, the garlic and rice thicken the broth and add exceptional creaminess, further augmented with a little heavy cream. Drizzling garlic-infused olive oil over the soup at the last minute provides the explosive garlic aroma essential to a bourride. Although it has only 2 teaspoons heavy cream and 1 teaspoon of olive oil per serving, this dish is truly luxurious.

Serve the soup with Rustic Garlic Toasts (page 368) and a fine chilled rosé from Provence.

Creamy Garlic Base

¼ **teaspoon saffron threads** (a large pinch)

1 **tablespoon hot water**

4 **heads** (8 ounces) **garlic,** separated into unpeeled cloves

1 **quart White Wine Fish Broth** (page 577)
or Shortcut Seafood Broth (page 578)

½ **cup finely chopped fennel** or ½ teaspoon fennel seeds

One **4-by-1-inch strip orange zest** (removed with a vegetable peeler)

½ **imported bay leaf**

¾ **to 1 teaspoon salt**

1 **cup water**

¼ **cup long-grain white rice**

3 **medium tomatoes,** peeled, seeded, and chopped

2 **tablespoons heavy cream or crème fraîche**

Garlic Oil

   1 teaspoon minced garlic

   ½ teaspoon salt

   1 tablespoon fruity extra-virgin olive oil

Six 6-ounce white-fleshed fish fillets, such as striped bass,
red snapper, sea bass, tilefish, halibut, or mahi mahi

Kosher salt and freshly ground black pepper

1 to 2 teaspoons fresh lemon juice

To make the creamy garlic base, combine the saffron and hot water in a small bowl. Set aside to steep for 15 minutes.

In a heavy medium saucepan, combine the garlic cloves, broth, fennel, orange zest, bay leaf, ½ teaspoon of the salt, and the 1 cup water. Bring to a boil over moderate heat. Stir in the rice, reduce the heat, partially cover, and simmer until the garlic is puree-soft, about 35 minutes.

Strain the broth; discard the bay leaf and orange zest. Pick out the garlic cloves with a fork. To squeeze the soft flesh out of the hot skins, place the garlic cloves on a work surface and press the flesh out with the side of a dinner knife. Scrape the flesh into a blender container, and discard the peels. (Alternatively, you can pass the garlic cloves through a food mill; add to the blender.)

Working in batches, if necessary, add the broth and any remaining solids to the garlic and blend until smooth and creamy. If you have less than 4 cups soup, add enough water or broth to make that amount.

Return the soup to the pan over moderate heat, and add the tomatoes, cream, and saffron with its liquid. Adjust the seasoning, but leave the base slightly undersalted, as it will reduce more when you cook the fish.

Shortly before serving, make the garlic oil: In a mortar, or on the work surface, pound or mash the minced garlic with the salt until pureed. Transfer to a small bowl and stir in the olive oil. Set aside to infuse for 10 minutes.

Bring the soup to a simmer over moderate heat. Arrange the fish fillets in the soup in a single layer, cover, and simmer gently (do not allow to boil!) until just cooked through, about 9 minutes; a two-pronged kitchen fork inserted in the thickest part should meet with no resistance.

Transfer the fillets to six warmed shallow soup bowls. Season the soup with salt and pepper and the lemon juice, and ladle it over the fish. Drizzle the garlic oil over the soup and serve at once.

You can prepare the base up to 1 day ahead; cover and refrigerate.   **IN ADVANCE**

Steamed Lobster with Vanilla Butter Sauce

SERVES 4

To mimic sea water for steaming or boiling lobsters, dissolve ¼ cup sea salt in each gallon of tap water.

I first had the astonishing pairing of lobster with vanilla butter at L'Archestrate, Chef Alain Senderens's restaurant in Paris; it was a revelation in the perfection of seemingly incongruous flavors. Serve this elegant sauce in small ramekins in place of melted butter when you are treating your guests to lobster.

Steaming is the best, simplest method of cooking whole lobsters, since it intensifies their pure flavor (boiling dilutes the flavor, as water seeps into the shells). Lobsters yield a little less than half their weight in meat, so I generally serve 1½-pound lobsters. For 4 lobsters, you'll need a tall, narrow 4- to 6-gallon pot. As a steaming rack, use a vegetable steamer or an upside-down colander, anything that will elevate the lobsters above 1 inch of salted water. If you are uncomfortable about cooking lobsters live, there is a way to kill them instantly (see page 678).

> **Four 1½-pound lobsters,** rinsed
> **Vanilla Butter Sauce** (page 644), kept warm in a double boiler

Add 1 inch of hot water to a narrow 4- to 6-gallon pot. Measure or roughly estimate the amount and stir in ¼ cup of salt per gallon. Arrange a rack in the pot and bring the water to a boil. Add the lobsters, cover, and cook for 14 minutes, rearranging the lobsters once during that time.

Place the cooked lobsters on a large cutting board. Holding one with a tea towel, cover its claws with a wet cloth, and rap with a hammer to crack the claws. Repeat with the remaining lobsters. With kitchen shears, make a vertical cut up the center of each tail shell. Place on four large platters and serve at once, accompanied by the sauce.

Note: If you are more comfortable boiling lobsters, boil them in plenty of boiling salted water, timing from the moment you add the lobsters, not when the water returns to a boil, for 11 minutes. To release the water trapped inside each lobster's shell, with the tip of a knife, punch a small hole between the cooked lobster's eyes; tilt the lobster head down until all the water drains out.

IN ADVANCE Prepare the sauce up to 30 minutes ahead and keep warm in a double boiler. You can set up your steamer, with the salted water and rack, up to several hours in advance.

ON THE STOVE TOP: PAN SMOKING. Pan smoking, a remarkably easy method of smoking foods at home, even in a city apartment, is one of the most exciting cooking techniques I've explored. It imbues foods with the sweet flavor of wood smoke, adding wonderful character with hardly any fat and no nitrites. It renders fish astonishingly succulent and sweet.

The method is simple. You add wood chips or dried ancho chiles to a hot cast-iron skillet or a wok, then place the food on a rack over them. When the pan is covered, the food cooks in the intense heat and is flavored by the smoke. Since you use only a small amount of chips, there is not enough smoke to worry about: Your kitchen simply takes on the pleasing smell of fragrant smoke. What I love most is that this method requires no special equipment and can be easily improvised anywhere. The spectacular results belie its ease.

SWEET SMOKE: WOOD CHIPS AND ANCHO CHILES

Many aromatic woods are available commercially as chips for smoking or grilling, either by mail or, during barbecue season, in supermarkets and specialty stores. Alder, apple, and cherry might be found in your own backyard or a nearby field (they must be dried before smoking) and make exceptionally sweet, mellow smoke, as do grapevines, my personal favorite. I buy grapevine wreaths for a few dollars at florists and garden stores, then break off pieces as I need it. Though mesquite's flavor is rather assertive, it goes well with most foods.

Surprisingly, ancho chile smoke surpasses even fruitwoods for subtlety and deliciousness, lending a mild sweet flavor to the food. (Hot chile peppers, on the other hand, produce an acrid smoke that will drive you out of the house.) Ancho chiles can be found in the Mexican food section of many supermarkets and in gourmet stores. To use, break 1 chile into 2 pieces, discarding the seeds and stem. If it is dry and brittle, rather than rubbery and pliable, place it in a bowl and pour boiling water over to cover. Let it soak for 1 minute or less, until pliable. Drain and pat dry.

You can order wood chips and ancho chiles by mail. See Sources, page 711.

Line a 10- or 11-inch cast-iron skillet or wok with aluminum foil. Tear a 1½-inch round out of the center so that the wood or chile will lie directly on the bottom of the pan; the foil will prevent dripping fat from burning on the bottom of the pan. Line a heavy lid to fit the skillet or wok with aluminum foil, to make cleanup easier. Place a round wire cake rack with 1-inch-high feet in the skillet. If necessary, roll 5 pieces of foil into tight 1-inch balls and place them under the edges of the rack to elevate it.

Pan-Smoked Fish

A GUIDE TO IMPROVISING

SERVES 4

To serve more or less than 4, figure on 2 teaspoons sugar, 1 teaspoon salt, and 1 teaspoon black pepper per pound of fish.

Once you get the hang of this simple method, you can experiment with many kinds of fish and shellfish. The secret is to cure the fish slightly with sugar, salt, and pepper to draw out some liquid and firm up the flesh before smoking it. The cure also seems to act as a wick for the smoke, drawing it into the flesh and mellowing it.

Curing Mixture

2½ teaspoons granulated or light brown sugar

1¼ teaspoons kosher salt

1¼ teaspoons freshly ground black pepper

1½ pounds fish fillets or steaks or shellfish, such as

Salmon, mackerel, or bluefish (fatty fish): one 1½-pound fillet or four 6-ounce steaks, at least 1¼ inches thick

Tuna and swordfish: one 1½-pound steak or four 6-ounce steaks, at least 1¼ inches thick

Sea scallops (at least ¾ inch thick)

Peeled and deveined jumbo shrimp

1 teaspoon vegetable or olive oil

Smoking medium, such as

1½ teaspoons wood chips

One 1-by-¼-inch chunk fruitwood or mesquite

Two 2-inch pieces grapevine

1 dried ancho chile, stemmed, seeded, and broken into 4 pieces

1. At least 1 but no more than 3 hours before smoking, make the curing mixture: Combine the sugar, salt, and pepper in a small bowl. Rub the mixture into the fish or shellfish. Place on a platter and cover with plastic wrap. Refrigerate if curing for more than an hour.

2. Blot the fish or shellfish dry with paper towels and brush lightly with the oil.

3. Set up your smoker, as directed on page 266. Heat over high heat for 5 minutes.

4. Add the chips, wood, or chile to the pan and place the metal rack in the skillet. Arrange the fish on the rack. When the wood or chile starts to smoke, after 2 to 3 minutes, cover the pan, placing a weight on the lid to seal it tight. Reduce the heat to medium, or so you just faintly smell smoke and see a little escaping from the pan. Cook the fish according to the guidelines below.

APPROXIMATE COOKING TIMES FOR PAN-SMOKED FISH

Adjust the cooking times as necessary according to the thickness of the fish. If you are unsure, test it early, then continue smoking until done.

Fatty Fish, such as salmon, mackerel, and bluefish: Cook until a two-pronged fork inserted into the fish meets with no resistance, about 10 to 12 minutes.

Rare-Cooked Fish, such as tuna and swordfish: Smoke the fish for 4 minutes. Turn it over and smoke until it is opaque and golden on the outside and springy to the touch, 4 to 8 minutes, depending on the thickness; an instant-read thermometer inserted into the thickest part should read 115°F.

Sea Scallops and Jumbo Shrimp: Cook until opaque throughout, 4 to 5 minutes.

Pan-Smoked Salmon

improvisation 1

This has become the favorite recipe of several bachelor friends because it is virtually foolproof and yields such dramatic results. Cooking the salmon in the intense enclosed heat and smoke seems to release the fat that marbles the flesh, basting it as it were from the inside and rendering it incredibly succulent with a smoky sweet flavor. It is magic with Yogurt Sauce with Toasted Spices, Lime Zest, and Basil (page 630). It is also great cold.

Following the Guide on pages 266 to 267, smoke the salmon for 10 to 12 minutes, or until a two-pronged fork inserted into a fillet or steak meets with no resistance. With a thin metal spatula, transfer the salmon to a serving platter and serve at once.

Pan-Smoked Rare Tuna

improvisation 2

The results of pan-smoking tuna are startling, yet it is almost as easy to do as pan-searing it. Although the tuna is smoked, it remains rare inside; when thinly sliced, it looks like filet mignon. For a lovely warm salad, serve the sliced warm tuna on a bed of mesclun or Herb Salad (page 415), with some Rustic Garlic Toasts (page 368). It also lends itself to improvised dishes: on a bed of buckwheat noodles with Ginger-Sake Broth (page 582), for example.

Following the Guide on pages 266 to 267, smoke the tuna for 4 minutes. Turn it over and smoke until it is opaque and golden on the outside and springy to the touch, 4 to 8 minutes. An instant-read thermometer inserted in the thickest part should read 115°F for rare. Transfer the tuna to a cutting board and allow it to rest for 3 minutes. Slice it as thin as possible and serve at once.

Traditionally, dishes made with flaked or shredded fish or shellfish, such as crab cakes and *brandade de morue*, the luxuriously creamy salt cod puree, require a lot of rich ingredients—whether cream, egg yolks, or mayonnaise—to moisten and bind them together. The trick is to figure out how to bind them without adding lots of fat and calories. The following recipes offer some simple solutions.

Ginger-and-Cilantro Crab Cakes

A good crab cake consists mainly of crabmeat, not breading, as is so often the case. It should taste of fresh crab, be well seasoned, and be bound just enough to hold the crabmeat together into a cake form, and be crisp on the outside, yet not greasy. This crab cake recipe fulfills these rigorous criteria. It is inspired by some silver dollar–sized crab cakes I had years ago at Barbara Tropp's inspired Chinese restaurant in San Francisco, China Moon, which were redolent with ginger and cilantro and had mild chile pepper heat.

Fat and calories are reduced by replacing the egg yolks with egg whites, trimming the traditional mayonnaise binder, and frying the cakes in the reduced amount of oil in a nonstick skillet. Serve the crab cakes with Cilantro and Coconut Chutney (page 665).

SERVES 4 AS A MAIN COURSE, 6 AS AN HORS D'OEUVRE

If you want to economize, you can make these cakes replacing up to one third of the crab with flaked cooked mild white fish.

2 slices (1½ ounces) **fresh white sandwich bread** (see Note)

Chinese Seasonings

> **1½ cups fresh cilantro leaves,** cleaned and spun dry in a salad spinner

> **2 tablespoons grated fresh ginger**

> **2 scallions,** cut into ¼-inch rings (about ¼ cup)

> **1 tablespoon plus 1 teaspoon Chinese or Thai chile paste** (available in the Asian food section of some supermarkets and in specialty markets), or to taste

1 tablespoon mayonnaise

2 teaspoons dry sherry or sake

½ teaspoon kosher salt

½ teaspoon sugar

1½ pounds fresh lump crabmeat

3 large egg whites, beaten

2 teaspoons Asian sesame oil

In a food processor, process the white bread to soft crumbs. (You should have 1 cup.) Scrape them into a medium bowl; set aside. Add the cilantro, ginger, scallions, chile paste, mayonnaise, sherry, salt, and sugar to the work bowl, and process to make a thick paste, about 15 seconds. Scrape into the bowl with the bread crumbs.

Blot the crabmeat dry with paper towels. Add the crabmeat and egg whites to the bowl and toss lightly with a fork to combine, taking care not to break up all the lumps of crabmeat. Shape the crab mixture into twelve 2½- to 3-inch patties and place on a baking sheet lined with waxed paper. Refrigerate for at least 30 minutes, and up to 4 hours, to dry the patties out slightly.

Preheat the oven to 200°F.

In a nonstick 10-inch skillet, heat 1 teaspoon of the sesame oil over moderate heat. Using a spatula, gently slide 6 of the crab patties into the pan. If they break apart, simply press them back together in the pan—they will set as they cook. Fry, turning once, until golden brown, about 3 minutes on each side. Transfer to an ovenproof platter and keep warm in a low oven while you fry the other 6, using the remaining 1 teaspoon oil. Serve at once.

Note: You can use 4 to 6 tablespoons dry bread crumbs instead of the fresh crumbs, though the crab cakes will not be quite as moist or as tender. Add only enough to absorb the excess moisture without the mixture becoming dry.

IN ADVANCE   You can make the patties up to a day ahead; cover and refrigerate. Let come to room temperature for 15 minutes before frying.

variation   **Classic Maryland Shore Crab Cakes.** Omit the Chinese Seasonings. Add to the bowl with the bread crumbs: 1¼ teaspoons paprika, ⅜ teaspoon curry powder, ⅜ teaspoon freshly ground black pepper, ⅜ teaspoon dry mustard, scant ¼ teaspoon ground allspice, scant ¼ teaspoon cayenne pepper, 3 tablespoons minced fresh flat-leaf parsley, 1 tablespoon mayonnaise, 1½ tablespoons fresh lemon juice, 1½ teaspoons Worcestershire sauce, 1 teaspoon dry sherry, and 3 drops Tabasco sauce; omit the salt and sugar. Stir in the crabmeat and egg whites and proceed as directed, using olive oil to fry the crab cakes. Serve with Curry Cream (page 628), Roasted Garlic Aïoli (page 618), or Rouille (page 619).

Tuna Burgers

SERVES 4

This recipe was inspired by the one served years ago at the Gotham Bar & Grill in New York, where it was cooked rare and served on a toasted roll with grilled onions, lettuce, and lemon-garlic mayonnaise. I like to garnish it with thinly sliced sweet onion or "Fried" Onions (page 62) and serve it with mesclun salad, with or without a bun. Serve with Yogurt Sauce with Toasted Spices, Lime Zest, and Basil (page 630), Roasted Garlic Aïoli (page 618), or Cilantro and Coconut Chutney (page 665).

- **One 3-inch piece fresh ginger,** peeled and cut in 3 pieces
- **1½ pounds tuna steaks**
- **3 tablespoons minced scallions**
- **1 tablespoon finely chopped fresh cilantro**
- **¼ teaspoon minced garlic**
- **1½ teaspoons minced jalapeño chile**
- **Pinch of sugar**
- **¼ teaspoon kosher salt**
- **Freshly ground black pepper**
- **1½ teaspoons low-sodium soy sauce**
- **2 teaspoons Asian sesame oil**
- **2 tablespoons sesame seeds** (optional)

With a chef's knife, finely chop the tuna on a cutting board.

Press the ginger in a garlic press, catching the pulp in a small bowl, or finely grate it. Add 1 teaspoon of ginger to the tuna, along with the scallions, cilantro, garlic, jalapeño, sugar, salt, pepper to taste, the soy sauce, and 1 teaspoon of the sesame oil.

With wet hands, shape the tuna into 4 equal patties. Place on a cookie sheet and freeze for 10 minutes to firm up the flesh.

Brush the patties with the remaining 1 teaspoon sesame oil. Sprinkle on both sides with the sesame seeds, if using, and pat them into the burgers.

To panfry the burgers: Heat a large nonstick skillet over high heat until very hot. Add the burgers and cook for 2 minutes on each side, or until deep brown on the outside but still rare on the inside.

To grill: Place on a grill over hot coals and cook for 1½ to 2 minutes on each side. Serve at once.

Garlic-Scented Salt Cod Puree

The coastal regions of France, Italy, and Spain share a love of salted cod that has been soaked, poached gently, and then beaten with garlic and large quantities of olive oil to make a thick, unctuous puree. The most famous permutation is from Provence, called *brandade de morue*.

In this leaner adaptation, the cod is poached in milk with potatoes, which provide the thickening normally achieved with quantities of olive oil, then beaten with garlic, anchovy, and the flavorful poaching liquid until it is the right creamy consistency. A small amount of extra-virgin olive oil is added at the end so that its flavor remains apparent.

Serve the brandade in its baking dish, with Rustic Garlic Toasts (page 368) and a lightly dressed salad or bitter greens or arugula. Or serve it as they do in Venice, mounded alongside crisp slices of Panfried, Roasted, or Grilled Polenta (page 201).

I prefer the mildly salted center-cut salt cod available in the frozen food section of many supermarkets; it needs only 8 hours of soaking time. The traditional dried board-like salt cod can be found at ethnic markets and many fish markets, but because it is more highly salted, you must soak it for at least 24 hours.

8 ounces dried salt cod, preferably frozen

5 ounces yellow or red waxy potatoes, peeled and cut into ½-inch-thick slices

1 ¼ cups low-fat (2%) milk

⅛ teaspoon dried thyme

1 imported bay leaf

1 garlic clove, cut in half, plus ½ to 1 teaspoon minced garlic

½ oil-packed anchovy, drained and mashed, or ½ teaspoon anchovy paste

2 tablespoons extra-virgin olive oil

Freshly ground black pepper

Place the salt cod in a medium bowl and add enough cold water to cover. Soak for at least 8 hours if frozen, 24 hours if dried, in the refrigerator, changing the water at least three times. Drain the cod.

In a medium saucepan, combine the cod, potatoes, milk, thyme, and bay leaf. Heat just to a simmer and cook over low heat until the potatoes are tender, about 15 minutes. Turn off the heat and let sit for 10 minutes. Remove the bay leaf and discard.

Preheat the oven to 400°F. Rub the inside of a 1-quart gratin dish with the cut garlic clove. Allow to dry for 2 minutes. Then oil the dish lightly.

With a slotted spoon, transfer the cod to a medium bowl. Set aside until cool enough to handle.

With your fingers, remove any membrane or bones from the cod. Break the cod into 1-inch pieces. Add the potatoes, garlic, and anchovy to the bowl (reserve the poaching liquid). With an electric hand mixer, beat the cod and potatoes until they are the consistency of tuna fish salad. Slowly dribble in ½ cup of the hot poaching liquid, until the mixture is creamy. Beat in 1 tablespoon of the olive oil and plenty of pepper.

Spoon the brandade into the gratin dish, smooth the top, and then create a rippled pattern by gouging the brandade lightly with the side of a large spoon. Drizzle the top with the remaining tablespoon olive oil.

Bake until the top is golden brown and the puree is heated through, 15 to 20 minutes. Serve at once.

IN ADVANCE You can prepare the brandade mixture up to 1 day ahead. Allow to come to room temperature for 15 minutes before baking.

COLD AND CURED SEAFOOD. These recipes are among the easiest, and most dramatic, ways I know of preparing cold fish and shellfish. Home-cured fish fillets have the added virtue of being versatile, transforming instantly into carpaccio, tartare, salads, or sandwiches.

Thai Seafood Salad with Lemongrass Dressing

SERVES 4 AS A
MAIN COURSE,
6 AS A FIRST
COURSE

Flavored with lime juice, lemongrass, chiles, cilantro, basil, and mint, this Thai-inspired seafood salad is wonderfully refreshing and flavorful, yet contains no added fat. You can make it with any combination of shrimp, calamari, scallops, or lobster you like.

Thai ingredients are increasingly available in supermarkets, as well as in Asian stores. Fish sauce and chile paste keep indefinitely refrigerated, so are easy to keep on hand. You can freeze fresh lemongrass and kaffir lime leaves. If you can't find fresh lemongrass, dried lemongrass is almost as good.

You could serve this salad with Rustic Garlic Toasts (page 368) or even add some cooked white beans to it; it is unorthodox but delicious.

Lemongrass Dressing

2 ½ tablespoons sugar

About ½ cup fresh lime juice (you can replace 1 tablespoon of the lime juice with an equal amount of rice wine vinegar for added pungency)

¼ cup Thai fish sauce (nam pla)

3 to 4 quarter-sized slices fresh ginger

1 tablespoon water

2 kaffir lime leaves (optional)

2 stalks fresh lemongrass or 1 tablespoon dried lemongrass

1 to 2 teaspoons Thai chile paste or 2 small serrano or jalapeño chiles, finely diced

1 small red onion, peeled

1 medium cucumber, peeled

1¼ pounds peeled and deveined shrimp or other shellfish, such as cleaned calamari cut into ½-inch rings, bay scallops, or cooked lobster, cut into bite-sized pieces

2 scallions, thinly sliced on the diagonal

¾ cup packed fresh Thai basil leaves or ½ cup regular basil leaves plus ¼ cup mint leaves

¾ cup packed fresh cilantro leaves

4 cups mixed lettuces, washed and dried

3 tablespoons roasted peanuts, chopped (optional)

To make the dressing, combine the sugar, ⅓ cup of the lime juice, the fish sauce, ginger, and water in a small saucepan. Bruise the kaffir lime leaves and the bulbs of the lemongrass, if using, by pressing them with the side of a chef's knife or something heavy. Trim the lemongrass stalks to 2½ inches and slice crosswise as thin as possible. (You should have about 3 tablespoons.) Add the fresh or dried lemongrass and the lime leaves to the saucepan. Bring to a simmer over moderate heat, stirring until the sugar is dissolved; simmer for 1 minute. Set aside to cool and infuse.

Strain the dressing. Stir in the chile paste.

Thinly slice the red onion lengthwise and place in a bowl of ice water for 15 minutes to draw out any bitterness.

Slice the cucumber lengthwise in half. With a teaspoon, remove the seeds. Cut each cucumber half crosswise into thin slices. Place in a medium bowl.

Steam the shrimp, calamari, or scallops, if using, covered, on a rack set over rapidly boiling water until just cooked through, 2 to 3 minutes. Plunge into a bowl of ice water to stop the cooking. Drain well and transfer to the bowl of cucumbers.

Drain the onions and pat dry with paper towels. Add to the bowl, along with the scallions and the lobster, if using. Drizzle the dressing over and toss to coat. Coarsely chop the herbs and mix into the salad. Add enough of the remaining lime juice to lift the flavors.

Divide the lettuces among four chilled dinner plates or place on a large platter. Spoon the seafood mixture over the lettuces, garnish with the peanuts, if desired, and serve.

You can prepare the Lemongrass Dressing up to 4 days ahead; cover and refrigerate.

IN ADVANCE

Home-Cured Salmon

SERVES 8

If you wish to cure
2 fillets, simply
double the amount
of cure and proceed
as directed, wrapping
each fillet separately.

The dense creamy texture and sweet concentrated flavor of both smoked salmon and Swedish gravlax are the result of a salt-and-sugar cure that draws out some of the fish's moisture. Home-cured salmon is easy to make and much less expensive than store-bought. It is wonderful to have on hand for a delicious first course or cold lunch. It is an ideal healthy food, rich in omega-3 fatty acids.

This simple method for curing one-pound fillets takes much less time than recipes for whole sides of fish. The delicate balance of salt and sugar lends itself to any number of flavorings, from aromatic pepper and fresh herbs to grappa and lemon zest to juniper berries and aquavit.

You can also use this method to cure other firm-fleshed fish, such as mahi mahi, red snapper, bluefish, or striped bass.

> **1 pound center-cut salmon fillet,** pinbones removed (see Note)
> **Curing Mixture**
>> **1 ½ tablespoons kosher salt**
>> **1 tablespoon light brown sugar**
> **Flavorings** (see suggested combinations that follow)

Place the salmon skin side down on a large piece of plastic wrap. Combine the salt and sugar in a small bowl. Rub evenly over both sides of the fish. Then add the flavorings that follow.

Double-wrap the salmon securely in plastic wrap. Sandwich it between two small cookie sheets or flat platters. Place a 4- to 5-pound weight on top. Refrigerate for 36 hours, turning the package once.

To serve, with a long narrow slicing knife held almost parallel to the fish, slice the fillet into slices about ⅛ inch thick.

Note: If you are concerned about the safety of eating raw fish, ask your fishmonger for fish that has been flash-frozen at sea; flash-freezing (at below −31°F) for 15 hours kills organisms with parasites without any change in flavor or texture.

Well-wrapped, the salmon will keep for 1 week in the refrigerator, and up to 2 months in the freezer (about 6 hours before serving, place in the refrigerator to defrost).

Salmon Cured with Aquavit and Juniper

flavoring combination 1

Aquavit is a strong Scandinavian liquor distilled from potatoes or grain. Its herbal caraway flavor marries wonderfully with juniper berries as a flavoring for salmon. I like to serve icy-cold aquavit alongside open-faced salmon sandwiches on buttered whole-grain bread.

- **1 teaspoon grated lime zest**
- **1 tablespoon plus 1 teaspoon aquavit**
- **1 tablespoon juniper berries,** finely crushed in a mortar or with a side of a chef's knife
- **1½ teaspoons coarsely ground black pepper**

Spread the lime zest over the skinless side of the salmon. Drizzle the aquavit over the salmon and sprinkle the juniper berries and pepper over both sides, pressing them in.

Salmon Cured with Pastis and Tarragon

flavoring combination 2

Although you might think tarragon would overpower the salmon, it imparts a mild anisy flavor to the fish.

- **1 teaspoon grated lemon zest**
- **1 tablespoon plus 1 teaspoon Pastis or Pernod**
- **1 teaspoon coarsely ground black pepper**
- **½ cup fresh tarragon leaves**

Spread the lemon zest over the skinless side of the salmon. Drizzle the Pernod over the salmon and rub the pepper over both sides. Press the tarragon leaves into both sides of the salmon.

Salmon Cured with Tequila and Cilantro

flavoring combination 3

Earthy tequila marries with cilantro's clean herbal flavor to delicately perfume the salmon.

- **1 teaspoon grated lime zest**
- **1 tablespoon plus 1 teaspoon gold tequila**
- **1 teaspoon coarsely ground black pepper**
- **1 cup fresh cilantro leaves**

Spread the lime zest over the skinless side of the salmon. Drizzle the tequila over the salmon and rub the pepper over both sides. Press the cilantro leaves into both sides of the salmon.

Salmon Cured with Aromatic Pepper and Herbs

This is my favorite basic "gravlax," seasoned with an aromatic pepper and herb mix.

1 teaspoon grated lemon zest

1 tablespoon plus 1 teaspoon cognac or Armagnac

½ teaspoon black peppercorns

½ teaspoon white peppercorns

6 allspice berries

¼ teaspoon coriander seeds

¼ cup finely chopped mixed fresh herbs, such as flat-leaf parsley, chervil, chives, and tarragon (with no more than 1½ teaspoons tarragon)

Spread the lemon zest over the skinless side of the salmon. Drizzle the cognac over the salmon. With a mortar and pestle, spice grinder, or blender, coarsely grind the black and white pepper, allspice, and coriander. Rub the spice mixture evenly over both sides of the fish, then press the herbs into both sides of the salmon.

Home-Cured Salmon is so rich a little goes a long way; a 4-ounce serving, at about 200 calories, is ample as a main course; 2 ounces generous as an appetizer.

As carpaccio: in paper-thin slices arranged in a single layer on each plate, then garnished with herbs and extra-virgin olive oil.

As tea sandwiches: on lightly buttered white bread with thin slices of cucumber.

As Asian open-faced tea sandwiches: on ⅓-inch-thick sheets of cooked sushi rice with chives.

As a salad: layered with thin slices of ripe avocado and watercress sprigs and dressed with lime juice and extra-virgin olive oil.

As a tartare: diced and tossed with a teaspoon or two of extra-virgin olive oil and a few tablespoons of chopped fresh herbs, such as chives, tarragon, basil, chervil, and flat-leaf parsley.

As a topping for Corn Blini (page 379) **or Chive French Toast** (page 381): with a drizzle of lime-flavored regular or low-fat sour cream.

On slices of hot corn bread: with chive-flavored regular or low-fat sour cream.

Spice–Rubbed
Duck Steaks with
Port Wine Sauce
(page 326), served
with Brown Butter
Orzo "Risotto"
(page 126)

POULTRY & MEAT

a guide to improvising

It might seem odd to include a chapter on red meat in a book about healthy eating. After all, so much has been written about the potentially deleterious effects of animal fats on health. Why include them at all?

To begin with, red meat is part of our culture, the vocabulary of flavors and ingredients that resonates for many people. I don't want to give up a rosemary-scented leg of lamb, a roast duck with crispy skin, or the occasional rare strip steak smothered in onions. Second, red meats are exceptionally rich in the protein, zinc, iron, and vitamins B_6 and B_{12} we need to thrive. It gives many people a boost that they can't get from any other kind of food. Red meat's dangers outweigh its benefits only when we consume too much of it.

I've taken a cue from the Mediterranean diet, in which meat is consumed only occasionally, and never in big portions. I limit portion size to about 4 ounces of cooked meat, a little more if it is an exceptionally lean cut, and I always serve it with appealing vegetable side dishes. This approach means changing the configuration of a traditional meal slightly to weight it more heavily with lighter plant-based foods that balance out the moderate but satisfying portion of meat. This differs from the currently popular notion of using meat as a condiment or flavoring element, which I feel is unrealistic. If you crave meat, that simply isn't going to satisfy you. It is better to eat a moderate serving of the meat you truly hunger for prepared in the leanest way possible.

In this chapter, I will show you the best ways I have found to cook meat and poultry leanly and flavorfully. The first section begins with oven methods, from the perfect roast chicken to traditionally taboo foods like roast duck and spareribs. The second section covers stove-top methods building on the technique of pan-searing to make simple quick meals and slow-cooked braises cloaked in their own pan sauce. The last section includes a lightened approach to recipes made with ground meats, like meat loaf, pâté, sausages, and burgers.

Foolproof Roast Chicken with Its Own Pan Sauce (page 291), served with Roasted Garlic (page 37) and roasted fingerling potatoes (page 34)

CHOOSING CUTS OF MEAT AND POULTRY

These recipes offer a choice of meat cuts you can use, ranging from lean to those more liberally marbled with fat. This is to allow you the greatest flexibility and enjoyment in cooking—and because there are times you want to splurge with a less lean piece of meat. So, for example, you could make Milanese Style Scaloppine with Peppery Greens (page 323) with either turkey breast, which is extremely lean, or traditional veal scallops, which have more fat but an incomparable flavor. Either necessitates some trade-offs. Which you opt for is your choice.

Consult the chart on page 688 for comparisons of the fat and calorie content of various cuts. Whatever cut you choose, be sure to trim off all the fat you can. The chart includes some less readily available meats that are extraordinarily low in fat. If you come across them, substitute buffalo or beefalo (a cross of buffalo and beef) for steak in any recipe.

SHOPPING FOR MEATS AND POULTRY

Whenever possible, buy meat and poultry that have been raised without the use of growth stimulants, hormones, or antibiotics, which can remain in the animal's flesh. Many supermarkets are stocking organically fed or hormone-and-antibiotic-free beef and poultry in response to consumer requests. If you are unable to purchase them locally, you can mail-order them and freeze them to keep on hand (see Sources, page 711).

Meat and poultry lose about 25 percent of their weight in cooking. When shopping, figure that 5 ounces of raw meat will yield 4 ounces cooked. For 4 people, 1¼ pounds, or 20 ounces, of raw meat will yield 16 ounces cooked, or 4 ounces per serving.

BIRDS: TO SKIN OR NOT

Most of the fat in a chicken resides in the skin and in the pockets around the tail end opening. For sautés and braises, you'll want to remove the skin, because in these cooking methods, a lot of fat is rendered out into the sauce. But I do roast and broil birds with the skin on, because it keeps the flesh moist during cooking; then I remove the skin before eating. Research has shown that cooking birds with the skin on does not add fat to the flesh itself.

IN THE OVEN: ROASTING. Roasting—cooking meats and poultry in the dry heat of an oven—is probably the easiest way to achieve dramatic results with little fat or effort. Once you have seasoned the roast, the oven does all the work, with little of the anxious activity that sometimes attends stove-top cooking. A roast can be as simple as an herb-and-lemon-scented chicken for Sunday supper or as elaborate as an elegant olive-stuffed leg of lamb for a dinner party. You can also cook side dishes, such as roasted root vegetables or potato gratins, right alongside.

SEASONING

Salt is the primary seasoning for roasts; it is essential for bringing out the true flavors of meat or poultry and can also improve its texture. If you salt meat and poultry an hour or more before cooking, the salt will penetrate the flesh, seasoning it more deeply and drawing some moisture out of the meat to firm it up and tenderize it. You can leave meats and poultry at room temperature up to 1 hour before cooking; longer than that, cover and refrigerate them. Be sure to pat the meat dry before cooking so that it browns nicely. If you don't have a chance to salt ahead, season immediately before cooking. In that case, also sprinkle the slices of cooked meat or poultry with a few grains of an excellent sea salt or fleur de sel to season the interior flesh. When salting roasts, sprinkle the entire surface with salt (as in all these recipes, use kosher salt).

In addition to salt, you can use any of the Flavor Essences, Dry Rubs, or Marinades on pages 541 to 563 to season a roast. (When using a dry rub, omit the preliminary salting.) You can coat a roast with a dry rub right before cooking, or up to a day ahead, so that its flavors penetrate the meat just like a wet marinade. Wet marinades need time to penetrate the meat: at least 6 hours, or overnight, in the refrigerator.

Figure on about 2 tablespoons Dry Rub or Flavor Essence and ¼ teaspoon sugar per pound of meat (the sugar rounds out the flavors).

Always bring a roast to room temperature for about 1 hour before roasting.

The biggest area of dispute in roasting is oven temperature. Each cook seems to have his or her own theories and favored uses of high and low heat. I've found that different combinations of heat work for specific situations and cuts of meat or poultry, as illustrated in the recipes that follow. If I had to reduce my thinking to a basic theory to use for improvising, it would be this:

Tender, well-marbled roasts that are no more than 4 inches thick and meant to be eaten rare or medium rare, such as rack or saddle of lamb and fillet of beef, are best cooked at a high temperature, around 450°F. The intense heat sears the outside so that it becomes brown and crusty in the relatively short time it takes to bring the inside to medium rare.

Tougher, leaner, or thicker cuts, such as leg of lamb, or cuts of meats that must be cooked completely, such as pork loin, rabbit, and chicken, do better at a moderate to low oven temperature, which ensures that the flesh will be tender and succulent. These should be subjected to high heat only for a short time, during the first or last 15 minutes or so of cooking, to brown the outside.

A FOOLPROOF WAY TO DETERMINE DONENESS

It is worth investing in an instant-read thermometer so that you can know exactly when your roast has come to the correct internal temperature. You simply insert it into the thickest part of the roast when the roast is approaching doneness. Bear in mind that it will keep cooking for a short while after it comes out of the oven, elevating the internal temperature by 5 to 10 degrees.

Poultry (Chicken, Game Hens, Pheasant): The breast should read 150°F; the part of thigh closest to the body should read about 170°F.

Rabbit: The thigh should read 150°F.

Pork Loin and Tenderloin: The center should read 145° to 150°F.

Leg of Lamb, Beef Roasts: The thickest part should read 120° for rare, 135° to 140°F for medium rare.

Roasts that have a tendency to dry out in the oven, such as chicken, turkey, game hens, pheasant, and pork loin and tenderloin, benefit immensely from brining—immersion in a solution of sugar, salt, and water. The brine draws out blood and seasons the flesh at the same time, giving it a fuller, cleaner flavor and moist, succulent flesh.

The amount of time a roast should spend in a brine depends on its size and thickness and the saltiness of the brine. Unfortunately, there are no cut-and-dried times, but the worst that can occur from overbrining is that the cut may be slightly salty; it will still be succulent and delicious. Thin cuts and small birds, like pork tenderloins and game hens, should spend no more than 6 hours in a brine. Larger cuts or birds, such as pork loin roasts and whole chickens, benefit from 8 to 12 hours in a brine. If you don't have that much time, even a couple of hours will have a beneficial effect. Turkeys need a longer, milder brine (see Foolproof Roast Turkey, page 302).

Basic Brine (enough to brine a 4½-pound roast or bird). In a large saucepan, bring 2 cups water to a boil, add 6 tablespoons kosher salt and 5 tablespoons sugar, and stir until dissolved. Pour into a deep bowl or plastic tub just large enough to hold the meat or poultry snugly and stir in 1½ quarts cold water. Cool to room temperature.

Add the meat or poultry and place a ceramic dish on top to keep it submerged. You can leave it at room temperature for up to 1 hour; for any longer than that, up to 24 hours, refrigerate.

Preheat the oven. Remove the meat or poultry from the brine, rinse under cold water, and pat dry. Discard the brine. Tie the roast or truss the bird as necessary and rub lightly with oil. Season with fresh herbs or a dry rub as desired. Place on a rack in a roasting pan and roast as directed in your recipe or following the guidelines on page 288.

BARDING MEATS TO PRESERVE SUCCULENCE

Very lean roasts that have no surface protection of skin or fat, such as pork loin or lean game birds like pheasant and guinea hen, will dry out in the hot, dry heat of the oven. Barding, that is, covering them with thin slices of fat such as fatback or bacon, is a traditional way of protecting the fragile meat. The fat forms a barrier around the flesh and, as it melts, bastes the surface with flavorful fat—most of which then drips into the pan. If the barding fat is removed before serving, very little additional fat will be consumed. The fatty skin of a chicken or duck acts in a similar way to protect the flesh during roasting while adding no additional calories if it is removed after cooking. My favorite bard is pancetta because its peppery flavor seems to enhance almost any meat or poultry.

ALLOW ROASTS TO REST

Letting roasts rest before you carve them (15 minutes for red meats, 10 for poultry) allows the juices that have been forced inward during the roasting to move back toward the surface; as they become evenly distributed throughout the flesh, they make it very juicy. If you carve the meat right after taking it from the oven, the juices will rush out and the meat will be dry. Don't worry about the meat getting cold; a roast retains heat for a long time.

Foolproof Roast Chicken with Its Own Pan Sauce

By some mysterious chemistry, roasting a chicken with a lemon in its cavity guarantees crisp skin, moist, flavorful flesh, and abundant pan juices, with no added fat—in short, everything one could ask of a roast chicken. The more "natural" the bird, the more flavor, so start with a hormone-free, free-range bird, increasingly available in supermarkets.

SERVES 4

Rubbing a chicken with a little grappa intensifies the chicken's natural flavor, making it taste more like a real farm bird.

¼ **teaspoon olive oil**

One 3-pound roasting chicken, rinsed and patted dry (neck and giblets reserved)

1 teaspoon kosher salt

1 teaspoon freshly ground black pepper

3 tablespoons fresh rosemary, thyme, and/or savory leaves, in any combination

3 garlic cloves: 1 crushed, 2 lightly smashed

1 large lemon, washed

2 medium carrots, coarsely chopped

2 shallots, cut lengthwise in half

3 sprigs fresh thyme

¼ **cup Madeira or dry white wine,** or a mixture of the two

Preheat the oven to 350°F. Place a 4-by-4-inch square of foil or parchment in a roasting pan and brush lightly with oil. Set aside.

With a thin sharp knife, cut the excess fat from the neck and hind cavity of the chicken and discard. Sprinkle the chicken evenly inside and out with the salt and pepper, rubbing it into the skin. Stuff the herb leaves and the crushed garlic clove into the cavity. Prick the lemon about 25 times with a toothpick or skewer. Stuff it into the cavity of the chicken. Using toothpicks or trussing needles, pin the neck and hind cavities closed, or truss the chicken with cotton string (see page 678).

Place the chicken breast side down on the foil in the roasting pan. Nestle the neck and giblets, carrots, shallots, smashed garlic cloves, and thyme sprigs around the chicken. Roast for 15 minutes.

Turn the chicken breast side up and carefully remove the foil. Roast for 20 minutes longer. Increase the oven temperature to 400°F. Roast the chicken for 20 to 25 minutes longer, until the skin is brown and crisp and the juices run clear when the part of the thigh nearest the body is pricked with a kitchen fork. An instant-read thermometer inserted in the thigh should read 160° to 170°F, in the breast, 150°F. Remove the toothpick or twine from the hind end. Lift the chicken with two wooden spoons and tilt it slightly so the juices run out of the cavity into the pan (discard the lemon and herbs). Place the chicken on a warm platter.

Pour the pan juices into a small measuring cup and let settle for 3 to 4 minutes. Carefully skim the fat off the surface with a tablespoon. Pour the juices back into the roasting pan, set it over moderate heat, and add the Madeira. Simmer, stirring to dissolve the browned bits on the bottom of the pan, until the alcohol has cooked off, about 5 minutes. Skim off any fat or scum that rises to the surface. Strain the sauce into a small bowl, and taste for seasoning. (You will have about ½ cup.)

Carve the chicken and pour any juices that have collected on the platter into the sauce. Spoon about 2 tablespoons of the sauce over each portion of chicken.

I always serve roasted chicken with the crisp skin and let my guests decide if they want to eat it or not. I personally like the option of indulging occasionally in the delicious skin. One ounce of cooked chicken skin (from about one quarter of a roasting chicken) adds an additional 110 calories per serving (most of it in fat).

variation **Butterflied Roast Chicken.** If you are in a hurry, you can butterfly the bird, removing the backbone and then opening the bird out and flattening it (see page 678). Omit the lemon and lay the chicken on a bed of the herb leaves (or place some under the skin) and the other aromatics. Place skin side up on a rack in a roasting pan and roast at 500°F for about 45 minutes.

ADDING FLAVORINGS UNDER THE SKIN

Sliding flavorings under the chicken skin is a great way to infuse a chicken with flavor. Leaves of soft fresh herbs, such as sage and tarragon, or whole imported bay leaves, spice pastes, and rubs (see Flavor Essences and Dry Rubs, pages 541–552) all work well.

Begin by working from the neck opening: With your fingers, gently pull the chicken skin away from the breast and legs, without tearing it. Then gently insert whatever flavorings you wish under the skin, over the breast and thigh meat. Be sure to season the cavity of the bird with salt and pepper and some of whatever you've placed under the skin, or some crushed garlic or grated ginger.

Herb-Scented Tuscan Pork Roast

SERVES 8

At Peggy Markel's cooking school, La Cucina al Focolore, eighteen miles southeast of Florence, a pork roast is boned and seasoned with sage-and-rosemary salt, then placed on a rack of the bones, which add flavor to the meat and pan juices. As it roasts, it is basted with white wine, both to build up a caramelized surface and to provide a pan sauce, a technique used for all manner of roasts in Tuscany. My American adaptation of this recipe is to cover the roast with thin slices of pancetta, which give it the juiciness and savor of Italian pork.

If you ask the butcher to saw through the chine bone that holds the ribs together, the ribs will roast into a rack of delectable spare ribs, which you can cut apart to nibble on. (Bear in mind that since ribs are quite rich, they will up the fat and calorie count.)

This is a wonderful dinner party dish, because it takes so little work for such a dramatic effect. It is also delicious cold.

> **One 7-pound pork loin,** boned (have the butcher do this, reserving the bones; see Headnote), fat trimmed
>
> **Tuscan Herb Salt** (page 549)
>
> **Four 10-inch-long rosemary branches**
>
> **1½ teaspoons kosher salt**
>
> **3 ounces** (4 to 5 thin slices) **lean pancetta**
>
> **1 teaspoon olive oil**
>
> **2 cups dry white wine**
>
> **Kosher salt and freshly ground black pepper**

Pat the pork loin dry. Using a knife-sharpening steel or a long-handled wooden spoon, pierce a hole lengthwise through the center of the loin. Working from either end of the loin, use your fingers to stuff all but 1 tablespoon of the herb salt into the hole. Insert 1 of the rosemary branches into each end so that it forms a tassle. Mix the remaining herb salt with the 1½ teaspoons salt and rub it all over the roast.

Arrange the pancetta slices, slightly overlapping each other, down the length of the roast. Arrange the 2 remaining rosemary sprigs on top. Tie the roast at 1-inch intervals with cotton string to give it a neat shape (see page 678). Transfer to a platter, cover with plastic wrap, and refrigerate for at least 2 and up to 24 hours. Bring to room temperature for 1 hour before roasting.

Preheat the oven to 450°F.

Place the rack of rib bones curved side down in a shallow roasting pan. Pat the roast dry with paper towels and rub with the olive oil. Place the roast on the rack and roast for 15 minutes. Remove the pan from the oven, turn the roast over, and baste with a few tablespoons of the wine. Return the roast to the oven and reduce the temperature to 350°F. Cook for 1¼ to 1½ hours longer, turning the roast and basting it with wine every 20 minutes; reserve ½ cup of wine for the sauce. The roast is done when an instant-read thermometer inserted in the center registers 145°F.

Transfer the roast to a platter and pour the pan juices into a measuring cup. If the meat on the rack of bones is still pink and you wish to serve the ribs, place on a baking sheet and return to the oven for about 15 minutes.

Meanwhile, place the roasting pan over two burners over moderate heat; when it starts to sizzle, add the reserved ½ cup wine and cook for 2 minutes, scraping up the drippings from the bottom of the pan. Add to the pan juices in the measuring cup; let the fat rise to the surface, about 5 minutes. Skim off the fat and season the sauce with salt and pepper.

Remove the strings and carve the roast into thin slices. If serving the ribs, remove the rack from the pan and cut through the ribs. Arrange the meat and ribs on a platter and serve the pan juices on the side.

IN ADVANCE You can wrap and tie the pork loin up to 1 day ahead; cover and refrigerate. Bring to room temperature for 1 hour before roasting.

Honey-Cured Pork Loin with Peppery Juniper and Fennel Seed Rub

SERVES 8 Rubbing a loin of pork with a highly spiced salt and honey rub a day before roasting it cures the flesh slightly, tenderizing it, and giving it a pleasing sweet "wild" flavor missing in today's commercial pork. The roast is delicious hot and even better cold.

The old recommendation for cooking pork to 180°F renders today's leaner meats dry and flavorless. Technically, pork is safe to eat when it has reached an internal temperature above 135°F, at which point the rare but dangerous trichinae parasite is killed. I like to cook it to an internal temperature of 150°F, when it is barely pink and still very juicy.

Peppery Juniper and Fennel Seed Rub

    3 to 4 cardamom pods

    30 black peppercorns

    18 juniper berries

    1 ½ teaspoons fennel seeds

    6 allspice berries

    1 tablespoon kosher salt

One 3½-pound boneless pork loin roast

3 tablespoons wildflower or tupelo honey

1 teaspoon olive oil

To make the peppery rub, press down on the cardamom pods with the side of a chef's knife to crack the husks. Break apart with your fingers and place the seeds in a mortar, blender, or spice grinder. Add the peppercorns, juniper berries, fennel seeds, and allspice berries and grind to a coarse powder. Transfer to a small bowl and stir in the salt.

Pat the pork loin dry and place on a platter. Massage 2 tablespoons of the honey into the loin, then rub the spice mixture over it to coat it completely. Cover with plastic wrap and refrigerate for at least 8 hours, or overnight. Let come to room temperature for 1 hour before roasting.

Preheat the oven to 450°F.

Pat the roast dry with paper towels. Tie it with cotton string at 1-inch intervals to give it a neat, compact shape (see page 678). Rub the loin with the olive oil. Place on a rack in a shallow roasting pan.

Roast the loin for 10 minutes. Reduce the heat to 350°F and roast for 40 minutes longer. Brush the pork with the remaining 1 tablespoon honey and roast for about 10 minutes longer, until a meat thermometer inserted in the center reads 150°F. Transfer the loin to a platter and let rest for 15 minutes before carving into thin slices.

You can marinate the pork loin up to 1 day ahead; cover and refrigerate. To serve it cold, you can prepare the roast up to 3 days ahead. **IN ADVANCE**

Leg of Lamb Roasted on a Bed of Herbs

SERVES 12 This foolproof recipe combines the lamb cooking methods of two great cooks. From my mother comes the traditional Greek way of marinating the lamb in lemon juice and olive oil, which tenderizes and sweetens the meat. From Lulu Peyraud, proprietor of the winery Domaine Tempier in the South of France, comes the technique of cooking lamb on a bed of fresh thyme, which delicately scents the flesh.

Because the lamb is roasted on a rack and there are no pan juices, I often serve a prepared sauce or condiment on the side, such as Red Wine Essence (page 639), Port Wine Sauce (page 637), Roasted Tomato Sauce (page 39), Onion Marmalade with Sherry Vinegar (page 667), Balsamic-Cooked Peppers (page 666), Charred Onion Salsa (page 662), or Cilantro and Coconut Chutney (page 665).

This recipe is for a whole leg of lamb to serve 12 people. If you wish to serve half a leg, buy the shank end, which is meatier and easier to carve. Cut the marinade ingredients in half.

Plan to marinate the lamb 8 to 48 hours ahead.

> **Juice of 2 lemons** (about 6 tablespoons)
> **⅓ cup extra-virgin olive oil**
> **2 garlic cloves,** lightly smashed
> **2 teaspoons kosher salt**
> **1 teaspoon freshly ground black pepper**
> **One 5-pound leg of lamb**
> **5 to 6 bunches** (about 4 ounces) **fresh thyme**

In a casserole just large enough to hold the lamb, combine the lemon juice, olive oil, garlic, ½ teaspoon of the salt, and the pepper. Turn the lamb several times in the marinade to coat it completely. Nestle 7 or 8 thyme sprigs around the lamb; cover and refrigerate for at least 8 hours and up to 48 hours, turning occasionally. Remove the lamb from the refrigerator 1 hour before roasting.

Preheat the oven to 450°F.

Place a rack in a shallow roasting pan and arrange the thyme on it to form a thick bed. Remove the leg of lamb from the marinade and blot it dry with paper towels. Place skin side up on the bed of thyme.

Roast for 10 minutes. Reduce the oven temperature to 350°F and roast for 20 minutes. Reduce the temperature to 275°F and roast for 30 minutes longer, or until the lamb reaches an internal temperature of 140°F, for medium rare. Transfer the lamb to a platter and allow to rest for 15 minutes before carving.

Boneless Leg of Lamb Stuffed with Crushed Olives

When a leg of lamb is boned, then opened up (that is, butterflied), it provides a large surface area that's ideal for rubbing with any number of flavorings. Then it can be rolled into a sausage shape and tied, so it will cook evenly and be easily sliced. When I tried a coarse paste of crushed olives flavored with orange peel and herbs, I did not realize that the salty olive paste would have such a tenderizing effect on the meat. Serve with Greek-Style Potatoes with Lemon and Thyme (page 49).

SERVES 12

If you are in a hurry, you can use ¾ cup prepared olive paste instead of the olive-herb mixture.

Crushed Herb-Scented Olive Paste

> **Scant ½ teaspoon minced garlic**
>
> **2 teaspoons fresh thyme leaves**
>
> **¾ teaspoon chopped fresh rosemary**
>
> **¾ teaspoon grated lemon zest**
>
> **Pinch of kosher salt**
>
> **1¼ cups** (8 ounces) **ripe, meaty brine-cured black olives,** such as Kalamata or Gaeta, pitted (see page 683) and coarsely chopped
>
> **1 teaspoon extra-virgin olive oil**

One 4½- to 5-pound leg of lamb, boned and butterflied (have the butcher do this, reserving the bones), trimmed of all visible fat

8 to 10 sprigs fresh thyme and/or rosemary

½ teaspoon kosher salt

½ cup dry white wine

To make the olive paste, in a mortar, pound together the garlic, thyme, rosemary, lemon zest, and salt. Gradually add the olives and olive oil, pounding to a coarse paste. Alternatively, you can combine the ingredients in a food processor and pulse until a chunky puree forms.

Open out the lamb, skin side down, on a work surface, with the grain of the meat running from right to left. Spread the olive paste over the lamb, working it into the seams. Working on a slight diagonal, roll the lamb lengthwise into a uniform sausage shape about 5 inches in diameter. Cut off the small, sinewy flap of skin left at the end. (You can sauté it up as a snack.) Tie the rolled lamb with cotton string at 1-inch intervals (see page 678). Wrap tightly in plastic wrap and refrigerate for at least 6 hours, and up to 2 days. Remove from the refrigerator 1 hour before roasting.

Preheat the oven to 450°F.

Place a rack in a shallow roasting pan and arrange the lamb bones on the rack. Place the lamb on the bones and tuck the herb sprigs under, around, and over it. Sprinkle with the salt.

Roast the lamb for 10 minutes. Reduce the heat to 350°F and pour the wine over the lamb. Roast for 20 minutes, basting it twice with the wine. Reduce the oven temperature to 275°F and roast for about 30 minutes longer, basting the lamb two more times, until the lamb reaches an internal temperature of 140°F, for medium rare. Transfer the lamb to a carving board and allow it to rest for 15 minutes.

Pour the pan drippings into a measuring cup and allow the fat to float to the surface. Skim off the fat and discard.

Remove and discard the strings and cut the lamb crosswise into ½-inch-thick slices. Arrange on a platter. Pour any lamb juices into the pan drippings, spoon them over the lamb, and serve.

IN ADVANCE You can prepare the olives up to 4 days ahead; cover and refrigerate. You can marinate the lamb up to 2 days ahead.

Rabbit Stuffed with Prunes

I got the idea for this recipe from *Lulu's Provençal Kitchen*, by cookbook author Richard Olney. Lulu stuffs her rabbit with prunes stuffed with foie gras. This version uses a simpler stuffing of prunes soaked in red wine, which become almost creamy, their winy flavor a classic complement to the rabbit. The recipe is quite easy to execute and a spectacular dinner party dish. Plan to soak the prunes 8 hours ahead.

SERVES 4

18 pitted prunes (6 ounces)

2 to 2½ cups dry red wine

One 2¾- to 3-pound cleaned rabbit, its liver reserved (or 3 chicken livers, cleaned)

1¼ teaspoons kosher salt

1¼ teaspoons freshly ground black pepper

1½ tablespoons fresh thyme leaves or 1½ teaspoons dried thyme

½ teaspoon olive oil

3 ounces (4 to 5 thin slices) **lean pancetta**

Several branches fresh thyme, tied together to use as a basting brush (optional)

At least 8 hours before cooking, combine the prunes and 2 cups of the red wine in a medium bowl; cover and let stand until the prunes are very soft and have absorbed most of the wine.

Preheat the oven to 450°F.

Drain the wine from the prunes into a cup; reserve. Dice the liver.

Lay the rabbit on its back on the work surface. Sprinkle the abdominal cavity with ¾ teaspoon each of the salt and pepper and half of the thyme leaves. Stuff the cavity with the prunes and diced liver. Drizzle about 1 tablespoon of the reserved wine over the prunes. With a large needle and heavy thread, sew together the abdominal flaps to enclose the stuffing.

Turn the rabbit over and rub it with the olive oil. Sprinkle with the remaining salt, pepper, and thyme leaves. Place 3 of the pancetta slices, slightly overlapping each other, along the back of the rabbit, and place 1 on each thigh (or, if you only have 1 slice of pancetta left, cut it in half and place half on each thigh). Tie cotton kitchen string around the rabbit at 1- to 2-inch intervals to secure the pancetta. Place the rabbit on a rack set in a shallow roasting pan.

Roast the rabbit for 30 minutes. Reduce the heat to 350°F and pour the reserved wine into the roasting pan. Roast, basting frequently, with the herb brush, if using, and adding more wine (or water) if the pan is getting dry, for 20 to 25 minutes longer, until an instant-read thermometer inserted in the thigh reads 150°F. Place the rabbit on a cutting board and let rest for 10 minutes.

Pour the pan juices into a small measuring cup and let settle for 3 to 4 minutes. Carefully skim the fat off the surface with a tablespoon.

To carve the rabbit, cut off the strings and discard. Place the pancetta on a serving platter for guests to eat if they wish. Cut off the legs; cut the hind legs in two at the joint. Cut down the sewn seam of the cavity and remove the string. Scoop out the stuffing and place it in the center of the platter. Cut the rabbit loin crosswise into uniform slices. Arrange the rabbit around the stuffing. Add the juices from the cutting board to the measuring cup, then pour them over the rabbit pieces and serve.

IN ADVANCE   You can stuff and truss the rabbit up to 4 hours ahead; cover and refrigerate. Let sit at room temperature for 1 hour before roasting.

variation   **Rabbit Roasted with Fennel and Juniper.** Instead of stuffing it with prunes, you can marinate the rabbit with a spicy rub redolent of fennel. Serve it with Basic Polenta (page 198), and pan juices.

Omit the prunes and red wine. Substitute the following spice rub for the salt, pepper, and thyme: In a blender, coarsely grind ¼ teaspoon each black and white peppercorns, 2 juniper berries, ¼ teaspoon fennel seeds, ¼ teaspoon salt, ½ small garlic clove, and ½ teaspoon grated lemon zest. Drizzle in 1 teaspoon each olive oil and lemon juice and blend to a paste.

Rub the paste all over the rabbit and inside the abdominal cavity. Place the rabbit in a bowl, cover, and refrigerate for at least several hours, or overnight. Bring to room temperature and rub with the oil. Proceed as directed above, wrapping the rabbit with the pancetta and roasting it.

The Ultimate Roast Duck

SERVES 5   Roast duck is not worth eating without its skin. But because duck skin has so much fat, it has been considered off limits to any health-conscious person. However, there is an intriguing theory that duck fat, though saturated, doesn't act like saturated fat in the body, but more like olive oil, and is protective rather than detrimental. Whether this is wishful thinking or not, a glut of delicious duck fat *will* add calories. So here is a simple method of cooking duck that renders out most of the fat, leaving breathtakingly crisp skin and succulent flesh, which I learned from my friend Mindy Heiferling. She simply seasons the duck and roasts it in a very low-temperature oven for 5 hours, checking it occasionally. The long slow cooking renders out the fat (about 2 cups' worth) and makes the flesh tender enough to eat with a spoon.

You can serve this with root vegetables braise-sautéed (page 64) with a little of the duck fat. To balance the richness of the duck, serve a simple salad of bitter frisée lettuce and walnuts, dressed with Everyday Vinaigrette (page 606). The duck would also be lovely with Cabbage Braised with Smoky Ham and Riesling (page 70).

One 5-pound Pekin (Long Island) duck
Kosher salt and freshly ground black pepper
3 garlic cloves, chopped
1 small bunch fresh thyme

Preheat the oven to 300°F.

Rinse the bird inside and out with cold water; pat dry with paper towels. With a thin sharp knife, cut the excess fat from the neck and hind cavity and discard. Cut off the wing tips (freeze the neck and wing tips for stock). Sprinkle the cavity with salt and pepper, then rub with the garlic. Stuff the cavity with the thyme. With a sharp paring knife, pierce the duck skin without cutting into the flesh, by inserting the tip of the knife on a sharp diagonal almost parallel to the bird; make dozens of slits all over the bird.

Place the duck breast side up on a rack set in a shallow roasting pan. Roast the duck for 1 hour. Remove the bird from the oven and carefully pour off the fat into a measuring cup, making sure to hold the bird and rack securely with a kitchen fork. Pierce the skin again and turn the bird over. Repeat this process every hour. After 4 hours, increase the oven temperature to 350°F. The bird, which should be breast side up at this point, should be golden brown. Season the skin liberally with salt and pepper and cook until the skin is browned and very crisp, about 1 hour longer. Remove from the oven and allow the duck to rest for 20 minutes.

To serve, remove the herbs from the cavity. With a sharp chef's knife, cut the duck into 2-inch pieces (use a cleaver if necessary to cut through the bones, though they will be quite soft). Arrange the duck on a warm platter and serve at once.

Duck fat is a delicious fat to cook with, for frying potatoes, root vegetables, or duck steaks. Strain the liquid fat into a clean glass jar. It will last indefinitely in the refrigerator.

Foolproof Roast Turkey

SERVES 16 I know of very few people who don't get anxious at the prospect of roasting a turkey. Because the breast cooks more quickly than the dark meat thigh, it is often dry and overcooked by the time the bird comes out of the oven. Nobody seems to be certain of what, exactly, the best roasting method is, whether high heat or low, tented with foil or roasted breast down.

Brining (submerging the bird in a salt-and-sugar solution before roasting it) is one of the best ways I know of to ensure a succulent, flavorful roasted turkey. And the best brine for turkey was created by Alice Waters, the inspired and inspiring founder of Chez Panisse in Berkeley, California, from whom this recipe was adapted. The seasonings in the brine bring out the turkey's natural flavor, making it taste more like a farm bird with subtle herbal overtones.

If you don't have a large (at least 16-quart) stockpot, you can use an inexpensive plastic bucket or new garbage pail. If necessary, adjust a rack in your refrigerator to make room for it.

If you wish, you can stuff the bird before roasting it; truss according to the directions on page 678 and roast the bird about 20 minutes longer.

Aromatic Brine

2 **gallons water**

¾ **cup plus 2 tablespoons kosher salt**

¾ **cup sugar**

2 **medium onions,** coarsely chopped

1 **carrot,** peeled and coarsely chopped

1 **celery rib,** coarsely chopped

1 **leek,** white and light green parts only, coarsely chopped and washed

3 to 4 **sprigs fresh thyme**

2 **imported bay leaves**

1 **tablespoon black peppercorns**

1 **tablespoon coriander seeds**

¼ **teaspoon fennel seeds**

¼ **teaspoon red pepper flakes**

2 **star anise** (optional)

One 12- to 14-pound organic free-range turkey, giblets, liver, and neck reserved for another use, if desired

1 tablespoon extra-virgin olive oil

6 large rosemary branches, tied together to make a brush for basting (optional)

To make the brine, in a large stockpot, bring 1 gallon of the water to a boil. Stir in the salt and sugar until completely dissolved. Turn off the heat and add the onions, carrot, celery, leek, thyme, bay leaves, peppercorns, coriander and fennel seeds, red pepper flakes, and star anise, if using. Stir in the remaining 1 gallon cold water. Let the brine cool completely, then refrigerate until cold.

Rinse the turkey inside and out with cold water. Carefully place the turkey in the brine. To keep the turkey submerged in the brine, place a weight such as a heavy plate or pot lid on top of the bird. Refrigerate for 72 hours.

Remove the turkey from the brine and pat dry (discard the brine). Place the turkey on a rack in a large roasting pan and rub all over with olive oil. Let sit for 1 hour to come to room temperature.

Preheat the oven to 425°F.

Roast until the turkey starts to brown, about 25 minutes. Turn down the oven to 350°F and roast about 10 minutes per pound, for a total of 2 to 2½ hours, until an instant-read thermometer inserted in the thickest part of the thigh reads 160°F. As the turkey roasts, baste frequently with the pan juices, with the rosemary brush, if using. If the bird begins to darken too much, cover loosely with foil.

Remove the turkey from the oven, transfer to a serving platter, and let rest for 20 minutes before carving.

You can make the brine up to 2 days ahead; cover and refrigerate. **IN ADVANCE**

IN THE OVEN: ENCLOSED CASSEROLE ROASTING.

When I first started cooking poultry and tough cuts of meat in foil packages, I thought I had devised a brilliantly innovative technique for achieving succulence and deep flavor with little fat and effort. Then I realized that I was only duplicating the age-old method of casserole roasting: sealing food in a heavy, tightly sealed vessel with aromatics and a little liquid and burying it in the embers of the cooking fire. The intense heat builds within the meat, creating steam and causing its tough collagen to break down. The pressure of the steam then opens up the meat fibers, causing the fat in the meat to melt and the juices to move from the center to the outside. The food essentially cooks in its own juices, yielding extraordinarily tender, juicy flesh and depth of flavor.

This method yields slightly different results depending on what you are cooking. I use it to cook chickens and guinea hens when I want to perfume their flesh with flavors—garlic, herbs, or truffles, for example—and have abundant juices. For fatty and tough cuts like spareribs and duck legs, this method renders out the fat while leaving the flesh succulent and tender.

THE PERFECT CONTAINER FOR ENCLOSED CASSEROLE ROASTING

Because it is essential that the container you use be snug, heavy-duty aluminum foil is the perfect answer, as you can cut and fold it to accommodate any cut of meat or amount you wish to cook. If you prefer to use a casserole, make sure it holds the meats or poultry snugly with a little air space. Cover with a double layer of foil and then a tight-fitting lid. Increase the baking time by 20 minutes.

Lacquered Baby Back Ribs

SERVES 4

Cooking spareribs (a dietarily "incorrect" meat) in a foil package as a preliminary step tenderizes them while rendering out most of their fat. Then you can roast or grill them slowly, basting them with a pungent marinade until their surface is lacquered and caramelized. These ribs are as free of fat as they can possibly be. Since they are still very rich, I like to serve them with a cool sauce such as Cilantro and Coconut Chutney (page 665) or Charred Onion Salsa (page 662), or a slaw such as Classic Coleslaw (page 423) or Southeast Asian Slaw (page 429).

3 tablespoons dark brown sugar

1 tablespoon Sandy's Curry Powder (page 548)
or commercial curry powder

1 teaspoon whole cloves

½ teaspoon cayenne pepper

½ teaspoon ground allspice

½ teaspoon kosher salt

¼ teaspoon coarsely ground black pepper

¼ cup plus 2 tablespoons reduced-sodium soy sauce or tamari

2 tablespoons fresh lime juice

2 tablespoons dark rum

1 tablespoon minced fresh ginger

2 garlic cloves, minced

4 racks baby back pork ribs (5 ribs per rack; 3½ to 4 pounds), trimmed of excess fat

In a large bowl, combine all the ingredients except the ribs, mixing well. Add the ribs and turn to coat. Cover and marinate for 2½ hours at room temperature. Or refrigerate for up to 12 hours; let sit at room temperature for 1 hour before roasting.

Preheat the oven to 325°F.

Remove the ribs from the marinade and brush off any cloves or pieces of ginger or garlic; reserve the marinade. Wrap each rack tightly in foil and place on a baking sheet. Roast the ribs for 1½ hours.

Meanwhile, if you wish to grill the ribs, light a charcoal or wood fire and allow it to burn down to white-hot coals. In a small saucepan, bring the marinade to a boil over moderate heat; boil for 30 seconds.

Remove the ribs from the foil, being careful of the escaping steam, and place on a rack on a baking sheet or on the grill rack. Roast or grill, brushing the ribs with the marinade every 10 minutes, for 30 minutes. Turn the ribs over and cook, basting every 10 minutes, until the ribs are brown and glazed, about 30 minutes longer. Cut the ribs apart through the joints and serve.

You can marinate the ribs up to 12 hours ahead.   **IN ADVANCE**

Chicken with Garlic, Thyme, and Olives

SERVES 4 Chicken with Forty Cloves of Garlic is a classic of French country cooking, in which a whole chicken is baked with whole garlic cloves, herbs, and lots of olive oil. The garlic becomes sweet and mild from the long, slow cooking and perfumes the chicken. The olive oil becomes in effect a flavorful, if caloric, sauce.

To get around using so much oil, you can seal the whole chicken tightly in foil (or a snug casserole) with garlic and herbs, white wine, and olive paste or chopped olives. The chicken cooks in the garlicky emulsion and produces an abundance of flavorful juices perfect for sopping up with thick slices of French bread that have been spread with the soft puree-like garlic.

Leave the chicken skin on to protect the flesh during the cooking. Since it doesn't crisp and has none of the appeal of roasted chicken skin, remove the skin before serving.

> **One 3-pound chicken,** preferably free-range, rinsed and patted dry
>
> **¾ teaspoon kosher salt**
>
> **1 teaspoon freshly ground black pepper**
>
> **10 sprigs fresh thyme** or 1 teaspoon dried thyme
>
> **½ cup dry white wine**
>
> **1 tablespoon green olive paste** (see page 683) or ¼ cup meaty black olives, such as Kalamata or Gaeta, pitted (see page 683) and coarsely chopped
>
> **2 teaspoons fruity extra-virgin olive oil**
>
> **2 large heads garlic,** separated into cloves but not peeled
>
> **2 imported bay leaves**

Preheat the oven to 325°F.

Rub the chicken inside and out with the salt and pepper. Place 4 thyme sprigs (or ½ teaspoon dried thyme) in the cavity. Place the chicken breast side down on one side of an 18-by-26-inch piece of heavy-duty foil. Turn up the edges of the foil slightly to contain the liquid you will be adding.

In a small bowl, combine the wine, olive paste, and olive oil, and pour the mixture over the chicken. Arrange the garlic cloves, the remaining 6 thyme sprigs, if using, and the bay leaves around and on top of the chicken (or sprinkle the remaining ½ teaspoon dried thyme over the chicken). Fold the foil over the chicken and, beginning at one folded corner, fold the edges over in neat pleats, being sure to fold each successive pleat so it overlaps the previous one to make a tight seal until you get to the opposite corner. Place on a baking sheet.

Bake the chicken for about 1 hour and 10 minutes, until the meat is very tender and the garlic very soft. Place the package on a serving platter and let rest for 10 minutes.

If you like, open the package carefully at the table to let everyone enjoy the fragrant steam. Transfer the chicken and garlic cloves onto the platter. Form the foil into a spout and pour the juices into a measuring cup. Let rest while you carve the chicken (discarding the skin), then skim off the fat and pour the juices over the chicken. (If you don't wish to go to the trouble of skimming the fat, you can simply pour the juices over the chicken. They will add only 1 scant teaspoon of fat [4 grams, at 40 calories] per serving.)

IN ADVANCE

You can prepare the chicken packet up to 4 hours ahead; refrigerate. Bring to room temperature for 1 hour before baking.

Chicken Breasts with Mexican Flavors

SERVES 2

In Mexico, a *mixiote* is a package made of a parchment-like skin of maguey cactus leaves—in essence, a papillote. Mixiotes can be made with various combinations of meat, poultry, or fish seasoned with herbs or chiles, as I learned from Felipe Quevodo's mother in Cuernavaca. She used foil rather than maguey leaves to make individual packages, which she steamed in a covered pot until the filling of pork chunks was meltingly tender, with an abundance of sauce, like an instant stew.

The mixiote uses the same principle as the French enclosed casserole and papillote methods, only with Mexican flavorings. Here Revisionist Mole (Ancho Chile Sauce) or even store-bought mole paste is used as a flavoring for chicken breasts for a quick, delicious meal. It is easier to bake the mixiotes in a low-temperature oven, which ensures the meat is tender, rather than to steam them in a pot on the stove; the food is essentially steaming in the tightly sealed packages anyway.

You can also make this mixiote with chicken thighs or legs; bake them for 15 minutes longer.

2 medium chicken breast halves on the bone, skin removed

1 teaspoon kosher salt, plus more to taste

1 teaspoon vegetable oil

2 medium Vidalia or Bermuda onions, thinly sliced lengthwise

¼ cup Revisionist Mole (Ancho Chile Sauce) (page 656) or 2 tablespoons prepared mole poblano paste (see Sources, page 711) plus 6 tablespoons unsalted homemade (page 574) or canned low-sodium chicken broth

2 pinches cumin seeds

3 tablespoons chopped fresh cilantro

½ lime, cut into wedges

Preheat the oven to 275°F.

Place the chicken on a platter and sprinkle with the salt.

In a medium nonstick skillet, heat the oil over moderate heat. Add the onions and sauté, tossing frequently, until soft and browned, about 7 minutes. Season with salt.

Meanwhile, if you are using prepared mole paste, in a small heavy saucepan over moderate heat, whisk together the paste and chicken broth. Boil until it has thickened to the consistency of sour cream, about 2 minutes. Salt to taste.

Lay two 18-inch squares of heavy-duty foil on the counter. Spoon one quarter of the onion mixture into the center of each. Coat the chicken with the mole and place on top of the onions. Spoon the remaining onions on top of the chicken and sprinkle with the cumin seeds. Pull up the four corners of each mixiote so they meet, crimp the edges of the foil tightly together, and twist the corners to seal them.

Place the mixiotes on a baking sheet and bake for 45 minutes.

Transfer the packets to plates, or carefully open them, avoiding the steam, and spoon the contents of each one into a shallow bowl. Serve with the cilantro and lime wedges on the side.

IN ADVANCE You can prepare the packets up to 6 hours ahead; refrigerate. Bring to room temperature for 30 minutes before baking.

Celebration Guinea Hen Cooked with Black Truffles

If you've never tasted—or smelled—a truffle, the homely fungus that grows underground at the base of certain trees, you might well find it difficult to imagine what all the fuss is about. Although its aroma is remarkable and so unlike anything else that it is virtually indescribable, it is really how a truffle makes you *feel* that is so extraordinary: transformed, as one food writer put it, "at one with nature." No wonder truffles are one of the most coveted foods in the world.

Fresh black truffles appear in the fall and winter and are a traditional part of holiday celebrations in France. Jim Peterson taught me this vastly simplified approach to the classic *poulet demi-deuil* ("Chicken in Half-Mourning"), in which a whole chicken is truffled under the skin, then poached in a rich stock. The bird is wrapped in a tightly sealed foil package with a little butter and Madeira and roasted in its own truffled juices. When you open the package at the table, the heady cloud of truffle steam engulfs you and your guests for an unforgettable presentation. It is one of the best ways to use a single modest truffle.

My only innovation to Jim's perfect recipe is to make it with guinea hen, which has a mildly gamy flavor (similar to pheasant) and tender flesh, but you can use chicken if you prefer.

Serve with Brown Butter Orzo "Risotto" (page 126), Buttermilk Mashed Potatoes (page 77), Mashed Potatoes and Root Vegetables (page 80), or simply steamed, crushed fingerlings or baby Yukon Gold potatoes. The abundant truffley juices are all the adornment necessary.

While considerably less expensive than white truffles, black truffles are nevertheless quite dear, costing about $30 per ounce. This recipe makes the most of a single fresh black truffle with dazzling effect. Do not even consider making it with a black truffle preserved in a jar, which will have no flavor.

One 3-pound guinea hen or organic free-range chicken,
rinsed and patted dry

1 fresh black truffle (1 ounce or more)

¾ teaspoon kosher salt

Freshly ground black pepper

1 garlic clove, cut lengthwise in half

2 teaspoons unsalted butter, softened

2 tablespoons Rainwater or Sercial (dry) Madeira

2 teaspoons Cognac

Working from the neck opening, with your fingers, gently loosen the skin from the guinea hen breast and legs, without tearing it. Slice the truffle into thin disks with a sharp paring knife, a vegetable peeler, or a mandoline or vegetable slicer. Place a few slices in the cavity of the bird. Slip most of the slices under the skin in a single layer, to cover as much of the flesh as possible. Rub the bird inside and out with the salt and pepper to taste.

Place an 18-by-26-inch piece of heavy-duty foil on the work surface. Rub the foil with the cut garlic clove; smear the butter over it, to within 2 inches of the edges. Turn the edges up slightly to contain the liquid you will be adding. Place the hen breast side down on one side of the foil. Pour half the Madeira and Cognac into the hen's cavity and half on the foil. Fold the foil over the hen and, beginning at one folded corner, fold the edges over in neat pleats, being sure to fold each successive pleat so it overlaps the previous one to make a tight seal, until you get to the opposite folded corner. Let sit for 1 hour at room temperature, or refrigerate for up to 5 hours, to let the truffle flavor permeate the flesh. If the bird has been refrigerated, bring to room temperature for 1 hour before baking.

Preheat the oven to 350°F.

Place the package on a baking sheet and bake for about 1 hour and 10 minutes for a 3-pound bird, 10 minutes longer for 3½ pounds. Place the package on a serving platter and let rest for 10 minutes.

Open the package carefully at the table to let everyone enjoy the fragrant steam. Transfer the hen and juices onto the platter. Carve the hen and spoon some of the juices over each serving. (The juices are not skimmed because it would be a waste to discard the fat, which has lots of truffle flavor.)

IN ADVANCE You can prepare the hen for roasting up to 5 hours ahead and refrigerate it.

A fresh truffle should be firm to the touch: Any "give" to pressure or sponginess indicates it has begun to deteriorate. It should be very fragrant. Flash-frozen black truffles have excellent flavor and are a reliable way to buy truffles if no good fresh ones are available (see Sources, page 711).

The fragrance of truffles permeates whatever they are close to. Before cooking with the truffle, you can impart its flavor to whole eggs or butter or cheese simply by locking them together in a jar in the refrigerator for a day. Then you can cook the truffle in this or another dish, and enjoy a bonus of truffle-flavored eggs, butter, or cheese.

Revisionist Confit of Duck Legs

For centuries, French farmers in Gascony have preserved goose, pork, duck, or rabbit by salting it to draw out the moisture, curing it slightly, and then cooking it slowly in melted fat. They then seal the cooked meat in the fat to protect it from the air and consequent spoilage, a way of preserving it for many months without refrigeration. The confit can be extracted from the fat at a moment's notice to fry and crisp in a hot skillet and serve with potatoes, cabbage or salads, or to use as a flavoring for cassoulets, hearty soups and stews, ravioli filling, and so on: a farmstead version of fast food.

SERVES 4

In this radical departure from traditional confit making, seal lightly cured and seasoned duck legs in a foil package and cook them in a low oven until they are tender and most of the fat has rendered out, so they cook in their own juices. This method takes only a few minutes of preparation, eliminates the need for quantities of fat, and guarantees a lean but tender confit. You can freeze the confit in individual portions to make quick meals. See page 681 for information on saving the rendered fat.

Meaty Moulard duck legs, which are two times larger than Pekin (Long Island) duck legs, can be ordered by mail (see Sources, page 711). Or you can have the butcher cut up several whole ducks, and use the leg and thigh portions for the confit, reserving the boned breasts for other recipes (see pages 326 and 329).

Confit Seasoning

2 tablespoons kosher salt

10 juniper berries

1½ teaspoons black peppercorns

2¼ teaspoons minced fresh thyme or ¾ teaspoon dried thyme

1 large imported bay leaf, crumbled

6 allspice berries

½ teaspoon coriander seeds

½ teaspoon sugar

1 teaspoon minced garlic

1 teaspoon grappa (optional)

4 Moulard duck legs/thighs or 8 Pekin (Long Island) duck legs/thighs (3 to 4 pounds), excess fat trimmed

To make the seasoning, in a mortar or spice grinder, combine all the ingredients except the garlic and grappa. Pound or grind to a coarse powder. (Use 1 tablespoon of the spice mixture per pound of meat.) Rub the spice mixture and the garlic and grappa into the duck legs and place in a ceramic dish. Cover with plastic wrap and refrigerate overnight.

Preheat the oven to 300°F.

Lay an 18-by-26-inch rectangle of heavy-duty foil shiny side up on a work surface. Pat the legs and thighs dry with paper towels. Prick the skin several times with a needle or the tip of a paring knife. Arrange the duck legs on one half of the foil. Fold the empty half of the foil over the legs and, beginning with one folded corner, crimp the edges together until you get to the opposite folded corner to make a neat, tightly sealed package.

Place the package on a baking sheet and bake for about 2 hours until the duck legs give easily when pressed. Remove from the oven and allow to rest for 10 minutes.

Carefully unfold the seams of the package, avoiding the steam, and open it up. With tongs, lift each duck leg out of the fat and pat dry with paper towels. You can use the confit immediately or refrigerate or freeze it.

IN ADVANCE Refrigerate the confit, well wrapped, for up to 5 days, or freeze for up to 2 months; defrost in the refrigerator.

Confit has many uses. You can shred it (discarding the fatty skin) to add to soups and stews. The whole legs can be crisped in a pan as described below and served with any of the following accompaniments. Pears in Fragrant Wine (page 668) and Prunes in Armagnac (page 473) make wonderful condiments to serve alongside the warm confit.

To Crisp Duck Confit. Place the legs skin side down in a dry nonstick skillet over moderate heat and cook until the skin is crisp and brown, about 7 minutes. Turn and crisp the other side. Although a great deal of the fat will have rendered out of the skin, it will still be quite fatty and caloric—but utterly delicious. If you don't wish to eat it, simply pull it off and discard. The flesh itself will be very lean.

Accompaniments for Confit

Revisionist Cassoulet (page 110)

Rustic Cassoulet Beans (page 107)

Gratin of Beans (page 100)

White Beans and Mellowed Garlic with Rosemary Oil (page 102)

Roasted Root Vegetable Hash (page 44)

Buttermilk Mashed Potatoes (page 77)

Roasted Garlic Mashed Potatoes (page 78)

Celery Root and Apple Puree (page 81)

Mashed Turnips with Crispy Shallots (page 82)

Mashed Potato Cake (page 54)

Herb Salad (page 415)

Celery Root "Rémoulade" (page 424)

Warm Frisée Salad with Bacon and Croutons (page 454)

Peppery or Bitter Greens with Seasonal Fruits and Roasted Nuts (page 417)

Warm Potato and Grilled Vidalia Onion Salad (page 440)

Warm Bean Salad with Balsamic-Bacon Vinaigrette (page 444)

Risotto Cake (page 189)

Risotto with Red Wine, Rosemary, and Champagne Grapes (page 188)

Risotto with Wild Mushrooms (page 193)

ON THE STOVE TOP: QUICK PAN-SEARED MEATS AND POULTRY. When you sear thin cuts of meat and poultry in a hot skillet, using very little fat, by the way, the surface caramelizes into a satisfying crust without any work on your part. You can flavor the crust by rubbing the meat with mixtures of ground spices, herbs, or flavoring powders such as smoky tea. Then serve a made-ahead sauce, salsa, or condiment with it, for an extraordinarily easy quick meal. Your creativity in using this approach comes in the way you combine the elements: a quick-cooking cut of meat or poultry + a seasoning or rub + a complementary sauce. For example:

> **Pork loin steaks + Mole Rub + Charred Onion Salsa**
>
> **Boneless chicken breasts + Rosemary Pepper Rub + Onion Marmalade with Sherry Vinegar**
>
> **Venison medallions + Wild Juniper Rub + Balsamic Syrup**

THE BEST CUTS FOR PAN-SEARING

Pan-searing is ideal for quick-cooking cuts less than 1 inch thick, such as:

Pork: medallions (steaks) cut from the loin or tenderloin or well-trimmed pork chops

Chicken: skinless, boneless breasts

Turkey: turkey steaks (from the breast) or scaloppine

Lamb: chops, steaks cut from the leg or loin medallions

Beef: flank, sirloin, strip, skirt, or hanger steak or filet mignon

Buffalo: sirloin or shell steaks

Duck: skinless, boneless breasts

Veal: medallions, chops, or scaloppine

Quail: backbone removed and butterflied

Venison: medallions, chops, or scaloppine

Crusting Meats with Dry Rubs

A GUIDE TO IMPROVISING

Rubbed onto the surface of a food before cooking, dry rubs made from ground spices, herbs, teas, or other flavorings form a flavorful crust when the food is pan-seared or grilled. You can also use dry rubs to marinate meats and poultry.

To use a Flavor Essence or other plain ground dried herbs or spices as a dry rub, mix in ½ teaspoon each of salt and pepper and a pinch of sugar per 2-teaspoon serving. (For 4 servings, that's 2 teaspoons each of salt and pepper and ¼ teaspoon sugar per 3 tablespoons Flavor Essence).

> **1 ¼ pounds meat or skinless poultry,** no more than 1 inch thick (see The Best Cuts for Pan-Searing, page 314)
>
> **1 teaspoon vegetable oil**
>
> **3 to 4 tablespoons Dry Rub** (pages 549–552), **Flavor Essence** (pages 542–548), **or ground herbs or spices** (mix Flavor Essences, herbs, or spices with 2 teaspoons each of salt and freshly ground black pepper and ¼ teaspoon sugar)
>
> **2 teaspoons grapeseed or olive oil** (if pan-searing in a nonstick skillet)

1. Blot any excess moisture from the meat or poultry with paper towels. If you are going to grill or broil it, rub it lightly with a little vegetable oil to prevent sticking. (This is not necessary if you are going to pan-sear it.)

2. Sprinkle the Dry Rub, Flavor Essence, or ground herbs or spices over both sides and rub or press it in to the flesh to make a thin, even coating. Alternatively, you can sprinkle the powder on a plate and dredge the food in it, shaking off the excess.

You can cook the meat immediately or marinate it, covered and refrigerated, for up to 2 days. Be sure to blot the meat dry again before cooking.

3. Grill, broil, or sear in a grill pan or nonstick skillet, as desired. If using a nonstick skillet, heat it over high heat, add the oil, and swirl to coat before adding the meat or poultry.

SERVES 4

Figure on 2 to 2½ teaspoons Dry Rub or Flavor Essence per 5-ounce portion of raw meat or poultry (about 3 tablespoons per 4 servings). Use half this amount for very spicy rubs made with peppercorns or chiles.

A grill pan is a heavy skillet with raised metal ridges across the bottom, used to simulate some of the effects of outdoor grilling on a stove top. The pan is heated until very hot so that when the meat is added, it sears it quickly. The ridges keep the meat elevated, allowing any fat to drain underneath it. A grill pan works best for meats that don't require long cooking, such as steaks, lamb chops, and pork chops up to 1½ inches thick; boneless duck breasts; or boneless chicken breasts, or cutlets. I find a grill pan to be preferable to broiling in achieving a good surface crust and moist interior since most home broilers cannot get hot enough to sear meat properly. I also often use one instead of a nonstick skillet to sear meats and poultry when I'm not planning to make a pan sauce.

Make sure the pan is clean and well seasoned. Place it over high heat for at least 5 minutes, until very hot. Rub the meat lightly with oil, then season with salt and a Flavor Essence or Dry Rub (pages 541–552), if desired. Cook until well browned and crusty on the bottom. For rare-cooked meats, you will want to turn the meat as soon as little drops of blood begin to pool on the surface. Turn the meat, and cook to desired doneness. If the fat in the bottom of the pan begins to smoke, sprinkle some kosher salt into the pan around the meat.

Transfer the meat to a carving board or platter to rest for at least 5 minutes before slicing.

Szechwan Pepper–Crusted Steak Smothered with Onions

SERVES 4

A crusty seared steak smothered with fried onions is one of the simplest and most satisfying combinations imaginable. I rub the steak with a mix of finely ground Szechwan, white, and black peppercorns, which imparts an aromatic, slightly floral yet peppery flavor that goes wonderfully with the onions. Although it is delicious as is, this combination sings when drizzled with a rich winy sauce and served with potatoes, such as Potato Chips (page 47) or Buttermilk Mashed Potatoes (page 77).

You can use many cuts of beef for this recipe, as long as they are tender enough to be served rare. The most flavorful steaks for pan-searing are at opposite ends of the spectrum in price—shell and strip steak of beef or buffalo are quite expensive; skirt and hanger steak are inexpensive.

Buffalo steaks, either shell or sirloin, are a great alternative to beef; they are flavorful and tender, yet spectacularly lean.

"Fried" Onions

> 1½ pounds Vidalia or Bermuda onions, peeled
>
> 2 teaspoons unsalted butter
>
> ¾ teaspoon kosher salt
>
> ½ teaspoon sugar
>
> 1 to 2 teaspoons balsamic vinegar
>
> Freshly ground black pepper

Szechwan Pepper Rub

> 1 teaspoon Szechwan peppercorns
>
> ½ teaspoon white peppercorns
>
> ½ teaspoon black peppercorns
>
> ¼ teaspoon allspice berries

1¼ pounds beef skirt, hanger, or strip steak or buffalo sirloin or shell steak, trimmed of all fat

> 1 teaspoon vegetable oil
>
> Kosher salt
>
> Scant 1 teaspoon finely grated ginger
>
> Port Wine Sauce (page 637), Balsamic Syrup (page 636), or Red Wine Essence (page 639) (optional)

To make the onions, slice the onions in half through the stem. With a mandoline or vegetable slicer or a thin sharp knife, cut lengthwise into ⅛-inch slices. (You should have about 6 cups.)

In a large nonstick skillet, melt the butter over moderately low heat. Add the onions, sprinkle with ½ teaspoon of the salt, and toss to coat. Cover and cook until the onions have released their liquid, about 13 minutes.

Uncover the pan, increase the heat to moderate, and cook slowly, stirring occasionally, until the liquid has evaporated, about 10 minutes. Sprinkle the onions with the sugar and continue cooking, stirring frequently, until they are golden brown and caramelized, about 10 minutes longer. Sprinkle with the balsamic vinegar and toss until the vinegar has evaporated. Add the remaining ¼ teaspoon salt, and season generously with pepper. Remove from the heat and cover to keep warm.

Meanwhile, prepare the pepper rub: In a small heavy skillet, toast the peppercorns and allspice over moderate heat, shaking the pan occasionally, until fragrant, about 3 minutes. Transfer to a blender or spice grinder and grind to a fine powder. Strain the spices into a small bowl and return the coarse bits to the blender. Blend again and strain.

Pat the steaks dry with paper towels; rub lightly with a little of the oil. Sprinkle lightly with salt and massage the ginger into the steak; then rub the pepper rub over them.

Heat a grill pan or heavy nonstick skillet over high heat. Lightly oil the grill pan, if using, or swirl the remaining oil in a nonstick skillet. Add the steaks to the pan and cook until little droplets of blood form on the surface, about 4 minutes. Turn the steaks over and continue cooking until droplets of blood form on the top again, another 3 to 4 minutes, for rare. Transfer the steaks to a cutting board and let rest for 5 to 10 minutes.

With a thin sharp knife, slice the steaks on a slight angle against the grain. Sprinkle the meat with a little salt and arrange the slices on four warm dinner plates. Nestle a mound of onions next to the steak, drizzle a little of the optional sauce around the meat, and serve at once.

IN ADVANCE You can prepare the Szechwan pepper rub up to 2 days ahead and the onions up to 6 hours ahead; cover and leave at room temperature. About 5 minutes before serving, sauté the onions in a hot pan until warm through.

variation **"Wood-Smoked" Steak Smothered with Onions.** Crust the steaks with Smoky Tea Essence (page 545) instead of the Szechwan Pepper Rub—to make the steak taste as though it was grilled over wood.

Cumin-Crusted Quail with Cilantro Gremolata

I keep quail, those tiny mild-flavored game birds, on hand in the freezer **SERVES 2** because they make easy, unusual meals in no time. So that both legs and breasts will cook evenly and quickly, butterfly the quail—that is, cut out the backbone, open the quail up, and press them flat. The crushed cumin seed forms an aromatic crust when the birds are browned in the hot pan. Instead of a sauce, I sprinkle the birds with a cilantro gremolata—minced garlic, lemon zest, and cilantro—whose flavor explodes on contact with the hot birds. Serve with Fresh Corn "Polenta" (page 82).

> **1 tablespoon plus 1 teaspoon cumin seeds**
>
> **½ teaspoon kosher salt**
>
> **¼ teaspoon freshly ground black pepper**
>
> **4 quail** (4 ounces each), cleaned
>
> **Gremolata**
>
>> **1 teaspoon finely minced garlic**
>>
>> **¼ teaspoon salt**
>>
>> **1½ teaspoons finely grated lemon zest**
>>
>> **¼ cup coarsely chopped fresh cilantro or flat-leaf parsley**
>
> **1½ teaspoons peanut or grapeseed oil**

In a small skillet, toast the cumin seeds over moderate heat, stirring occasionally, until fragrant. Transfer to a mortar, spice grinder, or blender and coarsely grind them. Stir in the salt and pepper. Transfer to a pie plate or dinner plate.

One at a time, place each quail breast side down on a work surface. With scissors, cut down one side of the backbone, then cut down the other side of the backbone to remove it. Open the quail out, turn it over, and press down with the palm of your hand to flatten it.

Press the quail breast side down into the cumin salt, so that they are completely coated. Sprinkle the remaining cumin salt onto the other sides of the quail. Arrange the quail breast side up on a platter to dry while you make the gremolata.

Place the garlic on a cutting board, add the salt and lemon zest, and mince together. Add the cilantro and continue chopping until finely chopped. Set aside.

Heat a large nonstick skillet over moderately high heat. Add the oil and swirl to coat. Working in batches if necessary, add the quail breast side up and cover with a heavy flat lid that sits directly on the quail. Cook for 1 minute. Turn the quail, cover, and cook for 1 minute. Uncover and cook until the breast skin is crisp and the quail are cooked, about 1½ minutes longer. The breasts should be medium rare and still somewhat springy when touched. If cooking in batches, transfer the cooked quail to a plate and cover loosely with foil.

To serve, place 2 quail on each dinner plate, and sprinkle with the gremolata. Serve at once.

IN ADVANCE You can butterfly the quail up to a day ahead; cover and refrigerate. You can toast and grind the cumin seeds up to 6 hours ahead; cover tightly.

Seared Lamb with Moroccan Spices and Tomato Jam

SERVES 8 The leg is one of the leanest, least expensive, and most flavorful cuts of lamb. If you have the butcher butterfly a whole leg—that is, bone it and open it out into a flat "sheet"—you will have, in essence, a large lamb steak that will feed about 14 people. You can then marinate it in sweet Moroccan spices and grill it, or broil under a hot broiler. The spice mixture caramelizes on the outside to make a delicious crust, while the interior becomes succulent and tender.

You can also view a butterflied leg as several smaller "steaks." A butterflied half leg from the meatier shank end will feed 8 people (or fewer, figuring in some wonderful leftovers). For a little steak for 3 or 4 people, divide the butterflied shank half into two steaks; cook one and freeze the second for another meal.

This recipe is for a butterflied half leg of lamb from the meaty shank end. But exact proportions of spice paste to meat are not critical. To serve a whole butterflied leg, double the Moroccan Spice Paste and the Tomato Jam; to serve a small steak (half the shank end), divide them in half. Figure on 5 ounces of raw lamb per serving if you have odd amounts. You can cook smaller cuts in a grill pan, set over high heat until searingly hot.

Serve the lamb with Farro Salad with Green Apple, Toasted Spices, and Pine Nuts (page 445), and Carrots in Chermoula (page 434) or Moroccan "Gazpacho" Salad (page 426).

Butterflied ½ leg of lamb from the shank end (2½ pounds), fat trimmed

Moroccan Spice Paste (page 560)

Tomato Jam

> **2 pounds ripe tomatoes,** grated (see page 683), or one 28-ounce can peeled plum tomatoes, drained and chopped (2 cups)
>
> **1 small Vidalia or Bermuda onion,** finely grated
>
> **2 teaspoons finely grated peeled fresh ginger**
>
> **1 small garlic clove,** minced
>
> **1 teaspoon extra-virgin olive oil**
>
> **Kosher salt**
>
> **1 tablespoon plus 1 teaspoon wildflower or tupelo honey**
>
> **1 tablespoon tomato paste**
>
> **½ teaspoon ground cinnamon**
>
> **½ teaspoon grated lemon zest**
>
> **1 to 2 teaspoons fresh lemon juice**

1 teaspoon olive or grapeseed oil

Place the lamb in a shallow dish. Rub the spice paste into it, cover, and refrigerate for at least 6 hours, or overnight.

Meanwhile, prepare the tomato jam: In a heavy medium saucepan, combine the tomatoes, onion, ginger, and garlic, oil, and ¼ teaspoon salt. Cook over moderate heat, stirring frequently, until the liquid has evaporated and the tomatoes have thickened, about 15 minutes. Stir in the honey, tomato paste, and cinnamon, and cook until the mixture has the consistency of a thick jam, about 10 minutes longer. Stir in the zest, lemon juice, and salt to taste. Set aside to cool. Cover and refrigerate until ready to serve.

Prepare a fire in a grill or preheat the broiler.

Blot the lamb dry with paper towels, being careful not to wipe off all the spices. Rub it with a little oil to keep it from sticking. Grill or broil the lamb for about 8 to 10 minutes on each side for medium rare, or until a meat thermometer inserted in the fleshiest part reads 140°F. Let the lamb rest for 10 to 15 minutes before carving.

Cut the lamb into thin diagonal slices across the grain. Serve the tomato jam on the side.

IN ADVANCE You can marinate the lamb up to 1 day ahead. You can prepare the Tomato Jam up to 3 days ahead; cover and refrigerate.

Six Simple Ways to Season Lamb. Instead of the Moroccan Spice Paste, you can season the lamb in any number of simple ways: with Smoky Tea Essence (page 545), Rosemary Pepper Rub (page 549), Aromatic Pepper and Tangerine Rub (page 552), or 3 tablespoons bruised fresh rosemary or savory leaves plus ½ teaspoon each salt and freshly ground black pepper. Or marinate it in Classic Greek Lemon and Olive Oil Marinade with Herbs (page 554) or Tandoori Marinade (page 558).

Seared Meats or Poultry Sauced with Broth

A GUIDE TO IMPROVISING

SERVES 4 When you sauce thinly sliced seared meat or poultry with an interesting broth, it becomes a sophisticated dish that also offers the comfort of a soup. The approach can be as simple or as complex as you wish. You can crust the meat with a dry rub, herbs, or spices, or simply season it with salt and pepper. You can simmer julienned or diced vegetables in the broth and use them as a bed for the meat, to make a complete meal. One of my favorite quick improvisations is buffalo sirloin steak crusted with Smoky Tea Essence (page 545), and sauced with Hearty Miso-Porcini Broth, garnished with snipped chives.

3 cups rich broth, such as

Faux Veal Broth (page 572)

Celery Root Broth (page 568)

Hearty Porcini-Miso Broth (page 573)

Curry and Fennel Seed Broth (page 581)

Star Anise Broth (page 581)

About 1 pound vegetables (optional), such as carrots, turnips, parsnips, leeks, celery root, or wild mushrooms, peeled or trimmed and cut into thin julienne or medium dice (about 3 cups)

1 ¼ pounds lean, boneless meat or poultry, such as beef or buffalo sirloin steak, skinless duck breasts or chicken cutlets, or pork or lamb medallions

Kosher salt and freshly ground black pepper or 3 to 4 tablespoons Dry Rub or Flavor Essence (pages 541–552) or ground herbs or spices (Flavor Essences, herbs, or spices should be mixed with 2 teaspoons each of salt and freshly ground black pepper and ¼ teaspoon sugar)

1 to 2 teaspoons olive or grapeseed oil

½ cup chopped fresh herbs, such as flat-leaf parsley, chives, basil, cilantro, or chervil

1. In a medium saucepan, bring the broth to a simmer. If using the vegetables, add them and simmer them until they are tender but still have a little crunch.

2. Meanwhile, dust the meat or poultry lightly with salt and pepper or a Dry Rub, Flavor Essence, or ground herbs or spices.

3. Heat a large nonstick skillet over high heat and add the oil. Add the meat and sear, turning once, until both sides are well browned and the meat is cooked to the desired doneness (do this in batches if necessary). Alternatively, rub the meat lightly with oil and cook it in a hot grill pan. Transfer to a cutting board and let rest for 5 minutes.

4. To serve, slice the meat against the grain into thin slices. Place a mound of the vegetables, if using, in the center of each shallow soup bowl and arrange the meat on top (or in the bowls). Add herbs to the broth and spoon the broth over the meat.

Milanese-Style Scaloppine with Peppery Greens

Veal cutlets, breaded and fried in an inch of olive oil, are deliciously satisfying but an extreme splurge, particularly since veal in itself is high in cholesterol. This version of the classic is considerably lighter but keeps the essential elements intact, a worthy everyday *scaloppine milanese*.

SERVES 2

Although veal cutlets have the best flavor, turkey cutlets make an admirable substitute with considerably fewer calories and less fat, cholesterol, and expense. You pound the cutlets thin, lightly coat them with beaten egg, then dip them in a mixture of bread crumbs and Parmesan cheese. When they are panfried in a small amount of olive oil, the cheese melts and fuses with the crisp bread crumbs to form a delicious coating. You can bread the cutlets without using the egg wash (the residual moisture on the meat will make the crumbs adhere), but the small amount of egg adds richness and crispness.

Traditionally, breaded cutlets are served with a juicy salad of arugula and tomatoes spooned on top. Since this coating would be rendered soggy by juicy tomatoes, I prefer to serve a lighter salad of peppery or tart greens, which provide pleasing contrast.

Peppery Greens

> 1 teaspoon extra-virgin olive oil
>
> 1 teaspoon balsamic vinegar
>
> 1 teaspoon orange juice or warm water
>
> Pinch of kosher salt
>
> Pinch of freshly ground black pepper
>
> **2 ounces** (about 4 cups) **peppery greens,** such as arugula, watercress, upland cress, or greens for Herb Salad (page 415) cleaned and dried

8 ounces boneless turkey breast or veal cutlets, sliced ⅓ inch thick

⅓ cup fine dried plain bread crumbs

2½ tablespoons freshly grated Parmigiano-Reggiano cheese

Pinch of kosher salt

Freshly ground black pepper

¾ teaspoon dried rosemary, crumbled (optional)

1 large egg

1 tablespoon water

2 teaspoons fruity extra-virgin olive oil

1 garlic clove, thinly sliced

½ lemon, sliced into wedges

To prepare the greens, in a medium bowl, whisk together the olive oil, balsamic vinegar, orange juice, salt, and pepper. Cross a serving fork and spoon in the bowl and rest the greens on top. Cover and refrigerate until ready to serve.

Place a cutlet on a work surface, cover it with plastic wrap, and pound it lightly with a meat pounder, the side of a heavy cleaver, or the bottom of a heavy skillet until it is a scant ¼ inch thick. Repeat with the remaining cutlets.

In a pie plate or shallow casserole, combine the bread crumbs, cheese, salt, pepper, and rosemary, if using. In a wide shallow bowl, beat the egg with the water. Dip one of the cutlets in the egg wash; allow any excess to drain off, then dredge it in the bread crumb mixture, patting them over it if necessary, so that both sides are coated. Shake off any excess and place on a plate to dry. Repeat with the remaining cutlets.

Heat a large nonstick skillet over moderate heat until very hot. Add 1 teaspoon of the oil to the pan and swirl to coat. Add half the garlic and allow to frizzle for about 30 seconds. Move the garlic to the edge of the pan and add half the cutlets. Cook for 30 to 45 seconds on each side, until golden and crisp. Transfer to a plate and keep warm. Wipe out the pan with paper towels and repeat the process, using the remaining 1 teaspoon oil and garlic.

Arrange the cutlets on two dinner plates. Quickly toss the salad and arrange half on top or on the side of each cutlet. Garnish with the lemon wedges and serve at once.

You can pound the cutlets up to a day ahead; cover tightly and refrigerate.   IN ADVANCE

BONELESS DUCK BREASTS, AN ALTERNATIVE TO STEAK

Three kinds of boneless duck breasts are available at specialty and many supermarkets and by mail-order (see Sources, page 711). The breasts from Pekin, or Long Island, duckling are small and the most delicately flavored, averaging about 6 ounces each (5 ounces, skinned). Muscovys, ducks of South American origin, are thin-skinned and 40 percent leaner than Pekin ducks, but the breasts have a fuller flavor and a steak-like texture. They average 12 ounces each (about 10 ounces, skinned). Magrets are the large breasts from the Moulard duck, a hybrid cross of female Pekin and male Muscovy, whose liver is used for foie gras. They are fed a corn-based diet and the breasts are aged for 1 week on the bone. They have a more complex, winy flavor and the denser, slightly tougher texture of a game meat. One boneless breast weighs about 1 pound (about 12 ounces, skinned). Since sizes and yields vary, figure on roughly 5 ounces raw skinned duck per serving, and gear cooking time according to the thickness of the breast. Then portion out 4-ounce servings of cooked duck, saving any leftovers for another meal. (See Spiced-Rubbed Duck Steaks with Port Wine Sauce, page 326.)

Spice-Rubbed Duck Steaks with Port Wine Sauce

SERVES 4

Duck is a surprisingly lean meat, with a rich, slightly winy flavor. More than half of its calories and most of its fat are in the skin, so once the skin is removed, duck flesh is among the leaner red meats. A skinless duck breast makes an ideal steak. Briefly marinating the breasts in a mixture of salt, pepper, allspice, thyme, and orange zest tenderizes the meat and accentuates the duck's natural flavor. Seared in a hot pan to crust the surface while cooking them rare, like steak, thinly sliced, and served with Port Wine Sauce, they make an elegant, easy meal. Brown Butter Orzo "Risotto" (page 126) is a perfect accompaniment.

Spice Rub

> ½ teaspoon kosher salt
>
> ¼ teaspoon black peppercorns
>
> ¼ teaspoon white peppercorns
>
> 4 allspice berries
>
> ¼ teaspoon sugar
>
> ½ teaspoon grated orange zest
>
> ¼ teaspoon fresh thyme leaves or ⅛ teaspoon dried thyme

2 boneless Moulard or Muscovy duck breast halves (¾ to 1 pound each) or 4 boneless Pekin duck breast halves (about 6 ounces each), skin and fat removed (you can reserve a little fat for cooking the breasts)

1 teaspoon peanut or grapeseed oil or reserved duck fat

Port Wine Sauce (page 637)

2 teaspoons roasted hazelnut or fruity extra-virgin olive oil, or unsalted butter

To make the spice rub, in a mortar and with a pestle, or in a spice grinder, coarsely crush the salt, peppercorns, and allspice with the sugar. Add the orange zest and thyme and grind as fine as you can; the mixture should look like sand.

Place the duck breasts on a platter and rub the spice mixture into them. Cover with plastic wrap and refrigerate for at least 4 hours, or overnight.

About 20 minutes before cooking, remove the duck breasts from the refrigerator to return to room temperature. Pat dry with paper towels. With a paring knife, remove the tenderloin, the thin strip of meat that runs lengthwise down the underside of each breast.

In a heavy medium skillet, heat the oil until hot. Add the duck breasts and cook until browned on both sides but still springy to the touch, about 3 to 4 minutes on each side for Moulard or Muscovy breasts, or about 2 to 4 minutes on each side for Pekin breasts, and about 1 minute per side for the tenderloins. Transfer to a cutting board and let rest for 5 minutes.

Meanwhile, in a small saucepan, bring the sauce to a simmer. Stir in the oil.

Using a thin sharp knife, slice each breast on a diagonal ⅛ inch thick. Fan the duck slices onto each plate and spoon the sauce over. Serve at once.

You can make the Port Wine Sauce and marinate the duck breasts up to IN ADVANCE 1 day ahead. Cover and refrigerate.

Ancho Chile–Rubbed Duck Steaks. A rub of mildly spicy variation Ancho Chile Essence accentuates the duck breast's affinity for fruit and herbs and Southwestern flavors. Serve them with Warm Mango Chutney (page 664) or Charred Onion Salsa (page 662) instead of the Port Wine Sauce.

Instead of the Spice Rub, use a mixture of 1 teaspoon kosher salt, ½ teaspoon sugar, and 1 tablespoon Ancho Chile Essence (page 543).

Hash

A GUIDE TO IMPROVISING

My favorite treatment for leftover roasted or grilled meat or poultry is hash, SERVES 4 dicing it and sautéing it with potatoes or root vegetables, onions, and herbs to make a deliciously comforting dish. This recipe marries the best of both worlds, pan cooking and roasting.

You can plug in just about any leftover roast, including chicken, turkey, beef, veal, venison, lamb, or pork. (If you have no leftovers, you can buy roasted meats by the pound.) You can even make it with just one kind of root vegetable or only potatoes. Some wonderful combinations are lamb with leeks, potatoes, parsnip, and celery root; the classic beef, potatoes, and onion; and turkey, parsnip, and parsley root. If you happen to have an abundance of leftover cooked root vegetables or potatoes, simply dice enough to make 4 cups and add them to the sautéed onions, omitting the raw vegetables.

2 ounces lean pancetta or thick-sliced bacon, cut into ¼-inch dice (scant ½ cup) or 1 tablespoon plus 2 teaspoons extra-virgin olive oil

1 cup coarsely chopped onions or leeks (white part only)

1¼ pounds root vegetables, singly or in combination, such as parsnips, celery root, parsley root, rutabagas, or turnips, peeled and cut into ½-inch dice (about 3 cups)

12 ounces red potatoes or Yellow Finns, peeled, cut into ½-inch dice (2 cups), rinsed in cold water, and dried with paper towels

¾ cup water

½ teaspoon kosher salt, plus more to taste

1 teaspoon minced garlic

2 teaspoons minced fresh pungent herbs, such as thyme, rosemary, savory and/or sage, in any combination

12 ounces cooked meat or skinless poultry, such as lamb, pork, beef, chicken, turkey, or duck, cut into ½-inch dice (2½ cups)

¼ to ½ cup chopped fresh flat-leaf parsley

Freshly ground black pepper

1. In a large nonstick skillet over moderate heat, cook the pancetta until it has rendered its fat and is crisp. With a slotted spoon, transfer the pancetta to a small bowl. Spoon 1 teaspoon of the fat into another small bowl and reserve. Alternatively, add 1 tablespoon plus 1 teaspoon of the olive oil to the pan and heat until hot.

2. Add the onions, cover the pan, and cook, stirring occasionally, until translucent, about 4 minutes. Uncover and sauté, stirring frequently, until the onions are tender and golden brown, about 4 minutes longer. Add the root vegetables, potatoes, and the reserved pancetta and toss to coat with the fat. Add the water and salt, cover the pan, and cook until the water has evaporated and the vegetables are tender but not mushy, 10 to 15 minutes. (If the water is evaporating too quickly, add a couple of tablespoons more to the pan.) Uncover and sauté the vegetables, tossing and stirring frequently, until well caramelized and browned, about 5 minutes.

3. While the vegetables are browning, in a medium nonstick skillet, heat the reserved 1 teaspoon pancetta fat or remaining 1 teaspoon oil over moderate heat. Add the garlic and minced herbs and sauté, stirring constantly, until the garlic is soft but not browned. Add the meat or poultry and sauté, tossing the pieces, until browned and just heated through. Sprinkle with a little salt.

4. Add the meat to the root vegetables, along with the chopped parsley, and toss to combine. Grind over plenty of fresh pepper to taste. Serve at once.

ON THE STOVE TOP: QUICK PAN SAUCES AND BRAISES. Quick pan sauces and braises are, in essence, variations on the basic approach to making sauced meat and poultry dishes in a single pan. The meats are browned first so the exterior caramelizes. Then a liquid is added, usually wine or broth, which dissolves the bits left in the bottom of the pan and boils down to make a rich sauce. The difference between them is that a quick pan sauce is made with tender cuts that require little cooking, such as duck or chicken breasts or veal or turkey scallops, and the sauce can be made within minutes; braising is for cuts that require longer cooking in liquid to tenderize them, such as bone-in chicken or rabbit parts and tougher cuts of meat, such as stewing beef and venison.

When making pan sauces and braises, use a heavy well-seasoned skillet rather than a nonstick one, which prevents caramelized bits from adhering to the bottom of the pan (when dissolved, these bits will add rich flavor to the sauce).

Duck Breasts with Thyme-Infused Honey and Balsamic Pan Sauce

You can take the basic method of searing meats a step further by using the bits left in the pan as the flavoring to make a rich sauce. Here the infused honey and balsamic vinegar—at once sweet, tart, floral, and herbal—enhance the winy flavor of the duck meat. Curing the duck steaks briefly with salt and sugar ensures that they will be tender. This sauce is also delicious with pork or lamb medallions.

SERVES 4

1¼ teaspoons kosher salt

½ teaspoon coarsely ground black peppercorns

¼ teaspoon sugar

2 boneless Moulard or Muscovy duck breast halves (¾ to 1 pound each) or 4 boneless Pekin (Long Island) duck breast halves (about 6 ounces each), skin and fat removed (you can reserve a little fat for cooking the breasts)

3 tablespoons lime blossom, thyme, or wildflower honey

1 tablespoon fresh thyme leaves (and flowers, if possible), plus sprigs for garnish

1 teaspoon reserved duck fat or olive oil

3 tablespoons balsamic vinegar

¼ cup veal demiglace (see note, page 331) or ½ cup unsalted homemade (page 574) or canned low-sodium chicken broth, reduced to ¼ cup

2 teaspoons cold unsalted butter

Kosher salt and freshly ground black pepper

In a small bowl, combine the kosher salt and peppercorns with the sugar. Place the duck breasts on a platter and rub the spice mixture into each one. Cover with plastic wrap and refrigerate for at least 4 hours, or overnight.

About 20 minutes before cooking, remove the duck breasts from the refrigerator to return to room temperature. Pat dry with paper towels. With a paring knife, remove the tenderloin, the thin strip of meat that runs lengthwise down the underside of each breast.

In a small saucepan, combine the honey and thyme leaves and bring to just a simmer over low heat, crushing the leaves with the back of a spoon; set aside to infuse for 5 minutes.

In a heavy medium skillet, heat the duck fat until hot and shimmering. Add the duck breasts and tenderloins and cook until browned and crusty on both sides but still springy to the touch, about 3 to 4 minutes on each side for the Moulard or Muscovy breasts, or 2 to 3 minutes per side for Pekin breasts, and about 1 minute per side for the tenderloins. Just before they are done, brush each duck breast with some of the thyme-infused honey and continue to cook until lightly caramelized. Transfer the breasts to a cutting board and let rest for 5 minutes. Discard the fat from the pan.

Add the balsamic vinegar to the pan and stir to loosen the browned bits on the bottom. Boil until the vinegar is very syrupy, about 1½ minutes. Stir in the remaining infused honey and the demiglace and return to a boil. Boil until thick and syrupy, about 1½ minutes longer. Stir in the cold butter and add the salt and pepper to taste.

Using a thin sharp knife, slice each breast on a diagonal ⅛ inch thick. Arrange the slices on four warmed dinner plates. Pour the duck juices left on the cutting board into the pan sauce, strain the sauce over the duck slices, and serve at once.

IN ADVANCE   You can marinate the duck breasts up to 1 day ahead.

The traditional way of giving pan sauces a rich, smooth quality is to swirl in butter or cream at the end. Reduced-fat pan sauces that leave out this step often have a rough, unfinished quality. One solution is to add a few teaspoons of *demiglace*, highly concentrated veal stock that gives deep meaty flavor and body to a sauce. Although demiglace was once solely in the realm of professional kitchens, commercial versions are now available to home cooks, either in the frozen food section of gourmet markets or by mail-order (see Sources, page 711). Although it may seem a bit expensive, demiglace is so highly concentrated that it takes only a little to enrich sauces. It lasts indefinitely in the freezer or refrigerator.

Scaloppine Marsala

SERVES 4

Veal Marsala is a holdover from old-style Italian restaurants that is still secretly loved by many as a great classic dish. This revised version, though lightened, has a more robust flavor than the original because of the highly concentrated Marsala wine and wild mushrooms. Although veal has a richer, more elegant flavor, I usually make this dish with thinly sliced turkey breast, an admirable and much leaner substitute.

Serve scaloppine with Classic Saffron Risotto (page 186) or roasted new potatoes.

1 ounce dried mushrooms, such as cèpe or morel

1 cup boiling water

1¼ pounds boneless turkey breast or veal cutlets, sliced about ⅓ inch thick

3 tablespoons all-purpose flour

1 teaspoon kosher salt

1 teaspoon freshly ground black pepper

1 tablespoon plus 1 teaspoon olive oil

1½ cups dry Marsala or Rainwater or Sercial (dry) Madeira

12 ounces fresh wild mushrooms, such as shiitake, oyster, morel, or chanterelle, tough stem ends removed and sliced

1 tablespoon demiglace (see above) (optional)

1 teaspoon arrowroot or potato starch, mixed with 2 teaspoons water

2 tablespoons minced fresh flat-leaf parsley or chervil

In a small bowl, combine the dried mushrooms and boiling water. Cover and set aside to let the mushrooms soften, about 15 minutes.

Place a turkey slice on a work surface, cover it with plastic wrap, and pound it lightly with a meat pounder, the side of a heavy cleaver, or the bottom of a heavy skillet until about ¼ inch thick. Repeat with the remainder.

Spread the flour in a shallow pan. Lightly sprinkle both sides of each slice with salt and pepper. Dredge in the flour and shake off the excess.

With a slotted spoon, transfer the mushrooms to a strainer and rinse well. Squeeze out the excess water. Coarsely chop the mushrooms.

In a large heavy well-seasoned or nonstick skillet, heat 1 teaspoon of the olive oil over moderate heat. When it is very hot, add only as many slices as will fit without crowding. Brown for about 2 minutes on each side; transfer the slices to a platter. Repeat until all the turkey slices are browned, adding as much of the remaining tablespoon of oil as necessary.

With paper towels, blot the fat from the pan. Add the Marsala to the skillet and pour in ½ cup of the mushroom soaking liquid, taking care not to disturb the sediment in the bottom of the bowl. Stir in the dried and fresh mushrooms and boil over high heat, scraping up the browned bits from the bottom of the skillet, until the mushrooms are tender and the liquid has reduced to about 1 cup, 8 to 10 minutes. Stir in the demiglace, if using, reduce the heat to moderately low, add the arrowroot mixture, and stir until the sauce thickens slightly. Return the turkey slices to the pan, spooning the sauce over them until they are hot. Serve at once, garnished with the herbs.

IN ADVANCE You can pound the cutlets up to 1 day ahead; cover tightly and refrigerate.

RABBIT, A PERFECT SUBSTITUTE FOR CHICKEN

For roasting and sautéing, rabbit requires 5 minutes (for pieces) to 8 minutes (whole) less cooking time than chicken. For braising, rabbit requires 7 to 8 minutes more.

Chicken is not often as flavorful as it should be, due to mass-farming methods. I find the flavor of a domestic rabbit closer to that of a "real" chicken, the kind you encounter on farms in Italy and France: still mild and lean, but with a fuller flavor. Because they grow so quickly, rabbits are generally not fed the usual doses of hormones and antibiotics that commercial chickens get. The cooking methods for both are virtually interchangeable, with only slight variations in cooking times. See page 679 for how to cut up a rabbit for sautéing or braising.

Chicken or Rabbit Braised in Wine

A GUIDE TO IMPROVISING

You can improvise any number of pan-braised chicken or rabbit dishes SERVES 4 using different combinations of wines and fruit, from rabbit with port and prunes or with dried cherries and Madeira to chicken with wild mushrooms and pearl onions.

When making a pan braise, include the bony parts of chicken and rabbit, which are usually discarded, such as forelegs or wing tips, neck, and rib cage. They add a lot of flavor to the sauce (discard before serving).

If using poultry, remove the skin before braising, since the fat from the skin would otherwise be rendered into the sauce. In order to brown skinned poultry and rabbit without drying them out, roll the pieces in flour, which will both create a crust and thicken the sauce slightly.

2 ounces lean thick-sliced bacon or pancetta, cut into ½-inch dice (scant ½ cup), or 1 tablespoon plus 1 teaspoon extra-virgin olive oil

3 tablespoons all-purpose flour

One 3-pound chicken or rabbit, skinned and cut into 8 pieces for sautéing

¾ teaspoon kosher salt

¾ teaspoon freshly ground black pepper

⅓ cup finely chopped shallots or leeks (white part only)

¾ cup dry fortified wine, such as Rainwater or Sercial Madeira, amontillado sherry, or ruby or tawny port (use to soak any dried fruits, then pour into the braise when called for)

Full-bodied wine, such as

>   **1½ cups dry red or white wine**

>   **1 cup sweet dessert wine,** such as Sauterne, Monbazillac, Barsac, Muscat de Beaumes-de-Venise (if using a sweet dessert wine, omit the fortified wine)

1½ cups unsalted homemade (page 574) **or canned low-sodium chicken broth**

2 sprigs fresh thyme

Flavorings (optional), such as

>   **1 to 2 sprigs fresh herbs,** such as rosemary, lavender, or basil, or 1 to 2 imported bay leaves (use sparingly, or remove when the flavor is as strong as you want)

>   **1 to 2 star anise, crushed juniper berries, cloves, allspice berries, or other spice**

Garnishes (optional), singly or in combination, such as

1 cup (6½ ounces) **dried cherries** (soaked for 1 hour in the Madeira; reserve the Madeira)

1 cup pitted prunes (soaked for 1 hour in the port; reserve the port)

2 medium Granny Smith apples, peeled, cored, cut into ⅛-inch-thick slices, and sautéed in 2 teaspoons unsalted butter until golden

Roasted Wild Mushrooms (page 40)

20 pearl onions, boiled and peeled (see page 678)

20 chestnuts, roasted and peeled (see page 684)

½ teaspoon sugar

1 to 2 teaspoons fresh lemon juice or balsamic vinegar

1 teaspoon brandy or eau-de-vie, such as cognac, Armagnac, Calvados, or kirsch

1. If using bacon, cook it in a small skillet, covered, over moderately low heat, until it has rendered its fat and is crisp, about 8 minutes. With a slotted spoon, transfer the bacon to paper towels to drain. Scrape the fat into a small bowl.

2. Sprinkle the flour on a dinner plate. Pat the chicken dry with paper towels and sprinkle evenly with about ½ teaspoon each of the salt and pepper. Roll the pieces in the flour to coat evenly; tap off the excess.

3. Measure 2 teaspoons of the reserved fat or the oil into a large heavy well-seasoned skillet and heat over moderate heat until hot. Sauté the chicken in batches, using another teaspoon of the fat, until golden, about 3 minutes on each side. Transfer to a platter. Reduce the heat to moderately low.

4. Add 1 teaspoon more fat and the shallots to the pan. Cook, covered, stirring occasionally, until the shallots have softened, about 5 minutes. Uncover, increase the heat slightly, and sauté the shallots until golden brown, about 3 minutes. Add the fortified wine, if using, to the pan (hold back any dried fruit you soaked in it) and boil for 1 minute, stirring up any brown bits. Add the full-bodied wine and cook for 5 minutes longer, or until slightly reduced. Stir in the broth, thyme, and any flavorings.

5. Nestle the legs and thighs in the pan (reserve the chicken breast or rabbit loin, which takes less time to cook). Bring to a simmer, cover, and cook chicken for 7 minutes, rabbit for 15 minutes. Add the reserved breast or loin portions, cover, and cook until tender, about 15 minutes longer; the sauce will reduce as they cook.

If you are using chicken, which cooks in less time, you will need to continue cooking the sauce to thicken it. Remove the chicken pieces and keep warm. Cook the sauce at a low boil until it has reduced and the flavors are rich and mellow, about 10 minutes. Return the chicken pieces to the pan.

6. Stir in the optional garnishes and simmer for about 5 minutes to heat through. Add the remaining salt and pepper to taste, along with the sugar and just enough lemon juice to heighten the flavors. Drizzle in the brandy and serve at once.

Rabbit with Dried Cherries and Madeira

improvisation 1

Madeira accentuates the winy flavor of dried cherries to make a sauce that complements rabbit perfectly.

Follow the Guide above, using Rainwater or Sercial (dry) Madeira and full-bodied red wine, 2 crushed juniper berries as the flavoring, and 1 cup dried cherries as the garnish. An hour before you begin the recipe, soak the cherries in the Madeira. In Step 6, drizzle in kirsch or cognac.

Rabbit Braised in Port

improvisation 2

Follow the Guide above, using ruby or tawny port and full-bodied red wine, 2 crushed juniper berries as the flavoring, and 1 cup pitted prunes as the garnish. An hour before you begin the recipe, soak the prunes in the port. In Step 6, drizzle in prune eau-de-vie or cognac.

Chicken in Red Wine with Mushrooms, Bacon, and Pearl Onions

SERVES 4 Coq au vin, chicken cooked in wine, is the quintessential French braise. It can be made with almost any kind of wine, whether a rich Burgundy, a fruity Bourgueil from the Touraine, a white Riesling from Alsace, or even a rosé from Provence. Mushrooms, pearl onions, and crisp pieces of lean bacon are the classic elements that remain consistent.

To achieve the extraordinarily rich, concentrated red wine sauce in this version, you fortify a full-bodied red wine with Madeira, port, and the flavorful juices from roasting the mushrooms. As in any coq au vin, the preparation of the garnishes is the real work. Only fresh pearl onions will do, and there is no way around peeling them, one by one. But the results are worth the effort.

You can also use rabbit instead of chicken, cooking it about 8 minutes longer.

Serve the chicken with lightly buttered egg noodles, Brown Butter Orzo "Risotto" (page 126), or steamed new potatoes.

Roasted Mushrooms

8 ounces button and/or shiitake mushrooms, tough stems trimmed and quartered lengthwise (about 3 cups)

1 sprig fresh thyme or ¼ teaspoon dried thyme

1 small shallot, finely chopped

1 small garlic clove, crushed and coarsely chopped

1 juniper berry, crushed

2 tablespoons dry white wine

1 teaspoon extra-virgin olive oil

⅛ teaspoon kosher salt

Freshly ground black pepper

About 1 cup unsalted homemade (page 574) **or canned low-sodium chicken broth**

20 pearl onions or small shallots

2 ounces thick-sliced lean bacon or pancetta, cut into ½-inch dice (scant ½ cup)

3 tablespoons all-purpose flour

One 3-pound chicken or rabbit, skinned and cut into 8 pieces for sautéing

¾ teaspoon kosher salt

¾ teaspoon freshly ground black pepper

⅓ cup finely chopped shallots

1 tablespoon tomato paste

½ cup ruby port

¼ cup Rainwater or Sercial (dry) Madeira

1½ cups dry red wine

2 sprigs fresh thyme or ½ teaspoon dried thyme

1 teaspoon cognac or other brandy

1 to 2 teaspoons fresh lemon juice

Preheat the oven to 325°F.

To roast the mushrooms, in a large nonstick ovenproof skillet, combine the mushrooms, thyme, the shallot, garlic, and juniper berry. Combine the white wine and olive oil and pour over the mushrooms. Sprinkle with the salt and pepper to taste. Cover and roast for 30 minutes.

Holding the mushrooms in the pan with a spatula, drain the mushroom juices into a measuring cup; set aside. Increase the heat to 450°F and roast the mushrooms, uncovered, for 10 to 15 minutes longer, until browned. Remove from the oven and set aside. Add enough chicken broth to the mushroom liquid to make 1⅓ cups.

Meanwhile, with scissors, cut the pointed tips off the onions. Place in a small saucepan with cold water to cover by 1½ inches, bring to a boil, and cook for 2 minutes. Drain, run cold water over the onions until they are cool, and drain again. Peel the onions, trimming off the stem ends. Set aside.

Cook the bacon in a small skillet, covered, over moderately low heat until it has rendered its fat and is crisp, about 8 minutes. With a slotted spoon, transfer the bacon to paper towels to drain. Scrape the fat into a small bowl.

Sprinkle the flour on a dinner plate. Pat the chicken dry with paper towels, then sprinkle evenly with about ½ teaspoon each of the salt and pepper. Roll the pieces in the flour to coat evenly; tap off the excess.

Measure 2 teaspoons of the bacon fat into a large heavy well-seasoned skillet and heat over moderate heat until hot. Sauté the chicken in batches, using additional bacon fat as necessary, until golden, about 3 minutes on each side. Transfer the chicken to a platter.

Reduce the heat to moderately low and add 1 teaspoon more bacon fat and the chopped shallots to the pan. Cook, covered, stirring occasionally, until the shallots have softened, about 5 minutes. Uncover, increase the heat slightly, and sauté the shallots until golden brown, about 3 minutes. Add the tomato paste and stir constantly until it has begun to caramelize on the bottom of the pan, about 1½ minutes. Add the port and Madeira and boil for 1 minute, stirring up the browned bits on the bottom of the pan. Add the red wine and cook for 5 minutes longer, or until slightly reduced. Stir in the mushroom-broth mixture, the 2 sprigs of thyme (or ½ teaspoon dried), and the remaining salt. Add the reserved bacon, the pearl onions, and chicken legs and thighs, partially cover, and cook for 7 minutes. Add the breasts and wings, cover, and simmer until cooked through, about 20 minutes. Transfer the chicken to a plate and keep warm.

Simmer the sauce until it is slightly thickened and the flavors are rich and mellow, about 10 minutes, stirring in the roasted mushrooms during the last 5 minutes. Return the chicken pieces to the pan, add the cognac, and cook for 30 seconds. Adjust the seasoning, adding pepper to taste and just enough lemon juice to heighten the flavors.

IN ADVANCE | You can prepare the braise up to 3 days ahead; cover and refrigerate. Reheat in a heavy covered saucepan over low heat until just heated through, about 15 minutes; do not allow the chicken to overcook.

Chicken with Sherry Vinegar Sauce

SERVES 4 | Although chicken *au vinaigre* is said to be of Lyonnaise origin, recipes for this delicious combination appear elsewhere throughout France, as well as in Spain, where it is made with sherry vinegar. Here the assertively flavored vinegar cooks slowly with sherry and plum tomatoes into a rich, concentrated sauce with very little fat. It is excellent for dinner parties because you can double or triple the quantities with ease, make it days ahead, or even freeze it. Serve with Brown Butter Orzo "Risotto" (page 126) or Mashed Potato Cake (page 54).

You can also use rabbit instead of the chicken, cooking it for about 8 minutes longer.

> **One 3-pound chicken,** skinned and cut into 8 pieces for sautéing
> ¾ **teaspoon kosher salt,** plus more to taste
> ¾ **teaspoon freshly ground black pepper,** plus more to taste
> **3 tablespoons all-purpose flour**
> **1 tablespoon plus 1 teaspoon olive, grapeseed, or peanut oil**
> ¼ **cup plus 2 tablespoons finely chopped shallots**

⅔ cup medium-sweet sherry, such as amontillado, or dry sherry mixed with 1 tablespoon honey

⅓ cup sherry vinegar, preferably aged

1 to 1½ teaspoons sugar

2 cups unsalted homemade (page 574) **or canned low-sodium chicken broth**

1 cup drained and coarsely chopped peeled plum tomatoes

1 tablespoon Dijon mustard

Pat the chicken dry with paper towels, then sprinkle evenly with ¾ teaspoon each salt and pepper. Spread the flour on a dinner plate and roll the pieces in the flour to coat evenly; tap off the excess.

Pour 2 teaspoons of the oil into a large heavy skillet and heat over moderate heat until hot. Sauté the chicken, in batches, until golden, about 3 minutes on each side, adding more oil by the teaspoon as necessary. Transfer the chicken to a platter.

Reduce the heat to moderately low and add the shallots to the pan. Cook, covered, stirring occasionally, until the shallots have softened, about 5 minutes. Uncover, increase the heat slightly, and sauté the shallots until golden brown, about 3 minutes. Add the sherry and increase the heat to moderately high, stirring up the browned bits on the bottom of the pan. Cook for 4 minutes until reduced by about half. Stir in the sherry vinegar and sugar and cook for 3 to 4 minutes longer, until reduced by half. Stir in the chicken broth, tomatoes, mustard, and salt and pepper to taste. Add the chicken legs and thighs, partially cover, and cook for 7 minutes. Add the breasts and wings, cover, and simmer until the chicken is cooked through, about 20 minutes. Transfer the chicken to a plate and keep warm.

Simmer the sauce until it is slightly thickened and the flavors are rich and mellow, about 10 minutes. Return the chicken pieces to the pan and heat through, then serve.

IN ADVANCE You can prepare the braise up to 3 days ahead; cover and refrigerate. Reheat over low heat in a heavy covered saucepan until just heated through, about 15 minutes; do not allow the chicken to overcook.

MEAT LOAVES, PÂTÉS, SAUSAGES, AND BURGERS.

Meat loaves, pâtés, sausages, and burgers are old-fashioned dishes traditionally made with ground scraps of meat or poultry and a good deal of fat to keep them from drying out. They are homey, practical, and delicious creations and, to many people nowadays, something of a taboo, due to the surfeit of fat and red meat they often contain. The following recipes illustrate several simple approaches to lightening these immensely satisfying foods.

Meat Loaf with Wild Mushrooms

SERVES 8

This recipe tries to make the best of a difficult situation—how to deal with ground beef and pork, which are fairly high in fat but have an inimitable flavor and texture—by using a few simple tricks (rather than substituting ground turkey, a common ploy, which many of us find lacking). I extend the lean meats with a mixture of caramelized onions and wild mushrooms, which adds rich flavors. A coarse puree of white bread and nonfat milk makes a creamy binder. The result is a hearty, moist, extremely flavorful meat loaf. I think it is even better served cold—thinly sliced, on toasted country bread with mustard.

Try hot meat loaf with Ancho Chile Ketchup: Dissolve 1 to 2 teaspoons of Ancho Chile Essence (page 543) or pure ancho chile powder in 1½ tablespoons boiling water, then stir in ½ cup tomato ketchup. Let stand for 15 minutes to develop the flavors.

½ cup (⅔ ounce) **dried porcini mushrooms**

½ **cup hot water**

12 ounces fresh wild mushrooms, such as shiitake, cremini, oyster, and/or portobello, in any combination

2 teaspoons olive oil

3 medium onions, finely chopped

1 tablespoon minced garlic

½ **cup dry white wine**

2 tablespoons tomato paste

1 teaspoon Smoky Tea Essence (page 545; optional)

5 slices (about 4¾ ounces) **white sandwich bread,** crusts removed, and torn into large pieces

⅓ cup nonfat milk

3 large egg whites

1½ pounds lean ground beef

12 ounces lean ground pork

3 tablespoons freshly grated Parmigiano-Reggiano cheese

2 to 3 teaspoons kosher salt

1½ teaspoons freshly ground black pepper

Place the dried mushrooms in a small bowl and cover with the hot water. Set aside to soak for 25 minutes.

Rinse the fresh mushrooms in cold water and drain. Remove and discard the tough stems. If you are using portobellos, remove the black gills with a paring knife. Coarsely chop the mushrooms by hand or in a food processor, pulsing it on and off.

With a slotted spoon, scoop the dried mushrooms out of their liquid; rinse them under cold water to remove any grit. Finely chop them; reserve the liquid.

Preheat the oven to 350°F.

In a large heavy skillet, combine the olive oil and onions, cover, and cook over moderate heat, stirring occasionally, until the onions have released their liquid, about 7 minutes. Stir in the garlic and cook for 1 minute longer. Add the fresh and dried mushrooms, cover, and cook until the fresh mushrooms have wilted and released some liquid. Uncover, increase the heat slightly, and cook, stirring frequently, until all the liquid has evaporated and the vegetables are nicely caramelized, about 15 minutes.

Stir in the wine, tomato paste, the tea powder, if using, and the mushroom liquid, taking care to leave any sediment behind. Simmer until the liquid has completely evaporated, about 8 minutes. Set aside to cool for 5 minutes.

In a large bowl, combine the bread and milk and, using a fork, mash together to make a paste. Stir in the egg whites. Add the beef, pork, and cheese, using a wooden spoon or your hands to blend them thoroughly. Stir in the mushroom mixture, salt, and pepper. Scoop the mixture onto the center of a large nonstick baking pan. Shape into a loaf about 10 by 5 inches.

Bake the meat loaf for 25 minutes. Increase the oven temperature to 400°F and bake for about 30 minutes longer, or until a meat thermometer inserted in the center reads 150°F.

Let the meat loaf cool slightly, and blot up the fat in the pan with paper towels before slicing.

IN ADVANCE The meat loaf can be refrigerated, well wrapped, for up to 5 days.

Country Terrine with Pistachios

SERVES 12 Many years ago, I worked as a chef in a charcuterie. Every week I turned out terrines of pork, veal, duck, rabbit, and venison. The terrines were delicious, but extremely rich. Traditionally, terrines contain about 45 percent pork fat. To create a lightened version that I could eat every day, I put everything I knew about terrines to work.

I use a *panade,* bread softened and mashed with milk, to form a binding moistening paste. I take care to grind the meat to different textures, adding some liquid to keep it moist, a small amount of gelatin to give it stability, and garlic, spices, and Calvados to lend an assertive flavor. I cook the terrine slowly to avoid toughening the meat, and then weight it with a brick to bind the ingredients.

This pâté is based on a classic *pâté campagne,* or country pâté, coarsely ground or chopped pork and veal seasoned with Cognac, herbs, spices, and pistachios. In reality, it is a meat loaf made with respect for the essential terrine notions of texture and seasoning. It is well flavored, coarsely textured, and moist.

The pork can be from either the loin or the shoulder, as long as it is trimmed of all fat and sinew. The loin, a solid piece of pure meat, requires the least amount of work, but it is more expensive than the shoulder. Prepare the terrine at least 24 hours before serving, to mellow the flavors (48 hours is even better). It will keep for up to 6 days refrigerated.

Serve it with cornichons, good bread, grainy mustard, and coarse salt.

1 **cup apple cider or unsweetened apple juice**

1½ **envelopes** (3½ teaspoons) **unflavored gelatin**

6 **slices** (about 5½ ounces) **white sandwich bread,** torn into small pieces

½ **cup low-fat** (2%) **milk**

2 **large eggs**

1 **teaspoon vegetable oil**

½ **cup chopped onions or shallots**

2 **garlic cloves,** finely chopped

1 **cup Calvados**

2 **pounds well-trimmed boneless lean pork loin** (about 2½ pounds, untrimmed) **or shoulder** (about 2¾ pounds, untrimmed), cut into 1-inch chunks

12 **ounces trimmed boneless veal shoulder** (about 1¼ pounds, untrimmed), cut into 1-inch chunks

4 **ounces Black Forest ham,** cut into small dice

1 **tablespoon kosher salt**

1¼ **teaspoons coarsely ground black pepper**

1½ **teaspoons dried thyme**

½ **teaspoon ground allspice**

½ **teaspoon ground coriander**

½ **teaspoon ground imported bay leaf** or 7 medium imported bay leaves ground in a spice grinder, plus 3 imported bay leaves

¼ **teaspoon ground cinnamon**

⅛ **teaspoon ground cloves**

2 **teaspoons balsamic vinegar**

3 **tablespoons coarsely chopped pistachios**

In a small saucepan, bring ¾ cup of the cider to a boil over high heat. Boil until reduced to ¼ cup, 8 to 10 minutes.

Meanwhile, in a small bowl, sprinkle the gelatin over the remaining ¼ cup cider and let soften, about 5 minutes. Add the hot cider and let stand, stirring once or twice, until the gelatin is completely dissolved, about 2 minutes. Let cool.

In a small bowl, using a fork, mash together the bread and milk to make a paste. Blend in the eggs.

In a small skillet, combine the oil, onions, and garlic, cover, and cook over low heat until the onions are translucent. Uncover and, holding the pan away from the heat, pour in the Calvados. Return to moderate heat and tilt the pan slightly, and ignite the Calvados (make sure there are no shelves or equipment hanging above the pan; the flames will shoot up about 1 foot). You can place the pan on a trivet on the counter while the flames burn off if you wish. Boil until the Calvados is reduced to about 2 tablespoons. Set aside.

Preheat the oven to 250°F.

In a food processor, working in small batches, chop the pork and veal, quickly pulsing the machine, until the meat is ground medium-coarse, with small chunks ¼ inch to ½ inch remaining. Pick out any sinews and discard. Transfer to a large bowl. Add the cider mixture, the onions, garlic, the bread-egg mixture, the ham, salt, pepper, 1 teaspoon of the thyme, the allspice, coriander, the ground bay leaf, cinnamon, cloves, balsamic vinegar, and pistachios and mix with your hands until well blended.

Spoon the mixture into a 9-by-5-inch (8-cup) terrine or loaf pan. Press it down firmly and smooth the top. Rap the terrine on a folded tea towel on the counter several times to eliminate any air pockets. Sprinkle the pâté with the remaining ½ teaspoon thyme and arrange the bay leaves on top.

Cover the pan with a double layer of heavy-duty aluminum foil and place it in a roasting pan. Set in the oven and fill the roasting pan with enough boiling water to reach halfway up the sides of the terrine. Bake for about 2½ hours, until a thermometer inserted into the center of the terrine reads 160°F. Let the terrine cool to lukewarm, then remove from the water bath.

Place the terrine in a rectangular cake pan to catch any juices. Press the foil down onto the top of the terrine and weight with a slightly smaller pan filled with heavy cans or other weights (about 4 pounds). Refrigerate for at least 12 hours.

To serve, pour off any unjelled liquid and invert the terrine onto a platter or cutting board. Slice the terrine into twelve ¾-inch slices.

IN ADVANCE The terrine can be refrigerated, well wrapped, for up to 6 days.

Chicken Liver Pâté
with Golden Raisins

Traditionally, smooth liver pâtés are bound with large quantities of pork fat, butter, cream, and egg yolks, which give them their rich and creamy consistency. The question is, what can be used in place of these saturated fats to achieve the same delicious effect?

MAKES ABOUT
2½ CUPS;
SERVES 10

Unsweetened chestnut puree proved to be an astonishing answer. Although it may seem a rather radical approach, the flavor of chestnuts is quite neutral and, like fat, the puree has an extremely fine texture.

You can use it to replace fats in savory mousses, ounce for ounce, without substantially altering the other ingredients. In this recipe, inspired by French chef Michel Guérard, I substitute chestnut puree for most of the fat—240 calories' worth per serving of fatback and crème fraîche—to achieve nearly the same rich texture and marvelous flavors of the original.

Unsweetened chestnut puree imported from France is available in cans from Minerve (see Sources, page 711). Check the ingredients of the type you buy to make sure that type includes only chestnuts and water, no sweeteners. If you can't get the puree, you can start with 8 ounces whole chestnuts (see page 684).

You can double the recipe if you wish. However, the pâté must not be more than 2 inches deep, or it won't cook properly.

1¼ teaspoons unflavored gelatin

¾ cup less 1 tablespoon whole milk

¼ cup golden raisins

About ½ cup boiling water

¾ cup (7 ounces) **unsweetened chestnut puree**

10½ ounces **chicken or duck livers**, trimmed

1½ teaspoons kosher salt

1½ teaspoons freshly ground black pepper

Pinch of ground allspice

4 large egg yolks

2½ tablespoons Armagnac or cognac

Preheat the oven to 300°F.

In a small saucepan, sprinkle the gelatin over ¼ cup of the milk; set aside to soften. Place the raisins in a small bowl and pour the boiling water over to cover. Let soften for 5 minutes, then drain well and pat dry on paper towels.

In a food processor, process the chestnut puree, chicken livers, salt, pepper, and allspice until creamy. Add the egg yolks and Armagnac and process to blend.

Over low heat, heat the milk mixture until the gelatin is dissolved. Stir in the remaining milk and add to the liver mixture. Process for at least 1 minute, until perfectly smooth. Pour the mixture through a fine strainer set over a bowl, rubbing and stirring with a rubber spatula to force it through the strainer, leaving the filaments behind in the strainer. Stir in the raisins.

Pour the mixture into a 1-quart baking or soufflé dish. Place the dish in a larger baking pan and set on the center rack of the oven. Add enough boiling water to the pan to come halfway up the sides of the baking dish. Cover loosely with a piece of aluminum foil. Bake until the pâté is set, about 1 hour and 15 minutes; a thermometer inserted into the center of it should read 140°F. Remove the dish from the water bath and allow to cool completely at room temperature.

Because the pâté has so little fat, it will darken if exposed to the air for too long; gently press plastic wrap directly against the surface to prevent this. Refrigerate overnight, to chill completely.

Serve the cold pâté on thin slices of toast. If you wish, you can pack the pâté into small ramekins for individual servings.

IN ADVANCE   You can prepare the pâté up to 4 days ahead; wrap well and refrigerate.

Homemade Sausages

Although there are many intriguingly flavored sausages now available, very few are made without preservatives, nitrites, and a lot of fat. These home-made sausage patties are a healthier alternative, flavorful and satisfying, with no synthetic additives or added fat. You can make them with either lean pork or duck. I like them for breakfast as an accompaniment to Rosemary Buttermilk Biscuits (page 374), Corn Blini (page 379), or French Toast (page 380).

2 slices (about 2ounces) **white sandwich bread,** torn into ½-inch pieces

2 tablespoons low-fat (2%) **milk**

1 pound lean pork loin or duck meat, cut into 1-inch chunks

2 tablespoons beaten egg white

1 ¼ teaspoons freshly ground black pepper, or more to taste

½ teaspoon kosher salt

Sausage Seasoning

   ½ teaspoon dried thyme

   ½ teaspoon ground coriander

   ¼ teaspoon ground allspice

   ⅛ teaspoon ground ginger

1 teaspoon olive oil or duck fat

In a medium bowl, toss the bread with the milk, breaking it apart further with your fingers. Set aside to soften.

Chop the meat in a food processor, pulsing it on and off, until coarsely ground. Do not overprocess; there should be some ¼-inch chunks of meat remaining. Pick out any sinews or bits of fat from the meat and discard. Transfer three quarters of the meat to a medium bowl, leaving the rest in the work bowl.

Add the bread mixture to the work bowl, along with the egg white, salt, pepper, and seasonings. Pulse until just combined, about 30 seconds. Add this mixture to the meat and knead it with your hands to combine.

With wet hands, divide the mixture into 16 equal portions. Shape each into a 2½-inch patty; place on a baking sheet. Cover with plastic wrap and refrigerate until shortly before you are ready to cook the patties; bring to room temperature before frying.

Heat a large heavy skillet or griddle over moderate heat until hot. Add ½ teaspoon of the olive oil to the pan. Arrange half the patties in the skillet, leaving 1 inch between them. Fry the patties until the undersides are brown, about 2 minutes. Flip the patties and cook until the juices run clear when pierced with a fork and the undersides are brown, about 2 minutes longer. Transfer to a platter and cover to keep warm. Repeat with the remaining patties, using the remaining ½ teaspoon oil. Serve hot.

IN ADVANCE   You can shape the patties up to a day ahead and refrigerate them. Or freeze them, well wrapped, for up to 2 months; defrost in the refrigerator.

variation   **Homemade Merguez.** To make a leaner version of the traditional spicy Moroccan lamb sausage, replace the pork with lean lamb. For the sausage seasoning, use 1¾ teaspoons sweet Hungarian paprika, ¼ teaspoon ground cumin, ¼ teaspoon ground coriander, ¼ teaspoon fennel seeds, ⅛ teaspoon ground cinnamon, ⅛ teaspoon cayenne, and 1 teaspoon minced garlic. This sausage is wonderful with bean dishes such as Chickpea Stew with Saffron and Winter Squash (page 99) and White Beans with Mellowed Garlic and Rosemary Oil (page 102).

variation   **Duck or Lamb Burgers.** Prepare the sausage mixture, using duck or Homemade Merguez as directed above, omitting the egg white. Wet your hands and shape the mixture into 4 patties, ¾ to 1 inch thick. Broil the patties, flipping once, for about 4 minutes on each side for medium rare. Serve on toasted buns or peasant bread, with Onion Marmalade with Sherry Vinegar (page 667).

Turkey Burgers with Apples, Onions, and Sage

SERVES 4   Because turkey is a very lean meat, it can become extremely dry when ground and cooked as a burger. A *panade* of bread and milk, along with sautéed onions and apple, acts like fat to bind the turkey and ensure it remains juicy and tender. Serve the burgers on good crusty buns, along with Onion Marmalade with Sherry Vinegar (page 667).

2 slices (about 2 ounces) **white sandwich bread,** torn into 1-inch pieces

3 tablespoons low-fat (2%) **milk**

2 teaspoons unsalted butter

½ cup finely chopped onions

Kosher salt

½ medium apple, finely chopped (⅓ cup)

1 ¼ teaspoons minced fresh sage or scant ½ teaspoon dried sage

1 teaspoon fresh lemon juice

1 pound ground turkey

½ teaspoon freshly ground black pepper

1 teaspoon extra-virgin olive oil

In a small bowl, soak the bread in the milk to soften it, about 5 minutes.

In a small nonstick skillet, melt 1 teaspoon of the butter over low heat. Add the onions, sprinkle lightly with salt, and toss to coat. Cover and cook until the onions have released some juices, about 5 minutes. Uncover, increase the heat to moderate, and cook, tossing occasionally, until the liquid has evaporated and the onions are golden brown, 10 to 12 minutes. Add the remaining 1 teaspoon butter, the apple, and sage and cook, stirring frequently, until the apple is soft, about 4 minutes. Sprinkle with the lemon juice and remove from the heat.

In a medium bowl, combine the turkey, soaked bread, ½ teaspoon apple mixture, salt, and the pepper, tossing well with your hands. Wet your hands and shape the mixture into four ¾-inch patties. (Do not make them any thicker than this, or the outside will dry out before the center is cooked.) Place the patties on a baking sheet, cover, and refrigerate until ready to cook.

Preheat the broiler. Brush the broiler rack lightly with oil and arrange the burgers on it; brush the tops of the burgers lightly with oil. Broil 4 inches from the heat for 5 minutes. Flip them, brush the tops lightly with oil, and broil until the juices run clear when pierced with a knife, about 7 minutes longer. Serve at once.

You can shape the patties up to 4 hours ahead.

IN ADVANCE

Wild Mushroom Turkey Burgers. In a small bowl, soak 1 ounce dried porcini mushrooms in ½ cup hot water until very soft, about 20 minutes. Scoop them out of the liquid with a slotted spoon, leaving any grit in the bottom of the bowl. Rinse the mushrooms under cool water. Drain and squeeze to extract as much water as possible. Finely chop the mushrooms.

variation

Proceed as directed above, adding the mushrooms along with the apple, and cook for 4 minutes. Then add 1 tablespoon plus 1 teaspoon cognac and cook for 1 minute longer. Stir in the lemon juice and continue as directed.

Rosemary, Lemon, and Pepper Focaccia (page 366)

QUICK BREADS

FROM PIZZA TO PANCAKES

The breads I make most often —Italian-style pizzas and old-fashioned American quick breads like buttermilk biscuits and muffins—have very different origins but much in common. They are eminently practical because they are easy to make, and at the same time they provide many of the pleasures of bread baking, the aromas and comfort of fresh-baked dough, and the satisfaction of baking "from scratch," with very little effort.

The recipes that follow are carefully lightened versions of popular quick breads that you can serve as hors d'oeuvres, accompaniments to meals, or warming snacks or breakfasts.

PIZZA. Although you can buy pizza on practically any street corner, it will most likely not be nearly as good, or as healthful, as the pizza you can make at home. Once you know the basic approach, it is easy to make pizzas with a chewy, yeasty crust, melty fresh mozzarella, and vibrantly flavored toppings without the surfeit of calories and fat of a pizza parlor pie, at upward of 700 calories per serving. After figuring out exactly how much of the fattening ingredients it took to make a delicious pizza, I paired them in judicious amounts with a simple yeast dough, building up flavor and satisfying texture with naturally lean vegetables.

CREATING A BAKER'S OVEN AT HOME

Professional bakers use brick-lined ovens to ensure a good pizza crust. You can easily fashion a makeshift baker's oven at home using a baking stone or quarry tiles, which can take intense heat for long periods. You can buy them at tile and housewares shops. Thirty minutes before baking, place the stone or tiles on the middle oven rack to heat. When you slide the risen dough directly onto the hot stone, it dries the bottom of the dough, creating a toothsome, well-cooked crust.

If you don't have a baking stone or tiles, the next best thing is an inverted large cast-iron skillet or griddle, or a heavy professional-gauge baking sheet that can withstand the heat without warping.

Free-form breads such as pizza and focaccia can be tricky to transfer onto a hot baking stone, since the dough often sticks to the surface it rose on. After shaping the dough, place it on a sheet of parchment paper on a baking peel, edgeless cookie sheet, or inverted sheet pan before setting it out to rise. Then you will be able to slide the dough on its parchment directly onto the stone. Once the crust is cooked, you can pull the parchment out from under the pizza and discard it.

Basic Pizza Dough

This dough is very easy to make and works well for either thin- or thick-crust pizza and focaccia. Letting the dough rise slowly, either all day on the counter or in the refrigerator overnight, will greatly improve both flavor and texture. (I like to mix the dough in the morning before work, to bake it that night.) If you are in a hurry, however, you can mix the dough and let it rise in a warm place; it will take about 1½ hours for it to double in bulk, so you can bake your pizzas within a couple of hours.

This recipe can easily be halved or doubled.

MAKES 1 ½ POUNDS

Because chlorine inhibits the action of yeast and can produce an off flavor, use filtered or, preferably, bottled spring water in bread doughs.

1 cup lukewarm water (105° to 110°F), preferably bottled spring water

Pinch of sugar

One ¼-ounce package (2 ½ teaspoons) **active dry yeast**

3 cups (1 pound total) unbleached all-purpose flour, plus 2 ½ tablespoons for kneading and shaping

2 ¼ teaspoons kosher salt

About 1 ½ tablespoons extra-virgin olive oil

Combine the water and sugar in a small bowl. Sprinkle the yeast over it and set aside for 5 minutes, or until foamy. Stir to dissolve completely.

To make the dough by hand: Combine the 3 cups flour and the salt in a large bowl. Gradually stir in the yeast mixture and 1 tablespoon plus 1 teaspoon of the olive oil until a stiff dough has formed. Turn the dough out onto a lightly floured work surface. Adding only enough flour to keep the dough from sticking to the work surface, knead it until smooth and elastic, about 6 minutes. (When you press your finger in the dough, it will immediately spring back.)

To make the dough in a food processor: Add the 3 cups flour and the salt to the work bowl. With the motor running, pour in the yeast mixture and 1 tablespoon plus 1 teaspoon of the olive oil. Process until the dough is uniform: It will either have the texture of coarse meal or will gather into one or two balls near the blade. Remove the dough and form into a ball, if necessary. (If bits of dough remaining in the processor cause the blade to stick, making it difficult to remove when cleaning the processor, pour some hot water into the work bowl and run the processor for a few minutes.)

To make the dough in an electric mixer: Add the 3 cups flour and the salt to the mixer bowl. Using the balloon whisk or paddle attachment on medium speed, drizzle in the yeast mixture and 1 tablespoon plus 1 teaspoon of the olive oil, mixing until the dough begins to pull away from the sides of the bowl. Change to the dough hook. Knead at medium speed, adding more flour as necessary to make a smooth dough, until the dough is very elastic, about 5 to 6 minutes. Turn the dough out onto a well-floured work surface and continue kneading a minute or two longer, until it is soft and velvety and does not stick at all to the work surface. (When you press your finger in the dough, it will spring back immediately.)

Place the dough in a lightly oiled bowl. Using a slightly dampened brush, brush the top of the dough lightly with oil. Cover with a damp tea towel and set aside in a warm place until doubled in bulk, 1 to 2 hours.

Punch down the dough. You can use it now or let it rise a second time, which will give it a finer texture and flavor: Cover the dough again with a damp tea towel and set in a warm place to rise for 40 minutes longer. Punch the dough down again.

Proceed as directed in the following recipes.

IN ADVANCE The dough can be covered and refrigerated for up to 4 days (just punch it down if it rises too high) or frozen, well wrapped, for up to 2 months. To freeze rolled-out dough for pizza and focaccia, see page 357.

variation **Sponge Dough.** Pizza dough made with a sponge—allowing a short preliminary fermentation of the yeast with some flour and water—has a chewier texture and more fully developed flavor than regular dough. Mix the yeast with ½ cup of the water, the sugar, and ¼ cup of the flour, cover, and set aside for 1 hour, or until the sponge is thick and foamy and has increased in volume. Then proceed as directed, mixing the sponge, the remaining ½ cup water, and the oil into the remaining 2¾ cups flour and salt.

Plan the Rising Time of Homemade Pizza Dough to Fit Your Schedule. You can speed up rising time by putting the dough in a warm place, slow it down by putting it in a cool place. (Freezing it suspends activity altogether, until the dough warms up again.) Letting dough rise in the refrigerator is a great technique for busy people. The cold temperature makes the dough rise more slowly than it would at room temperature, so it can be left on its own while you do other things. A slow rise actually yields a better crust, with a much more developed flavor. So you could mix up the dough early one morning and leave it to rise in the refrigerator all day. Then you can make a pizza that night for dinner.

Use Commercial Pizza Dough. For times when I am just too busy to make my own pizza dough, I buy a few pounds of raw dough from a local pizza parlor to have on hand. Before you settle on a source, first taste pizza from several neighborhood pizza parlors to determine the quality of their crust. Look for a crust that is chewy and yeasty, not the soft insipid dough of chain pizza parlors. Commercial dough can be substituted for home-made dough in any of the recipes in this book. If not using the dough right away, freeze, well wrapped, in 1-pound balls; thaw in the refrigerator for about 4 hours before using.

Freeze Rolled-Out Dough. You can freeze rolled-out pizza and focaccia dough for up to 2 months to defrost and bake on the spur of the moment. On a lightly floured surface, roll the dough into the desired round or free-form shape. Place on a cookie sheet and freeze until the dough is frozen solid, at least 45 minutes. Carefully pry the dough off the baking sheet without cracking it, wrap it well in plastic wrap, and freeze it until ready to use. About 1½ hours before baking, unwrap the dough and place it on a piece of parchment on a baking sheet. Cover lightly with plastic wrap and let it thaw in the refrigerator. Top as desired and bake.

Thick-Crust Pizza

A GUIDE TO IMPROVISING

MAKES ONE 6-INCH PIZZA

To cut down on the olive oil, brush on rather than drizzle just enough oil before baking the pizza so that it bakes properly. Then, just before serving, brush it again, toppings and all, so the flavor of the oil hits the palate with each bite, making it seem as though there is a lot more oil than there really is.

An abundance of dough and cheese makes traditional thick-crust pizzas among the most satisfying of foods—and extremely caloric. My solution is to spread the dough with a generous topping of cooked vegetables—such as roasted tomatoes, sautéed greens, or a vegetable stew—which are low in calories and fat and rich in flavor and substance.

The following formula provides the right balance of dough, cheese, oil, and toppings for a single serving. By multiplying it by the number of people you want to serve, you can make any size pizza. For example, 12 ounces dough will make an 11-inch pizza that serves 4; 1 pound 2 ounces dough will make a 15-inch pizza to serve 6.

Flour for shaping the pizza

3 ounces (a 2¼-inch ball) **Basic Pizza Dough** (page 355)

½ teaspoon extra-virgin olive oil or Flavored Oil (pages 588–597)

Fresh herbs (optional), such as

> **10 to 15 fresh basil leaves**
>
> **5 to 6 fresh sage leaves**
>
> **¼ to ½ teaspoon finely chopped fresh rosemary or thyme**

⅓ to ½ cup cooked vegetable topping, such as

> **Tomato Sauce** (page 652) **or any variation**
>
> **Slow-Roasted Tomatoes** (page 38)
>
> **Peperonata** (page 63)
>
> **Wild Mushroom Ragù** (page 151)
>
> **"Fried" Onions** (page 62)
>
> **"Fried" Eggplant** (page 42)
>
> **Steam-Roasted Fennel with Pancetta and Juniper** (page 58)
>
> **Roasted Wild Mushrooms** (page 40)
>
> **"Fried" Artichokes with Crispy Garlic and Sage** (page 67)
>
> **Tender Greens Sautéed with Garlic and Olive Oil** (page 74)

Freshly ground black pepper

1½ ounces soft, mild cheese, singly or in combination, such as salted fresh mozzarella (plain or smoked), Fontina, ricotta salata, or goat cheese, thinly sliced or shredded

1½ tablespoons grated hard pungent cheese, such as Parmigiano-Reggiano, pecorino Romano or Toscano, or an aged goat cheese

1. Thirty minutes before baking, preheat the oven to 450°F and place a pizza stone or baking tiles, an inverted large cast-iron skillet, or a heavy baking sheet on the middle rack of the oven to heat. If the dough has been refrigerated, bring to room temperature 15 to 20 minutes before shaping.

2. On a lightly floured surface, with floured hands, stretch and roll the dough into a rough 6-inch circle. Place a sheet of parchment paper roughly the size of the dough on a wooden peel, a rimless cookie sheet, or an inverted baking sheet. Transfer the dough to the parchment and reshape it with your fingers, building up the edges so they form a ½-inch lip. Prick the dough every inch or two with a fork and, using a slightly dampened brush, brush lightly with a little of the olive oil. Cover the dough loosely with plastic wrap and set in a warm place to rise for 15 minutes.

3. Spread the topping evenly over the dough, leaving a 1-inch border uncovered. If the topping is not very liquid, brush it lightly with a little of the olive oil. Sprinkle with pepper and with herbs, if desired. Scatter the cheeses evenly over the topping.

4. Slide the pizza, on the parchment, onto the hot stone in the oven. Bake until the crust is golden brown and the cheese is bubbly, 15 to 20 minutes. Brush or drizzle the remaining oil over the top. Serve at once.

Wild Mushroom and Smoked Mozzarella Pizza

improvisation 1

Follow the Guide above, using ⅓ cup Wild Mushroom Ragù for the topping and shredded smoked mozzarella and grated Parmigiano-Reggiano for the cheeses.

Garlic Greens, Ricotta Salata, and Pecorino Pizza

improvisation 2

Follow the Guide above, using ⅓ cup Tender Greens with Garlic and Oil for the topping and 1¼ ounces ricotta salata cheese, thinly sliced, and grated Fiore Sardo or a hard aged goat cheese for the cheeses.

Artichoke Pizza

improvisation 3

Follow the Guide above, using ⅓ cup Panfried Artichokes with Crispy Sage, thinly sliced, for the topping and thinly sliced or shredded smoked mozzarella and grated Parmigiano-Reggiano for the cheeses.

Thin-Crust Pizza

A GUIDE TO IMPROVISING

In thin-crust pizzas, the dough is rolled out too thin to accommodate heavy toppings without becoming soggy. These pizzas are best made with a thin layer of cheese and just a few elements scattered on top, such as thinly sliced vegetables such as tomatoes or roasted peppers. (The topping is placed on top of the cheese to give it a chance to cook during the short baking time.) The resulting pizzas are much lighter and more delicate than thick-crust pizzas, and the flavor of each element remains distinct.

I invariably use fresh mozzarella cheese on thin-crust pizzas because it becomes molten and gooey in the oven, a pleasing counterpoint to the crisp crust. A little Fontina cheese mixed in adds flavor and creaminess.

I usually serve individual thin-crust pizzas rather than one big one. Three ounces of Basic Pizza Dough will roll out to be about 25 percent larger in diameter than thick-crust pizzas, so they seem quite luxurious and abundant. Multiply the proportions below to serve as many people as you wish.

3 ounces (a 2¼-inch ball) **Basic Pizza Dough** (page 355)

1 teaspoon extra-virgin olive oil or Flavored Oil (pages 588–597)

1¼ ounces salted fresh or smoked mozzarella, thinly sliced or shredded

¼ ounce Fontina cheese, shredded (1 tablespoon)

Fresh herbs (optional), such as

  10 to 15 fresh basil leaves

  5 to 6 fresh sage leaves

  ¼ to ½ teaspoon finely chopped fresh rosemary or thyme

Toppings (optional), singly or in combination, such as

  ½ cup thinly sliced vegetables, such as raw sweet onion, roasted or raw bell pepper, or wild mushrooms

  3 to 4 slices ripe tomato or 5 cherry or grape tomatoes, cut into quarters and seeds removed

  ¼ cup chopped pitted (see page 683) **meaty Kalamata olives**

  One ½-ounce slice prosciutto, torn into ½-inch-wide strips

  3 to 5 oil-packed anchovies, drained and sliced lengthwise in half

1½ teaspoons minced shallot

1. Thirty minutes before baking, preheat the oven to 450°F and place a pizza stone or baking tiles, an inverted large cast-iron skillet, or a heavy baking sheet on the middle rack of the oven to heat. If the dough has been refrigerated, bring to room temperature 15 to 20 minutes before shaping.

2. On a lightly floured work surface, with floured hands, stretch and roll the dough into a rough 8-inch circle. Place a sheet of parchment paper roughly the size of the dough on a wooden peel, a rimless cookie sheet, or an inverted baking sheet. Transfer the dough to the parchment and reshape it with your fingers, building up the edges so they form a ½-inch lip. Prick the dough every inch or two with a fork and, using a slightly dampened brush, brush lightly with a little of the olive oil. Cover the dough loosely with plastic wrap and set in a warm place to rise for 15 minutes.

3. Spread the cheese over the dough, leaving a 1-inch border uncovered. Arrange the optional herbs and/or topping on top of the cheese. Scatter the shallots over the top. Using a slightly dampened brush, brush lightly with half the remaining olive oil.

4. Slide the pizza, on the parchment, onto the hot stone in the oven. Bake until the crust is golden brown and the cheese is bubbly, 7 to 10 minutes. Brush or drizzle the remaining oil over the top. Serve at once.

Tomato and Basil Pizza
improvisation 1

Following the Guide above, on the rolled and risen dough, arrange the cheeses, 10 to12 fresh basil leaves, 4 or 5 thin slices of ripe tomato or 6 or 7 cherry tomatoes, cut into quarters; sprinkle with 1 tablespoon minced red onion or shallot and brush lightly with oil. Proceed as directed.

Onion and Rosemary Pizza
improvisation 2

Following the Guide above, on the rolled and risen dough, arrange the cheeses, ½ cup thinly sliced Vidalia onions, and ½ teaspoon minced fresh rosemary. Proceed as directed.

Anchovy Pizza
improvisation 3

Following the Guide above, lightly rub the rolled and risen dough with a halved garlic clove; arrange the cheeses and 3 or 4 oil-packed anchovies, drained and sliced lengthwise in half. Proceed as directed. Garnish with coarsely chopped fresh flat-leaf parsley.

Pizza and focaccia are wonderful cooked on a grill, especially over hard-wood charcoal, for the dough absorbs the flavor of the sweet smoke. While it is easy to do, it is important to follow certain guidelines.

About 30 minutes before grilling, prepare a hot fire, with the rack about 4 inches above the coals. The fire is ready when the coals are coated with white ash and burn red-hot when you blow on them, or when you can hold the palm of your hand 5 inches above them for only 3 to 4 seconds.

Roll the pizza dough no less than ¼ inch thick and no more than 10 to 12 inches in diameter; individual rounds are easier to manage. Prepare the toppings and have them ready on a tray next to the grill.

Brush or rub a little oil on the grill rack just before grilling. Using both hands, lift the dough gently by one edge and drape it over the grill. When the dough has puffed slightly and the underside has stiffened enough so that it no longer sticks—about 1 minute—slide the pizza or focaccia toward the cooler edge of the grill and flip the dough over using a pair of tongs. Quickly arrange the toppings on the dough. Push the pizza or focaccia back into the center of the grill and cook, moving it around frequently so that the bottom does not burn, until the toppings are heated through and/or the cheese is melted, 5 to 7 minutes. If you are using a grill with a lid, you can close it to encourage the cheese to melt. Just before serving, brush the pizza with olive oil and sprinkle with herbs, if desired.

HORS D'OEUVRES AND SIDE BREADS. Hors d'oeuvre breads such as focaccia and bruschetta, enriched with olives, herbs, pungent cheeses, and vegetables, serve several delicious purposes. Their slightly salty, savory flavors stimulate the appetite and complement aperitifs or cocktails. They stave off hunger until the meal starts, while fueling anticipation of good things to come. Many are marvelous as snacks and as accompaniments to soups, salads, and stews.

The recipes that follow include such classics as *pissaladière*, the French onion and olive tart, rustic garlic-rubbed toasts, and innovative savory biscotti, scented with rosemary. In addition to making them more healthful, lightening these delightful breads ensures that they won't be too filling.

Focaccia

A GUIDE TO IMPROVISING

This focaccia is no more than Basic Pizza Dough, rolled or patted flat, brushed with oil, and scattered with the simplest flavorings—from olive oil and sea salt to more esoteric combinations of herbs and fruit—just enough to adorn but not obscure the bread. These quickly made breads are some of my favorite hors d'oeuvres.

MAKES ONE 12-INCH ROUND FOCACCIA; SERVES 6 AS AN HORS D'OEUVRE

This is the basic method for making one 12-inch focaccia, for 6 people. This classic focaccia, dressed only with olive oil and sea salt, is the base to which a variety of other toppings, such as rosemary, garlic, and olives, can be added. The only fixed quantity is the oil. If you wish to make focaccia to feed more or less people, or make individual ones, figure on 2½ ounces of dough and ½ teaspoon olive oil per person. Increase or decrease the topping amounts listed below accordingly.

You can roll out the dough in advance of assembling the focaccia. Arrange it on parchment, wrap well in plastic wrap, and freeze until ready to use. Thaw in the refrigerator for 1 hour before baking.

1 pound Basic Pizza Dough (page 355)

About 1 tablespoon all-purpose flour for shaping the dough

1 tablespoon fruity extra-virgin olive oil

Toppings (optional), singly or in combination, such as

> **3 to 4 garlic cloves,** thinly sliced
>
> **1 cup thinly sliced Vidalia or Bermuda onions**
>
> **Fresh herbs,** such as 3 tablespoons fresh rosemary leaves or 50 small fresh sage leaves
>
> **1 cup pitted** (see page 683) **and coarsely chopped meaty black olives,** such as Kalamata or Gaeta
>
> **1 teaspoon fennel seeds or crushed black peppercorns**
>
> **1 ounce aged grating cheese,** such as Parmigiano-Reggiano or Manchego, grated or thinly shaved

½ teaspoon flaked sea salt, such as Maldon, **or kosher salt,** or more to taste

1. Thirty minutes before baking, preheat the oven to 450°F and place a pizza stone or baking tiles, an inverted large cast-iron skillet, or a heavy baking sheet on the middle rack of the oven to heat. If the dough has been refrigerated, bring to room temperature 15 to 20 minutes before shaping.

2. On a floured work surface, flatten the dough into a disk and roll it, or press, pat, and stretch it into a rough circle, about 12 inches in diameter, adding a little more flour if necessary to keep it from sticking. Place a sheet of parchment paper roughly the size of the dough on a peel, rimless cookie sheet, or an inverted baking sheet. Transfer the dough to the parchment. Prick the dough all over with a fork and brush it with 1½ teaspoons of the oil. Cover loosely with plastic wrap and set in a warm place to rise until puffy, 15 to 20 minutes.

3. Arrange the optional toppings over the dough; if using cheese, add it after the dough has baked for 4 to 5 minutes and is just beginning to puff and brown. Using a slightly dampened brush, brush lightly with oil. Sprinkle with the salt.

4. Slide the dough, still on the parchment, onto the hot pizza stone. Bake for 15 to 20 minutes, until the bubbles that formed on the surface are golden and the edges of the dough are browned. Remove the focaccia from the oven and slide it off the parchment; brush with the remaining oil. With a heavy chef's knife, cut the focaccia into wedges. Serve at once.

Classic Rosemary Focaccia

improvisation 1

Follow the Guide on pages 363 to 364, using 3 tablespoons fresh rosemary leaves or 1 tablespoon dried crumbled rosemary as the topping.

Garlic and Sage Focaccia

improvisation 2

Follow the Guide on pages 363 to 364, using the sage leaves and garlic cloves as the topping.

Onion and Fennel Seed Focaccia

improvisation 3

Follow the Guide on pages 363 to 364, using onions as the topping. After brushing them lightly with oil, sprinkle with the salt, a pinch of sugar, freshly ground black pepper, and ¼ teaspoon ground coriander. Scatter 1 teaspoon fennel seeds over the top.

Black Olive and Herb Focaccia

improvisation 4

Follow the Guide on pages 363 to 364, using olives as the topping. Sprinkle the oiled dough with about 1 tablespoon minced fresh thyme or rosemary, then scatter the olives over and press them gently into the dough.

Parmesan and Black Pepper Focaccia

improvisation 5

Follow the Guide on pages 363 to 364, omitting the salt. Bake the plain oiled dough as directed in Step 4 for about 5 minutes, until bubbles form in the dough and it is just beginning to brown. Scatter 1 ounce Parmigiano-Reggiano cheese, grated or thinly shaved, over the focaccia. Bake for about 10 minutes, until the cheese is melted and the focaccia is golden, with browned edges. Brush with the remaining oil and sprinkle generously with freshly ground black pepper.

Rosemary, Lemon, and Pepper Focaccia

SERVES 6 AS AN
HORS D'OEUVRE

When chef Kevin Taylor told me about this intriguing focaccia he had served at the Zenith American Grill in Denver, I could not imagine how lemons would work on a bread. So I adapted it to my standard focaccia method to try it; it remains one of the most dramatic and delicious focaccias I know, never failing to surprise and delight me or my guests.

Flour for rolling

1 pound Basic Pizza Dough (page 355)

1 tablespoon fruity extra-virgin olive oil

2 teaspoons finely chopped fresh rosemary

Freshly ground black pepper

1 lemon, scrubbed and dried

1 tablespoon freshly grated Parmigiano-Reggiano cheese
or ½ teaspoon flake sea salt, such as Maldon, or kosher salt

Thirty minutes before baking, preheat the oven to 425°F and place a pizza stone, or baking tiles, an inverted large cast-iron skillet or griddle, or a heavy baking sheet in the oven to heat.

Flour the work surface lightly and roll the dough into a rough circle 11 inches in diameter. Place a sheet of parchment paper roughly the size of the dough on a wooden peel, a rimless cookie sheet, or an inverted baking sheet. Transfer the dough to the parchment and reshape it with your fingers.

Prick the dough with a fork and brush it lightly with some of the olive oil. Sprinkle evenly with the rosemary and grind pepper over it. Cut the lemon in half through the stem (reserve one half for another use). Slice the remaining half crosswise as thin as you can. Remove any seeds. Arrange the lemon slices in a single layer over the dough. Brush them lightly with olive oil. Cover loosely with plastic and set aside to rise for 15 minutes.

Slide the focaccia, still on the parchment, onto the hot stone. Bake until the crust is golden brown and puffed, about 20 minutes. Brush the dough with the remaining oil and sprinkle with the cheese or salt. Cut into wedges and serve at once.

IN ADVANCE You can roll out the dough well in advance of assembling the focaccia. Arrange it on a baking sheet on the parchment, wrap well in plastic wrap, and freeze until ready to use. Thaw in the refrigerator for 1 hour before baking.

Pissaladière (Provençal Onion Tart)

Pissaladière, a yeast dough topped with long-cooked sweet onions, anchovies, and tiny Niçoise olives, is sold by the slice in most bakeries in Nice and eaten out of hand as a snack or quick lunch. Classically the onions are cooked very slowly in a lot of olive oil until they melt to a near puree. To cut the oil to less than half the traditional amount, use sweet onions that have a naturally high water content: They literally melt as if they were steeped in oil. Once it has been baked, it can sit for several hours and be served at room temperature.

SERVES 8 AS AN APPETIZER, 4 AS A LIGHT LUNCH (WITH A SALAD)

- **2 tablespoons extra-virgin olive oil**
- **2 pounds Bermuda or Vidalia onions,** thinly sliced (7 cups)
- **2 large sprigs fresh thyme** or ½ teaspoon dried thyme
- **½ teaspoon kosher salt**
- **Freshly ground black pepper**
- **⅓ cup Niçoise olives,** pitted (see page 683)
- **1 pound Basic Pizza Dough** (page 355)
- **12 to 16 oil-packed anchovy fillets,** drained and sliced lengthwise in half

In a large heavy sauté pan, combine 1 tablespoon of the olive oil, the onions, thyme, and salt, cover, and cook over low heat, stirring occasionally, until the onions are a pale golden color and meltingly soft, almost a puree, about 1 hour. Uncover and continue to cook, stirring occasionally, until all of the liquid has evaporated. Remove the thyme sprigs, pepper generously, and set aside.

Preheat the oven to 375°F.

On a floured work surface, roll and pat the dough into a rough rectangle approximately 11 by 14 inches. Transfer it to an 11-by-14-inch baking pan and press it into the pan, making a slight lip at the edges. Prick the dough with a fork. Cover loosely and let rest for 15 minutes.

Spread the onions evenly over the dough. Arrange the anchovies in a criss-cross pattern on the onions. Place the olives decoratively on top.

Bake the pissaladière until the crust is crisp and golden, about 30 minutes. Drizzle with the remaining 1 tablespoon olive oil. Serve warm or at room temperature.

IN ADVANCE The onions can be cooked up to 2 days ahead; cover and refrigerate. The dough can be pressed into the pan and frozen, well wrapped, for up to 2 months. Thaw in the refrigerator for 1 hour before baking.

Rustic Garlic Toasts

SERVES 4 Coarse bread, grilled and rubbed with a cut clove of garlic and drizzled with extra-virgin olive oil, is a staple of Mediterranean cooking. It is the perfect accompaniment to soups, stews, and salads and can also be used as a base for Bruschetta (see page 369).

There are several methods of toasting the bread, depending on how many people you are serving and whether or not you want to heat up the oven. Brush the olive oil onto the bread rather than drizzling it on, a method that leaves flavor without excess. You could also use a flavored oil, such as Rosemary Oil (page 592), or melted butter.

4 ounces crusty peasant bread or baguette, sliced ¼ inch thick

1 tablespoon extra-virgin olive oil or unsalted butter, melted

2 garlic cloves, halved

½ teaspoon kosher salt

Oven method: Preheat the oven to 425°F. Arrange the bread slices on a baking sheet and, using a slightly dampened brush, brush both sides with the olive oil. Toast the bread in the oven for 2 to 3 minutes on each side, until browned. Rub each slice lightly with the garlic and sprinkle the salt on top.

Stove-top method: Heat a large cast-iron skillet over medium heat for 5 minutes, or until very hot. Using a slightly dampened brush, brush both sides of the bread slices with the olive oil. Arrange the bread in the pan and toast until the bottom side is golden, about 2 minutes. (Press the slices down if necessary with a metal spatula to brown the bottoms evenly.) Turn the bread over and toast the other side. Brush both sides of each toast lightly with the garlic and sprinkle with the salt.

Pan-grilled bread: This simple variation of the stove-top method re-creates the flavor, texture, and satisfaction of bread grilled over a wood fire (see page 265 for a discussion of different smoking media). When the pan is hot, sprinkle a scant 1 tablespoon smoking chips or place a 1-inch piece of grapevine in the bottom. Place a round footed rack in the skillet. When the chips or grapevine begins to smoke, arrange the oil-brushed bread on the rack, cover, and toast for about 3 to 4 minutes on each side, until golden. Brush the toasts with the garlic and sprinkle with the salt.

Bruschetta

Bruschetta are thick slices of grilled peasant bread rubbed with garlic and drizzled with olive oil, usually eaten with a savory topping such as fresh tomato sauce or a bean puree made from leftover beans as an hors d'oeuvre or snack. When I have leftover corn bread, I slice and toast it the same way I do the garlic toasts to make a sublime but unorthodox bruschetta spread with black olive paste.

To make bruschetta, prepare Rustic Garlic Toasts (page 368) and top each toast with one of the following:

Up to ¼ cup of
> **Uncooked Fresh Tomato Sauce** (page 654)
> **White Beans and Mellowed Garlic with Rosemary Oil** (page 102)
> **Roasted Wild Mushrooms** (page 40)
> **Tender Greens Sautéed with Garlic and Oil** (page 74)
> **Warm Olivada (Warm Crushed Olives)** (page 655)
> **Roasted Garlic** (page 38)
> **Slow-Roasted Tomatoes** (page 37)

or up to 2 ounces of
> **Thinly sliced prosciutto or bresaola (air-dried beef)**
> **Thinly sliced smoked salmon**
> **Ricotta salata cheese,** thinly shaved

Parmesan Crisps

These paper-thin wafers, based on the *frico* of Friuli, Italy, are spectacular appetizers. Grated Parmigiano-Reggiano cheese, stabilized with a minute amount of flour, is sprinkled into a hot nonstick pan to form a thin pancake of melted cheese that hardens into a lacy wafer with the clear, delicious flavor of the cheese. There is no added fat, and the cheese goes a long way: A single ounce yields a dramatic 9-inch disk that is wonderful with Champagne, wine, or cocktails. Broken up, it can also garnish salads, soups, and vegetable stews.

As with pancakes or crepes, it is best to experiment with the first one or two crisps, until you get a feel for the correct heat of the pan. Once you get the hang of it, you can make a whole batch in ten minutes. Use only real Parmigiano-Reggiano or another hard aged grating cheese, such as Montasio. Under no circumstances use domestic Parmesan.

8 ounces Parmigiano-Reggiano or aged Montasio cheese, grated (about 3 cups)

2 tablespoons plus 2 teaspoons all-purpose flour

1 teaspoon freshly ground black pepper or Ancho Chile Essence (page 543) or ½ teaspoon ground cumin or dried rosemary, or to taste

In a medium bowl, combine all the ingredients. Heat a heavy 10-inch nonstick skillet over moderate heat until hot but not smoking. Reduce the heat slightly. Using a soupspoon, a measuring cup, or a coffee cup, sprinkle 1 ounce (about ⅓ cup) of the cheese mixture evenly over the bottom of the skillet to make a thin lacy pancake: You should not be able to see the bottom of the skillet. You may have to adjust the heat; the cheese should sizzle when it hits the pan, but it should not smoke. Cook the crisp until the fine grains of cheese have melted together and the edges are just beginning to brown. Remove the pan from the heat and let sit for 30 seconds to 1 minute to set. If the crisp hardens too much, return the pan to the burner for a few seconds to warm it.

With a plastic spatula, gently lift the crisp up by one edge and slide it onto a wire rack to cool until hardened, about 3 minutes. Repeat with the remaining cheese mixture. When the crisps are completely cool, they can be carefully stacked and stored in a tin or box.

Serve the crisps whole or broken into large irregular quarters and arranged standing in a basket.

Free-form Parmesan crisps (oven method): This method is a little easier than the stove-top method, though the crisps aren't quite as charming looking. Success depends on using Silpat bakeware liners or other silicone baking mats (see page 27) to keep them from sticking to the baking sheet.

Preheat the oven to 400°F.

Place a 16½-by-11½-inch Silpat liner on each of two 17-by-13-inch baking sheets. Sprinkle the cheese mixture evenly over the liners to form a large sheet of cheese on each. Bake for 8 to 9 minutes, or until the crisps are bubbling and slightly puffy and the edges are golden. Let cool a minute or two, until the crisps are firm enough to slide off the liners onto a cutting board to cool. Cut into squares or rectangles with a chef's knife, or you can break the crisps into free-form shapes.

The crisps will keep for about 1 week in an airtight tin.

IN ADVANCE

Savory Rosemary Biscotti

MAKES 64 BISCOTTI

Biscotti, the hard lightly sweetened cookies meant for dipping in strong espresso, have gained enormous popularity during the past few years, in part because they contain little fat and are immensely satisfying. This recipe translates the basic notion of biscotti into a savory version using pine nuts, Parmigiano-Reggiano cheese, rosemary, and grappa—an adult biscotti that is perfect with cocktails.

4 ounces pine nuts (1 cup) **or walnuts** (about 1 cup)

2 teaspoons fruity extra-virgin olive oil

1 tablespoon plus 1 teaspoon minced fresh rosemary
or 1¼ teaspoons dried rosemary, crumbled

2 cups plus 2 tablespoons unbleached all-purpose flour

½ cup freshly grated Parmigiano-Reggiano cheese

¼ cup cornmeal

1 tablespoon plus 1 teaspoon sugar

1½ teaspoons baking powder, preferably nonaluminum

1 teaspoon baking soda

1½ teaspoons kosher salt

¼ teaspoon cayenne pepper

2 large eggs

3 tablespoons buttermilk or low-fat yogurt

1½ tablespoons grappa or cognac

Preheat the oven to 375°F.

Place the nuts on a baking sheet and roast them, tossing occasionally, until they are fragrant, about 7 minutes. Set aside to cool. Leave the oven on.

In a small skillet or saucepan, combine the oil and rosemary, cover, and heat over low heat until the oil is fragrant, about 2 minutes. Set aside.

Chop the pine nuts medium fine and transfer to a medium bowl. Stir in 2 cups of the flour, the cheese, cornmeal, sugar, baking powder, baking soda, salt, and cayenne.

In a small bowl, beat the eggs lightly with the buttermilk, grappa, and reserved rosemary oil. Make a well in the center of the flour mixture and pour in the egg mixture. With a fork, stir the mixture until a coarse dough forms. Using your hands, knead the dough until almost uniform.

Divide the dough into 4 parts. Cover 3 of them with plastic wrap.

Using just enough of the remaining 2 tablespoons flour to keep the dough from sticking to a work surface, roll the remaining piece of dough under your palms into a thin log, about 14 inches long. Transfer it to a nonstick cookie sheet, placing it on a diagonal if necessary to make it fit. Repeat with the remaining pieces of dough, spacing the logs 2 inches apart; use two cookie sheets if necessary.

Bake the logs for 20 minutes, or until lightly browned. Cool for 2 minutes.

With a serrated knife, slice the logs on a sharp diagonal into ½-inch slices. The biscotti will be chewy and somewhat crumbly at this point. You can leave them as is or bake them again to dry them out and make them brittle and crunchy. To do so, reduce the oven temperature to 200°F. Leave the oven door ajar for about 4 minutes to cool it down.

Arrange the slices on the cookie sheets, place in the oven, and let dry for 30 minutes, or until hard to the touch but not browned. Set the biscotti aside to cool and dry further for several hours, or overnight.

IN ADVANCE The biscotti will keep for several weeks in an airtight tin.

Rosemary
Buttermilk Biscuits
(page 374)

OLD-FASHIONED QUICK BREADS.

Biscuits, scones, muffins, and pancakes are immensely useful in our busy lives. Leavened without yeast, they need no rising time; you can mix their batters in minutes and bake them immediately.

Traditionally, quick breads are made of flour, flavorings, and egg in tandem with lots of butter, which gives them inimitable flavor and moist texture. To cut down on the butter, I generally rely on an old-fashioned technique: using buttermilk—a low-fat cultured milk product—which, teamed with baking soda, provides leavening and produces a very tender crumb. Buttermilk has a creamier flavor than low-fat milk, providing richness with few calories.

Rosemary Buttermilk Biscuits

**MAKES TWELVE
2½-INCH BISCUITS**

Because buttermilk stays fresh for many weeks when refrigerated, it can easily be kept on hand. Transfer it from the carton to a clean glass bottle to prevent it from picking up any off flavors. (For alternatives, see page 685.)

Good biscuits are fluffy and tender, qualities that comes from the special chemistry of butter, flour, and buttermilk. I cut the butter down to the minimum amount necessary—about a third that of traditional recipes—by adding a little sour cream to provide richness. To make up for the loss of some of the buttery flavor, I scent the biscuits with fresh rosemary. Serve these biscuits with baked ham, roast chicken, or corn chowder, or split and fill with savory fillings such as country ham and Cheddar cheese with chutney, or with honey, or use as a base for shortcake (with or without the rosemary). For classic buttermilk biscuits, just omit the rosemary.

2 cups sifted all-purpose flour, plus a little for rolling

2 teaspoons baking powder, preferably nonaluminum

½ teaspoon baking soda

1 teaspoon kosher salt

1 teaspoon minced fresh rosemary

2 ½ tablespoons cold unsalted butter

2 tablespoons regular sour cream

¾ cup buttermilk

In a medium bowl, combine the flour, baking powder, baking soda, salt, and rosemary. With a pastry cutter or 2 table knives, cut in the butter and sour cream until the mixture resembles very coarse meal. Make a well in the center and pour in the buttermilk. With a fork, stir until it just holds together. Gather the dough together and knead it in the bowl six or seven times.

On a lightly floured work surface, pat or roll the dough to a ½-inch thickness. Cut into rounds with a floured 2¼-inch cookie cutter or a thin inverted glass. Place the biscuits about 1 inch apart on an ungreased cookie sheet. Reroll the scraps and cut out more biscuits. Cover with waxed paper, refrigerate, and let rest for 20 minutes, or up to 2 hours.

Preheat the oven to 450°F.

Bake the biscuits for 12 to 14 minutes, until lightly browned. Serve hot.

IN ADVANCE Although they won't be quite as good as when fresh-baked, leftover biscuits can be stored for a day or two in a tightly sealed plastic bag. Reheat, wrapped in foil, in a 350°F oven for 15 minutes; or split and toast them. You can also freeze uncooked biscuits on a baking sheet, then store in a plastic bag for up to 1 month. Bake frozen biscuits 4 to 5 minutes longer.

Coriander-and-Orange-Scented Scones

These fragrant scones employ the technique of using buttermilk to achieve a tender crumb while using a good deal less butter than usual. Coriander and fresh orange zest, along with the small amount of butter, ensure lovely flavor.

MAKES 8 SCONES

Oil for the baking sheet

2 cups unbleached all-purpose flour, plus extra for kneading

2 teaspoons baking powder, preferably nonaluminum

½ teaspoon baking soda

2½ teaspoons ground coriander or 2 teaspoons coriander seeds, crushed in a mortar or spice grinder

1 teaspoon kosher salt

3 tablepoons sugar

4 tablespoons cold unsalted butter

¾ cup dried cherries, blueberries, or currants

1½ to 2 tablespoons grated orange zest

¾ cup buttermilk

Preheat the oven to 425°F. Brush a baking sheet lightly with oil and set aside.

In a medium bowl, combine the flour, baking powder, baking soda, coriander, salt, and sugar. With a pastry blender or two knives, cut in the butter until the mixture resembles coarse meal. Scatter in the cherries and orange zest. With a fork, stir in the buttermilk until just combined. Turn the dough out onto a floured work surface and knead it three or four times with floured hands.

Divide the dough into 8 equal portions and shape each into a ball. Place the balls of dough on the baking sheet with at least 2 inches between them. With a sharp knife, cut a cross in the top of each ball. Refrigerate for 15 minutes.

Bake the scones for 13 to 15 minutes, until golden brown.

IN ADVANCE

The scones are best when freshly baked, but they will keep, well wrapped, for up to 2 days. To refresh them, wrap in foil and heat in a 350°F oven for 15 minutes, or until warm. Or split and toast them.

Oat Bran Muffins with Dried Pears

Several years ago, oat bran had its fifteen minutes of fame when researchers thought they'd discovered its ability to lower cholesterol. Although many of the claims were exaggerated, oat bran has proven to be an excellent source of fiber, easily assimilated when baked in quick breads like these tender muffins redolent of spices, cider, and dried fruit.

When egg whites replace whole eggs in a batter, they often render baked goods rubbery and wan tasting. Here, however, a highly flavored batter with several tenderizing ingredients—honey, buttermilk, and oat bran—makes up for what the egg whites lack.

About 1 teaspoon oil for brushing the muffin cups

1¾ cups oat bran

¾ cup unbleached all-purpose flour

2 tablespoons granulated or light brown sugar

2 teaspoons baking powder, preferably nonaluminum

¾ teaspoon baking soda

1¼ teaspoons ground cinnamon

¼ teaspoon grated nutmeg

½ teaspoon kosher salt

½ cup finely chopped dried pears (5 to 6 halves, chopped with 1 teaspoon of the flour to keep them from sticking) or 1 small apple, peeled, cored, and cut into small dice

½ cup apple cider or orange juice

½ cup buttermilk

3 tablespoons wildflower or tupelo honey

3 large egg whites

2 tablespoons roasted hazelnut, walnut, or grapeseed oil

1 teaspoon pure vanilla extract

Preheat the oven to 375°F. Lightly grease eight ¾-cup muffin cups or line them with paper liners. Set aside.

In a medium bowl, combine the oat bran, flour, sugar, baking powder, baking soda, cinnamon, nutmeg, and salt. Add the dried pears (or apple) and toss to coat with the flour.

In a small bowl, combine the cider, buttermilk, honey, egg whites, oil, and vanilla. Whisk this mixture into the dry ingredients until just combined. Divide the batter equally among the prepared muffin cups.

Bake the muffins until they are golden brown, about 30 minutes; cover them with foil if they begin to brown too quickly. A knife inserted in the muffins should come out clean except for a few moist crumbs clinging to it; it should not be wet. Cool the muffins in the pans for about 10 minutes. Run a knife around the edges to release them if necessary and invert them onto a cooling rack; turn right side up and let cool for 5 minutes. Serve warm.

IN ADVANCE These are best when freshly baked, but they will keep, well wrapped, for up to 3 days. To refresh them, wrap them in foil and heat in a 350°F oven for about 15 minutes, or until warm.

Irish Brown Bread

MAKES 2 LOAVES, EACH SERVING 8 Throughout the southwestern part of Ireland, thick slices of coarse, chewy brown bread are served daily in pubs, restaurants, and homes to accompany meals and for tea. The bread has an immensely satisfying flavor and texture that belies its simple elements: a coarsely milled whole wheat flour called graham flour, buttermilk, and baking powder. Because the bread is made without yeast, it takes only a few minutes to make.

Although graham flour is not readily available in America, a combination of whole wheat and unbleached all-purpose flours, rolled oats, and oat bran approximates the Irish flour (this trick was devised by my mother, who has lived in Ireland for many years). It yields a flavorful bread that is high in fiber and low in calories and fat.

Brown bread is a lovely accompaniment to smoked salmon or Home-Cured Salmon (see page 276), salads, and soups. It is also delicious toasted for breakfast or tea.

> **About 2⅓ cups whole wheat flour**
>
> **1 cup unbleached all-purpose flour**
>
> **⅓ cup old-fashioned rolled oats**
>
> **⅓ cup oat bran**
>
> **2 teaspoons dark brown sugar**
>
> **1½ teaspoons kosher salt**
>
> **1 teaspoon baking powder,** preferably nonaluminum
>
> **1 teaspoon baking soda**
>
> **1¾ cups buttermilk**
>
> **3 tablespoons unsalted butter,** melted
>
> **About 1/2 teaspoon vegetable oil** to coat the pan or baking sheet

Preheat the oven to 400°F.

In a large bowl, stir together 2¼ cups of the whole wheat flour, the all-purpose flour, rolled oats, oat bran, brown sugar, salt, baking powder, and baking soda. With a fork, stir in 1½ cups of the buttermilk and the melted butter. Add more buttermilk, little by little, just until a soft but not too wet dough forms. (The amount of buttermilk needed will vary with the moisture content of the flour.) Knead the dough in the bowl until smooth, about 2 minutes. If the dough is too wet, knead in up to 4 teaspoons more whole wheat flour, 1 teaspoon at a time.

Divide the dough into 2 equal portions. You can bake the bread in traditional round loaves or in loaf pans, which make for more uniform slices.

For round loaves: Shape each portion of dough into a ball. Place 4 inches apart on a lightly oiled baking sheet and flatten slightly. Using a thin sharp knife, make 2 crisscrossing slashes on top of each loaf. (This allows the dough to expand evenly as it bakes.)

For rectangular loaves: Using a slightly dampened brush, brush about ¼ teaspoon oil into each of two 8-by-4-inch loaf pans, coating the bottoms and sides of the pans evenly. Shape each portion of dough into a log about the size of the loaf pans. Place a log of dough in each pan, patting it down gently to fill the pan. With a thin sharp knife, cut 3 or 4 lengthwise slashes, ½ inch deep, in the top of each loaf.

Bake the loaves for 30 to 35 minutes, or until a cake tester inserted in the middle comes out clean and, after the loaves have been removed from the pans, the bottom of the loaves sounds hollow when tapped. Place on a rack to cool.

To serve, slice into ¼-inch-thick slices.

IN ADVANCE Store the bread, well wrapped, at room temperature for up to 5 days. Or freeze in a heavy-duty plastic bag for up to 2 months.

The problem with most pancake and French toast recipes is the quantity of fat used both in the batter and in cooking. Some butter is essential, but the following guidelines make it easy to cut it to a minimum:

- Use a nonstick pan or griddle.
- Use clarified butter rather than plain melted butter to prevent it from burning.
- Use a brush to brush only a small amount of butter over the pan.
- Brush the tops of the cooked pancakes with a little melted butter rather than melting pats of butter on them.

Corn Blini

These light, crispy cornmeal cakes are my all-time favorite pancake. They have an affinity with both savory and sweet accompaniments. For breakfast, they are wonderful with maple syrup or a fruit sauce, along with some panfried country ham. Served as an hors d'oeuvre with sour cream and caviar or smoked fish and a glass of Champagne, they are celestial, the ideal festive snack on New Year's Eve.

MAKES 24 BLINI; SERVES 6

If possible, use a good stone-ground cornmeal or polenta meal, available at Italian markets. Using bacon fat instead of butter adds a wonderful down-home flavor.

> **1 cup stone-ground yellow cornmeal**
>
> **⅓ cup all-purpose flour**
>
> **1¼ teaspoons baking powder,** preferably nonaluminum
>
> **¼ teaspoon baking soda**
>
> **1 teaspoon sugar**
>
> **Scant ½ teaspoon kosher salt**
>
> **1½ cups buttermilk,** plus more if desired
>
> **1 large egg**
>
> **2 tablespoons plus 2 teaspoons melted unsalted butter or rendered bacon fat** (see page 681)

In a medium bowl, combine the cornmeal, flour, baking powder, baking soda, sugar, and salt. In a small bowl, beat together the buttermilk, egg, and 2 teaspoons of the melted butter. Whisk into the cornmeal mixture until very smooth. (For thinner blini, add a tablespoon or two more buttermilk to the batter.)

Heat a large heavy griddle or skillet over moderate heat until a drop of water bounces across the surface. Brush the surface lightly with melted butter. Drop the batter, 2 tablespoons at a time, onto the surface, leaving enough room for the pancakes to spread (the blini will be about 2 to 3 inches in diameter). Adjust the heat if necessary to keep butter from burning. Cook the blini until the surface is bubbled and set and the edges of the undersides are brown. Flip the blini and cook until the second side is browned.

Serve the blini as they come off the griddle, or keep them warm, layered in (and covered with) clean tea towels in a low (200°F) oven; just before serving, brush them with a little melted butter. Repeat until all the batter is used, brushing the pan with butter before each batch.

IN ADVANCE You can make the blini batter up to 2 hours ahead; cover and refrigerate.

variation **Cornmeal and Wild Rice Cakes.** Use the bacon fat rather than butter. Stir ⅔ cup cooked wild rice, blotted dry on paper towels, into the batter.

variation **Blueberry Cornmeal Cakes.** Add ½ cup blueberries to the batter.

French Toast

SERVES 2 French toast is panfried bread that is saturated in what is basically an egg-and-milk custard. The flavor of the egg custard is essential to the character of this simple preparation. When I read recipes that omit the eggs and milk by adding fruit juice to the batter, or use only egg whites, I rebel.

The abundance of fat and calories in French toast actually comes mostly from frying it in too much fat, then dousing it with butter and syrup—and eating slice after slice of it. In fact, 1 serving contains only about ½ egg and a couple of tablespoons of milk, which add a nice amount of protein to breakfast.

You can lighten French toast by using 2% fat milk and flavoring the egg-and-milk mixture with vanilla, orange zest, and a little cinnamon. Using a nonstick pan, you will need only 1 teaspoon of butter to fry the bread.

French toast is good with any number of toppings and syrups, from powdered sugar and lemon to crushed fresh raspberries.

The key to great French toast is exceptional bread, whether peasant bread, sourdough, or a good homemade sandwich loaf. The texture of the bread affects the outcome: Coarse peasant bread needs time to soak up the custard and will produce a toast that is appealingly chewy and robust. A softer bread will soak up the custard quickly and make a more traditional French toast with a creamy center.

> **1 large egg**
>
> **⅓ cup low-fat** (2%) **or whole milk**
>
> **½ teaspoon pure maple syrup**
>
> **½ teaspoon pure vanilla extract**
>
> **¼ teaspoon grated orange zest**
>
> **⅛ teaspoon kosher salt**
>
> **Pinch of ground cinnamon**
>
> **Four ⅓- to ½-inch-thick slices bread** (2 ounces)
>
> **2 teaspoons unsalted butter** or 1½ teaspoons clarified butter (see page 681)

In a shallow pan, combine the egg, milk, maple syrup, vanilla extract, orange zest, salt, and cinnamon and beat lightly with a fork to mix. Place the bread in the batter and poke holes in it with a fork to help it to absorb the liquid. Let sit for a minute or two, until the bottom is soft, then carefully flip the slices to coat and soak the other side. You may need to repeat the process with coarser breads and let them soak longer.

Heat a large nonstick skillet over moderately high heat. Add 1 teaspoon of the butter and tilt to coat the pan. When the butter stops sizzling and is fragrant, arrange the soaked bread in the pan. (You may need to fry the toast in batches, using more butter as necessary.) When the underside is cooked and brown, after 2 to 3 minutes, turn the slices over with a spatula, adding ¼ teaspoon of butter to the pan as you lift each one to flip it. Cook until the underside is deep brown, 2 to 3 minutes longer. Serve at once.

Chive French Toast. It occurred to me one day that French toast might | variation be just as delicious a savory as a sweet. So I tried adding minced chives to the unflavored egg-and-milk mixture and using challah, the soft Jewish egg bread. It was like the most wondrous of onion breads, crispy and fried on the outside, eggy and delicious inside. I serve it with lime-flavored sour cream and Home-Cured Salmon (page 276) for an unexpected brunch, or as is, cut into squares as an hors d'oeuvre to serve with drinks. It is also delicious made with coarser bread.

Replace the maple syrup, orange zest, and cinnamon with 1 tablespoon minced fresh chives. Increase the salt to ¼ teaspoon.

French Winter
Vegetable Soup
(page 402)

SOUPS

Even at their most refined, soups are nurturing. They provide a brand of comfort and nourishment like no other food. The following recipes are for some of my favorite soups. They use many techniques explained elsewhere in this book, such as pureeing roasted vegetables to achieve a creamy texture or infusing a broth with unexpected ingredients to deepen flavor. In several that traditionally have an abundance of cream and butter, I've reworked their chemistry to achieve a luxurious effect with much less fat. These soups range from simple to complex, thin to thick, subtle to intense; they illustrate, in a delicious way, the endless possibilities for improvising soups. All are substantial enough to be eaten as a main course.

CREAMY AND PUREED SOUPS. Cream soups, which classically contain upward of ½ cup of heavy cream (and 400 calories) per serving, are among the most luxurious savory foods. The abundance of cream illuminates flavors, as well as adding inimitable richness. Unfortunately, however, cream in such quantity not only contains a great deal of saturated fat, but it can be overwhelmingly filling. I prefer to make lighter versions of creamy soups by using a smooth, concentrated vegetable puree that is delicious as is. Adding a small amount of real cream gives the impression of a great deal more.

Leek, Potato, and Sometimes Sorrel or Watercress Soup

SERVES 4 This recipe makes one of the world's great soups—leek and potato—with the cream and butter pared down to a sane amount, just enough to lend the characteristic flavor and creaminess. The leek and potato base offers many options for improvisation. You can enjoy it as is, or flavor it further with fresh greens such as tart sorrel or peppery watercress. Adding the greens at the very last minute rather than cooking them with the base preserves their vivid green color and fresh flavor.

1 teaspoon unsalted butter

2 medium leeks (8 ounces), white and tender green parts only, thinly sliced, rinsed in several changes of water to remove the grit, and drained (1½ cups)

4 cups unsalted homemade (page 574) **or canned low-sodium chicken broth**

1 large white boiling potato (8 ounces), peeled and cut into ½-inch dice

¼ teaspoon sugar

Kosher salt

4 cups lightly packed sorrel leaves or 1½ cups lightly packed watercress leaves (optional)

2½ tablespoons heavy cream or crème fraîche

Freshly ground white pepper

⅛ teaspoon grated nutmeg

2 tablespoons chopped fresh chervil or flat-leaf parsley

1 tablespoon chopped fresh chives

Melt the butter in a heavy medium saucepan. Add the leeks, cover, and cook over low heat, stirring, until softened, about 5 minutes. Add the broth, potato, sugar, and salt to taste, partially cover, and bring to a boil. Reduce the heat and simmer until the potato is soft, 15 to 20 minutes. Remove from the heat.

In a food processor or blender, puree the soup in two batches, adding half the sorrel, if using, with each batch. Return the soup to the saucepan and whisk in the heavy cream, white pepper, and nutmeg. Reheat over moderate heat, stirring frequently. Sprinkle each serving with some of the herbs.

IN ADVANCE You can prepare the basic leek and potato puree, without the greens or cream, up to 4 days ahead; cover and refrigerate. Or freeze it for up to 2 months. Bring to a simmer and puree with the greens. To serve, return to the pan, add the cream, pepper, and nutmeg, and reheat.

Potato Soup with Cilantro and Cumin. This basic premise variation offers many possibilities for using different combinations of soft greens and herbs. Pureeing the leek and potato base with 1 cup packed fresh cilantro leaves and ¼ teaspoon ground cumin gives it a surprising and delicious flavor. Bear in mind that the intensity of herbs can vary greatly depending on the season—it's best to start with a smaller amount and add more to taste.

Root Vegetable Crema

This puree of root vegetables is adapted from one by Paul Bertolli when he SERVES 4 was chef at Chez Panisse in Berkeley, California. The root vegetables are slowly braised in water with a little butter, so the small amount of fat gives them a rich texture.

Although this soup is delicious as is, an optional tablespoon of heavy cream or crème fraîche per serving gives it a luxurious finish (even with this splurge, a serving weighs in at under 150 calories).

2 teaspoons unsalted butter

1 medium yellow or red waxy potato, thinly sliced (¾ cup)

1 small celery root, finely diced (¾ cup)

1 medium leek, white part only, thinly sliced and rinsed (¼ cup)

2 small parsnips, halved lengthwise, woody core removed, and finely sliced (½ cup)

2 garlic cloves, thinly sliced

1 sprig fresh thyme

¼ teaspoon kosher salt

¼ teaspoon sugar

⅔ cup water

3 cups unsalted homemade (page 574) **or canned low-sodium chicken broth**

Freshly ground white pepper

A few gratings of nutmeg (optional)

¼ cup heavy cream or crème fraîche, lightly whipped (optional)

Melt the butter in a medium saucepan over moderate heat. Add the potato, celery root, leek, parsnips, garlic, thyme, salt, sugar, and water and bring to a simmer. Cover and cook for 15 minutes, or until almost all the water has evaporated. Add the chicken broth, bring back to a simmer, cover, and cook for an additional 15 minutes, or until the vegetables are soft.

For the finest texture, puree the soup, in batches, in a blender. If you are using a food processor, let it run for at least 2 minutes. Strain the soup back into the saucepan. Season to taste with white pepper, nutmeg, and additional salt, if necessary. Swirl some of the cream, if using, into each serving.

IN ADVANCE You can prepare the soup 3 days ahead; cover and refrigerate. Or freeze it for up to 2 months.

variation **Root Vegetable Soup with Truffles.** Root vegetables have a special affinity for truffles. Pound all or part of a fresh black truffle to a paste in a mortar and add to the soup. A drizzle of white truffle oil is also divine.

Garlic Soup with Pasta and Ham

SERVES 4 Although I can't prove it, I am sure that garlic is a healing food, a balm to the soul when one's spirits are low, a strengthening blast to the immune system when getting a cold. This soup is garlic at its very best: elemental, deliciously mellow, and wondrously fortifying. If you have no truck with any of these rather personal notions of the healing properties of garlic, this soup, with its origins in French country cooking, will still prove a delight.

Masses of garlic are cooked in chicken broth until soft enough to puree. The soup is then garnished with some small pasta, country ham, and Parmigiano-Reggiano cheese. I sometimes drizzle it with a little heavy cream or crème fraîche or olive oil, for an additional 25 calories per serving (since the soup is extremely low in fat, this addition is still moderate). To make a thicker soup with a more delicate flavor, add ¼ cup of white rice to the broth once it comes to a boil; puree the soup in a food processor.

Alone, the mellow Garlic Broth makes an excellent soup base for bitter greens, beans, or potatoes (see Composed Soups, pages 396–400).

Garlic Broth

3 to 4 heads (8 ounces) **garlic**

7 to 8 sprigs fresh thyme or 4 fresh sage leaves

1 imported bay leaf

4 cups unsalted homemade (page 574) **or canned low-sodium chicken broth**

2 teaspoons fruity extra-virgin olive oil

¼ teaspoon sugar

Kosher salt

4 ounces small pasta shapes, such as shells, orecchiette, or gemelli

Freshly ground black pepper

1 to 2 tablespoons fresh lemon juice (optional)

2 ounces lean country-style ham or prosciutto, cut into thin slivers

1 ounce Parmigiano-Reggiano cheese, cut into thin slivers

1½ tablespoons heavy cream or crème fraîche or 2 teaspoons fruity extra-virgin olive oil (optional)

To make the broth, press down on the garlic to break the heads apart. Skin but don't peel the cloves. Tie the herbs together with a piece of kitchen string.

In a heavy medium saucepan, combine the garlic, herb bundle, broth, olive oil, sugar, and a pinch of salt. Bring to a boil over moderate heat. Reduce the heat, cover, and simmer until the garlic is puree-soft, about 35 minutes. Strain the soup, reserving the broth, and discard the herbs. Transfer the garlic to a plate and let cool.

Meanwhile, bring a medium pot of water to a boil. Salt well, add the pasta, and boil until it is al dente (tender but still slightly firm to the bite). Drain and cool down under cold running water. Drain again. Reserve.

To puree the soup, pass the soup and unpeeled garlic through a food mill. Or squeeze the soft garlic flesh out of the husks and process to a fine puree in a food processor or blender, gradually adding the reserved cooking liquid, and letting the processor or blender run until the puree is perfectly smooth.

If you have less than 4½ cups soup, add enough water to make that amount. Return the soup to the pan and adjust the seasoning, adding pepper and some lemon juice if necessary to sharpen the flavors. Bring the soup to a simmer. Add the ham and the reserved pasta, and heat through. Serve at once, adding the cheese to each bowl at the very last minute. Drizzle a little cream (or olive oil) over each serving, if desired.

You can prepare the soup, without the pasta, ham, cheese, or cream, up to 4 days ahead; cover and refrigerate. Or freeze it for up to 2 months. Just before serving, bring it to a boil, reduce to a simmer, and add the garnishes. **IN ADVANCE**

Garlic Soup with Poached Eggs and Other Savory Embellishments. *variation* This soup takes well to tortellini, baby ravioli, or gnocchi, or slices of toasted country bread lightly brushed with olive oil. You can add a large pinch of saffron, crumbled, when you are making the broth. Sometimes I omit the pasta and poach eggs (1 per serving) right in the soup.

Corn Soup with Chiles, Lime, and Cilantro Cream

SERVES 4 This is a wonderful soup for the height of summer, when corn is sweet and tender. The Mexican-inspired flavorings, including fragrant toasted cumin, chiles, and cilantro, seem magically to heighten its flavor. It is as thick and as rich as a stew, yet very low in fat. Its creaminess results from cooking the corn in a milk-based broth and pureeing some of the kernels at the end. Adding the scraped corncobs to the soup as it cooks extracts all the milky corn juice and adds more corn flavor.

6 ears fresh corn, shucked, or two 10-ounce packages frozen corn kernels, thawed

2 teaspoons olive oil

2 medium onions, chopped (2 cups)

3 to 4 garlic cloves, minced

2 serrano or jalapeño chiles, seeded and minced

1½ teaspoons cumin seeds

¾ teaspoon kosher salt

½ teaspoon sugar

2 cups unsalted homemade (page 574) **or canned low-sodium chicken broth**

2 cups whole milk

1½ ounces lean smoky ham, cut into 4 chunks

Cilantro Cream

> **¼ cup regular or reduced-fat sour cream**
>
> **¼ cup buttermilk**
>
> **¼ cup finely chopped fresh cilantro**
>
> **1 teaspoon minced fresh chives or scallions**
>
> **¼ teaspoon kosher salt**
>
> **¼ teaspoon sugar**

2 to 3 tablespoons fresh lime juice

Freshly ground black pepper

1 lime, sliced into 8 wedges

If using fresh corn, with a thin sharp knife, slice the corn kernels off the cobs into a large bowl. Scrape the cobs lengthwise to extract the juices. You should have 5 cups corn kernels. Reserve the cobs.

In a large heavy saucepan, combine the olive oil and onions, cover, and cook over low heat, stirring occasionally, until the onions are translucent, about 10 minutes. Stir in the corn kernels, cover, and cook for 4 minutes longer. Stir in the garlic, chile peppers, and cumin seeds and cook, stirring occasionally, for 2 minutes, or until the garlic is soft and the cumin is fragrant. Add the salt, sugar, chicken broth, and milk and nestle the ham and corncobs, if you have them, into the mixture (if the cobs are very large, break them in half). Bring to a boil, reduce the heat to moderately low, cover, and simmer for 20 to 30 minutes, until the corn is very tender. (Older or winter corn will take considerably longer than young summer corn.)

While the soup is cooking, prepare the cilantro cream: In a small bowl, whisk together the sour cream, buttermilk, cilantro, chives, salt, and sugar. Cover and refrigerate until ready to use.

Remove the corncobs and ham from the soup and discard.

In a food processor, process half of the soup to a fine puree. Add it to the remaining soup. Heat the soup, stirring, over moderate heat until it just reaches the boiling point. Add lime juice and pepper to taste. Serve at once, spooning about 2 tablespoons of the cilantro cream into the center of each serving. Pass the lime wedges separately.

IN ADVANCE You can make the soup, without the lime juice or Cilantro Cream, up to 5 days ahead; cover and refrigerate. Or freeze it for up to 3 months.

Spicy Coconut Milk Soup

SERVES 6 In this Thai-inspired soup, unsweetened coconut milk is infused with pungent Southeast Asian flavors—lemongrass, kaffir lime leaf, and ginger—to make a spicy aromatic base that can be embellished any number of ways at the last minute. You can cook shrimp, squid, scallops, or chicken breasts right in the broth, or simmer shards of leftover roasted pork, or grilled poultry or seafood in it with some cooked noodles. With the addition of potatoes, leeks, and other root vegetables, it makes a wonderful vegetable soup.

In Southeast Asian dishes, coconut milk plays a role similar to heavy cream to make them rich and satisfying, while providing subtle coconut flavor, at 23 calories per tablespoon, about half the calories of heavy cream.

Although some of these ingredients seem exotic, they can be found at almost any Asian grocery and many supermarkets. If you can't find fresh lemongrass and kaffir lime leaf, dried versions work fine in this soup; or lime zest can be substituted for the kaffir lime. Thai fish sauce and chile paste are condiments that keep indefinitely.

4 cups unsalted homemade (page 574) **or canned low-sodium chicken broth or bottled clam juice**

1½ cups canned unsweetened coconut milk (not coconut cream)

½ cup water

¼ cup Thai or Vietnamese fish sauce (nam pla or nuoc nam)

¼ cup fresh lime juice

2 tablespoons plus 1 teaspoon sugar

1½ stalks fresh lemongrass, white bulb only, bruised and thinly sliced, or 3½ tablespoons dried lemongrass, in a tea infuser

2 kaffir lime leaves or 2 teaspoons grated lime zest

One 2-inch piece fresh ginger, peeled and thinly sliced

2 to 3 teaspoons Thai or Chinese red chile paste or 1 small serrano or jalapeño chile, minced

1 pound raw shellfish or poultry, such as peeled and deveined medium shrimp or shucked scallops, or skinless boneless chicken breasts, sliced crosswise into ½-inch strips, or squid, cleaned and cut into ¼-inch rings, tentacles left whole

½ cup fresh cilantro leaves

In large saucepan set over moderate heat, combine the chicken broth, coconut milk, water, fish sauce, lime juice, sugar, lemongrass, lime leaves, and ginger. Bring to a simmer, cover partially and cook for 15 minutes.

If using dried lemongrass, remove the tea infuser. Add the chile paste and the shellfish or poultry, and simmer until tender, 3 to 5 minutes. Garnish with the fresh cilantro.

You can make the coconut milk base up to 4 days ahead; cover and refrigerate. Just before serving, bring to a simmer and finish the recipe. IN ADVANCE

Roasted Pumpkin and Garlic Soup

Here is an utterly simple recipe using the concentrated flavors and intense, melting texture of roasted pumpkin, and which yields an exceptionally creamy soup when pureed with chicken broth. It is delicious as is, sublime with the addition of a small amount of heavy cream or crème fraîche. SERVES 4

When I can find it, I like to use kabocha squash, a squat striated green winter squash increasingly available in supermarkets, for this recipe. Its flesh is extremely creamy.

> **2 pounds sugar pumpkin or winter squash,** such as kabocha, butternut, or acorn
>
> **½ teaspoon olive oil**
>
> **1 head garlic**
>
> **2 cups unsalted homemade** (page 574) **or canned low-sodium chicken broth**
>
> **3 tablespoons heavy cream or crème fraîche** (optional)
>
> **¾ teaspoon kosher salt**
>
> **Freshly ground black pepper**
>
> **1 to 2 teaspoons fresh lemon juice**
>
> **¼ cup chopped fresh flat-leaf parsley or basil**

Preheat the oven to 350°F.

Cut the pumpkin in half and scoop out the seeds. Brush the cut sides with oil and place cut side down on a heavy baking sheet. Sprinkle 2 tablespoons water onto the pan. Pull the loose papery skin off the garlic, keeping the head intact, and wrap it in a sheet of foil. Place the baking sheet and the foil packet in the oven and bake for 40 minutes, or until the squash is puree-tender and the garlic gives when the package is pressed. Set aside until cool enough to handle, about 20 minutes.

With a spoon, scoop the flesh out of the pumpkin into the bowl of a food processor. Separate the garlic cloves and squeeze the soft pulp into the work bowl. Process the mixture to a fine puree. With the motor running, drizzle in the chicken broth and process until perfectly smooth.

Transfer the soup to a medium heavy saucepan set over moderate heat and bring to a simmer, stirring frequently. Whisk in the cream, salt, and pepper to taste. Stir in enough lemon juice to taste to balance the flavors. Simmer for 1 minute, and serve. Scatter the herbs over each serving.

IN ADVANCE The soup will keep, covered, in the refrigerator for about 1 week and can be frozen for up to 2 months.

variation **Herbed or Spiced Pumpkin and Garlic Soup.** The soup takes well to many flavorings, such as spice mixtures or herbs. Heat the puree with any of the following: 2 to 3 teaspoons Sandy's Curry Powder (page 548) or commercial garam masala, or 1 to 2 teaspoons ground cumin, or a mix of: 1 teaspoon each ground coriander and sweet paprika, ½ teaspoon ground cumin, and ¼ teaspoon ground caraway seeds. Garnish with ¼ cup chopped fresh cilantro instead of the parsley.

Roasted Tomato Soup with Herb Cream

SERVES 4 When tomatoes are roasted slowly at a low temperature, their flavor becomes very concentrated and their texture dense and creamy. When they are pureed, even mediocre dead-of-winter plum tomatoes make a smooth rich soup that tastes like summer. The cool herb cream mellows the intense flavor of the soup.

Herb Cream

½ cup regular or reduced-fat sour cream

2 tablespoons minced fresh herbs, such as chives, basil, cilantro, or tarragon

2 teaspoons vinegar: cider, white wine, or Champagne

Pinch of kosher salt

Freshly ground black pepper

3 tablespoons finely chopped shallots

1 teaspoon extra-virgin olive oil

1¾ cups Slow-Roasted Tomatoes (page 38)

About 2¾ cups unsalted homemade (page 574) **or canned low-sodium chicken broth**

Kosher salt and freshly ground black pepper

To make the herb cream, combine the sour cream, herbs, vinegar, salt, and pepper in a small bowl. Cover and refrigerate for at least 30 minutes to mellow the flavors.

In a small skillet set over low heat, cook the shallots, covered, in the oil until they are soft and just beginning to brown, about 7 minutes. Remove from the heat.

Combine the tomatoes and shallots in a blender or food processor (you may have to work in two batches) and, with the motor running, drizzle in the chicken broth until the soup is as thick as you like, with a vibrant tomato flavor. Strain, if desired, through a coarse strainer. (Alternatively, you can pass the tomatoes through a food mill, then blend in the shallots and chicken broth.)

Pour the soup into a medium saucepan and heat over moderate heat until hot. Season to taste with salt and pepper.

Ladle the soup into four warm soup bowls, and swirl the herb cream into the center of each.

The soup (without the herb cream), can be refrigerated, covered, for up to 4 days or frozen for up to 2 months. IN ADVANCE

COMPOSED SOUPS. A composed soup is a broth to which a variety of elements is added. You can make marvelous composed soups by pairing any of the broths on pages 568 to 582 (such as quickly made fennel broth or curry-infused chicken broth) with roasted vegetables, pasta, cooked dried beans, herbs, greens, or cooked meat, poultry, or seafood. The possibilities are endless; the resulting soup will be determined by the amount of time you have and what ingredients are on hand.

Composed Soups

A GUIDE TO IMPROVISING

SERVES 4

This method suggests the approximate proportions for a soup for 4 people. The quantity of broth will depend upon the kinds of elements you are adding. Soups containing a protein and some greens will need only about 1 cup broth per serving. Soups with starchy ingredients like beans, grains, pasta, and root vegetables, which will absorb a good amount of the broth, need 1½ to 2 cups broth per serving.

If you don't have time to make a broth, you can just simmer low-sodium canned chicken broth with a rind from Parmigiano-Reggiano cheese, smashed garlic cloves, or herbs (see Infused Broths, page 578).

4 to 8 cups broth of your choice (pages 568–582), such as Fennel Broth, Garlic Broth, Curry and Fennel Seed Broth, or Celery Root Broth

4 to 8 cups raw or cooked vegetables, beans, or grains, in any combination, such as diced fresh tomatoes, wild mushrooms, roasted peppers, roasted vegetables, or sautéed onions, leeks, or garlic; up to 4 cups can be drained cooked beans, pasta, or coarse kernel grains such as barley, farro, or wild rice

8 ounces to 1 pound cooked lean protein (optional), such as chicken, beef, lamb, shrimp, ham, or roast pork or lamb, shredded or cut into bite-sized pieces

4 cups coarsely chopped cleaned greens (optional), such as spinach, arugula, Swiss chard, tatsoi, Chinese cabbage, mizuna, or watercress

Garnishes (optional), singly or in combination, such as

2 to 4 tablespoons minced fresh herbs, such as flat-leaf parsley, basil, cilantro, chives, or chervil

1 tablespoon or more extra-virgin olive oil or Flavored Oil (pages 588–597), about ¾ teaspoon to drizzle over each serving

1 to 2 teaspoons fennel or cumin seeds, toasted in a small skillet until fragrant

1 to 2 ounces aged cheese, such as Parmigiano-Reggiano, pecorino Toscano, Manchego, or Fiore Sardo, thinly shaved

Rustic Garlic Toasts (page 368)

1. In a large heavy saucepan, bring the broth to a simmer over moderate heat.

2. Add the additional components—vegetables, protein, and greens—in order, according to how much time they will need to cook or heat through.

3. Garnish each serving as desired.

Miniature Ravioli, Olives, and Herbs in Celery Root Broth

improvisation 1

I made this simple, satisfying soup one day with what I had in an almost empty fridge. Leftover Celery Root Broth, an unexpected treasure, became the catalyst for some long-keeping foods I always have on hand: olives, Parmigiano-Reggiano cheese, and frozen miniature cheese ravioli.

In a medium saucepan, bring 5 to 6 cups Celery Root Broth (page 568) to a boil over high heat. Add 8 ounces miniature cheese ravioli and simmer until tender. Add ½ cup chopped fresh flat-leaf parsley, chives, basil, or chervil and 12 black olives, such as Kalamata, pitted (page 683) and coarsely chopped. Scatter shaved Parmigiano-Reggiano (2 ounces total) over each serving.

Impromptu Roasted Vegetable Soups

improvisation 2

Roasted vegetables, with their rich caramelized flavors, give character to a soup, making it hearty and comforting. Of the many possible combinations of roasted vegetables and complementary broths, the following are my favorites. Follow the Guide above, figuring on about 1 cup of broth and 1 cup roasted vegetables per serving.

Roasted Winter Squash Slices (page 35) in **Star Anise Broth** (page 581)

Roasted Wild Mushrooms (page 40) in **Garlic Broth** (page 580)

Sweet onions roasted with thyme (page 34) in **Faux Veal Broth** (page 572), with shredded or shaved Gruyère cheese

Peppers Roasted with Garlic and Anchovies (page 42) in **Fennel Broth** (page 568)

Roasted Root Vegetable Hash (page 44) in **Curry and Fennel Seed Broth** (page 581)

Steam-Roasted Fennel with Pancetta and Juniper (page 58) in **Parmesan Broth** (page 580)

Soothing Japanese Noodle Soup

SERVES 4

Flavorful dashi, made from two long-keeping Japanese pantry staples, can be used as a quickly made broth to improvise simple seafood soups, embellished with snipped fresh herbs.

This soup is based on dashi, the delicate Japanese broth made from shavings of dried bonito (a small tuna) and kombu, a flavorful seaweed. It is both sustaining and comforting. This is an easy soup to make and a great staple recipe, since almost all the ingredients are dried and can be kept on hand in the pantry. Stripping it down to its bare bones, you could even get by without the ginger and lemon. If you don't want to make the dashi from scratch, you can buy decent instant dashi, although it tends to be somewhat saltier than homemade.

This soup is wonderfully mutable. You can use many kinds of Japanese noodles, and add many other elements as you want: cooked sliced chicken, salmon, shrimp, spinach, or vegetables such as carrots and turnips, as well as tofu.

Kombu, dried bonito shavings, instant dashi, tamari, mirin, Japanese noodles, and shiso leaves are available at health food stores and Asian grocery stores.

Dashi

1 ounce kombu (kelp)

5 cups water

1 ounce dried bonito shavings

¼ **cup tamari or other mild soy sauce,** preferably reduced-sodium

2 tablespoons mirin (sweet cooking wine)

One 1-inch knob fresh ginger, peeled and thinly sliced

2 teaspoons sugar

Kosher salt

8 ounces dried buckwheat or green tea noodles

2 to 3 ounces shiitake mushrooms tough stems removed and thinly sliced, **or enoki mushrooms,** tough stem ends removed (optional)

1 to 2 tablespoons fresh lemon juice, or more to taste

4 thin lemon slices

2 scallions, thinly sliced on a diagonal

2 tablespoons slivered Japanese shiso leaves or a combination of fresh basil and mint or flat-leaf parsley (optional)

To make the dashi, place the kelp and water in a medium saucepan and slowly bring to a simmer over medium-low heat, about 10 to 15 minutes.

Remove the kelp with tongs and discard. Remove the pan from the heat and add the bonito shavings. Do not stir. When the bonito has sunk to the bottom, after a minute or two, strain the broth through a fine strainer. Press the bonito to extract all the liquid, then discard.

Return the dashi to the saucepan. Stir in the tamari, mirin, ginger, and sugar. Bring to a simmer over low heat and keep warm.

Meanwhile, bring a large pot of water to a boil. Salt well, add the noodles, and boil until the noodles are al dente (tender but still slightly firm to the bite). Drain and rinse quickly with cold water to remove excess starch; drain again.

Add the noodles to the broth, along with the mushrooms, if desired. Simmer for 1 to 2 minutes to heat through. Stir in the lemon juice.

Divide the soup evenly among 4 warm soup bowls. Garnish each with a lemon slice, some scallions, and herbs, if desired.

You can make the dashi up to 4 days ahead; keep it, covered, in the refrigerator. **IN ADVANCE**

Beans and Wild Mushrooms in Fennel Broth

SERVES 4 In this splendid hearty soup, the aromatic Fennel Broth mellows the earthiness of the wild mushrooms, pancetta, and beans. Many other broths work well here too, such as simple chicken or veal broth, Celery Root Broth (page 568), Faux Veal Broth (page 572), or Garlic Broth (page 580).

1 ounce pancetta or thick-sliced bacon, cut into ¼-inch dice (scant ¼ cup) or 1 tablespoon extra-virgin olive oil

1 large onion, quartered lengthwise, then thinly sliced crosswise (2 cups)

3 small parsnips, peeled and diced (optional)

5 to 6 cups Fennel Broth (page 568) **or other broth of your choice**

2 ounces wild mushrooms, such as oyster, shiitake, bluefoot, chanterelle, or morel, stems trimmed, sliced or quartered

2 cups drained cooked white beans, such as navy, Great Northern, baby limas, or flageolets (see page 92)

¼ cup minced fresh herbs, such as flat-leaf parsley, basil, chervil, or chives

In a medium nonstick skillet set over low heat, cook the pancetta slowly, covered, stirring occasionally, until it has rendered its fat and is crisp, about 8 minutes. With a slotted spoon, remove the pancetta and drain on paper towels.

Add the onion to the pan, cover, increase the heat slightly, and cook until it has released its liquid, about 5 minutes. Uncover and sauté until the liquid has evaporated and the onion is golden, about 5 minutes longer. If you are using parsnips, add them now with ½ cup water, cover, and simmer until they are tender, about 6 minutes. Add the broth, mushrooms, and beans, bring to a simmer, and cook until the mushrooms are tender and the beans are hot, about 7 minutes.

Just before serving, stir in the herbs.

IN ADVANCE The soup will keep, covered, in the refrigerator for about 5 days.

RUSTIC SOUPS. These one-pot soups are the kind you might find while traveling through the countryside of Italy, southern France, or Latin America: unfussy combinations of coarsely cut vegetables, beans, and herbs, whose rich juices and abundant fiber coalesce into something akin to a stew. They are easy to make, at once comforting and nourishing, and perfect for feeding a crowd.

Simple Summer Soup with Pesto

This lovely soup is a pared-down version of the elaborate vegetable soups of the Italian and French Riviera. Made with water rather than broth, it retains the very clear, fresh flavor of each vegetable. Pesto, made without pine nuts, is added at the last minute, for an explosion of fragrance.

SERVES 4 AS A (GENEROUS) MAIN COURSE, 8 AS A FIRST COURSE

> **1 pound fresh shell beans,** shelled (1 cup), or 4 ounces (½ cup) dried cannellini or Great Northern beans, soaked overnight in warm water
>
> **1 shallot,** peeled
>
> **3 sprigs fresh thyme**
>
> **1 imported bay leaf**
>
> **2 quarts water**
>
> **2 teaspoons kosher salt,** plus more to taste
>
> **3 large leeks** (about 1 pound), white and pale green parts only, thinly sliced and rinsed to remove any grit (2 cups)
>
> **1 pound zucchini and/or yellow summer squash,** cut into ½-inch dice (3½ cups)
>
> **12 ounces green beans,** ends removed and cut into ¾-inch pieces (about 3 cups)
>
> **Pinch of sugar**
>
> **1 pound** (4 medium) **ripe tomatoes,** peeled, seeded, and diced (1½ cups)
>
> **Freshly ground black pepper**
>
> **Pesto Sauce for Soups** (page 623)

In a large heavy saucepan, combine the beans, shallot, thyme, bay leaf, and water. Bring to a simmer over moderate heat and cook, adding the salt halfway through, until the beans are tender, about 30 minutes for fresh shell beans, 45 to 60 minutes for dried beans.

Holding a strainer over a large measuring cup, drain the beans, reserving the cooking liquid.

Return the cooking liquid, along with the bay leaf, to the pan and add enough water to make 6 cups. Bring to a simmer. Add the leeks, zucchini, green beans, and sugar and simmer for 10 minutes. Add the tomatoes and continue cooking until the vegetables are tender, about 10 minutes longer. Stir in the cooked beans and simmer for 5 minutes. Add salt and pepper to taste.

Ladle the soup into large soup bowls. Invite your guests to spoon some of the pesto into their soup.

IN ADVANCE Because the green vegetables fade, the soup is best the day it is made. You can, however, cook the beans up to 2 days ahead; reserve the cooking liquid and the beans separately, covered, in the refrigerator. About 30 minutes before serving, bring the cooking liquid to a simmer and proceed as directed.

French Winter Vegetable Soup

SERVES 6 This recipe is a model for a classic winter vegetable soup. It has a purity of flavor that can be achieved only by using water as the cooking medium, rather than broth. After half an hour or so of cooking together, the flavors of the vegetables coalesce into a thick savory soup that is both nourishing and comforting. A little olive oil is incorporated to add body and harmonize flavors.

This recipe has infinite permutations: You can include or substitute other vegetables or add a chunk of smoky ham or herbs. I often add shredded cooked chicken or lamb, thin slices of smoked duck, or cooked dried beans to make it more substantial. You can also pass grated sheep's milk cheese or Parmigiano-Reggiano on the side. Sometimes I pound fresh herbs, such as basil, chervil, and flat-leaf parsley, with small amounts of stronger herbs, such as thyme and rosemary, in a mortar with a little olive oil to spoon into the soup rather than the plain olive oil (see Guide, page 589).

Serve the soup with pan-grilled Rustic Garlic Toasts (page 368) and mesclun salad.

6 cups water

3 tablespoons extra-virgin olive oil

2 teaspoons kosher salt

1 medium onion, cut into ¼-inch dice

2 medium Yellow Finn or Yukon Gold potatoes (about ¾ pound), peeled and cut into ¼-inch dice

3 medium leeks, white and pale green parts only, thinly sliced and rinsed to remove grit

3 to 4 medium carrots (8 ounces), peeled and cut into ¼-inch dice

3 medium parsnips (6 ounces), peeled and cut into ¼-inch dice

2 medium turnips or ½ rutabaga (8 ounces), peeled and cut into ¼-inch dice

1 small celery root (8 ounces), peeled and cut into ¼-inch dice

1 small fennel bulb, trimmed, cored, and cut into ¼-inch dice

2 garlic cloves, smashed

Freshly ground black pepper

In a large heavy saucepan, bring the water, 2 tablespoons of the olive oil, and salt to a boil. Add the vegetables and garlic and simmer, half covered, until the vegetables are very tender, about 30 to 35 minutes. Pepper liberally.

Ladle into bowls and drizzle about ½ teaspoon of the remaining olive oil over each serving.

The soup will keep for up to 4 days, covered, in the refrigerator.

IN ADVANCE

Basic Bean Soup and Many Embellishments

A GUIDE TO IMPROVISING

You can make this classic bean soup with just about any bean, from white beans, such as baby limas and navy beans, to hearty red beans, such as rattlesnake beans and Jacob's cattle. Each serving contains very little fat, since it takes only a small amount of pancetta or bacon to flavor 8 servings.

The soup is delicious as is, although I like to use it as a base for further embellishments. Less assertively flavored soups made with tender beans, for instance, white beans, such as cannellini or navy, combine best with many kinds of flavorings and garnishes that also provide a visual contrast. For an exciting garnish, spoon some chopped cooked vegetables, such as Slow-Roasted Tomatoes (page 38) or "Fried" Artichokes with Crispy Garlic and Sage (page 66), into the center of each serving.

SERVES 8

No matter how simply or elaborately you embellish a bean soup, adding a drizzle of fruity extra-virgin olive oil and a few shavings of aged sheep's milk cheese to each serving will always bring it to new heights.

Basic Bean Soup

1 ounce lean pancetta or thick-sliced bacon, cut into ¼-inch dice (scant ¼ cup) or 1 tablespoon extra-virgin olive oil (you can add a chunk of lean smoked ham or prosciutto for flavor, if desired)

1 medium onion, finely chopped

1 medium carrot, peeled and finely chopped

2 garlic cloves, chopped

1 pound (about 2½ cups) **dried beans,** such as baby limas, navy, cannellini, flageolets, pinto, rattlesnake, Jacob's cattle, or borlotti, soaked overnight in water to cover by 2 inches

6 to 8 cups unsalted homemade (page 574) **or canned low-sodium chicken broth**

1 small serrano or jalapeño chile, seeded and deribbed, or ¼ teaspoon red pepper flakes

2 imported bay leaves

½ teaspoon sugar

1½ teaspoons fine sea salt

Flavorings (optional), such as

2 to 3 tablespoons chopped pungent fresh herbs, such as rosemary, thyme, savory, or sage

½ cup Roasted Garlic Puree (page 38)

1 pound peppery greens, such as mustard, turnip, or arugula, tough stems removed, cleaned, and dried

Freshly ground black pepper

Embellishments (optional), singly or in combination, such as

2 tablespoons fruity extra-virgin olive oil or Flavored Oil (pages 588–597)

1 cup chopped mild fresh herbs, such as basil, cilantro, chives, flat-leaf parsley, or chervil

2 ounces aged hard cheese, such as Parmigiano-Reggiano, Fiore Sardo, or Manchego, thinly shaved or grated

2 cups cooked vegetables (to be spooned into the center of each serving), such as

Slow-Roasted Tomatoes (page 38)

Roasted Root Vegetable Hash (page 44)

"Fried" Artichokes with Crispy Garlic and Sage (page 66)

Peperonata (page 63)

Steam-Roasted Fennel with Pancetta and Juniper (page 58)

Roasted Wild Mushrooms (page 40)

"Fried" Onions (page 62)

1. In a large heavy saucepan or a Dutch oven, over low heat, cook the pancetta, if using, covered, stirring occasionally, until it has rendered its fat and is fairly crisp, about 15 minutes; with a slotted spoon, transfer the pancetta to a bowl. Or, if using olive oil, heat it over low heat.

2. Add the onion, carrot, and garlic to the pan, cover, and cook, stirring frequently, until the vegetables are soft but not browned, about 15 minutes. Drain the soaked beans and add to the pan, along with 6 cups of the broth, the chile pepper, bay leaves, sugar, and cooked pancetta, if using.

3. Bring to a simmer, partially cover, and cook until the soup begins to thicken and the beans are soft, about 1¼ to 1½ hours, adding as much additional chicken broth as necessary to achieve the consistency you prefer. After 1 hour of cooking, stir in the salt. During the last half hour of cooking, stir in any flavorings you wish. Season the soup with pepper.

4. To serve, ladle the soup into warm soup bowls. Add any embellishments as desired.

Herb-Infused "Crema" with Olive Paste

improvisation 1

Basic Bean Soup is easily transformed into a velvety "crema" by pureeing it until perfectly smooth in a food processor or blender. Simmer the pureed soup with 4 imported bay leaves, soaked in lukewarm water for 5 minutes, or 4 sprigs fresh rosemary, until it is pleasantly perfumed with the herbs; then remove the herbs. Swirl about 1 teaspoon of commercial or homemade black olive paste (see page 683) into each serving at the last minute. Pass freshly grated Parmigiano-Reggiano on the side and serve with Rustic Garlic Toasts (page 368).

Lentil Soup with Ginger

improvisation 2

Substituting lentils for the beans changes Basic Bean Soup into a classic lentil soup. I like to use the tiny French lentilles du Puy, which keep their shape and add a more interesting texture than standard brown lentils. There is no need to soak them. To make an unusual gingered lentil soup, in Step 2, use olive oil (with no ham) to sauté the onions and carrots. After 7 minutes, add 2 tablespoons or more minced fresh ginger. In Step 3, use 8 cups chicken broth and 2 cups water. Cook until the soup is thick and the lentils are very tender, 45 minutes to 1 hour. As the lentils absorb the liquid, stir in enough hot water to keep them soupy. If you want a more intense ginger flavor, add another tablespoon or two of minced ginger in the last 5 minutes of cooking.

Chicken and Vegetable Stew
with Cilantro, Cumin, and Saffron

SERVES 4 Maria Robledo, whose photographs grace this book, is from Manizales, Colombia. Her mother, Letitia, taught me to make this stew, called *sancocho*, during one of her visits to New York. Infused with cilantro, cumin, and saffron, it is truly the national dish of Colombia. Families commonly eat it at least once a week and on holidays, often cooking it outdoors over a wood fire. It is rich, filling, and rather caloric due to the starchy yuca, potato, and plantain. It is also extremely healthful, high in fiber, vitamins, minerals, and protein. The soup is made entirely without fat except for the chicken's skin (which adds flavor to the stew and is removed after cooking). Sliced ripe avocado, the traditional garnish for sancocho, adds the only other fat, but one that's extremely healthful. Fresh plantains and yuca are available at Latin American groceries and some supermarkets. Frozen yuca, from Goya, is sold in some supermarkets.

Letitia leaves the chicken pieces whole when she serves the soup. Some of my guests have found it easier to eat if the meat is pulled off the bone, although you can skip that step if you wish.

Saffron-Cilantro Broth

9 cups unsalted homemade (page 574) **or canned low-sodium chicken broth**

1 large onion, thinly sliced

5 garlic cloves, smashed

1 large bunch fresh cilantro (about 6 ounces), ¾ cup leaves removed and reserved for garnish, the remaining sprigs tied together with kitchen string

½ teaspoon cumin seeds, crushed

Large pinch of saffron threads

Kosher salt and freshly ground black pepper

One 3-pound chicken, cut into 8 pieces, back and neck reserved

4 to 5 small new potatoes (12 ounces), peeled and cut into ¾-inch slices

12 ounces fresh or frozen yuca, peeled and cut into ¾-inch slices

12 ounces carrots, peeled and cut into ¾-inch slices

1 green or barely yellow plantain (with no black spots), peeled and cut into ¾-inch slices

2 ears corn, shucked and cut into 1½-inch rounds

1 ripe avocado, peeled, seeded, and sliced (optional)

To make the broth, in a large heavy pot, combine the chicken broth, onion, garlic, tied cilantro, and cumin. Crumble in the saffron and bring to a boil. Reduce the heat to low and simmer for 10 minutes. Season with salt and pepper. Add the chicken thighs, legs, back, and neck and simmer for 15 minutes (do not allow the broth to boil). Add the breasts and wings and simmer until all the meat is barely cooked through, about 10 minutes longer. Remove from the heat and remove the chicken pieces from the broth; set aside until cool enough to handle. Discard the cilantro and chicken back and neck.

Skin the chicken. If desired, pull the meat off the bones; reserve. Skim the fat from the broth. Coarsely chop the reserved cilantro leaves.

Bring the broth to a simmer. Add the potatoes, yuca, carrots, and plantain and simmer over moderate heat for 10 minutes. Add the corn and chicken and simmer until the vegetables are tender and the chicken is heated through, about 8 minutes longer (if the chicken is off the bone, add it 3 minutes after adding the corn). Adjust the seasoning.

Ladle the soup into large bowls, and garnish with the avocado, if using, and the chopped cilantro.

IN ADVANCE The broth (without the vegetables) and the chicken can be prepared up to 4 hours ahead. Cover the broth and wrap the chicken well; refrigerate. Let the chicken come to room temperature for 1 hour before finishing the soup. The sancocho will keep for 4 days, covered, in the refrigerator.

Farm-stand salad of mild, peppery and bitter greens, herbs, and edible flowers (page 413), dressed with Lemon Vinaigrette with a Little Garlic (page 607), Niçoise olives, and sheep's milk cheese

SALADS

Many people see salad as their dietary salvation. Greens and vegetables, a salad's most basic ingredients, are generally so healthful, so low in calories and fat, so full of fiber and vitamins, and their texture is so satisfying to eat that we think, "This is something I can eat with abandon." And it is, almost. The danger is the dressing, the very element that makes a salad complete and ties all the elements together into a delicious whole. A good dressing makes a salad sing; without one, it is dry and dull. So, we pile the dressing on, not realizing that 1 tablespoon can add 100 calories to the 25 of the virtuous vegetables we thought we were consuming.

Making healthful salads with dressings that impart the most flavor possible means using fats judiciously and creatively. In this chapter are my solutions for a broad range of salads, from simple mixed greens and vegetable salads to main-course salads. They are the salads I rely on and eat on almost a daily basis because I can, truly, eat them with abandon.

LEAFY SALADS. Every day in my supermarket it seems another lettuce becomes available. I can buy organically grown mesclun—the mélange of baby lettuces so beloved in France—peppery watercress and arugula, mild Buttercrunch, and even mâche, the delicate lettuce that tastes faintly of rose petals, as well as herbs such as mint, basil, tarragon, and chives. Because many of these greens are grown hydroponically or in greenhouses, they are available year-round. There is no reason not to be eating marvelous salads every day, especially if you know a few tricks for selecting and caring for greens.

If you were to separate out the different leaves in a bowl of mesclun, you would find an array of lettuces and herbs, each of which provides a distinct flavor and texture. The list below gives you an idea of the range of possibilities you have to make your own mixes. You might use just two or three lettuces, or a mélange of herbs (page 415).

Mild and Tender Lettuces. Oak-leaf lettuce, lollo rossa, Bibb, Boston, crisphead (homegrown iceberg), mâche (corn salad), spinach, romaine, amaranth, tatsoi.

Peppery or Pungent Greens. Arugula, watercress, garden cress, baby turnip or mustard greens, radish sprouts, Chinese cabbage, mizuna, shungiku, Tuscan kale, Russian kale.

Bitter Greens. Radicchio (both red and Treviso), chicory, curly endive and frisée, Belgian endive, escarole, Sugarloaf, baby beet, dandelion.

Herbs. Basil, flat-leaf parsley, mint, cilantro, chervil, tarragon, borage, hyssop, lovage.

Special Greens. Fennel tops, nasturtium leaves, purslane (miner's lettuce), pea shoots.

Edible Flowers. Nasturtium, violet, pansy, borage, pot marigold, lavender, chrysanthemum, hollyhock, daisy, daylily, geranium, English primrose, rose, clary sage, European elder.

From spring through autumn, local farmers' markets and farm stands, and even some supermarkets, are great sources for unexpected greens that can jazz up just about any salad. When I feel like improvising, I toss whole leaves, flowers, or bite-sized sprigs of exotic greens into basic mesclun or mixed green salads.

HOW TO CLEAN SALAD GREENS

A salad spinner is absolutely essential to making a good salad. Watery greens dilute flavors and become soggy. A water bath followed by a vigorous spin, though, can revive even tired wilted greens and make them taste fresh-picked.

Pick over the greens, removing and discarding tough stems or blemished or wilted leaves. Wash in several changes of water. The best way to do this is to place a colander, or the perforated bowl of a salad spinner, in a large bowl. Fill the bowl with water, add the lettuces, and swish them gently around. Then lift the colander out of the bowl, so that you leave the grit behind in the water. Rinse out the bowl and repeat as often as necessary until the greens are perfectly clean. Drain the greens, then spin them dry in a salad spinner.

Loosely wrap the greens in lightly dampened paper towels or a clean tea towel, place in a plastic bag, and seal it. Refrigerate. The greens will keep from 5 to 14 days, depending on how fresh they were to begin with.

Many people, including professional cooks, overdress salads. Heavy-handedness with salad dressing obscures the clear flavors of the salad itself and adds unnecessary fat, negating the salad's low-fat virtues. Generally speaking, it takes only about 1½ to 2 teaspoons of a vinaigrette to dress 2 cups of greens. In this quantity, even a standard full-fat vinaigrette will add only 45 to 50 calories.

For salads composed of delicate greens, choose a dressing that won't overwhelm them, such as Champagne Herb Vinaigrette (page 608), Classic Mustard Vinaigrette (page 608), or Everyday Vinaigrette (page 606). With salads made up mainly of lettuces with peppery or bitter flavors, use more robust, intensely flavored dressings, such as Nut Oil Vinaigrette (page 607), Rustic Olive Vinaigrette (page 609), or warm Vinaigrette with Roasted Poultry, Meat, or Game Juices (page 607). Other vinaigrette recipes can be found on pages 603 to 617.

To Dress a Salad for Four. Place the prepared salad ingredients in a large bowl. Figure on 8 cups washed and dried greens or herbs. Drizzle with 2 to 3 tablespoons of a vinaigrette and toss to coat. Add enough salt and pepper so that the salad has a vivid flavor, without being salty. Serve at once.

Herb Salad

This tart salad of pungent herbs and peppery and bitter greens tastes like the salads you find in Greece and Turkey, where wild herbs and dandelion grow in abundance. They are always dressed with lemon and good olive oil, which harmonize the flavors into a refreshing and immensely satisfying salad. I make this in spring and summer when young tender-leafed greens are available. Embellished with black olives, sharp sheep's milk cheese such as feta or ricotta salata, and Rustic Garlic Toasts (page 368), it makes a lovely first course or light lunch.

Because herbs are so intensely flavored, an abundance of one or another in a salad can throw off the flavor balance. Follow the proportions in this recipe to get the hang of it, then improvise on your own. A general approach to improvising is to start with a base of tender, moderately peppery and bitter greens, for example, frisée and arugula (about 8 cups total), to which you can add ⅓ cup or more snipped herbs, such as tarragon, parsley, chervil, chives, sorrel, and dill, tasting as you go along until you get the flavors right.

Garlic Dressing

1 garlic clove, cut lengthwise in half

2 teaspoons fresh lemon juice

Pinch of kosher salt

1 tablespoon plus 1 teaspoon fruity extra-virgin olive oil

1 teaspoon hot water

4 cups (2 ounces) **arugula leaves,** torn into bite-sized pieces

1½ cups (1½ ounces) **watercress leaves and tender stems**

1½ cups (2 ounces) **escarole,** torn into bite-sized pieces

½ cup packed mizuna or frisée leaves

½ cup packed fresh flat-leaf parsley leaves

¼ cup packed small fresh basil leaves

¼ cup bite-sized sorrel leaves

¼ cup (2 ounces) **purslane sprigs,** tough stems discarded (optional)

20 fresh tarragon leaves

10 whole small fresh sage leaves or 5 large, torn into small pieces

5 chives, cut into ⅛-inch pieces

Freshly ground black pepper

Rub the cut side of one of the garlic halves over the inside of a large salad bowl. Add the lemon juice and salt. Spear both garlic halves on a dinner fork. Using this as a whisk, drizzle in the olive oil and then the hot water, whisking constantly until it is an intensity of garlic you like. Discard the garlic.

Add the greens and herbs and toss well. Grind some black pepper over the salad, toss again, and serve.

IN ADVANCE You can prepare the greens up to 4 hours ahead. Wash, spin dry, and store in a plastic bag in the refrigerator.

Classic Green Salad with Russian or Blue Cheese Dressing

You can make this 1950s and 1960s American classic with a creamy blue cheese or Russian dressing that doesn't add hundreds of calories to the meal. My versions of these dressings are based on sour cream and buttermilk.

Separate the leaves of 1½ pounds Bibb (Buttercrunch) lettuce or romaine hearts (the tender pale green leaves in the center of the head). Wash and spin dry. Arrange the leaves on four chilled salad plates. Drizzle 3 tablespoons Russian Dressing (page 631) or Roquefort or Maytag Blue Cheese Dressing (page 632) over each and top with chopped fresh chives, flat-leaf parsley, or chervil. (Serves 4.)

Peppery or Bitter Greens with Seasonal Fruits and Roasted Nuts

A GUIDE TO IMPROVISING

Tender greens with somewhat assertive flavors, such as peppery arugula and watercress or bitter endive, young dandelion, or the Herb Salad mixture (page 415), go wonderfully with sweet citrus fruits like oranges, mandarins, and blood oranges, ripe pears or crunchy apples, and figs. Roasted nuts bring out the sweetness in the greens. There are endless possible variations on this theme. One of my favorites is arugula, blood oranges, and roasted pine nuts. Or, for an easy main-course luncheon salad, combine frisée, quartered ripe figs, and walnuts, then top it with thin sheets of prosciutto or smoked goose breast.

8 cups (about 12 ounces) **trimmed, cleaned, and dried peppery or bitter greens,** such as arugula, watercress, frisée, Belgian endive, or radicchio

Fruits, such as

1 medium ripe pear or apple, peeled, cored, and sliced

4 ripe figs, cut into quarters

2 navel or blood oranges, peeled and sectioned (see page 677)

3 mandarin oranges, tangerines, or clementines, peeled and sectioned

8 kumquats, sliced crosswise into paper-thin slices

Sherry Vinaigrette

1 teaspoon sherry vinegar

½ teaspoon balsamic vinegar

Pinch of kosher salt

1 tablespoon plus 1 teaspoon extra-virgin olive oil

2 teaspoons water or juice from sectioned citrus fruits

Freshly ground black pepper

2 to 4 tablespoons coarsely chopped roasted nuts, such as pine nuts, pecans, walnuts, or hazelnuts

1. Put the greens in a large bowl and scatter the fruit over them.

2. In a small bowl or a jar with a lid, combine the sherry vinegar, balsamic vinegar, salt, olive oil, and water. Stir or shake vigorously to emulsify. Drizzle the dressing over the salad and toss to coat, seasoning liberally with pepper.

3. Scatter the nuts over the top. Serve at once.

Belgian Endive with Apples, Walnuts, and Blue Cheese

SERVES 4 Bitter Belgian endive, tart-sweet apples, and walnuts have great affinity for blue cheeses such as French Roquefort or our own Maytag Blue, made in Wisconsin. This elegant salad can be served as a first course or as a salad and cheese course after the entrée. Because the cheese is very pungent, only a very small amount is necessary.

> **6 heads** (about 1½ pounds) **Belgian endive,** cleaned and dried
>
> **1 medium tart apple or ripe pear,** peeled and cored
>
> **3 tablespoons Nut Oil Vinaigrette** (page 607) made with roasted walnut oil
>
> **Freshly ground black pepper**
>
> **1 ounce blue cheese,** such as Roquefort or Maytag, crumbled (¼ cup)
>
> **1 ounce roasted walnuts,** coarsely chopped (⅓ cup)

Remove any browned outer leaves from the endive heads. Slice each head lengthwise in half; then slice each half lengthwise in half again. Cut out the core at the base of each wedge, separate the leaves, and place in a salad bowl. Slice the fruit lengthwise into quarters, then slice each quarter crosswise into thin slices and add to the endive.

Drizzle the dressing over the endive and fruit and toss. Pepper generously. Sprinkle the crumbled blue cheese over the salad, followed by the walnuts. Serve at once.

RAW VEGETABLE SALADS AND SLAWS. Raw vegetable salads include simple summer tomato salads, slaws, chopped salads, and creamy cucumber salads. They are among the most refreshing and healthful of salads, due to the crisp textures, natural juiciness, and abundance of fiber of cut vegetables. In fact, their juices become part of the dressing, eliminating the need for a lot of oil or cream. They can often do double duty in a meal, acting both as a sauce to grilled meats, poultry, and fish and as a side dish.

Salads with Shaved Parmesan

SERVES 4

Paper-thin shavings of excellent Parmigiano-Reggiano atop thinly sliced raw vegetables lightly dressed with lemon, garlic, and olive oil is a common antipasto in northern Italy. The cheese not only enhances the flavors of the vegetables, like some extraordinarily delicious salt, but "completes" the dish with flavorful protein. A half ounce per serving is ample.

Many vegetables are wonderful dressed this way, alone or in combination, but my favorites are fresh fava beans, thinly sliced celery or raw fennel, and arugula. You can also add thinly sliced red radishes for color. Because these salads are so simple, every ingredient must be perfect—especially the olive oil. The same approach also works well with cooked vegetables and beans.

Lemon-Garlic Dressing

1 garlic clove, cut lengthwise in half

1 tablespoon plus 1 teaspoon fresh lemon juice

Pinch of kosher salt

Pinch of sugar

2 tablespoons fruity extra-virgin olive oil

2 teaspoons water

4 cups (about 12 ounces) **prepared raw vegetables or greens** (see page 420), such as

2 large fennel bulbs

1 bunch celery

3 pounds fava beans

2 large bunches arugula

Freshly ground black pepper

2 ounces Parmigiano-Reggiano or pecorino Romano cheese

Rub a medium bowl with the cut garlic clove; discard. Add the lemon juice, stir in the salt and sugar, then whisk in the olive oil and water. Add the vegetables or greens and toss to coat. Pepper generously. Divide the salad among four salad plates. Shave the cheese directly over each and serve at once.

To prepare fennel: Using scissors, snip enough fine feathery fronds from the fennel stalks to measure 6 tablespoons. Cut off and discard the green stalks, or save for another use (see Fennel-Roasted Fish, page 219). Quarter each fennel bulb lengthwise through the root. Cut out the core. Using a thin sharp knife or a mandoline or vegetable slicer, cut each fennel quarter lengthwise into paper-thin slices.

To prepare celery: Pull the stalks apart and trim the ends. With a vegetable peeler, remove the tough strings. Using a thin sharp knife or a mandoline or vegetable slicer, thinly slice the celery on an extreme diagonal.

To prepare fava beans: Use your thumb to break open the pods along the seam and dislodge the beans inside. The beans have a thin membrane that can easily be removed if you first loosen the skins by blanching them. Cook the beans in rapidly boiling water for 2 to 3 minutes, depending on the size. Drain the beans and cool them under cold running water to stop the cooking. Use your thumbnail to break open the skin at one end of each bean and peel it back. Press the bean gently and the bean will pop right out. Discard the skins.

To prepare arugula: Because commercially grown arugula has very soft leaves, it deteriorates quickly once washed, so be sure to wash it within 1 hour of serving. Remove the tough stems and bathe it gently in several changes of cold water to remove any grit. Spin dry in batches in a salad spinner. Place in a serving bowl and cover with a damp towel until ready to use.

IN ADVANCE You can prepare the vegetables (not the arugula) up to 3 hours ahead; cover and refrigerate. Prepare the dressing up to 1 hour before serving.

Julienned or Grated Raw Vegetable Salads

A GUIDE TO IMPROVISING

The classic French grated vegetable salads called *râpes* are kin to American slaws. Traditionally these are made from julienned or grated crunchy vegetables such as carrots, celery root, and beets, dressed with a vinaigrette. The basic formula invites improvisation: combining several kinds of vegetables, using jazzy vinaigrettes or flavored oils, or adding nuts, apples, or herbs. You can taste and add elements as you go.

A mechanical slicer such as a mandoline or Benriner with a julienning blade makes quick work of cutting the vegetables.

About 5 cups julienned or shredded raw crunchy vegetables, singly or in combination, such as celery root, parsnips, turnips, rutabaga, fennel, carrots, cabbage (green, red, or Chinese), red or yellow bell peppers, or beets (beets are best used alone, as they will color other vegetables)

3 tablespoons vinaigrette (pages 603–617), such as Everyday Vinaigrette, Nut Oil Vinaigrette, Citrus Vinaigrette, Classic Mustard Vinaigrette, or Lemon Vinaigrette with a Little Garlic, or a vinaigrette made with Flavored Oil (pages 588–597) and cider vinegar

Kosher salt and freshly ground black pepper

Handful of chopped fresh flat-leaf parsley

Additions (optional), singly or in combination, such as

 ¼ **cup finely chopped red onion,** soaked in ice water for 10 minutes and drained

 1 crisp tart apple, peeled, cored, and julienned (toss with a few teaspoons fresh lemon juice to prevent browning)

 ½ **cup** (2½ ounces) **roasted nuts,** such as pecans, walnuts, or hazelnuts, coarsely chopped

 2 to 3 teaspoons finely julienned or grated orange or lemon zest (Meyer lemons are particularly lovely)

 2 to 3 tablespoons chopped fresh herbs, such as chives, basil, or tarragon

1. In a large bowl, toss the julienned vegetables together with the vinaigrette and salt and pepper to taste. Let stand for 30 minutes.

2. Adjust the seasoning. Stir in the parsley and any optional additions, tasting as you add to determine quantities.

Celery Root, Fennel, and Apple Salad with Slivered Lemon Zest and Hazelnuts

improvisation 1

This is one of my favorite raw vegetable salads, which I make when fragrant Meyer lemons are in season. In addition to the zest, I add little pieces of the sweet-tart flesh—bitter white pith removed. Follow the Guide on page 421, using roughly 4 cups julienned celery root and 1 cup julienned fennel. Use Nut Oil Vinaigrette (page 607) made with hazelnut oil. Add the apple and hazelnuts.

Grated Summer Beet Salad

improvisation 2

Make this delicate salad in late summer with the different kinds of young beets that appear in the market then, from classic purple to yellow to rosy Chioggia. If you are using several colors of beets, dress them and arrange them in separate piles on a platter so the colors don't bleed together. Omit the vinaigrette and season them simply with 2 tablespoons fine extra-virgin olive oil and salt and pepper, adding lemon juice to taste. This salad is best eaten within an hour of grating the beets, because some beets become bitter upon standing.

AN INSTANT ANTIDOTE FOR WINTER SALAD DOLDRUMS

Winter can be the doldrums for making salad. Herbs and lettuces are but shadows of their summer selves, and there is a limited range of great raw ingredients to choose from. From November to May, I rely on a treasure that sporadically appears in produce markets to inspire my winter salads. California-grown Meyer lemons, intensely perfumed, taste like an exotic lemony tangerine and have a mildly tart flesh, far sweeter than regular lemons. You can use their juice in place of all or part of the vinegar or citrus juice in salad dressings; mixed with some fine extra-virgin olive oil or nut oil, kosher salt, pepper, and a pinch of sugar, it makes an utterly simple and delicious dressing that is good on just about any salad. The best part is the zest, where most of the fragrance resides. Strip it off with a vegetable peeler and slice into thin slivers with a paring knife. Toss the slivers and juice with cooked drained beans and grains, julienned root vegetable and cabbage slaws, roasted vegetables and greens, both raw and cooked. Meyer lemons will keep for 2 weeks stored uncovered in the refrigerator.

Classic Coleslaw

SERVES 6

This coleslaw recipe rolls several Southern slaws into one, while fudging the fattening ingredients. Most slaw recipes feature dressings with at least ½ cup mayonnaise, close to 1,000 calories in fat alone. This recipe uses less than 1 tablespoon of sour cream per person and low-fat buttermilk to produce a creamy slaw at enormous savings of calories and fat. You can flavor the slaw in any number of ways, from the classic celery seed to horseradish or fresh herbs.

Serve this slaw as a cool counterpoint to rich ham or pork dishes, as well as with grilled seafood or poultry.

Buttermilk Slaw Dressing

> ¼ cup plus 1 tablespoon regular or reduced-fat sour cream
>
> ¼ cup buttermilk
>
> 1 tablespoon cider vinegar
>
> 1 teaspoon Worcestershire sauce
>
> 2 to 4 dashes hot sauce
>
> 1 ¼ teaspoons sugar
>
> ½ teaspoon kosher salt
>
> ½ teaspoon freshly ground black pepper

1 small head cabbage (1 pound), tough outer leaves removed

¼ cup chopped Vidalia or Bermuda onion

¼ cup chopped fresh flat-leaf parsley

Flavorings (optional), such as

> **1 teaspoon celery seed or caraway seed**
>
> **½ to 1 tablespoon prepared horseradish,** drained
>
> **2 tablespoons chopped fresh basil or chervil**

In a small bowl, whisk together the sour cream, buttermilk, vinegar, Worcestershire sauce, hot sauce, sugar, salt, and pepper. Set aside.

Quarter the cabbage; cut out the core. With a mandoline or vegetable slicer, or a thin sharp knife, slice lengthwise into ¼-inch-wide shreds.

In a large bowl, toss the cabbage with the onion, parsley, and dressing, adding any flavoring you wish. Serve, or cover and refrigerate.

IN ADVANCE

You can make the dressing up to 1 day ahead; cover and refrigerate. You can shred the cabbage up to 5 hours ahead; cover and refrigerate. The slaw can be assembled up to 1 hour ahead.

Celery Root "Rémoulade"

SERVES 6

This adaptation of one of the most famous and beloved of French salads, *céleri rémoulade*—shredded or julienned raw celery root dressed with a mustardy mayonnaise—uses a low-fat base of buttermilk and sour cream, with no loss in flavor.

Although traditionally served as a first course, this also makes an unusual main-course salad when topped with rich meats and seafood, such as thin slices (3 to 4 ounces per serving) of cured ham, smoked duck breast, or smoked salmon, or chunks of chilled steamed lobster or crabmeat. You can also make a lovely and surprising variation of this salad by replacing the celery root with 4 chayote squashes, peeled, seeded, and julienned on a mandoline or vegetable slicer.

> **1 medium celery root** (about 1¼ pounds)
> **1 small green apple**
> **2 tablespoons fresh lemon juice**
> **Double recipe Mustard Cream** (page 628)
> **Freshly ground black pepper**

Pare the celery root and cut it into quarters. Peel, halve, and core the apple. Using the large holes on a hand grater, or a mandoline or vegetable slicer with a fine julienne blade, or a food processor, coarsely grate or julienne the celery root and apple. Immediately toss with the lemon juice in a medium bowl to coat completely and prevent browning. Stir in the dressing and toss to coat. Pepper liberally. Serve, or cover and refrigerate.

IN ADVANCE Store the salad, covered, in the refrigerator for up to 2 days.

Cucumbers with Curry Cream

SERVES 4

This salad can double as a cool sauce for delicate dishes, such as Slow-Roasted or Pan-Smoked Salmon (page 224 or 268), or cold grilled chicken, shrimp, lobster, and crabmeat.

2 seedless cucumbers (1½ pounds), peeled and thinly sliced (about ⅛ inch thick)

2 teaspoons kosher salt

Curry Cream

> **1 tablespoon Sandy's Curry Powder** (page 548) **or commercial curry powder**
>
> **1 tablespoon hot water**
>
> **¼ cup regular or reduced-fat sour cream**
>
> **¼ cup buttermilk**
>
> **1 to 2 teaspoons vinegar:** cider, white wine, or Champagne
>
> **¼ teaspoon grated fresh ginger** (optional)
>
> **½ to 1 teaspoon sugar,** or to taste
>
> **⅛ teaspoon kosher salt**
>
> **Freshly ground black pepper**
>
> **¼ cup chopped fresh cilantro**

Place the cucumbers in a colander set in a bowl and toss gently with the 2 teaspoons salt. Cover with ice cubes and refrigerate for 1 hour, or until the cucumbers have released some of their water.

To make the curry cream, in a small heavy skillet, toast the curry powder over low heat until fragrant, about 1 to 2 minutes. Transfer to a small bowl and stir in the hot water. Let sit for 5 minutes.

Toasting curry powder and other dry spices gently in a dry skillet heightens their flavors.

Whisk in the remaining ingredients, except the cilantro. Refrigerate for at least 30 minutes to mellow the flavors.

Discard the ice cubes and rinse the cucumbers in cold water to remove the salt; pat dry with paper towels.

Arrange the cucumber slices on a platter. Spoon the curry cream over them and garnish with the cilantro.

You can prepare the Curry Cream up to 1 day ahead; cover and refrigerate.

IN ADVANCE

Cucumbers with Chive Cream. Omit the curry powder, ginger, and cilantro and stir 2 tablespoons finely minced fresh chives (or other minced fresh herbs, such as basil, tarragon, or mint) into the sour cream.

variation

The Best Tomato Salad

In the height of summer, when tomatoes are at their best at farmers' markets and farm stands, you can make salads using several kinds of tomatoes: red beefsteaks, yellow tomatoes, and an array of cherry and grape tomatoes, some as small as peas.

Slice 1 pound ripe tomatoes (halve cherry or grape tomatoes) and arrange them on a platter. Up to 20 minutes before serving (but no longer, or the tomatoes will lose too much of their juices), season the tomatoes with a scant ½ teaspoon kosher salt (if the tomatoes are not quite ripe, use ¼ teaspoon sugar as well). Just before serving, drizzle with 1½ tablespoons excellent fruity extra-virgin olive oil. If you like, add some snipped fresh herbs, such as basil, tarragon, cilantro, chervil, chives, or flat-leaf parsley, in any combination, and/or 2 tablespoons balsamic vinegar. (Serves 4.)

Moroccan "Gazpacho" Salad

SERVES 4

This refreshing chopped salad shares many ingredients and a juicy crunch with a Spanish gazpacho, but with Moroccan flavors. If you pulse it a few times in a food processor with a splash of sherry or red wine vinegar (without feta cheese), it does, in fact, become a great soup.

1 garlic clove, smashed and halved lengthwise

3 tablespoons fresh lemon juice

1 teaspoon kosher salt, or more to taste

½ teaspoon sugar

1½ tablespoons fruity extra-virgin olive oil

1 pound cucumbers: 4 medium kirby cucumbers or 1 English seedless cucumber

1½ pounds ripe red and/or yellow tomatoes

2 red or yellow bell peppers or 1 of each (¾ pound), seeded, cored, and cut into ¼-inch dice (2 cups)

1 small Vidalia or Bermuda onion or red onion, finely diced (⅔ to ¾ cup)

¾ cup chopped fresh cilantro, basil, mint, and/or flat-leaf parsley, in any proportion

Pinch of crushed toasted cumin seeds

2 ounces (¼ cup) **green olives,** pitted (see page 683) and chopped (optional)

1½ ounces feta cheese, crumbled (optional)

Freshly ground black pepper

Rub a medium bowl with the cut clove of garlic and leave the garlic clove in the bowl. Add the lemon juice, salt, and sugar. Whisk in the olive oil. Let steep until the dressing tastes as garlicky as you like, then discard the garlic. (You can leave the garlic in the bowl when you add the vegetables to flavor it more; just remember to discard it so that you won't bite into raw garlic when eating the salad.)

Peel the cucumbers, halve lengthwise, and scoop out the seeds with a teaspoon. Slice the halves lengthwise into ¼-inch strips and then crosswise into ¼-inch dice. Add to the bowl.

Cut the tomatoes crosswise in half. Squeeze out the juices and seeds. Cut the tomatoes into ¼-inch dice. Add to the bowl, along with the peppers, onion, cilantro, cumin seeds, and olives and feta, if using. Toss to coat. Season liberally with pepper and adjust the salt. Serve, or let stand at room temperature until ready to serve.

IN ADVANCE You can dice the cucumbers and peppers up to 1 day ahead; store them separately in a plastic bag in the refrigerator. The salad can be assembled up to 2 hours before serving.

Chopped Salad from the '21' Club

SERVES 6 When I was growing up in the 1950s my mother used to make a salad that was served at New York's '21' Club: diced vegetables—carrots, celery, cucumbers, tomato, onion, and peppers—mixed with Russian dressing and tossed with little bits of American cheese. She always served the salad with hamburgers or the mammoth two-inch-thick sirloin steaks my father used to grill on the hibachi. Like a fifties version of salsa, it was a perfect accompaniment to the sauceless steak.

More than forty years later, I still find this salad wonderful, with its slightly corny flavors. Instead of the mayonnaise-based Russian dressing, I substitute one with much less fat, made with sour cream and buttermilk. Extra-sharp Vermont Cheddar has such an intense flavor that much less cheese is required. The salad is also good with Dry Jack cheese.

The recipe can easily be multiplied many times.

¼ cup regular or reduced-fat sour cream

3 tablespoons buttermilk

3 tablespoons prepared chili sauce

½ teaspoon prepared horseradish, drained

¾ teaspoon kosher salt

2 large carrots, peeled and cut into ⅓-inch dice (1 cup)

1 red or yellow bell pepper, cored, seeded, and cut into ⅓-inch dice (1 cup)

1 medium cucumber, peeled, seeded, and cut into ⅓-inch dice (1 cup)

2 celery ribs, peeled to remove tough strings and cut into ⅓-inch dice (1 cup)

2 medium tomatoes, halved crosswise, seeds and juice squeezed out, and cut into ⅓-inch dice (1 cup)

1 small Vidalia or Bermuda onion, cut into ¼-inch dice (½ cup)

2 ounces extra-sharp Vermont Cheddar cheese or Dry (aged) Jack cheese, cut into ⅛-inch dice (½ cup)

Freshly ground black pepper

In a small bowl, stir together the sour cream, buttermilk, chili sauce, horseradish, and salt. Cover and refrigerate until you are ready to mix the salad.

Toss the vegetables and cheese together in a medium bowl. Cover and refrigerate until ready to serve.

Just before serving, spoon the dressing over the salad and toss to coat. Adjust the seasoning to taste.

IN ADVANCE You can make the dressing, dice the cheese, and prepare all the vegetables except the onion and tomato up to 1 day ahead; cover and refrigerate. (You can store the vegetables together in a plastic bag.)

Southeast Asian Slaw

Here is a kind of Asian slaw that Margot Wellington, a fearless, intuitive cook, SERVES 8 uses as sauce, condiment, and salad with grills or roasts, to cool and refresh the palate. The lemongrass-flavored dressing of pungent Thai fish sauce tempered by sugar, rice vinegar, and lime juice is a perfect balance of salty, sweet, and acid that seems to enhance any combination of the vegetables listed below. The vegetables should be shredded or finely julienned; a food processor or a mandoline or vegetable slicer makes this quick work. This recipe can be scaled up or down to serve more or fewer people. Figure on about 2 teaspoons dressing and 1 tablespoon cilantro for every cup of vegetables.

Lemongrass Dressing

2½ to 3 tablespoons fresh lime juice (juice of 1 to 2 limes)

2 tablespoons Thai or Vietnamese fish sauce (nam pla or nuoc mam)

1 tablespoon rice wine vinegar

1½ teaspoons Asian sesame oil

1 tablespoon plus 1 teaspoon sugar

1½ teaspoons grated fresh ginger

1 teaspoon minced fresh lemongrass (inner white bulb only) or 1 tablespoon dried, soaked in a little water for 1 hour, drained, and minced (optional)

Pinch of cayenne pepper

10 cups shredded or finely julienned vegetables and fruits, such as

Green or napa cabbage, tough outer leaves removed and cored

Bean sprouts

Daikon radish, peeled

Cucumber, peeled; squeezed after slicing to remove water

Red or yellow bell pepper, cored and seeded

Carrot, peeled (this can then be shaved with a vegetable peeler)

Snow peas, strings and stems removed

Jicama, peeled

Scallions, trimmed

Endive, trimmed

Radicchio, cored

Green mango or papaya, peeled and seeded

½ cup finely chopped fresh cilantro (you can also mix in some basil or mint)

2½ ounces (½ cup) **chopped roasted unsalted peanuts**

To make the lemongrass dressing, in a small bowl, combine the lime juice, fish sauce, rice wine vinegar, sesame oil, sugar, ginger, lemongrass, and cayenne. Stir until the sugar is dissolved. Let sit for at least 2 hours before using to allow the flavors to develop.

At least 30 minutes before serving, toss together the vegetables, cilantro, and dressing. As the salad sits, the vegetables will give off their own liquid and dilute the dressing. When you are ready to serve, if the dressing is still too intense, simply add a little water to dilute it.

Garnish the salad with the peanuts and serve.

IN ADVANCE You can prepare the dressing up to 1 week ahead. You can julienne the vegetables (except the scallions) up to 1 day ahead and store them, separately, in plastic bags in the refrigerator until you are ready to dress them. The salad gets even better with age; store, covered, in the refrigerator for up to 4 days.

variation **Vietnamese Chicken Salad.** Make a simple slaw using green or napa cabbage. Add 3 ounces of shredded cooked chicken per person (1½ pounds total for 8) and dress and garnish the salad as directed.

COOKED VEGETABLE SALADS. With a vinaigrette dressing, just about any cooked vegetable can be turned into a delicious chilled or room-temperature salad. From classics such as asparagus vinaigrette to an esoteric Chayote Squash Salad with Lime and Peanuts (page 433), these healthful salads can be served as a first course or light lunch in tandem with some protein. As with leafy salads, the key is in not overdressing the vegetables, which would obscure their bright flavors.

Simple Cooked Vegetable Salads

A GUIDE TO IMPROVISING

Pairing the vegetables and vinaigrette is where your creativity comes in. There are endless possibilities using the vinaigrettes on pages 603 to 617, such as green beans with cilantro and Lemon Vinaigrette with a Little Garlic; broccoli with Warm Anchovy and Olive Oil Sauce; parsnips with Nut Oil Vinaigrette; or roasted peppers, onions, and eggplant with Everyday Vinaigrette and shavings of ricotta salata cheese. One of my favorites is a salad of early spring vegetables—new potatoes, asparagus, French beans, and fava beans or sugar snap peas—dressed with Champagne Herb Vinaigrette (page 608) and garnished with fresh chervil and chives.

SERVES 4

> **1 to 1¼ pounds vegetables,** such as green beans, broccoli, carrots, parsnips, eggplant, onions, leeks, bell peppers, or beets trimmed or peeled and cut into bite-sized pieces (4 cups)
>
> **2 tablespoons vinaigrette** (pages 603–617), such as Everyday Vinaigrette, Nut Oil Vinaigrette, Citrus Vinaigrette, or Classic Mustard Vinaigrette
>
> **¼ to ½ cup minced fresh herbs,** such as cilantro, basil, chives, chervil, or flat-leaf parsley
>
> **Kosher salt and freshly ground black pepper**

1. Cook the vegetables by steaming, boiling, or roasting them until they are just tender. If you steamed or boiled them, stop the cooking by cooling them down under cold running water. Drain well and pat dry.

2. Toss the vegetables with the vinaigrette. Toss with the herbs, salt, and pepper to taste and serve.

French Beans with Tarragon Cream Dressing and Hazelnuts

SERVES 4 I've always loved the classic French salad of green beans in a lemony, heavy cream dressing. I replaced some of the heavy cream with sour cream and milk but still preserved the inimitable taste of cream. Since the dressing is quite thick and rich, you need only a small amount to coat the beans. Roasting intensifies the flavor of hazelnuts dramatically, so only a few per serving are needed to provide flavor—and crunch. This salad contains about half the calories of the classic version.

This dressing is also delicious on mild lettuces such as Buttercrunch and Boston.

½ **ounce** (12 to 15) **hazelnuts**

Tarragon Cream Dressing

    1 tablespoon plus 1 teaspoon heavy cream

    1 tablespoon plus 1 teaspoon regular or reduced-fat sour cream

    1 tablespoon plus 1 teaspoon whole milk

    1½ teaspoons fresh lemon juice

    1½ teaspoons minced fresh tarragon

    1 teaspoon minced fresh chives

    ¼ teaspoon kosher salt

½ **teaspoon kosher salt**

½ **teaspoon sugar**

1 pound haricots verts or young green beans, stem ends snapped off

Freshly ground black pepper

Fresh tarragon or chive sprigs for garnish (optional)

Preheat the oven to 400°F.

Spread the nuts on a small baking sheet or pie pan and roast, stirring them occasionally, until very fragrant and golden brown, 7 to 10 minutes. If it's possible, mist once or twice with a water spritzer to loosen the skins. Allow to cool slightly.

To remove the skins from the hazelnuts, pile them in a tea towel and rub them between your hands to remove the skins. Coarsely chop the hazelnuts and set aside.

To make the dressing, in a medium bowl, whisk together the heavy cream, sour cream, milk, lemon juice, tarragon, chives, and the ¼ teaspoon salt. Refrigerate for 1 hour before serving to let the flavors marry.

Bring a large pot of water to a boil over high heat. Stir in the ½ teaspoon salt and the sugar, add the beans, and boil until crisp-tender, about 5 minutes. Drain the beans and place them in a bowl of cold water. Run cold tap water over the beans until they are thoroughly cool. Drain well. Pat dry with paper towels.

Place the beans in a bowl and toss them with the dressing until completely coated. Add pepper to taste. Divide among four salad plates or shallow bowls and sprinkle with the hazelnuts. Garnish, if desired, with tarragon sprigs.

You can make the dressing and prepare the beans up to 6 hours ahead; cover and refrigerate. **IN ADVANCE**

Chayote Squash Salad with Peanuts and Lime

Chayote is a pale green pear-shaped squash of Caribbean origin with a delicate flavor and texture that is like a cross between a zucchini and an apple. Here it is gently cooked, cooled, and dressed with lime, basil, cilantro, and peanuts—no oil is used—an approach I learned from Marcia Kiesel, a master of Vietnamese cooking. This salad can also act like a salsa, adding refreshing, cool, crunchy elements to a meal. In place of chayote, you can make the salad with 5 cups peeled, seeded, and diced raw cucumber. **SERVES 4**

- **2 pounds** (3 or 4) **chayote squash**
- **¾ teaspoon kosher salt**
- **1 shallot,** minced (about 1½ tablespoons)
- **½ teaspoon sugar,** or more to taste
- **½ teaspoon freshly ground black pepper**
- **½ teaspoon finely grated lime zest**
- **¼ cup fresh lime juice**
- **¼ cup minced fresh cilantro and basil,** in any proportion (with a small portion of mint, if desired)
- **¼ cup** (2 ounces) **chopped roasted cashews or peanuts**

With a vegetable peeler, peel the tough outer skin off the squash. Slice the squash lengthwise in half and remove the flat pit. Cut each half lengthwise in two, then slice each quarter crosswise into ⅛-inch-thick slices.

Bring a medium saucepan of water to a boil and add ½ teaspoon of the salt. Blanch the squash until it becomes just barely translucent but is still crunchy. Drain and plunge it into a bowl of cold water; run cold water over it until it is completely cold. Drain well and pat dry.

In a medium bowl, stir together the shallot, sugar, the remaining ¼ teaspoon salt, the pepper, lime zest, and lime juice. Add the chayote and toss to coat. Just before serving, sprinkle with the herbs and chopped nuts.

IN ADVANCE You can assemble the salad, minus the herbs and nuts, up to 1 day ahead; cover and refrigerate.

Carrots in Chermoula

SERVES 4

Fragrant Moroccan chermoula sauce is marvelous on all manner of simply cooked fish and shellfish, chicken, grains, cooked dried white or split fava beans, and roasted peppers, onions, or squash.

In this recipe, warm steamed carrots are tossed with *chermoula*, a spicy, fragrant Moroccan sauce made from olive oil that has been briefly infused with toasted cinnamon, cumin, paprika, and cilantro. The oil is so fragrant that only a little is necessary to vividly flavor the carrots. It can be served as an hors d'oeuvre with an array of Mediterranean salads.

Other root vegetables also work well in this recipe, such as Yellow Finn potatoes, sweet potatoes, or parsnips. You could roast the vegetables instead of pan-braising them.

Chermoula Sauce

¾ **teaspoon cumin seeds**

1½ **teaspoons sweet Hungarian paprika**

Scant ½ **teaspoon ground cinnamon**

1 **tablespoon plus 1 teaspoon extra-virgin olive oil**

2 **small garlic cloves,** peeled

⅛ **teaspoon kosher salt**

¾ **teaspoon sugar**

3 **tablespoons chopped fresh cilantro**

3 **tablespoons chopped fresh flat-leaf parsley**

Juice of 1 lemon (4 to 5 tablespoons)

2 **pounds medium or small carrots or parsnips,** peeled and cut on the diagonal into ½-inch ovals

½ **cup water**

¼ **teaspoon kosher salt**

To make the sauce, in a small heavy skillet, toast the cumin seeds over moderately low heat, tossing frequently, until very fragrant and slightly darkened. Turn off the heat and stir in the paprika and cinnamon, to toast them slightly. Then stir in the olive oil. Set aside to steep for 10 minutes.

In a mortar, mash the garlic with the salt and sugar. Add the cilantro and parsley and pound to a coarse paste. Drizzle in all but 1 teaspoon of the spice oil and pound the mixture to crush the cumin seeds coarsely. Drizzle in the lemon juice. Alternatively, mince the garlic with the salt and sugar. Placing the flat side of a chef's knife almost parallel to the work surface, mash the garlic a little at a time by crushing and smearing it against the cutting board until it is completely reduced to a paste. Add the herbs and cumin, alternately chopping and mashing them into the garlic; drizzle with all but 1 teaspoon of the spice oil and work it into the mixture with the side of the knife. Then transfer to a small bowl and stir in the lemon juice.

Combine the carrot slices, the remaining 1 teaspoon spice oil, the water, and salt in a skillet. Toss to coat the carrots, cover the pan, and cook over moderately high heat, tossing occasionally, until the water has evaporated and the carrots are crisp-tender, about 5 to 7 minutes: Do not overcook. If the water evaporates too quickly, add about 2 tablespoons more to the pan; if there is still water left in the pan when the carrots are almost tender, uncover and boil it off over high heat, tossing the carrots so they don't stick. Transfer the carrots to a serving dish and let cool slightly.

Scrape the sauce over the carrots and toss to coat. Serve warm or at room temperature.

You can prepare the Chermoula Sauce, without the lemon juice, up to 4 hours **IN ADVANCE** ahead; cover and refrigerate. You can assemble the dish up to 2 hours ahead. Set aside at room temperature.

Beet Salad

Fresh beets are a convenience food in Italy and France, where you can buy them already cooked and peeled, ready to be sliced and dressed for a salad. Their sweet earthy flavor complements a range of lettuces and greens, from peppery watercress and bitter chicories to delicate mâche and mesclun; endive is perhaps the most famous. Beets also have an affinity for apples, pears, citrus fruits, and for all kinds of roasted nuts.

To bring out their sweetness, season peeled and sliced beets with some vinegar and salt while they are still warm. Then, just before serving, dress them with a little oil and toss with lightly dressed greens, fruits, or nuts. You can strip this recipe down to a minimum and serve the beets alone if you like as part of an antipasto platter. The lightly dressed beets are fabulous served with Greek Garlic Sauce (page 623).

In the summer, farmers' markets offer several kinds of beets in addition to the familiar dark purple variety: golden beets and candy-striped Chioggia beets. Beet greens, if they are in good shape, can be trimmed and cooked as Tender Greens Sautéed with Garlic and Olive Oil (page 74).

1 pound beets, just cooked (see page 683)

1 tablespoon balsamic vinegar

1 tablespoon sherry vinegar

1 teaspoon fresh lemon juice

½ plus ⅛ teaspoon kosher salt

1 tablespoon plus 1 teaspoon extra-virgin olive, walnut, or hazelnut oil

Freshly ground black pepper

1 teaspoon hot water

6 cups (about 9 ounces) **cleaned and dried lettuces,** such as mesclun, frisée, or mâche, or 6 heads Belgian endive, trimmed and sliced crosswise on a diagonal

1 ripe apple or pear, peeled, cored, and diced, or 1 small blood or navel orange, peeled and sectioned (see page 677) (optional)

2 tablespoons coarsely chopped roasted pecans, walnuts, hazelnuts, or pine nuts (optional)

Cut off the stem and root ends of the beets and scrape off the thin layer of skin. Slice the beets into half moons, disks, or ⅛-inch julienne. Place in a medium bowl. Add 2 teaspoons each of the balsamic and sherry vinegars, the lemon juice, and ½ teaspoon salt and toss. Set aside to marinate for at least 10 minutes, or until ready to serve. Then toss them with 2 teaspoons of the oil and freshly ground black pepper to taste.

In a medium bowl, combine the remaining 1 teaspoon each of the balsamic and sherry vinegars the remaining ⅛ teaspoon salt, the remaining 2 teaspoons oil, and hot water. Add the lettuces, the fruit, if desired, and pepper to taste and toss well.

Place a mound of greens on each of four salad plates. Place the beets on top. Garnish with the nuts, if desired, and serve.

You can dress the cooked beets up to a day ahead; cover and refrigerate. IN ADVANCE

Grilled Corn, Poblano, and Tomato Salad

This is the perfect salad for summertime grilling. Slightly smoky and juicy, it **SERVES 4** rolls side dish, salad, and salsa into one. Once you've fired up the grill, you can grill the various elements before cooking a main course of meat, poultry, or fish. Then toss the salad together while the rest of the meal cooks. The ripe tomatoes and grilled peppers exude flavorful juices that become part of the dressing. You can substitute, or add, other grilled vegetables, such as zucchini or summer squash, eggplant, or portobello mushrooms.

3 poblano or 2 red or yellow bell peppers (12 ounces), cored, seeded, and sliced into 2-inch-wide strips

1 medium Vidalia or Bermuda onion, sliced lengthwise through the core into ¼-inch-thick slices; do not separate

4 ears fresh corn, shucked

1½ tablespoons extra-virgin olive oil

1 pound very ripe red and/or yellow tomatoes, cored and diced (about 2¾ cups)

⅓ cup chopped fresh cilantro

2 tablespoons chopped fresh basil

1½ tablespoons balsamic vinegar or fresh lime juice

⅛ teaspoon kosher salt, or more to taste

Freshly ground black pepper

¼ teaspoon ground cumin (optional)

Prepare a fire in a grill.

When the coals are white-hot, brush the peppers, onions, and corn with 2 teaspoons of the oil. Sandwich the onion and pepper slices in a hinged grill rack or arrange directly on the grill and cook until tender, 4 to 5 minutes on each side. Transfer to a platter and add the corn to the grill. Cook, turning frequently, until beginning to brown on all sides, about 5 minutes.

With a serrated knife, slice the corn kernels off the cobs directly into a large bowl. Dice the peppers and onions. Add the peppers, onions, tomatoes, cilantro, and basil to the corn; pour over the juices from the platter. Drizzle with the balsamic vinegar, the remaining 2½ teaspoons oil, the salt, pepper to taste, and the cumin, if desired; toss to coat. Adjust the seasoning and serve.

IN ADVANCE You can assemble the salad up to 6 hours ahead; cover and refrigerate. Bring to room temperature before serving.

Warm Potato Salad with Olives, Lemon Zest, and Thyme

SERVES 4 Unadorned, a potato is all virtue, full of good things for body and soul. Its starchy flesh, however, has a propensity for absorbing fat, making potato salads amply dressed in mayonnaise or oil sublime but fattening.

To make light, delicious potato salads, first season boiled potatoes while they are still warm with something flavorful and fat-free—a reduced broth or wine, or only salt—which saturates the bland flesh and amplifies its flavor. Once the potatoes are cool and no longer so absorbent, dress them with fruity olive oil that has been emulsified and extended with a piquant liquid—reduced broth or wine again, or lemon juice—so that the oil remains on the surface of the potatoes, where its taste lingers.

Try combining different types of small new potatoes in salads for more interest and color. Golden Bintjes and oddly shaped fingerlings are increasingly available in supermarkets, as are occasionally the garish purple Peruvians. Yellow Finns, whose slices are a little larger than I like, have a good texture and appealing buttery flavor.

1½ pounds russet or Yellow Finn potatoes, scrubbed

1 small serrano chile, split in half

2 ounces (about 10) **Kalamata olives**

1 cup dry white wine or white vermouth

1 medium shallot, minced (1 tablespoon)

½ teaspoon sugar

½ teaspoon kosher salt, or more to taste

1 tablespoon Champagne vinegar or white wine vinegar

1¼ teaspoons minced fresh thyme

1¼ teaspoons grated lemon zest

1 tablespoon plus 1 teaspoon extra-virgin olive oil

Freshly ground black pepper

Place the potatoes in a medium saucepan with enough water to cover, add the chile pepper, and bring to a boil. Partially cover and cook for 30 to 35 minutes, until tender. Drain and set aside to cool slightly.

Meanwhile, place the olives on a work surface and tap each one lightly with a heavy can or meat pounder or the side of a chef's knife. Remove and discard the pits. Coarsely chop the olives and set aside.

In a small saucepan, combine the wine, shallots, sugar, and salt. Bring to a boil over moderately high heat and boil for about 4 minutes, until the wine is reduced by half. Stir in the vinegar and remove from the heat.

Peel the potatoes, if desired. Cut into 1-inch slices and place in a medium bowl. Spoon half the wine mixture over the potatoes and toss to coat. Set aside for 15 minutes; the potatoes will absorb the mixture as they stand.

Toss the potatoes with the thyme and lemon zest.

Bring the remaining wine mixture to a boil and add the olives and olive oil. Boil vigorously until the oil and wine are blended, about 1 minute.

Pour the dressing over the salad and toss to coat. Add plenty of freshly ground pepper and adjust the salt. Serve.

IN ADVANCE You can assemble the salad up to 6 hours ahead; cover and keep at room temperature.

variation **Plain Potato Salad for Embellishing.** If you leave out the olives, thyme, and lemon zest, you will have a still delicious "plain" potato salad. You can flavor it any way you want: with chopped herbs such as basil, chives, flat-leaf parsley, tarragon, or cilantro, for example, or bits of chopped sweet pickle or capers.

variation **Warm Potato and Grilled Vidalia Onion Salad.** One of my favorite embellishments for the Plain Potato Salad is grilled Vidalia onions and walnuts. (If you have walnut oil, use it instead of the olive oil in the dressing.) Preheat the broiler. Slice 1 medium Vidalia or Bermuda onion (about 7 ounces) into ⅛-inch rings. Brush the broiler pan or rack lightly with olive oil. Arrange the onion slices on the rack and brush the top of each lightly with olive oil. Season with ⅛ teaspoon kosher salt. Broil as close to the heat as possible until the onions are soft and just beginning to char, 3 to 5 minutes. Add the onions to the potatoes along with ¼ cup coarsely chopped roasted walnuts.

variation **Salade Niçoise with Fresh Tuna.** Warm Potato Salad with Olives, Lemon Zest, and Thyme makes a perfect base for a superb Niçoise salad. Prepare the potato salad as directed on page 438 to 439 and toss with 8 ounces cooked, chilled French string beans and 4 sliced plum tomatoes. Arrange on 4 cups (6 ounces) mesclun salad. Top with 8 drained oil-packed anchovies and 2 teaspoons drained capers. Season two 8-ounce tuna steaks with kosher salt and pepper and 1 teaspoon minced fresh rosemary. Sear (as directed on page 241) or grill. Slice the tuna thinly and arrange on top of the salad; serve at once.

BEAN AND GRAIN SALADS. The usual way to make a salad with starchy ingredients such as beans and grains is to toss them with a lot of vinaigrette, which keeps them from tasting dry and bland but adds unnecessary calories and fat. Instead, start with a small amount of extra-virgin olive oil and extend it with a few tablespoons of a liquid such as reduced wine and vinegar, which also provides acidity that heightens the beans' or grains' flavors. Beans and grains absorb some of the dressing and are coated by the rest, so that the taste of the fat remains vibrant. You can use this approach on all kinds of bean and grain salads, from quinoa dressed with coconut milk and lemongrass to black-eyed peas dressed with bacon and balsamic vinegar.

Simple Salads Made with Beans, Grains, and Other Starchy Ingredients

A GUIDE TO IMPROVISING

This Guide gives a simple approach to dressing all kinds of beans and kernel grains. You can also use it on starchy cooked vegetables, such as potatoes and yuca, that have been peeled and cut up.

SERVES 4 TO 6

Once you've made the basic salad, you can add other interesting elements, such as roasted peppers, olives, lemon zest, or grilled vegetables. Grain salads are delicious with a tablespoon or two of chopped roasted nuts or dried cherries, currants, or cranberries.

Boiling (rather than the pilaf method) is the best way to cook grains for salads, so that they remain light and fluffy (see page 174). You can add herbs and spices to the cooking water to give them a subtle layer of flavor. When served cool, grains can be somewhat stodgy; they benefit from a good deal more acid—vinegar, lime, lemon, or orange juice—than other salads. Finely chopped shallot, red onion, or scallion adds a savory note that also seems to heighten the grains' flavors. To reduce salt, add a pinch of cayenne.

Dressing

1 cup dry white wine or white vermouth or mild broth, such as unsalted homemade (page 574) or canned low-sodium chicken broth or Leek Broth (page 569)

2 teaspoons minced shallots

1 tablespoon fat, such as fruity extra-virgin olive oil, roasted nut oil, Flavored Oil (pages 588–597), or rendered bacon fat (see page 681)

1 tablespoon plus 1 teaspoon vinegar or fresh lemon juice, or more to taste

½ teaspoon sugar

Kosher salt

3 cups warm, drained just-boiled beans, peas, lentils, kernel grains, or potatoes

Additions (optional), singly or in combination, such as

¾ to 1 cup chopped roasted peppers (see page 683) **or raw bell peppers**

1 cup "Fried" Onions (page 62)

1 cup diced tomatoes

¼ cup pitted (see page 683) **olives,** halved or slivered

2 tablespoons capers, drained

2 to 3 teaspoons slivered lemon or orange zest

2 to 4 tablespoons roasted pine nuts or walnuts

Kosher salt and freshly ground black pepper

Chopped fresh herbs, such as

3 tablespoons chopped mild herbs, such as basil, chives, cilantro, or flat-leaf parsley

2 teaspoons chopped pungent herbs, such as rosemary, thyme, savory, oregano, or tarragon

1. To make the dressing, in a small saucepan, simmer the wine and shallots until the liquid has reduced to about ¼ cup, about 20 minutes. Add the oil, vinegar, sugar, and salt and bring to a boil over moderate heat, then turn off the heat.

2. Place the beans in a medium bowl, add the dressing, and toss to coat. Stir in any optional additions. Season with salt and pepper and toss with the herbs.

Warm Bean Salad with Fresh Herbs and Olives

I love to serve pale beans like cannellini or baby white limas as a warm salad, SERVES 4 dressed with an emulsion of rosemary-and-thyme-infused olive oil, a little of their cooking liquid, and olives. Lemon juice and chopped fresh parsley and basil add another layer of summery flavor. The beans make a delicious accompaniment to grilled or roasted lamb, chicken, and seafood, or a light meal unto themselves with some shaved goat cheese or ricotta salata or cooked shrimp. I often make this recipe with pale green dried flageolets; their pea-like flavor reminds me of fresh shell beans.

3 cups drained cooked white beans, such as cannellini, navy, baby white limas, or flageolets (see page 92; reserve about ⅓ cup of the cooking liquid) or canned beans, drained and rinsed well

Herb Dressing

1 tablespoon plus 1 teaspoon fruity extra-virgin olive oil

2 garlic cloves, minced

½ teaspoon finely chopped fresh rosemary

½ teaspoon finely chopped fresh thyme

Scant ⅓ cup bean cooking liquid, unsalted homemade (page 574) **or canned low-sodium chicken broth, or water**

½ cup black olives, such as Kalamata or Gaeta, pitted (see page 683) and chopped, **or green olives,** such as a picholine or Barese, if using flageolets

3 tablespoons chopped fresh flat-leaf parsley

4 large fresh basil leaves, torn into ⅛- to ¼-inch pieces

2 to 3 tablespoons fresh lemon juice

½ teaspoon kosher salt, or to taste

Freshly ground black pepper

Place the beans in a medium nonstick skillet and set aside.

To make the dressing, in a small skillet, combine the olive oil and garlic over low heat, cover, and cook until the garlic is soft, about 3 minutes. Uncover, increase the heat to moderate, and add the rosemary and thyme. Cook until the herbs begin to sizzle and little bubbles dance around them; do not let the garlic brown. Add the bean cooking liquid and olives, increase the heat to high, and boil for 30 seconds.

Scatter the parsley and basil over the beans and pour over the dressing, tossing to coat. Place the beans over high heat and toss frequently until they are hot and have absorbed most of the dressing. Remove from the heat and add the lemon juice, salt, and pepper to taste. Serve warm.

IN ADVANCE You can cook the dried beans up to 3 days ahead; cover and refrigerate. You can sizzle the garlic and herbs in the oil up to 4 hours ahead; let sit at room temperature until you are ready to finish the dressing. Although the salad is best served warm, you can refrigerate it, covered, for up to 2 days.

Warm Bean Salad with Balsamic-Bacon Vinaigrette

SERVES 4   Beans love bacon; its rich smoky pork flavor brings out their best flavors without masking them. You can dress many different kinds of beans—including scarlet runners, flageolets, black-eyed peas, and lentils—with this vinaigrette made from rendered bacon fat and sweet balsamic vinegar. When boiled with a little water or bean cooking liquid, the small amount of flavorful fat emulsifies to become a limpid sauce that coats the beans. Caramelized onions and the crisp bacon add contrasting texture.

Think of this as a base recipe to which you can add herbs and spices, depending on the kind of bean you are using. Black beans are much enhanced by adding a teaspoon of cumin seeds to the onions as they cook. Try white beans with a little minced fresh rosemary, or lentils with slivered lemon zest and flat-leaf parsley.

Balsamic-Bean Vinaigrette

1 ounce lean smoky thick-sliced bacon or pancetta, cut into ¼-inch dice (scant ¼ cup)

3 medium onions, halved and thinly sliced lengthwise

2 imported bay leaves

⅓ cup balsamic vinegar

2 tablespoons water or reserved bean cooking liquid

3 cups drained cooked beans or lentils (see page 92) **or canned beans,** rinsed well and drained

Kosher salt and freshly ground black pepper

¼ cup chopped fresh flat-leaf parsley

To make the dressing, put the bacon in a medium heavy nonstick skillet set over moderately low heat, cover, and cook until it is crisp and browned and has rendered all its fat, about 8 minutes. Add the onions, cover, and cook until they are wilted, about 5 minutes, adding 1 tablespoon of water if necessary to prevent sticking. Remove the lid and continue cooking until the onions are golden brown, about 8 minutes. Add the bay leaves, balsamic vinegar, and water and simmer for 30 seconds. Stir in the beans and salt to taste. Simmer for 5 to 10 minutes, tossing occasionally, until the beans are heated through. Pepper generously and stir in the parsley. Serve warm.

You can prepare the beans up to 2 days ahead; cover and refrigerate. Reheat in a nonstick skillet over moderate heat, adding a tablespoon or two of water if they are dry.

IN ADVANCE

Farro Salad with Green Apple, Toasted Spices, and Pine Nuts

SERVES 6

Farro, which looks like pale wheat berries, is an ancient Roman grain that is popular in many regions of Italy. It has a pleasingly chewy texture and a mildly nutty flavor that is marvelous in salads such as this one, accented with fennel seeds, coriander, and roasted pine nuts. This is an excellent treatment for many other hearty grains such as wild rice, wheat berries, or brown rice. Although this rustic salad is best served at room temperature, I also like to serve it warm, as a bed for seared quail, duck breast, or grilled chicken.

⅔ **cup pine nuts**

1½ **teaspoons coriander seeds**

¼ **teaspoon fennel seeds**

1 **tablespoon plus 1 teaspoon extra-virgin olive oil**

1½ **cups coarsely chopped onions** (2 medium onions)

Kosher salt

3 **tablespoons vinegar:** aged sherry, Banyuls, or white wine

4 **cups drained cooked farro** (see chart, page 170)

1 **cup coarsely chopped fresh flat-leaf parsley**

1 **medium Granny Smith apple,** peeled and finely diced (about ¾ cup)

1 **teaspoon finely slivered lemon zest** (optional)

2 **to 3 tablespoons fresh lemon juice**

About ½ **teaspoon freshly ground black pepper**

Preheat the oven to 350°F.

Spread the pine nuts on a baking sheet and roast, tossing occasionally, until fragrant and golden, about 7 minutes. Set aside to cool.

In a medium nonstick skillet over low heat, gently toast the coriander and fennel seeds until fragrant. Transfer to a mortar and crush with a pestle, or place on a cutting board and crush the seeds with the side of a chef's knife, then chop them finely.

Add 1½ teaspoons of the oil and the onions to the skillet and sprinkle lightly with salt. Cover and cook over moderately low heat until the onions are translucent and have released some of their liquid, about 5 minutes. Uncover, increase the heat slightly, and cook, stirring occasionally, until the onions are golden brown, about 5 minutes longer. Stir in the vinegar and cook until reduced by half. Add the remaining 2½ teaspoons oil and the reserved spices. Remove from the heat.

Place the farro in a bowl. Coarsely chop the pine nuts and add them, along with the onion mixture, the parsley, apples, and the lemon zest, if desired, and 2 tablespoons of the lemon juice. Toss to combine, seasoning with salt, additional lemon juice, and plenty of freshly ground black pepper. Serve warm or at room temperature.

IN ADVANCE Although the salad is best the day it is made, you can store it for up to 2 days in the refrigerator. Bring to room temperature before serving.

Quinoa Salad with Lemongrass, Cilantro, and Mint

SERVES 4

Toast quinoa in a dry pan before boiling it to bring up its flavor and ensure that the kernels remain separate when cooked.

Although it looks like a delicate cereal grain, quinoa is really a member of the goosefoot family of herbs. It tastes something like a cross between millet and wild rice, with a faint hint of mustard, a flavor that sings with assertive treatment. Because quinoa has such exceptional nutritional properties—one cup has more calcium than a quart of milk, and it is exceptionally high in protein and lysine—this salad is well worth adding to your repertoire. It makes a delectable bed for grilled shrimp, squid, or fish or roasted chicken.

Here quinoa is cooked in spicy lemongrass-flavored water to give it an underlying aromatic sweetness that will amplify the dressing of cilantro, mint, and lime juice. A few tablespoons of unsweetened coconut milk instead of the usual oil in the dressing ensures that the salad stays moist. Roasted peanuts balance the flavors and add crunch.

You can make this recipe with other mild-flavored grains, such as millet, couscous, and white rice—including basmati and jasmine. You will need about 3½ cups cooked grain; figure the dry amount from the package information or the chart on pages 170 to 173 and add the flavorings to the cooking liquid.

1 cup quinoa

2 cups water

1 bulb lemongrass, bottom 2½ inches only, finely chopped (1½ tablespoons), or 1½ teaspoons dried lemongrass, placed in a tea ball or tied in cheesecloth

1 kaffir lime leaf, finely chopped (optional)

1 small serrano or jalapeño chile, finely chopped

¼ teaspoon kosher salt

¾ cup chopped fresh cilantro

¼ cup chopped fresh mint

2 tablespoons finely chopped red onion

3 to 4 tablespoons fresh lime juice

3 tablespoons unsweetened coconut milk or 2 teaspoons peanut oil

3 tablespoons (¾ ounce) **dry-roasted peanuts,** chopped

6 to 8 fresh basil leaves (optional)

Place the quinoa in a medium, heavy nonstick skillet and toast over medium heat, tossing and stirring, until it is golden brown and fragrant, about 6 minutes. Transfer to a medium saucepan.

Add the water, lemongrass, kaffir lime leaf, if desired, chile pepper, and salt. Bring to a boil over moderate heat, reduce the heat to a simmer, cover tightly, and cook until all the liquid is absorbed, about 12 minutes. Transfer to a medium bowl and fluff with a fork. Let cool completely.

Add the cilantro, mint, and red onion to the quinoa and toss to combine.

In a small bowl, combine the lime juice and coconut milk. Drizzle it over the quinoa and toss again. Cover and refrigerate until ready to serve.

Just before serving, stir in the peanuts (if you add them more than an hour ahead, they will lose their crunch). Garnish, if desired, with torn or thinly sliced basil leaves.

Store the salad, covered, in the refrigerator for up to 2 days.

IN ADVANCE

MAIN-COURSE SALADS. In *Simple French Food,* Richard Olney wrote eloquently about improvised salads that he called composed salads because they do just that, compose whatever is at hand into a harmonious whole. Ingredients might include anything you feel works well together or have left over from other meals: meat, poultry, seafood, pasta, beans, grains, raw or cooked vegetables, herbs, greens, nuts—few foods are inappropriate.

The addition of few ounces of cooked meat, poultry, seafood, or cheese can elevate a simple appetizer salad into a main course. For example, you might arrange some grilled shrimp on a bed of Warm Potato Salad with Olives, Lemon Zest, and Thyme (page 438) or embellish Celery Root, Fennel, and Apple Salad with Slivered Lemon Zest and Hazelnuts (page 422) with thin slices of smoked duck breast.

You can compose main-course salads by layering two or three simple recipes such as the following:

Warm Goat Cheese Salad (page 451)
on **Peppers Roasted with Garlic and Anchovies** (page 42)

Salmon Cured with Aromatic Pepper and Herbs (page 278)
on **Cucumbers with Curry Cream** (page 425) and mesclun salad

Cumin-Crusted Quail with Cilantro Gremolata (page 319)
on **Herb Salad** (page 415) with **Parsnip Fries** (page 46)

Quinoa Salad with Lemongrass, Cilantro, and Mint (page 446)
with **Curry-Crusted Shrimp** (page 242) and **Crispy Shallots** (page 48)

Warm Main-Course Salads

This is a model for an easy-to-make warm main-course salad: a bed of leafy greens or mesclun topped with slices of warm, quickly cooked meats, poultry, game, or seafood, for protein. These wilt the greens slightly, and their natural juices form part of the dressing, fusing the two elements together.

SERVES 2
(4 AS A FIRST COURSE)

In addition to pan-seared meat or poultry, you can use such recipes as Spice-Rubbed Duck Steaks (page 326), Pan-Smoked Salmon (page 268), or The Best Way to Grill Shrimp (page 237). You can also elaborate by adding other elements such as olives, roasted peppers, tomatoes, other cooked or raw vegetables, nuts, or fruits. Or use other salads instead of the greens.

Figure on about 3 to 4 ounces of protein per person, thinly sliced or artfully cut. Or if using cheese, limit to 2 ounces per serving.

> **4 cups cleaned and dried greens, lettuces, and herbs,** in any combination
>
> **Additions** (optional), such as
>
>> **1 ounce** (¼ cup) **roasted walnuts, pecans, or hazelnuts,** broken into pieces
>>
>> **1 tomato,** seeded and diced
>>
>> **Thinly sliced Vidalia or Bermuda onion or fennel**
>>
>> **1 small pear, apple, or orange,** peeled and sliced, **or 1 fig,** sliced
>>
>> **½ cup cooked green beans, beets, or roasted peppers**
>
> **1 tablespoon plus 2 teaspoons vinaigrette** (pages 603–617)
>
> **Kosher salt and freshly ground black pepper**
>
> **6 to 8 ounces lean boneless meat, poultry, or seafood,** such as flank or sirloin steak, loin of lamb, pork tenderloin or medallions, skinless duck or chicken breast, fillet of salmon, tuna steak, or peeled and deveined shrimp
>
> **1 teaspoon olive oil** for sautéing or grilling

1. In a large bowl, combine the greens and any optional additions. Drizzle with the vinaigrette and toss to coat. Season with salt and pepper and toss again.

2. Arrange the salad on each of two dinner plates (or four salad plates).

3. Brush the meat, poultry, or seafood lightly with the olive oil. Sear in a hot grill pan or a nonstick skillet until browned on each side and cooked as you like it. Transfer to a cutting board to rest for a few minutes before slicing.

4. Slice the meat, poultry, or seafood into thin slices as appropriate. Place slightly askew on the greens. Drizzle any juices over the salad. Serve at once.

Pan-Seared Quail over Greens

SERVES 4 This dish is the kind of simple main-course salad my friend Josh Eisen, a wine writer and inspired cook, frequently makes for impromptu dinners. Quail are quickly seared, then placed on raw greens. Their juices dress and wilt the greens slightly and marry their flavors with the quail. Because of the fat in their skin, quail, like other game birds, are a bit of a splurge nutritionally. Leaner cuts of meats, such as trimmed lamb chops, loin of lamb, or skinless boneless duck or chicken breasts, make delicious substitutes.

The quality of the mesclun salad is critical for this dish. It should be very fresh and crisp with the right balance of mild and peppery greens. Frisée lettuce makes a good addition if you want sturdy greens.

If you don't have two skillets, cook the quail in two batches.

Herb Rub
  1 teaspoon dried sage
  ¾ teaspoon dried rosemary
  ½ teaspoon dried thyme
  ¼ teaspoon dried savory
8 medium quail (4 ounces each)
2 garlic cloves, sliced
1 teaspoon vegetable oil
Kosher salt and freshly ground black pepper
2 teaspoons balsamic vinegar
2 teaspoons sherry vinegar
1½ teaspoons water
2 tablespoons extra-virgin olive oil
8 cups (about 12 ounces) **cleaned and dried mesclun salad**

To make the rub, place the dried herbs in a mortar and crush with a pestle until they are the texture of coarse sand. You can also crush them in a small bowl with the back of a wooden spoon. Do not allow them to become powdery, or they will burn and turn bitter.

To butterfly the quail: Holding 1 quail breast side down in your hand, with scissors, cut along either side of the backbone and remove it. Cut off the wing tips at the first joint. Open the quail out and place skin side up on the work surface. Press down sharply on the breastbone with the heel of your hand to crack the wishbone and flatten the quail. Repeat with the remaining quail.

Rub the quail on both sides with the cut garlic cloves. Rub lightly with the oil. Season on both sides with the herb mixture and salt and pepper.

In a small bowl, combine the balsamic and sherry vinegars, water, olive oil, and a generous pinch of salt. Place the greens in a large bowl and drizzle the dressing over. Toss to coat, adding salt and pepper to taste. Arrange the greens on a large serving platter.

Heat two large heavy nonstick skillets over high heat. When they are very hot, add the quail skin side up and place two heavy flat lids smaller than the skillets on top of the quail to keep them flat. Cook for 1 minute, then remove the lids and cook for 1 minute longer for medium-rare (add 30 seconds more if you like them more well done). Turn the quail over, weight them again with the lids, and cook for 1 minute. Cook for another minute, or until the skin is crisp and brown (add 30 seconds more if you like them more well done).

Arrange the quail on the greens. Let the juices and heat of the quail wilt the salad slightly, about 2 minutes, then serve.

IN ADVANCE You can make the herb rub, butterfly the quail, and prepare the dressing up to 1 day ahead; cover and refrigerate.

Warm Goat Cheese Salad

SERVES 4 The flavor and creaminess of goat cheese are accentuated when it is warmed, making it delicious served with any number of vegetables and greens, such as roasted potatoes, peppers, or onions or mixed slightly bitter greens dressed with walnut or olive oil. Because the cheese is very rich, about 2 ounces per person is ample. Be sure to serve slices of an interesting bread, such as crusty sourdough or walnut bread, or Rustic Garlic Toasts (page 368), on which to spread the warm cheese. A variety of aged goat cheeses works well. Pyramids, cones, or three-sided logs also lend themselves to appealingly shaped portions.

8 cups (about 12 ounces) **cleaned and dried mesclun or greens for Herb Salad** (page 415) **or other green salad**

3 tablespoons Everyday Vinaigrette (page 606)

Kosher salt and freshly ground black pepper

8 ounces mild goat cheese, such as Lingot or Montrachet, cut into 4 equal portions

½ teaspoon fresh thyme leaves or ¼ teaspoon dried thyme

Preheat the oven to 400°F.

Place the mesclun in a large salad bowl. Drizzle the dressing over and toss to coat. Season with salt and pepper. Divide the salad among four dinner plates.

Place the goat cheese in a small cast-iron skillet or a heavy baking pan and sprinkle on the thyme and pepper to taste. Bake until the cheese is warmed through and soft but not collapsing, about 3 minutes. Using a thin metal spatula, place one slice of cheese on each portion of the greens and serve.

IN ADVANCE Prepare the dressing up to 1 week ahead; cover and refrigerate. Up to 6 hours ahead, clean and dry the greens and place in a bowl. Store, covered with plastic wrap, in the refrigerator. Up to 2 hours ahead, place the cut slices of goat cheese in the pan, season, cover, and refrigerate. If necessary, bake the cold cheese a few minutes longer.

Warm Wild Mushroom Salad

SERVES 2 (4 AS A FIRST COURSE)

Years ago, at Jim Peterson's restaurant Le Petit Robert in New York City, the signature dish was a sublime wild mushroom salad—mushrooms quickly sautéed in goose fat, finished with sherry vinegar, and tossed with mesclun.

Although mushrooms themselves contain little fat or calories, their porous texture soaks up the fat when they are sautéed, making them extremely caloric. By roasting the mushrooms in a little oil and white wine or sherry, you can produce a texture similar to that of sautéed mushrooms, with much less fat. The mushrooms release flavorful juices, which become part of the dressing. Sometimes I add bits of prosciutto, confit of duck or goose, or roasted dark meat chicken to the salad for protein.

12 ounces wild mushrooms, such as chanterelle, shiitake, oyster, or hen of the woods

3 tablespoons finely chopped shallots

1 garlic clove, crushed and chopped

2 sprigs fresh thyme

1 juniper berry, crushed with the side of a chef's knife and chopped

Scant ½ teaspoon kosher salt

⅓ cup dry sherry or dry white wine

1 tablespoon plus ½ teaspoon extra-virgin olive oil

1½ tablespoons balsamic vinegar

¼ teaspoon water

½ teaspoon roasted hazelnut or walnut oil (optional)

4 to 5 cups (3 to 4 ounces) **cleaned and dried salad greens,** such as mesclun

Freshly ground black pepper

2 tablespoons finely chopped fresh flat-leaf parsley or chervil

Preheat the oven to 350°F.

Trim the tough stems off the mushrooms and discard. Cut the mushrooms lengthwise into halves, quarters, or eighths to make bite-sized pieces that still retain some of the mushroom's shape.

In a large shallow baking dish, toss together the mushrooms, 1 tablespoon of the shallots, the garlic, thyme, juniper berry, and ¼ teaspoon of the salt. Combine the sherry and 1 teaspoon of the olive oil and pour over the mushrooms. Cover with foil and bake until the mushrooms are tender and have released a lot of juices, about 30 minutes.

In a salad bowl, combine 1½ teaspoons of the olive oil, 1½ teaspoons of the balsamic vinegar, the water, and a pinch of salt. Set aside.

Holding the mushrooms in the pan with a slotted spoon or spatula, drain the juices into a small bowl. Return the mushrooms, uncovered, to the oven, increase the heat to 450°F, and roast for 10 to 15 minutes longer, until the mushrooms have glazed and browned lightly on top.

Meanwhile, in a small saucepan or skillet, cook the remaining 2 tablespoons shallots in the remaining 1 teaspoon olive oil, covered, over moderately low heat, stirring occasionally, until they are soft, about 5 minutes. Uncover and sauté, stirring frequently, until golden, about 2 minutes. Add the reserved mushroom cooking liquid, increase the heat to high, and boil to reduce it to ¼ cup. Stir in the remaining 1 tablespoon balsamic vinegar and boil for 30 seconds. Stir in the nut oil, if desired.

Add the salad greens to the bowl with the dressing and toss to coat. Season with pepper and additional salt if necessary. Arrange the salad on individual plates. Remove the mushrooms from the oven and toss with the reduced cooking liquid and some pepper. Adjust the seasoning and spoon over the greens. Sprinkle with the herbs and serve at once.

IN ADVANCE You can clean the mushrooms and greens up to 6 hours ahead; store in a loosely closed plastic bag in the refrigerator. You can make the dressing up to 4 hours ahead.

Warm Frisée Salad with Bacon and Croutons

SERVES 4
(8 AS A FIRST
COURSE)

The classic French *frisée au lardons*, a salad of bitter greens doused with a warm bacon fat dressing, cracklings, and crisp fried croutons, is divine but unnerving in its richness. Here's how to make it without the surfeit of fat.

Use slab bacon that has been double-smoked over sweet wood, such as apple or hickory, because it has a much more intense flavor than commercial sliced bacon. Render the fat from 6 ounces of the diced bacon to make crisp lean lardons—the delicious little smoky nuggets that are essential. You need only a small amount of the intensely smoky fat—about one quarter of the usual amount—to make the dressing and to brown the croutons. (If there is any leftover bacon fat, pour it into a small jar and refrigerate to use as a flavorful cooking fat.) Balsamic vinegar balances the smoky richness with sweetness and acidity, and a little water extends the fat to coat every leaf.

1 garlic clove, halved lengthwise

1 pound frisée, curly endive, or young dandelion greens
(or a mixture), cleaned and dried (16 packed cups)

6 ounces lean double-smoked slab bacon, sliced ⅓ inch thick
and cut into ⅓-inch dice

Extra-virgin olive oil (optional)

1 cup (2 ounces) **diced** (⅓-inch) **crustless bread**
(French or Italian baguette or peasant loaf)

3 tablespoons balsamic vinegar

1 tablespoon water

Pinch of sugar

Kosher salt and freshly ground black pepper

Rub the inside of a large salad bowl with the cut sides of the garlic clove; discard the garlic. Tear the greens into 2-inch pieces and add to the bowl. Cover with plastic wrap and refrigerate until you are ready to make the salad.

In a medium, heavy skillet over moderately low heat, cook the bacon, covered, until it is crisp and browned and has rendered all its fat, 8 to 10 minutes. With a slotted spoon, transfer the bacon to paper towels to drain. Pour the rendered fat into a small bowl. You should have 2 tablespoons; if you don't, add enough olive oil to make that amount.

Pour 2 teaspoons of the fat back into the skillet. When it is hot, add the bread and sauté, stirring occasionally, until golden brown, about 4 to 5 minutes. Transfer the croutons to a plate to cool.

Add the remaining 1 tablespoon plus 1 teaspoon of fat to the skillet and heat over moderate heat until hot. Add the bacon, balsamic vinegar, water, and sugar and bring to a boil.

Pour half the dressing over the greens and toss. Add the remaining dressing, the croutons, and salt and pepper to taste and toss again. The greens should be lightly wilted. If they are not, toss them into the skillet set over moderate heat to wilt them slightly, no more than 30 seconds. Mound the salad on serving plates and serve at once.

You can cook the bacon and fry the croutons up to 4 hours ahead. Reserve IN ADVANCE the croutons, crisp bacon, and fat separately at room temperature.

Rustic Free-form
Fruit Tarts made
with apricots,
raspberries,
blackberries, and
blueberries
(pages 481–485)

DESSERTS

a guide to improvising

a guide to improvising

T

he hunger for dessert is for the soothing comfort of sweet things that has little to do with nutritional needs. Rather, scientists suspect, it is linked to opiate-like receptors in the brain, to a different order of satisfaction.

Dessert is also the area where the greatest dietary taboos prevail, and, commonly, an attendant mix of pleasure and guilt—perhaps because dessert often is made up of everything we are told is ill-advised: butter, sugar, cream, chocolate in abundance.

I believe in dessert, in its importance at the end of the meal. I believe also in eating full-tilt no-holds-barred desserts here and there, when you are in a great restaurant, or are served something the likes of which you will never find again: a fresh coconut layer cake made by your Aunt Tilly in Georgia or a lemon meringue pie at a truck stop in Texas.

The desserts in this book are for an everyday sort of eating and entertaining, to provide the full pleasure of a dessert with less of a caloric wallop. I use the traditional ingredients of good dessert making, but I use them in novel ways, putting small amounts to best use.

SIMPLE FRESH FRUIT DESSERTS. Fresh fruit is the obvious choice for healthy desserts because fruit has no fat and only natural sugars. Yet everyone knows just how unsatisfying fresh fruit desserts can be. However, with care, fresh fruits can be a revelation of subtle flavor and fragrance.

The cardinal rule is that the fruit be ripe, so that its flavors and sweetness are fully developed. To tell if fruit is ripe and worth eating, sniff it; it should smell like itself. If fruit has no fragrance, it will have no flavor.

Chocolate
Malted Pudding
(page 504)

There are many simple ways to embellish fruits, such as tossing them with a fruit sauce, Flavored Syrup, or a fragrant wine to add a contrasting flavor. Even a few teaspoons of an eau-de-vie—a fruit brandy—can add surprising dimension to a simple bowl of fruit.

The great virtues of these embellishments are that they not only contain little sugar and yet are very satisfying, but they are easy to execute. Exact amounts are not critical, and there is lots of room for improvisation.

Fruits in Fragrant Wines

A GUIDE TO IMPROVISING

SERVES 4 You can improvise endless delightful and sophisticated desserts by splashing wine over ripe fresh fruits and garnishing them with citrus zest, herbs, or spices. Choose wines that will enhance the flavors of the fruit, from spicy Gewürztraminer, Riesling, and rosé to dessert and fortified wines. Some of my favorite combinations are:

Raspberries and strawberries in a fruity red wine with a pinch of ground cinnamon and a sprinkling of slivered basil leaves.

Strawberries in dry Marsala or Banyuls.

Peaches, preferably white-fleshed ones, with Prosecco (an Italian sparkling wine), Spanish Cava, or Champagne (this combination is the basis for the famous Bellini cocktail served at Harry's Bar in Venice).

Mangoes with Sauternes and grated lime zest.

Macerating the fruit in sugar for a few hours first brings out its full flavor and causes it to release some juices, forming a natural syrup that further perfumes the wine.

1 tablespoon sugar, or more to taste (depending on the ripeness of the fruit)

4 cups fruit (peeled, pitted, and/or sliced, as appropriate), singly or in combination, such as strawberries, raspberries, blackberries, peaches, nectarines, or mangoes

1 cup chilled wine, such as fruity red or white wine, Champagne, Prosecco, or a dessert (sweet) wine, such as Muscat de Beaumes-de-Venise, Sauternes, Marsala, or Banyuls

2 to 4 teaspoons fresh lemon juice (to taste)

Flavorings (optional), such as

¼ **teaspoon ground spices,** such as cinnamon, cloves, or cardamom

8 fresh basil or rose geranium leaves, left whole or torn

1 tablespoon finely slivered orange, lemon, or lime zest

1. In a medium bowl, sprinkle the sugar over the fruit and toss to coat. Marinate for 2 hours at room temperature or up to 6 hours in the refrigerator. The fruit will release some of its juices to form a syrup.

2. Up to 1 hour before serving, divide the fruit and syrup evenly among four goblets. Add ¼ cup of the wine, ½ to 1 teaspoon of the lemon juice, and any flavorings to each goblet; toss the fruit to coat.

Frozen Lychees

In late June in New York's Chinatown, the sidewalks are strewn with the brittle rose-brown shells of fresh lychees: telltale evidence of impromptu open-air snacking on this beloved fruit. Wrapped in a thin, pliable shell, the silky opalescent fruit has an intoxicatingly exotic aroma. Lychees have increased so much in popularity among Westerners of late that I have found them in many supermarkets as well as gourmet and Asian markets.

My friend Anne Disrude had the inspired idea to freeze lychees whole in their shells. She places a bowl of them on the dinner table for guests to peel themselves and enjoy the frozen sorbet-like flesh within for an effortless and dramatic dessert, especially when paired with homemade cookies.

Buy lychees by the pound, and still on their branches if possible. No ripening is required. They will keep for 2 to 3 weeks under refrigeration. Stored in a plastic bag in the freezer, they will keep for 2 to 3 months.

Tropical Fruits with Passion Fruit Sauce

Inside the homely, puckered brown shell of the passion fruit is a bright orange pulp with a marvelous flavor that mingles pineapple, orange, and banana. It makes a lovely instant sauce for a variety of fruits, particularly tropical ones such as mango, papaya, banana, and pineapple, although peaches and strawberries also go well with it.

One passion fruit will yield enough pulp to dress 1 serving (about 1 cup) of fruit.

Simply slice the passion fruit crosswise in half and scoop out the pulp. Strain, if desired, although the seeds can be eaten and add a pleasant crunch. Toss the pulp with fresh-cut fruits.

White Peaches with Crushed Raspberry Sauce

At Le Merenda, a tiny restaurant near the Cours Saleya market in Nice that is renowned for the simple preparation of perfect ingredients, I tasted as lovely a dessert as I have ever encountered: an ordinary-sounding "compote" of raspberries and peaches. The raspberries were crushed with a fork rather than pureed, leaving their texture intact. The perfectly ripe white peaches with their characteristic haunting fragrance were simply tossed with the raspberry sauce, whose slight acidity enhanced their extraordinary flavor.

In a medium bowl, with a fork, mash 2 cups fresh raspberries with 2 tablespoons sugar and 1 teaspoon fresh lemon juice until coarsely crushed. Just before serving, peel 6 ripe peaches, preferably white, cut into ½-inch slices, and toss with the crushed raspberries. Serve at once. (Serves 6.)

FRUITS IN FRAGRANT SYRUPS.

Figure on about ¼ cup flavored syrup per 1-cup serving fresh fruit.

Many years ago, at Restaurant l'Archestrate in Paris, I was served a simple dessert of beautifully cut tropical fruits in a syrup infused with vanilla bean, lemongrass, coriander seeds, five-spice powder, ginger, and lime, orange, and lemon zests. Of that entire meal of many courses, that is what I remember most vividly, for its elemental beauty and surprising flavors.

Syrups flavored with delicate and unusual combinations of spices, citrus zest, herbs, eau-de-vie, or flower water can turn simple fresh-cut fruits into memorable desserts that belie their ease of preparation. You can also use these syrups to moisten plain uniced cakes and as a poaching liquid for sturdy fruits, such as pears, peaches, and apricots or dried fruit.

Though flavored syrups are typically 50 percent sugar, I find that much lighter syrups provide enough sweetness to enhance the fruits' natural flavors and to carry flavorings without being cloying or adding unnecessary calories. I often add a split vanilla bean to the syrup because it amplifies the natural sweetness and perfume of the fruit, making it possible to use less sugar.

The following recipes illustrate some of the possible combinations of herbs, spices, and eaux-de-vie you can use to flavor syrups. These syrups can be made up to a week ahead and refrigerated, to create lovely impromptu desserts.

Basic Vanilla Bean Syrup

Vanilla is one of the prime movers in fruit desserts because it heightens the natural flavors of fruits as it sweetens. This syrup has the sweet, rather floral flavor of vanilla beans that complements just about any fruit. You can add other flavors to the basic syrup, such as 1 tablespoon of an eau-de-vie such as Poire William or Calvados, strips of lemon or orange zest, spices, or herbs such as basil or rosemary.

MAKES 1 CUP; SERVES 4

Even after they have been cooked, scraped vanilla bean pods have a lot of flavor. To make vanilla sugar, dry them well and place in a jar of sugar for at least 2 weeks, adding more as you have them.

> 1½ cups water
>
> 3 tablespoons sugar
>
> 1 moist vanilla bean, preferably Mexican or Bourbon (Madagascar)

In a small saucepan, combine the water and sugar. With a thin sharp paring knife, split the vanilla bean lengthwise in half. Scrape out the seeds and add the seeds and bean to the pan. Simmer over moderate heat until reduced to 1 cup, about 10 minutes. Let cool, then discard the bean.

You can make the syrup up to 1 week ahead; cover and refrigerate.

IN ADVANCE

Kirsch Syrup. The combination of intensely flavored kirsch (cherry eau-de-vie) and vanilla is especially good with honeydew melon, pineapple, apricots, peaches, and of course, cherries.

variation

Add two 2-by-½-inch strips lemon zest along with the vanilla. When the syrup is cool, stir in 1 tablespoon kirsch.

Rose Water Syrup. This syrup, scented with a fragrant distillation of damask roses, is lovely on lush fruits such as strawberries, blackberries, raspberries, melon, and lychees. In Morocco, it is poured over oranges sprinkled with a pinch of cinnamon. My favorite combination is sliced fresh black figs and cherries.

variation

The best rose waters are from France or the Middle East, available at Mediterranean, gourmet, and herb stores. Avoid synthetically derived rose water, which has chemical overtones.

Add 1 cinnamon stick along with the vanilla. When the syrup is cool, stir in 2 teaspoons rose water.

variation **Rosemary and Lavender Syrup.** Use a mild, fragrant honey to sweeten the syrup and act as a wine-like base for the herbs. You could also use a fragrant sweet dessert wine mixed with an equal amount of water as a base. This syrup goes well with peaches, nectarines, apricots, cherries, berries, and very ripe figs. Lavender flowers can be found at herb markets as well as stores that sell flowers for sachets (make sure they are unsprayed).

Substitute 3 tablespoons mild, fragrant golden honey (preferably lime blossom) for the sugar. Omit the vanilla bean, and add ½ teaspoon lavender blossoms and a sprig of fresh rosemary. When the syrup is cool, remove the rosemary sprig.

variation **Basil and Cinnamon Syrup.** This syrup is lovely on peaches, nectarines, and all kinds of berries. Omit the vanilla bean and add ½ cup finely shredded fresh basil and a 2-inch piece of cinnamon stick. When the syrup is cool, strain and stir in 1 tablespoon fresh lemon juice.

variation **Whiskey and White Peppercorn Syrup.** This syrup is wonderful on orange sections, sliced bananas, and fresh cherries. Use only ½ vanilla bean, and add 16 white peppercorns. After the syrup has reduced to 1 cup, add ¼ cup slivered lemon zest and simmer for 2 minutes longer. Add 1 tablespoon Irish whiskey, cool to room temperature, and remove the vanilla bean.

Alain Senderens's Syrup for Tropical Fruits

MAKES 1 CUP;
SERVES 4

This delicate, highly perfumed syrup is like an essence of exotic flowers. It goes particularly well with fruits such as mango, pineapple, kiwi, papaya, and passion fruit.

1 cup plus 3 tablespoons water

3 tablespoons sugar

1 bulb fresh lemongrass, smashed and chopped (1½ tablespoons), or 1½ teaspoons dried lemongrass plus 2 grinds of fresh black pepper

3 coriander seeds

1 whole clove

¼ teaspoon five-spice powder

Three 2-by-¾-inch strips lime zest (removed with a vegetable peeler)

Three 2-by-¾-inch strips orange zest (removed with a vegetable peeler)

Three 2-by-3¾-inch strips lemon zest (removed with a vegetable peeler)

½ teaspoon chopped fresh ginger

1 vanilla bean

1 tablespoon fresh lime juice

In a small saucepan, combine the water, sugar, lemongrass, coriander seeds, clove, five-spice powder, zests, and ginger. With a thin sharp paring knife, split the vanilla bean lengthwise in half. Scrape out the seeds and add the seeds and bean to the pan. Bring to a boil and remove from the heat. Let cool.

Strain the syrup and stir in the lime juice.

You can make the syrup up to 1 week ahead; cover and refrigerate.   IN ADVANCE

Berry Elixir

This syrup, created by pastry chef Rhona Lauvand, is less an adornment than a magic elixir; it will coax superb flavor from even less-than-perfect berries, especially useful in winter when only out-of-season berries are available.   MAKES 1½ CUPS, ENOUGH FOR 8 CUPS BERRIES

Let the berries macerate in the syrup for at least 1 hour, or overnight in the refrigerator. To dress smaller amounts of fruit, figure on 2 to 3 tablespoons elixir per cup of fruit.

⅔ cup water

⅔ cup sugar

Four 3-by-¾-inch strips lemon zest (removed with a vegetable peeler)

Two 3-by-¾-inch strips orange zest (removed with a vegetable peeler)

⅓ vanilla bean

⅓ cup fresh or frozen unsweetened raspberries

¼ cup fresh orange juice

2 tablespoons fresh lemon juice, or to taste

In a small saucepan, combine the water, sugar, and the citrus zests. With a thin sharp paring knife, split the vanilla bean lengthwise in half. Scrape out the seeds and add the seeds and bean to the pan. Simmer over moderate heat for 5 minutes. Set aside to cool and infuse.

Strain the syrup into a food processor or blender. Add the raspberries and puree until smooth. Strain the puree, then add the orange juice and enough lemon juice to create a balance of tart and sweet.

You can make the elixir up to 5 days ahead; cover and refrigerate.   IN ADVANCE

BOWL AND SPOON DESSERTS. My taste in desserts leans toward rather sloppy warm desserts I can eat out of a wide shallow soup bowl with a large soupspoon. I call them bowl and spoon desserts: free-form assemblages of cooked or roasted fruits with various embellishments, such as sauces or ice cream. They can be as simple as Warm Fresh Cherries with Kirsch (page 472) with a small scoop of vanilla ice cream, or Caramelized Roasted Pears (page 476) with a saffron custard sauce (page 530). If you take them a step further and add phyllo pastry lids or cookie-cutter shapes of a rich nut pastry, they provide all the satisfaction of a tart. These are really the most spectacular and rewarding desserts for the amount of work involved, at once homey and elegant, inventive but unfussy. They are wonderful dinner party fare; the component parts can all be made ahead and assembled at the last minute.

The recipes in this section illustrate simple ways to cook the fruits that are the basis for bowl and spoon desserts. Recipes for complementary sauces, ice creams, and pastries can be found elsewhere in the chapter.

This blueprint illustrates the basic approach to constructing Bowl and Spoon Desserts. The possible combinations are endless.

Base of cooked or roasted fruits, such as

Warm Fresh Cherries with Kirsch (page 472)

Inside a Blueberry Pie (page 473)

Prunes in Armagnac (page 473)

Roasted Fruit (page 475)

Caramelized Roasted Pears (page 476)

Apricots Roasted with Cardamom (page 478)

Slow-Roasted Peaches (page 476)

PLUS

Saucy or creamy embellishments, such as

Warm Spilling Fruit (page 472)

Fruit Coulis (page 528)

Strawberries in Beaujolais Sauce (page 529)

Basic Vanilla Custard Sauce (page 529) or variations

AND/OR

Quick Sorbets and Faux Ice Creams (page 525)

Real Whipped Cream or Crème Fraîche (page 533)

Rich Faux Cream (page 534)

Yogurt Cream (page 535)

AND

A pastry lid or crunchy topping, such as

Foolproof Flaky Butter Pastry (page 490)

Individual Phyllo Disks (page 495)

Thin Phyllo Wafers (page 496)

Earl Grey Tea Wafers (page 516)

Clove and Lemon Wafers (page 517)

Apple, Pear, Banana, or Mango Chips (page 519)

Roasted nuts (see page 676)

Warm Spilling Fruit

A GUIDE TO IMPROVING

SERVES 4 Ripe fruit gently cooked with a small amount of sugar and a little water releases its juices and melts slightly. A vanilla bean amplifies the fruit's own sweetness and perfume. The effect is like a pie filling and has many uses, both as filling and as sauce. The fruit is delicious served warm, with or without a small scoop of ice cream or a tablespoon of crème fraîche. It can be spooned into a wide shallow bowl and topped with a baked pastry "lid" or used as a rustic sauce for Roasted Fruit (page 475) and plain cakes.

This method works wonderfully for many kinds of fruits, including pears, apples, peaches, nectarines, mangoes, plums, cherries, and berries, such as strawberries, raspberries, and blackberries.

3 cups fresh fruit (peeled, pitted, and/or sliced ½ inch thick, as appropriate), singly or in combination, such as strawberries, raspberries, blackberries, blueberries, peaches, nectarines, or plums

2 tablespoons water

1 to 4 tablespoons sugar, honey, or maple syrup (depending on the sweetness of the fruit)

1 vanilla bean

1 to 2 teaspoons fresh lemon juice

1 to 3 teaspoons eau-de-vie, such as kirsch, framboise, or Poire William (optional)

1. In a medium saucepan, combine the fruit, water, and 1 tablespoon of the sugar. With a thin sharp knife, split the vanilla bean lengthwise in half. Scrape out the seeds and add the seeds and bean to the pan. Cover and cook over moderate heat until the fruit releases its juices, 2 to 4 minutes.

2. Taste the fruit for sweetness and add more sugar if necessary. Stir in the lemon juice. Uncover and cook over high heat until the fruit is tender and the juices are syrupy, about 2 minutes longer. Discard the vanilla bean and stir in the eau-de-vie, if desired. Serve warm.

Warm Fresh Cherries with Kirsch

improvisation 1

Pitting cherries seems like such a daunting task that people rarely eat fresh cherries these days any way other than out of hand. So we miss the extraordinary pleasure of cooked fresh cherries, when their fragrance is released in all its glory.

In this warm compote, pitted cherries are cooked with a vanilla bean and sugar just until they release their juices. A drizzle of kirsch (cherry brandy) accentuates their marvelous flavor. They are best eaten warm, spooned into shallow soup bowls, with a Scented Custard Sauce (page 530), Real Whipped Cream or Crème Fraîche (page 533), ice cream, ice milk, or frozen yogurt. They also make an extraordinary sauce for plain cakes such as Fresh Lemon Cake (page 506) or Pistachio and Almond Cake (page 514).

Follow the Guide on page 472 using 3 cups pitted fresh cherries (see page 677) and 3 tablespoons sugar or honey. When the cherries are tender, discard the vanilla bean and stir in 2 to 3 teaspoons kirsch, rum, or cognac.

Inside a Blueberry Pie

improvisation 2

This wonderful stew of blueberries is indeed like the inside of a blueberry pie. Sprigs of fresh thyme make the blueberries taste like wild ones. Served warm, the sauce is particularly good with baked fruits such as Slow-Roasted Peaches (page 476) or Caramelized Roasted Pears (page 476) or with vanilla ice cream or frozen yogurt. The sauce can also be made with black or red raspberries or blackberries. (The frozen sugarless blackberries available in supermarkets work wonderfully.)

Follow the Guide on page 472, using fresh or frozen unsweetened blueberries, 1½ tablespoons honey, 1 tablespoon water, and ½ vanilla bean. Add 2 to 3 sprigs fresh thyme, cover, and cook over moderate heat until the berries have released their juices but are still whole, about 5 minutes. Remove the vanilla bean.

Prunes in Armagnac

These boozy prunes are a classic of Southwest France, land of confit, pâté, and foie gras. They are steeped in a syrup spiked with Armagnac, the region's delicious brandy. Since the prunes are pitted, they release some of their sweet juices to make a syrup, making little sugar necessary. The prunes are so intensely flavored they can be eaten almost as a candy, to finish off a meal. The Armagnac in the syrup tends to sneak up on people, rendering them as giddy as children. The prunes are sublime served over vanilla and coffee ice cream and as an ingredient in pear, apple, or quince tarts. Prepare at least 1 week before serving to allow the prunes to mellow. Since they last indefinitely, you can keep them on hand for instant desserts. Packed in a pretty jar, they make a welcome gift.

MAKES ABOUT 3 CUPS

1 ½ cups water

2 tablespoons sugar

1 vanilla bean

12 ounces large pitted prunes

½ cup Armagnac or Bas Armagnac, or more to taste

In a small nonreactive saucepan, combine the water and sugar. With a thin sharp knife, split the vanilla bean lengthwise and scrape out the seeds. Add the seeds and bean to the pan and bring to a boil over moderately high heat, stirring until the sugar dissolves.

Place the prunes in a clean dry jar and pour the syrup over them. Allow to cool completely, then stir in the Armagnac. Refrigerate for at least 1 week before serving.

IN ADVANCE Refrigerated, the prunes will keep indefinitely.

variation **Prune Croustade.** Arrange 5 Prunes in Armagnac in each shallow dessert bowl and top with a tablespoon of crème fraîche and an Individual Phyllo Disk (page 495).

Warm Sautéed Fresh Figs with Raspberry Coulis and Cream

SERVES 4 Sliced figs are sautéed in butter and sugar until they are just caramelized and warmed but not cooked through. The slight heating releases their fragrance. Served in a pool of pureed raspberries with a drizzle of cream, they make an intoxicating dessert. To gild the lily, top with a Thin Phyllo Wafer (page 496).

½ cup Raspberry Coulis (page 528)

2 tablespoons heavy cream or crème fraîche, stirred to loosen it

1 tablespoon plus 1 teaspoon unsalted butter

2 tablespoons plus 1 teaspoon sugar

6 medium figs, halved through the stem

Just before cooking the figs, spoon 2 tablespoons of the coulis into each of four shallow soup bowls. Drizzle ½ tablespoon of the cream over each pool of coulis.

In a large nonstick skillet, heat the butter and sugar over moderately high heat, stirring occasionally, until golden brown and bubbly. Add the figs cut side down to the pan and shake the pan vigorously until the figs just begin to release their juices, about 1 minute. Turn the figs over and cook for 1 minute longer, or until they are coated with the butter and sugar and warm but not really cooked or soft. Arrange 3 fig halves in each bowl and serve at once.

Roasted Fruit

A GUIDE TO IMPROVISING

SERVES 4

Roasting tends to bring out the best in fruits. The dry heat concentrates the flavors and caramelizes the natural sugars. A small amount of butter brushed on roasted fruits tastes like a great deal more.

This method works for many kinds of fruits, including plums, apricots, peaches, pears, apples, pineapples, and mangoes. Extremely soft, skinless fruits such as strawberries or peeled bananas need no water at all. Although the basic mixture of vanilla, lemon juice, and sugar will heighten the fruit's flavors, you can also dust it with a pinch of ground spices such as cinnamon, allspice, or cardamom, or even fresh herbs. A teaspoon of fresh thyme leaves gives roasted plums a somewhat wild flavor.

You can combine roasted fruits with a sauce of Fruit Coulis (page 528), a custard sauce (pages 529–530), or with tiny scoops of vanilla ice cream. Roasted peaches are lovely with Inside a Blueberry Pie (page 473).

> **3 to 4 tablespoons sugar, honey, or maple syrup**
>
> **½ vanilla bean**
>
> **2 tablespoons water**
>
> **1½ pounds fruit,** peeled, pitted, and halved or sliced (no more than ¾ inch thick) as appropriate such as pears, fresh peaches, apricots, nectarines, apples, pineapple, mangoes, strawberries, or bananas
>
> **2 teaspoons fresh lemon juice**
>
> **2 teaspoons unsalted butter** (optional)

1. Preheat the oven to 375°F.

2. If using the sugar, place it in a small bowl. With a thin sharp knife, split the vanilla bean lengthwise in half and scrape out the seeds. Stir the seeds into the sugar. Or, if you are using honey or maple syrup, combine it with the water, then add the vanilla seeds. Cut the vanilla bean into 2-inch pieces.

3. Arrange the fruit in a large baking dish, cut side up if halved. Drizzle the lemon juice evenly over the fruit, then drizzle the vanilla sugar or sweetener over. Nestle the vanilla bean among the fruit. If using sugar, add the water to the dish. If desired, cut the butter into small pieces and distribute it over the fruit.

4. Roast the fruit, brushing it occasionally with the pan juices, until it is tender and glazed and the juices are thick and syrupy. If the syrup evaporates too quickly, add a tablespoon or two more water to the dish. If the fruit is halved, turn over halfway through the cooking time. Softer fruits, such as plums, apricots, or peaches, will take about 20 to 25 minutes. Harder fruits, such as pears and apples, will take about 40 minutes. Serve warm.

an improvisation

Slow-Roasted Stone Fruits

When I have time, I like to slow-roast stone fruits such as peaches and plums at 275°F. It renders the flesh extraordinarily creamy and concentrated.

Follow the Guide above, using peaches or plums. Use only 1 teaspoon sugar and omit the water and lemon juice; melt the butter. Cut the fruit through the stem along the natural seam and remove the pits. Roast the fruit cut side up, brushed with the lemon juice, butter, and a sprinkle of sugar, until very tender, 2 to 2½ hours.

Caramelized Roasted Pears

SERVES 4

Pears roasted with a sweet fragrant dessert wine and a little butter become dense and glazed, as though they were cooked with a lot of butter. They are delicious as is or with Saffron Custard Sauce or Raspberry Coulis.

When I make this dessert, I usually open a half bottle of a good dessert wine, using some to roast the pears and serving the rest chilled with the dessert. If you don't have dessert wine, mix ⅔ cup Riesling with 1½ tablespoons wildflower honey.

> **4 large not-quite-ripe pears** (1½ pounds), preferably Comice
>
> **¾ cup sweet dessert wine,** such as Muscat de Beaumes-de-Venise, Sauternes, Barsac, or Monbazillac, plus more if needed
>
> **½ vanilla bean**
>
> **2 teaspoons unsalted butter**
>
> **1½ tablespoons sugar**
>
> **Saffron Custard Sauce** (page 530), **Raspberry Coulis** (page 528), **or 4 small scoops vanilla ice cream** (optional)

Preheat the oven to 375°F.

Peel the pears. Cut them lengthwise in half and scoop out the cores and seeds, leaving the stems intact if possible. Arrange the pear halves cut side down in a large ovenproof skillet or flameproof baking dish. Pour ½ cup of the wine over the fruit. With a sharp paring knife, split the vanilla bean lengthwise in half. Scrape out the seeds and add to the wine. Nestle the bean among the pears. Dot the pears with the butter. Bring to a boil over moderate heat.

Cover loosely with foil and roast for 35 minutes, brushing the pears occasionally with the wine. Turn the pears over, cover loosely, and bake for 15 minutes longer, brushing them frequently.

Set the skillet over moderate heat and add the remaining ¼ cup wine. Simmer until the liquid is syrupy, about 3 minutes. Turn the pears over so they are again cut side down, and sprinkle with the sugar.

Return to the oven and roast for an additional 10 to 15 minutes, brushing the pears frequently, until they are tender and nicely glazed. If the wine evaporates too quickly, add a little more wine or warm water to the skillet to dissolve the caramelized juices into a thick glaze. Set aside to cool slightly.

To serve, arrange 2 pear halves in each of four shallow soup bowls and brush with the syrup. Spoon the sauce around the pears or place a small scoop of vanilla ice cream between them.

IN ADVANCE You can roast the pears up to 2 hours before serving. Rewarm them in a 250°F oven for about 20 minutes, adding a little water to the pan if necessary to dissolve some of the juices so you can brush the pears 2 or 3 times.

variation **Roasted Pear and Raspberry Napoleon.** Assemble these at the last minute to keep the pastry from getting soggy.

Roast the pears as directed above. Slice each pear half crosswise into ¼-inch-thick slices. In a small bowl, coarsely mash 1 cup fresh raspberries with 2 teaspoons sugar. Place 1 Thin Phyllo Wafer (page 496) on each of eight dessert plates. Arrange one half of a sliced pear on each wafer. Spoon a little of the crushed raspberries over each pear, then top with 2 tablespoons Real Whipped Cream or Crème Fraîche (page 533) or Rich Faux Cream (page 534). Arrange another phyllo wafer on top of each. Strain confectioners' sugar over them.

Apricots Roasted with Cardamom

Because I so rarely find fresh apricots with really good flavor and texture, I often use dried apricots in desserts. Once reconstituted, they can be roasted just like fresh ones, and yield an intense true apricot flavor. (Dried apricots keep indefinitely, so have them on hand for times when you have no fresh fruit.) Here they are flavored with cardamom and vanilla, inspired by a recipe from Paula Wolfert. They are great with Yogurt Cream (page 535), Real Whipped Cream or Crème Fraîche (page 533), or ice cream.

Use California dried apricots, which are more tart and have a more consistent texture than Turkish apricots.

If you should happen upon great fresh apricots, roast them as directed below, using 1 pound apricots, halved and pitted, and only ½ cup water (soaking is not necessary).

> **8 ounces large California dried apricot halves** (about 30)
> **2 cups water**
> **2 tablespoons plus 2 teaspoons sugar**
> **½ vanilla bean**
> **3 cardamom pods**
> **2 teaspoons fresh lemon juice**

Place the dried apricots in a medium bowl and pour the water over them. Set aside to soak for at least 6 hours or overnight.

Preheat the oven to 400°F.

Drain the apricots, reserving ½ cup of the soaking liquid. Arrange the apricots skin side down in a baking dish.

Place the sugar in a small bowl. With a sharp paring knife, split the vanilla bean lengthwise in half. Scrape out the seeds and stir them into the sugar. (Place the pod in a jar of sugar to make vanilla sugar if you like.) Crush the cardamom pods and stir the black seeds into the sugar; discard the pods.

Sprinkle 2 tablespoons of the vanilla sugar over the apricots. Reserve the rest. Drizzle 6 tablespoons of the reserved soaking liquid and the lemon juice over the fruit; reserve the rest.

Roast the apricots until they are tender, about 30 minutes, spooning the juices over them twice. (If the juices are evaporating too quickly, add some of the reserved soaking liquid to the dish.)

Sprinkle the apricots with the remaining 2 teaspoons vanilla sugar and roast for 10 minutes longer, or until the apricots are well glazed and tinged with brown and almost all of the liquid has evaporated. Serve warm or at room temperature.

You can roast the apricots up to 5 hours before serving. To serve warm, heat gently in a shallow pan on the stove top.

variation

Apricots Roasted with Kirsch. Use either dried or fresh apricots. Omit the cardamom and add 1½ tablespoons kirsch (cherry eau-de-vie) during the last 30 minutes of cooking.

Strawberry-Rhubarb Crumble

SERVES 6

A crumble is a fine quick solution when you hunger for a tart: It is nothing more than fruit topped with a mixture of sugar, flour, butter, and ground almonds, which bakes into a crisp buttery topping that offers many of the satisfactions of a piecrust with much less work. You can substitute many kinds of fruits for the strawberry-rhubarb mixture; figure on about 5 cups sliced fruit (peeled if desired) and add sugar and lemon juice according to its sweetness; for juicy fruits such as peaches and berries, add 2 tablespoons flour.

I also like to use other kinds of nuts. Hazelnuts, roasted, peeled, and thinly sliced (see page 676), are marvelous.

Topping

¼ **cup plus 2 tablespoons** (1½ ounces) **sliced almonds**

¼ **cup plus 2 tablespoons unbleached all-purpose flour**

¼ **cup plus 2 tablespoons packed dark brown sugar**

Pinch of kosher salt

3 tablespoons cold unsalted butter, cut into ¼-inch pieces

1½ **pounds rhubarb,** ends trimmed, sliced into ½-inch chunks (4 cups)

1½ **cups ripe strawberries,** hulled and halved, or quartered if large

2 tablespoons unbleached all-purpose flour

3 tablespoons granulated sugar

2 tablespoons dark brown sugar

1 tablespoon fresh lemon juice

Preheat the oven to 350°F.

To make the topping, spread the almonds on a baking sheet. Roast until they are just golden and fragrant, 6 to 7 minutes; do not allow them to brown. Set aside to cool.

In a food processor, grind the almonds, flour, sugar, and salt to a medium-fine meal. Transfer to a medium bowl. With your fingers, work in the butter by pinching and rubbing the mixture until it is very crumbly. Refrigerate for 15 minutes.

In a 10-inch gratin dish, combine the rhubarb with the strawberries. Toss with the flour and both sugars. Sprinkle the lemon juice over the fruit and toss again. Spread the fruit evenly in the dish and spread the topping evenly over it.

Bake until the fruit is bubbling and the top is browned, about 40 minutes. If the top is browning too quickly, cover loosely with foil. Serve warm or at room temperature.

IN ADVANCE You can prepare the topping up to 4 days ahead; cover and refrigerate. You can prepare the filling up to 2 hours ahead; add the topping just before baking. The crumble is best eaten within 2 hours of baking.

variation **Pear or Apple Crumble.** Proceed as directed, but prepare the filling using 4 large pears or apples, peeled, cored, and thinly sliced, 2 tablespoons dark brown sugar, ½ teaspoon ground cinnamon (optional), and 2 tablespoons fresh lemon juice. Bake for 50 to 60 minutes, until the fruit is tender.

variation **Peach-Blackberry Crumble.** Proceed as directed, but prepare the filling using 3 cups blackberries or blueberries, 2 cups sliced peeled peaches, preferably white-fleshed, 2 tablespoons unbleached all-purpose flour, 2 tablespoons sugar, and 1½ teaspoons fresh lemon juice. Bake for about 40 minutes, until the fruit is tender and the top is browned.

FRUIT TARTS AND FREE-FORM PASTRIES. I love fruit tarts and pies for the great variation in flavors and texture they provide in one fell swoop, from flaky crust to tender, juicy fruit filling. In addition, they evoke plenty of childhood memories—blueberry pies at the beach and apple pies at Thanksgiving—and rather primitive feelings of safety. My pies and tarts must satisfy the criteria of childhood memory (my mother was a consummate pie maker) while being low enough in sugar and fat to satisfy my dietary needs and easy to accomplish.

You can cut back on the amount of sugar and butter in most recipes by following these tips: Use fragrant ripe fruit; add a vanilla bean, split and scraped, lemon juice, and/or eau-de-vie to heighten the sense of sweetness; and add a small amount of butter on top of the fruit, where it will be immediately tasted.

Rustic Free-form Fruit Tarts

A GUIDE TO IMPROVISING

Here is a rustic European hybrid of tarts and pies reminiscent of the galettes found all over France. Their charm lies in their imperfection.

SERVES 6

All of these tarts rely on one simple dough that's rolled into a rough free-form round. The fruit is piled in the middle and the edges are folded up around it. This method eliminates much of what can be daunting about making tarts and pies: the time-consuming task of crimping dough into a tart tin or pie plate. This is the quickest method I know to create a great fruit pie-tart, about 20 minutes once the pastry is made. (Make up batches of the pastry and freeze for when you are pinched for time.)

You can prepare variations of this tart throughout the year with whatever fruits are in season. The only variables are the way the fruit is cut and the amount of sugar. See the improvisations that follow for specific combinations.

Foolproof Flaky Butter Pastry (page 490)

1 tablespoon sugar

2 to 2½ tablespoons unbleached all-purpose flour for thickening the juices, plus extra for rolling the dough

Fruit Filling

> **3 cups ripe fruit** (peeled, pitted, and cut into ¼-inch-thick slices as appropriate), such as pears, plums, peaches, apricots, bananas, berries, cherries, or rhubarb
>
> **1 to 2 tablespoons fresh lemon juice**
>
> **3 tablespoons to ½ cup sugar** (depending on the sweetness of the fruit)

Flavorings (optional), singly or in combination, such as

> **½ vanilla bean,** split lengthwise in half, seeds scraped out and mixed with the sugar, or 1 to 2 teaspoons pure vanilla extract
>
> **½ to ¾ teaspoon ground spices,** such as cinnamon or cloves, or a few gratings of nutmeg
>
> **1 to 3 teaspoons eau-de-vie,** such as framboise, Poire William, or kirsch
>
> **1 to 1½ teaspoons minced fresh thyme or rosemary**

1 teaspoon unsalted butter

2 teaspoons confectioners' sugar

1. Preheat the oven to 400°F.

2. On a lightly floured surface, roll the dough into a rough circle 14 or 15 inches in diameter. Transfer the dough to a baking sheet and refrigerate it while you prepare the fruit.

3. In a small bowl, combine the 1 tablespoon sugar with 2 tablespoons flour (or 2½ tablespoons for very juicy fruits, such as berries, rhubarb, and cherries).

4. Place the fruit in a bowl and toss it with the lemon juice, sugar, and any flavorings. Remove the dough from the refrigerator and sprinkle the flour/sugar mixture evenly over it, leaving a 2-inch border uncovered. Arrange the fruit evenly over the flour/sugar mixture. Fold the edges of the dough over the fruit. Moisten your fingers with water and gently press the pleats so that they hold together. Shave the butter over the fruit.

5. Bake the tart until the crust is golden brown, the fruit is tender, and the juices syrupy, about 40 minutes, covering the tart halfway through the cooking time if the crust is browning too rapidly. Let cool for 10 minutes, then slide the tart onto a serving platter.

6. Just before serving, sift the confectioners' sugar evenly over the crust.

Miniature rustic
free-form fruit tarts
(page 481–485)

MAKING RUSTIC FREE-FORM TARTLETS

You can make tartlets in a variety of sizes by making the following simple adjustments to the Guide on pages 481 to 482:

- **For two 7-inch tarts,** divide the dough in half and roll each portion into a circle about 9 inches in diameter. Proceed as directed, using half of the filling for each tart. Bake for about 25 minutes.

- **For four 5-inch tarts,** divide the dough into quarters and roll each portion into a circle about 7 inches in diameter. Proceed as directed, using one quarter of the filling for each tart and leaving a 1½-inch border of dough uncovered to fold over the fruit. Bake for about 20 minutes.

- **For eight 3-inch tarts** (especially appealing with berries), divide the dough into 8 pieces and roll each portion into a circle about 4 inches in diameter. Proceed as directed, using one eighth of the filling for each tartlet and leaving a 1-inch border of dough uncovered to fold over the fruit. Bake for about 15 minutes.

improvisation 1 ## Pear Tart

Follow the Guide on pages 481 to 482, using the following filling: In a small bowl, combine ¼ cup sugar with the seeds scraped from ½ vanilla bean, split lengthwise (alternatively, use ¾ teaspoon pure vanilla extract). Peel and core 1½ pounds ripe, fragrant pears and cut into ¼-inch slices (about 3 cups). Place in a bowl and toss with 1 tablespoon fresh lemon juice, 1 teaspoon Poire William (optional), and the vanilla sugar.

improvisation 2 ## Plum Tart

Follow the Guide on pages 481 to 482, using the following filling: Cut 1½ pounds ripe plums into ¼-inch slices (about 3 cups) and place in a bowl. Toss with 1 tablespoon fresh lemon juice, 1 teaspoon pure vanilla extract or framboise, and ¼ cup plus 2 tablespoons sugar.

improvisation 3 ## Peach Tart

Follow the Guide on pages 481 to 482, using the following filling: In a small bowl, combine ¼ cup sugar with the seeds scraped from ½ vanilla bean, split lengthwise (alternatively, use ¾ teaspoon pure vanilla extract). Peel and pit 1½ pounds ripe peaches or nectarines and cut into ¼-inch slices (3 cups). Place in a bowl and toss with 1 tablespoon fresh lemon juice, 1 teaspoon framboise or kirsch (optional), and the vanilla sugar.

improvisation 4 ## Apricot Tart

It is rare even in summer to find good apricots in this country. More often than not, they have little flavor and a mealy texture. Oddly enough, though, you can make lovely tarts using apricots canned in extra-light syrup. Baking them with kirsch and vanilla completely transforms them, bringing out a lovely fresh apricot flavor.

Follow the Guide on pages 481 to 482, using the following filling: Drain two 16-ounce cans apricot halves in extra-light syrup. In a small bowl, combine 2 tablespoons sugar with the seeds scraped from ½ vanilla bean, split lengthwise (alternatively, use ¾ teaspoon pure vanilla extract). Place the apricots in a bowl and toss them with 1 tablespoon kirsch, 1 teaspoon fresh lemon juice, and the vanilla sugar.

Banana Tart

improvisation 5

Follow the Guide on pages 481 to 482, using the following filling: Slice 3 medium ripe bananas (1½ pounds) ¼ inch thick on a diagonal. Place in a bowl and toss gently with 1 teaspoon dark rum, 1 teaspoon pure vanilla extract, and 2 tablespoons sugar. Bake the tart for only 30 minutes.

Raspberry, Blackberry, or Blueberry Tart

improvisation 6

Follow the Guide on pages 481 to 482, using 2½ tablespoons flour for thickening and the following filling: In a medium bowl, toss 1½ pints (about 3 cups) raspberries, blackberries, and/or blueberries (in any combination), 1 tablespoon fresh lemon juice, 1 teaspoon framboise or kirsch (optional), and ¼ cup sugar.

Cherry Tart

improvisation 7

Follow the Guide on pages 481 to 482, using 2½ tablespoons flour for thickening and the following filling: In a small bowl, combine 3 tablespoons sugar with the seeds scraped from ½ vanilla bean, split lengthwise (alternatively, use ¾ teaspoon pure vanilla extract). Pit 1½ pounds cherries (see page 677) and place in a medium bowl. Toss with 2 teaspoons fresh lemon juice, 2 teaspoons kirsch (optional), and the vanilla sugar.

Rhubarb Tart

improvisation 8

Dried strawberries or cherries add sweet, fruity notes that balance the rhubarb's tart, wild flavors. Instead of dried fruit, you can substitute 1 cup quartered fresh strawberries for 1 cup of the rhubarb.

Follow the Guide on pages 481 to 482, using 1 tablespoon flour for thickening and the following filling: Cut 1¼ pounds trimmed, fresh rhubarb crosswise into ½-inch chunks (be sure to cut off and discard any leafy portions; they are poisonous). Place in a medium bowl and toss with 2 teaspoons pure vanilla extract or kirsch, 2 tablespoons all-purpose flour, ¾ cup sugar, and 2 tablespoons chopped dried strawberries or cherries (optional).

Rustic Rosemary-Apple Tart

SERVES 6 Apple tarts lend themselves to exotic flavorings beyond the classic American cinnamon-scented pies of my childhood. My favorite is rosemary, which gives a unexpectedly lovely herbal flavor to the tart.

Foolproof Flaky Butter Pastry (page 490)

2 tablespoons all-purpose flour for thickening the juices, plus extra for rolling the dough

¼ cup packed light brown sugar

1½ pounds apples, such as Granny Smith, Golden Delicious, Stayman, Macoun, or Winesap

2 tablespoons fresh lemon juice

1½ teaspoons minced fresh rosemary (do not substitute dried) or ¾ teaspoon ground cinnamon

1 teaspoon unsalted butter

2 teaspoons confectioners' sugar

Preheat the oven to 400°F.

On a lightly floured surface, roll the dough into a rough circle about 14 inches in diameter. Transfer the dough to a baking sheet and refrigerate while you prepare the apples.

In a small bowl, combine the flour with 1 tablespoon of the brown sugar; reserve. Peel and core the apples. Slice them into ¼-inch-thick slices. (You should have about 3 cups.) Place the apples in a bowl and toss them with the lemon juice, the remaining 3 tablespoons sugar, and the rosemary.

Remove the dough from the refrigerator and sprinkle the reserved flour/sugar mixture evenly over it, leaving a 2-inch border uncovered. Arrange the apples evenly over the flour mixture. Fold the edges of the dough over the apples. Moisten your fingers lightly with water and gently press the creases so that they hold together. Shave the butter over the fruit.

Bake the tart for about 40 minutes, until the crust is golden brown, the apples tender, and the juices syrupy, covering the tart halfway through the cooking time if the crust is browning too rapidly. Let cool for 10 minutes, then slide the tart onto a serving platter.

Just before serving, sift the confectioners' sugar evenly over the crust.

IN ADVANCE You can bake the tart up to 3 hours before serving.

Shaker Rose Water Apple Tart. Traditional Shaker flavorings— variation rose water and nutmeg—make an unusual and somehow poetic apple pie. Replace the rosemary with 1½ teaspoons rose water and ⅛ teaspoon freshly grated nutmeg.

Upside-Down Red Wine–Pear Tart

When I started to experiment with a lightened tarte Tatin, I remembered a SERVES 6 recipe I had learned almost twenty years ago from the late food writer Richard Olney, in which he cooked pears in red wine before baking them in an upside-down tart. This is my version of his inspired idea, which makes a very sophisticated tart.

- **2½ cups dry red wine**
- **¼ cup sugar**
- **½ vanilla bean**
- **4 large or 5 medium-small pears** (about 2 pounds)
- **2 teaspoons unsalted butter**
- **Flour for rolling**
- **Foolproof Flaky Butter Pastry** (page 490)

In a heavy ovenproof 10-inch nonstick skillet, combine the wine and sugar. With a sharp paring knife, split the vanilla bean lengthwise in half. Scrape out the seeds and add the seeds and bean to the wine. Bring to a boil over high heat and simmer until the sugar has dissolved and the wine has reduced slightly, about 5 minutes. Remove from the heat and let cool.

Peel the pears and slice them lengthwise into quarters. Remove the cores. Arrange as many of the pear quarters as will fit in a circle, stem ends toward the center, core side up, in the skillet. Cut the remaining pear quarters lengthwise in half and place 1 slice cut side down between each of the quarters. Cutting the remaining pear slices to fit if necessary, arrange them in the center of the pan and in any open spaces between the pear slices.

Set the skillet over moderate heat and bring to a boil. Reduce the heat slightly and cook at a low boil, brushing the pears frequently with the wine, until they are tender when pierced with a knife but still hold their shape and the wine is reduced and very syrupy, 40 to 45 minutes. Slip little bits of the butter down the sides of the pan and into the center of the pears. Set aside to cool.

While the pears are cooking, roll the dough out on a lightly floured surface into a circle 10 inches in diameter. Prick the dough all over with a fork. Gently roll the dough up over the rolling pin and unroll it on a baking sheet. Cover with plastic wrap and refrigerate until you are ready to bake the tart.

Preheat the oven to 400°F.

Just before baking the tart, slide the pastry on top of the pears. Bake the tart until the pastry is golden brown, 25 minutes. Set aside to cool. Do not remove the tart from the pan until you are ready to serve it, or the pastry will get soggy.

To remove the tart from the pan, set the pan over moderate heat to melt the syrup and loosen the pears. Cover the pan with a flat serving platter and invert the tart onto the platter in one quick motion. Brush the pears with the juices that remain in the pan. Serve warm.

IN ADVANCE You can cook the pears and roll out the dough up to 4 hours ahead; cover both but refrigerate just the dough. You can bake the tart up to 2 hours ahead.

Lemon Curd Tart

SERVES 8

Dried beans and grains (about 1 or 2 cups' worth) make excellent pie weights to keep an unfilled crust from losing its shape when you bake it. After using, cool them and store in a a plastic bag for the next time you need them.

This makes a thin, ethereal lemon tart very similar to the traditional French-style lemon tart—a prebaked buttery crust filled with tart lemon curd—with a great deal less calories and fat.

> **Flour** for rolling
>
> **Foolproof Flaky Butter Pastry** (page 490) **or Rich Nut Pastry** (page 491)
>
> **1 cup Tart, Ethereal Lemon Curd** (page 532)
>
> **½ cup regular or reduced-fat sour cream**

On a lightly floured work surface, roll the dough into a circle about 12 inches in diameter. Gently roll the dough up over the rolling pin and transfer it to a 10- or 10½-inch tart pan with a removable bottom. Press the edges of the dough into the sides of the pan and crimp them with a fork to make a ½-inch-high rim. Prick the pastry all over with a fork. Chill for 20 minutes.

Preheat the oven to 375°F.

Crumple a 12-inch square of waxed paper into a tight ball, then carefully uncrumple it, without ripping it. Place it in the tart shell, then fill it with pie weights, rice, or dried beans to hold the pastry in place while it bakes and sets. Bake the tart shell for 10 minutes; carefully lift up the edges of the waxed paper and remove it and the pie weights. Bake for 5 to 10 minutes longer, or until the pastry is lightly browned. Cool the tart shell on a rack, then remove the sides of the tart pan and transfer the tart shell to a serving platter.

Meanwhile, in a medium bowl, fold together the lemon curd and sour cream. Cover with plastic wrap and refrigerate until ready to use.

To serve, spread the lemon curd evenly into the tart shell.

IN ADVANCE You can bake the tart shell and prepare the lemon curd mixture up to 6 hours before serving; cover and refrigerate the curd. You can assemble the tart up to 1 hour before serving.

Lime Curd Tart. Substitute Lime Curd (page 533) for the lemon curd. variation

Lemon (or Lime) Curd Tart with Berries or Mangoes. variation To make an instant fresh berry tart, arrange 3 cups raspberries, blueberries, blackberries, or sliced strawberries on the lemon curd. The lemon curd acts like pastry cream to meld the berries with the pastry. For a spectacular tropical tart, substitute Lime Curd (page 533) for the lemon curd and arrange thin slices of ripe mango over it.

PASTRY DOUGHS.

A good pastry dough is by definition made with fat. Fat tenderizes the dough, traps air in its layers to create flakiness, and provides flavor.

I believe there is just so far you cut back on fat in pastry before the chemistry will break down, despite claims to the contrary. Witness a particularly flavorless, wooden pastry crust based on part-skim ricotta cheese, skim milk, and egg whites taught by an esteemed cooking school. Margarine is also often used in reduced-calorie or reduced-fat crusts instead of butter in the mistaken belief that it is healthier and lower in fat (see page 14). Crusts made with margarine invariably have a flat taste and cardboard texture.

To me, a crust is not worth eating unless it has the essential qualities that give satisfaction and pleasure, as important to health and well-being as vitamins and minerals. Why eat something that is only a shadow of the real thing, that forces one to pretend that it is something it is not? I make my doughs with unsalted butter, because of its inimitable flavor and the flakiness it contributes, and because I think it is healthier than hydrogenated shortenings or lard.

Foolproof Flaky Butter Pastry

MAKES
8 OUNCES
(ENOUGH FOR
ONE 9- TO
10-INCH TART)

For many people, pastry dough is one of the most fearsome tasks in cooking. All the talk of cutting in the butter just so, adding the exact amount of water, of needing just the right touch has fueled this fear. As it turns out, in the process of manipulating pie dough recipes to reduce the fat, I inadvertently created a recipe that is hard to mess up.

This is an easy-to-make crust that is flaky and tender and tastes like butter. The butter is pared down to what I consider to be the minimum amount possible. The flour/butter mixture is chilled midway through the process so that when the dough is rolled, the hard butter forms flat sheets, increasing the flakiness of the dough. Some of the usual butter is replaced with sour cream, which has less fat and calories but adds to the tenderness and richness of the crust. A pinch of baking powder adds a degree of lightening.

This crust has many possible permutations, as the variations that follow illustrate. You can use it in both sweet and savory dishes.

1 cup unbleached all-purpose flour

1 teaspoon sugar

½ teaspoon kosher salt

¼ teaspoon baking powder, preferably nonaluminum

4 tablespoons cold unsalted butter, cut into ½-inch bits

3 tablespoons regular or reduced-fat sour cream

To make the dough in a food processor: In a food processor, combine the flour, sugar, salt, and baking powder, and process to mix. Add the butter and process until the mixture resembles a coarse meal. Put the work bowl in the refrigerator to chill for 15 minutes.

Add the sour cream to the flour mixture and process until the dough comes together in the bowl. Gather the dough into a ball and knead it several times on a lightly floured surface. Form it into a 1-inch-thick disk, wrap it in plastic, and chill for at least 30 minutes before rolling.

To make the dough by hand: In a medium bowl, combine the flour, sugar, salt, and baking powder. Add the butter and cut it into the flour with a pastry cutter or two knives until it resembles a very coarse meal. Alternatively, using a pinching motion, mix the butter into the flour with your fingers, then rub the butter and flour between the palms of both hands to blend it until the mixture is the texture of coarse meal. Chill the dough in the refrigerator for 15 minutes.

Add the sour cream and blend it in with the pastry cutter or a fork. Knead and squeeze the dough 7 or 8 times to incorporate any loose bits. Gather the dough together into a rough ball (it will be a coarse mass), flatten it into a 1-inch-thick disk, and wrap in plastic wrap. Refrigerate at least 30 minutes before rolling.

Roll out the dough as directed on page 492.

IN ADVANCE The dough can be refrigerated, well wrapped in plastic wrap, for up to 3 days or frozen for up to 1 month. (I like to make a double or triple recipe and freeze part of the dough.) Defrost in the refrigerator for several hours before using.

Sweet Pastry. This variation produces a pastry that is sweeter and crisp like a sugar cookie. variation

Increase the sugar to 3 tablespoons and add ½ teaspoon pure vanilla extract or grated lemon zest.

Cornmeal Pastry. Replacing some of the flour with cornmeal adds a pleasing slight grittiness and corn flavor. Cornmeal crusts are especially good in pear, apple, and blueberry or blackberry desserts. A mixture of fine and coarse cornmeals, like those used for polenta, produces the most interesting texture. variation

Replace ⅓ cup of the flour with cornmeal and substitute 1 tablespoon light brown sugar for the granulated sugar.

Rich Nut Pastry. Roasted almonds and lemon zest turn classic Foolproof Flaky Butter Pastry into a rich crumbly pastry, for an additional 30 calories per serving. variation

Reduce the flour to ¾ cup and add ⅓ cup roasted blanched almonds (1¼ ounces). Grind the nuts into a fine meal in a food processor with a few tablespoons of the flour. Process with the remaining flour before blending in the butter. Increase the salt by ⅛ teaspoon and add ½ teaspoon grated lemon zest.

To make cookies, increase the sugar to 1 tablespoon. Roll out the dough and cut into decorative shapes as directed on page 492. Bake and cool, then sift 2 tablespoons confectioners' sugar over the cookies.

Rolling Pastry Dough and Cutting It into Shapes

This is the basic method for handling, rolling, and cutting pastry dough. You can use the rolled-out dough for tart shells or cut it into shapes to bake and use as lids or platforms for free-form tarts (see Bowl and Spoon Desserts, pages 472–480).

You can roll and cut the dough into shapes up to one week ahead of baking, arrange on a baking sheet, wrap well, and freeze. There is no need to defrost them before baking.

> **Pastry dough,** such as 8 ounces Foolproof Flaky Butter Pastry (page 490) or any variation, or 10 ounces all-butter puff pastry
>
> **Flour** for rolling

1. **To roll out the dough:** Let the dough sit at room temperature for about 15 minutes before rolling. Sprinkle the work surface lightly and evenly with a little flour. Rub the rolling pin with flour as well. Place the dough in the middle of the work surface.

2. Beginning at one edge, press the rolling pin down onto the dough to flatten it, moving it across the dough in increments. Then, moving from the center of the dough outward, begin to roll the dough, adding more flour as necessary to keep the dough from sticking. Roll the dough gradually in all directions, flattening as you go, to form a large circle about 14 inches in diameter; do not roll it thinner than ⅛ inch. If the dough cracks or pulls apart, moisten the torn edges with a little water (using your finger or a brush) and press together to seal. Dust lightly with flour if the surface of the dough is sticky.

3. The dough is ready to use in a tart or to cut out. To transfer the dough to a 9-by-10-inch tart tin or baking sheet, place the rolling pin gently on one edge of the dough and roll the dough up over the pin—then you can move it wherever you want.

To cut the dough into decorative shapes, such as circles, hearts, and animals: Lightly flour a cookie or biscuit cutter and press into the rolled circle of dough to make cutouts. With a thin metal spatula, transfer the cutouts to a baking sheet. Gather the scraps of dough together, press into a ball, wrap in plastic wrap, and refrigerate for 30 minutes to relax the gluten. Then roll out and cut more shapes.

To cut the dough into free-form geometric shapes, such as squares, diamonds, strips, or rectangles: These are the simplest shapes to make, and, if you roll the dough into a square to start, they require no rerolling of the dough and result in no waste. When making the dough, press it into a block roughly 5 inches square instead of a disk. In Step 2, roll it into a 10-inch square. Using a floured chef's knife, cut the dough into long strips, then cut the strips crosswise into squares or rectangles, or on a diagonal to make diamond shapes. With a thin metal spatula, transfer the shapes to a baking sheet.

To bake the dough: Refrigerate the cutout dough for at least 10 minutes before baking. Preheat the oven to 375°F. Bake until the dough is golden brown and crisp, about 10 minutes. Let cool until warm or room temperature before serving.

USING PUFF PASTRY IN PLACE OF FOOLPROOF FLAKY BUTTER PASTRY

Puff pastry is a classic French pastry dough made by interleaving thin layers of a flour-and-water dough with thin layers of butter. When baked, it puffs to many times its volume to make wonderful, ethereal flaky pastries like napoleons and apple tarts. Since all-butter puff pastry is commercially available and quite easy to handle, it is worth knowing how to use it to make spectacular desserts in a pinch.

No matter how you slice it, puff pastry is about 50 percent butter. However, a small amount of puff pastry goes a long way, permitting the occasional indulgence. One and a quarter ounces of puff pastry per serving looks paltry in its uncooked state, but as it bakes, it puffs up to make an ample serving of flaky, buttery pastry, at about 165 calories. Fruit fillings or toppings rarely amount to more than 100 calories, so a whole individual dessert will weigh in at about 265 calories per serving, still low for a puff pastry dessert. (Note: A piece of puff pastry that weighs less than 1¼ ounces won't cook properly.)

With the few caveats on page 494 in mind, puff pastry can be used instead of Foolproof Flaky Butter Pastry in any of the recipes in this chapter, figuring on 25 percent more than the recipe calls for. So if it calls for 8 ounces of dough, you will need 10 ounces of puff pastry. It can be topped with fruit to make an open-faced tart, or split and filled with roasted fruits and whipped cream, or used as a lid for a fruit filling such as Warm Spilling Fruit (page 472).

- Defrost frozen puff pastry in the refrigerator for 1 hour before rolling.

- After rolling and cutting the dough into the desired shapes, chill in the refrigerator for 30 minutes.

- Bake the pastry in a preheated 375°F oven until it is firm and dry to the touch and deep golden brown in color.

- Save scraps of pastry to reroll later. Layer and then press them into a 1-inch-thick disk. Wrap in plastic and refrigerate for several hours before rerolling, or freeze.

WORKING WITH PHYLLO PASTRY

Phyllo (also called filo dough), the tissue-like pastry sheets used in Middle Eastern desserts, is wonderful for dramatic-looking pastries that are actually easy to make. Because the dough has hardly any fat, each sheet of phyllo must be brushed with melted butter to give it flavor and help it to brown properly. The sheets are usually stacked on top of each other to create flaky layers when baked. If you don't overbutter the phyllo, it makes an excellent low-fat pastry dough, containing only about 1 teaspoon of fat per serving.

Phyllo is readily available, packed in long narrow boxes, in the dairy or frozen food section of most supermarkets. If you can, buy phyllo dough directly from Greek or Middle Eastern markets or bakeries where they make it themselves, because it has a better flavor and texture.

Phyllo dough is easy to use as long as a few precautions are followed:

- If the phyllo is frozen, allow it to defrost in the refrigerator overnight. Defrosting it too quickly at room temperature can cause the sheets to stick together.

- Have all the ingredients assembled before you open the package and expose the phyllo to air.

- Phyllo dries out very quickly, becoming too brittle to work with. While working with it, always keep it covered with a sheet of plastic wrap topped with a damp towel.

Brown Butter for Brushing Phyllo. As a general rule, you will need 1 teaspoon melted butter and ¾ teaspoon sugar per sheet of phyllo. Browning the butter first will give the baked dough a much deeper buttery flavor. For 2 tablespoons brown butter, place 3 tablespoons unsalted butter in a small heavy saucepan or skillet over moderately low heat. Cook slowly until the butter smells like roasting nuts and the solids in the bottom of the pan are golden brown. Tilt the pan, carefully skim off the white residue on the surface of the butter and discard. Spoon the clear butter into a small bowl, leaving the solids behind.

Individual Phyllo Disks

This is the simplest way I know to make a dramatic pastry lid for free-form fruit desserts: Butter a sheet of phyllo, crumple it, press it into a round mold, and bake. The chewy-crisp phyllo disks are best eaten the day they are made.

MAKES FOUR
4-INCH DISKS

4 sheets phyllo dough

4 teaspoons Brown Butter for Brushing Phyllo (see above) **or melted butter**

1 teaspoon sugar

Preheat the oven to 375°F.

Unroll the phyllo dough on the counter. Cover with a sheet of plastic wrap, then place a damp tea towel over it to keep the phyllo from drying out as you work.

Brush four 4-inch tart tins or ramekins lightly with some of the butter. Lay 1 sheet of phyllo on the work surface and brush it with butter. Gently gather it in your hands and crumple it into a loose ball. Press it into a tin until it is compacted to about ⅓ inch high. Sprinkle with ¼ teaspoon of the sugar. Repeat with the remaining phyllo.

Place the tins on a baking sheet and bake until the phyllo is golden brown and crisp, about 16 minutes. Allow to cool for a few minutes, then run a knife around the edge of the tins to release the pastry. Cool on a rack.

You can prepare the phyllo disks without baking them up to 1 day ahead. Wrap well and refrigerate.

IN ADVANCE

Thin Phyllo Wafers

MAKES 16;
SERVES 8

In this method used by chefs, buttered, sugared, and stacked sheets of phyllo are sandwiched between baking pans, which both keep them flat during baking and conduct heat that caramelizes the sugar. The result is crisp phyllo wafers that can be layered with fillings to make napoleon-like desserts. I like to use roasted fruits such as pears or peaches with thin layers of whipped crème fraîche and crushed raspberries.

You can also use the thin wafers in savory dishes, brushing them with fats, such as olive oil or rendered bacon or pancetta fat, and omitting the sugar. You can sprinkle chopped herbs and spices on each sheet to add flavor. Curry powder makes a particularly appealing pastry in which to sandwich barely cooked salmon or goat cheese.

6 sheets phyllo dough

2 tablespoons Brown Butter for Brushing Phyllo (see page 495)
or melted butter

1 ½ tablespoons sugar

Preheat the oven to 375°F.

Unroll the phyllo dough on the counter. Cover with a sheet of plastic wrap, then place a damp tea towel over it to keep the phyllo from drying out as you work. Line a baking sheet—large enough to lay 1 sheet of phyllo flat—with a sheet of parchment paper or a silicone liner.

Place 1 sheet of phyllo on a cutting board. Using a slightly dampened brush, lightly brush with butter and sprinkle with ¾ teaspoon of the sugar. Place another phyllo sheet on top of it, brush with butter, and sprinkle with another ¾ teaspoon sugar. Repeat with the remaining 4 sheets of phyllo. With a long sharp or serrated knife, cut the stack of dough lengthwise in half, then cut each half into 4 squares. Cut each square crosswise in two to make 2 rectangles or on a diagonal to make 2 triangles. With a metal spatula, transfer the shapes to the prepared baking sheet. Cover with a sheet of parchment and place a second baking sheet on top.

Bake for 14 to 16 minutes, until the pastry is golden brown. Remove the top pan and paper and allow the pastry to cool.

IN ADVANCE You can prepare the phyllo wafers without baking them up to 1 day ahead. Cover tightly and refrigerate.

SERIOUS CHOCOLATE. Chocolate is the acid test for cooks attempting to reduce fat and sugar in desserts. About three quarters of its calories are fat in the form of cocoa butter, and it traditionally requires cream, egg yolks, and butter to bring it to fruition. The epitome of chocolate confections is the truffle, which rolls all these forbidden goodies into one small caloric bite of chocolate heaven. It is no mean feat to create a chocolate dessert that has the good winy flavor and rich texture of chocolate but is low in calories, fat, and sugar.

For starters, you should use the best chocolate, or cocoa, you can find. Those with more intense flavor and perfume will go farther and have more impact than ordinary ones. I generally combine small amounts of fine bar chocolate with unsweetened cocoa powder. The chocolate, which is rich in cocoa butter and chocolate solids, adds depth to the cocoa powder base, making for a truly satisfying experience. Then I add flavorings that amplify the chocolate: vanilla bean, cognac, and espresso powder.

For chocolate truffles and mousse-like desserts, I use chestnut puree as the medium for the chocolate in place of egg yolks, cream, and butter, because its finely textured starch imitates these high-fat ingredients.

Beyond these, I use standard tried-and-true techniques for cutting down fat and sugar.

The better the chocolate you use, the better the result will be. Because fine chocolate is the result of blending various kinds of chocolate beans and precise proportions of cocoa liquor and cocoa butter, the flavor of different brands of chocolate can differ radically, as can confections made with them. Valrhona, a French chocolate favored by chefs, categorizes its chocolates by the percentage of cocoa solids and cocoa butter, known as chocolate mass, in the formula: Its different chocolates have very different perfumes and flavors. Because I use small amounts of chocolate in my desserts, I like to use imported semi- and bittersweet chocolates with a high degree of chocolate mass, which are more intensely flavored and go further. Other excellent brands include Callebaut from Belgium and Lindt Excellence from Switzerland.

Cocoa powder is chocolate liquor with about 75 percent of the cocoa butter removed, so it is used often in healthful and low-fat cooking—often without great success. Cakes and cookies made with cocoa alone do not have the full flavor of baked goods made with bar chocolate, and I recommend a combination of fine bitter- or semisweet chocolate and cocoa. Cocoa powders can also vary considerably. Some have extraordinary perfume and great chocolate intensity; others have a hollow, almost dusty flavor and little aroma. Among the best I've found are Bendsorp, Pernigotti, Lindt, Valrhona, and Van Houten, all Dutch-processed, which means they have been treated with a mild alkali to make them more soluble and mellow the flavor (they also contain a slightly higher percentage of cocoa butter).

Chocolate Chestnut Truffles

MAKES 40

Peeled whole roasted chestnuts are available frozen or in vacuum-packed bottles at fine gourmet stores (see Sources, page 711).

This truffle recipe, a product of much rumination, has a base of pureed chestnut, a finely textured starch closer to a potato than a nut. It's the perfect medium for the chocolate, replacing the usual egg yolks, cream, and butter at many fewer calories. Using the best chocolate and cocoa possible, flavored with good French cognac and vanilla bean, this truffle easily competes with a classically made truffle.

35 to 40 (1½ cups) **peeled whole roasted chestnuts** (one 7.4-ounce jar)

1 cup whole milk

1 vanilla bean

5 ounces semisweet chocolate, finely chopped

2 tablespoons light corn syrup

1½ to 2 tablespoons cognac or Armagnac

Pinch of kosher salt

1½ tablespoons unsweetened cocoa powder, preferably Dutch-processed

In a small heavy saucepan, combine the chestnuts and milk. With a sharp paring knife, split the vanilla bean lengthwise and scrape out the seeds. Add the seeds and bean to the chestnut mixture, partially cover, and bring to a simmer. Simmer over low heat, stirring occasionally, until the chestnuts are very soft and the milk has reduced to about ¼ cup, about 30 minutes. (Don't worry if the milk looks curdled.)

Discard the vanilla bean. Reduce the heat to very low and add the chopped chocolate, stirring until melted. Transfer the mixture to a food processor and puree, scraping down the sides occasionally, until the mixture is perfectly smooth, at least 4 minutes. Remove the plunger from the feed tube to allow steam to escape as you puree the chestnuts. Add the corn syrup, cognac, and salt and process for 1 minute longer. If you have time, let the mixture cool in the work bowl with the cover off for 30 minutes, then process for 2 minutes. This makes the mixture fluffier but is not essential.

Transfer the truffle mixture to a bowl, cover, and refrigerate until firm, at least 4 hours.

To shape the truffles, scoop up about 2 heaping teaspoons at a time of the truffle mixture and roll it into a rough ball about 1 inch in diameter with your fingers. Working with a few at a time, roll the truffles in the cocoa until they are completely coated. Transfer to a plate as they are finished, then sprinkle any remaining cocoa over them. Seal in a plastic container and refrigerate until ready to serve.

The unrolled truffle mixture can be frozen for up to 1 month; thaw in the refrigerator. The prepared truffles will keep sealed in a plastic container in the refrigerator for up to 2 weeks.

IN ADVANCE

Truffles Stuffed with Candied Chestnuts or Roasted Pecans. I sometimes like to embed a chunk of *marron glacé*—candied chestnut—or a roasted pecan in the center of each truffle before rolling it in cocoa. You will need 10 marrons glacé, cut into ½-inch pieces, or 20 roasted pecans, cut crosswise in half. (Pecan truffles should be made no more than 2 hours ahead, or the pecans will lose their crispness.) When you are rolling the truffle mixture into balls, press 1 piece of marron glacé or ½ roasted pecan into the center of each truffle and smooth the truffle mixture around it.

Chocolate Mousse Cake

SERVES 12   For chocolate lovers, chocolate mousse cake is the epitome of a forbidden dessert. In this recipe, an amalgam of chestnut puree and dark chocolate is blended with meringue, and barely stabilized with gelatin, to form an incredibly rich truffle-like cake with an intense chocolate flavor at less than half the calories of the full-fat version. Using the best possible chocolate, cocoa, and flavorings such as French cognac and vanilla bean is crucial.

Because of the controversy around eating uncooked eggs (see page 16), I include two methods here: one using a regular meringue and one using a cooked Italian meringue—egg whites beaten with sugar in a double boiler—which is a little trickier. Since the second method requires more sugar, the cake will be slightly sweeter.

Unsweetened chestnut puree imported from France is available in the gourmet food section of many supermarkets, at specialty food stores, and by mail order. You can easily make your own chestnut puree (see page 684) using frozen or vacuum-packed bottled chestnuts.

> ¾ **cup whole milk**
>
> 1¼ **teaspoons unflavored gelatin**
>
> 1⅓ **cups packed unsweetened chestnut puree** (see Headnote)
>
> ¾ **vanilla bean**
>
> 8¼ **ounces semisweet chocolate,** finely chopped
>
> 1 **tablespoon plus 2 teaspoons cognac**
>
> 3 **large egg whites,** preferably organic, at room temperature
>
> ⅛ **teaspoon kosher salt**
>
> ⅛ **teaspoon cream of tartar**
>
> ¼ **cup superfine sugar,** plus an additional 3 tablespoons for the cooked meringue
>
> 1 **teaspoon unsweetened cocoa powder** for dusting

Pour ¼ cup of the milk into a small bowl; sprinkle the gelatin over. Set aside to soften.

In a small heavy saucepan, combine the chestnut puree and the remaining ½ cup milk. Using a thin sharp knife, split the vanilla bean lengthwise and scrape out the seeds. Add the seeds and bean to the chestnut mixture. Cook over low heat, stirring frequently, until hot, about 10 minutes. Remove from the heat and stir in the chocolate until melted. Discard the vanilla bean.

Transfer the mixture to a food processor, add the cognac, and process, scraping down the sides occasionally, until the mixture is very thick and creamy, at least 5 minutes. Add the reserved gelatin mixture and process to blend, scraping the sides down once. Transfer the mixture to a large bowl and set aside.

To make the cake with a cooked meringue: In a double boiler, combine the egg whites, salt, and cream of tartar over barely simmering water. (The top of the double boiler should be about 1 inch above the water.) Using a hand-held electric mixer, beat the mixture at medium speed until soft peaks form, about 1 minute. Gradually beat in the sugar until the meringue is shiny and forms stiff upright peaks when the beater is lifted out of them, about 5 minutes. The temperature should register 150°F on a candy thermometer or instant-read thermometer. Remove from the heat and continue beating for 1 minute longer.

To make the cake with an uncooked meringue: In a perfectly clean medium bowl, combine the egg whites, salt, and cream of tartar. Using a handheld electric mixer, beat the mixture at medium speed until soft peaks form, about 1 minute. Gradually beat in the sugar until the meringue is firm and shiny and forms stiff upright peaks when the beater is lifted out of them.

Using a rubber spatula, fold one third of the meringue into the chocolate mixture to lighten it. Gently fold in the remaining meringue until incorporated. Scrape the mousse into an 8- or 9-inch springform pan and refrigerate until set, at least 5 hours.

Sift the cocoa over the top of the cake. Unmold it and transfer it to a platter. Serve chilled.

You can prepare the mousse cake up to 1 day before serving. Cover and refrigerate. **IN ADVANCE**

Chocolate Angel Food Cake

SERVES 12

Before whipping egg whites, make sure the mixing bowl and beaters are perfectly clean and dry; any trace of fat will prevent the whites from whipping.

Angel food cake is an old-fashioned American cake, made from beaten egg whites, sugar, and flour, that people seem to love or hate. Those who dislike it are often put off by its intense sweetness, from the quantity of sugar needed to stabilize the egg whites. Those who love it respond with child-like delight to the airy texture of the cake, and to its affinity with crushed strawberries and ice cream.

This recipe, based on master baker Rose Levy Beranbaum's almost-foolproof method, is one of the best I know. The sweetness of a classic angel food cake is tempered by a powerful dose of cocoa powder. I boosted the chocolate flavor by adding other slightly bitter and aromatic components—espresso, vanilla, and cognac—which result in a sophisticated cake.

Using a high-quality fragrant cocoa powder such as Pernigotti, Valrhona, or Bensdorp will ensure a deep chocolate flavor.

¼ cup plus 2 tablespoons unsweetened cocoa powder, preferably Dutch-processed

2 teaspoons instant espresso powder

Pinch of ground cinnamon (optional)

¼ cup boiling water

2 teaspoons pure vanilla extract

1 teaspoon cognac or Armagnac

1 cup sifted cake flour (not self-rising)

1¾ cups sugar

¼ teaspoon kosher salt

16 large egg whites (2 cups)

2 teaspoons cream of tartar

Preheat the oven to 350°F.

In a large bowl, combine the cocoa, espresso powder, and cinnamon, if using. With a small whisk or a fork, gradually blend in the boiling water to make a paste, then blend in the vanilla and cognac. Press a piece of plastic wrap against the surface of the paste to keep it from drying out.

In a small bowl, combine the flour, ¾ cup of the sugar, and the salt. Blend well.

In a large bowl, beat the egg whites at high speed with an electric mixer until frothy. Add the cream of tartar and continue beating until soft peaks form.

Gradually beat in the remaining 1 cup sugar. Continue beating until the whites form stiff upright peaks when the beater is lifted out.

Sift about ¼ cup of the flour mixture over the egg whites. With a balloon whisk, fold in the flour mixture. Fold in the remaining flour, ¼ cup at a time. Gently whisk 1 cup of the batter into the cocoa paste to lighten it. Then scrape the egg white mixture over the cocoa mixture and fold them together, using a rubber spatula, until the batter is fairly uniform.

Pour the batter into an ungreased 10-inch tube pan. Rub a knife through the batter several times to remove any air pockets. Bake for 50 minutes, or until the cake springs back when pressed and a knife inserted into the center comes out clean.

Invert the pan over the neck of an empty wine bottle. (Letting it cool upside down prevents it from collapsing like a soufflé.) Let cool completely, 1½ to 2 hours.

To unmold the cake, run a thin knife around the sides of the pan and around the center tube. Invert onto a serving plate.

You can bake the cake up to 3 days ahead. Wrap well in plastic wrap.

IN ADVANCE

Individual Chocolate Angel Food Cakelets. To make 12 miniature angel food cakelets, use two jumbo (1-cup) muffin tins. Proceed as directed above, baking the cakelets for 30 to 35 minutes. Position four inverted mugs or ramekins at the corners of each inverted pan to elevate them off the counter while they cool upside down.

variation

Chocolate Malted Pudding

SERVES 8 This extremely rich pudding tastes like a malted milk ball and is always greatly appreciated by both children and adults. Chocolate and cocoa powder fortified by espresso and vanilla provide intense chocolate flavor, while the malted milk gives it a creaminess despite the low-fat milk. For classic chocolate pudding, simply omit the malted milk powder.

4 cups low-fat (1%) **milk**

¼ **cup cornstarch**

1 cup malted milk powder

¼ **cup unsweetened cocoa powder,** preferably Dutch-processed

¼ **teaspoon kosher salt**

2 ounces unsweetened chocolate, coarsely chopped

¼ **cup plus 2 tablespoons sugar**

1 teaspoon pure vanilla extract

In a small bowl, blend ½ cup of the milk with the cornstarch.

Combine the malted milk powder, cocoa, and salt in a small heavy saucepan; slowly whisk in the remaining 3½ cups milk, the chocolate, and sugar. Heat over moderate heat, stirring occasionally, until the chocolate is melted. Whisk in the cornstarch mixture. Cook, stirring frequently, over very low heat until very thick and just beginning to boil, about 10 minutes. Remove from the heat and stir in the vanilla extract. Let cool, stirring occasionally, until the custard is just warm.

Pour the pudding into individual ½-cup custard cups or small bowls. Cover with plastic wrap and refrigerate until chilled and set.

IN ADVANCE You can prepare the pudding up to 3 days ahead.

CAKES AND COOKIES. I have tried many of the techniques touted as solutions for reducing the fat in cakes and cookies— usually substituting prune or banana puree or applesauce for the much demonized butter and eggs—hoping to learn something new about the chemistry of baking. The outcomes were, for the most part, mediocre, at best just okay. Most of the resulting cakes or cookies suffered from the rubbery texture and oversweet one-dimensional flavor that often characterizes low-fat baked goods.

A certain amount of fat is necessary in baking, although it may be only a fraction of what has traditionally been called for if one is creative with other ingredients. Making cakes and cookies with less fat than the classic versions, yet with all the flavor and textures, is a sane and realistic compromise, a way to have your cake and eat it, too.

OLD-FASHIONED BUTTERMILK CAKES.

To bake traditional butter or chiffon-style cakes with less fat and sugar, I rely on buttermilk, an ingredient that was often used in farmstead cake made long ago. Modern buttermilk is low-fat milk that has been treated, or cultured, with lactic acid bacteria (buttermilk was originally the milky whey left over from churning butter). It is very creamy and has a tart, rich flavor. In my lightened cake formula, buttermilk supplies gloss and moistness, as well as a tender crumb, making it possible to greatly reduce the amount of butter and eggs. This technique produces truly delicious cakes without the rubbery texture caused by replacing fat with fruit pulp or other sugary substances. Since buttermilk lasts for a couple of months refrigerated, I always keep some on hand, stored in a glass bottle.

Another trick for ensuring a tender crumb is to use cake flour rather than all-purpose flour. Cake flour is made from finely ground soft winter wheat, which is low in gluten-forming proteins, which can make cakes tough. But all-purpose flour will work well in these recipes too, though the cakes will have a slightly coarser texture. In general, for every 1 cup sifted cake flour, substitute ¾ cup plus 2 tablespoons sifted all-purpose flour.

Your choice of cake pan will determine the look of your finished cake. You can bake these in an 8-inch round pan to be sliced into wedges. Or you can bake them in a 9-inch square pan and slice them into the elongated wedges you might see in the windows of pâtisseries in France.

To slice a 9-inch square cake: Invert the cake onto a flat surface and trim off the tough edges. Cut the cake into 3 equal rectangles, then halve each one on the diagonal to form 6 thin triangles.

Arrange the cake slices on a platter. Sift confectioners' sugar over the top, if desired.

Fresh Lemon Cake

SERVES 6

Although it has a much lighter texture, this reminds me of the lemon pound cakes of my childhood. It is moistened with a clove-scented lemon syrup.

Lemon Syrup

3 medium lemons

6 tablespoons granulated sugar

4 whole cloves

2 tablespoons plus ½ teaspoon unsalted butter, softened

1¾ cups sifted cake flour or 1½ cups sifted unbleached all-purpose flour

1¾ teaspoons baking powder, preferably nonaluminum

½ teaspoon baking soda

Pinch of kosher salt

⅓ cup buttermilk

¼ cup water

7 tablespoons granulated sugar

1 large egg

2 teaspoons confectioners' sugar

For the lemon syrup, grate the zest of the lemons; you should have 2 tablespoons. Juice the lemons; you should have ½ cup plus 1 tablespoon. In a small saucepan, combine the zest, juice, sugar, and cloves. Bring to a boil over moderate heat and cook for 1 minute, stirring to dissolve the sugar. Set aside to cool, then discard the cloves.

Preheat the oven to 350°F. Grease an 8-inch round cake pan or a 9-inch square pan with ½ teaspoon of the butter. Dust the pan with 2 teaspoons of the flour and set aside.

Sift together the remaining flour, the baking powder, baking soda, and salt. In a measuring cup, combine 6 tablespoons of the lemon syrup and the buttermilk. Add the water to the remaining lemon syrup and reserve.

In a large bowl of an electric mixer, beat the remaining 2 tablespoons butter and the sugar until light and fluffy. Add the egg and beat well to combine. Add the dry ingredients alternately with the lemon-buttermilk mixture in three additions, mixing until just incorporated; do not overmix.

Pour the batter into the prepared pan. To distribute the batter evenly in the pan, beginning at the edge of the pan, move your index finger in a spiral through the top ¼ inch of the batter until you reach the center, or zigzag back and forth if using a square pan. Rap the pan on the counter a few times to remove any air bubbles.

Bake for 30 minutes if using an 8-inch pan, 25 minutes if using a 9-inch pan, or until a thin sharp knife or cake tester inserted in the center comes out clean. Cool the cake on a wire rack for about 10 minutes.

Run a knife around the edges of the pan and invert the cake onto the rack. Let cool completely.

Pour the reserved syrup onto a large plate with a lip. Place the cake upside down on the syrup. Sift the confectioners' sugar over the top.

IN ADVANCE The cake is best the day it is baked, but it will keep, well wrapped, for up to 3 days.

variation **Filled Lemon Cake.** Sometimes I layer this lemon cake with a tart, creamy lemon curd. Split the cooled cake layer horizontally in half and spread the bottom layer with Tart, Ethereal Lemon Curd (page 532). Replace the top layer and sift the confectioner's sugar over the top. When serving, pour some of the lemon syrup around each slice.

Gingerbread

It took some time to devise a really satisfying gingerbread, one as rich and moist as traditional recipes, which are extremely liberal with molasses and butter, often at upward of 500 calories per slice. This lightened version has all the elements of an old-fashioned gingerbread: molasses, mustard, strong coffee, and a host of spices. Lots of grated fresh ginger, which, curiously, you don't often find in gingerbread recipes, enlivens the spices and makes the cake extremely moist. This gingerbread relies on buttermilk to tenderize it and lend richness, in tandem with baking soda, which acts as leavening, and counteracts the acidity of the molasses.

> **3 tablespoons plus ½ teaspoon unsalted butter**, softened
>
> **1¾ cups sifted cake flour** or 1½ cups sifted unbleached all-purpose flour
>
> **1 teaspoon baking soda**
>
> **1 teaspoon ground ginger**
>
> **½ teaspoon ground cinnamon**
>
> **½ teaspoon dry mustard**
>
> **⅛ teaspoon ground cardamom**
>
> **Pinch of kosher salt**
>
> **3 tablespoons packed dark brown sugar**
>
> **1 large egg**
>
> **¼ cup plus 2 tablespoons unsulfured molasses**
>
> **3 tablespoons grated fresh ginger**
>
> **2 tablespoons strong brewed coffee**
>
> **1 teaspoon pure vanilla extract**
>
> **½ cup buttermilk**
>
> **1 tablespoon confectioners' sugar**

Preheat the oven to 350°F. Grease an 8-inch round cake pan or a 9-inch square pan with ½ teaspoon of the butter. Dust the pan with 1 teaspoon of the flour. Set aside.

Sift together the flour, baking soda, spices, and salt.

In a large bowl, combine the remaining 3 tablespoons butter and the brown sugar. With a handheld electric mixer or a wooden spoon, cream the mixture until it is light and fluffy. Add the egg, molasses, fresh ginger, coffee, and vanilla extract and beat well to combine. Add the flour mixture alternately with the buttermilk in three additions, beating well after each addition.

Pour the batter into the prepared pan. To distribute the batter evenly in the pan, beginning at the edge of the pan, move your index finger in a spiral through the top ¼ inch of the batter until you reach the center, or zigzag back and forth if using a square pan.

Bake for 30 minutes if using an 8-inch pan, 25 minutes if using a 9-inch pan, or until a thin sharp knife or cake tester inserted in the center comes out clean. Cool the cake on a wire rack for about 10 minutes.

Run a knife around the edges of the pan and invert the cake onto the rack. Let cool completely.

Place the cake upside down on a plate. Sift confectioners' sugar over the top.

The gingerbread will keep, well wrapped, for up to 4 days. **IN ADVANCE**

Applesauce Cake

This applesauce cake is almost identical in taste and texture to one I **SERVES 8** remember from my childhood, taken from the 1952 *Joy of Cooking*. It was moist and tender, made with cinnamon and allspice and lots of nuts and raisins. Here, applesauce, honey, and buttermilk provide the moist crumb that butter and a large number of eggs did in the original.

2 tablespoons plus ½ teaspoon unsalted butter, softened

1¾ cups sifted cake flour or 1½ cups plus 1½ teaspoons sifted unbleached all-purpose flour

⅔ cup sweetened chunky applesauce

½ cup golden raisins

1½ teaspoons baking powder, preferably nonaluminum

½ teaspoon baking soda

1 teaspoon ground cinnamon

¼ teaspoon ground cloves

¼ teaspoon kosher salt

⅓ cup buttermilk

⅓ cup packed dark brown sugar

3 tablespoons honey

1 large egg

1 teaspoon pure vanilla extract

1½ teaspoons grated lemon zest

½ cup (2 ounces) **roasted walnuts,** coarsely chopped

2 teaspoons confectioners' sugar

Preheat the oven to 350°F. Grease an 8-by-4-inch loaf pan with ½ teaspoon of the butter. Dust the pan with 2 teaspoons of the flour and set aside.

In a small saucepan, simmer the applesauce over low heat, stirring frequently, until reduced by half, about 10 minutes. Set aside to cool.

Meanwhile, place the raisins in a bowl and pour about ¾ cup boiling water over them. Allow to plump for 10 minutes. Drain well and pat dry.

Sift together the remaining flour, the baking powder, baking soda, cinnamon, cloves, and salt. Stir the buttermilk into the applesauce.

In a large bowl, with an electric mixer, beat the remaining 2 tablespoons butter with the brown sugar and honey until smooth. Add the egg, vanilla, and lemon zest and beat well to combine. Add the dry ingredients alternately with the applesauce mixture in three additions, mixing until just incorporated; do not overmix. Fold in the raisins and nuts.

Pour the batter into the prepared pan. To distribute the batter evenly in the pan, beginning at one end of the pan, move your index finger in a zigzag back and forth through the top ¼ inch of the batter until you reach the other end. Rap the pan on the counter a few times to remove any air bubbles.

Bake the cake for 50 to 55 minutes, until a knife, or cake tester inserted in the center comes out clean. Cool the cake on a wire rack for about 10 minutes.

Run a knife around the edges of the pan and invert onto the rack. Let cool completely before serving.

IN ADVANCE The cake is best the day it is baked, but keeps, well wrapped, for up to 3 days.

Nuts are very high in calories because they contain so much fat, an average of 83 percent. Although their fat is highly nutritious, I try to find a middle ground when cooking with nuts, to enjoy their good nutrition and flavor without excessive calories. This is something of a challenge when it comes to nut cakes, where a nutty texture is as important as the flavor. I've tried all kinds of permutations, including substituting bread crumbs for some of the nuts, which tend to weaken the flavor of more subtly flavored nuts like almonds and pistachios. Finally, I devised a solid formula out of the classic sponge cake method: The yolks and whites are each beaten separately with sugar, forming an airy batter in which to suspend the ground nuts, stabilized by a little flour to prevent collapse. The result is moist, rich, and chewy, easy to make, and still low in calories, with little added fat.

Nut Cakes

A GUIDE TO IMPROVISING

In this method, ground roasted nuts are folded into an airy batter of separately beaten egg whites and yolks that have been stabilized with a little sugar and flour, then baked into a fragrant nut cake. Endless variations are possible simply by changing the flavorings and the type of nuts you use.

SERVES 8

To make a 10-inch cake to serve 16 people, double the recipe

It is essential to roast the nuts to bring out their fullest flavor, making it possible to use the minimum amount. If you have a roasted nut oil that complements the nuts you are using, such as a hazelnut oil for a hazelnut cake, you can brush the top of the baked cake with 1 teaspoon of it to intensify the flavor (adding as few as 5 calories per serving).

Have all the ingredients measured out and the equipment ready when you make this cake. You need to work quickly once you have beaten the eggs so that they don't deflate.

½ teaspoon unsalted butter, softened

2 tablespoons fine dried bread crumbs

1¼ cups (5 ounces) roasted nuts, such as pecans, almonds, pistachios, walnuts, or hazelnuts (see page 676)

3 tablespoons unbleached all-purpose flour

½ teaspoon baking powder, preferably nonaluminum

Dry flavorings (optional), singly or in combination, such as

1 to 2 tablespoons unsweetened cocoa powder

1 tablespoon instant espresso powder

¼ to ½ teaspoon ground spices, such as cinnamon, allspice, cardamom, or coriander

3 large eggs, separated, at room temperature

½ cup plus 2 tablespoons granulated sugar

¼ teaspoon kosher salt

Liquid flavorings (optional), singly or in combination (but no more than 1½ tablespoons total), such as

1 to 1½ tablespoons cognac, bourbon, or kirsch

½ to 1½ teaspoons grated orange or lemon zest

2 teaspoons pure vanilla extract

1 tablespoon roasted nut oil, such as walnut, hazelnut, or almond

¼ teaspoon cream of tartar

2 teaspoons confectioners' sugar

1. Preheat the oven to 350°F. Line an 8-inch round cake pan with a round of waxed paper or parchment cut to fit. Grease the paper and the sides of the pan with the butter. Dust with the bread crumbs, tapping and rotating the pan to coat it evenly. Set aside.

2. In a food processor, combine the nuts with the flour, baking powder, and any dry flavorings and grind to a fine meal. Set aside.

3. In a medium bowl, with an electric mixer, beat the egg yolks with ½ cup of the sugar and ⅛ teaspoon of the salt at high speed until the mixture is thick and pale and forms a ribbon when the beaters are lifted, 4 to 5 minutes. Beat in any liquid flavorings; set aside. Wash and dry the beaters.

4. In a clean dry medium bowl, beat the egg whites with the cream of tartar and the remaining ⅛ teaspoon salt until soft peaks form. Gradually beat in the remaining 2 tablespoons sugar until stiff peaks form. Push the whites to one side of the bowl with a rubber spatula, and pour the egg yolk mixture into the other. Fold them together three or four times. Sprinkle the nut mixture on top and fold until just combined.

5. Scrape the mixture into the prepared pan. To evenly distribute the batter in the pan, beginning at the edge of the pan, move your index finger in a spiral through the top ¼ inch of the batter until you reach the center.

6. Bake the cake on the center rack of the oven until the top is springy, the sides pull away from the pan, and a knife or cake tester inserted in the center comes out clean, 30 to 35 minutes. Let the cake cool on a rack for 15 minutes.

7. Invert the cake onto the rack and let cool completely. Just before serving, sift the confectioners' sugar over the top.

Individual Nut Cakelets

improvisation 1

Follow the Guide above, but use a 12-cup muffin pan or twelve 2¼-inch ramekins. To prepare the muffin pan (or ramekins), in a small saucepan, cook 1½ teaspoons butter over low heat until it is lightly brown and smells like roasted nuts. Remove from the heat and grease the cups with the butter. Spoon ½ teaspoon flour into each cup and tilt and tap the cups, to lightly coat them with the flour. Turn over and tap out any excess flour. Set aside.

Proceed as directed, but bake the cakelets for 15 to 16 minutes.

Mocha Pecan Cake

improvisation 2

Cocoa and espresso are a delicious mocha background for the roasted pecans.

Follow the Guide on pages 511 to 513, using pecans for the nuts, 1 tablespoon each of cocoa powder and instant espresso powder for the dry flavorings, and 1 tablespoon bourbon for the liquid flavoring.

Hazelnut Cake

improvisation 3

It is said that the very best hazelnuts in the world are grown in the Piedmont region of Italy, home also of white truffles and some of Italy's greatest wines. The hazelnuts are used to make extraordinary local confections, like the famous *gianduotti*—chocolate and hazelnut candies—of Turin, and the flat chewy hazelnut cakes found in Alba and the region's small villages. This cake emulates those divine cakes. Its intense hazelnut perfume comes from the combination of freshly roasted nuts, fine imported hazelnut oil, and unsweetened cocoa.

Follow the Guide on pages 511 to 513, using hazelnuts for the nuts, 2 tablespoons cocoa powder for the dry flavoring, and roasted hazelnut oil and vanilla extract for the liquid flavoring.

Pistachio and Almond Cake

SERVES 8

This unusual cake was inspired by a recipe Richard Olney published in *Simple French Food*. It has a lovely, almost floral quality and is moist and chewy. Serve with Basic Vanilla Custard Sauce (page 529), whipped cream, or Warm Fresh Cherries with Kirsch (page 472).

Have the ingredients measured out and the equipment ready when you begin; you must work quickly once you beat the eggs so that they don't deflate.

Candied Fruit Zest

1 orange (for the zest only)

1 lemon (for the zest only)

⅓ cup water

1 tablespoon sugar

½ teaspoon unsalted butter, softened

2 tablespoons unflavored dried bread crumbs

¾ cup (3½ ounces) **shelled undyed unsalted pistachios**

½ cup (2 ounces) **blanched whole or sliced almonds**

½ cup plus 2 tablespoons granulated sugar

2 tablespoons unbleached all-purpose flour

½ teaspoon baking powder, preferably nonaluminum

3 large eggs, separated, at room temperature

¼ teaspoon kosher salt

1½ teaspoons grated lemon zest (you can use the lemon from above)

1½ tablespoons kirsch

¼ teaspoon cream of tartar

2 teaspoons confectioners' sugar

To candy the zest, with a vegetable peeler, remove three ½-by-1-inch-long strips of zest from the orange and lemon, taking care to avoid the white pith. With a sharp paring knife, slice the strips into thin slivers; you should have 1 tablespoon each orange and lemon zest slivers. Bring a small saucepan of water to a boil. Add the zest and boil for 5 seconds. Drain well and rinse in cold water. Return the orange and lemon zest to the pan, add the water and sugar, and bring to a boil. Simmer until almost all the liquid is evaporated, about 25 minutes; do not allow the zest to caramelize. Remove the peel to a cake rack to dry.

Preheat the oven to 325°F. Line an 8-inch round cake pan with waxed paper or parchment cut to fit. Grease the paper and the sides of the pan with the butter. Dust evenly with the bread crumbs. Set aside.

Spread the pistachios on a baking sheet and roast until fragrant, about 5 minutes. (Do not brown; they will lose their green color.) Transfer to a bowl to cool. Increase the oven temperature to 350°F. Spread the almonds on the baking sheet and roast until golden, 4 to 5 minutes. Set aside to cool.

In a food processor, combine the nuts, candied zest, and 1 tablespoon of the sugar. Pulse to process to a coarse meal. Add the flour and continue processing to a fine meal. Add the baking powder and process 5 seconds more to combine. Set aside.

In a small bowl, with an electric mixer, beat the egg yolks with 7 tablespoons of the sugar and ⅛ teaspoon of the salt at high speed until the mixture is thick and pale and forms a ribbon when the beaters are lifted, 4 to 5 minutes. Beat in the lemon zest and kirsch. Set aside. Wash and dry the beaters.

In a clean dry medium bowl, beat the egg whites with the cream of tartar and the remaining ⅛ teaspoon salt until soft peaks form. Gradually beat in the remaining 2 tablespoons sugar until stiff peaks form. Push the whites to one side of the bowl with a rubber spatula, and pour the egg yolk mixture into the other. Fold them together three or four times. Sprinkle the nuts on top and fold in until just combined.

Scrape the mixture into the prepared pan. To distribute the batter in the pan evenly, beginning at the edge of the pan, move your index finger in a spiral through the top ¼-inch of the batter until you reach the center.

Bake the cake on the center rack of the oven until the top is springy, the sides pull away from the pan, and a knife or cake tester inserted in the center comes out clean, about 30 to 35 minutes.

Let the cake cool on a wire cake rack for 10 minutes. Then run a knife around the edges of the pan and invert the cake onto the rack; let cool completely.

Just before serving, transfer the cake to a plate or platter, still upside down, then sift confectioners' sugar over the top.

The cake is best the day it is baked, but keeps, wrapped, for up to 3 days. **IN ADVANCE**

Shortcut Pistachio and Almond Cake. Omit the candied fruit zest and increase the grated lemon zest to 2 teaspoons. variation

A cookie by any name—*biscotto* in Italy, *biscuit* in France—is very simply a little cake. Marcel Proust wrote better than anybody did about the profound effect a simple cookie could have, of the *madeleines* and *macarons* that so powerfully stirred his senses, emotions, and memories.

We all have memories of cookies, of warm chocolate chips or brownies made on a rainy afternoon. My childhood associations are of the anise-and-bitter-almond-scented cookies in the Italian cafés my father used to take me to during our walks around downtown New York...perhaps the reason I prefer a plate of cookies to almost any dessert or other sweet. I like to have several little cakes to eat lingeringly, dipped in strong coffee, rather than a full-blown dessert that too often overwhelms. They are also lovely for afternoon tea.

Earl Grey Tea Wafers

MAKES ABOUT 6 DOZEN COOKIES

These unusual paper-thin, buttery wafers have a delicate fragrance of bergamot from the Earl Grey tea that is ground with the sugar. Around Christmastime, I make big batches of them to give as gifts.

> **5 teaspoons Earl Grey Tea** (or the tea from 4 tea bags)
> **¾ cup boiling water**
> **⅓ cup packed light brown sugar**
> **5 ⅓ tablespoons plus 1 ½ teaspoons unsalted butter,** softened
> **⅓ cup granulated sugar**
> **1 large egg**
> **¼ teaspoon pure vanilla extract**
> **¼ teaspoon kosher salt**
> **¾ cup unbleached all-purpose flour**

In a measuring cup, steep 1¼ teaspoons of the tea in the boiling water for 5 minutes. Strain and discard the tea leaves. Place the tea in the refrigerator to cool.

In a blender, combine the remaining 3¾ teaspoons tea and the brown sugar and blend to a fine powder.

In a medium bowl, using a handheld electric mixer, beat together 5⅓ table-spoons of the butter, the granulated sugar, and the tea sugar at high speed until the mixture is pale yellow and fluffy. Beat in the egg, 3 tablespoons of the brewed tea (use the remainder for iced tea), the vanilla extract, salt, and flour. Cover with plastic wrap and let rest for 30 minutes to let the tea flavor develop.

Preheat the oven to 350°F. Lightly grease two large nonstick or heavy regular cookie sheets with a little of the remaining butter.

Drop scant teaspoonfuls of the batter onto one of the prepared sheets, spacing them 2 inches apart. Using the back of a spoon or your finger, spread the cookies out to make 2-inch circles.

Bake for 9 to 10 minutes, until the edges are just beginning to brown. While the cookies are baking, drop the batter onto a second lightly buttered baking sheet. Place in the oven when you remove the first pan. Let the cookies cool on the pan for 1 minute to firm them up. Using a thin metal spatula, carefully transfer the cookies to wire racks. Wipe the sheet clean and repeat using the remaining butter and batter.

IN ADVANCE

Store the cookies for up to 3 weeks in an airtight tin.

variation

Clove and Lemon Wafers. These delicate wafers have an intense lemon flavor that will complement many desserts; they are also lovely on their own. You can use orange zest and juice instead of the lemon to make orange-scented cookies.

Omit the tea and boiling water. Omit the brown sugar and use ⅔ cup white sugar. When you beat in the egg, add 2½ teaspoons grated lemon zest, 3 tablespoons fresh lemon juice, and a scant ¼ teaspoon ground cloves, along with the remaining ingredients.

variation

Ginger and "Yuzu" Wafers. The combination of lemon and tan-gerine closely approximates the lovely complex flavor of yuzu, a Japanese citrus fruit that is difficult to come by in this country. These cookies are wonderful with jasmine tea.

Omit the tea and boiling water. Omit the brown sugar and use ⅔ cup white sugar. Beat the butter and sugar with 1¼ teaspoons grated lemon zest, 1¼ teaspoons grated tangerine, tangelo, or clementine zest, and 1 teaspoon grated fresh ginger. When you beat in the egg, add 1½ tablespoons fresh tangerine, tangelo, or clementine juice and 1½ tablespoons fresh lemon juice, along with the remaining ingredients.

Anne's Spicy Ginger Cookies

My friend Anne Disrude keeps the cookie jar in her Catskill country house full of these crisp spicy cookies. She makes up big batches of dough, which keep for weeks in the fridge or can be frozen. She rolls it out as needed, cuts it into squares or triangles, and bakes them. Use the maximum amount of cayenne for a thrillingly spicy cookie.

For an instant dessert, roll some dough out, cut it into shapes, and arrange it on cookie sheets so the cookies are ready to bake near the end of your meal. Place the cookie sheet of warm just-baked cookies in the center of the dinner table with a thin metal spatula and a bowl of whipped cream. Invite your guests to slide off cookies, spoon whipped cream onto them, and enjoy. (You could, of course, turn any cookie recipe into an instant dessert this way.)

1 cup sugar

1 teaspoon baking soda

½ cup ground ginger

1 tablespoon finely ground black pepper

2 teaspoons ground allspice

2 teaspoons ground cloves

1 teaspoon freshly grated nutmeg

Pinch (or up to ⅛ teaspoon) cayenne pepper

12 tablespoons (1½ sticks) unsalted butter, softened

¾ cup plus 2 tablespoons pure maple syrup

2 tablespoons unsulfured molasses

4 cups unbleached all-purpose flour, plus more for rolling

2 tablespoons low-fat (2%) milk (optional)

In a large bowl, combine the sugar, baking soda, ginger, black pepper, allspice, cloves, nutmeg, and cayenne. Add the butter and, with an electric mixer, beat until the mixture is pale and fluffy. Beat in the maple syrup and molasses. Beat in the flour 1 cup at a time. Stir in the milk if the dough is too dry.

Divide the dough into 4 equal portions. Shape into four 1-inch-square bricks, wrap well in plastic wrap, and refrigerate for at least 1 day and up to 3 days to mellow the flavors.

Remove the dough from the refrigerator 30 minutes before rolling. Preheat the oven to 350°F. Lightly butter 2 baking sheets, or use nonstick sheets.

Sprinkle a work surface lightly with flour. One at a time, roll each block of dough into an 11-inch square, a scant ⅛ inch thick. With a chef's knife, trim the edges of dough to make a 10-inch square. Cut the dough into sixteen 2½-inch squares. With a metal spatula, transfer the squares to a baking sheet. Reroll the scraps into a 5-inch square. Cut it into four 2½-inch squares and transfer to the baking sheet. Bake until the cookies are firm and just beginning to brown, 9 to 11 minutes. Transfer to a cooling rack and allow to cool.

This dough freezes beautifully, so you can bake some and freeze the rest for later. Wrap well and freeze for up to 2 months. The cookies will keep for up to 1 month in an airtight tin. IN ADVANCE

Cookie-Cutter Ginger Cookies. You can also cut out the dough with cookie cutters to make stars, hearts, or animal shapes. variation

Proceed as directed, rerolling the scraps to make more cookies.

Quick Ginger Cookies. For quick-to-bake cookies that require no rolling, form the dough into four 9-by-1½-inch logs before wrapping and refrigerating. When you wish to bake cookies, use a thin sharp knife to slice the dough into ⅛-inch-thick disks. Bake as directed. variation

Apple, Pear, Banana, and Mango Chips

Paper-thin slices of fruit, oven-dried at a very low temperature, make delicate, chewy, intensely flavored fruit wafers, very different from the usual thickly cut commercial dried fruits. I like to slice whole uncored pears and apples to get cross sections of the fruits that remind one of a botanical print. Although they are not technically cookies, you can serve them as if they were, at the end of a meal, to accompany sorbets or ice cream or garnish Bowl and Spoon Desserts (pages 472–480). YIELD WILL VARY

These chips have a tart, concentrated flavor that intensifies as you chew them. Because they are sliced so thin, you can eat many more than the usual dried fruit halves, which are very caloric. They make lovely snacks as well.

The fruit should be fragrant and ripe, but still firm enough to slice. If the fruit isn't very fragrant or sweet, brushing it with a light sugar syrup before drying will intensify the flavor. In a small saucepan, heat ¼ cup sugar in ½ cup water until dissolved. Remove from the heat and stir in 1 teaspoon fresh lemon juice. Dip each fruit slice in the syrup, shaking off the excess before arranging them on the baking sheet.

The amounts below fill 1 large baking sheet (or 2 smaller ones). You can multiply the recipe, for as many racks as you have in your oven.

For best results, slice the fruit on a mandoline or vegetable slicer.

For each 18-by-13-inch baking sheet

Fruits, cleaned and prepared as directed below, such as

    1 medium pear or apple

    1 medium mango (about 12 ounces)

    4 medium bananas or 2 very ripe (black) plantains

To prepare pears or apples: Slice lengthwise ⅛ inch thick (20 to 25 slices).

To prepare mangoes: Peel with a vegetable peeler. Using a thin sharp knife, slice parallel to the flat pit to cut the flesh off in two large ovals. Then slice along the edges of the pit to remove the thin strips of flesh. Slice the flesh lengthwise into ⅛-inch-thick crescents (about 50 slices).

To prepare bananas or plantains: Peel and slice crosswise on a diagonal into slices a little more than ⅛ inch thick (about 60 slices). Alternatively, do not peel first. Slice lengthwise through the skin into long thin slices, then remove the skin.

For chewy fruit chips: Preheat the oven to 150° to 165°F. (If the pilot light keeps your oven quite warm, there is no real need to light the oven.) Place a large wire cooling rack, a silicone liner, or a sheet of parchment on a large baking sheet. Arrange the fruit on the pan so the slices are barely touching, fitting them like a puzzle to get on as much fruit as possible. Place in the oven and leave overnight. If using more than one pan, switch them several times from upper to lower oven racks (the oven is hotter at the top). After 8 hours or so, the fruit will be dry and leathery. Transfer the wafers to an airtight container.

For crisp fruit chips: Preheat the oven to 200°F. Proceed as directed above, but bake until the fruit is crisp and dry, 2 to 2½ hours. If using more than one pan, after 1 hour switch the position of the pans so the fruit dries evenly.

IN ADVANCE   You can store the chips for up to 1 month in an airtight tin.

OLD-FASHIONED COMFORTS. Some sweets, such as Jell-O, rice pudding, and pears poached in wine, offer such comfort with so little fanfare that they are clearly of another time. Their style is old-fashioned, originally meant as everyday family desserts. Most people I know secretly adore these foods, that is, when they are lucky enough to find true, homemade versions—such as the recipes that follow. These have the added virtue of being skillfully lightened so they are, truly, as healthful as they seem.

Real "Jell-O"

A homemade gelatin dessert without artificial flavors and synthetic dyes is a great thing that almost nobody gets to experience anymore. It is simple— a good fruit juice jelled with unflavored gelatin.

SERVES 4

An easy way to make real "Jell-O" is to buy some high-quality fruit juice, such as imported pear, peach, passion fruit, or cassis, available at specialty and gourmet markets, or guava nectar from Goya, with its tropical flavor and lovely coral color. Or, juice fresh fruits with an electric juicer and sweeten to taste.

For a thicker, less limpid gelatin, puree the fruit in a food processor, strain out any seeds, and use the puree instead of juice. Frozen juice concentrates, especially purple grape juice, make great "Jell-O." I reconstitute them in a proportion of 1 part concentrate to 2 parts water.

Certain raw fruits have an enzyme that will prevent gelatin from setting. Pineapple, mango, kiwi, and ginger must all be cooked for 5 minutes to destroy the enzyme before using. Fructose is available at health food stores.

> **2 cups fresh or good-quality bottled fruit juice or puree**
>
> **1 envelope** (¼ ounce) **unflavored gelatin**
>
> **2 to 3 teaspoons fresh lemon juice** (optional)
>
> **Sugar, honey, maple syrup, or fructose to taste** (optional)

Pour ½ cup of the fruit juice into a medium glass bowl or measuring cup and sprinkle the gelatin over it. Let stand for 1 minute.

In a medium saucepan, bring the remaining 1½ cups fruit juice to a boil. Stir into the gelatin mixture until dissolved. Add the lemon juice and sweetener to taste, if desired. Pour into individual bowls or into one bowl. Let cool, then refrigerate for several hours, until set.

variation **Stripes and Shapes.** There are endless possibilities for creating colorful patterns using different fruit juice "Jell-Os." For layers in a glass container, pour one color "Jell-O" into the container to the desired depth and refrigerate until it is completely set. Then pour another color on top and let it set. Repeat, using as many colors as you wish.

To make "Jell-O" that can be unmolded, use an additional 1½ teaspoons gelatin. When the gelatin is set, dip the mold in hot water to the depth of the gelatin for about 10 seconds. Loosen the edges with a thin knife. Wet a plate with cold water (this will allow you to position the unmolded gelatin), invert the plate over the mold, and, holding them together, turn them upside down. The gelatin should slip out.

IN ADVANCE You can prepare the "Jell-O" up to 5 days ahead.

Risotto Rice Pudding

SERVES 6 In experimenting with different rices, I discovered that Arborio and baldo rice (see page 183), the more tender cooking rices for risotto, are perfect in rice puddings. Their abundant starches bind with milk to make a custardy sauce that makes eggs unnecessary, and the rice retains a pleasing texture. Baldo rice is available at some gourmet stores and by mail order (see Sources, page 711).

> 4½ cups low-fat (1%) milk
>
> 1 vanilla bean
>
> 1 cup water
>
> 1 cup Arborio or baldo rice
>
> ½ cup sugar
>
> Small pinch of saffron threads
>
> ½ teaspoon kosher salt
>
> ¾ to 1 cup boiling water if using baldo rice
>
> 3 to 5 tablespoons whole milk
>
> Cinnamon for dusting (optional)

In a heavy medium saucepan, bring the low-fat milk to a simmer over moderate heat. Meanwhile, using a thin sharp paring knife, split the vanilla bean lengthwise in half. Scrape out the seeds and add the seeds and bean to the milk; keep hot over low heat.

In another heavy medium saucepan, bring the 1 cup water to a boil. Stir in the rice and simmer over moderate heat until the water is completely absorbed, about 2 minutes. Stir in the sugar, saffron, salt, and hot milk and cook over moderately low heat, stirring often, until the rice is very tender and suspended in a thick custard-like sauce, 30 to 35 minutes for Arborio rice, 40 to 45 minutes for baldo. (If using baldo rice, add boiling water as necessary to keep it from getting too dry.)

Pour the rice into a serving dish and set aside to cool, uncovered, stirring occasionally. Discard the vanilla bean.

Stir in the whole milk by tablespoons until the rice is creamy. Cover with plastic wrap and refrigerate until ready to serve. Just before serving, dust with cinnamon, if desired.

IN ADVANCE

You can make the pudding up to 3 days ahead.

variation

Scented Rice Pudding. You can embellish the basic recipe with any number of flavorings. During cooking, add one 3-inch strip orange or lemon zest or a single bay leaf, which will add a haunting flavor. Discard the zest or bay leaf once the rice is cool. Or, before serving, stir in a few drops of orange flower water, or rose water, to taste, or dust with chopped pistachios.

Pears, Peaches, or Quinces in Fragrant Red Wine Syrup

SERVES 4

I can think of no dessert more reminiscent of French country cooking than pears poached in red wine, the perfect refreshing dessert after a rich meal. This recipe is based on one I learned from my friend Maxime Deferts's mother at lunch at her house in Vézelay, Burgundy, many years ago. It works wonderfully not only with pears, but with peaches (preferably white-fleshed) and small quinces. Cooking the fruit whole with the stems intact is more charming visually than using cut fruit. You can, however, halve or slice the fruit before cooking to make it easier to handle (in which case, it will require less cooking time).

Collect the "ends" or leftovers of bottles of red wine in a single bottle and store, corked, in the refrigerator to use as a poaching liquid for fruit.

One 750-milliliter bottle full-bodied red wine, plus more if needed

1 cup sweet fortified wine, such as ruby port or Malmsey Madeira, or an additional ½ cup sugar

½ cup sugar

One 3-by-¾-inch strip orange zest (removed with a vegetable peeler)

½ cinnamon stick

¼ teaspoon coriander seeds

1 whole clove

1 vanilla bean

4 slightly underripe Comice or Bartlett pears, peaches, or quinces, peeled, stems left intact

In a nonreactive saucepan large enough to hold the fruit in one layer, combine the wine, sugar, orange zest, cinnamon stick, coriander seeds, and clove. With a sharp paring knife, split the vanilla bean lengthwise in half and scrape out the seeds. Add the seeds and bean to the pan. Bring to a boil over moderate heat, stirring to dissolve the sugar.

If the fruit won't stand upright, cut a thin slice off the flower end of each to make a flat bottom. Arrange the fruit in the syrup. Cut a circle of parchment to fit the diameter of the pan and place over the fruit. Place a pot lid or plate slightly smaller than the saucepan on top of the parchment to hold the fruit below the surface of the liquid as it cooks.

Return the wine to a simmer. Cook, rearranging the fruit occasionally, until a skewer passes to the cores with little resistance, 35 to 40 minutes for pears or peaches, up to 1½ hours for quinces. If the wine evaporates to below the top of the fruit, add a little wine or water to bring the level up.

Gently transfer the fruit to a serving bowl. Boil the wine over moderate heat until reduced to a syrup, about 1 cup. Strain it over the fruit. Serve at room temperature or chilled.

IN ADVANCE You can poach the fruit up to 4 days ahead; cover and refrigerate in the syrup.

variation **Pears in Spiced Wine Syrup.** My friend Josh Eisen poaches pears in an unusual mixture of fragrant exotic spices. Replace the orange zest, cinnamon stick, clove, and vanilla bean with 1 tablespoon black peppercorns, 6 lightly crushed cardamom pods, 1 star anise, and 1 bay leaf; increase the coriander seeds to 1 tablespoon.

Quinces in White Wine and Honey. variation When you cook whole quinces in white wine and honey, they turn a lovely rosy color and their floral flavor really comes through. Substitute dry white wine for the red wine and ¾ to 1 cup wildflower honey for the sugar. Omit the cinnamon stick, coriander, clove, and fortified wine. Add enough water to the saucepan to cover the quinces.

Quick Sorbets and Faux Ice Creams

A GUIDE TO IMPROVISING

SERVES 4

Fruits that are truly ripe are not only more fragrant, sweet, and flavorful, but have a creamier texture. When frozen, they can be pureed in a food processor to make instant low-sugar sorbets with a lovely texture and much fresher and more vivid flavor than commercial versions. With the addition of a little cream or coconut milk, they become surprisingly rich faux ice creams. This method also works wonderfully with roasted fruits, which have a more concentrated caramel flavor. In a pinch, you can use packaged frozen berries in light syrup (defrost slightly before pureeing).

4 cups ripe, fragrant fruit (peeled, seeded or cored, and cut into ½-inch chunks, as appropriate), such as

> **2 pints strawberries, raspberries, or blackberries**
>
> **2 pounds peaches,** preferably white-fleshed
>
> **2 pounds Bartlett or Comice pears**
>
> **3 medium mangoes** (12 ounces each)
>
> **2 pounds papaya** (preferably red papaya)
>
> **Roasted Caramelized Pears** (page 476) **or roasted peaches** (page 475)

1 tablespoon fresh lemon or lime juice

1 tablespoon honey or sugar

1 to 2 teaspoons eau-de-vie or other liqueur (optional), such as rum, framboise, kirsch, Poire William, or Grand Marnier

Creamy enrichment (optional), such as

> **¼ cup heavy cream mixed with ¼ cup buttermilk**
>
> **½ cup unsweetened coconut milk**

1. In a medium bowl, combine the fruit, lemon juice, and honey. Let sit at room temperature until the fruit has released its juices, about 1 hour.

2. Pour the fruit mixture onto a rimmed baking sheet, cover with plastic wrap, and freeze until solid, at least 2 hours.

3. Break up the fruit with a kitchen spoon and transfer to a food processor. Pulse until the fruit has reduced to the texture of a crystalline meal, stopping frequently to scrape down the sides (if the fruit is frozen too hard to process, allow it to soften for 1 to 2 minutes before continuing).

4. Add the eau-de-vie to taste and pulse a few times more. Add the optional creamy enrichment and continue processing until creamy.

5. Serve at once, or transfer to a serving bowl, cover with plastic wrap, and freeze up to 1 hour (after that it becomes too hard to serve).

SERVING ICE CREAM AND SORBET

Supermarkets now offer a vast array of appealing sorbets, frozen yogurts, and lightened ice creams with a smooth creamy texture that are low in fat. Flavors run the gamut from dark chocolate to flower petal. But often a small scoop of full-fat egg-yolk-and-cream ice cream is all that is needed on special occasions to add a sense of indulgence to a slice of cake or pie or a bowl of roasted fruit. Because the way an ice cream or sorbet is scooped can greatly affect both calorie count and visual appeal, I have ice-cream scoops in a wide range of sizes, from a hilarious, tiny ½-ounce scoop, which is only about 1 inch in diameter, increasing by 1-ounce intervals up to 4 ounces (3 inches in diameter).

Use a small (½- or 1-ounce) scoop to adorn a homemade dessert such as a pie or Bowl and Spoon Dessert (pages 472-480) with a full-fat ice cream. (A 1-ounce scoop of Häagen-Dazs adds only 68 calories.) Use a medium (2-ounce) scoop when serving several kinds of low-calorie frozen desserts at the same time. Use a large (3- or 4-ounce) scoop when serving a low-calorie frozen dessert, such as Banana and Coconut Milk Ice Cream (page 527) or a sorbet.

Banana and Coconut Milk Ice Cream

SERVES 4

Very ripe bananas frozen and then pureed in a food processor achieve the texture of light ice cream. It makes a delightful dessert on its own, but the addition of some coconut milk gives it an extraordinarily lush flavor and the texture of a full-fat ice cream. Sometimes I top it with a sprinkling of toasted shredded coconut.

You can make this with other creamy tropical fruits, such as papaya, mango, and golden pineapple.

> **2 very ripe large bananas**
>
> **¼ cup shredded sweetened coconut** (optional)
>
> **½ cup unsweetened coconut milk**
>
> **1 tablespoon superfine sugar**
>
> **Squeeze of lime juice**
>
> **A few drops of dark rum**

Peel the bananas. Slice crosswise ½ inch thick and place on a rimmed baking sheet. Freeze until solid, about 1 hour.

Meanwhile, if using the coconut, preheat the oven to 375°F.

Place the coconut in a pie plate, and toast in the oven, tossing occasionally, until golden, about 4 minutes; watch carefully so it does not burn. Set aside to cool.

In a food processor, puree the frozen banana slices for about 2 minutes, scraping the sides down occasionally. Although at first the mixture will be very granular, as the bananas thaw slightly, it will become very creamy. Drizzle in the coconut milk, sugar, lime juice, and rum and process until it is the consistency of soft ice cream. Serve at once, or transfer to an airtight container and freeze for up to 30 minutes before serving. Garnish with the toasted coconut, if using.

DESSERT SAUCES. A good sauce can transform the simplest dessert. It is an added touch that can heighten or mellow flavors, harmonize disparate textures, and intensify effect. It is the key to making Bowl and Spoon Desserts (pages 472-480). The recipes that follow are the best and most versatile sauces I know.

Fruit Coulis

A GUIDE TO IMPROVISING

MAKES 1 CUP

A coulis is simply a smooth sauce made from pureed fruit. You can make coulis from strawberries, raspberries, blackberries, pineapple, or mangoes, and use them to embellish practically any dessert, from cut raw fruit or roasted fruits to cake to rice pudding and ice cream. The basic method is simple; the only real variable is the amount of sweetening. I like to add a little rum or eau-de-vie such as framboise (raspberry) to heighten the flavors and perfume. Kirsch (cherry) goes particularly well with pineapple.

Of all the frozen foods available, raspberries and strawberries frozen in light syrup are to my mind the most useful and true to their fresh counterpart. They are perfect for making vividly flavored coulis out of season, when fresh berries don't have much flavor.

> **2 cups ripe, fragrant fruit,** such as strawberries, blackberries or raspberries, or 1-inch chunks peeled pineapple or mangoes, or one 10-ounce package frozen raspberries or strawberries in light syrup, thawed
>
> **Confectioners' or superfine sugar or mild wildflower honey to taste**
>
> **2 to 3 teaspoons fresh lemon or lime juice**
>
> **Eau-de-vie or other clear alcohol** (optional), such as framboise, kirsch, or rum

1. Puree the fruit in a food processor, letting the motor run until you have a very smooth puree. Add sugar to taste and just enough lemon juice to heighten the flavors.

2. Strain through a fine strainer into a bowl. Stir in the eau-de-vie, if using.

Strawberries in Beaujolais Sauce

MAKES 2½ CUPS; SERVES 6

The intense fruitiness of the Beaujolais in this simple sauce marries well with the berries. The sauce is an excellent way to use up an open bottle of Beaujolais. Served hot or cold, it is wonderful on ice cream, plain cakes, and pancakes or French toast, as well as many Bowl and Spoon Desserts (pages 472–480).

1½ cups Beaujolais or other very fruity young wine

⅓ cup sugar

4 cups strawberries, hulled and halved, or quartered if very large (you can substitute up to 1 cup raspberries for some of the strawberries if you like)

2 to 3 teaspoons lemon juice

In a medium saucepan, combine the wine and sugar and boil over high heat, stirring occasionally, until reduced by half and beginning to get syrupy. Stir in the berries and boil, stirring occasionally, until they just collapse.

Remove the berries with a slotted spoon and set aside. Boil the sauce until syrupy again. Let cool slightly, then add the lemon juice and berries. Serve the strawberries warm or cold.

The sauce will keep for 5 days, covered and refrigerated.

IN ADVANCE

Basic Vanilla Custard Sauce

MAKES 1 GENEROUS CUP

This pouring custard is modeled after the classic French dessert sauce *crème anglaise,* an egg yolk–thickened milk-based sauce infused with vanilla. It makes the plainest cake or poached pear memorable. In this version, the sugar and fat have been cut back, producing a light sauce that is intensely flavored with vanilla bean.

Egg yolks are essential to the taste of a custard sauce. I reduce the usual number of eggs, using only one egg yolk per cup of milk for flavoring and richness. Gentle thickening is achieved by the use of arrowroot. I use whole milk because it has the necessary body and creaminess.

It is important to use a real vanilla bean rather than extract, for it has a much more profound and satisfying flavor, which makes up for the reduction of egg yolks.

The recipe can easily be doubled.

1 teaspoon arrowroot

1 cup whole milk

⅓ vanilla bean

1 large egg

3 tablespoons sugar

In a medium bowl, combine the arrowroot with 1 tablespoon of the milk, stirring until completely dissolved.

Pour the remaining milk into a small heavy saucepan. With a thin sharp paring knife, split the vanilla bean lengthwise, scrape out the seeds, and add the seeds and bean to the pan. Bring to a simmer over moderate heat.

While the milk is heating, whisk the egg and sugar into the arrowroot mixture.

Whisk the hot milk into the arrowroot mixture. Pour the mixture back into the saucepan and cook, whisking constantly, over very low heat until the sauce has thickened enough to coat the bowl of a spoon, about 7 minutes; do not allow it to boil. Strain the sauce into a medium bowl and let cool to room temperature, stirring occasionally.

Cover with plastic wrap and refrigerate. Serve chilled.

IN ADVANCE   The sauce will keep for up to 3 days refrigerated. Stir before serving.

variations   ## Scented Custard Sauces.   In addition to the classic vanilla flavoring, you can flavor custard sauce with spices, citrus zest, honey, brandies and eau-de-vie, even herbs or passion fruit. Proceed as directed, adding the flavorings as indicated below to the milk. Bring to a simmer and remove from the heat. Let the flavors steep until you get the intensity you like, then strain them out. Reheat the milk and proceed.

- **Fresh herbs,** such as lavender, basil, verbena, thyme, or rose geranium, make unexpectedly delicious custards. Omit the vanilla bean and add several sprigs or large leaves.

- **Saffron** makes a deep yellow, delicately perfumed sauce that is particularly lovely with warm apple and pear desserts, and sublime with slow-roasted nectarines, peaches, or apricots. The red saffron threads in the pale yellow sauce are beautiful. Omit the vanilla bean and add 8 saffron threads and 1 cardamom pod, crushed. Return the threads to the sauce after straining, if desired.

- **Honey or maple syrup.** There are as many flavors of honey as there are flowers, which you can use alone or in tandem with other flavorings. My favorite is tilleul honey from Provence, which has a rich floral aroma that works well with lavender and thyme. Similarly, maple syrup will add its inimitable flavor to a custard sauce, and is the perfect complement to warm apple and pumpkin desserts. Add 3 or 4 tablespoons, to taste, instead of the sugar.

- **Orange, lemon, tangerine, or lime zest.** Add two or three 2-by-1-inch strips of zest. Meyer lemons make a particularly appealing custard.

- **Fennel seeds.** Add ¾ teaspoon.

- **Cinnamon stick.** Add one 3-inch piece; Mexican cinnamon is exceptionally fragrant.

- **Allspice berries.** Add ½ teaspoon, crushed.

- **Cardamom pods.** Add 4 pods, crushed, the seeds removed and lightly crushed.

- **Fresh ginger.** Add 4 or 5 quarter-sized slices.

You can also add any of the following flavorings to the cooled custard sauce.

- **Cognac, Armagnac, bourbon, Poire William, framboise, kirsch, or rum.** Add 2 to 3 teaspoons, to taste.

- **Flower waters,** such as rose or orange flower water. Add 2 to 3 teaspoons, to taste.

- **Passion fruit.** The intensely flavored orange pulp of this fruit adds a tropical flavor to a custard sauce. It goes particularly well with desserts made with mango, pineapple, orange, or papaya. Halve 2 or 3 passion fruits, scoop out the pulp, and strain to remove the seeds. Stir the puree into the cold custard.

A BREATHTAKING SAUCE FOR DESSERT

Artisan-made balsamic vinegar from Modena or Reggio Emilia, Italy, makes a great dessert sauce. It doesn't taste like a vinegar at all, but rather a rich condiment with a deeply complex, luscious flavor that is magic on desserts with fruit, caramel, or creamy flavors. It is so concentrated that you need only a drizzle—½ teaspoon at most to make a celestial dessert out of the most humble elements: good vanilla ice cream, roasted fruits such as Caramelized Roasted Pears (page 476) or Slow-Roasted Stone Fruits (page 476), or a Rustic Free-form Fruit Tart (pages 481–487). Although real artisanal balsamics are very expensive, a small bottle will last a long time. It is worth every penny (see page 640 for more about artisanal balsamics).

Tart, Ethereal Lemon Curd

MAKES 1 CUP,
ENOUGH FOR A
10-INCH TART

Classic lemon curd is basically a custard made of egg yolks, sugar, and lemon juice, enriched with lots of butter. It has the consistency of a thick jam and is inordinately rich. This curd is based on one I used to make many years ago at Le Petit Robert, owned by my friend James Peterson. We left out the butter intentionally and added some whipped crème fraîche to the cooled curd to make a filling for delicious lemon tarts.

To make up for using one less egg yolk than is usual, in my revised curd I add a touch of unflavored gelatin to give it more body. It is delectable just the way it is, although you can fold in some regular or reduced-fat sour cream before filling tarts.

½ **teaspoon unflavored gelatin**

½ **cup fresh lemon juice**

7 tablespoons sugar

1 large egg

1 egg white

One 3-by-1-inch strip lemon zest (removed with a vegetable peeler)

In a small bowl, sprinkle the gelatin over 2 tablespoons of the lemon juice. Set aside to soften.

In a medium stainless steel bowl, or the top of a double boiler, combine the remaining lemon juice and the sugar, egg, egg white, and zest. Set the bowl over, but not in, simmering water. (Although the curd could be cooked directly over low heat in a heavy saucepan, using a water bath ensures that it doesn't overcook.) Whisk constantly until the curd is thick and coats the back of a spoon, about 5 minutes. Stir in the gelatin mixture and cook for 1 minute longer. Strain into a medium bowl and allow to cool to room temperature, whisking occasionally. Transfer the curd to a jar, cover, and refrigerate until ready to use.

IN ADVANCE | The curd will keep for about 1 week.

Meyer Lemon Curd. Fragrant Meyer lemons, which grow in abundance in California but are only sporadically available nationally, make a spectacular curd. Since they are sweeter than regular lemons, you will need only ⅓ cup sugar. variation

Lime Curd. Replace the lemon juice with an equal amount of fresh lime juice (Key limes are particularly fragrant) and add 2 teaspoons rum. variation

Real Whipped Cream or Crème Fraîche

MAKES ¾ CUP

In the same way that air causes a small amount of puff pastry to expand to many times its volume, it works a similar miracle with cream. One tablespoon of cream whips to two tablespoons, at 50 calories. Three or four tablespoons of real whipped cream makes a healthy dollop, enough to give the inimitable satisfaction and pure flavor of the real thing without overdoing it.

Whipped cream that has been delicately scented with spices or alcohol lends a lovely touch to a dessert, such as espresso sorbet with cinnamon-scented whipped cream or a warm cherry pie with kirsch-scented whipped cream.

> ¼ **cup plus 2 tablespoons heavy cream or crème fraîche**
> ¾ **teaspoon sugar**
> **Optional flavoring,** such as
> > **Tiny pinch of ground allspice, cinnamon, cardamom, or cloves**
> > ¼ **to** ½ **teaspoon alcohol,** such as cognac, bourbon, or scotch
> > **any eau-de-vie,** such as Poire William, framboise, kirsch, or grappa
> > **pure vanilla or almond extract** (just a few drops)
> > **rose water**
> > **orange flower water**

Pour the cream into a chilled medium bowl. Using a chilled whisk, beat the cream until soft mounds form. Beat in the sugar and any flavoring and continue beating until the cream is stiff. Refrigerate until ready to use.

You can whip the cream up to 4 hours ahead; cover and refrigerate. IN ADVANCE

Rich Faux Cream

MAKES 1 CUP Here is a low-fat dessert cream that is a delicious and realistic alternative for those who should not have the real thing. It has nearly the consistency and flavor of lightly whipped cream, although it is somewhat more dense. Low-fat, salt-free cottage cheese is pureed to a perfectly smooth creamy base with a neutral flavor. A small amount of sour cream and heavy cream, vanilla, and sugar add the flavoring elements and some of the richness of real whipped cream. A half cup of this cream contains only 4 grams of fat, as compared to 24 grams in ½ cup of real whipped cream. It can be flavored in the same way as Real Whipped Cream.

> 1 cup no-salt low-fat (1%) **cottage cheese**
>
> 2 teaspoons **superfine sugar**
>
> ¼ teaspoon **pure vanilla extract**
>
> 2 teaspoons **regular or reduced-fat sour cream**
>
> 2 teaspoons **heavy cream**

Puree the cottage cheese, sugar, and vanilla in a food processor until perfectly smooth, about 1 minute. Scrape the mixture into a small bowl and fold in the sour cream and heavy cream. Serve as is, or flavor as suggested on page 533. Cover and refrigerate until ready to use.

IN ADVANCE The cream will keep, covered and refrigerated, for about 1 week.

Yogurt Cream

Yogurt cream—yogurt from which much of the watery whey has been drained—makes an excellent mildly tangy, thick cream that is wonderful with roasted fresh fruit or cooked dried fruit, such as Apricots Roasted with Cardamom (page 478). Yogurt cream must be made with whole-milk yogurt rather than low-fat, which is very acidic, or it will not have the appealing sweet creamy flavor.

MAKES ABOUT 1⅓ CUPS

1 quart plain whole-milk yogurt

Line a large colander or conical strainer with 3 layers of cheesecloth (or use a yogurt cheese funnel) and place over a bowl. Spoon the yogurt into the cheese-cloth and cover lightly with plastic wrap. Refrigerate for at least 6 hours, or overnight. The liquid will drain from the yogurt, causing it to thicken like cream cheese; discard the liquid.

Transfer the cream to a clean jar or bowl, cover, and refrigerate.

You can store the yogurt cream, covered and refrigerated, for up to 1 month.

IN ADVANCE

FLAVOR CATALYSTS

- FLAVOR ESSENCES,
  DRY RUBS, AND MARINADES
- BROTHS
- FLAVORED OILS
- SAUCES

Lack of time seems to characterize our age. Although many of us adore cooking, we don't often have the time or the energy to do it the way we did in the past on a daily basis. Yet we love to eat, while our pragmatic sides demand that we eat healthfully. To accommodate these conflicting realities, I've learned to think strategically about how to make simple foods taste more elaborate than they really are.

I rely on what I call Flavor Catalysts, simple make-ahead preparations that can transform the simplest foods into deeply satisfying dishes. They fall into three categories: preparations to apply to foods before cooking, Flavor Essences, Dry Rubs, and Marinades; Broths, to be used in cooking and as the base for many dishes; and preparations to embellish foods after they are cooked, Flavored Oils and Sauces. All these catalysts have affinities for a wide variety of foods, so they continue to inspire me to improvise new combinations. Their effect is always a great deal more than the sum of their parts. And many have a long shelf life, so you can keep them on hand to use at a moment's notice.

Red miso and sweet white miso pastes form the base of glazing marinades, such as Red Miso Glaze (page 559) and Miso-Sake Glaze (page 236)

FLAVOR ESSENCES,

DRY RUBS,
AND MARINADES

FLAVOR ESSENCES AND DRY RUBS. Flavor Essences
are fine powders made from ground dried flavorings such as wild
mushrooms, chiles, lemongrass, spices, and even certain teas.
Unlike my Dry Rubs, they do not contain salt or sugar, so you
can use them in just about every aspect of your cooking to quickly
flavor soups, sauces and stews, oils, and marinades. A pinch of
Smoky Tea Essence gives an instant bacony flavor to baked beans,
or a smoky grilled flavor to seared steaks, and it even makes commercial ketchup taste like homemade. Use Sweet, Hot, Smoky
Pepper to add piquant flavor to Parmesan Crisps (page 370), to
fortify commercial chili powder, and to season pork chops,
roasted peppers, and onions. When mixed with salt and sugar,
Flavor Essences become Dry Rubs.

Dry Rubs can be made from Flavor Essences or can be combinations of ground spices and herbs that are mixed with salt and sugar. They are used to coat meats, fish, or poultry before pan searing, grilling, or roasting. When cooked, they form a crust, providing texture as well as subtle strata of flavors that surprise the palate while illuminating those inherent in the food. You can also use them as a marinades to imbue foods with flavor; the salt will help to tenderize them. See Crusting Meats with Dry Rubs (page 315) and Pan-Seared Crusted Fillets, Steaks, and Shellfish (page 241).

Because they make dramatic results so easy to achieve, you should keep an array of these specially made seasonings on hand.

Making Flavor Essences and Dry Rubs

A GUIDE TO IMPROVISING

MAKES ABOUT ⅓ CUP

If the ingredients are not brittle enough to grind, spread them on a baking sheet and dry them in a 200°F oven for 30 minutes to 1 hour, until very brittle.

You can make Flavor Essences and Dry Rubs with an enormous variety of dried ingredients, such as spices, herbs, chile peppers, mushrooms, cocoa, even certain teas, alone or in combination. The possible permutations and blends are endless. Use a blender or a spice grinder (or a perfectly clean coffee grinder). A food processor will not create a fine-enough powder.

In Dry Rubs, salt and sugar act as an essential link between the powder and the food itself; without them, they taste flat. The exact quantity of salt and sugar depends on the balance of flavors in the mix: Hot chiles need less salt, for example; dried herbs need more. If you are not sure of how much to add when improvising a dry rub, start with 1½ teaspoons kosher salt and a scant ½ teaspoon sugar per ⅓ cup ground spices, herbs, or other ingredients. Trial and error will tell you what adjustments to make.

> **⅓ to ½ cup dried flavoring** (broken or cut into ½-inch pieces if appropriate), singly or in combination, such as spices, herbs, chiles, wild mushrooms, or tea
>
> **1½ to 2 teaspoons kosher salt and scant ½ teaspoon sugar** (for Dry Rubs)

1. Place the dry ingredients in a blender container or spice grinder. Let the motor run for 1 minute or longer at high speed to achieve the finest-possible powder. Allow the mixture to settle for about 30 seconds before removing the cover, so the fine powder does not fly into the air.

2. Use a dry pastry brush to push the powder through a strainer into a clean dry container. Blend and strain the larger bits again.

3. If making a dry rub, stir in the salt and sugar.

Store in a tightly sealed jar away from light for up to 3 months. To revive a powder that has lost some of its freshness, warm it in a small heavy skillet over low heat until fragrant.

IN ADVANCE

Ancho Chile Essence

Ancho chiles—dried poblano chiles—have a mild sweet flavor with just a slight spiciness that complements many foods. I find myself using this essence frequently, as a dry rub for pan-seared and grilled meats and poultry, as a seasoning in Parmesan Crisps (page 370), and when I want an underlying sweet chile flavor for Southwestern-style foods, such as Ancho Chile–Rubbed Duck Steaks (page 327) and Ancho Chile Ketchup (page 340). I also often use it as the base when I am improvising dry rubs such as Mexican "Mole" Rub (page 551).

MAKES ABOUT ⅓ CUP

3 dried ancho chiles (1½ to 2 ounces)

Break the chiles apart. Remove the stems and seeds. If the chiles are still pliable, dry them in a warm oven (200°F) for about 1 hour, until they are very brittle.

Transfer the chiles to a blender or spice grinder. Blend at high speed for at least 1 minute, until you have the finest-possible powder. Let the mixture settle for about 30 seconds before removing the cover, so the powder does not fly into the air. Use a dry pastry brush to push the powder through a strainer into a clean, dry container. Blend and strain the larger bits again.

Store in a tightly sealed jar away from light for up to 3 months.

IN ADVANCE

Wild Mushroom Essence

MAKES ABOUT
⅓ CUP

Wild Mushroom Essence can be used to give an earthy flavor to hearty broths such as Roasted Vegetable Broth (page 571) and Classic Rich Poultry, Meat, or Game Broth (page 574) or to tomato-based soups and pasta sauces like Wild Mushroom Ragù (page 151). Use a teaspoon or two to punch up the flavor of mushroom or meaty-tasting recipes such as Roasted Wild Mushrooms (page 40), Mushrooms with Madeira and Shallots (page 61), The Best Part of a Potato Gratin (page 50), Gratin of Pasta with Leftover Meat Juices (page 152), or Classic Game Ragù (page 148). It makes an excellent rub for meat, poultry, and, surprisingly, meaty firm-fleshed fish, particularly those that will be served with a red wine or port wine sauce. For an example of how to use it as a crust for fish, see Mushroom-Crusted Bass with Port Wine Butter Sauce (page 246).

You can make this essence with many kinds of dried wild mushrooms. Porcini, also called cèpes, have an exceedingly rich flavor that makes a wonderful all-purpose powder. They are imported from Italy (porcini) and France (cèpes), along with less expensive versions from Poland. Morel mushrooms also make a delicious powder. The best are from France, where they are dried over wood fires, giving them an appealing faintly smoky flavor. Dried wild mushrooms are generally quite expensive, but their flavor is so intense you only need a little. It is cheaper to buy them loose, by the ounce, than in small packages. The dried button mushrooms commonly sold in supermarkets do not have enough flavor to make a good powder.

1 ounce (about ⅓ cup) **dried wild mushrooms,** such as porcini or morel

Break the mushrooms into ½-inch pieces and place in a blender or spice grinder. Blend for at least 1 minute at high speed, until you have the finest-possible powder. Let the mixture settle for about 30 seconds before removing the cover, so the powder does not fly into the air.

Use a dry pastry brush to push the powder through a strainer set into a clean dry container. Blend and strain the larger bits again.

IN ADVANCE Store in a tightly sealed jar away from light for up to 3 months.

Tomato-based sauces such as ketchup, pasta, and barbecue take especially well to instant seasoning with Ancho Chile or Wild Mushroom essences, making them taste homemade. For 1 cup sauce: In a small bowl, moisten 2 to 3 tablespoons Flavor Essence with an equal amount of water and allow to sit for a few minutes. Stir the paste into the sauce until you have the desired intensity.

Smoky Tea Essence

This powder, my most exciting discovery with rubs, is made from Lapsang Souchong or Hu-Kwa, a smoked tea from China's Fukien province. It imparts a sweet, bacony, smoky flavor to foods. You can use it in just about any dish where a slight hint of wood smoke is desired. I've rubbed it on steaks to give them a grilled flavor, infused it into broths to impart a bacony flavor to soups, and added it to pots of beans or to roasted peppers. When I am cooking for vegetarians, I use it instead of bacon or ham to impart a smoky flavor. While it is great as a rub on its own, I often use it in tandem with many other Flavor Essences and Dry Rubs.

MAKES ABOUT ⅓ CUP

Smoky teas are readily available in supermarkets and gourmet stores.

> ½ **cup** (1½ ounces) **loose Lapsang Souchong tea** or 20 tea bags

If you are using tea bags, cut them open. Empty the tea into a blender or spice grinder. Blend the tea for at least 1 minute at high speed, until you have the finest-possible powder. Let the mixture settle for about 30 seconds before removing the cover, so the fine powder does not fly into the air.

Use a dry pastry brush to push the powder through a strainer set into a clean dry container. Blend and strain the larger bits again.

Store in a tightly sealed jar away from light for up to 3 months.

IN ADVANCE

Lemongrass Essence

MAKES ABOUT
⅓ CUP

Lemongrass
Essence is good to
keep on hand for
use when you can't
find fresh lemon-
grass to infuse
broths and soups.
One teaspoon
equals 1 stalk of
fresh.

Lemongrass is a tall, fibrous, pale green grass with a scallion-like bulb. It has a bright, lemony herbal flavor that is key to Thai and Vietnamese cooking. This essence makes a lovely rub for seafood, shellfish, squid, chicken, and quail. It also makes a lovely iced tea.

8 stalks fresh lemongrass (about 1 ounce) or ½ cup dried lemongrass

If using fresh lemongrass, preheat the oven to 200°F.

With a thin sharp knife, slice the white bulb of each stalk as thin as possible, just up to the point where the leaves begin to branch. Discard the tough upper branches. Scatter the lemongrass on a baking sheet and place in the oven until completely dry, about 30 minutes.

Place the lemongrass in a blender or spice grinder and blend for at least 1 minute at high speed, until you have the finest-possible powder. Let the mixture settle for about 30 seconds before removing the cover, so the fine powder does not fly into the air.

Use a dry pastry brush to press the powder through a strainer into a clean dry container. Return the coarse chaff to the blender and blend again for 2 minutes. Strain again and discard the tough chaff that remains.

IN ADVANCE   Store in a tightly sealed jar away from light for up to 3 months.

variation   **Lemongrass Rub.** Add 2 teaspoons salt and ½ teaspoon sugar.

Sweet, Hot, Smoky Pepper

MAKES ABOUT
¼ CUP

This is a facsimile of a marvelous ground chile powder from Spain that has a sweet, resonant flavor like good paprika, yet is quite spicy with an underlying smoky flavor. Because it is quite hot, use this versatile powder sparingly, or in tandem with other flavorings, wherever you want a hit of sweet hot smoke. It is especially delicious on pork chops or tenderloin, and as a seasoning for roasted red bell peppers, giving them some of the piquant smoky flavor of the famous piquillo peppers of Spain.

3 tablespoons sweet paprika, preferably Hungarian

2¼ teaspoons loose smoky tea, such as Lapsang Souchong or Hu-Kwa (about 2 tea bags, cut open)

1 teaspoon cayenne pepper, or more to taste

Place the paprika, tea, and cayenne pepper in a blender or spice grinder and blend for at least 1 minute at high speed, until you have the finest-possible powder. Let the mixture settle for about 30 seconds before removing the cover, so the fine powder does not fly into the air.

Use a dry pastry brush to push the powder through a strainer into a clean dry container.

Store in a tightly sealed jar away from light for up to 3 months.

IN ADVANCE

Moroccan Spice Essence

MAKES ABOUT ½ CUP

This mix endows foods with the warm spicy flavors found in many Moroccan dishes. It is especially good rubbed into lamb or chicken and dusted on sliced eggplant, peppers, potatoes, tomatoes, and onions before roasting. It perks up tomato-based sauces and stews. I also use it to season dried white and split fava beans. Try garnishing foods flavored with this mix with chopped fresh cilantro just before serving.

> **2 tablespoons coriander seeds**
> **2 tablespoons cumin seeds**
> **2 tablespoons black peppercorns**
> **2 tablespoons sweet paprika,** preferably Hungarian
> **1 tablespoon ground cinnamon**

In a small heavy skillet, combine the coriander, cumin seeds, and peppercorns and toast over moderate heat, stirring constantly, until fragrant. Remove from the heat and stir in the paprika and cinnamon.

Scrape the spices into a blender container or spice grinder and blend for at least 1 minute at high speed, until you have the finest-possible powder. Let the mixture settle for about 30 seconds before removing the cover, so the fine powder does not fly into the air.

Use a dry pastry brush to press the powder through a strainer into a clean dry container.

Store in a tightly sealed jar away from light for up to 3 months.

IN ADVANCE

Sandy's Curry Powder

MAKES ABOUT
⅓ CUP

Unable to find a great commercial curry powder, talented cook and friend Sandy Gluck divined her way thorough an array of spices to make this curry powder, with its lovely balance of sweet pungent flavors. Use it in any recipe that calls for curry powder, or to crust panfried shrimp and scallops.

When I do stumble across a decent commercial curry powder, usually at an Indian food market or from a fine spice store like Penzey's (see Sources, page 711), I note that invariably, the list of spices on the label begins with either coriander or cumin seeds. I have found that turmeric is usually the main ingredient in inferior curry powders. This inexpensive, rather one-dimensional spice with an appealing yellow color is often used to extend more expensive ones.

2 tablespoons coriander seeds

2 teaspoons cumin seeds

1 teaspoon black peppercorns

1 ½ teaspoons fennel seeds

1 teaspoon ground turmeric

1 teaspoon ground mustard

1 teaspoon ground ginger

1 teaspoon ground cinnamon

In a small heavy skillet, combine the coriander, cumin, and peppercorns and toast over moderate heat, stirring constantly, until fragrant. Remove from the heat and stir in the remaining spices.

Scrape the spices into a blender container or spice grinder and blend for at least 1 minute at high speed, until you have the finest-possible powder. Let the mixture settle for about 30 seconds before removing the cover, so the fine powder does not fly into the air.

Use a dry pastry brush to press the powder through a strainer into a clean dry container. Blend and strain the larger bits again.

IN ADVANCE Store in a tightly sealed jar away from light for up to 3 months.

variation **Fiery Curry Powder.** Increase the peppercorns to 2 teaspoons and add ½ teaspoon red pepper flakes after the spices are toasted.

Tuscan Herb Salt

In Tuscany, this vibrantly flavored herb salt is used to season all kinds of roasts, from pork to guinea hen (see Herb-Scented Tuscan Pork Roast, page 293). While it is best fresh, you can also let it dry out in an uncovered container—the salt will preserve the herbs' and garlic's clear flavor—to use as a versatile seasoning. I love to toss some with sautéed vegetables like green beans or potatoes. You can also vary the combination of herbs, using thyme or savory in the same way. You will need about ¼ cup herb leaves in all.

MAKES ABOUT
¼ CUP

> 1 garlic clove
> 1 tablespoon kosher salt
> 1 small bunch fresh sage (about 30 leaves)
> 2 sprigs fresh rosemary

On a cutting board, mince the garlic with the salt. Place the herbs in a mound and coarsely chop them. Add the garlic salt and chop them together to make a coarse rub. Use the salt right away, or let it dry, uncovered, in a bowl for a few days.

The dried salt rub can be stored indefinitely in a clean dry jar.

IN ADVANCE

Rosemary Pepper Rub

Because rosemary has an affinity for so many foods, this is one of the most useful rubs. It's great for lamb, chicken, duck, rabbit, tuna, swordfish, and quail, as well as for grilled or roasted portobello mushrooms, peppers, eggplant, and onions.

MAKES ABOUT
⅓ CUP

> ¼ cup plus 2 tablespoons dried rosemary
> 1 tablespoon freshly ground black pepper
> 1 teaspoon kosher salt
> ¼ teaspoon sugar

Place the rosemary and pepper in a blender or spice grinder and blend for at least 1 minute at high speed, until you have the finest-possible powder. Let the mixture settle for about 30 seconds before removing the cover, so the fine powder does not fly into the air.

Use a dry pastry brush to push the powder through a strainer set into a clean dry container. Stir in the salt and sugar.

Store in a tightly sealed jar away from light for up to 3 months.

IN ADVANCE

Szechwan Pepper Rub and Dipping Salt

MAKES ABOUT
⅓ CUP

Szechwan peppercorns are berries from the prickly ash tree that are widely used as a flavoring in Chinese and Japanese cooking. Although they are not in fact a member of the pepper family, they have a mild peppery flavor, with overtones of anise. This makes an excellent rub for shrimp, quail, and pork and, surprisingly, for beef steaks instead of traditional black peppercorns. You can also use the rub as a dipping salt for grilled shrimp and squid and Shellfish Cooked in an Iron Skillet (page 250).

Szechwan peppercorns can be found in well-stocked supermarkets and any Asian market.

> ¼ cup Szechwan peppercorns
> ½ teaspoon black peppercorns
> 2½ teaspoons sugar
> 1½ teaspoons kosher salt

In a small heavy skillet, toast the Szechwan and black peppercorns over moderate heat, shaking the pan occasionally, until fragrant, about 3 minutes.

Transfer them to a blender or spice grinder and blend for at least 1 minute at high speed, until you have the finest-possible powder. Let the mixture settle for about 30 seconds before removing the cover, so the fine powder does not fly into the air.

Use a dry pastry brush to push the powder through a strainer into a clean dry container. Blend the larger bits for 2 minutes and strain again. Stir in the sugar and salt.

IN ADVANCE Store in a tightly sealed jar away from light for up to 3 months.

Wild Juniper Rub

MAKES ABOUT
⅓ CUP

This highly aromatic rub imparts a wild, somewhat gamy flavor to foods. It is good on venison, pork, duck, game birds like quail and pheasant, and oily fish like salmon. Or try it on grilled mushrooms, particularly meaty ones such as portobellos.

3 tablespoons juniper berries

1 tablespoon dried rosemary

1 ½ teaspoons dried thyme

¾ teaspoon ground allspice

1 ½ teaspoons kosher salt

1 ½ teaspoons sugar

Place the juniper berries, rosemary, thyme, and allspice in a blender or spice grinder and blend for at least 1 minute at high speed, until you have the finest-possible powder. Let the mixture settle for about 30 seconds before removing the cover, so the fine powder does not fly into the air.

Use a dry pastry brush to push the powder through a strainer into a clean dry container. Stir in the salt and sugar.

Store in a tightly sealed jar away from light for up to 3 months.

IN ADVANCE

Mexican "Mole" Rub

Taking a cue from the Mexican mole sauce, I added cocoa powder to a rub with traditional Mexican flavors. It provides a faint chocolaty undercurrent that mellows the chile and pepper and gives it an unusually deep resonant flavor. It is wonderful on pork, chicken, meaty fish like swordfish, salmon, and tuna, and roasted or grilled portobello mushrooms and bell peppers. Or add it to red or black beans.

MAKES ABOUT
⅓ CUP

1 tablespoon Ancho Chile Essence (page 543)

1 tablespoon sweet paprika, preferably Hungarian

2 teaspoons ground cumin

1 teaspoon freshly ground black pepper

1 teaspoon dried oregano, preferably Mexican

1 teaspoon cocoa powder

1 ½ teaspoons dark brown sugar

1 teaspoon granulated sugar

1 teaspoon kosher salt

Combine all the ingredients in a small jar. Shake to blend.

Store in a tightly sealed jar away from light for up to 3 months.

IN ADVANCE

Aromatic Pepper

MAKES ABOUT
⅓ CUP

This mix of black, white, and pink peppercorns, allspice berries, and coriander seeds can be used as a delicious seasoning or as the base of a dry rub such as the tangerine-scented version below. I often use it instead of ordinary pepper when I want a more complex seasoning to perk up dishes.

2 tablespoons black peppercorns

2 tablespoons white peppercorns

2 tablespoons pink peppercorns

1 tablespoon allspice berries

1 tablespoon coriander seeds

Combine the peppercorns, allspice, and coriander seeds in a blender or spice grinder. Using an on-and-off motion, blend the spices just until they are like a coarse meal. Transfer to a clean dry container. Cover tightly. To use as a seasoning, place in a peppermill to grind as you need it.

IN ADVANCE Store in a tightly sealed jar away from light for up to 3 months.

variation

When improvising dry rubs made with citrus zest, it's important to mix in the finely grated zest just before applying the rub. When dried, citrus zest can impart a cloying candy-like quality to a rub.

Aromatic Pepper and Tangerine Rub. To turn the Aromatic Pepper into a rub, I mix it with freshly grated tangerine or orange peel, sugar, and salt, which balance and mute the pepperiness. The rub is delicious on beef, game, lamb, pork, seafood, and shellfish. It was inspired by Gray Kunz, formerly of Lespinasse in New York City.

Just before using, mix together 1½ tablespoons of the aromatic pepper with 1 teaspoon kosher salt, ½ teaspoon sugar, and 1½ teaspoons finely grated tangerine or orange zest. (Makes about ¼ cup.)

Miso-Sake–Glazed Fish Fillets and Steaks (page 236), served with steam-sauteed baby bok choy (page 71)

MARINADES AND PASTES. In addition to dry rubs, I use various kinds of "wet rubs," better known as marinades or pastes, to flavor foods. They include a wide range of seasoning elements, from garlic and ginger to coconut milk and Southeast Asian fish sauce. As foods soak in these liquid flavorings, they absorb their flavors. The acid, salt, and sugar in them often act as a tenderizing agent. Unlike dry rubs, the effect of these wet flavorings is not instant—they need time to penetrate food, usually a minimum of 6 hours.

The definitions of marinades and pastes are not exact. The difference between them has to do with their texture and how that texture carries flavors.

Marinades are generally composed of an acid, such as citrus juice or wine, a fat, such as olive oil or coconut milk, and spices or herbs, and are quite liquid. Pastes are like a cross between a dry rub and a marinade. Since they are thicker, their flavorings adhere to form a light coating when cooked. Many have some sort of sugar in them, which will lacquer foods with a deliciously caramelized surface.

Since pastes are thicker and adhere to foods better than marinades, you will need less of them. Figure on roughly ⅓ cup of a paste or ¾ cup marinade to coat 3 pounds of meat, poultry, or seafood.

1. Place the meat, poultry, or seafood in a shallow glass, ceramic, or stainless steel container. Coat it completely with the marinade or paste. Cover with plastic wrap and refrigerate for up to 4 hours for seafood and at least 6 hours, or up to 1 day, for poultry and meats, turning a couple of times.

2. Let the food come to room temperature for about 1 hour before cooking.

3. Remove the food from the container and pat dry with paper towels, scraping off any large pieces of herbs or spices (which would burn during cooking). Rub or brush lightly with oil and season with salt and pepper. Cook as directed.

Unless otherwise specified, most unused marinades will keep for several days in a sealed jar in the refrigerator. Marinades and pastes that have come into contact with meat, fish, or poultry should be discarded, since blood and other uncooked juices will have seeped into them.

Classic Greek Lemon and Olive Oil Marinade with Herbs

MAKES ABOUT ½ CUP (ENOUGH TO MARINATE 3 POUNDS OF FOOD)

Marinating lamb for at least a day in olive oil, lemon juice, and herbs renders the flesh tender and succulent and heightens the flavors of the herbs. In Greece, wild oregano, which has a sweeter, less sharp flavor than American, is traditionally used. I prefer Provençal herbs: thyme, rosemary, and savory and occasionally a bit of dried lavender flowers, which add a floral note.

I use this marinade for just about any cut of lamb I plan to cook medium rare, such as the rack, chops, or leg of lamb, whole or boned and butterflied (see Leg of Lamb Roasted on a Bed of Herbs, page 296). It is also delicious with chicken, poussin, venison, and whole fish.

You can purchase dried lavender flowers from herb stores and wherever potpourri is sold. (Be sure it is unsprayed.) Look for dried Greek oregano in markets specializing in Mediterranean foods; if using, replace the herbs below with 1 tablespoon.

2 tablespoons fresh thyme leaves or ¾ teaspoon dried thyme

2 tablespoons fresh rosemary leaves or 1½ teaspoon dried rosemary

1 tablespoon fresh savory leaves or 2 teaspoons dried savory

½ teaspoon dried lavender flowers (optional, for lamb only)

1 garlic clove, thinly sliced

3 tablespoons olive oil

Juice of 1 lemon

½ teaspoon kosher salt

In a shallow casserole just large enough to hold the food you wish to marinate, combine the herbs, garlic, olive oil, lemon juice, and salt. Use as directed on page 554, marinating meat or poultry for at least 12 hours, and up to 3 days.

The marinade is best made just before you use it.

IN ADVANCE

Rosemary and Orange Zest Marinade

Use this cross between a paste and a marinade, fragrant with fresh rosemary and orange zest, to flavor and tenderize lamb, duck, pork, quail, and chicken.

MAKES ABOUT ¾ CUP (ENOUGH TO MARINATE 3 POUNDS FOOD)

⅓ cup fresh rosemary leaves

¾ teaspoon unsprayed dried lavender flowers (optional)

3 garlic cloves, sliced

1½ teaspoons slivered orange zest

¾ teaspoon kosher salt

⅓ cup plus 2 teaspoons extra-virgin olive oil

3 tablespoons fresh lemon juice

3 tablespoons fresh orange juice

In a mortar with a pestle or in a blender, blend the rosemary, lavender, if using, garlic, orange zest, and salt to a coarse paste. (Alternatively, place the ingredients on a cutting board and chop them together, then mash them into a coarse paste with the side of your chef's knife. Transfer to a small bowl.) Gradually blend in the olive oil and the fruit juices. Use as directed on page 554.

The marinade is best made just before you use it.

IN ADVANCE

True grappas from Italy are clear alcohols distilled from the fermented grape pressings, skins, and pits left from wine making. They have an earthy, musky aroma and flavor. In cooking, grappas give a marvelous wild flavor to certain foods. Use just a tiny amount, a drizzle or so, to enhance the flavor of cooked wild mushrooms. A teaspoon drizzled over a cup of olives will bring out their flavor. Grappa imparts a delicious aged flavor to beef and makes a whole roasted chicken taste more like a farm bird. I once rubbed a teaspoon into a defrosted shell steak that had a freezer odor and left it overnight in the fridge. When I cooked it, the off flavor was gone. Note that some clear alcohols distilled from fruits such as pears and raspberries are not really grappas, even though they are called grappas. Their fruit flavors are best in desserts and fruit sauces.

Southeast Asian Marinade

MAKES ABOUT ¾ CUP (ENOUGH TO MARINATE 3 POUNDS OF FOOD)

This marinade produces the most succulent and delicious grilled, pan-seared, or broiled red meats and game, such as beef, duck, and quail, and oily fish, such as mackerel and bluefish, and imbues them with a blend of sweet, pungent, and piquant flavors typical of Southeast Asian cooking. It is based on the central seasoning of Thai and Vietnamese cuisine, fish sauce, (nam pla or nuoc mam), a liquid condiment made from fermented fish that seems to intensify the flavors of whatever it touches. Don't be put off by its aroma; it disappears when it is mixed with other ingredients.

You will find fish sauce in the Asian section of most supermarkets. Because it contains a lot of salt, it will keep indefinitely in the refrigerator, or up to 3 months unrefrigerated.

¼ **cup rice vinegar**

3 **tablespoons Thai or Vietnamese fish sauce (nam pla or nuoc mam)**

2 **tablespoons low-sodium soy sauce**

1 **tablespoon water**

2 **teaspoons sugar**

3 **large garlic cloves,** minced

3 **medium shallots,** minced

1 **jalapeño chile,** minced

In a small bowl, combine the rice vinegar, fish sauce, soy sauce, water, sugar, garlic, shallot, and chile. Use as directed on page 554.

IN ADVANCE The marinade will keep in a tightly sealed jar in the refrigerator for up to 1 month.

Sesame-Ginger Marinade

MAKES ABOUT
¾ CUP (ENOUGH
TO MARINATE
3 POUNDS FOOD)

You can use this sesame-based marinade as is, or flavor it with either the light citrusy flavor of lemongrass or the warm sweet flavor of anise. Both are good on poultry and game birds such as chicken and quail, as well as on fish. The honey in the marinade will caramelize on the outside of the food to form a delicious glaze. I like to sprinkle on sesame seeds during the last few minutes of cooking to add an appealing crunch.

Sesame-Ginger Marinade Base
  2 tablespoons honey
  2 tablespoons low-sodium soy sauce
  2 tablespoons dry sherry
  2 tablespoons Asian sesame oil
  2 tablespoons chopped scallions
  2 teaspoons minced fresh ginger
  1 teaspoon grated orange zest
  1 teaspoon minced serrano or jalapeño chile
  3 tablespoons minced fresh lemongrass or ½ teaspoon Lemongrass Essence (page 546), soaked in 1 tablespoon boiling water (optional)

To make the marinade base, in a small bowl, combine the honey, soy sauce, sherry, sesame oil, scallions, ginger, orange zest, and chile. Use as is or stir in the lemongrass.

Use as directed on page 554. Brush the food with the marinade several times during cooking to build up a glaze.

IN ADVANCE The marinade will keep for up to 3 days, covered and refrigerated.

variation **Sesame-Ginger Marinade with Five-Spice Powder.** Instead of the optional lemongrass, stir in ½ teaspoon five-spice powder, 4 star anise left whole, and ¼ teaspoon ground coriander.

Chipotle Adobo Marinade

MAKES ABOUT ¾ CUP (ENOUGH TO MARINATE 3 POUNDS FOOD)

Chipotle *chiles en adobo* are smoked jalapeños canned in a thick tomato-based sauce. The fiery, smoky chiles are used in many Mexican dishes. The adobo sauce has a mellower flavor and is an excellent condiment in itself. In this marinade, the acidic yogurt base tenderizes the meat while the adobo imparts a spicy, smoky flavor. It is an excellent way to use leftover adobo sauce. Use it for beef or chicken.

Chipotles are packed in small cans, for a little goes a long way. Leftovers can be refrigerated for up to a week. Since I never use very much at one time, I often divide the contents of a can among small plastic containers and freeze them.

½ cup low-fat yogurt

2 tablespoons adobo sauce from canned chipotles

1 tablespoon fresh lime juice

½ teaspoon minced garlic

⅜ teaspoon kosher salt

In a small bowl, combine the yogurt, adobo sauce, lime juice, garlic, and salt. Use as directed on page 554.

IN ADVANCE   The marinade will keep for up to 2 days, covered and refrigerated.

Tandoori Marinade

MAKES 1 CUP (ENOUGH TO MARINATE 3 POUNDS FOOD)

Tandoor is the name of the Indian clay oven in which meat, poultry, or fish is cooked in searing heat after it has been marinated in a mixture of spices and yogurt. This marinade both tenderizes and suffuses the food with classic Indian flavors: curry, cardamom, chile, and ginger. Tandoori-marinated foods are most delicious grilled, but they can be roasted or broiled as well. You can improvise on this recipe by varying the proportion of spices, substituting or adding others, such as garam masala or another prepared Indian spice mix.

¼ cup finely chopped onion

1 large garlic clove, minced

1 tablespoon minced fresh ginger (a 1-inch piece)

1 small serrano or jalapeño chile, minced

½ cup plain yogurt

1 tablespoon plus 2 teaspoons Sandy's Curry Powder (page 548) **or commercial curry powder**

¾ teaspoon kosher salt

¼ teaspoon sugar

⅛ teaspoon ground cardamom or 1 pod crushed, seed discarded

In a small bowl, stir together the onion, garlic, ginger, chile, yogurt, curry powder, salt, sugar, and cardamom. Cover and refrigerate for 1 hour before using to let the flavors marry. Use as directed on page 554.

The marinade will keep for up to 2 days, covered and refrigerated.

IN ADVANCE

Red Miso Glaze

This paste, made with miso, the fermented soybean paste that is the cornerstone of Japanese cooking, is delicious on red meats and poultry. It firms the flesh slightly, making it more succulent, and slightly caramelizes and glazes the outside. It intensifies natural flavors and makes red meats taste aged.

Because it lasts indefinitely, you can keep a batch on hand to use for an instant flavor enhancer. For a version of this marinade to use with fish, see page 236.

Miso is available at health food stores and Asian markets (see Sources, page 711). It will keep for several months, refrigerated, in a covered container.

MAKES ABOUT
1 ¼ CUPS (ENOUGH
TO MARINATE
3 POUNDS FOOD)

Mild, sweet white miso and heartier red miso are useful long-keeping refrigerator staples. Mixed with simmering water, they make excellent quick broths and soup bases.

½ cup sweet white miso

½ cup red (aka) miso or country-style barley miso

3 tablespoons dark brown sugar

¼ cup sake

¼ cup mirin (Japanese rice wine) or medium-dry sherry

1 teaspoon olive oil

In a medium saucepan, combine all the ingredients and bring to a simmer over moderate heat. Reduce the heat to low and cook for 2 minutes. Set aside to cool.

Use as directed on page 554. There is no need to salt the meat before cooking.

The glaze will keep indefinitely in a covered container in the refrigerator.

IN ADVANCE

Moroccan Spice Paste

MAKES ABOUT
½ CUP (ENOUGH
TO MARINATE
3 POUNDS FOOD)

In this recipe, the traditional spices of a Moroccan *mechoui*—slow-cooked lamb scented with coriander, cumin, paprika, and garlic—make a paste to use on fast-cooking tender cuts that will be cooked medium rare. It takes very little work, yet has a dramatic impact. Try it on butterflied leg of lamb (see page 320) and lamb chops, or on chicken.

1 tablespoon plus ¼ teaspoon coriander seeds

2 teaspoons cumin seeds

2 teaspoons sweet paprika, preferably Hungarian

½ teaspoon kosher salt

¼ teaspoon sugar

4 to 5 garlic cloves, coarsely chopped

2 tablespoons olive oil

1½ tablespoons water

In a small skillet, toast the coriander and cumin seeds over moderate heat, shaking occasionally, until fragrant, about 2 minutes.

Transfer to a blender or spice grinder and add the paprika, salt, and sugar. Blend at high speed until reduced to a powder. Add the garlic, olive oil, and water and blend to a thick paste. Use as directed on page 554.

IN ADVANCE   The paste will keep for up to 2 days, covered and refrigerated.

Thai Green Curry Paste

This is one of my favorite pastes. Unsweetened coconut milk mellows the intense flavors of the curry spices, lemongrass, and cilantro and provides enough fat to keep food moist during cooking.

MAKES ABOUT ¾ CUP (ENOUGH TO MARINATE 3 POUNDS FOOD)

It is marvelous on chicken, quail, duck, or pork, shrimp or scallops, and meaty white-fleshed fish. Use it in The Best Way to Grill Shrimp (page 237) and Fillets in Green Curry Sauce (page 228). It can also be used as an instant flavoring for brothy dishes. I often stir a couple of tablespoons into coconut milk–based sauces or steamed shellfish dishes, or into broth to make soups.

If you are in a hurry, you can substitute 2 to 3 teaspoons prepared curry powder for the dry spices. Leftover coconut milk will keep for 1 week in a plastic container in the refrigerator. Or you can freeze it for up to 2 months.

¼ **cup minced fresh lemongrass** (4 to 5 stalks, white bulbs only)

3 garlic cloves, crushed

2 small serrano or jalapeño chiles, minced (about 2½ teaspoons)

⅔ **cup fresh coriander leaves**

¾ **teaspoon grated lime zest**

1 tablespoon fresh lime juice

1½ **tablespoons minced fresh ginger**

1½ **teaspoons ground coriander**

¾ **teaspoon ground cumin**

½ **teaspoon kosher salt**

¼ **teaspoon ground cinnamon**

¼ **teaspoon freshly ground white pepper**

⅛ **teaspoon ground cardamom**

¼ **cup stirred unsweetened coconut milk**

Combine all the ingredients except the coconut milk in a food processor and process until the mixture resembles very coarse meal. With the motor running, slowly drizzle in the coconut milk and process to a fairly fine puree. Use as directed on page 554.

The curry paste will keep for up to 1 week, covered and refrigerated, or frozen for up to 2 months.

IN ADVANCE

Hoisin Barbecue Sauce

MAKES ¾ CUP
(ENOUGH TO
MARINATE 3
POUNDS FOOD)

Like a traditional Southern barbecue sauce with an exotic spin, this unusual sauce has a base of hoisin, the thick, sweet garlicky sauce made from soybeans, red beans, and chiles, used as a seasoning and condiment in Chinese cooking. The sweetness of the hoisin is balanced by the addition of balsamic vinegar and ginger. I use this both as a marinade and as a glaze for cooking meats. It is excellent on grilled or roasted poultry, duck, pork, and shrimp, as well as on eggplant. For a more peppery sauce, increase the amount of pepper to 2 teaspoons.

Hoisin sauce is available in the Asian section of most supermarkets.

- **⅓ cup hoisin sauce**
- **3 tablespoons fresh orange juice**
- **2 tablespoons ketchup,** preferably low-sodium
- **1 tablespoon plus 1 teaspoon rice vinegar**
- **1 tablespoon plus 1 teaspoon Asian sesame oil**
- **2 teaspoons balsamic vinegar**
- **1 teaspoon grated fresh ginger**
- **1½ teaspoons grated garlic**
- **1 teaspoon coarsely ground black pepper**

In a small bowl, combine the hoisin sauce, orange juice, ketchup, rice vinegar, sesame oil, and balsamic vinegar.

Add the ginger to the bowl, along with the garlic and pepper, and stir to blend. Cover and refrigerate for 1 hour to let the flavors develop. Use as directed on page 554.

IN ADVANCE The marinade will keep for up to 1 week, covered and refrigerated.

variation **Smoky Fusion Barbecue Sauce.** To give the sauce a Southwestern twist with slight undertones of star anise and sesame, add 1½ teaspoons Smoky Tea Essence (page 545) and 1 teaspoon Ancho Chile Essence (page 543).

Jamaican Jerk Paste

"Jerk" refers to the elaborate seasoning blends of Jamaica, which usually include chiles and warm spices, such as ginger, cinnamon, and, especially, allspice, in tandem with an acid element such as vinegar or lime juice. Sweet, pungent, and assertive, this paste makes a wonderful rub for grilled pork and chicken.

MAKES ABOUT
½ CUP (ENOUGH
TO MARINATE
3 POUNDS FOOD)

¼ **cup minced scallions**

2 **tablespoons minced fresh ginger**

2 **garlic cloves,** mashed to a paste

½ **jalapeño chile,** minced (½ teaspoon), or more to taste

1 **tablespoon dark brown sugar**

1 **teaspoon ground allspice**

1 **teaspoon ground cinnamon**

¾ **teaspoon kosher salt**

¼ **teaspoon freshly ground black pepper**

⅛ **teaspoon cayenne pepper**

2 **teaspoons olive oil**

2 **teaspoons red wine vinegar**

2 **teaspoons fresh lime juice**

In a small bowl, combine all the ingredients. Let sit for 1 hour to blend the flavors. Remove the garlic. Use as directed on page 554.

The marinade will keep for up to 3 days, covered and refrigerated.

IN ADVANCE

Composed Soup
(page 396)
made with Hearty
Porcini-Miso Broth
(page 573),
baby vegetables,
and herbs

BROTHS

The traditional long-cooked meat-based stocks of twenty years ago hold little appeal in our busy lives, except on special occasions. Today I rely on quickly made broths based on vegetables or infusions of spices, herbs, aromatics, and other flavorings to do double work as sauces and soup bases, to turn whatever is on hand into a complete delicious dish. A broth can as easily be a sauce for a seared fish fillet as it can be the base for a hearty bean-and-roasted-vegetable soup. Often distinctions blur: A dish of grilled chicken and vegetables sauced with a fragrant broth shares the soothing qualities of a soup. Because broths can be frozen for an indefinite period of time, you can always have some on hand.

Vegetable broths are particularly easy to make with ingredients from any corner market, and offer a vast range of possibilities, from single flavors, such as celery root and fennel, to "meaty" broths made with wild mushrooms and roasted vegetables.

The recipes in this chapter illustrate essential, often innovative, broth-making techniques. You'll find ways to use them as sauces and liquid flavor bases scattered throughout the book. To use them for improvising soups, see page 396.

Because vegetable-based broths often lack the body and roundness of flavor of broths made with meat or poultry, which contain collagen from the bones, cartilage, and fat, I add a small amount of fat, such as butter or olive oil, to a vegetable broth as it cooks. Using the fat to create a light emulsion disperses the flavorful fat molecules throughout the broth and adds a pleasing subtle viscosity.

Fennel and Other Vegetable Broths

A GUIDE TO IMPROVISING

MAKES 2 CUPS You can make many different vegetable broths using this basic model, simmering cut-up vegetables in water with other flavorings until they have given all their flavors to the broth. The addition of a small amount of butter gives the broth more body for very few extra calories. Fennel broth's sweet, anisey flavor makes it a lovely sauce for fish, shellfish, and pasta, especially cheese-filled pastas, such as ravioli and tortellini. Celery root broth makes a wonderful sauce for pastas filled with wild mushrooms, as well as roasted or grilled meats, poultry, and game.

You can create interesting broths by combining 2 or 3 vegetables, such as celery root, fennel, and leeks, or peas, leeks, and asparagus. Bear in mind that sweet vegetables, such as parsnips and peas, make a rather sweet broth that is best balanced with herbs or spices. Very strongly flavored vegetables, such as cabbage, broccoli, eggplant, and collard and dandelion greens, can produce off-putting broths and should be used with discretion.

This recipe gives rough proportions of vegetables to water. If a broth is a bit weak, you can always boil it down to concentrate the flavors. Be sure to pare off any brown, bruised, dirty spots or bitter skins from vegetables before making your broth. You can, however, use inedible trimmings such as shell pea pods, corncobs, and asparagus stems to mix flavors into a broth. Adding a peeled potato will give it greater body.

About 4 cups cut-up vegetables, singly or in combination, such as

Fennel bulb (about 1¼ pounds) stalks and all, coarsely chopped)

Celery root, parsley roots, or parsnips (about 1½ pounds) peeled and coarsely chopped

Leeks (about 2 pounds), trimmed, rinsed, and coarsely chopped

Shell peas (about 2 pounds), shucked, pods reserved, chopped, and added to the broth, or 1 pound sugar snap peas, coarsely chopped (this is good with some asparagus trimmings)

1 small potato (about 3 ounces) (optional), peeled and cut into 1-inch chunks

4 garlic cloves, thinly sliced

4 shallots, thinly sliced

Flavorings (optional), singly or in combination, such as

    1 teaspoon fennel seeds plus 1 allspice berry (for fennel broth)

    1 teaspoon curry powder plus 1 kaffir lime leaf or strip of orange or lemon zest (for parsnip broth)

    2 sprigs fresh mint or tarragon (for pea broth)

    Pinch of saffron (for leek broth)

¾ **teaspoon kosher salt**

¾ **teaspoon sugar**

1 teaspoon unsalted butter or extra-virgin olive oil

4 cups cold water

1. Place all the ingredients in a large saucepan. Bring to a boil over moderate heat. Reduce the heat to a simmer and simmer for 30 to 45 minutes, until the vegetables are soft and the broth is reduced to about 2 cups and intensely flavored.

2. Strain the broth through a fine sieve set over a bowl, pressing on the solids to extract all the liquid; discard the solids.

The broth can be refrigerated, covered, for 5 days or frozen for up to 2 months.   **IN ADVANCE**

Leek Broth

This subtle, easy-to-make essence of leeks is the vegetable broth I rely on most in cooking for risotto, soups, and sauces, particularly beurre blanc–style sauces (see pages 640–645). It is a good substitute for chicken broth and makes a simple embellishment to pasta, especially filled pastas, as well as seafood dishes, such as pan-smoked salmon or tuna (page 268).   **MAKES 1 QUART**

3 medium leeks, trimmed, coarsely chopped, and rinsed in several changes of cold water

1 small potato (about 3 ounces), peeled and cut into 1-inch chunks

1 medium shallot, thinly sliced

1 ounce dry-cured unsmoked country ham, such as prosciutto or jambon de Bayonne

2 teaspoons unsalted butter or extra-virgin olive oil

6 cups cold water

½ **teaspoon kosher salt**

¼ **teaspoon sugar**

In a large heavy saucepan, combine all the ingredients. Bring to a boil over moderate heat, reduce the heat, and simmer until the liquid is reduced to 4 cups, about 45 minutes.

Strain the broth through a fine sieve set over a bowl, pressing on the vegetables to extract as much liquid as possible; discard the solids.

IN ADVANCE The broth can be refrigerated, covered, for about 5 days or frozen for up to 2 months.

Basic Vegetable Broth

MAKES 1½
TO 2 QUARTS This recipe is only a rough guide, for the ingredients are endlessly variable according to the balance of flavors you wish to achieve and what you have on hand. The small amount of oil in the broth gives it a pleasing body as well as flavor. Use this rich vegetable broth as you would chicken broth.

> **12 ounces leeks** (2 to 3), trimmed, thinly sliced, and washed in several changes of water
>
> **1¼ pounds celery root** (1 large), peeled, quartered, and coarsely chopped
>
> **8 ounces carrots,** peeled and sliced
>
> **1 medium onion,** coarsely chopped
>
> **1 cup coarsely chopped mushrooms**
>
> **½ teaspoon black pepppercorns**
>
> **2 imported bay leaves**
>
> **4 sprigs fresh flat-leaf parsley**
>
> **2 sprigs fresh thyme**
>
> **1 tablespoon extra-virgin olive or vegetable oil**
>
> **1 gallon cold water**
>
> **Kosher salt** (optional)

In a large pot, combine all the ingredients except the salt and bring to a boil over high heat. Reduce to a simmer and cook until the liquid is reduced to 2 quarts, about 1 hour.

Strain the broth through a sieve over a large bowl, pressing on the vegetables with a wooden spoon to extract all the liquid. Discard the vegetables. Use as is or return the broth to the pot and boil until it has reduced to the desired strength. Season the broth lightly with salt if desired.

The broth can be refrigerated, covered, for about 5 days or frozen for up to 2 months. IN ADVANCE

Roasted Vegetable Broth. You can make vegetable broth as you would a brown meat stock by browning the vegetables in the oven to deepen their flavor before simmering them in water. The resulting broth is dark, rich, and flavorful, with good body. variation

Preheat the oven to 450°F. With some of the oil, lightly rub a baking sheet pan just large enough to hold the vegetables in a 1-inch layer.

Place the vegetables on the pan and toss to coat with the remaining oil. Roast, tossing once or twice, until the vegetables are a deep golden brown, about 1¼ hours. During the last 5 minutes, stir 1 tablespoon tomato paste into the vegetables.

Transfer the vegetables to a large pot. Sprinkle the baking sheet with ½ cup dry white wine and stir to loosen the caramelized bits on the bottom. Pour into the pot. Add the peppercorns, bay leaves, parsley, thyme, and water to cover by 2 inches (about 7 cups). Bring to a boil, then reduce the heat and simmer for 45 minutes to 1 hour, until the broth is reduced to about 4 to 5 cups and is full-bodied.

Strain through a sieve set over a bowl, pressing on the vegetables with a wooden spoon to extract all the liquid. Discard the solids. (Makes about 1 quart.)

Faux Veal Broth

MAKES
1¾ TO 2 CUPS

I was skeptical when chef Jean-Georges Vongerichten claimed that his mush-room broth tastes like veal stock. How could something so easy to make duplicate a classic stock that takes hours and a stockpot full of bones? Happily, though, it is true. Although it does not have the clear, limpid quality of veal stock, it has an exceptionally rich meaty flavor and body, achieved with a fraction of the effort and time—less than forty-five minutes.

In the original recipe, the mushrooms are sautéed in several tablespoons of butter or oil. I cook them in an emulsion of water and just 1 tablespoon butter, which coats them with the fat and helps them cook evenly. Once the liquid boils away, the mushrooms caramelize, their natural sugars becoming concentrated. When then simmered in water, they impart a deep color and richness to the resultant broth.

Use this extremely versatile broth in place of veal or beef broth. It makes an excellent deglazing liquid for meat and game pan sauces, a broth for risotto, or sauce for pasta, particularly filled pastas, as well as hearty fish like salmon and swordfish. Figure on about ⅓ to ½ cup per person.

> 1 tablespoon unsalted butter, or olive, walnut, or hazelnut oil
>
> About 4 cups cold water
>
> 1¼ pounds (two 10-ounce containers) white button or cremini mushrooms, thickly sliced or quartered (about 10 cups)
>
> Scant ½ teaspoon kosher salt
>
> Freshly ground black pepper
>
> 2 tablespoons chopped fresh flat-leaf parsley
>
> 2 shallots, sliced
>
> 1 garlic clove, halved
>
> 1 to 2 teaspoons low-sodium soy sauce, or to taste

In a heavy nonstick skillet large enough to hold the mushrooms in a layer no more than 1½ inches deep (or use two 10-inch skillets), bring the butter and 3 tablespoons water to a boil over high heat. Stir in the mushrooms, salt, and pepper to taste and cook until the mushrooms have released their juices, 10 to 12 minutes. Continue to cook, stirring frequently, until the juices have evaporated, 5 to 7 minutes. Reduce the heat to moderate and cook, tossing frequently, until the mushrooms have caramelized to a deep brown, 20 to 25 minutes longer.

Stir in the parsley, shallots, and garlic. Add enough water to just cover the mushrooms; stir and scrape up the browned bits clinging to the bottom of the pan with a wooden spoon. Bring to a boil, then reduce to a simmer and cook until the liquid has reduced by about half and the broth has a deep brown color, about 25 minutes.

Strain the broth through a fine sieve set over a bowl, pressing firmly on the mushrooms to extract as much liquid as possible; discard the mushrooms (which will have lost their flavor). Season to taste with soy sauce and pepper.

The broth can be refrigerated, covered, for about 5 days or frozen for up to 2 months.

IN ADVANCE

Hearty Porcini-Miso Broth

I wanted to make a vegetarian friend a meatless soup that was as hearty and earthy as a rich meat broth. My solution was to use dried wild mushrooms and Madeira in league with miso paste to give the broth body. Since all of these elements can be kept on hand almost indefinitely, you can forge this rich broth at a moment's notice. Use it to make composed soups (pages 396–400), potato or bean gratins (pages 50 and 102), and pilafs (pages 174–181).

MAKES ABOUT 1 QUART

Sweet white miso and red miso paste are available at health food stores and Asian grocery stores. They will keep for at least three months in the refrigerator.

1 ounce dried mushrooms, such as porcini

6 cups hot water

1½ teaspoons unsalted butter

½ teaspoon vegetable oil

½ cup coarsely chopped shallots (4 shallots)

⅓ to ½ cup Rainwater or Sercial (dry) Madeira

1 tablespoon sweet white miso

1 tablespoon red (aka) miso

Place the dried mushrooms in a large bowl and cover with the water. Let steep for 20 minutes.

In a small heavy saucepan, heat the butter over moderate heat until it is amber colored and smells like roasted nuts. Add the oil and shallots, cover, and cook over low heat, stirring frequently, until the shallots are translucent and golden brown, about 5 minutes.

Add the Madeira and bring to a boil over high heat. Boil until reduced by half, about 5 minutes. Add the mushrooms and their liquid and simmer for 20 minutes, or until reduced to 1 quart.

Strain the broth through a fine sieve set over a bowl, pressing on the mushrooms to extract all the liquid; discard the solids. The miso will have the freshest flavor if you whisk it into the broth just before you serve it. Strain again if desired.

IN ADVANCE The broth will keep, covered, in the refrigerator for about 5 days. Reheat gently, without boiling, before using.

Classic Rich Poultry, Meat, or Game Broth

MAKES ABOUT 1 TO 1½ QUARTS

To ensure as clear and lean a broth as possible, before cooking, remove as much fat and skin as possible from meat trimmings and cuts.

Homemade poultry, meat, or game broths are like gold in the kitchen, a source of unparalleled flavor and body for use in sauces, stews, and soups. The secret to making rich and concentrated broths is to first roast the vegetables and bones or meat trimmings until they brown, then add wine or water to dissolve the flavorful caramelized juices. (If the bones are already roasted—for example, a roast chicken carcass—roast the vegetables alone.)

The more meat, as opposed to bones, you use in the broth, the richer the broth will be. Freeze trimmings from other recipes until you have enough for a broth. You can buy cheap meaty cuts such as chicken legs, backs, and thighs; lamb shanks; veal breast; or pork shoulder to make broth or to augment trimmings you already have. Or ask your butcher for any cheap, bony extras. To extract all their flavor, cut the trimmings into 1- or 2-inch pieces with kitchen shears or a cleaver.

It is not necessary to make huge pots of broth. Simply adjust the quantity of vegetables and water for the amount of trimmings you have. You can brown the small amount of trimmings in a heavy saucepan on top of the stove in a little olive oil rather than roasting them. Then brown the aromatics, deglaze with a little water, wine, or chicken broth, and simmer for about 20 minutes.

To make a clear broth, what is called a white stock rather than brown stock, skip the roasting and just simmer the ingredients in the water.

1 medium onion (skin on)

1 carrot

1 rib celery

3 to 4 pounds poultry, meat, or game trimmings and bones, skin and fat trimmed

1 cup dry white wine

About 3 quarts cold water

1 imported bay leaf, crumbled

4 sprigs fresh thyme or 1 teaspoon dried thyme

¼ bunch fresh flat-leaf parsley, coarsely chopped

½ teaspoon kosher salt

Preheat the oven to 450°F.

Coarsely chop the onion, carrot, and celery. Spread the trimmings and bones and vegetables in a large roasting pan. Roast until well browned and the juices have begun to caramelize in the pan, 30 to 50 minutes. Check after 20 minutes and add a few tablespoons of water if the juices are threatening to burn on the bottom of the pan.

Transfer to a 4-quart stockpot. Place the roasting pan over moderate heat, add the wine to the pan, and stir with a wooden spoon to scrape up and dissolve the browned bits on the bottom. Add to the pot. Pour over enough water to cover the contents by 1 inch and add the herbs and salt.

Bring to a simmer over moderate heat. Reduce the heat to maintain a bare simmer. Using a large spoon, periodically skim off the scum on the surface of the water until the liquid is almost clear. Simmer the stock for 2½ to 3 hours, or until it has a rich flavor and deep brown color. Do not stir or boil. If the liquid evaporates to below the ingredients during the first 2 hours, add just enough water to cover. During the last hour, let it evaporate to concentrate the flavor.

Set a fine-mesh strainer or cheesecloth-lined colander over a bowl and ladle the stock through the strainer. Transfer the bones and trimmings to the strainer and let drain; discard the solids.

Freeze the stock for about 20 minutes, until the fat rises to the surface and congeals. Skim off the fat with a spoon. If you want a more concentrated flavor, pour the stock into a saucepan and simmer to reduce it.

The stock can be refrigerated, covered, for 3 to 4 days or frozen for up to 2 months. **IN ADVANCE**

Shortcut Poultry, Meat, or Game Broth

MAKES 1 QUART When I am in a hurry and need a flavorful broth for risotto, paella, or certain sauces, I simmer good-quality commercial broth with trimmings to give it a homemade flavor. Match the broth and the trimmings, using unsalted or low-sodium chicken broth for mildly flavored meats and poultry, such as veal, rabbit, duck, pork, squab, or chicken trimmings. Fortify commercial beef broth with trimmings from red meats like beef or lamb.

4 cups canned low-sodium chicken broth (for poultry, pork, or game) **or beef broth** (for red meats)

2 cups water

¼ cup dry white wine

About 12 ounces poultry, meat, or game trimmings and bones, skin and fat trimmed

½ teaspoon kosher salt

In a large saucepan, combine the broth, water, wine, trimmings, and salt. Bring to a boil over moderately high heat. Reduce the heat to low and simmer for about 45 minutes, until reduced to 4 cups, skimming off the scum from the surface with a large spoon.

Strain the broth through a fine-mesh sieve set over a bowl; discard the solids.

IN ADVANCE The broth can be refrigerated, covered, for 3 to 4 days or frozen for up to 2 months.

White Wine Fish Broth

Full flavored white-fleshed fish such as striped bass, sea bass, or red snapper MAKES 1 QUART make the most delicious fish broths. Oilier fish such as salmon or mackerel are too strong. You can use carcasses, heads, and trimmings from whole fish from which you've removed the fillets, or you can buy fish carcasses and heads to make the broth. Use this broth for poaching fish and shellfish, and as a base for fish soups and stews. You can cook just about any fish fillet in it, including fattier salmon or tuna.

- **1 medium onion,** coarsely chopped
- **¾ cup sliced leek greens** (optional)
- **4 sprigs fresh flat-leaf parsley**
- **3 fresh thyme sprigs** or ½ teaspoon dried thyme
- **1 imported bay leaf**
- **2 pounds fish trimmings, heads, and bones,** gills removed, well rinsed and coarsely chopped
- **¾ cup dry white wine**
- **About 5 cups cold water**

In a large saucepan, combine all the ingredients except the water. Add enough cold water to cover the bones by 2 inches. Bring to a simmer over moderate heat, periodically skimming off the froth that floats to the top with a large spoon. Simmer the broth gently until reduced to 4 cups, about 30 minutes.

Strain the broth through a fine-mesh sieve set over a bowl; discard the solids.

The broth can be refrigerated, covered, for up to 3 days or frozen for up to **IN ADVANCE** 2 months.

Shortcut Seafood Broth

MAKES 4 TO 5
CUPS

Bottled clam juice simmered with fresh clams or mussels and white wine acquires a surprisingly fresh sea flavor. You can also use fish trimmings or shrimp shells from seafood you are preparing. Use this quickly made broth anywhere you would use White Wine Fish Broth (page 577).

Four 8-ounce bottles clam juice

1 pound clams or mussels, scrubbed, or about 8 ounces lean white fish trimmings or shrimp shells, in any combination

4 cups cold water

¼ cup dry white wine

½ teaspoon kosher salt

In a large saucepan, combine all the ingredients and bring to a boil over moderately high heat. Reduce the heat to moderate and simmer for 15 to 20 minutes, until reduced by about half.

Strain the broth through a fine-mesh sieve set over a bowl; discard the solids.

IN ADVANCE The broth can be refrigerated, covered, for up to 3 days or frozen for up to 2 months.

Infused Broths

A GUIDE TO IMPROVISING

MAKES ABOUT
1 QUART

A whole world of broth possibilities opens up when you know how to infuse basic broths with aromatic flavorings. By simmering spices or herbs in a broth, as you would prepare an herb tea, you release their flavor into the broth. The flavorings you can use are endless—fresh herbs, spices, lemongrass, dried wild mushrooms, garlic, kaffir lime leaves, ginger, chiles, and orange zest, to name a few—determined by their affinity for the foods the broth will be paired with. For example, you might infuse fennel broth with saffron to complement grilled shrimp or squid, or infuse chicken broth with fresh basil leaves for a vegetable soup. Ever-innovative chef Charlie Trotter uses the skin from sides of smoked salmon to infuse fish broth (along with sweet onions and white peppercorns) to make a smoky fish broth. Similarly, you can use smoky ham to infuse chicken or vegetable broths.

Because the intensity of spices and herbs varies dramatically, it is difficult to give exact amounts for infusing broth. To control the intensity of flavor in an infused broth, I like to place loose spices or other flavoring in a metal tea ball or tie them in muslin or cheesecloth so that I can remove them once the broth has achieved the desired depth of flavor. Similarly, bunches of fresh herbs can be tied with string for easy removal. Of course, if you put loose flavorings directly into the broth, you can always simply strain the broth when it reaches the desired intensity.

4 cups broth (pages 568–578), such as Classic Rich Poultry, Meat, or Game Broth, Leek Broth, White Wine Fish Broth, Faux Veal Broth, Roasted Vegetable Broth, Shortcut Seafood or Poultry Broth, or canned low-sodium chicken broth

½ to 2 cups water (to allow for evaporation)

Flavorings, singly or in combination (amounts are rough estimates), such as

> **Garlic cloves** (from 4 and 5 cloves, peeled and mashed, to up to 4 heads, broken apart, cloves left unpeeled) **or shallots**

> **Whole spices,** such as

>> **1 to 2 teaspoons cloves, cumin, fennel seeds, or coriander seeds**

>> **1 or 2 cinnamon sticks**

>> **1 to 2 star anise**

>> **1 to 2 large pinches saffron threads,** crumbled

>> **5 to 6 cardamom pods,** crushed

> **Ground spices:** from 2 teaspoons for sharp spices, such as cloves or allspice, to ¼ cup for milder, sweeter spices, such as curry powder

> **Fresh herbs**

>> **About 4 ounces mild soft herbs,** such as basil, cilantro, or chervil

>> **About 1 ounce more pungent herbs,** such as rosemary, thyme, tarragon, or sage

> **About 1 ounce dried wild mushrooms**

> **4 ounces Parmigiano-Reggiano rinds** or 2 ounces Parmigiano-Reggiano cheese

> **3 ounces smoky ham**

> **Other aromatic flavorings,** such as

>> **3 to 4 tablespoons chopped fresh ginger**

>> **2 or 3 bulbs lemongrass,** smashed and coarsely chopped

>> **3 to 4 kaffir lime leaves**

>> **4 to 5 imported bay leaves**

>> **4 or 5 strips orange or lemon zest** (removed with a vegetable peeler)

>> **1 to 2 dried chiles**

½ to 1 teaspoon unsalted butter or extra-virgin olive oil (optional)

1. Combine the broth, water, and flavorings in a medium heavy saucepan. To mellow sharper flavors, such as spices or garlic, add the butter or oil, if desired. Bring to a simmer over moderately low heat. Simmer, tasting the broth frequently, until it is flavored the way you like.

2. Strain through a fine-mesh sieve set over a bowl; discard the solids.

3. If you wish to concentrate the broth, return the broth to the saucepan and boil gently until it has reduced to the desired amount. If it is too strong, add a little more water.

IN ADVANCE The broth can be refrigerated, covered, for up to 3 days or frozen for up to 2 months.

improvisation 1 ## Parmesan Broth

In Italy, cooks use the rinds of chunks of Parmigiano-Reggiano cheese to flavor soup the way we use ham bones in America. This trick also works miracles in doctoring canned chicken broth to make a wonderful soup base or sauce for pasta or beans, with the addition of herbs and vegetables. It is also a delicious liquid in which to cook potatoes for mashing.

Following the Guide above, combine 4 cups homemade or canned low-sodium chicken broth, 2 cups water, 4 ounces Parmigiano-Reggiano rinds (or 2 ounces Parmigiano-Reggiano cheese), a 2-ounce chunk prosciutto (optional), 7 sprigs fresh thyme, and 5 garlic cloves, peeled. Simmer until liquid is reduced to about 4 cups, about 1 hour. Strain. Let cool, then chill for several hours; discard the fat that has congealed on the surface.

improvisation 2 ## Garlic Broth

Just as garlic seems to complement just about every savory food, so too does this mellow Garlic Broth. I especially like to use it as a soup base for bitter greens, dried beans, or potatoes.

Press down on 4 heads of garlic to break the cloves apart. Don't peel them, but simply discard the papery skin that holds the heads together. Following the Guide above, combine the garlic, 4 cups homemade or canned low-sodium chicken broth, 1 cup water, 8 sprigs fresh thyme or 4 fresh sage leaves or a large pinch of saffron threads, 1 imported bay leaf, and 1 teaspoon olive oil. Simmer until the garlic is puree-soft, about 35 minutes. Strain.

Smoky Broth

improvisation 3

To give a broth an appealing smoky flavor usually due to lightly grilled bones and meat, infuse some smoky tea such as Lapsang Souchong or Hu-Kwa in any poultry, meat, game, or mushroom-flavored broth.

Place ½ teaspoon loose smoky tea in a tea ball or use a tea bag. Following the Guide on pages 578 to 580, place in 1 quart of simmering broth; turn off the heat and infuse until the broth has a subtle smoky flavor, about 5 minutes. Remove the tea ball. Another way to achieve smoky flavor is to simmer a chunk of lean smoky ham in the broth.

Star Anise Broth

improvisation 4

Star anise–flavored broth is particularly good used as a sauce or soup base for roasted root vegetables and winter squashes.

Following the Guide on pages 578 to 580, bring 4 cups meaty broth such as Roasted Vegetable Broth (page 571), Classic Rich Poultry, Meat, or Game Broth (page 574), Shortcut Poultry, Meat, or Game Broth (page 576), or Faux Veal Broth (page 572), 2 cups water, and 2 star anise to a simmer; cook until the broth has reduced to 4 cups, about 45 minutes.

Curry and Fennel Seed Broth

improvisation 5

I love to use this broth with Indian flavors as a sauce or soup base for seafood, chicken, and potatoes.

In a medium saucepan over moderately low heat, toast 1 tablespoon fennel seeds, stirring, until they are fragrant. Add 3 tablespoons Sandy's Curry Powder (page 548) or commercial curry powder and stir for 20 seconds. Add 4 cups homemade (page 574) or canned low-sodium chicken broth, Shortcut Poultry Broth (page 576), or Leek Broth (page 569), 1 cup water, and ¾ teaspoon butter. Following the Guide on pages 578 to 580, simmer until reduced to about 4 cups, about 30 minutes. Strain.

Ginger-Sake Broth

This spicy broth is good with seafood and any Asian treatments or seasonings for poultry and pork. For a Southeast Asian flavor, add 2 stalks lemongrass, coarsely chopped, and 1 kaffir lime leaf.

Following the Guide on pages 578 to 580, combine 4 cups homemade (page 574) or canned low-sodium chicken broth, Shortcut Poultry Broth (page 576), or White Wine Fish Broth (page 577); ¼ cup peeled, chopped fresh ginger; 1 leek, trimmed and chopped, or 2 shallots, chopped; 1½ teaspoons coriander seeds; ½ teaspoon sugar; ¾ teaspoon unsalted butter; and 1 cup water and 1 cup sake. Simmer until reduced to 4 cups, about 30 minutes. Strain. (Makes 1 quart.)

Using Broths as Sauces

A GUIDE TO IMPROVISING

SERVES 4 Broths make excellent light sauces for grilled, pan-seared, and roasted meats, poultry, and seafood; for boiled ravioli and for tortellini; and for grilled and roasted vegetables. To stand up as a sauce, however, a broth must be quite concentrated. Boiling it down to evaporate some of its water will intensify the flavors and give it a more limpid texture.

Although you can serve any well-flavored broths unadorned for virtually fat-free sauces, I like to enrich them at the last minute with a small amount of fat, such as sour or heavy cream, butter, or a flavorful oil. For just a few additional calories, they gain immeasurably in luxuriousness.

2 cups broth (pages 568–578)

Creamy enrichment, such as

¼ **cup regular or reduced-fat sour cream**

2 tablespoons plus 2 teaspoons heavy cream or crème fraîche

1 tablespoon plus 1 teaspoon unsalted butter, extra-virgin olive oil, nut oil, or Flavored Oil (pages 588–597)

¼ **cup chopped fresh herbs** (optional), such as flat-leaf parsley, basil, chives, chervil, or cilantro

1. Pour the broth into a small saucepan. Boil it down over moderately high heat until it has the desired intensity of flavor.

2. To enrich the broth with sour cream, remove it from the heat and whisk in the sour cream. Then heat gently over low heat; do not allow it to boil or it will curdle. To enrich the broth with heavy cream or crème fraîche, or butter or oil, bring it to a full boil, then add the fat. Boil for about 30 seconds to disperse the fat throughout the broth and make the sauce creamy. Stir in the herbs, if using.

3. To serve, pour the sauce into four warmed shallow soup bowls. Arrange the cooked meat, poultry, seafood, pasta, or vegetables in the center.

From left to right: Saffron Oil, Chive Oil, Olive-Infused Olive Oil, Basil Oil, and Lemon Olive Oil

FLAVORED OILS

In Italy, fine extra-virgin olive oil is commonly drizzled over simply prepared grilled fish and meats, vegetables, even soups, acting as a sauce to enrich, moisten, and add flavor. It is the ultimate convenience food because it makes so many foods instantly delicious.

Taking the idea a step further, many chefs infuse oils with flavorings such as herbs, spices, garlic, or truffles, to add concentrated hits of flavor. You can use these oils as quick sauces for pasta or polenta, instead of butter on mashed potatoes or boiled grains, and as an embellishment for grilled foods or vegetable dishes. You can also use these flavored oils in place of usual fats in your cooking, particularly in salad dressings and sauces.

Stored in the refrigerator, most flavored oils will last for two months or more, ready to use on a moment's notice. Basil oil drizzled over soups and on mashed potatoes gives them the bright flavor of summer in the dead of winter. Sauté vegetables in Chinese Five-Flavor Oil for a quick lunch. Or use Chive Oil to embellish grilled fish.

The possibilities for basic flavored oils are endless—from saffron to fennel seed—as are the combinations of flavorings you can improvise. For example, you might infuse Basil Oil with orange zest to make a Basil-Orange Oil, or fortify the flavor of Curry Oil with caramelized shallots.

Although the oils are made with olive or vegetable oil and thus contain no saturated fat, they are quite caloric—120 calories per tablespoon. But their flavor is so concentrated, you need use only a little to dazzling effect. One teaspoon per serving (40 calories' worth) is ample.

The method for making a flavored oil varies slightly according to the flavoring agent used. Soft mild flavorings such as chives, fruit zest, and truffles need to be handled a little differently from tougher herbs such as thyme and rosemary, dried spices, and seeds.

Choose the oil according to the flavoring you are using, either to enhance it or to provide a neutral medium.

Extra-virgin olive oil goes well with Mediterranean flavorings, such as herbs, garlic, roasted peppers, wild mushrooms, and truffles.

Neutral vegetable oils that have little character of their own, such as canola and grapeseed oil, are best whenever the fruity flavor of extra-virgin olive oil is not appropriate, for spices, and for Flavor Essences.

Toasted sesame seed oil is most appropriate for Asian flavorings, such as ginger, Szechwan peppers, and hot chiles.

Olive-Infused Olive Oil

I adore olives and olive oil and use them almost daily, but it is not always easy to find a well-flavored but economical extra-virgin olive oil for every-day use. So I use a technique learned from Anne Disrude, a truly inspired cook. I fill a jar half full with olives, then cover the olives with an average extra-virgin olive oil. The olives flavor the oil, giving it a truer flavor, and the oil in turn preserves the olives, which I scoop out as needed to serve as an hors d'oeuvre or use for focaccia, pizza, pastas, stews, and sauces. With this simple technique, you will never have unexceptional oil again.

You can make the oil with many different kinds of (unpitted) olives. Generally, I like to use a combination of brine-cured black and green olives that I buy at my local Italian market. Avoid olives that have been highly flavored with herbs, garlic, or wine, because they can overpower the oil.

Store the oil (with or without olives) in a tightly stoppered jar at room temperature, but away from heat, up to 6 months. The olives on their own are best eaten within 2 months—after that, they begin to soften too much for eating, but they are still good for cooking or to use in Warm Olivada (page 655).

Making Flavored Oils
by Simple Infusion

A GUIDE TO IMPROVISING

MAKES ABOUT
½ CUP

Although most flavorings used to make flavored oils generally need coaxing with heat to release their true flavor, certain soft, fragrant ingredients, such as tender, mild herbs, garlic, grated citrus zests, or truffles, need only be chopped or pounded in a mortar to release their flavors quickly into the oil. The latter is an excellent way to make small amounts of flavored oils for use at the last minute as embellishments for soups, vegetables, and simple fish dishes.

There is no exact formula for making these oils—the ratio of flavoring to oil depends on the intensity of the ingredients you choose. Taste the oil as it infuses and add more flavoring if you wish. If the oil is starting to get too strong, simply strain out the flavoring.

Flavoring, singly or in combination, such as

> **Up to 2 cups tender, mild herbs or greens,** such as basil, cilantro, or arugula

> **Up to ¼ cup strongly flavored herbs,** such as tarragon, rosemary, savory, thyme, or sage (leaves only) or chives

> **Zest of 1 lemon, lime, or small orange** (removed in strips with a vegetable peeler)

> **1 garlic clove,** peeled

> **¼ ounce fresh white or black truffle**

Pinch of kosher salt

½ cup oil, such as extra-virgin olive or grapeseed oil

1. Thinly slice or finely chop the flavoring. Place it in a mortar or heavy bowl, add the salt, and pound to a coarse paste with a pestle, or mash with the back of a spoon.

2. Continue to stir and mash the flavorings as you drizzle in the oil. Set aside to infuse until the flavor reaches the desired intensity, 30 minutes to 1 hour before using. It is not necessary to strain these quickly made oils. In fact, it can be quite charming to serve them directly from a mortar.

IN ADVANCE

Most of these oils can be refrigerated for up to 1 week in a tightly sealed container; after that, strain out and discard the flavorings and refrigerate for up to 3 weeks longer.

Lemon Olive Oil

At olive oil–making time in the Abruzzo and Molise regions of Italy, lemons are often added to the last pressing to clean and freshen the press for the next season. The resulting oil, called *limonato,* is intense and redolent of lemon. Since the real thing is both expensive and hard to find, I make my own version by grinding lemon zest in a mortar with gutsy olive oil. It is splendid on practically anything you would dress with olive oil—especially vegetables such as roasted peppers, fennel, and eggplant and fish. It is great for improvising quick pasta dishes such as fresh fettuccine with chopped arugula, Parmigiano-Reggiano, and pepper. It is a superb salad dressing mixed with a dry, fragrant vinegar such as Banyuls or Cava.

Follow the Guide on page 589, using lemon zest and a fruity extra-virgin olive oil. Combine the lemon zest and salt in a mortar or a medium stainless steel or wooden bowl and pound and crush the peel with the pestle or the back of a wooden spoon for several minutes to extract its oils. Use a circular motion to crush the zest against the bottom of the bowl as you dribble in the olive oil a little at a time, then continue working the zest this way for about a minute. Let the oil infuse for at least 1 hour before serving, but no longer than 8 hours (if you let it steep too long, it will begin to taste like candy). Strain into a clean dry jar.

Chive Oil

Chive oil is one of the easiest oils to make, since tender chives release their flavor very quickly. Its delicate oniony flavor complements many foods, especially fish and shellfish dishes and vegetables. A teaspoon of the oil will go a long way to dress a baked potato, eliminating the need for butter. Simply thinly slice or snip ¼ cup fresh chives and mix with ½ cup extra-virgin olive oil; omit the salt. Set aside to infuse for 30 minutes before serving.

Cilantro, Mint, and Basil Oil

This oil adds a bright fresh flavor to vegetable soups, roasted peppers, tomatoes, and seafood. The quantities are approximate, and you can use any combination or just a single one. Follow the Guide on page 589, using 1 cup cilantro leaves, ½ cup basil leaves, and ¼ cup mint leaves, pounded, for the flavoring. Increase the salt to ¼ teaspoon and use ⅓ cup extra-virgin olive oil. Let infuse for 1 hour.

White Truffle Oil

One of the ways to make a white truffle go further is to use part of it to make a flavored oil to drizzle on just about anything to give it the heady aroma of truffles: fresh fennel and country bread, or fresh pasta, risotto, polenta, mashed potatoes, wild mushrooms, carpaccio, or grilled or poached salmon and lobster. Follow the Guide on page 589, using a white truffle and first rubbing the mortar or bowl with a cut clove of garlic. The exact amount of extra-virgin olive oil you need will depend on how potent the truffle is.

Making Flavored Oils with Fresh Herbs and Pungent Aromatics

A GUIDE TO IMPROVISING

The traditional way of making a flavored oil with fresh herbs such as thyme, rosemary, savory, basil, or sage or pungent aromatics such as garlic, ginger, or shallots is to steep them in the oil for several weeks. I find this method produces an oil with a hollow flavor, lacking the natural depth and sweetness of these ingredients. Gently heating them in the oil quickly extracts and mellows their sometimes sharp flavors, producing an intensely flavorful oil.

MAKES ABOUT 1 CUP

1 cup extra-virgin olive oil

Fresh herbs or pungent aromatics, singly or in combination, such as

> ½ **packed cup leaves pungent, strong herbs,** such as rosemary, thyme, savory, sage, or oregano
>
> 1½ **packed cups leaves tender, soft herbs,** such as basil, cilantro, or tarragon, coarsely chopped
>
> **5 garlic cloves,** thinly sliced
>
> **10 quarter-sized slices fresh ginger**
>
> **6 shallots,** thinly sliced

1. Combine the oil and herbs or aromatics in a small heavy pan and heat the oil over low heat until tiny bubbles dance around the herbs. Reduce the heat to very low and heat tender herbs for 1 minute longer, strong herbs for 3 minutes longer, or until their color begins to fade, or aromatics for about 4 minutes, until they are soft.

2. Remove from the heat and let steep for at least 2 hours, or overnight, before using. Strain into a clean dry jar.

The oil will keep in a tightly sealed jar in the refrigerator for up to 3 months. **IN ADVANCE**

Basil Oil

Basil is one of the most versatile and appealing of flavored oils because it has an affinity with a multitude of foods. In the colder months, I use basil oil to impart a vivid summery flavor to mashed potatoes, pan-seared fish, roasted onions, and tomatoes and pasta. It's especially good with winter squashes and pumpkins. Although basil oil is available commercially, it has none of the intense herbal flavor of the homemade oil. I make big batches of it in the summer when fresh basil is plentiful and give bottles of it to friends. To make 1 quart, follow the Guide on page 591, using about 6 cups packed fresh basil leaves (from 5 or 6 bunches, or about 1 pound basil) and 4 cups oil. Allow to steep for at least 24 hours and up to 3 days before straining.

Rosemary Oil

In addition to being an extremely useful oil for seasoning lamb, poultry, and all manner of vegetables, rosemary oil makes a delicious dip for country bread, and it can be brushed on focaccia. You can also use it to flavor Niçoise olives to serve as an hors d'oeuvre.

Follow the Guide on page 591, using fresh rosemary.

Roasted Garlic Oil

This oil is a way to keep the deep caramelized flavor of roasted garlic on hand. I particularly like it on mild goat cheeses and on pizza, focaccia, and polenta.

Follow the Guide on page 591, using 2 tablespoons Roasted Garlic Puree (page 38) for flavoring and heating it in the oil for 1 minute.

Provençal Herb Oil

Thyme, rosemary, and savory grow wild all over Provence and are used extensively in the region's cooking because they complement the local foods. I keep this oil on hand to have instant access to those flavors. Use it to season lamb chops, chicken, or game birds before grilling them, drizzle it on white beans and polenta, or use it to dress steamed or roasted vegetables like potatoes, zucchini, tomatoes, and green beans.

Follow the Guide on page 591, using ¼ cup fresh thyme leaves, 2 tablespoons each fresh rosemary and summer savory leaves, and ½ cup fresh flat-leaf parsley leaves.

Sage and Garlic Oil

This oil captures the sweet garlic and sage flavors of Tuscany, which perfume local specialities such as cannellini beans, crostini, or plump wild quail grilled over grapevines. Drizzle this oil over pasta, polenta, potatoes, white beans, and focaccia or brush vegetables and small game birds or chicken with the oil before roasting or grilling them.

> **1 cup extra-virgin olive oil**
> **5 garlic cloves,** thinly sliced
> **½ cup lightly packed fresh sage leaves**
> **Pinch of kosher salt**

In a small heavy saucepan, combine the oil and garlic and cook, covered, over moderately low heat, stirring frequently, until the garlic is just barely golden, about 5 minutes. Remove the garlic with a slotted spoon and drain on paper towels.

Add the sage leaves to the oil and heat, uncovered, until tiny bubbles surround the leaves; continue until the leaves release their fragrance and darken somewhat. Cover and set aside to steep for several hours.

Strain the oil into a clean dry jar, reserving the sage leaves. Drain them on paper towels.

The oil will keep in a tightly sealed jar in the refrigerator for up to 3 months.

Garlic Oil. Garlic oil made with sliced fresh garlic that has been gently simmered in oil has a mellow sweet flavor that is completely different from the harsh flavor of oils made with raw garlic. It makes a great staple oil for sautéing vegetables or dressing pasta, eliminating the chore of peeling and slicing garlic at the last minute.

Omit the sage leaves and double the garlic. Add a pinch of hot pepper flakes or a small piece of peperoncino if you like.

The by-product of this recipe is deliciously crisp garlic and sage leaves. Once you have strained the oil, blot them on a paper towel. Sprinkle them with a little sea salt and use them as a garnish for the dish you've flavored with the oil—or eat them as is.

IN ADVANCE

variation

Chinese Five-Flavor Oil

MAKES ¾ CUP

This powerfully flavored oil combines the essential flavors of Chinese cooking—ginger, Szechwan peppercorns, chile pepper, scallion, and sesame oil. Keep this versatile oil on hand for busy times, to make quick stir-fries and sautés and to drizzle on tofu and grilled or steamed fish. Because the oil is so aromatic, you only need three quarters of a teaspoon to season one serving, keeping calories to a minimum.

I use this oil often in place of olive oil to give steam-sautéed green vegetables (page 71) and greens (page 74) an Asian flair. It also makes a delicious dressing for Cold Spicy Sesame Noodles (page 127) instead of the traditional highly caloric version made with sesame paste or peanut butter.

> **2 scallions**, white and pale green parts only
> **8 quarter-sized slices fresh ginger**
> **1 tablespoon Szechwan peppercorns**
> **½ cup plus 1 tablespoon Asian sesame oil**
> **3 tablespoons peanut oil**
> **1 teaspoon red pepper flakes**

With the flat side of a chef's knife, lightly smash the scallions. Slice into 1-inch pieces. Smash the ginger slices and quarter them. Combine the scallions, ginger, and Szechwan peppercorns in a bowl and set aside.

In a small heavy saucepan, heat the sesame and peanut oils over moderate heat. Drop a few hot pepper flakes into the oil. When the flakes begin to sizzle and are surrounded by rings of tiny bubbles, the oil is hot enough. Reduce the heat slightly and add the remaining pepper flakes. Count 5 seconds, then remove the pan from the heat.

Stir in the scallions, ginger, and peppercorns. Cover the pan loosely and set aside to steep for at least 1 hour, or, preferably, overnight, at room temperature.

Pour the oil through a fine strainer into a clean dry jar.

IN ADVANCE The oil will keep in a well-sealed jar in the refrigerator for about 3 months.

Making Flavored Oils with Spices, Seeds, and Other Dry Flavorings

A GUIDE TO IMPROVISING

Dry, brittle flavorings—such as fennel, cumin, and anise seeds, dried chiles, ground spices, curry powder, or Flavor Essences—need special treatment to coax the flavor out of them. By first toasting them, then steeping them in boiling water, you "waken" their flavor before infusing them in warm oil. These oils add dimension to many dishes: Fennel seed oil is marvelous on grilled fish and shellfish and white beans. Curry oil seasons lentils and rice; wild mushroom oil, pasta, polenta, pizzas, or hearty broths and soups.

Because ground flavorings have varying levels of flavor, the amounts given here are approximate. Taste the oil as it steeps. When it reaches the strength you like, strain it. More earthy flavorings, such as Wild Mushroom Essence or Ancho Chile Essence, benefit from the addition of garlic.

The oil will keep in a well-sealed jar, refrigerated, for up to 3 months.

MAKES 1 CUP

To intensify the flavor of spices and seeds before steeping, toast them in a dry skillet, over low heat, until they release their fragrance.

Flavorings, singly or in combination, such as

> **2 tablespoons ground spices,** such as cloves, cinnamon, coriander, or juniper berries

> **2 tablespoons Flavor Essence** (pages 542–548), such as Sandy's Curry Powder, Wild Mushroom Essence, or Ancho Chile Essence

> **⅓ cup fennel, anise, or cumin seeds**

> **Up to 2 large pinches of saffron threads,** crushed

Hot water

1 cup extra-virgin olive, grapeseed, or canola oil

1 garlic clove, thinly sliced (optional)

1. In a small skillet, toast the spices, Flavor Essence, or seeds, stirring over low heat until fragrant. Transfer to a small bowl.

2. Add enough boiling water to make a sandy paste. Let sit for 10 minutes.

3. In a small saucepan, heat the oil over low heat. If using garlic, add it now and simmer for about 3 minutes, or until soft but not brown. Whisk the steeped flavorings into the hot oil. If using a ground spice or flavor essence, immediately remove from the heat. Cover and set aside to steep for 2 days. If using seeds, cook at a bare simmer over low heat for 3 minutes. Set aside, covered, to infuse.

4. Ladle the clear oil into a clean dry jar, leaving the sediment behind.

Saffron Oil

This golden oil is so intensely flavored you need only a few drops per serving. Drizzle over seafood or tomato dishes, into soups and broths, or over pasta or potatoes and beans.

In a small jar, crush 2 large pinches of saffron threads with the back of a spoon (you should have about 1 teaspoon crushed saffron). Stir in 2 teaspoons hot water. Let sit for 10 minutes.

In a small saucepan, heat ½ cup each grapeseed and extra-virgin olive oil over low heat until hot. Pour over the saffron, cover, and shake the jar. Set aside to infuse for at least 24 hours before using.

Hot (and Smoky) Chile Oil

In Italy, *olio infernale,* an elemental hot pepper oil, is used to enliven all kinds of foods, from tomato sauces to sautéed vegetables. I like to make it with chipotle chiles—dried smoked jalapeño peppers—because they have an appealing smoky flavor. Use either 4 canned chipotles in adobo, chopped, with 2 tablespoons of their sauce, or 4 dried chipotles, broken apart, stemmed, seeded, and soaked in boiling water to cover for 30 minutes. If you just want heat without the smoky flavor, replace the dried chipotles with 4 dried Italian red peppers (peperoncini), crumbled, or ¼ cup red pepper flakes.

In a small saucepan, heat 1 cup canola or grapeseed oil and the chiles over low heat until the oil is hot. Cover and set aside to infuse for 5 days. Strain into a clean dry jar.

BUYING AND STORING NUTS

Nuts become rancid quickly because their oils are so volatile. Fresh nuts should smell and taste sweet; rancid nuts have a harsh, somewhat acrid aroma and flavor. Buy fresh nuts from a vendor who has a large turnover. Store nuts in a sealed plastic container for up to 1 month in the refrigerator or 2 months in the freezer. Roast them to bring out their flavor.

Roasted Nut Oils

I use hazelnut and walnut oils when I want to impart the concentrated flavor of freshly roasted nuts into all kinds of preparations, from simple Belgian endive salads to steamed asparagus and mashed potatoes. They can even boost the flavor of chocolate in desserts.

MAKES 1 CUP

First-rate nut oils can be both costly and hard to find. I have lost count of the times I've opened a bottle of expensive nut oil from a producer I don't know to find it is bland or rancid. To make a flavorful nut oil, apply the same technique you use to make oils from seeds and coarse herbs—steeping them in hot oil. Also, you can use the same method to punch up the flavor of bland nut oil.

> **1 cup** (4 ounces) **hazelnuts, walnuts, or pecans**
> **1 cup grapeseed or canola oil**

Preheat the oven to 400°F.

Spread the nuts on a baking sheet and roast, rearranging them occasionally, until very fragrant, 7 to 10 minutes. If using hazelnuts, spray them with water once or twice during roasting; remove the skins by piling them in a tea towel and rubbing them between your hands to rub off the skins. Allow the nuts to cool slightly.

Place the nuts in a food processor or blender, and finely chop them. Drizzle in the oil, then let the motor run a couple of minutes if necessary, scraping down the sides occasionally, until you have a very smooth puree.

Transfer the oil to a small saucepan and heat it slowly over the lowest heat possible until it is very hot but not boiling, about 10 minutes. Remove from the heat, cover, and set aside to steep for 2 days.

After the oil has steeped, the solids should have sunk to the bottom. Carefully spoon the oil (do not pour!) into a clean dry jar, taking care not to disturb the solids. Discard the nuts (all of their flavor will have gone into the oil).

Nut oils are as volatile as nuts. Store them in a well-sealed jar in the refrigerator for up to 3 months.

IN ADVANCE

Pan-seared
shrimp (page 241),
served with
Pumpkin Seed
Sauce (page 658)
and warm
corn tortillas

SAUCES

Sauce making today encompasses a broad range of techniques and ingredients from the world's cuisines. In fact, it has no strict parameters: A sauce can be any liquid "dressing" that will add the right counterpoint of flavor, piquancy, or surprise to bring a dish to fruition, from salsas and chutneys to warm vinaigrettes, flavored oils, and vegetable juice reductions. It is a far cry from yesterday's images of stockpots and cream- and butter-laden recipes that take a lot of time, energy, and knowledge to prepare.

Sauces are powerful catalysts—separately made components with the ability to transform simply prepared foods into complex dishes, such as Port Wine Sauce (page 637) embellishing a roast chicken, or Cilantro and Coconut Chutney (page 665) served with grilled shrimp. Often these sauces can be made ahead of time, eliminating the anxiety of making one at the last minute. Most can be paired with many different foods, encouraging a freer, more improvisational way of cooking.

The recipes in this chapter show you new ways of making and using sauces that are immensely flavorful yet low in fat and calories.

VINAIGRETTES. It used to be that a vinaigrette dressing—classically, a mixture of oil and wine vinegar—was used exclusively to dress cold salads, in particular, greens. Over the past twenty years, though, vinaigrettes have come to include any number of combinations of different fats—from rendered bacon fat and brown butter to flavored oils—in tandem with a wide range of acidic components, such as fifty-year-old sherry vinegar, citrus juice, or a wine reduction. Vinaigrettes can sauce many kinds of savory dishes—grilled and spice-crusted fish, meat, or poultry or roasted vegetables anytime you want a mild acid counterpoint.

Vinaigrettes are quite caloric because they are made with a high percentage of fat, albeit often virtuous olive or vegetable oils. These fats provide most of the deliciousness and pleasing texture in a vinaigrette. My solution to lightening vinaigrettes has been to find ways to extend the essential fat rather than trying to eliminate it—a tack that I find unsatisfying.

A VINAIGRETTE LESSON

Generally speaking, it takes 1½ to 2 teaspoons of vinaigrette to dress 2 cups of raw or cooked food, about 1 tablespoon of warm vinaigrette to sauce 1 serving.

Vinaigrettes are all about balance, both of oil to vinegar or other acidic ingredients, and of the vinaigrette to the food to be dressed. Making a vinaigrette demands that you use your senses and make some judgments.

The trick to making a great vinaigrette is to start with the best ingredients—flavorful fats and well-made vinegars whose flavors are complex and balanced. Using such ingredients lessens the possibility of producing a bitingly acidic vinaigrette and also means you can use a greater proportion of vinegar to oil, thereby reducing the amount of fat in the dressing. For example, a fine fruity extra-virgin olive oil has far more flavor than a mediocre one. And an aged balsamic vinegar will be smoother and more intensely flavored than a watery, astringent red wine vinegar, so you won't need to rely on oil to smooth the vinegar out. On the contrary, you can use the vinegar to extend the oil. (For a discussion of oils and vinegars, see pages 8 to 10.)

To extend the fat in a vinaigrette, blend in a small amount of liquid—water, vegetable or fruit juice, or skimmed meat juices—which will emulsify the oil into a homogenous dressing that coats foods evenly. In effect, this trick "spreads" the oil farther so that you use less.

Basic Vinaigrette

A GUIDE TO IMPROVISING

The ratio of oil to acid in a vinaigrette is to a degree a matter of personal preference. Some chefs prefer a dressing as strong as 2:1, some like it as mild as 4:1. I generally prefer a ratio of about 3 parts oil to 1 part vinegar or lemon juice, because I always mix in a little hot water to make the vinaigrette mix more uniformly and coat foods. Adjust this balance according to the strength and flavor of the vinegar and the food you are dressing. For example, balsamic vinegar has such a sweet mellow flavor, and far less acidity than other vinegars, that it is possible to use a much larger proportion of vinegar to oil, even 1 to 1. (This is why balsamic vinegar is used so often in low-fat dressings.) Sharper vinegars, such as sherry vinegar, should be used more sparingly.

The vinaigrette can be stored in a tightly sealed jar in the refrigerator for up to 1 week. (If the vinaigrette separates upon standing, mix again.)

MAKES SCANT
½ CUP

Remember that the more sharply flavored the vinegar, the greater proportion of oil you will need.

1 to 1½ teaspoons finely chopped shallots (optional)

Vinegar, such as

> **1½ to 2 tablespoons "sharpish" vinegar:** Champagne, apple cider, or sherry

> **Up to 4 tablespoons mellow balsamic vinegar**

> **1½ to 3 tablespoons of a combination of vinegars**

Good pinch of kosher salt

¼ cup oil, such as extra-virgin olive oil, roasted nut oil, or Flavored Oil (pages 588–597)

1½ to 2 teaspoons hot water (or up to 3 tablespoons fruit juice, meat or poultry juices, or broth)

1. If you are using the shallots, place them in a jar or bowl, add the vinegar and salt, and allow to stand for 10 minutes. Otherwise, just combine the vinegar and salt in a jar or bowl. Cover the jar and shake vigorously, or stir to dissolve the salt.

2. Add the oil and hot water. Cover the jar and shake vigorously, or stir, until the mixture is uniform. Taste and adjust the balance of oil to vinegar, if desired. Use at once.

You can jazz up a vinaigrette by adding any of the following flavorings. If you are unsure of amounts, stir in the flavoring and let the vinaigrette stand, tasting it periodically, until it is the way you like it, then strain out the flavoring.

- **Minced fresh herbs,** such as basil, chives, chervil, cilantro. (Pungent herbs such as rosemary and thyme should be used sparingly.) Never use dried herbs, as they have a musty flavor.

- **Grated fresh ginger** or minced fresh lemongrass.

- **Grated citrus zest:** orange, tangerine, lemon, or lime.

- **Spices,** such as finely crushed juniper berries, cumin or coriander seeds, or curry powder.

- **You can also combine flavorings,** such as citrus and ginger, basil and orange, or curry and lime.

Garlic is wonderful in vinaigrettes, but it must be used with care or it will be harsh. For a mild garlic flavor, rub a salad bowl with a cut clove of garlic before adding the greens or the dressing or spear a cut or smashed garlic clove with a fork and whisk it around the dressing until the desired flavor is achieved; then discard it.

essential recipe

Everyday Vinaigrette

MAKES SCANT
½ CUP

This is the dressing I use most. It goes with just about any food without overwhelming it. It is a mix of a high-quality balsamic vinegar—often called balsamic condiment—with an aged sherry vinegar. Because these aged vinegars are exceptionally mellow, you can use equal amounts of oil and vinegar, rather than the usual 3 to 1 ratio. You can use this formula with other mellow vinegars and oils. My favorite is Banyuls vinegar (in place of the sherry vinegar) mixed with Lemon Olive Oil (page 590).

> **3 tablespoons aged balsamic vinegar** (see page 640)
> **1 tablespoon aged sherry vinegar,** preferably 50 years old
> **Good pinch of kosher salt**
> **¼ cup extra-virgin olive oil**
> **2 teaspoons hot water**

Combine the balsamic and sherry vinegars and the salt in a small jar or bowl. Cover the jar and shake vigorously, or stir, to dissolve the salt. Add the oil and hot water, cover the jar, and shake vigorously, or stir until the mixture is uniform. Use at once.

IN ADVANCE Store in a tightly sealed jar in the refrigerator for up to 2 weeks. If the vinaigrette separates upon standing, mix again.

variation **Nut Oil Vinaigrette.** Nut oil vinaigrettes are delicious on assertively flavored, somewhat bitter greens, such as Belgian and curly endive, as well as on hearty root vegetables like beets and celery root. Use 1 tablespoon sherry or red wine vinegar and 2 teaspoons balsamic vinegar. Replace the olive oil with a very fragrant hazelnut or walnut oil made with roasted nuts. (See Roasted Nut Oils, page 597, to make your own.)

variation **Vinaigrette with Roasted Poultry, Meat, or Game Juices.** When I am serving a leafy green salad alongside roasted poultry, meat, or game, I add a couple of tablespoons of the skimmed meat juices to Everyday Vinaigrette to tie all the flavors together. This also makes a delicious dressing for boiled or roasted potatoes.

Lemon Vinaigrette with a Little Garlic

MAKES ¼ CUP This is a great dressing for chilled raw or cooked vegetable or bean salads, from wilted greens to shaved fennel (especially if garnished with finely shaved Parmigiano-Reggiano cheese), as well as carpaccio of thinly sliced raw beef or fish.

1 garlic clove, cut lengthwise in half

1 tablespoon plus 1 teaspoon fresh lemon juice

Pinch of kosher salt

2 tablespoons plus 2 teaspoons fruity extra-virgin olive oil

Rub the cut side of one of the garlic halves over the inside of a small bowl. Add the lemon juice and salt. Spear both garlic halves on a dinner fork. Using this as a whisk, drizzle in the olive oil until the vinaigrette thickens slightly; discard the garlic. Use at once.

IN ADVANCE Since its fresh flavor deteriorates on standing, make it in small amounts and use within 1 day.

Classic Mustard Vinaigrette

MAKES SCANT
⅔ CUP

Whisking the vinegar and oil into prepared mustard results in a thicker, creamier dressing. Since mustard contains vinegar, you need to use slightly less vinegar (or more oil) in the dressing. In addition to greens, this is particularly good on cold vegetable salads, such as those of asparagus, potatoes, or beets.

For a sweeter but more robust dressing, use balsamic vinegar instead of white wine vinegar and omit the shallot. Spear a lightly smashed garlic clove with a fork, whisk it in the dressing, then discard it.

> 1 teaspoon Dijon mustard
> 2 tablespoons white wine vinegar or Champagne vinegar
> Pinch of kosher salt
> 1 to 1½ teaspoons minced shallot (optional)
> ¼ cup plus 2 tablespoons extra-virgin olive oil
> 2 teapoons hot water
> ⅛ to ¼ teaspoon sugar

Combine the mustard, vinegar, salt, and shallot, if using, in a small jar or bowl. Cover the jar and shake vigorously, or stir, to blend. If using the shallot, allow to stand for 20 minutes in the jar to let it mellow.

Add the oil, hot water, and sugar and shake vigorously or stir until the mixture is uniform. Use at once.

IN ADVANCE The shallots become bitter if left in the dressing for more than 1 day; strain them out for longer storage. The vinaigrette will keep in a sealed jar for up to 2 weeks. (If it separates upon standing, mix again.)

variation **Champagne Herb Vinaigrette.** Mellow Champagne vinegar makes a delicate vinaigrette that is good on a variety of milder greens and baby lettuces, as well as on cold steamed spring vegetables, such as asparagus and baby carrots, as it will not obscure their flavor.

Omit the mustard and use 1½ teaspoons minced shallot and Champagne vinegar. Just before using, add 2 tablespoons minced fresh herbs, such as cilantro, basil, flat-leaf parsley, or chervil, or 1 tablespoon fresh tarragon, in any combination.

variation **Honey-Mustard Vinaigrette.** Increase the mustard to 1 tablespoon plus 2 teaspoons. When you combine the mustard and vinegar, add 1 tablespoon wildflower honey. Omit the sugar. (Makes about ¾ cup.)

Rustic Olive Vinaigrette. When I want to create a dressing with an variation intense olive flavor for more rustic dishes (or boost the flavor of a bland olive oil), I blend in a little olive paste, either commercial or homemade (page 683). This vinaigrette is wonderful on cold cooked vegetables and greens, octopus, and shrimp.

Omit the mustard and shallot. Add 1 tablespoon black or green olive paste to the vinegar (use green olive paste with white wine or Champagne vinegar, black olive paste with balsamic vinegar).

Citrus Vinaigrette

The flavors of oranges and tangerines marry wonderfully with olive and nut MAKES ABOUT ½ CUP oils. I use both zest and juice with mellow balsamic vinegar and herbs; the juice acts as the extending liquid the way water does in the other dressings. This is especially good on bitter greens, such as endive, radicchio, and arugula, grilled chicken or fish, and roasted root vegetables.

> 1 tablespoon plus 1 teaspoon fresh navel or blood orange, tangerine, or clementine juice
>
> 1 tablespoon plus 1 teaspoon balsamic vinegar
>
> Large pinch of kosher salt
>
> 2 tablespoons extra-virgin olive oil or hazelnut or walnut oil
>
> 2 to 3 teaspoons finely slivered or grated orange, tangerine, or clementine zest
>
> 3 to 4 grindings of black pepper
>
> 1 tablespoon minced fresh basil (optional)
>
> 1 teaspoon minced fresh tarragon (optional)

Combine the juice, vinegar, and salt in a small jar or a bowl. Cover and shake vigorously, or stir, to dissolve the salt. Add the oil, zest, and pepper. Cover the jar again and shake vigorously, or stir, until the mixture is blended. Just before serving, add the fresh herbs and shake again.

The vinaigrette can be stored, tightly sealed, in the refrigerator for up to 3 days. IN ADVANCE (If the vinaigrette separates on standing, shake again.)

Dieter's Balsamic Dressing

MAKES ABOUT
½ CUP

I created this dressing for those times when I have to lose a few pounds, but am tired of using plain balsamic vinegar to dress my salads. It is a smooth emulsion of commercial green olive paste with orange juice or unsalted chicken broth and some balsamic vinegar. The olive paste provides the flavor, and some of the viscous texture, of a fruity olive oil. While this is one of the best low-calorie dressings I've tasted, it does not have that mellow quality of an oil-based vinaigrette, but at 14 calories per tablespoon, it is a worthy substitute.

> **2 tablespoons plus 2 teaspoons commercial green olive paste**
>
> **¼ cup fresh orange juice or unsalted homemade** (page 574) **chicken broth or canned low-sodium chicken broth**
>
> **2 tablespoons balsamic vinegar,** or more to taste
>
> **Freshly ground black pepper**

In a blender, combine the olive paste, orange juice, balsamic vinegar, and pepper and blend at high speed until the dressing is smooth. Use at once, or transfer to a clean dry jar so that you can shake the dressing to emulsify it again before using.

IN ADVANCE The dressing can be stored, tightly sealed, in the refrigerator for up to 5 days. (If the dressing separates upon standing, shake vigorously before serving.)

Roasted Sesame Seed Dressing

Instead of sesame oil, roasted sesame seeds impart a fresh sweet sesame flavor MAKES ⅔ CUP and slightly thicken the base of fresh ginger, soy sauce, and rice vinegar for an oil-less dressing. The fragrant dressing is excellent on delicate small Japanese eggplants, sliced lengthwise in half and roasted (see "Fried" Eggplant, page 42). It is also ideal on all manner of vegetables and crunchy salads such as julienned cucumbers, shredded raw vegetables such as daikon, carrots, and cabbage, and watercress, as well as on tofu. Or try it as a sauce for grilled fish and duck breasts.

- ¼ cup white sesame seeds
- 1 teaspoon sugar
- Pinch of red pepper flakes
- ¼ cup plus 1 tablespoon rice vinegar
- ¼ cup low-sodium soy sauce
- 2 to 3 teaspoons fresh lime juice
- 1 teaspoon grated fresh ginger
- 2 tablespoons water

In a medium skillet, toast the sesame seeds over low heat, stirring frequently, until fragrant and golden. Transfer to a blender, add the sugar and pepper flakes, and grind to a fine powder. Add the vinegar, soy sauce, lime juice, ginger, and water and blend for several minutes until the mixture is uniform. Use at once, or transfer to a clean dry jar so that you can shake the dressing to emulsify it again before serving.

The dressing can be stored, tightly sealed, in the refrigerator for up to 2 weeks. IN ADVANCE (If the dressing separates upon standing, shake vigorously before serving.)

WARM VINAIGRETTES.

When warmed, vinaigrettes gain another dimension that makes them seem more substantial, a perfect light, savory sauce for many cooked foods. I use them to dress peppery or bitter greens, cooked vegetables, and tofu, and as a sauce for meat, poultry, seafood, and starchy foods such as potatoes and beans, which normally soak up a lot of fat.

Any vinaigrette, including those on pages 605 to 611, can be warmed over low heat to be used as a sauce. You can also create warm vinaigrettes using the Guide to Improvising and the recipes that follow.

Impromptu Warm Herb Vinaigrettes

A GUIDE TO IMPROVISING

MAKES ABOUT
⅓ CUP

You can quickly devise any number of delicious warm piquant sauces by first making a quick flavored oil—garlic and herbs cooked in olive oil—and then splashing balsamic vinegar into it. Use a single herb or a combination, depending on what you wish to serve it on. This dressing is good on warm steamed root vegetables, such as potatoes, parsnips, and turnips, as well as on grilled fish, poultry, and lamb.

> **3 tablespoons plus 1 teaspoon extra-virgin olive oil**
>
> **2 garlic cloves,** quartered lengthwise
>
> **2 teaspoons minced fresh herbs,** such as rosemary, thyme, savory, sage, or oregano
>
> **3 tablespoons balsamic vinegar**
>
> **Pinch of kosher salt**
>
> **Freshly ground black pepper**

1. In a small skillet, combine the olive oil, garlic, and herbs. Cook gently over moderately low heat until the garlic is just beginning to brown. Discard the garlic and remove from the heat.

2. Pour in the balsamic vinegar, taking care to stand back, as the mixture will splutter. Stir in the salt and pepper. Serve hot.

IN ADVANCE
These vinaigrette are best used as soon as they are made, but any leftovers can be stored in a sealed jar in the refrigerator. Warm, if desired, before using, adding a teaspoon or two of water.

Warm Sesame, Ginger, and Scallion Vinaigrette with Salted Black Beans

This is a play on the classic Chinese sauce of ginger, scallions, sesame oil, and soy sauce that I use for grilled, roasted, or pan-seared fish, sea scallops, and shrimp, as well as steamed broccoli and tofu. First, a small amount of sesame oil is seasoned with ginger and scallions to make a quick flavored oil. Then it is boiled with chicken broth to mellow and extend it. Fermented black beans add a marvelous pungency.

2 tablespoons unsalted homemade (page 574) **or canned low-sodium chicken broth**

2 tablespoons low-sodium soy sauce

2 tablespoons Chinese rice wine vinegar or white wine vinegar

¾ teaspoon sugar

Ginger-Scallion Oil

> **1 tablespoon vegetable oil,** such as canola or grapeseed
>
> **1 tablespoon Asian sesame oil**
>
> **¼ cup finely minced fresh ginger**
>
> **6 scallions,** thinly sliced on a diagonal (½ cup)
>
> **3 tablespoons minced garlic**
>
> **⅛ teaspoon red pepper flakes**

1½ tablespoons Chinese salted black beans, rinsed well and drained (optional)

Combine the chicken broth, soy sauce, vinegar, and sugar. Set aside.

For the oil, heat a large nonstick skillet over medium heat. Add the oils and swirl to coat the pan. Add the ginger and stir constantly with a wooden spoon for 30 seconds. Add the scallions and stir for 30 seconds more. Reduce the heat to moderate. Add the garlic and pepper flakes and sauté, stirring constantly, until the garlic is soft and barely golden, about 2 minutes.

Add the chicken broth mixture and the black beans, if using. Bring to a boil and simmer for 2 minutes to reduce the sauce slightly. Serve warm.

You can make the flavored oil up to 4 hours ahead; set aside at room temperature. Reheat before finishing the sauce.

Any leftover sauce can be kept in a sealed container in the refrigerator for up to 1 week. Reheat gently before serving.

Warm Anchovy and Olive Oil Sauce

Bagna cauda, literally, "warm bath," is the classic Italian dip for raw vegetables and bread. It is a warm infused oil made with the staple ingredients of the peasant kitchens in which it evolved: olive oil, butter, garlic, and anchovies. It is utterly elemental, satisfying, and caloric. In this bagna cauda–inspired version, I have used traditional ingredients to make an intensely flavored olive oil, which I then boil with broth to carry those flavors further, to use less oil.

You can use this versatile sauce to dress cooked and raw vegetables, such as potatoes, asparagus, fennel, and peppers. It tempers the sharp qualities of cruciferous vegetables, such as cauliflower, broccoli, and cabbage. It is especially delicious on the unusual chicory from Italy called puntarella, becoming increasingly available here, served sliced as a salad. You can even use it as a sauce for linguine or spaghetti. Or wilt fresh greens, such as beet greens, spinach, arugula, or Swiss chard, in it: Figure on 1 tablespoon sauce for each 2 cups of cleaned dried greens, and quickly toss together in a skillet over high heat.

½ cup fruity extra-virgin olive oil

2 garlic cloves, minced

¼ teaspoon red pepper flakes

2 ounces oil-packed anchovies (about 10), drained, patted dry, and finely chopped or mashed

½ teaspoon dried savory

¼ cup unsalted homemade (page 574)
or canned low-sodium chicken broth or Garlic Broth (page 580)

Up to 1 tablespoon fresh lemon juice, to taste

¼ cup minced fresh flat-leaf parsley

In a small heavy saucepan, heat the oil, garlic, and red pepper flakes over low heat, stirring occasionally, until the garlic is very soft, about 5 minutes. Stir in the anchovies and savory and cook for 1 minute longer. Add the broth, increase the heat to high, and bring to a boil. Boil for 30 seconds, or until the sauce is emulsified. Stir in the lemon juice and parsley and serve warm or at room temperature.

The sauce can be kept in a sealed container in the refrigerator for up to 1 week. Reheat gently before serving, if desired.

Warm Curry Vinaigrette

Use the complex sweet spice flavors of this curry vinaigrette to dress grilled fish, poultry, and lamb or steamed or roasted starchy vegetables, such as potatoes and parsnips. Chilled, it makes an unusual dressing for slaw; potato, chicken, and rice salads; and grated vegetables. Garnish with chopped cilantro.

MAKES ½ CUP

1 tablespoon plus 1 teaspoon extra-virgin olive oil

1 medium shallot, minced (about 1 tablespoon)

½ small green apple, peeled and finely diced (¼ cup)

2 teaspoons Sandy's Curry Powder (page 548)
or commercial curry powder

¼ cup apple cider or juice

¼ cup unsalted homemade (page 574)
or canned low-sodium chicken broth

1 tablespoon plus 1 teaspoon cider vinegar
or Champagne vinegar

Pinch of kosher salt

Freshly ground white pepper

1 to 2 teaspoons fresh lime juice

In a small nonstick skillet, combine the oil, shallot, and apple, cover, and cook over low heat, stirring occasionally, until the shallot is just softened, about 2 minutes. Uncover, increase the heat to moderate, and sauté until the shallot is golden brown, about 3 minutes. Add the curry powder and cook, stirring, for 1 minute, or until fragrant.

Add the cider, chicken broth, and vinegar and boil until reduced to ½ cup, about 6 minutes. Stir in the salt, white pepper to taste, and the lime juice. Serve warm.

The vinaigrette can be kept in a sealed jar in the refrigerator for 4 days. Reheat gently before serving. **IN ADVANCE**

Warm Vermouth and Shallot Dressing

MAKES ½ CUP This is an all-purpose dressing for pasta, beans, grains, root vegetables, potatoes, and other starchy foods that are absorbent and take a great deal of fat to coat. It has a base of reduced white vermouth and shallots, so the food absorbs the delicious reduction rather than lots of fat. You can use many different kinds of fat in this recipe: Extra-virgin olive oil goes with just about everything from dried beans to potatoes. Try nut oils with roasted root vegetables or boiled artichokes. Made with butter, this is a great dressing for grains.

1 cup white vermouth

1 tablespoon minced shallots

¼ to ½ teaspoon kosher salt, to taste

½ teaspoon sugar

2 teaspoons Champagne vinegar or white wine vinegar

1 tablespoon plus 1 teaspoon fruity extra-virgin olive oil, roasted walnut or hazelnut oil, Flavored Oil (pages 588–597), **or unsalted butter**

1 tablespoon minced fresh herbs, such as flat-leaf parsley, chervil, basil, or tarragon (optional)

Freshly ground black pepper

In a small heavy saucepan, combine the vermouth, shallots, and salt and bring to a boil over moderately high heat. Carefully tilt pan or use a long match to ignite the vermouth, and cook until the flames die down and the vermouth has reduced to about ¼ cup.

Add the sugar, vinegar, and oil and boil vigorously until the oil and vermouth are combined, about 30 seconds. Stir in the herbs and pepper to taste. Spoon half the dressing over the warm food you wish to dress; toss occasionally until it has cooled slightly and absorbed most of dressing. Then spoon the rest over.

IN ADVANCE The vinaigrette can be kept in a sealed jar in the refrigerator for 1 week. Reheat gently before serving.

Fruit Juice Vinaigrettes

A GUIDE TO IMPROVISING

You can make quick fragrant jewel-like sauces from fruit juices with clear, strong flavors, such as orange, cranberry, black currant, tangerine, and pink grapefruit. You simply boil the juice until it becomes highly concentrated and more acidic, then blend in a complementary fat—extra-virgin olive oil, flavored oil, or fragrant roasted nut oils—to make a slightly tart, fruity vinaigrette-like sauce.

MAKES ABOUT ½ CUP; SERVES ABOUT 6

These sweetly perfumed sauces are particularly good with simple poultry and seafood dishes. They can add surprising counterpoints of flavor to root vegetables, onions, and grains. A vinaigrette of black currant juice and hazelnut oil is marvelous with warm beets and farro, a coarse grain that looks like wheat berries. A blood orange vinaigrette makes a fine sauce for grilled fennel, Vidalia onions, and red peppers.

Because these have such intense flavor, about 1½ tablespoons will amply sauce 1 serving—a 5-ounce fish fillet or 1 cup of grains or vegetables, for example. When it is spooned onto the plate, the oil and juice will separate, creating a beautiful mottled effect.

The beauty of these sauces is that you can make them with store-bought fresh, frozen, or bottled juices.

> **2 cups unsweetened fruit juice,** such as regular or blood orange, cranberry, black currant, tangerine, or pink grapefruit
>
> **2 tablespoons oil,** such as fruity extra-virgin olive oil, Flavored Oil (pages 588–597), or roasted nut oil
>
> **2 to 3 teaspoons fresh lemon or lime juice** (optional)

1. In a small saucepan over moderately high heat, bring the juice to a boil, and boil until it is syrupy and reduced to a scant ½ cup, 25 to 30 minutes. Taste the juice to determine if it has a good, concentrated flavor; if not, continue boiling a few minutes longer.

2. Add the oil and boil for 30 seconds, or until blended. If you find the juice reduction not quite tart enough to be a vinaigrette, add lemon or lime juice to taste. Allow to cool slightly before using.

The vinaigrettes can be kept in a sealed jar in the refrigerator for up to 1 week. Reheat gently before serving.

IN ADVANCE

COLD MEDITERRANEAN-STYLE SAUCES FROM AÏOLI TO PESTO. The Mediterranean is known for its wondrous olive-oil-and-garlic sauces: rouille in Provence, allioli in Catalonia, skordalia in Greece, and pesto in Italy.

Although they can be shockingly high in calories and fat, I would never call these sauces unhealthy. They are made with olive oil, which is an exceedingly healthful fat (see pages x–xiv), and the quantity of egg yolk they contain per serving is negligible. These oil-thickened sauces are so delectable that it is my firm conviction that when you are offered the real thing, made by a great cook, you should indulge in it wholeheartedly. I devised my lightened versions for everyday purposes, to be enjoyed in between occasional hedonistic revels.

These classic sauces are traditionally made in a mortar with a pestle; the pounding coaxes out flavors in an entirely different way from the chopping action of a food processor. I usually use both tools, beginning with the food processor, to break down the more fibrous ingredients and whip them into a thick puree. Then, because garlic becomes bitter when chopped in the processor, I pound it to a paste in a mortar (or right on the work surface), which gives it a sweet, round flavor, and add it to the sauce.

Use only fresh, firm garlic cloves for these sauces. Before smashing, cut each lengthwise in half. If there is a green sprout, remove it with the point of a knife to avoid making the sauce bitter.

Roasted Garlic Aïoli

MAKES ABOUT 1 ¼ CUPS

Here is a lightened version of the French aïoli using roasted garlic puree and a paste made of milk-soaked bread to provide the thickening normally achieved by an emulsion of egg yolks and olive oil, at a savings of hundreds of calories of oil. You need only a quarter of the usual amount of extra-virgin olive oil to give it the requisite unctuous texture and olivey flavor. Adding a little raw garlic that has been mashed in a mortar gives the sauce the fresh, pungent garlicky flavor of true aïoli.

3 to 5 garlic cloves, peeled

About ½ teaspoon kosher salt

1 slice white bread, torn into 1-inch pieces

¼ cup unsalted homemade (page 574)
or canned low-sodium chicken broth or fat-free milk

½ cup plus 2 tablespoons Roasted Garlic Puree
(from 3 large heads garlic; page 38)

¼ cup fruity extra-virgin olive oil, or more to taste

Freshly ground black pepper

Squeeze of fresh lemon juice

Put the garlic in a mortar, sprinkle with the salt, and mash to a smooth paste. Alternatively, mash the garlic to a paste right on the work surface. Using a chef's knife, mince the garlic with the salt: Placing the flat side of the knife almost parallel to the work surface, mash the garlic a little at a time by crushing and smearing it against the cutting board until it is completely reduced to a paste. Set aside.

In a food processor, reduce the bread to fine crumbs. Remove the lid, drizzle the chicken broth over the bread crumbs, and toss with a fork—do not process—until they are just moistened. Let sit for a few minutes, until the crumbs become soft paste.

Add the roasted garlic puree and process the mixture to a fine puree, about 1 minute. With the motor running, add the reserved garlic, then dribble in 3 tablespoons of the olive oil. Add pepper to taste and the lemon juice. Transfer to a bowl.

Just before serving, stir in the remaining olive oil, without incorporating it completely.

IN ADVANCE The aïoli can be kept in a tightly sealed container in the refrigerator for up to 4 days.

variation **Rouille.** This garlicky red pepper and saffron sauce from the South of France is traditionally spooned into bouillabaisse or smeared on the toasted bread that accompanies it. It is marvelous served that way in any number of simpler fish stews or Shellfish Steams (see page 254), or as a sauce for grilled or roasted fish and shellfish.

Reduce the garlic puree to ¼ cup and add 1 roasted red bell pepper, peeled, seeded, and diced (see page 683). Use only 2 garlic cloves, and mash them with 1 small hot chile pepper, chopped, and ½ teaspoon saffron threads.

Romesco

Romesco is one of Spain's greatest sauces. It is said that if you were to walk through the region of Tarragona in Catalan Spain, asking people about the "true" romesco sauce, you would get a different recipe from each person you spoke to—and the philosophy behind it.

Romesco is, in its most fundamental form, garlic, roasted almonds, a special mildly spicy pepper *(nyora)*, bread that has been fried in olive oil, tomato, and olive oil, all pounded together in a mortar to make a thick emulsion. It is marvelous with cold seafood, as well as with steamed new potatoes and grilled vegetables such as baby leeks, fennel, and peppers. In Catalunya, romesco is eaten with grilled spring onions at local festivals. I use Roasted Garlic Puree to reduce much of the fat while maintaining the luxurious texture.

Mildly spicy dried ancho chiles are the closest chile available in this country to the Spanish nyora. They are available in many supermarkets and at Latino and specialty markets.

2 ancho chiles

20 blanched whole almonds

1 thick slice white peasant bread, crusts removed (about ¾ ounce trimmed)

¼ cup fruity extra-virgin olive oil

3 garlic cloves, peeled

About ½ teaspoon kosher salt

½ cup plus 2 tablespoons Roasted Garlic Puree (from 3 large heads garlic; page 38)

1 medium tomato (about 6 ounces)

2 to 3 teaspoons red wine vinegar or balsamic vinegar

Pinch of cayenne pepper

Freshly ground black pepper

Preheat the oven to 375°F.

Break the ancho chiles into several pieces. Remove the stems and seeds and discard, then tear them into strips. In a large heavy skillet, toast the chile strips over moderate heat, turning occasionally with a spatula to prevent them from burning, until they begin to darken and smell pungent, about 3 minutes. Transfer to a medium bowl and cover with about 1 cup boiling water. Let soak for 20 minutes.

Meanwhile, spread the almonds on a baking sheet and roast, rearranging occasionally, until golden and fragrant, about 10 minutes. Set aside.

While the almonds are roasting, brush the bread with 1 teaspoon of the olive oil. Place on a small baking sheet and toast till dry and golden. Slice one of the garlic cloves lengthwise in half and rub both sides of the bread with the cut sides of the garlic. Sprinkle with salt. Set aside; reserve the garlic. Drain the chiles and pat dry on paper towels.

In a food processor, finely chop the almonds, scraping the sides down occasionally. Break the bread into 1-inch pieces, add to the work bowl, and process to fine crumbs. Add the ancho chiles and garlic puree.

Slice the tomato crosswise in half. Squeeze out the juice and seeds and discard. Working directly over the work bowl, rub the cut sides across the large holes of a metal grater so that the flesh is coarsely grated but the skin remains intact in your hand. Discard the skin.

With the motor running, drizzle in all but 1 tablespoon of the remaining olive oil. Add the vinegar, cayenne, and pepper to taste, and transfer to a bowl.

In a mortar, mash the fresh garlic, including the cut clove, and ½ teaspoon salt to a paste. Alternatively, mash the garlic to a paste right on the work surface: Using a chef's knife, mince the garlic with the salt. Placing the flat side of the knife almost parallel to the work surface, mash the garlic a little at a time by crushing and smearing it against the cutting board until it is completely reduced to a paste. Stir into the sauce.

Just before serving, stir in the reserved 1 tablespoon oil, without totally incorporating it.

IN ADVANCE You can make the Roasted Garlic Puree up to 3 days ahead and store, covered, in the refrigerator until you are ready to make the sauce. The sauce can be kept in a tightly sealed jar in the refrigerator for up to 5 days.

Mortar-Made Pesto Sauce

MAKES ABOUT
½ CUP; SERVES 4

Liguria's famous sauce has great character and finesse, with many permutations, depending on the sensibilities of the cook. Made as it should be in a mortar with a pestle, pesto is a very different sauce from the one most Americans know: The flavor of each element remains clear and distinct within a mellow, sweet, and creamy whole. This version, modeled closely after Ligurian sauces, uses a little less oil, pine nuts, and cheese than the classic but retains the richness and clarity of flavor. Surprisingly, it takes hardly any more time in a mortar than it does using a food processor.

In Liguria, pesto is made with small tender basil leaves, which give the sauce a finer texture and sweeter flavor. Here, where a lot of basil is sold in big bunches of huge tough leaves, there are several strategies for finding tender-leafed basil: Look for early-season (June and July) small-leaf basil in farmers' markets, or buy young basil plants (you can even find them in supermarkets), or buy several big-leafed bunches and pull off the small tender leaves that are hidden among them. (Use the tough leaves for making Basil Oil, page 592.) If you can find only very large or very tough leaves, remove the spine from the leaves by pulling the stem backward against the leaf; discard.

2 large bunches of small-leafed basil (see Headnote for other options)

1 garlic clove

¼ teaspoon kosher salt, or more to taste

3 tablespoons Italian pine nuts (pignoli)

3 tablespoons finely grated Parmigiano-Reggiano cheese

¼ cup fruity extra-virgin olive oil

Remove enough of the smallest and most tender basil leaves to make 4 cups loosely packed. If the leaves are gritty, wash them gently in several changes of water and dry them well in a salad spinner.

Cut the garlic clove lengthwise in half and remove the green sprout in the center, if any. In a large heavy mortar, combine the garlic and salt and crush to a paste. Gradually add the basil and, using a circular stirring motion, grind the leaves until they are almost a paste. Add the pine nuts and continue grinding the mixture against the sides and bottom of the mortar until it is a coarse puree. Work in the cheese; the mixture should have the texture of a thick paste. Dribble in the olive oil a little at a time, using the same circular motion, until the pesto is creamy. Adjust the salt if necessary.

The pesto is best when freshly made, but it can be refrigerated, with a sheet of plastic wrap pressed directly against the surface, for up to 3 days. IN ADVANCE

Pesto Sauce for Soups. Pesto is marvelous when spooned into hot vegetable soups, such as Simple Summer Soup with Pesto (page 401). Its flavor and perfume are released when it hits the hot liquid. variation

Omit the pine nuts and add 1 more tablespoon of oil.

Greek Garlic Sauce

Skordalia is Greece's version of the garlic sauce beloved in all Mediterranean countries. Because it is commonly made with a base of mashed potatoes, it has a fluffier texture and somewhat earthier flavor than garlic sauces, such as aïoli, that are based on egg yolks. It is one of life's perfect foods, combining the simplest elements—potatoes, garlic, and olive oil—into a hauntingly flavored sauce. **MAKES ABOUT 3 CUPS; SERVES 8**

My favorite ways of eating skordalia are as a sauce for cold sliced beets or with giant white lima beans, as they do in Greece, or on grilled peasant bread. It is equally good with any number of other vegetables, such as asparagus, cherry tomatoes, bell peppers, fennel, or artichoke hearts.

This recipe is roughly based on one my great-grandmother used to make, pounding the garlic in a mortar with an old wooden pestle. The challenge for me was to try to reduce the amount of olive oil she used (normally around 1 cup) while retaining the character of the sauce. My solution was to first mash the starchy potatoes with their flavorful cooking water, rather than olive oil, then drizzle in a small amount of fruity olive oil at the end. Since the potatoes have already absorbed all the liquid they need, the oil coats the potatoes giving them the desired texture and flavor.

Use fresh, firm garlic when making skordalia. Garlic that has sprouted will give it a bitter flavor.

> 1½ **pounds red or yellow waxy potatoes,** peeled and sliced
> into 2-inch chunks
>
> **1 teaspoon kosher salt,** or more to taste
>
> **5 garlic cloves,** or more to taste, peeled
>
> ⅓ **cup extra-virgin olive oil**
>
> **Freshly ground black pepper**

Place the potatoes in a medium saucepan with enough water to cover them by ½ inch, add ½ teaspoon of the salt, and bring to a boil over high heat. Cover, reduce the heat, and boil gently until the potatoes are tender, about 25 minutes. As the water evaporates, add enough to keep the potatoes covered.

While the potatoes are cooking, mash the garlic: With a chef's knife, mince the garlic with the remaining ½ teaspoon salt, then scrape and crush the garlic against the cutting board with the side of the knife until it is reduced to a paste. (Alternatively, the garlic and salt can be pounded in a mortar with a pestle.)

With a slotted spoon, transfer the cooked potatoes to a medium bowl; reserve the cooking water. Beat with an electric mixer on low speed until the potatoes are broken apart and look like a coarse meal. Add the mashed garlic. Gradually beat in up to 1 cup of the cooking water, until the potatoes are reduced to a loose, rather soupy puree. Stir in ¼ cup plus 1 teaspoon of the olive oil, salt to taste, and plenty of pepper.

Serve the skordalia warm or at room temperature. The intensity of the garlic and the balance of salt will change as the skordalia sits. If you find the garlic or salt flavor has diminished, add a little more to taste. You can also add more olive oil if you wish (at an additional 40 calories per teaspoon). Just before serving, drizzle the remaining 1 tablespoon olive oil over the puree.

IN ADVANCE The skordalia is best within 24 hours of being made, but it will keep for about 4 days, covered and refrigerated. Allow it to stand at room temperature for 2 hours before serving.

Everyday Mayonnaise

MAKES 1 CUP Real mayonnaise, made in a mortar with egg yolks, lemon juice, and very good oil, is an immensely satisfying sauce. It tastes of the egg yolks and the oil, yet has a flavor that is far more than the sum of these parts, at about 100 calories per tablespoon. Commercial mayonnaise, with the same amount of calories, pales by comparison. So-called light mayonnaise and the soy-based mayonnaises sold in health food stores often have an insipid chalky flavor (and 35 calories per tablespoon).

This alternative mayonnaise is made with silken tofu, lemon juice, and excellent extra-virgin olive oil. Tofu has a neutral flavor and provides the necessary creamy thickening that comes from the egg yolk emulsion and oil in the original. This mayonnaise has the flavor of good olive oil and about one third the calories and fat of classic mayonnaise. It is fine for everyday purposes, such as sandwiches and salads, and takes readily to any number of flavorings: for instance, fresh herbs, olive paste, and garlic.

If you cannot find silken tofu, you can make the recipe using soft tofu, which is slightly firmer. The mayonnaise will be denser, slightly less delicate in flavor, and more caloric. Rinse the tofu well, then blot dry on paper towels. Proceed as directed, using 3 tablespoons more oil.

You can find silken and soft tofu packaged in airtight plastic tubs in the produce section of most supermarkets (see page 115).

6 ounces silken tofu (¾ cup)

2 teaspoons fresh lemon juice

¼ teaspoon kosher salt, or more to taste

3 tablespoons extra-virgin olive oil or neutral vegetable oil, such as canola or grapeseed

Freshly ground black pepper

Rinse the tofu gently and blot dry with paper towels.

Spoon the tofu into a food processor, along with the lemon juice and salt. Process to a fine puree, about 1 minute. With the motor running, drizzle in the olive oil. Puree until the mayonnaise is perfectly smooth. Add pepper to taste and more salt if necessary.

The mayonnaise will keep for 1 week, covered and refrigerated.   IN ADVANCE

Herb Mayonnaise. Add 2 to 4 tablespoons minced fresh herbs, such   variation
as chives, basil, cilantro, or tarragon, or a combination.

Olive Mayonnaise. Olive paste, made from pounded, pitted green or   variation
black olives, adds an earthy Mediterranean flavor to mayonnaise. Add about
2 tablespoons olive paste, either homemade (page 683) or commercial, or
to taste.

Garlic Mayonnaise. Add 1 to 2 teaspoons smashed (not pressed)   variation
garlic (page 676) to taste.

CREAMY SAUCES.

COOL CREAMY SAUCES AND DRESSINGS.

One of the great fallacies of healthy cooking is that low-fat yogurt is a good substitute for heavy cream and crème fraîche. I've lost count of the recipes I've tried that play on this hopeful notion. Invariably, yogurt's assertive tang and milky texture can't live up to the luxurious expectations we have of real cream.

My compromise solution is a cold creamy sauce that has some fat, though much less than one made with real cream. I make a creamy base with regular or reduced-fat sour cream—which has at most half the calories and fat of heavy cream—and buttermilk, which is creamy, with less tang than yogurt, and very little fat. Flavored with fresh herbs, horseradish, or curry, the sauce has a true delicious satisfying flavor and texture.

Cool Creamy Sauces

A GUIDE TO IMPROVISING

MAKES ABOUT ½ TO ¾ CUP; SERVES ABOUT 4

Once you make up the base, you can flavor it with herbs, citrus zest, spices, even grated horseradish. The exact proportion of buttermilk to sour cream in the Creamy Base varies according to the flavors you add and what the sauce will be used for. For a thick, stand-alone sauce to serve alongside cooked poultry, meats, seafood, and vegetables, use twice as much sour cream as buttermilk. For a salad dressing, which will be a little thinner, use equal amounts of each.

Because the base will thicken slightly and become noticeably creamier after 24 hours, you can mix up a cupful to keep for quick sauces.

Reduced-fat sour creams contain starches and thickeners to give them a texture similar to full-fat sour cream, with varying degrees of success. I never use nonfat sour cream, because it has a gluey texture and off flavor. If you can't get a reduced-fat sour cream that tastes good, use real sour cream. It will add only a few more calories per serving.

If you have a source for quark, the soft unripened cheese with a sour cream–like texture and flavor yet remarkably low in calories and fat, use it instead of the sour cream and buttermilk.

Creamy Base

   ¼ to ½ cup regular or reduced-fat sour cream

   ¼ cup buttermilk

Flavorings, singly or in combination, such as

   1 to 2 tablespoons minced fresh herbs

   1 tablespoon dried spices or Flavor Essence (pages 542–548) plus 1 tablespoon hot water

   2 to 3 teaspoons grated citrus zest

   ¼ cup grated horseradish, well drained and juices pressed out

2 to 3 teaspoons vinegar or fresh lemon or lime juice

½ teaspoon sugar

Pinch of kosher salt

Freshly ground black pepper

1. To make this creamy base, combine the sour cream and buttermilk in a small bowl.

2. If you are using dried spices or a Flavor Essence, toast them in a small heavy skillet over low heat until fragrant. Moisten with the hot water and let steep for 5 minutes.

3. Stir the flavorings, vinegar, sugar, salt, and pepper to taste into the creamy base. Refrigerate for at least 30 minutes before serving to let the flavors marry.

You can make the base up to 5 days ahead and store, covered, in the refrigerator. These sauces will keep for up to 3 days.   **IN ADVANCE**

Herb Cream

This creamy herb sauce is a model for many sauces you can improvise using equal parts buttermilk and sour cream. You can use just about any combination of fresh herbs, although soft-leafed herbs like basil, cilantro, flat-leaf parsley, chervil, tarragon, and chives work best.   **MAKES ABOUT ⅔ CUP; SERVES 4**

A cream of mixed herbs—such as basil, chives, and tarragon—is wonderful on juicy vegetables like tomatoes, cucumbers, or roasted peppers. Tarragon cream with a teaspoon of roasted walnut oil mixed in is delicious on thinly shaved raw fennel. A chive cream is perfection on sliced cucumbers, and a dollop of cilantro cream is lovely in corn soups.

Creamy Base

¼ cup regular or reduced-fat sour cream

¼ cup buttermilk

Pinch of kosher salt

Freshly ground black pepper

2 to 3 teaspoons vinegar: cider, white wine, or Champagne

½ to 1 teaspoon sugar, or to taste

2 tablespoons minced fresh chives, basil, or cilantro
or 1 tablespoon minced fresh tarragon

To make this creamy base, in a small bowl, whisk together the sour cream, buttermilk, salt, and pepper to taste.

Whisk in the vinegar and sugar. Stir in the herbs. Cover and refrigerate for 30 minutes before using to mellow the flavors.

IN ADVANCE   You can make the base up to 5 days ahead and store, covered, in the refrigerator. The Herb Cream will keep for up to 3 days refrigerated.

variation   **Curry Cream.** Mildly spicy Curry Cream is especially good on thinly sliced, lightly salted peeled cucumbers, potatoes, warm oysters or mussels (see Shellfish Cooked in an Iron Skillet, page 250), cold shrimp, and Slow Roasted (page 224) or Pan-Smoked Salmon (page 268).

In a small heavy skillet, toast 1 tablespoon Sandy's Curry Powder (page 548) or commercial curry powder over low heat until fragrant. Transfer to a small bowl and stir in 1 tablespoon hot water to moisten. Let sit for 5 minutes. Stir this into the creamy base. Omit the herbs; reduce the vinegar to 1 to 2 teaspoons (or omit) and reduce the sugar to ¼ teaspoon. Add ½ teaspoon minced shallots or fresh chives and ¼ teaspoon grated fresh ginger.

variation   **Mustard Cream.** This sauce is especially good on grated celery root, boiled potatoes, brisket, cold roast beef, and smoked fish. Omit the herbs. Use 1 to 2 teaspoons cider or Champagne vinegar (or fresh lemon juice) and ½ teaspoon sugar. Add 1 tablespoon Dijon or grainy mustard and ½ teaspoon minced shallot.

variation   **Chipotle Adobo Cream.** Flavored with adobo, the pungent, slightly smoky tomato sauce that accompanies canned chipotle chiles, this cream is at once cooling and fiery. It is a perfect accompaniment to Mexican and Southwestern foods, such as Corn Soup with Chiles, Lime, and Cilantro

Cream (instead of the cream) (page 390), or tacos, as well as steak or roast pork sandwiches. Or use it as a dressing for roasted onions, grilled shrimp, or fresh sliced tomatoes. Its heat depends on how much adobo you add. (See page 558 for information on chipotles in adobo sauce.)

Omit the vinegar and herbs and reduce the sugar to a pinch. Add 2 to 3 teaspoons adobo sauce.

Apple, Cucumber, or Green Mango Raita

Raitas are Indian yogurt sauces that, in a hot climate with a spicy cuisine, are meant to be cooling and refreshing. There are many kinds of raitas. Most are based on some kind of mild juicy vegetable or fruit, such as cucumber, green apples, or underripe mangoes, and herbs. Sometimes I use only cilantro as the herbal component; more often, a combination of cilantro, mint, and basil. Serve raitas with spicy foods, and grilled fish, shrimp, and lobster.

MAKES ABOUT 1 ½ CUPS; SERVES 6

½ **teaspoon cumin seeds**

1 cup plain whole-milk or sheep's milk (see Headnote, page 630) **yogurt**

⅛ **to** ¼ **teaspoon kosher salt**

Pinch of cayenne pepper

¼ **teaspoon grated fresh ginger**

1 medium Granny Smith apple, peeled, cored, and cut into ¼-inch dice, **or 1 medium cucumber,** peeled, seeded, and cut into ¼-inch dice, **or 1 green mango,** peeled, pitted, and cut into ¼-inch dice

2 tablespoons minced fresh cilantro, mint, or basil, in any combination

Kosher salt and freshly ground black pepper

A few drops fresh lemon juice

In a small skillet, toast the cumin seeds over low heat until very fragrant. Transfer to a mortar, spice grinder, or blender, and coarsely grind. In a medium bowl, combine the yogurt, pinch of salt, cayenne, ginger, and toasted cumin. Fold in the apple. Up to 3 hours before serving, stir in the fresh herbs. Adjust the seasonings and add a little lemon juice to lift the flavors, if necessary.

Store the raita in a covered bowl in the refrigerator for up to 2 days.

IN ADVANCE

Yogurt Sauce with Toasted Spices, Lime Zest, and Basil

MAKES 1 CUP

This deceptively simple recipe from chef Gray Kunz is an example of the magic of a few well-chosen ingredients artfully combined. The flavor of the yogurt is essential to the sauce and provides the base for an unusual combination of flavors: cumin, coriander, and cardamom in league with fresh basil, lime, and jalapeño.

This sauce is wonderful on fresh or cooked vegetables and grilled seafood and spectacular with Pan-Smoked Salmon (page 268); a cup would be enough for 4 to 6 servings. For an unusual dessert, serve it on sliced ripe honeydew or Persian melon.

To duplicate whole-milk yogurt, mix equal parts low-fat yogurt and regular or reduced-fat sour cream.

Use whole-milk yogurt for this sauce, preferably sheep's milk yogurt, which is extremely creamy and luxurious. The acidity and lack of body typical of nonfat and many low-fat yogurts would undermine the sauce.

Scant ½ teaspoon cumin seeds

4 coriander seeds

Seeds from 1 cardamom pod

1 cup whole-milk or sheep's milk yogurt

8 fresh basil leaves, finely chopped

½ small serrano or jalapeño chile, seeded and minced

1 teaspoon finely grated lime zest

⅛ teaspoon sugar

Pinch of kosher salt

Freshly ground black pepper

In a small skillet, toast the cumin, coriander, and cardamom seeds over moderate heat until fragrant. Set aside to cool slightly.

In a blender or a spice grinder, grind the toasted spices to a fine powder. Strain the powder through a fine sieve into a small bowl.

In a medium bowl, combine the yogurt, basil, jalapeño, lime zest, sugar, and ½ teaspoon of the spice powder or more to taste. Stir in the salt and pepper to taste. Refrigerate for 30 minutes before serving to let the flavors marry.

IN ADVANCE This sauce is best served the day it is made, but it will keep for up to 2 days in the refrigerator, with a slight fading of flavor.

Russian Dressing

This radically lightened Russian dressing is wonderful on old-fashioned salads, such as hearts of romaine or iceberg, on sliced tomatoes, and on turkey or roast beef sandwiches.

MAKES 1¼ CUPS

½ **cup regular or reduced-fat sour cream**
½ **cup buttermilk**
¼ **cup plus 1½ teaspoons chili sauce**
1 teaspoon minced shallot or scallion, white part only
¼ **to 1 teaspoon prepared horseradish,** drained and liquid squeezed out
¼ **teaspoon kosher salt**

In a small bowl, whisk all the ingredients together. Cover and refrigerate for at least 1 hour to let the flavors meld.

The dressing can be kept in a tightly sealed jar in the refrigerator for up to 1 week.

IN ADVANCE

Louis Dressing. Crab Louis, created in San Francisco at the turn of the nineteenth century, is one of the most delicious of crab salads, dressed with a mayonnaise spiked with chili sauce and scallions. For a lovely light Louis dressing to use on 2 pounds cooked shelled crab, shrimp, or lobster, omit the buttermilk and horseradish, use the scallion, and increase the sour cream to ¾ cup. Stir in 3 tablespoons chopped fresh flat-leaf parsley and 2 teaspoons finely chopped fresh tarragon.

variation

Roquefort or Maytag
Blue Cheese Dressing

MAKES ¾ CUP Bottled blue cheese dressing averages about 70 calories per tablespoon. My alternative is made with fine aged blue cheese—real French Roquefort or American Maytag Blue—and scented with sherry vinegar and walnut oil. It is slightly thinner than the old-fashioned thick "bleu cheese dressing," but the flavor is much better.

2 ounces crumbly aged blue cheese, such as Roquefort or Maytag Blue

⅓ **cup buttermilk**

¼ **cup reduced-fat sour cream**

¾ **teaspoon sherry vinegar**

½ **teaspoon roasted walnut oil** (optional)

Freshly ground black pepper

In a food processor or blender, combine the cheese, buttermilk, and vinegar, and process until the mixture is smooth and creamy, about 1 minute. Transfer to a jar and stir in the sour cream, walnut oil, if using, and pepper to taste. Cover and refrigerate until ready to use.

IN ADVANCE The dressing will keep, refrigerated, for up to 1 week.

WARM CREAMY SAUCES.

Warm creamy sauces are all about indulgence and the soothing comforts of cream and butter, which provide inimitable flavor and richness. Removing them altogether, as some cooks are wont to do, seems like a false economy, stripping away the true pleasures of a dish in the name of health.

My solution is compromise, not austerity. To reduce the amount of fat in a warm creamy sauce to sane levels, you can use mild-flavored vegetables that puree into a creamy sauce, or a starch, such as rice, which, when cooked in milk, purees into a creamy liquid with a buttery flavor. I never eliminate fat altogether; some is essential to achieve the satisfactions of real cream sauce. This might mean using whole milk or stirring in a tablespoon or two of cream at the end—whatever it takes to make it wonderful.

Rice Cream

The idea for a rice-based "cream" came out of a conversation with Margaret Fox, of Café Beaujolais in Mendocino, who has devised many innovative techniques for heart-healthy cuisine. She found that pureed rice, with its fine starch, works well as a thickener for soups, imparting a suave texture with a creamy effect and a surprisingly buttery flavor. I used rice flour—made from finely ground white rice—in milk to create a creamy sauce that is buttery and light, yet has enough body to coat foods like a traditional flour-thickened cream sauce without the butter.

Use Rice Cream in recipes where a classic béchamel sauce or cream reduction is called for, such as Macaroni and Cheese (page 153) and creamed pearl onions, or make a creamed spinach by heating steamed spinach (with all water squeezed out) with some Rice Cream and a few scrapings of nutmeg.

A ½ cup of plain Rice Cream will sauce a 1-cup serving of cooked pasta, vegetables, or poultry. When Rice Cream is enriched with roasted garlic, cheese, or cream, ¼ cup is enough to sauce 1 cup. I use whole milk rather than low-fat milk because it gives so much more creaminess to the sauce for only a few additional calories—a worthwhile compromise. If you wish to use low-fat milk, bear in mind that it will produce a sweeter sauce.

There is no limit to the ways you can flavor Rice Cream—from minced herbs, such as tarragon, chives, and basil to spices such as curry powder or nutmeg.

White rice flour is available at health food stores and can be kept in a plastic bag in the freezer for up to 6 months.

MAKES 2 CUPS; SERVES 4 TO 8

You can enrich Rice Cream with a little heavy cream or crème fraîche and use it like heavy cream, at half as many calories. Add 1 tablespoon cream per ¼ cup Rice Cream.

> 2 tablespoons plus 1 teaspoon white rice flour
>
> 2 ¼ cups whole milk
>
> 1 small shallot or onion, peeled and stuck with 1 whole clove
>
> ¼ teaspoon kosher salt
>
> 1 small imported bay leaf
>
> Freshly ground white pepper

Rinse out a small saucepan with cold water. (This keeps the milk from sticking.) Add the rice flour. With a whisk, gradually whisk in enough milk to make a thick paste. Then continue to whisk in the remaining milk until smooth. Add the shallot, salt, and bay leaf. Bring to a boil over very low heat, whisking frequently. Simmer for 10 minutes, or until the mixture has the consistency of thick cream. Strain through a fine sieve. Stir in white pepper to taste. Cover and refrigerate until ready to use.

Alternatively, to substitute long-grain white rice for the rice flour, cook it in the milk until it is very soft, about 45 minutes. Strain, reserving the milk. Puree the rice in a blender, adding the milk a little at a time and then letting the machine run 1 minute, until you have a perfectly smooth sauce. Strain the sauce through a sieve and proceed as directed above.

IN ADVANCE Rice Cream will keep for 5 days refrigerated. (It does not freeze well, because the starch breaks down, thinning out the sauce.)

variation **Roasted Garlic Cream.** This cream is especially good on filled pastas, such as ravioli and tortellini, and in pasta and vegetable gratins.

In a food processor or blender, blend 1 cup Rice Cream with ½ to ⅔ cup Roasted Garlic Puree (page 38), 1 teaspoon fresh lemon juice, and kosher salt and pepper to taste. (Makes 1½ cups.)

variation **Cheese Sauces.** You need only a little of a strongly flavored cheese such as Gorgonzola, Parmigiano-Reggiano, Dry (aged) Jack, or sharp Cheddar or a goat cheese such as Bûcheron to turn Rice Cream into a rich cheese sauce. Gorgonzola sauce is spectacular on pumpkin-filled ravioli and roasted polenta (page 201), and Dry Jack or sharp Cheddar cheese sauces are wonderful on cooked broccoli and cauliflower.

In a small saucepan, combine 1 cup Rice Cream and 2 ounces cheese, grated, shredded, or crumbled. Pepper generously. Heat over low heat until hot but not boiling. (Makes 1½ cups.)

Leek and Saffron Cream

MAKES 2 CUPS;
SERVES ABOUT 10 There are several techniques at work in this velvety sauce. First, the leeks are cooked slowly in milk with a little butter until they melt; when pureed, they both thicken and flavor the sauce. Then rice flour or white rice is added, lending further creaminess and a buttery flavor. The fats are carefully chosen to achieve the maximum effect with a minimum of fat and calories: in this case, a little butter and crème fraîche in fractional amounts.

This sauce is so rich that a 3-tablespoon serving—at an astonishing 60 calories—is ample to sauce a 6-ounce portion of seafood. It is perfect with pan-seared sea scallops and poached, grilled, or pan-seared fish fillets. Nap a dinner plate with the sauce and then arrange the fish or seafood on top.

4 medium leeks, white and pale green parts only

1 tablespoon water

1 teaspoon unsalted butter

Large pinch of saffron (about 1 teaspoon)

1 tablespoon rice flour or long-grain white rice

2 cups whole milk

¼ to ½ cup unsalted homemade (page 574)
or canned low-sodium chicken broth

3 tablespoons crème fraîche or heavy cream

½ teaspoon kosher salt

Freshly ground white pepper

Slice the leeks crosswise into very thin circles (you should have about 2½ cups). Separate them and rinse them in several changes of cold water to remove any grit. Drain well.

Place the leeks in a heavy medium saucepan, add the water, butter, and saffron, cover, and cook over moderately low heat, stirring occasionally, until the leeks are wilted and soft, about 10 minutes.

If you are using rice flour, place it in a small bowl and whisk it with a little of the cold milk to make a smooth paste. Add the remaining milk, ¼ cup of the chicken broth, and the rice or rice flour mixture to the leeks, increase the heat to moderate, and bring to a boil, stirring frequently. Reduce the heat to a bare simmer, partially cover, and cook for 30 minutes, stirring frequently, until the leeks and rice are puree-tender. Don't worry if the sauce looks curdled. Remove from the heat.

In a blender, blend half the leek mixture to a fine puree with the consistency of heavy cream, at least 1 minute. If the sauce is too thick, add a little of the remaining chicken broth. Transfer to a bowl and then puree the remaining leek mixture for 1 minute. Add the first puree and blend for 1 or 2 minutes longer. Return the sauce to the saucepan and reheat gently. Stir in the crème fraîche and season with the salt and white pepper to taste. Serve warm.

IN ADVANCE You can slice the leeks and cook them in the butter up to a day ahead. Store in a covered container in the refrigerator. Reheat before proceeding. The prepared sauce will keep for up to 5 days covered and refrigerated. Reheat before serving, allowing the sauce to boil for 1 minute.

WINE SAUCES.

RICH RED WINE AND VINEGAR SAUCES.

For years I rarely bothered to make the red wine sauces at home I had made routinely as a cook in French restaurants because I lacked long-cooked veal stock, the essential ingredient that gives many of these sauces their silky texture and resonant flavor. Then I learned some radical new techniques from professional chefs for making rich, winy sauces at home. They all are variations on a theme: highly reducing full-bodied wines, such as red wine or port, or balsamic vinegar, to a syrup with an extremely concentrated flavor. In some, chicken broth or aromatic vegetables are added to temper the roughness of the wine and mellow the sauce. All have the limpid syrupy texture of traditional red wine sauces, with deep concentrated flavor. All are extraordinarily easy to make.

These go with many foods, especially grilled, roasted, or pan-seared meats and game. Even when I have the energy only to pan-sear some lamb chops or a steak, I'll warm a tablespoon of Port Wine Sauce to accompany them, and make a simple, elegant meal. I also use these with more robustly flavored vegetable and pasta dishes.

Balsamic Syrup

MAKES ABOUT ½ CUP

This is the simplest sauce I know. It has only one ingredient and requires no effort other than pouring liquid into a pan. When boiled down to a concentrated syrup, ordinary supermarket balsamic vinegar is transformed into a luscious sauce with a caramelized sweet-and-sour flavor that goes well with many foods. Serve it with grilled sirloin steak or pork chops, pan-seared salmon, and roasted vegetables. Or drizzle a little over a food—from grilled cheese sandwiches to a tomato-based pasta sauce to a rich stew—to give it a little hit of piquant flavor. Many chefs swirl unsalted butter or olive oil into reduced balsamic to further mellow it and give it body, but I think it is fine without this embellishment.

If you don't want to reduce a whole bottle, reduce any quantity down to one quarter of the amount you start with: For example, reduce 1 cup to ¼ cup.

One 16.9-ounce bottle balsamic vinegar

In a heavy 1-quart saucepan, bring the balsamic vinegar to a boil over moderate heat. Boil until the vinegar has reduced to about ½ cup. It will be very syrupy, with big shiny bubbles. Watch it carefully as it approaches this point, as it can burn easily. Remove from the heat. Serve warm. (If the reduced vinegar gets too thick as it cools, heat it slowly with 1 to 2 tablespoons water until it is the right consistency.)

The syrup will keep indefinitely in a tightly closed jar at room temperature.   IN ADVANCE

Port Wine Sauce

This concentrated essence of port wine tastes as if it took many hours to make, yet it is actually very simple and versatile, since it goes with many grilled, roasted, or seared meats, poultry, or game, as well as risottos and salmon. It is so intense that 2 tablespoons is an ample serving.   MAKES ½ TO ⅔ CUP; SERVES ABOUT 4

To finish the sauce, you can add 1 teaspoon per serving of a Flavored Oil (pages 588–597), brown butter (page 681), or hazelnut oil. This will cause the sauce to separate on the plate, forming a beautiful "broken" pattern.

> **One 750-milliliter bottle imported ruby port**
> **2 shallots,** thinly sliced
> **½ cup unsalted homemade** (page 574)
> **or canned low-sodium chicken broth**

In a heavy medium saucepan, combine the port and shallots and bring to a gentle boil over moderately low heat. Cook until the port has reduced to 1 cup, about 30 minutes.

Strain into a small saucepan and add the chicken broth. Bring to a boil, reduce the heat to a simmer, and cook until reduced to ½ to ⅔ cup, about 15 minutes longer. Serve hot.

The sauce will keep up to 1 month refrigerated in a tightly closed jar.   IN ADVANCE

Port and Olive Sauce. Adding pitted chopped olives to the sauce makes a version of a classic red wine–olive sauce that goes well with duck breasts and lamb.   variation

Add 4 ounces Kalamata or Gaeta olives (about ½ cup), pitted (see page 683) and sliced, 2 crushed juniper berries, and 1 sprig fresh thyme during the last 5 minutes of cooking. Discard the thyme before serving.

variation **Port and Dried Cherry Sauce.** This sauce goes well with game birds, such as quail and guinea hen, duck, and pork.

Add 4 ounces dried cherries (about ¾ cup), 1 juniper berry, crushed, and 1 sprig of fresh thyme during the last 10 minutes of cooking. Discard the thyme before serving.

Brown Butter and Balsamic Sauce

MAKES ¼ CUP;
SERVES 4

I am a big fan of brown butter: sweet butter that is cooked slowly in a heavy pan until it gradually begins to "toast." It gains a rich nutty flavor and seems somehow more buttery. To make it into a quick savory sauce, I splash in some balsamic vinegar, which caramelizes slightly, and whose sweet mild acidity balances the richness of the butter. Because the sauce has such a concentrated flavor, I add a little chicken broth, which forms an emulsion that extends the small amount of butter.

Use this to sauce roasted or pan-seared fish, cooked beans, polenta, wild rice, and just about any cooked vegetable, including leeks, potatoes, beets, parsnips, string beans, and sweet potatoes.

> **2 tablespoons unsalted butter**
>
> **2 tablespoons balsamic vinegar**
>
> **2 tablespoons unsalted homemade** (page 574) **or canned low-sodium chicken or vegetable broth**
>
> **Pinch of kosher salt**
>
> **Freshly ground black pepper**

In a small heavy skillet, cook the butter over moderate heat until it takes on a rich golden brown color and smells of roasted hazelnuts, about 2 minutes. Remove from the heat and add the balsamic vinegar; stand back, as the butter will splutter violently.

When the butter stops spluttering, return it to the heat and add the chicken broth. Increase the heat and boil for 30 seconds to emulsify the sauce. Add the salt and pepper to taste and serve hot.

IN ADVANCE

You can store the sauce, covered, in the refrigerator up to 1 week. Before serving, bring to a simmer in a small heavy saucepan.

Red Wine Essence

This extravagant and delicious sauce is adapted from one created by chef Charlie Trotter. It is extravagant because it calls for two bottles of red wine and one bottle of port. It is worth every penny. The resulting reduction yields a rich, mellow essence of wine so highly concentrated that only a small amount— a tablespoon or two—is necessary to sauce a serving. It can transform simple foods such as roasts of lamb, beef, or venison or chicken. It never fails to wow my guests and make them think it required hours—and immense skill— to make. Yet the sauce is simple to prepare and can be made ahead of time.

Use a medium-bodied wine with good fruit and little tannin, such as a Pinot Noir.

MAKES 1 CUP

This sauce is a good way to make use of the "ends" of leftover bottles of red wine. Collect them in a single bottle and store, corked, in the refrigerator to use in cooking.

1 medium onion, coarsely chopped

1 carrot, peeled and coarsely chopped

1 rib celery, coarsely chopped

2 garlic cloves, smashed

1 apple, coarsely chopped

2 teaspoons flavorless vegetable oil, preferably grapeseed

Two 750-milliliter bottles dry red wine

One 750-milliliter bottle ruby port

1 cup unsalted homemade (page 574) **or canned low-sodium chicken broth**

In a heavy large saucepan, combine the onion, carrot, celery, garlic, apple, and oil, cover, and cook, stirring occasionally, until the vegetables have begun to release their juices, about 8 minutes. Uncover, increase the heat to moderate, and sauté the vegetables, stirring frequently, until caramelized to a deep golden brown.

Add the wine and port, increase the heat to high, and bring to a boil. Turn the heat down to a low boil and reduce the wine, to about 1 cup, about 2 hours.

Strain the wine into a small saucepan and add the chicken broth. Bring to a boil, reduce the heat to a simmer, and cook until reduced to 1 cup, about 45 minutes longer. (Or, for an even more concentrated flavor, reduce the sauce to ½ cup.) Serve hot.

The sauce will keep for up to 1 month refrigerated in a tightly closed jar.

IN ADVANCE

Distinct from the *vin ordinaire* balsamic vinegars commonly used in vinaigrettes are the rarified artisan-made balsamics, so intense and rich that a few drops are all that you need as a perfect finishing touch to any number of foods. The flavor is deeply complex and luscious, resembling old port with suggestions of caramel and wood, yet with a subtle acidity and sweetness. A small bottle can cost from $75 for twelve-year-old balsamic to $175 for Extra Vecchio, aged at least twenty-five years. Since you use so little, a bottle lasts a long time.

These true balsamic vinegars are made only in Emilia-Romagna's provinces of Modena and Reggio by traditional methods that date back a thousand years. A concentrate of must from wine grapes is fermented and mellowed for many years in progressively smaller wooden barrels made of different woods, each of which imparts its own flavor.

These great balsamics are never cooked. They are best used sparingly on simple foods: deep-fried fish and vegetables, grilled and roasted meats and game, steamed or roasted lobster, beans, polenta, risotto, roasted peppers, tomatoes, and, more remarkably, sweets such as caramelized custards, apple tarts, and vanilla ice cream. They are sublime on fresh fruits, such as ripe melons, peaches, pears, and, especially, cherries. Small chunks of young Parmigiano-Reggiano cheese and thin slices of prosciutto di Parma adorned with a few drops of aged balsamic make a lovely hors d'oeuvre.

BEURRE BLANC–STYLE BUTTER SAUCES.

In the classic French sauce beurre blanc, cold sweet butter is whisked into a concentrated essence of white wine, vinegar, and shallots to form a luxuriously creamy emulsion. However, the sauce has an inordinate amount of fat, about 100 calories per tablespoon. After many experiments, I developed a lighter version that uses the technique for making another classic sauce, beurre fondu—boiling cold butter with a liquid to form a light creamy sauce that has about one quarter of the calories of beurre blanc.

The quality of the butter is essential to its success. Use only unsalted butter that has a fresh, sweet aroma. You might splurge on small-batch "artisanal" butter, such as an organic cultured butter, or Normandy butter imported from France. These butters contain less water than commercial butters and tend to have a clearer, creamier flavor.

Arrowroot, powdered starch from a tropical tuber, is the only thickener I have found that can closely achieve the texture of a true beurre blanc. It stabilizes the sauce and makes it much less prone to separating on standing, a common problem with the classic version.

Beurre Blanc–Style Butter Sauces

A GUIDE TO IMPROVISING

This basic formula can be followed using many combinations of broths, wines, and vinegars. See the Port Wine Butter Sauce on page 644, for example, made with wild mushroom broth, port, and aged sherry vinegar. There is no limit to possible flavorings you can add; saffron, ginger, vanilla, curry powder, citrus zest, or fresh herbs. The Shallot-and-Vinegar Butter Sauce (page 643) is close to a classic beurre blanc. It makes an excellent base for many flavorings.

MAKES 1 CUP;
SERVES 6

1½ teaspoons arrowroot

1½ cups broth, such as Quick Leek Broth (see page 642) or any of the broths on pages 568–578

3½ tablespoons cold unsalted butter

2 to 4 tablespoons minced shallots

1½ cups wine (dry white wine is the norm, but dessert and fortified wines like port and Madeira are also possibilities)

Up to ¼ cup good-quality vinegar, such as Champagne, white wine, sherry, or Banyuls (the amount will depend on the acidity of both wine and vinegar)

Flavorings (optional), singly or in combination, such as

    Large pinch of saffron threads, crumbled

    1 vanilla bean, split lengthwise in half

    2 teaspoons minced fresh ginger

    Dried spices, such as 2 cardamom pods, crushed, or 1 teaspoon curry powder

    2 strips orange, tangerine, or lemon zest (removed with a vegitable peeler)

1 tablespoon heavy cream

Kosher salt and freshly ground white pepper

About ½ teaspoon honey or sugar

2 to 3 tablespoons finely chopped fresh herbs (optional), such as basil, chervil, tarragon, or cilantro

1. In a small bowl, combine the arrowroot with 2 tablespoons of the broth, stirring until smooth. Reserve.

2. In a small saucepan, combine 1½ teaspoons of the butter and the shallots, cover, and cook over low heat until very soft, about 5 minutes. Pour in the wine, the remaining broth, and the vinegar and add any flavorings. Bring to a boil and cook until the liquid has reduced to 1 cup, about 25 minutes. Remove the vanilla bean or citrus zest, if you used it.

3. Stir ¼ cup of the hot broth into the arrowroot mixture, then whisk this into the pan. Simmer for 2 minutes, or until thickened. Whisk in the remaining 3 tablespoons butter and the heavy cream and cook until the sauce is thick enough to coat the back of a spoon. Season to taste with salt and white pepper, and stir in enough honey to round out the acidity without adding any sweetness. Serve at once, or keep warm in a double boiler. Stir in the herbs, if desired, just before serving.

an improvisation
Leftover Butter Sauces

When chilled, this sauce thickens to the consistency of a mayonnaise and its flavor greatly intensifies. A little goes a long way. Spooned into the center of omelets, it melts to make a delicious quick filling. It is a great spread for sandwiches or dipping sauce for cold shellfish. Or use it instead of butter to dress noodles or vegetables or to mix into mashed potatoes. I usually allow about 1 teaspoon for each serving.

QUICK LEEK BROTH FOR BEURRE BLANC–STYLE BUTTER SAUCES

Although you can use many different broths when improvising a beurre blanc–style butter sauce, this quick leek broth works with a wide range of flavorings. In a small heavy saucepan, combine 1 large leek, white and pale green part only, thinly sliced and thoroughly rinsed, 1 shallot chopped, ½ ounce prosciutto, ½ teaspoon unsalted butter, and 2½ cups water. Bring to a boil, reduce the heat to a simmer, and cook until reduced to 1½ cups, 35 minutes. Strain. The broth can be made ahead and refrigerated for up to 2 days or frozen for up to 2 months.

Shallot-and-Vinegar Butter Sauce

This adaptation of the classic beurre blanc will turn any mild, light-fleshed fish, such as trout, Chilean sea bass, striped bass, grouper, or pike, and shellfish such as scallops or lobster—poached, roasted, or pan-seared—into a marvelous and very complete dish. Try it with Slow-Roasted Fish (page 224), Shellfish Cooked in an Iron Skillet (page 250), Roasted or Grilled Whole Fish (page 217), or Oven-Seared Thick Fish Fillets (page 222). It is also a lovely sauce for Steam-Roasted Leeks (page 58). It lends itself to endless flavorings and elaborations, as the variations that follow illustrate.

1½ teaspoons arrowroot

Quick Leek Broth (page 642)

3½ tablespoons cold unsalted butter

3 tablespoons minced shallots (2 medium)

1½ cups dry full-boiled white wine

3 tablespoons Champagne vinegar or fine white wine vinegar

1 tablespoon heavy cream or crème fraîche
(or 1½ teaspoons additional cold butter)

About ½ teaspoon honey or sugar

¼ teaspoon kosher salt

Freshly ground white pepper

Combine the arrowroot and 2 tablespoons of the broth in a small bowl, stirring until smooth. Set aside.

In a small saucepan, combine 1½ teaspoons of the butter and the shallots, cover, and cook over low heat until very soft, about 5 minutes. Add the wine, the remaining broth, and the vinegar and bring to a boil over high heat. Reduce the heat slightly and boil until the sauce reduces to 1 cup, about 25 minutes.

Stir ¼ cup of the hot broth into the arrowroot mixture, then whisk this mixture into the saucepan. Simmer for 2 minutes, or until the sauce has thickened enough to lightly coat the back of a spoon. Whisk in the remaining 3 tablespoons butter and the heavy cream. Stir in the sugar, salt, and white pepper to taste.

IN ADVANCE The sauce can be made up to 30 minutes ahead and kept warm in the top of a double boiler over hot, not boiling, water. See page 680 for improvising a double boiler. For using any leftovers, see page 642.

variation **Vanilla Butter Sauce.** This sauce, surprisingly, is the ultimate dipping sauce for cooked crustaceans such as steamed lobster (see page 264), crayfish, shrimp, and crab. The vanilla brings out the sweetness of their flesh.

Split 1 vanilla bean lengthwise in half and scrape out the seeds. Add the seeds and pod to the saucepan along with the wine, broth, and vinegar. Use honey instead of sugar. Remove and discard the vanilla pod before serving.

variation **Sorrel Butter Sauce.** Sorrel, a tender green herb with a tart lemony flavor, has an affinity for seafood, particularly salmon. When cooked, it falls apart into a suave puree that melts into any sauce.

Wash and dry 3 cups sorrel leaves. Cut them crosswise into the thinnest possible strips. Just before adding the cold butter to the sauce, stir in the sorrel and simmer until it has reduced to a puree, about 1 minute. Finish the sauce as directed, adding 2 to 3 teaspoons fresh lemon juice if desired to accentuate the tart flavor of the sorrel.

variation **Herb Butter Sauce.** The floral flavors of Gewürztraminer wine in tandem with fresh herbs make a butter sauce that is particularly good with shellfish, such as oysters and shrimp, and seafood sausages.

Substitute Gewürztraminer for the dry white wine. Add 2 tablespoons minced fresh chives, basil, flat-leaf parsley, and/or chervil, in any combination, just before serving.

Port Wine Butter Sauce

**MAKES 1 CUP;
SERVES 6**

A sauce created by the late Gilbert Le Coze of Le Bernardin in New York City was the inspiration for this combination of wild mushroom broth, port wine, and aged sherry vinegar. Far more robust than white wine-based butter sauces, it can stand up to heartier flavors, from grilled portobello mushrooms to chicken and mild-flavored game such as pheasant, guinea hen, and rabbit. It is especially delicious with meaty seafood, such as salmon, striped bass, sea bass, or sea scallops, that has been crusted with spices or wild mushrooms. Le Coze served his full-tilt version of this sauce with striped bass fillets that had been crusted with Chinese five-spice powder, a startling combination. I love it with Mushroom-Crusted Bass (page 246).

Quick Mushroom Broth (or substitute 1½ cups Faux Veal Broth, page 572)

> **2 cups unsalted homemade** (page 574) **or canned low-sodium chicken broth**
>
> **1 small shallot,** thinly sliced
>
> **½ ounce** (about ½ cup) **dried wild mushrooms,** preferably porcini

2 tablespoons minced shallots

4 tablespoons cold unsalted butter

1½ cups imported ruby port

3 tablespoons sherry vinegar, preferably aged

1½ teaspoons arrowroot

½ teaspoon sugar

Kosher salt and freshly ground white pepper

½ to 1 teaspoon fresh lemon juice

To make the mushroom broth, in a heavy medium saucepan, combine the chicken broth, shallot, and dried mushrooms. Bring to a boil over moderate heat, reduce the heat, and simmer until reduced to 1½ cups, about 20 minutes.

Strain the broth through a fine strainer into a measuring cup or a bowl; discard the solids. Let the broth sit undisturbed for 5 minutes to let any grit from the mushrooms settle to the bottom. Transfer 2 tablespoons of the broth to a small bowl, and set aside.

In a small saucepan, combine the shallots with 1 teaspoon of the butter, cover, and cook over low heat until very soft, about 5 minutes. Add the port and vinegar. Slowly pour in the mushroom broth from the measuring cup, leaving any grit in the bottom of the cup. Bring to a boil over high heat, reduce the heat slightly, and boil until the liquid has reduced to 1 cup, about 25 minutes.

Meanwhile, stir the arrowroot into the reserved 2 tablespoons broth until smooth. Stir ¼ cup of the hot broth mixture into the arrowroot mixture, then whisk this into the pan. Simmer for 2 minutes, or until the sauce has thickened. Whisk in the remaining 3 tablespoons plus 2 teaspoons butter. Stir in the sugar and salt, white pepper, and lemon juice to taste.

IN ADVANCE You can make the mushroom broth up to 2 days ahead and refrigerate it. Heat just before finishing the sauce. The sauce can be made up to 30 minutes ahead and kept warm in the top of a double boiler over hot, not boiling, water. See page 680 for improvising a double boiler. For using any leftovers, see page 642.

VEGETABLE SAUCES.

VEGETABLE JUICE SAUCES.

Ideas and trends in cooking often seem to explode on the scene in a kind of a culinary spontaneous combustion, "discovered" by many cooks simultaneously. In the 1980s, suddenly it seemed as if chefs all across the country were juicing vegetables as a base for sauces. Jean-Georges Vongerichten was the one who really put these sauces on the map, with the highly innovative dishes he was serving at Lafayette Restaurant in New York. Because these sauces are based on vegetable juices, they were hailed as being low-fat, which, in fact, they were not. They are enriched with quite a bit of butter—usually about 1 tablespoon (100 calories) per serving. The butter enrichment thickens the sauces slightly while mellowing their flavor. But all that butter, while delicious, is not really necessary. I discovered that it is possible to make leaner vegetable juice sauces by thickening the juice ever so slightly with arrowroot to provide body, then blending in tiny amounts of butter or extra-virgin olive oil at the last minute. This method works well with juices that naturally have a round sweet flavor, such as beet, carrot, and pepper juices. More aggressively flavored juices, such as broccoli or endive, tend to need more butter to mellow them and so don't take well to this method.

If you do not own a vegetable juicer, you can buy fresh vegetable juices at health food stores, juice bars, and some greengrocers. Carrot and beet are the most commonly available.

Vegetable Juice Sauces

A GUIDE TO IMPROVISING

MAKES 1 TO 2 CUPS; SERVES 4

A variety of juices and flavor combinations can be used for making the sauces. Generally speaking, sweeter vegetables such as carrots, beets, red and yellow peppers, and tomatoes work best, but you can combine more assertive ones such as celery root and fennel with a base of sweeter ones.

2 ½ to 3 ½ pounds vegetables, such as carrots, beets, red peppers, tomatoes, parsnips, celery root, fennel, or cucumber, peeled and cut into chunks as necessary

1 to 1 ½ teaspoons arrowroot

Flavorings (optional), singly or in combination, such as

> **2 teaspoons grated fresh ginger**
>
> **4 to 5 sprigs fresh herbs,** such as thyme, savory, or rosemary
>
> **1 imported bay leaf**
>
> **3 kaffir lime leaves**
>
> **1 to 2 teaspoons Sandy's Curry Powder** (page 548) **or commercial curry powder**

1 to 2 tablespoons flavorful fat, such as cold unsalted butter, extra-virgin olive oil, roasted walnut or hazelnut oil, or Flavored Oil (pages 588–597)

¼ teaspoon kosher salt

Freshly ground white pepper

¼ to ½ cup chopped fresh herbs (optional), such as basil, chives, cilantro, tarragon, or chervil, or a combination

1. Process the vegetables in a juice extractor to make 2 cups juice (3 cups for more watery vegetables, such as red peppers or cucumber).

2. In a small bowl, combine the arrowroot with 2 tablespoons of the juice, stirring until smooth.

3. Pour the remainder of the juice into a medium heavy saucepan. Add the optional flavorings, if desired. Bring to a boil over moderate heat and cook until the juice has reduced to the desired intensity of flavor. (You can reduce the juice by as much as one third; certain juices, such as carrot, will need no reduction.) Reduce the heat to a simmer.

4. Stir ¼ cup of the hot juice into the arrowroot mixture, then stir this back into the saucepan. Simmer for 2 minutes, or until thickened. Whisk in the fat until thoroughly combined. Season to taste with the salt and white pepper. Stir in the herbs just before serving, if desired.

IN ADVANCE Because it is stabilized with arrowroot, this sauce can sit at room temperature for up to 1 hour before serving. Reheat gently just until it comes to a boil, then immediately remove from the heat.

Beet Juice and Walnut Sauce

This sweet, earthy, deep purple sauce is delicious with firm white-fleshed fish such as black bass or red snapper and with pan-seared sea scallops.

Follow the Guide on pages 646 to 647, using 2½ pounds medium beets, peeled and cut into 1-inch chunks. Use only 1 teaspoon arrowroot, blending it with 1 tablespoon of the juice. In Step 3, add 1 tablespoon fresh lime juice to the beet juice and boil until it has reduced to 1 cup, about 20 minutes. Use 1 tablespoon roasted walnut oil in Step 4, and garnish with 2 tablespoons snipped fresh chives.

Spicy Carrot Juice Sauce

Jean-Georges Vongerichten's carrot juice sauce is perhaps the most famous of all juiced vegetable sauces. Aromatic kaffir lime leaf, hot chile, and lime juice balance the intense sweetness of carrots. To cut down on the butter, in my version I thicken the juice gently with a little arrowroot and then whisk in a small amount of butter for flavor at the last minute. You can replace the lime leaf with fresh ginger for a different but still delicious effect.

Although the sauce is good with many kinds of fish and shellfish, I particularly like to serve it as Vongerichten did, with sautéed or steamed jumbo shrimp. Because the sauce is brothy, serve it in large shallow soup bowls, and arrange the fish or shellfish in the center.

15 medium carrots (about 2¾ pounds), peeled

1½ teaspoons arrowroot

3 kaffir lime leaves, finely chopped, or 2 teaspoons grated fresh ginger

¼ teaspoon minced small serrano or jalapeño chile

2 tablespoons fresh lime juice

2 tablespoons cold unsalted butter

1 teaspoon heavy cream (optional)

¼ teaspoon kosher salt

Freshly ground white pepper

2 tablespoons chopped fresh cilantro

2 teaspoons chopped fresh mint (optional)

Process the carrots in a juice extractor, to make 2 cups juice.

In a small bowl, whisk the arrowroot with 2 tablespoons of the juice until smooth.

Pour the remainder of the juice into a heavy medium saucepan, add the kaffir lime leaves, chile, and lime juice, and bring to a boil over moderate heat. Reduce the heat to a simmer.

Whisk ¼ cup of the hot juice into the arrowroot mixture, then stir this back into the saucepan. Simmer until thickened, about 2 minutes. Whisk in the butter and cream, if using, until thoroughly combined and the sauce is glossy. Add the salt and white pepper to taste. Stir in the cilantro and mint, if using, just before serving.

IN ADVANCE You can juice the carrots and boil down the juice up to 2 days ahead; cover and refrigerate. The sauce can be made up to 1 hour before serving. Reheat gently just until it comes to a boil, then immediately remove from the heat.

Red Pepper–Juice Sauce

MAKES ABOUT
2 CUPS; SERVES 4 This pure essence of red pepper sauce comes from chef Kevin Taylor. Because the addition of even the barest thickening seems to mask the flavor of the peppers, I just serve it as a brothy sauce, unlike the thickened carrot juice and beet juice sauces. It is sublime on stuffed pastas such as agnolotti, ravioli, and tortelloni—especially if you add the optional olives. If you cook it down until it's reduced to 1 cup, it becomes a perfect partner for grilled fish, shellfish, and lamb. This sauce is gorgeous when made with yellow peppers.

- **3½ pounds** (about 8) **red or yellow bell peppers**
- **1 cup dry white wine**
- **2 tablespoons fruity extra-virgin olive oil**
- **1 tablespoon fresh lemon juice**
- **Kosher salt**
- **½ to ¾ cup chopped fresh herbs,** such as flat-leaf parsley, basil, cilantro, or chives
- **8 Kalamata olives,** pitted (see page 683) and sliced (optional)

With a sharp paring knife, cut the peppers in half and remove the stems, ribs, and seeds. Slice into 2-inch pieces, then juice the peppers in a juice extractor, to make 3 cups juice.

In a medium saucepan, combine the pepper juice with the wine and bring to a boil over moderately high heat. If you are serving it as a pasta sauce, boil until reduced to 2 cups, about 35 minutes. Or, if you want to serve the sauce with fish, shellfish, or lamb, boil it until reduced to 1 cup, about 50 minutes.

Whisk in the olive oil and lemon juice and season with salt. Just before serving, add the herbs and olives, if desired.

IN ADVANCE You can juice the peppers and boil down the juice up to 2 days ahead; cover and refrigerate. The sauce can be stored, covered, in the refrigerator for up to 3 days. Reheat gently.

Warm Beet Juice Vinaigrette

MAKES ⅔ CUP;
SERVES 6 Like fruit juices, fresh vegetable juices make delectable and unexpected warm vinaigrettes. You can use this beet juice vinaigrette as a basic model for other vegetable juice vinaigrettes, using different vinegars and oils. I boil the beet juice down to a concentrated essence but do not thicken it. Then I add balsamic vinegar and lime juice for acidity and nut or olive oil to give it another layer of flavor and enhance the texture. It is delicious with grilled, roasted, or sautéed fish or sea scallops, braised leeks, sliced warm new potatoes, roasted onions, and buckwheat noodles.

Because the vinaigrette has a vivid purple color that stains food quickly, I prefer to spoon the vinaigrette onto the plates and place the food on top of it.

1½ pounds (3 to 4) **medium beets,** peeled and cut into 1-inch chunks

2 tablespoons balsamic vinegar

2 tablespoons roasted walnut oil, extra-virgin olive oil, or Asian sesame oil

Fresh lemon or lime juice, to taste

Pinch of kosher salt

Freshly ground black pepper

Process the beets in a juice extractor, to make 1 cup juice.

In a small saucepan, boil the beet juice over high heat until it is reduced to ½ cup, about 10 minutes.

Stir in the vinegar and boil for 30 seconds. Add the oil and boil for 30 seconds, or until emulsified. Stir in the lime juice, salt, and pepper to taste and serve at once.

IN ADVANCE You can juice the beets and boil down the juice up to 2 days ahead; cover and refrigerate. The sauce will keep, covered and refrigerated, for up to 4 days. Reheat gently before serving.

Warm Tomato or Sweet Pepper Vinaigrette. You can use variation the same method to make vinaigrettes with fresh tomato juice or red or yellow bell pepper juices. These vinaigrettes have a sweet summery flavor that complements just about any kind of seafood; smoked fish, such as sturgeon, sable, and trout; grilled chicken and lamb; and roasted vegetables, such as eggplant, zucchini, sweet onions, and potatoes.

Substitute 2 cups fresh tomato or red or yellow pepper juice for the beet juice. (You will need to juice 2 to 2½ pounds of tomatoes or peppers.) Boil it down until it has a very rich concentrated flavor, to about ½ cup. Use a fruity extra-virgin olive oil and a mellow vinegar that won't alter the color of the juice dramatically as balsamic will, such as aged sherry, Banyuls, Cava, or cider vinegar. Use lemon juice, not lime.

RUSTIC VEGETABLE SAUCES.

Vegetables are your greatest ally in making boldly flavored sauces that are immensely satisfying and yet lean. Their abundance of naturally low-calorie fiber yields filling body and distinctive texture whether you serve them chunky or pureed into a smooth cream. Because vegetables contain their own natural sweetness and savor, intense flavor is easy to achieve with a minimum of effort.

Ever-popular and versatile tomato sauces, both cooked and raw, are the most obvious examples of rustic vegetables sauces. In Mexican mole-style sauces (page 656), chile peppers and onions provide texture and flavor; in Pumpkin Seed Sauce (page 658), tomatillos, the tart green herbal-flavored "tomato" related to the gooseberry, marries with the pumpkin seeds to achieve extraordinary creaminess. The possibilities are endless, as long as the vegetables are soft enough to meld together or be pureed. As in the Rustic Slow-Roasted Tomato Sauce (page 39), appealing rustic vegetable sauces can be made by pureeing or thinning certain cooked vegetable dishes with a little chicken broth. For example, you can try this with Peperonata (page 63) or White Beans and Mellowed Garlic with Rosemary Oil (page 102). Even some soups, such as Roasted Pumpkin and Garlic (page 393), can be used as a sauce, say for Swiss chard–filled pasta or for duck. Root Vegetable Crema (page 387) makes a marvelous cream sauce for chicken pot pies.

Tomato Sauce

Tomato sauces are perhaps the most commonly made savory sauces for good reasons: They have a flavor that we never seem to tire of. They take well to being matched with other savory elements—garlic, onions, herbs, spices, wine, and olives—without losing their essential nature. They have infinite applications, from pasta and pizza to saucing fish, chicken, and meat. And good canned tomatoes, which are fine for sauces, are available all year round.

This is my standard tomato sauce recipe. It is delicious as is but can be embellished in any number of ways, as the variations below illustrate. Many tomato sauces are prepared with a lot of oil. Here I use the smallest amount possible.

Because the sauce has so few ingredients, it is important to use excellent canned tomatoes if you are not using fresh. There is enormous variation in the quality of canned tomatoes. I find imported Italian San Marzano tomatoes to be superior in both color and flavor. Of domestic brands, Red Pack and Muir Farm, available nationally in supermarkets, are among the best I've tasted.

1½ pounds ripe plum tomatoes or one 28-ounce can plum tomatoes, seeded and coarsely chopped (2 cups)

2 teaspoons extra-virgin olive oil

¾ cup finely chopped onions

1 garlic clove, slivered

¼ to ½ teaspoon kosher salt

¼ teaspoon sugar

⅛ teaspoon freshly ground black pepper

If using fresh tomatoes, bring a large pot of water to a boil and add the tomatoes. When you see their skins split, drain them and cool down under cold running water. Slip the skins off the tomatoes and discard. Halve the tomatoes crosswise, squeeze them to remove the seeds, and core them. Coarsely chop the tomatoes and transfer to a medium bowl. If using canned tomatoes, drain, seed, and coarsely chop; transfer to a medium bowl. Set aside.

In a large skillet, combine the oil and onions, cover, and cook over medium-high heat, stirring occasionally, until the onions are very soft but not browned, about 10 minutes. Stir in the garlic and cook for 2 minutes longer.

Stir in the tomatoes, salt, sugar, and pepper and simmer for 10 minutes, or until the sauce is thick. Taste for seasoning.

The sauce can be refrigerated, covered, for up to 1 week or frozen for up to 2 months.

Twelve Tomato Sauce Variations

- Add strong herbs, such as thyme, oregano, savory, or, my favorite, rosemary. Stir in 2 large sprigs or 1 teaspoon chopped fresh herbs or ½ teaspoon dried with the tomatoes. (Remove herb sprigs before serving.)

- Add fresh leafy herbs, such as basil, flat-leaf parsley, chives, or cilantro. Stir in 2 to 4 tablespoons chopped herbs during the last few minutes of cooking.

- To make a quick puttanesca sauce, add ¼ cup pitted (see page 683) black olives, 1 tablespoon drained small capers, and 2 teaspoons fresh oregano with the tomatoes.

- To make a heartier sauce, replace the olive oil with 3 tablespoons finely diced bacon or pancetta cooked slowly in a covered skillet until crisp (see page 681).

- For a smoky flavor, add ½ to 1 teaspoon Smoky Tea Essence (page 545) with the tomatoes.

- To add a sweet, mildly spicy flavor, sprinkle 1 tablespoon Ancho Chile Essence (page 543) over the onions as they cook.

- To give the sauce the bosky flavor of wild mushrooms, add 1 tablespoon Wild Mushroom Essence (page 544) with the tomatoes.

- Add ½ cup coarsely chopped pitted (see page 683) black or green olives with the tomatoes.

- To add a subtle olive flavor at many fewer calories than olive oil, stir in 1 tablespoon black or green olive paste during the last 5 minutes of cooking.

- To add both chile heat and smoky flavor, stir in 1 or more canned chipotle chiles in adobo, minced, and a tablespoon or two of the adobo sauce with the tomatoes. Garnish the sauce with chopped fresh cilantro.

- For a piquant note, stir in 1 to 2 tablespoons balsamic vinegar during the last 5 minutes of cooking.

- To give the sauce a slightly smoky flavor and a chunkier texture, add 2 roasted bell peppers (see page 683), chopped, with the tomatoes.

Uncooked Fresh Tomato Sauce

MAKES 2 CUPS

A few drops of kirsch, the cherry brandy, will intensify the tomato flavor.

Fine ripe summer tomatoes are treasures in these days of famously wooden supermarket tomatoes. Their natural flavor needs almost no embellishment, so I make this uncooked sauce, enhanced with herbs and balsamic vinegar, and just add a little salt and sugar to draw out their juices. It tastes incredibly lush and fresh. Rather than mixing oil into the sauce, I drizzle it over the top just before serving so that its flavor hits the palate immediately, and less is necessary.

This sauce is dazzling splashed on hot pasta; its herbal perfume is released on contact with heat. It is also wonderful spooned onto grilled bread that has been rubbed with olive oil and garlic, to make classic Bruschetta (page 369). It is perfect for grilled fish, shrimp, and scallops, as well as warm goat cheese.

If you are in a hurry, or if you don't mind the skins, you can skip peeling the tomatoes.

> **1 pound ripe tomatoes**
>
> **¼ teaspoon kosher salt**
>
> **¼ teaspoon sugar**
>
> **¼ cup minced shallots,** rinsed in a strainer under cold water and drained well
>
> **2 tablespoons balsamic vinegar**
>
> **2 tablespoons minced fresh herbs,** such as thyme, tarragon, cilantro, fennel tops, and/or flat-leaf parsley, in any combination
>
> **Freshly ground black pepper**
>
> **¼ teaspoon kirsch** (optional)
>
> **1 tablespoon extra-virgin olive oil,** or more to taste

To peel, seed, and chop fresh tomatoes: Bring a large pot of water to a boil and add the tomatoes. When you see their skins split, drain them and cool down under cold running water. Slip the skins off the tomatoes and discard. Halve the tomatoes crosswise, squeeze them to remove the seeds, and core them. Dice them and transfer to a medium bowl. Toss with the salt and sugar and allow to sit for 10 minutes.

Stir in the shallots, vinegar, herbs, pepper to taste, and kirsch if desired. Drizzle the olive oil over the top.

IN ADVANCE Make the sauce, without the herbs and olive oil, up to 3 hours ahead. Cover and leave at room temperature. Just before serving, add the herbs and olive oil.

Warm Olivada
(Warm Crushed Olives)

MAKES 1½ CUPS

I first made this coarse olive paste as a way of using some olives that had been languishing in my refrigerator and were a little past their prime. Warmed and spooned onto peasant bread as an hors d'oeuvre, it was a revelation: The flavor of olives changes when they are heated, somehow becoming wilder.

Make the paste in a mortar or on the work surface rather than in a food processor, to produce a coarser texture that leaves the flavors of the mixed black and green olives distinct. In addition to the garlic, thyme, and orange zest, you could include other flavoring elements, such as chopped herbs, lemon zest, or toasted coriander seeds.

Put the skillet of warm olivada right on the table, along with sliced bread, for guests to serve themselves. You can also use it to sauce pasta and polenta.

> **1 garlic clove,** peeled
>
> **Pinch of kosher salt**
>
> **¾ teaspoon finely chopped or grated orange zest**
>
> **1 tablespoon plus 1 teaspoon chopped fresh thyme**
>
> **12 ounces** (2 cups) **mixed green and black olives,** pitted (see page 683) and coarsely chopped
>
> **Freshly ground black pepper**

In a mortar, pound the garlic clove and salt with the pestle until reduced to a puree. Add the orange zest and thyme and pound to a coarse paste. Add the olives and continue pounding until they are reduced to a very coarse mash. Add pepper to taste.

Alternatively, make the olivada right on the work surface. Using a chef's knife, mince the garlic with the salt. Placing the flat side of the knife almost parallel to the cutting board, mash the garlic a little at a time by crushing and smashing it against the work surface until it is reduced to a paste. Add the orange zest, thyme, and olives and continue working the knife in this way until they are reduced to a coarse mash.

To serve, spoon the olivada into a small skillet, add a tablespoon or two of water, and heat, stirring frequently, over moderate heat, until hot. Serve at once.

The paste will keep, covered and refrigerated, for about 3 weeks.

IN ADVANCE

Revisionist Mole
(Ancho Chile Sauce)

MAKES 1 QUART

Mole, perhaps Mexico's most famous sauce, is really a whole family of sauces based on varying proportions of chiles, spices, seeds, nuts, fruits, and, famously but not invariably, chocolate. Because moles are time-consuming to make from scratch—it is not uncommon for one to have thirty ingredients—I devised this rich, satisfying, but simplified sauce that uses many classic mole techniques: toasting the chiles and garlic in a hot skillet, soaking and pureeing the chiles, frying the sauce to develop its flavors. Based on sweet, mildly spicy ancho chiles, it is a thick pureed sauce with resonant flavor, though it is lighter and has much less fat than traditional moles.

This sauce is so versatile I often double this recipe, divide it among 1- or 2-cup containers, and freeze it. You can use it to season bean soups, doctor up canned beans, or braise pot roast and chicken. Use it in Fat Beans with Mole (page 106) or Chicken Breasts with Mexican Flavors (page 307). Toss it with shredded leftover pork or chicken or with shrimp and roll up in hot tortillas for a quick lunch or snack. Made ahead, it can become a splendid last-minute sauce for any number of roasted or grilled meats—it needs only to be heated and enriched by the juices released from the meats after slicing.

You can also make a marvelous chili by stewing 2 pounds of ½-inch chunks of trimmed stewing beef or venison in the sauce until it is very tender, about 1½ hours over low heat. Brown the meat in 2 teaspoons rendered bacon fat (see page 681) or peanut oil first. Add dark beer, ¼ cup at a time, to the sauce to replenish the level as it cooks.

Mexican chocolate, made by grinding cocoa beans with sugar and often with cinnamon, almonds, and milk solids, is available at specialty food shops.

> **6 dried ancho chiles**
>
> **5 garlic cloves,** unpeeled
>
> **1 teaspoon ground cinnamon**
>
> **¼ teaspoon dried basil**
>
> **¼ teaspoon dried oregano**
>
> **¼ teaspoon cumin seeds**
>
> **1½ cups unsalted homemade** (page 574) **or canned low-sodium chicken broth**
>
> **1 tablespoon balsamic vinegar**

1½ teaspoons vegetable oil or rendered bacon fat (see page 681)

2 medium onions, chopped medium fine

One 28-ounce can crushed tomatoes or whole plum tomatoes, pureed, with their juices, in a blender

One 1-ounce chunk smoked ham, cut into 4 pieces

¾ ounce Mexican chocolate or 1 tablespoon unsweetened cocoa powder

1 to 2 teaspoons sugar

Kosher salt

With scissors, split open the chiles, and discard the stems and seeds. Cut the chiles into large flat pieces. In a large heavy skillet, toast the chile strips over moderate heat, turning occasionally with a spatula to prevent them from burning, until they begin to darken and smell pungent, about 3 minutes. Transfer to a medium bowl. Cover with about 2 cups boiling water and let soak for 20 minutes, or until softened.

Meanwhile, add the garlic cloves to the skillet and toast for about 15 minutes, turning occasionally, until the skins have blackened in spots and the garlic has softened somewhat. Remove from the heat.

In a blender, combine the garlic, cinnamon, basil, oregano, cumin seeds, chicken broth, and vinegar. Drain the ancho chiles and add to the mixture. Blend at high speed until smooth, about 1 minute.

In a large nonstick skillet, combine the oil and onions, cover, and cook over low heat until the onions have begun to release some liquid, about 5 minutes. Uncover, increase the heat to moderate, and sauté the onions until golden brown, 10 to 15 minutes.

Add the ancho chile mixture and cook, stirring, for 5 minutes. Stir in the tomatoes and ham, partially cover, and simmer until the sauce is very thick, about 25 minutes.

Add the chocolate and simmer until the sauce is very thick and has reduced to about 4 cups, about 10 minutes longer. Discard the ham (which will have given up its flavor) and add the sugar and salt to taste.

IN ADVANCE The sauce can be refrigerated, covered, for up to 1 week or frozen for up to 3 months.

Pumpkin Seed Sauce

MAKES 1½ CUPS

Roasted tomatillos—small green tomato-like members of the gooseberry family—pureed with pumpkin seeds give this classic Mexican sauce a surprising creaminess and a delicate herbal flavor that is fortified with chiles and cilantro. It is excellent served with grilled shrimp, or you can simmer peeled shrimp right in the sauce. It also goes well with mild seafood such as grilled snapper, seared sea scallops, or squid and with chicken or quail. At room temperature, it makes a satisfying creamy dip for tortilla chips or raw vegetables, and leftover sauce mixed with shredded chicken is a tasty filling for hot tortillas.

Shelled pumpkin seeds are available at health food stores and at well-stocked supermarkets.

> **Scant 8 ounces** (6 to 8) **tomatillos,** husked, rinsed, and patted dry
>
> **¼ cup** (1 ounce) **shelled pumpkin seeds**
>
> **1 teaspoon vegetable oil**
>
> **1 small onion,** finely chopped (½ cup)
>
> **3 small serrano or jalapeño chiles,** seeded and minced
>
> **1 garlic clove,** minced
>
> **2½ tablespoons minced fresh cilantro**
>
> **⅔ to 1 cup unsalted homemade** (page 574) **or canned low-sodium chicken broth**
>
> **½ teaspoon kosher salt**
>
> **Pinch of sugar**
>
> **1 tablespoon regular or reduced-fat sour cream** (optional)

Preheat the broiler.

Broil the tomatillos as close to the heat source as possible until the tops are blistered with black spots and begin to soften, about 5 minutes. Turn them over and broil until they are well blistered again and beginning to exude some juices, about 4 minutes longer. Set aside to cool.

Meanwhile, in a small heavy skillet over moderate heat, toast the pumpkin seeds: After the first one pops, shake or stir the pan constantly until most of the seeds are toasted and popped, about 5 minutes. Set aside.

In a medium nonstick skillet, combine the oil, onion, chiles, and garlic, cover, and cook over low heat, stirring once or twice, until the onion has begun to soften, about 5 minutes. Uncover the pan, increase the heat to moderate, and cook, stirring frequently, until the onion is golden brown and caramelized. Stir in the cilantro and cook, stirring for 1 minute. Add the tomatillos and ⅔ cup of the broth and simmer for 4 minutes, or until the tomatillos have fallen apart. Stir in the pumpkin seeds.

Transfer the mixture to a blender or food processor (the blender will produce a much creamier sauce). Blend until the mixture is smooth, about 1 minute. Stir in the salt and sugar, transfer the sauce to a bowl, and stir in the sour cream, if using. (If you don't plan to serve the sauce right away, reserve the sour cream, then add it at the last minute.) If the sauce seems too thick, thin it out with some or all of the remaining ⅓ cup stock. Serve warm.

Broil the tomatillos and toast the pumpkin seeds up to 1 day ahead. Cover and refrigerate the tomatillos. The sauce is best eaten the day it is made, while the herbal flavors are still at their brightest, but it will keep, covered and refrigerated, for 4 days. Reheat gently before serving.   **IN ADVANCE**

SALSAS, CHUTNEYS, AND OTHER SWEET, SAVORY
SAUCES. Americans have always loved cool, sweet fruit sauces
with savory foods—beach plum jelly with roast chicken, cranberry
sauce with turkey, applesauce with pork—but during the past two
decades, we have widened our palate to include the fresh vibrant
chile-spiked salsas of Latin America, Indian chutneys, and the
sweet-and-sour condiments of Europe.

The great virtue of all these sauces is that they provide so much
flavor for few calories and little or no fat—not to mention the
obvious benefits of vegetables and fruit: fiber, vitamins, and minerals. They are also easy to make and extremely versatile.

Salsa

A GUIDE TO IMPROVISING

MAKES 2 CUPS

Salsa is the Spanish word for "sauce." In Latin America and the American
Southwest, it has come to mean something that is at once a spicy sauce and
a juicy chopped salad, made from a fresh, often somewhat sweet vegetable
or fruit—tomatoes and mangoes are the most common—spiked with chile
peppers, onions, and cilantro. Because the juices act as a dressing, salsas are
by nature low in calories and fat.

The beauty of salsas is that you can make many different ones just by changing the main ingredient and adjusting the balance of flavorings. This is the
basic formula I use to improvise salsas, sometimes adding other herbs such
as basil and flat-leaf parsley, or a little minced garlic, or orange juice in place
of some of the lime. Aside from classic tomato salsa, some of my favorite
combinations are papaya and black beans; fresh cherries with orange zest,
basil, and cilantro; and mango and tomatillo. The Charred Onion Salsa on
page 662 is a good example of a radical improvisation in the spirit of salsas.

2 cups ripe fruit or vegetables, singly or in combination, such as peeled, diced tomatoes, mangoes, papayas, pineapple, halved and pitted cherries, cooked drained black beans, diced roasted red peppers, or tomatillos

½ medium red onion, finely chopped

1 to 2 serrano or jalapeño chiles, seeded and minced

¼ cup chopped fresh herbs, singly or in combination, such as cilantro, basil, flat-leaf parsley, or chives

1 teaspoon olive oil (optional)

1 to 2 tablespoons fresh lime juice

½ teaspoon kosher salt

Drizzle of tequila (optional)

In a medium bowl, combine all the ingredients. Allow to stand for 30 minutes before serving to mellow the flavors.

Most salsas are best eaten the day they are made, but they will keep for several days, covered and refrigerated, their flavors fading somewhat.

IN ADVANCE

Roasted Tomatillo Salsa

Mildly spicy salsas made from tomatillos, green chiles, garlic, and onions are ubiquitous in Cuernavaca, in southern Mexico, for their tart herbal flavor seems to complement just about everything, even scrambled eggs. This recipe is an adaptation from the justifiably famous restaurant Las Mañanitas, where it is served, along with hot tortillas and guacamole, to accompany the seasonal delicacy called *escamoles*: sautéed ant larvae.

MAKES ABOUT 2 CUPS

Roasting tomatillos, chiles, and garlic concentrates and mellows their flavor and gives a pleasing subtle smokiness to the sauce.

1 pound (about 16 to 18) **tomatillos,** husked, rinsed, and patted dry

4 serrano chiles

2 garlic cloves, unpeeled

1 small onion, chopped

⅓ cup chopped fresh cilantro

Scant 1 teaspoon kosher salt

¾ teaspoon sugar

⅓ cup water

Preheat the broiler. Broil the tomatillos as close to the heat source as possible until the tops are blistered with black spots and beginning to soften, about 5 minutes. Turn them over and broil until they are well blistered all over and beginning to exude some juices, about 4 minutes longer. Set aside to cool.

Heat a small cast-iron skillet over moderate heat for 5 minutes. Add the chiles and garlic and toast, turning occasionally, until softened and blistered all over with dark brown spots, about 10 minutes for the chiles, 15 for the garlic. Let cool slightly. Peel the garlic and coarsely chop. Cut the stems off the chiles and coarsely chop.

Place the garlic, chiles, and tomatillos, with any juices, in a blender or food processor and pulse to a coarse puree. Scrape into a bowl.

Place the onion in a strainer and rinse under cold water for 1 minute; drain well. Stir the onion, cilantro, salt, sugar, and water into the tomatillo mixture. Let sit for 1 hour at room temperature to let the flavors marry, then adjust the seasoning.

IN ADVANCE | The salsa is best the day it is made, but it can be refrigerated, covered, for up to 3 days. Bring to room temperature before serving.

Charred Onion Salsa

MAKES 1½ CUPS | I serve this salsa, an earthy mix of slightly charred sweet yet savory onions balanced by tart lime juice and cilantro, with hearty fare, such as roast pork or grilled beef, game, or chicken, and meaty fish, such as tuna, swordfish, and bluefish.

When you have an outdoor grill fired up to make dinner, char the onions while getting the main course ready to grill, then toss together the salsa while it is cooking.

> **1 pound Vidalia or Bermuda onions**
> **1 tablespoon extra-virgin olive oil**
> **¾ teaspoon kosher salt**
> **⅓ cup chopped fresh cilantro**
> **3 to 4 tablespoons fresh lime juice**
> **¾ teaspoon sugar**
> **Freshly ground black pepper**

To char the onions, preheat the broiler or prepare a fire in a grill.

Peel the onions and slice crosswise, into ¼-inch-thick rounds, keeping the slices together. Using a slightly dampened brush, brush the slices lightly with 2 teaspoons of the olive oil and arrange on a broiler pan or in a hinged grill rack, or directly on the hot grill. Sprinkle with ¼ teaspoon of the salt. Broil or grill for 5 to 8 minutes, until the onions are just beginning to blacken, brushing them again with oil as they dry out. Turn the onions and broil or grill for 5 minutes longer, brushing again with the remaining oil, until soft and beginning to char.

Chop the onions into a rough ¼-inch dice. Place them in a bowl and add the cilantro, lime juice, sugar, the remaining ½ teaspoon salt, and plenty of freshly ground pepper. Toss to mix thoroughly. Let sit for 30 minutes before serving to allow the flavors to marry.

Note: You can also char the onions on the stove top. Heat a large heavy nonstick skillet over moderately high heat until very hot. In batches if necessary, brush the onion slices lightly with oil and arrange them in the pan in a single layer. Cook, brushing occasionally with oil, until browned and caramelized, with tinges of black, on the bottom. (If some of the outer onion rings contract and char more quickly than the inner rings, keeping the onion slices from lying flat, you can lift them off the slice and push them to the side of the pan to finish cooking.) Keeping the slices intact, turn them over and continue cooking, basting again with oil, until soft and browned. Transfer to a cutting board and sprinkle them with ¼ teaspoon of the salt.

Cook the onions up to 1 day ahead; cover and refrigerate. Although the salsa is best the day it is made, it can be refrigerated, covered, for up to 3 days. Bring to room temperature before serving. **IN ADVANCE**

Warm Mango Chutney

MAKES 2 CUPS Chile peppers, sweet onion, coriander, and basil are cooked gently with fragrant ripe mangoes until they begin to meld together. When served warm, this simple sauce has overtones of a chutney with the fresh flavors of a salsa. It is a versatile accompaniment to roasted or grilled poultry, game, pork, and seafood, and especially Curry-Crusted Shrimp (page 242). It is almost as delicious served cold.

> ½ **cup finely chopped Vidalia or Bermuda onions**
>
> 1 **teaspoon minced serrano or jalapeño chiles**
>
> ½ **teaspoon extra-virgin olive oil**
>
> 2 **ripe medium mangoes,** peeled and diced (2 cups)
>
> ¼ **cup fresh lime juice**
>
> ¼ **cup chopped fresh cilantro**
>
> 1 **tablespoon chopped fresh basil**

In a medium saucepan, cook the onions and chiles in the oil, covered, over moderately low heat until the onions are soft and just beginning to brown, about 7 minutes.

Reduce the heat, add the mangoes and half the lime juice, and cook, covered, stirring frequently, until the fruit begins to release some of its juices and softens slightly, without losing its shape, about 3 minutes. Remove from the heat and allow to cool slightly before stirring in the cilantro, basil, and remaining lime juice. Serve warm.

IN ADVANCE Prepare the chutney up to 4 days ahead; cover and refrigerate. Serve it cold, or warm it gently in a small saucepan with a tablespoon or so of water.

Cilantro and Coconut Chutney

This refreshing uncooked chutney is one step beyond the cool cilantro sauce I MAKES 1 CUP find myself spooning onto every dish at Indian restaurants. The vibrant flavor of fresh cilantro and hot chiles is mellowed and cooled by unsweetened coconut milk, which provides creaminess. Shredded coconut gives it a pleasingly coarse texture. This sauce is perfect with grilled chicken and seafood, particularly shrimp, lobster, and salmon.

> **1 large bunch cilantro** (about 4 ounces)
>
> **1 teaspoon cumin seeds**
>
> **1 jalapeño or 2 serrano chiles,** quartered lengthwise, seeded, and deveined
>
> **½ plus ⅛ teaspoon kosher salt**
>
> **¾ teaspoon sugar**
>
> **½ cup canned unsweetened coconut milk**
>
> **1 tablespoon fresh lime juice**
>
> **½ to 1 teaspoon white wine vinegar**
>
> **2 tablespoons shredded coconut**

Cut the tough stems off the cilantro at the point where the leaves begin, and discard. Wash the cilantro sprigs and dry well in a salad spinner. Coarsely chop them and set aside.

In a small heavy skillet, toast the cumin seeds over low heat, stirring, until fragrant and slightly darkened. Crush the seeds in a mortar and pestle. Or place on a cutting board and crush with the side of a chef's knife.

In a food processor, combine the jalapeño, cilantro, cumin seeds, salt, and sugar and pulse until chopped medium fine, about 1 minute. Add the coconut milk, lime juice, and vinegar and process it to a medium-coarse puree. Scrape into a bowl, stir in the coconut, and serve.

Although it is best freshly made, the chutney will keep, covered and refriger- IN ADVANCE ated, for 2 to 3 days.

Balsamic-Cooked Peppers

This endlessly useful condiment, courtesy of my friend Mary Rower, is nothing more than diced red peppers cooked in balsamic vinegar and a little olive oil until they become soft and glazed with the syrupy reduced vinegar. They have that tart, sweet winy flavor the French call *aigre-doux*, sour-sweet.

This is a great sauce to make when you have weekend guests, because it is so easy and you can fall back on it to make all kinds of impromptu dishes, depending on what you find at the market. On its own, it is a wonderful salsa-like accompaniment for any manner of grilled or roasted fish, poultry, and meats. It doubles as a sauce that can turn simple ingredients into quick delicious dishes. Mixed in equal parts with diced summer tomatoes or warm diced potatoes, it becomes a salad. Stirred into sautéed onions and corn kernels and served warm, it is a delicious succotash. Tossed with cooked pasta, diced tomatoes, ricotta salata, mozzarella, and minced fresh herbs, it becomes a summer pasta.

> **5 red bell peppers,** cored, seeded, and cut into ½-inch dice
>
> ½ **cup balsamic vinegar**
>
> ½ **teaspoon kosher salt**
>
> **2 tablespoons extra-virgin olive oil**
>
> **Freshly ground black pepper**

In a heavy medium nonreactive saucepan, combine the peppers, balsamic vinegar, and salt. Bring to a simmer, cover, and cook, stirring occasionally, until the vinegar has reduced to a thick glaze and the peppers are tender, about 25 minutes (if the vinegar evaporates too quickly, stir in a few tablespoons of water). Transfer to a bowl and allow the peppers to cool.

Stir in the olive oil and pepper to taste, and serve.

The peppers will keep, covered, in the refrigerator for about 2 weeks.

Onion Marmalade
with Sherry Vinegar

MAKES 1 CUP

When thinly sliced onions are cooked in butter over very low heat for a very long time, they "melt," becoming almost jam-like. With the addition of a little sugar, the onions caramelize slightly; a sprinkling of sherry vinegar turns them into a marvelous sweet-and-sour onion marmalade. Although similar recipes call for a great deal of butter, I find 2 teaspoons is sufficient to melt 6 cups of sweet onions down to 1 cup.

Serve this marmalade warm with grilled pork chops or steak. Cold, it is delicious on sandwiches, with pâtés, and on cold meats and poultry. It also makes a lovely omelet filling.

> 1 ¼ pounds Vidalia or Bermuda onions
>
> 2 teaspoons unsalted butter
>
> ½ teaspoon kosher salt
>
> ½ teaspoon sugar
>
> 1 tablespoon sherry vinegar, preferably aged
>
> 1 teaspoon balsamic vinegar
>
> Freshly ground black pepper

Peel the onions and slice lengthwise in half. Using a mandoline or a vegetable slicer, or a thin sharp knife, cut them lengthwise into ⅛-inch-thick slices. (You should have about 6 cups.)

In a large nonstick skillet, melt the butter over moderately low heat. Add the onions and sprinkle with the salt, tossing well. Cover and cook until the onions have released some liquid, about 13 minutes. Uncover and continue to cook slowly, stirring occasionally, until the liquid has evaporated, about 10 minutes.

Sprinkle the onions with the sugar and continue cooking, stirring frequently, until golden brown and caramelized, about 10 minutes longer. Increase the heat slightly, add the sherry and balsamic vinegars, and stir to dissolve the juices that have caramelized on the bottom of the pan. Cook for about 3 minutes longer, until it is the consistency of a thick marmalade. Season with pepper and additional salt if necessary. Serve warm or cold.

The jam will keep, covered and refrigerated, for about 2 weeks.

IN ADVANCE

Pears in Fragrant Wine

MAKES ABOUT
1 CUP

I devised this cool, ethereal pear sauce for an American-style Thanksgiving in Paris, where there were no cranberries. Cooked in dessert wine and spiked with a little Poire William, a clear brandy distilled from pears, the sliced pears have a sophisticated flavor that's more savory than sweet. Nowadays, I serve the pears with rich meats such as roast goose, duck, and pork, as well as preserved ones such as confit, ham, and sausages.

Choose a pear that is fragrant and just ripe—not dead ripe—so that the slices will hold their shape when cooked.

> **1 Bosc or Comice pear,** peeled, quartered, cored, and sliced crosswise ¼ inch thick
>
> **½ cup white dessert wine,** such as Sauternes, Barzac, or Monbazillac
>
> **1 vanilla bean**
>
> **1 teaspoon Poire William**

In a small nonreactive saucepan, combine the pear slices and wine. Split the vanilla bean lengthwise in half, scrape the seeds into the pan, and add the bean. Cook over moderate heat until the pear slices are quite tender but still hold their shape, about 5 minutes. Let cool slightly, then cover and refrigerate until chilled.

Just before serving, remove the vanilla pod and stir in the Poire William.

IN ADVANCE The sauce will keep for at least 2 weeks, covered, in the refrigerator.

variation **Star Anise–Scented Pears.** The addition of 1 star anise gives a lovely and unusual perfume to the pears. Add it with the vanilla bean and remove it when it has imparted a faint licorice-spice flavor.

Eleanor's Applesauce

MAKES ABOUT
1 ½ CUPS

Eleanor Mailloux owns a restaurant deep in the West Virginia Appalachians, where she serves the food of her forebears, the Swiss immigrants who settled the small town of Helvetia. This recipe chases after the flavors of her applesauce, whose recipe is a secret. I've always suspected that horseradish is what gives it its elusive flavor. But even without the horseradish, this sauce—flecked with tart bits of lemon flesh—is delicious and unique. I use light brown sugar, rather than white, because it brings out the flavor of the apples.

3 medium apples, peeled, cored, and diced (about 3 cups)

2 tablespoons light brown sugar

¼ lemon (cut lengthwise as a wedge), sliced crosswise into paper-thin slices

1 cinnamon stick

2 tablespoons water

2 to 3 teaspoons freshly grated or prepared horseradish, drained and liquid squeezed out, or more to taste (optional)

In a small heavy saucepan, combine the apples, brown sugar, lemon, cinnamon stick, and water. Cover and cook over medium heat, stirring often, until the apples have broken down into a coarse mush and the lemon slices are tender, about 5 to 8 minutes. If the sauce is still too lumpy, mash it coarsely with a fork or a potato masher.

Stir in the horseradish. Serve warm or chilled.

The sauce will keep, covered and refrigerated, for up to 2 weeks. IN ADVANCE

Red Wine–Cranberry Sauce

Cooking cranberries in red wine, rather than water or fruit juice, adds a wilder, more sophisticated flavor than that of the traditional cranberry sauce. MAKES ABOUT 1¾ CUPS

⅔ cup sugar

¾ cup dry red wine

½ cinnamon stick (about 1½ inches)

1 package fresh or frozen cranberries (about 3 cups)

1 tablespoon slivered tangerine, clementine, or orange zest, or more to taste

In a saucepan over moderate heat, combine the sugar, red wine, and cinnamon stick; bring to a boil. Reduce the heat and simmer for about 4 minutes, stirring occasionally, until the sugar is dissolved and the wine has reduced slightly. Add the cranberries and zest. Simmer for 10 minutes, or until the cranberries are soft and the sauce has thickened. Serve at room temperature or chilled.

The sauce will keep for 2 months in a covered container in the refrigerator. IN ADVANCE

Cranberry-Walnut Conserve

**MAKES ABOUT
2 QUARTS**

This unusual conserve is roughly adapted from *The Mennonite Cookbook,* one of those honest, old-fashioned community cookbooks that gives the name of the contributor after each recipe. It is immensely satisfying, tart and sweet, with a chunky texture from an abundance of nuts and raisins. It is delicious with roast chicken, turkey, and pork. (I like it best on its own, eaten with a spoon as a sweet snack.) It contains only the beneficial fat from the nuts.

Around Christmastime, I make this chutney in great quantities and pack it into jars to give as gifts.

> 1½ **cups** (6 ounces) **walnuts**
> 3 **navel oranges,** well washed
> 5 **cups fresh or frozen cranberries**
> ⅔ **cup wildflower honey,** or more to taste
> 1½ **cups hot water**
> 1¼ **cups dark raisins or currants**
> 2 to 3 **teaspoons fresh lemon juice** (optional)

Preheat the oven to 375°F.

Spread the walnuts on a baking sheet and roast, tossing occasionally, until fragrant, about 9 minutes. Set aside to cool.

With a sharp knife, cut the ends off the oranges and discard. Slice the oranges lengthwise into quarters. Slice each quarter crosswise into very thin slices, discarding the seeds as you work.

In a large heavy nonreactive saucepan, combine 4 cups of the cranberries, the oranges, honey, and water and bring to a boil over moderately high heat. Reduce the heat to moderate and cook, stirring occasionally, until the mixture has thickened and the cranberries are soft, about 15 minutes.

Stir in the raisins and the remaining 1 cup cranberries and cook until the raisins are plump, about 5 minutes. Remove the pan from the heat and allow to cool.

Coarsely chop the walnuts and stir them into the conserve, along with lemon juice if needed to bring out the flavors. Transfer to clean dry jars, cover, and refrigerate.

IN ADVANCE The conserve will keep for up to 1 month in the refrigerator.

"Wild" Plum Sauce

MAKES ABOUT
3 CUPS

During summer vacations at the beach, few people bothered to make beach plum jelly. Except my mother. She would return from forays to neighbors' properties, laden with wild beach plums, arms and hands dotted with tiny cuts from the thorny bushes, yet sure that her efforts would be worth the sacrifice. They were.

I discovered that I could make ordinary plums taste close to beach plums by cooking them in red wine with an infusion of juniper and fresh thyme. A friend who grew up on Cape Cod (where beach plums grow in profusion) tasted this sauce and said, "It tastes like August." It is delicious with poultry, particularly roast chicken and milder game birds, such as guinea hen and quail, as well as with pork.

1 cup dry red wine

¼ cup sugar

2 juniper berries, crushed

1 sprig fresh thyme

A 2½-by-¾-inch strip lemon zest
(removed with a vegetable peeler)

Pinch of ground allspice

1 pound red or purple plums,
pitted and cut into sixths

In a medium nonreactive saucepan, combine the red wine, sugar, juniper berries, thyme sprig, lemon zest, and allspice and bring to a boil over moderate heat. Reduce the heat and simmer for 4 minutes.

Add the plums and cook until they have fallen apart, about 7 to 10 minutes. Reduce the heat to a simmer and continue cooking, stirring frequently, until most of the liquid has evaporated. Discard the thyme and lemon zest. You can leave the sauce chunky or transfer it to a food processor and puree until smooth. Let cool, then pack into jars and refrigerate.

The sauce will keep for at least 1 month in the refrigerator.

IN ADVANCE

Roasted Peppers
(page 683)

BASIC TECHNIQUES

AND STANDARD PREPARATIONS

BASIC TECHNIQUES.

How to Toast Spices: Toasting dry spices in a skillet heightens their flavor. It also revives faded spices.

Scatter the spices over the bottom of a small skillet. Toast over moderately low heat, shaking the pan frequently, until their fragrance is released.

How to Roast Nuts: Roasting nuts sweetens and intensifies their flavor, which makes it possible to use less of them (they are very caloric) in recipes.

For most nuts, preheat the oven to 375°F. Scatter the nuts over a baking sheet and roast until they are very fragrant and deep golden brown, 6 to 9 minutes, watching carefully toward the end to be sure they don't burn.

Roast pistachios in a 300°F oven until fragrant, not brown, to preserve their green color.

Since hazelnuts have a papery brown skin that must be removed, you need to take them a step further. Roast the hazelnuts at 375°F for 2 minutes. With a water sprayer, mist them with water several times. Continue roasting until the nuts are brown and very fragrant, about 10 to 12 minutes. Rub the nuts in a tea towel to remove most of the skins.

How to Mash Garlic to a Paste: Use mashed garlic to flavor sauces and other preparations where you don't want to taste bits of raw minced garlic. It has a much mellower flavor than garlic pureed in a food processor or blender.

The easiest way to mash garlic to a paste is to pound it right on the work surface with a pestle. Alternatively, you can use a chef's knife: Mince the garlic with the salt in the recipe. Placing the flat side of the knife almost parallel to the work surface, mash the garlic a little at a time by crushing and smearing it against the cutting board until it is completely reduced to a paste.

How to Cool Down Blanched Vegetables or Just-Boiled Pasta: Instead of trying to cool drained, cooked vegetables or pasta down by covering them with ice cubes, try this easier method. Toss them into a bowl in the sink. Turn the cold water tap on high and let the water flood over until they are completely cool. Then drain well again.

How to Split and Scrape a Vanilla Bean: Vanilla beans give a deeper, more complex vanilla flavor to foods than extract, bringing out their inherent sweetness and lessening the amount of sweetener required.

Place the bean on the work surface. With a sharp paring knife, split it lengthwise in half. With the tip of the knife, scrape out the black paste from each half (the seeds). Add it, along with the scraped part, to your preparation.

You can also add the scraped pods to a canister of confectioner's sugar to make vanilla-scented confectioner's sugar to sprinkle over pastries and cakes.

How to Peel and Section Citrus Fruit: With a thin sharp knife, cut the stem and flower ends off the fruit. Stand the fruit on the work surface. Working from top to bottom, carefully cut away the skin and white pith in strips, leaving the flesh intact. Holding the peeled fruit over a bowl, cut between the membranes to release the sections, and place the sections in a small bowl. Squeeze the membranes to extract the remaining juice and discard.

How to Sliver Citrus Zest: Use a vegetable peeler to remove strips of the colored zest with as little of the bitter white pith as possible. Place the strips on a cutting board and, using either a chef's knife or a thin sharp paring knife, slice into fine slivers. You can also use a zester, a little tool with five small holes lined up across a flat end. When you pull it across citrus rind, fine threads of peel come off. Use the slivers as is, or finely chop to use in place of grated zest.

How to Pit Cherries: There are several well-designed cherry pitters on the market that can pit a pound of cherries in just a few minutes. I own a simple hand-held pitter made in West Germany that has a metal ring that holds the cherry in place and a spike-like protrusion that pushes the pit through the fruit.

When caught without a cherry pitter, you can pit cherries the same way you pit olives: by smashing them lightly with a can or jar. The flesh breaks open so the cherry is no longer a neat shape, but it makes it easy to take out the pit. Place the cherries in a baking dish with at least 2-inch-high sides when doing this, to prevent the juice from squirting on your clothes. Alternatively, you can cover them with paper towels to catch the spray.

How to Peel Fava Beans: To remove the beans from the pods, use your thumb to break open each pod along the seam and dislodge the beans inside. The beans have a thin skin that can be removed if you first loosen it by blanching the beans. Cook the beans in rapidly boiling water for 2 to 3 minutes, depending on the size. Drain and cool them under cold running water to stop the cooking. Use your thumbnail to break open the skin at one end of each bean and peel it back. Press the bean gently, and the bean will pop right out. (There is no need to cook the beans further.)

How to Peel Pearl Onions: With scissors, cut the pointed tips off the onions. Place in a small saucepan with cold water to cover by 1½ inches, bring to a boil, and boil for 2 minutes. Drain and cool under cold running water. Peel the onions, trimming off the root ends.

How to Debeard Mussels: The "beard" of a mussel is a fibrous tuft that the mussel uses to anchor itself to rocks. To remove it, grasp it tightly, as close to the shell as possible, with your thumb and forefinger and pull it off.

How to Kill a Live Lobster: Place the lobster belly down on the work surface. Place the point of a chef's knife against the lobster's head, between the eyes, and the sharp edge of the knife facing away from the tail. Push the knife forcefully straight down to the cutting board to split the head in half vertically. Any twitching is the result of posthumous muscle spasms.

How to Truss Chicken and Other Birds for Roasting: Cut a 40-inch length of cotton kitchen string. Place the bird on the work surface with the legs pointing toward you. Place the string, centered horizontally, across the breast. Pass the right half of the string down to the underside of the breast, pinning the wing to the body, then run the string diagonally under the bird so that it emerges under the left leg. Repeat with the left half of the string, pinning the other wing and running the string diagonally under the bird and out under the right leg. Lift up the ends of the string and wrap them around the ends of the legs, pulling them so that the legs are drawn together, and tie the string into a bow. Trim the ends of the string if necessary.

How to Butterfly Chicken and Other Birds: Place the bird on a work surface. With kitchen shears, cut through the bones along both sides of the backbone and remove it. Spread the bird open, skin side up, on the counter and press down against the breastbone with the palms of your hands to flatten it.

How to Tie a Boneless Roast: Place the roast on the work surface. Beginning 1 inch from one end of the roast, start to tie the string around the roast, leaving 5 inches free at one end and the ball of string still attached to the other. Unrolling the string from the ball as you go, wind the string around the roast in a spiral fashion, and leaving about 1-inch intervals between the coils of string. When you get to the other end of the roast, unroll enough string to run three times around the length of the roast. Run the end several times around the last coil of string to make a knot. Then wrap the string around the length of the roast and tie the two ends of string together to secure.

Alternatively, place the roast on the work surface. Beginning ¾ inch from one end of the roast, tie a length of string around the roast and knot it. Repeat at ¾-inch intervals, until you reach the other end.

How to Cut Up a Whole Duck (or Other Bird): If you can't easily find duck legs and breasts, the alternative is to buy a whole duck and cut it up yourself (or have your butcher do the work). This is also more economical—ducks are like pigs in that every part, even fat and skin (see page 681), can be used.

Cut off the wings (save for stock). If you wish to remove the skin, using a thin sharp knife and your fingers, pull off the skin, removing it entirely. Make a cut along each side of the breastbone from wishbone to tail. Pressing the knife against the rib cage as you slice, carefully slice each breast away from the ribs. Cut through the joint that connects the thigh to the body and remove both legs. (With kitchen shears, cut up the carcass for broth.)

How to Cut Up a Rabbit: Remove the liver, if any, and reserve. With a sharp heavy knife, separate the forelegs from the body. With kitchen shears, cut crosswise through the spine at the point where the hind legs attach. Cut through the joint connecting the legs to the spine. Cut crosswise through the spine to remove the whole rib cage and neck section just above the saddle, the midportion of the spine, and the two meaty loins that run along it. Cut the rib-cage portion crosswise in two. Cut the saddle crosswise into 3 sections.

How to Reduce Salt in a Recipe: If you are concerned about your intake of sodium, several techniques can help increase the perceived saltiness of a dish.

One is to add a little hot chile pepper. Add a pinch of red pepper flakes or minced fresh chile pepper when sautéing garlic or onions at the beginning of a recipe. A smidgen of cayenne (not enough to add real heat) can heighten the flavors of purees and soups.

The addition of an acid can also sharpen flavors: A few drops of vinegar or citrus juice, such as lemon or lime, are just enough to heighten flavors without being tart.

Use sea salt, which tastes much saltier than ordinary table salt or kosher salt. To avoid accidentally oversalting, reduce the salt called for in the recipe by half, then add more sea salt to taste if necessary.

How to Age and Store Cheese: My friend Joshua Eisen devised this simple way to age cheeses in the refrigerator so that the flavors continue to develop and they neither dry out nor turn moldy from their own moisture. (The worst way to keep cheese is wrapped in plastic; it suffocates the cheese, which needs air to age.) This method is useful both for aging small whole cheeses and for storing cheeses that have already been cut.

Line the bottom of a plastic container with a tight-fitting lid with a double layer of paper towels. If you have a wire cake rack that will fit in the container, place it on the paper towels. If the cheeses are cut, wrap them in parchment or wax paper, and place them in the container so they don't touch each other or the sides of the container. There is no need to wrap uncut whole cheeses. Place another folded paper towel on top and put the lid on. Every 4 or 5 days, wipe away the moisture that has condensed on the underside of the lid and the sides of the container and replace the paper towels with dry ones. This step is essential, since a buildup of moisture will cause the cheese to deteriorate. Stored this way, cheese will last many weeks, its flavor developing as it ages.

How to Season Cast-Iron Pans: Seasoning a cast-iron pan seals the iron and creates a smooth surface that food won't stick to. If your skillet is new, scrub it with soapy water to remove factory oil and dry completely. To season the pan, place it over medium heat. Cover the bottom of the pan completely with a thin layer of salt and heat for several minutes, until the salt begins to darken. Remove the pan from the heat and, using paper towels, scrub the pan with the salt; discard the salt. Rub the inside of the hot pan liberally with vegetable oil and set it aside to cool and absorb the oil; wipe out any excess.

Never use soaps or abrasives to wash cast iron. Simply use warm water and a brush, and dry well to prevent rusting.

Rub with a thin coat of oil. Gradually, a patina will begin to build up in the pan, developing into a smooth, black surface. If food ever begins to stick to the pan, reseason it as directed above.

How to Improvise a Double Boiler or Bain-Marie: Double boilers or bains-marie are useful to keep delicate foods warm and to cook custards and other egg dishes that can curdle if they become too hot. Fill a saucepan with 1 inch of water. Choose a heatproof bowl slightly larger than the saucepan, so that when you place it in the saucepan, the bottom of the bowl is suspended from ½ to 1 inch above the water. Bring the water to a boil and add the food to be heated to the bowl; replenish the water as necessary. If you wish to cover it, set a lid or plate slightly ajar.

STANDARD PREPARATIONS.

Clarified Butter: Clarified butter is pure butterfat, from which the milk solids have been removed. It is useful for high-heat cooking because it can be heated to much higher temperatures than regular butter without burning.

Melt ½ pound unsalted butter in a small saucepan over low heat until it begins to boil and a white foam has risen to the surface. With a tablespoon, skim off the foam and discard. Tilt the pan and spoon the clear yellow fat into a clean dry jar, taking care not to disturb the white milk solids in the bottom of the pan. Discard the solids. Refrigerate until ready to use. It will keep in the refrigerator for 2 months. (Makes ¾ cup.)

Brown Butter: Cooked slowly over low heat, whole unsalted butter will gradually "toast," turning golden brown and developing a sweet flavor with the fragrance of roasted nuts.

Melt ½ pound unsalted butter in a medium skillet over moderately low heat until it begins to boil and a white foam has risen to the surface. With a tablespoon, skim off the foam and discard. Continue cooking until the solids on the bottom of the pan have turned dark brown and the clear butter is amber colored and smells like roasted nuts. Remove from the heat and strain through a fine strainer into a clean dry jar. Refrigerate until ready to use.

(Makes about ⅔ cup.) If you need only a small quantity, figure that 3 tablespoons of unsalted butter will yield about 2 tablespoons brown butter.

Rendered Bacon, Pancetta, Ham, Duck, or Goose Fat: To render means to cook a fatty meat, or skin, slowly until the fat liquifies and separates from any flesh, skin, or cartilage. Then the fat can be strained into a clean jar and kept on hand (in the refrigerator) for use in cooking. You only need a little fat rendered from bacon, pancetta, a real cured ham such as prosciutto or Smithfield, or a goose or duck to add marvelous flavor to a dish.

The yield of different meats varies greatly. 1 pound bacon or pancetta yields about 1 cup fat; 1 ounce (about ¼ cup diced) yields about 1 tablespoon fat.

One pound double-smoked bacon yields ⅔ to ¾ cup fat; 1 ounce (about ¼ cup diced) yields about 2 teaspoons.

Cut the bacon or pancetta or the duck, ham, or goose fat or skin to be rendered into ¼-inch dice. In a heavy nonstick skillet, cook the fat, covered, over low heat, stirring occasionally, until the fat is liquid and the remaining meat or skin is crisp and brown. Strain into a clean dry jar, cool, and refrigerate. You can use the crisp rendered bits in recipes or as a garnish. Freeze them for up to 2 months and reheat them in a covered skillet with a little fat.

Homemade "Margarine": My sister Susy devised this homemade "margarine," which rolls the virtues of butter (flavor) and margarine (low saturated fat) into one (I love it made with fine French butter and great olive oil). It is a fine alternative to commercial margarine, whose hydrogenated fats are unhealthy. Because this "margarine" is not hydrogenated, it melts easily in a warm room. Keep refrigerated until just before serving.

In a small bowl or food processor, blend together 8 tablespoons (1 stick) softened unsalted butter, ½ cup grapeseed, canola, or mild extra-virgin olive oil, and ¾ teaspoon kosher salt until completely homogenized and liquid. Transfer to a container, cover, and refrigerate. The margarine will firm up as it chills. It will keep for several weeks. (Makes about 1 cup).

Crème Fraîche: You can use this rich fermented cream with a slightly sour, nutty flavor in place of heavy cream. Warm 1 cup heavy whipping cream (not ultrapasteurized) to about 100°F, then stir in 2 tablespoons cultured buttermilk or plain yogurt (make sure it contains active cultures). Cover loosely and allow the mixture to sit at room temperature for at least 8 hours, or overnight, before refrigerating.

Fresh Bread Crumbs: Soft white bread crumbs make the most delicate and appealing gratin topping and result in much lighter, airier sausages, pâtés, and fish cakes. Any good white bread will do except sourdough, which is often too dense to process and has too assertive a flavor.

To make about 1 cup fresh bread crumbs, you need 4 to 5 slices of white bread. If the bread is fresh, place it in a warm oven to dry out slightly, until it has the consistency of stale bread. Break the bread into pieces and process to crumbs in a food processor. Store in a sealed plastic bag in refrigerator for up to 5 days or freeze for up to 2 months.

To make garlic bread crumbs, rub both sides of the dried bread with a cut garlic clove and sprinkle with salt before processing.

Peeled, Seeded Tomatoes: Because tomato skins and seeds can turn harsh and bitter when cooked, it is always best to remove them.

To peel 1 or 2 tomatoes: Spear the tomato with a two-pronged kitchen fork. Holding it directly over a burner turned on high, rotate the tomato slowly as the skin splits open and chars slightly, about 1 minute. Allow to cool for a few minutes, then slip the skin off. To peel a lot of tomatoes: Plunge the tomatoes into a pot of rapidly boiling water. As soon as the skin splits, after about 30 seconds, drain the tomatoes and cool under cold running water. Remove the skins. **To seed a tomato:** Slice it crosswise in half and gently squeeze out the seeds.

Grated Tomatoes: Use this quick Catalan method of grating tomatoes when you need fresh tomato pulp for sauces. You don't have to peel the tomatoes first.

Halve and seed the tomatoes (see above). Rub the cut sides across the large holes of a metal grater so that the flesh is coarsely grated but the skin remains intact in your hand. Discard the skin.

Roasted Peppers: Roast peppers directly over a gas flame or under a broiler as close to the heat source as possible, turning frequently, until charred all over and softened. Enclose the peppers in a paper bag and let steam for 10 minutes.

Using a thin sharp knife or your fingers, scrape the skin off the peppers and remove the core, seeds, and ribs. Rinse if desired, although the charred bits will add flavor. (Wear rubber gloves to work with hot peppers.)

Cooked Beets: When whole beets are dry-roasted, they take so long to cook that the outer surface becomes tough and inedible, causing waste. When beets are boiled, their flesh becomes slightly watery. Roasting the beets in a loosely covered pan with a little water combines the best of the two, producing beets that are moist and tender yet with a concentrated roasted flavor. These beets are delicious as is as a side dish, or as a component in recipes.

One pound cooked beets = 2 cups sliced beets = 2 servings.

Trim the greens of 1 bunch of beets (1⅓ pounds) to within 1 inch and scrub the beets. Arrange the beets in a small roasting pan, add ⅛ inch water, and cover loosely with foil. Roast at 450°F for 30 to 45 minutes, until they are tender when pierced with a knife. To clean the cooked beets, cut off the stem and root ends and scrape the thin layer of skin off with a knife.

Pitted Olives: Place the olives on a work surface and tap each one lightly with a heavy can or meat pounder, or the side of a chef's knife, to split them open, revealing the pits. Remove the pits with your fingers.

One pound olives = 2 cups pitted = about 1½ cups finely chopped or pureed olives.

If you want to pit a lot of olives, sandwich them between two pieces of cheesecloth, to keep them from sliding around on the work surface, and then crack them all at once. Lift off the cheesecloth and remove the pits.

Olive Paste: Pounding or grinding pitted meaty black brine-cured olives reduces them to a thick paste, an olive pesto really. At once sweet, salty, and piquant, it goes a long way. It is indispensable for quickly transforming simple ingredients: Spread it on slabs of grilled polenta, on crusty bread, mozzarella, tomatoes, fennel, or sweet peppers. Add it to boiled, baked, or even mashed potatoes. Stir into risotto, bowls of boiled grains, beans, or pasta, mayonnaise or aïoli. It will keep for at least 6 weeks.

To make the paste in a food processor, combine 1¼ cups pitted meaty ripe black olives, such as Kalamata (see Pitted Olives, page 683), 2½ teaspoons minced fresh oregano or 1 teaspoon dried oregano, 1¼ teaspoons minced fresh basil or ½ teaspoon dried basil, ½ to 1 teaspoon balsamic vinegar, and ¾ teaspoon sugar in the work bowl and process for several minutes, scraping the sides down frequently, until reduced to a paste. With the motor running, drizzle in 2 to 3 teaspoons extra-virgin olive oil. Alternatively, for a slightly coarser texture, in a mortar, pound the olives to a paste with a pestle. Add the remaining ingredients and continue pounding and mashing to a coarse paste. Pack the olive paste into jars and refrigerate. (Makes 1 cup.)

Roasted and Peeled Fresh Chestnuts: Peeling the tough skin off chestnuts can be a tedious task and every cook seems to have his or her own method for doing it.

I score the chestnut peels first and soak the chestnuts in water before roasting. The residual water left in the drained chestnuts creates steam in the hot pan, keeping the chestnuts from drying out and making them easier to peel.

For 1 pound peeled chestnuts, start with 1½ pounds chestnuts in the shell. Using a thin sharp knife, carve an X on the flat side of each chestnut. Put the chestnuts in a large bowl and add enough water to cover by 1 inch. Let soak for at least 30 minutes and up to 1 hour. Drain the chestnuts and pat dry.

Spread the chestnuts in a roasting pan and roast in a preheated 400°F oven for 15 to 20 minutes, or until the shells are brittle and have curled back somewhat at the X. Remove from the oven.

As soon as the chestnuts are cool enough to handle, use a knife to peel off both the hard outer shells and the inner brown skins.

Chestnut Puree: If you cannot find commercial chestnut puree, it is easy to make your own using vacuum-packed bottled peeled chestnuts, frozen peeled chestnuts, or peeled fresh chestnuts.

Combine 1 pound vacuum-packed peeled chestnuts or peeled frozen or fresh chestnuts (see Peeled Fresh Chestnuts, page 684) and 1 cup water in a medium saucepan. Bring to a simmer over moderate heat, cover, and simmer for about 25 minutes, stirring occasionally, until the chestnuts are puree-tender. Drain the chestnuts well, reserving about ½ cup of the cooking water.

Process the chestnuts in a food processor, stopping frequently to scrape down the sides of the bowl, until they are reduced to a stiff, rather dry puree. If necessary, add a little of the cooking water to loosen the puree. Pack into a bowl and press plastic wrap directly against the surface of the puree to prevent it from discoloring. Refrigerate for up to 4 days or freeze up to 2 months. (Makes a scant 2 cups.)

IN A PINCH.

Dessert Wine: Sweet, fragrant dessert wines such as Sauternes, Monbazillac, Barsac, or Muscat de Beaumes-de-Venise are wonderful to cook with. But in a pinch, you can make the following substitution: 1 cup Riesling or fruity white wine plus 3 tablespoons golden honey.

Buttermilk: For baking recipes, and in sauces that call for a mixture of buttermilk and sour cream, whisk 1⅓ cups plain yogurt with ⅔ cup whole milk. For baking recipes only, combine 2 cups whole milk and 2 teaspoons cider vinegar or white wine vinegar or 1 tablespoon plus 1 teaspoon fresh lemon juice in a clean jar. Set aside until the milk curdles and thickens, about 10 minutes. Refrigerate until ready to use. (Makes 2 cups.)

You can also keep powdered buttermilk, which lasts for months, in your pantry, and reconstitute just as much as you need for any baking recipe.

Nonaluminum Baking Powder: Combine 1 teaspoon cream of tartar, ½ teaspoon baking soda, and ½ teaspoon cornstarch and sift together three times. Store in a tightly capped jar. (Makes 2 teaspoons.)

Rough Conversions and Equivalents

EGGS
1 large egg = ¼ cup = 2 oz = 60 g
1 egg yolk = 1 Tbs = 15 ml
1 egg white = 2 Tbs = 30 ml

BUTTER
1 stick = 4 oz = 115 g
1 tablespoon = ½ oz = 15 g

FLOUR
AMERICAN ALL-PURPOSE FLOUR IS A MIXTURE OF HARD AND SOFT WHEAT.
BRITISH PLAIN FLOUR IS A NEAR EQUIVALENT TO AMERICAN ALL-PURPOSE FLOUR.
1 cup all-purpose American flour = 5 oz = 160 g

SUGAR
AMERICAN SUGAR IS FINELY GRANULATED. BRITISH COOKS SHOULD USE CASTER SUGAR.
1 cup granulated sugar = 7 oz = 200 g
1 cup packed brown sugar = 6 oz = 175 g
1 cup confectioners' (icing) sugar = 4½ oz = 130 g

TEMPERATURES

	°F	°C	OVEN	°F	°C	GAS MARK
freezer storage	-10	-23	very cool	250–275	130–140	½–1
	0	-17.7	cool	300	148	2
water freezes	32	0	warm	325	163	3
room temperature	68	20	moderate	350	177	4
water simmers	205	96	moderately hot	375–400	190–204	5–6
water boils	212	100	hot	425	218	7
			very hot	450–475	232–245	8–9

VOLUME

AMERICAN	METRIC	IMPERIAL
¼ tsp	1.25 ml	
½ tsp	2.5 ml	
1 tsp	5 ml	
½ Tbs (1½ tsp)	7.5 ml	
1 Tbs (3 tsp)	15 ml	
¼ cup (4 Tbs)	60 ml	2 fl oz
⅓ cup (5 Tbs)	75 ml	2½ fl oz
½ cup (8 Tbs)	125 ml	4 fl oz
⅔ cup (10 Tbs)	150 ml	5 fl oz
¾ cup (12 Tbs)	175 ml	6 fl oz
1 cup (16 Tbs)	250 ml	8 fl oz (½ pint)
1¼ cups	300 ml	10 fl oz
1½ cups	350 ml	12 fl oz
1 pint (2 cups)	500 ml	16 fl oz (1 pint)
1 quart (4 cups)	1 liter	2 pints

WEIGHTS

AVOIRDUPOIS	METRIC	AVOIRDUPOIS	METRIC	AVOIRDUPOIS	METRIC
¼ oz	7 g	8 oz (½ lb)	225 g	1 lb	450 g
½ oz	15 g	9 oz	250 g	1 lb 2 oz	500 g
1 oz	30 g	10 oz	300 g	1½ lb	750 g
2 oz	60 g	11 oz	325 g	2 lb	900 g
3 oz	90 g	12 oz	350 g	2¼ lb	1 kg
4 oz	115 g	13 oz	375 g	3 lb	1.4 kg
5 oz	150 g	14 oz	400 g	4 lb	1.8 kg
6 oz	175 g	15 oz	425 g	4½ lb	2 kg
7 oz	200 g	16 oz (1 lb)	450 g		

COMPARATIVE NUTRITIONAL ANALYSES. These nutritional analyses are meant to be a resource for people wishing to gear their diets in specific ways. The data include calories, protein, carbohydrates, total fat, saturated fat, fiber, and sodium. I must stress, however, that rigid focus on numbers, particularly those of fat, takes the joy and spontaneity out of eating and is often misguided in its logic. A good diet is all about an *overall balance* of nutrients, fat, and calories in your way of eating over time, say, a week or a month, and not about making single recipes now and then. Occasional splurges balance out in the scheme of a consistent moderate diet.

You will find an analysis of each main recipe, though not for variations because they are usually similar. The Guides to Improvising are so mutable it is virtually impossible to run an accurate nutritional analysis on them. But since they are almost always followed by a derivative recipe, you can use its data as a ballpark figure for any improvisation you make using a Guide. In the cases where a Guide is not followed by a derivative recipe, I've included a very rough analysis to give an idea of the nutrition.

There are three useful tables comparing various cuts of meat, poultry, and game; flavorful cooking fats; and different kinds of creamy dairy products—the food categories that create the most concern for people trying to forge a healthful diet. Knowing the relative values of interchangeable ingredients, for example, veal cutlets and turkey breast, will allow you to make informed choices about which ones you wish to use in a recipe.

MEAT, POULTRY, GAME

PER 4-OUNCE COOKED, TRIMMED, SKINLESS PORTION	CALORIES (kcal)	PROTEIN (gm)	TOTAL FAT (gm)	SATURATED FAT (gm)	SODIUM (mg)
Beef, strip (shell)	209	32.4	7.8	2.9	77
Beef, sirloin	216	34.4	7.7	3.0	75
Beef, tenderloin (filet mignon)	233	32.0	10.7	4.0	71
Beef, flank	235	30.6	11.5	4.9	94
Beef, skirt steak	252	35.7	10.9	3.6	71
Beefalo	213	34.6	7.2	3.0	92
Buffalo	148	30.3	2.4	0.6	63
Chicken, breast	187	35.0	4.0	1.1	84
Chicken, leg/thigh	216	30.1	9.5	2.6	103
Chicken skin, roasted	129	5.8	11.5	3.2	19
Duck, breast	159	31.0	2.8	0.7	119
Duck, leg/thigh	202	33.0	6.8	1.6	122
Lamb, leg	216	32.0	8.7	3.1	77
Lamb, loin	245	33.9	11.0	3.9	95
Lamb, rib	266	31.4	14.7	5.3	96
Pork, tenderloin	186	31.8	5.4	1.9	63
Pork, loin	225	31.2	10.2	3.7	75
Rabbit	221	33.0	9.1	2.7	53
Turkey, breast	153	34.0	0.8	0.3	58
Turkey, leg/thigh	211	32.0	8.1	2.7	89
Veal, leg	230	41.6	5.8	2.1	76
Venison	179	34.2	3.6	1.4	61

CREAMY DAIRY PRODUCTS

PER 1 TABLESPOON	CALORIES (kcal)	PROTEIN (gm)	CARBOHYDRATES (gm)	TOTAL FAT (gm)	SATURATED FAT (gm)	SODIUM (mg)
Heavy Whipping Cream and Crème Fraîche	52	0.3	0.4	5.6	3.5	5.6
Sour Cream, regular	26	0.4	0.5	2.5	1.6	6.0
Sour Cream, reduced-fat	20	0.4	0.6	1.8	1.1	6.0
Sour Cream, light	20	1.0	1.0	1.3	0.8	10.0
Quark	20	1.3	0.5	1.5	0.8	20.0

Source: Nutritionist Five, First DataBank

FLAVORFUL COOKING FATS

PER 1 TEASPOON	CALORIES (kcal)	TOTAL FAT (gm)	SATURATED FAT (gm)	MONO- UNSATURATED FAT (gm)	POLY- UNSATURATED FAT (gm)
Butter	34	3.8	2.3	1.1	0.1
Canola Oil	41	4.7	0.3	0.0	1.4
Duck Fat	38	4.2	1.4	0.3	0.5
Grapeseed Oil	40	4.5	0.4	0.7	3.2
Olive Oil	40	4.5	0.6	3.3	0.4
Pancetta/Bacon Fat	38	4.2	1.6	1.9	0.5
Walnut Oil	40	4.5	0.4	1.0	2.8

RECIPES.

VEGETABLES

	CALORIES (kcal)	PROTEIN (gm)	CARBO- HYDRATES (gm)	TOTAL FAT (gm)	SATURATED FAT (gm)	FIBER (gm)	SODIUM (mg)	
Roasted Garlic	149	5.5	29.0	2.7	0.4	1.8	14	page 37
Slow-Roasted Tomatoes	68	1.8	10.0	3.2	0.4	2.3	91	page 38
Roasted Wild Mushrooms	110	6.0	14.0	3.8	0.5	4.5	176	page 40
"Fried" Eggplant	68	1.9	11.0	2.6	0.4	3.0	226	page 42
Peppers Roasted with Garlic and Anchovies	112	4.0	12.0	6.0	0.9	3.6	367	page 42
Roasted Root Vegetable Hash	206	4.0	37.0	6.3	0.8	9.0	371	page 44
Roasted Asparagus with Brown Butter and Pecorino	98	5.6	5.7	6.7	4.0	2.5	255	page 45
Parsnip Fries	184	2.3	34.6	5.0	0.7	9.4	406	page 46
Potato Chips	109	1.6	17.0	4.1	2.5	1.2	295	page 47
Greek-Style Potatoes with Lemon and Thyme	237	3.8	44.0	5.8	0.8	3.8	233	page 49
The Best Part of a Potato Gratin	180	6.4	28.7	4.2	2.5	2.6	467	page 50
Sweet Onion and Tomato Gratin	180	6.8	21.9	8.1	2.4	3.4	392	page 52
Mashed Potato Cake	236	7.6	34.1	7.9	4.9	2.6	562	page 54
Steam-Roasted Fennel with Pancetta and Juniper	107	3.7	19.0	3.0	1.0	7.8	298	page 58
Mushrooms with Sake and Lemon	115	6.2	15.3	2.4	1.3	3.6	415	page 60
"Fried" Onions	79	1.8	13.7	2.3	1.3	2.8	226	page 62
Peperonata	143	3.8	18.7	7.2	1.0	4.0	82	page 63
"Fried" Artichokes with Crispy Garlic and Sage	106	4.2	14.6	4.8	0.7	6.2	247	page 66

		CALORIES (kcal)	PROTEIN (gm)	CARBO-HYDRATES (gm)	TOTAL FAT (gm)	SATURATED FAT (gm)	FIBER (gm)	SODIUM (mg)
page 68	Spring Vegetable Ragout	135	6.6	17.2	5.3	0.7	6.0	282
page 70	Cabbage Braised with Smoky Ham and Riesling	149	4.7	17.9	5.7	1.3	6.7	642
page 74	Tender Greens Sautéed with Garlic and Olive Oil	90	4.6	6.8	6.2	0.8	4.1	265
page 75	Mature Greens with Bacon and Balsamic Vinegar	93	4.0	13.0	3.4	1.1	2.3	255
page 77	Buttermilk Mashed Potatoes	162	3.4	29.4	3.6	2.2	2.3	276
page 81	Celery Root and Apple Puree	115	3.7	20.0	3.1	1.7	2.2	350
page 82	Fresh Corn "Polenta"	209	9.0	33.0	7.2	3.6	4.5	327
page 83	Chestnut Puree with Fennel Seed	192	4.8	35.7	3.7	0.9	0.9	248

BEANS AND OTHER LEGUMES

		CALORIES (kcal)	PROTEIN (gm)	CARBO-HYDRATES (gm)	TOTAL FAT (gm)	SATURATED FAT (gm)	FIBER (gm)	SODIUM (mg)
page 92	Basic Cooked Beans, Peas, and Lentils	173	10.6	32.4	0.6	0.2	6.4	149
page 96	Tuscan Beans with Sage and Garlic	259	13.7	36.0	7.4	1.1	8.6	308
page 97	Beans with Pancetta and Sherry	265	14.4	38.0	5.8	2.3	9.3	240
page 98	Flageolets with Tomatoes and Herbs de Provence	271	12.9	41.9	6.5	0.8	4.3	312
page 99	Chickpea Stew with Saffron and Winter Squash	356	12.9	67.0	6.8	0.8	13.0	317
page 100	Gratin of Beans	221	16.0	34.0	2.7	1.5	8.5	260
page 101	Hummus (Chickpea Puree)	125	5.6	17.0	4.3	0.5	4.9	374
page 102	White Beans and Mellowed Garlic with Rosemary Oil	174	8.2	23.8	3.5	0.5	8.6	105
page 104	Red Lentil Stew with Caramelized Onions	343	19.6	56.0	5.0	1.1	2.0	351
page 106	Fat Beans with Mole	447	18.3	82.7	6.7	1.5	13.0	555
page 107	Rustic Cassoulet Beans	210	13.1	32.3	3.4	1.1	9.6	253
page 110	Revisionist Cassoulet (without meats or poultry)	360	22.4	55.1	5.9	1.9	16.0	486
page 111	Bourbon Baked Beans	262	14.4	48.8	1.9	0.4	14.2	196
page 113	Rustic Chickpea-Flour Pancake	127	3.8	11.2	7.5	0.9	2.2	116
page 114	Fresh Soybeans with Extra-Virgin Olive Oil and Shaved Cheese	399	36.8	27.8	15.5	3.9	3.0	756

PASTA

	CALORIES (kcal)	PROTEIN (gm)	CARBO-HYDRATES (gm)	TOTAL FAT (gm)	SATURATED FAT (gm)	FIBER (gm)	SODIUM (mg)	
Ravioli with Garlic, Olive Oil, and Crispy Sage	461	19.6	43.3	24.0	9.7	2.8	769	page 124
Brown Butter Orzo "Risotto"	238	7.3	42.4	3.9	2.0	1.4	295	page 126
Cold Spicy Sesame Noodles	240	8.4	35.6	7.1	1.0	2.5	491	page 127
Lasagna Noodles with Pesto and Summer Vegetables	518	19.8	65.5	20.3	3.4	7.8	318	page 129
Tortelloni with Red Pepper–Juice Sauce, Olives, and Ricotta Salata	488	18.0	50.0	21.3	8.3	4.0	1,181	page 132
Gyo's Chilled Noodles with Dipping Sauce and Embellishments	394	29.3	61.0	4.6	1.2	3.8	1,600	page 134
Pasta with Quickly Cooked Green Vegetables in Garlicky Olive Oil (Guide: rough average)	363	13.9	52.1	11.9	2.3	5.7	354	page 136
Tubetti with Asparagus, Morels, and Fava Beans	417	20.2	62.7	9.5	4.0	6.5	556	page 139
Pasta with Leeks, Pepper, and Aged Goat Cheese	357	12.0	55.5	9.7	4.7	3.0	293	page 140
Fresh Pasta with Cauliflower, Currants, and Pine Nuts	466	20.1	57.3	18.4	4.8	4.4	753	page 142
Pasta with Rosemary-Roasted Eggplant and Ricotta Salata	481	18.0	59.8	19.4	7.4	4.0	1,087	page 144
Pappardelle with Classic Game Ragù	532	51.5	39.0	16.7	6.0	2.0	501	page 148
Baked Penne with Wild Mushroom Ragù and Ricotta Salata	472	21.6	74.6	11.0	5.7	5.7	1,058	page 150
Gratin of Pasta with Leftover Meat Juices	265	11.5	43.2	4.6	1.8	1.4	266	page 153
Macaroni and Cheese	483	24.2	54.7	18.2	11.0	1.7	642	page 153
Crispy Saffron Noodle Gratin	208	7.7	26.9	7.7	4.2	0.7	268	page 155
Egg Pasta	194	7.9	31.6	3.6	0.9	0.0	104	page 159

GRAINS

		CALORIES (kcal)	PROTEIN (gm)	CARBO-HYDRATES (gm)	TOTAL FAT (gm)	SATURATED FAT (gm)	FIBER (gm)	SODIUM (mg)
page 178	Foolproof Rice	184	3.3	37.0	2.0	0.3	0.6	148
page 178	Rice (or Mild Grains) with Ginger and Curry	247	5.7	43.3	4.3	2.0	1.9	145
page 180	Rustic Pilaf with Madeira	219	8.2	35.6	5.6	2.4	5.6	272
page 181	Mozzarella Rice	449	18.0	54.2	17.0	10.3	2.0	661
page 182	Wild Rice with Leeks and Wild Mushrooms	919	5.8	32.9	4.8	2.6	3.6	313
page 184	Simple Risotto (Guide: rough average, without embellishments)	410	15.2	61.2	10.5	5.5	1.9	402
page 188	Risotto with Red Wine, Rosemary, and Champagne Grapes	475	15.6	74.1	9.4	5.0	1.6	389
page 189	Risotto Cake	334	11.8	48.9	8.6	4.8	1.0	396
page 191	Spring Risotto with Asparagus and Peas	381	15.1	56.4	9.3	4.9	3.2	369
page 193	Risotto with Wild Mushrooms	248	9.3	37.5	5.9	3.1	1.4	201
page 198	Basic Polenta	110	2.5	23.5	1.1	0.2	2.2	301
page 200	Polenta with Fragrant Herb Oil and Caramelized Garlic	229	7.2	26.6	11.0	3.0	2.6	489
page 201	Panfried, Roasted, or Grilled Polenta	130	2.5	23.5	3.3	0.5	2.2	301
page 202	Polenta Cake with Olive Paste and Mozzarella	300	12.6	26.1	16.4	8.0	2.6	684
page 203	Polenta "Gnocchi" Gratin	208	6.2	24.7	9.9	5.0	2.4	747

FISH AND SHELLFISH

		CALORIES (kcal)	PROTEIN (gm)	CARBO-HYDRATES (gm)	TOTAL FAT (gm)	SATURATED FAT (gm)	FIBER (gm)	SODIUM (mg)
page 219	Citrus and Olive Oil Sauce for Roasted or Grilled Fish	89	0.9	9.5	6.1	0.8	2.1	24
page 219	Fennel-Roasted Fish	327	35.3	13.3	14.3	2.1	3.1	827
page 223	Salt-Roasted Shrimp	143	27.4	1.2	2.3	0.4	0.0	345
page 225	Slow-Roasted Striped Bass with Olive Paste and Thyme	174	28.3	0.8	5.7	1.1	0.2	289
page 228	Fillets in Green Curry Sauce	289	35.4	4.8	13.2	9.9	1.2	828
page 232	Oven-Steamed Whole Fish with Chinese Flavors	176	22.7	5.3	6.0	1.1	0.8	309

	CALORIES (kcal)	PROTEIN (gm)	CARBO-HYDRATES (gm)	TOTAL FAT (gm)	SATURATED FAT (gm)	FIBER (gm)	SODIUM (mg)	
Oven-Steamed Red Snapper with Fennel and Curry	227	32.8	10.9	5.5	2.3	4.1	423	page 234
Miso-Sake–Glazed Fish Fillets and Steaks	286	28.4	2.6	17.0	3.3	0.1	196	page 236
The Best Way to Grill Shrimp	151	28.3	1.9	2.5	0.5	0.3	234	page 237
Grilled Whole Fish Wrapped in Pancetta and Herbs	191	35.0	0.0	3.9	1.1	0.0	369	page 238
Curry-Crusted Shrimp	255	30.1	12.1	10.5	1.6	4.7	265	page 242
Sesame-Crusted Swordfish with Cilantro and Coconut Chutney	398	36.1	7.7	25.0	10.4	3.3	638	page 243
Crispy Salmon with Warm Lentils and Balsamic Essence	446	37.1	32.6	17.5	4.8	13.1	425	page 244
Mushroom–Crusted Bass in Port Wine Butter Sauce	301	30.5	7.0	15.0	5.6	0.3	514	page 246
Panfried Skate with Brown Butter and Capers	304	42.8	10.6	9.9	5.8	0.6	429	page 248
Shellfish Cooked in an Iron Skillet	152	14.9	5.7	7.3	1.1	0.1	561	page 250
Coriander-Crusted Scallops in Fennel Broth	239	24.0	8.6	12.7	1.9	3.2	983	page 252
Clams Steamed in Sake	259	15.2	9.2	3.1	1.4	0.1	139	page 256
Mussels or Clams with Lemongrass, Ginger, and Chiles	237	16.9	10.6	12.4	9.0	1.5	633	page 257
Saffron Fish Stew	281	33.1	11.3	7.7	1.4	1.3	694	page 260
Creamy Garlic Fish Soup After a Bourride	253	26.6	22.5	5.9	2.1	1.8	482	page 262
Steamed Lobster with Vanilla Butter Sauce	240	18.2	5.6	13.6	8.0	0.0	625	page 264
Pan-Smoked Fish (Guide: rough average)	310	39.8	2.9	14.2	3.1	0.2	682	page 266
Ginger-and-Cilantro Crab Cakes	283	38.9	10.0	8.8	1.2	1.4	895	page 269
Tuna Burgers	261	38.4	0.9	10.4	2.4	0.2	213	page 271
Garlic-Scented Salt Cod Puree	270	37.6	7.9	8.9	1.7	0.6	1,000	page 272
Thai Seafood Salad with Lemongrass Dressing	228	31.9	19.1	2.9	0.5	2.8	1,685	page 274
Home-Cured Salmon	97	12.1	1.7	4.4	1.0	0.0	463	page 276

	CALORIES (kcal)	PROTEIN (gm)	CARBO-HYDRATES (gm)	TOTAL FAT (gm)	SATURATED FAT (gm)	FIBER (gm)	SODIUM (mg)
page 291 Foolproof Roast Chicken with Its Own Pan Sauce	220	32.9	0.5	8.4	2.3	0.1	389
page 293 Herb-Scented Tuscan Pork Roast	255	32.0	1.2	11.2	4.1	0.1	759
page 294 Honey-Cured Pork Loin with Peppery Juniper and Fennel Seed Rub	296	29.9	6.9	15.9	5.8	0.2	508
page 296 Leg of Lamb Roasted on a Bed of Herbs	281	28.7	0.2	17.5	7.9	0.0	244
page 297 Boneless Leg of Lamb Stuffed with Crushed Olives	230	30.9	1.2	10.3	3.2	0.5	257
page 299 Rabbit Stuffed with Prunes	518	55.6	30.8	16.7	4.9	3.0	475
page 300 The Ultimate Roast Duck	424	32.4	0.6	31.0	11.0	0.0	449
page 302 Foolproof Roast Turkey	224	41.8	1.1	4.6	1.3	0.0	750
page 304 Lacquered Baby Back Ribs	347	40.7	7.1	16.5	5.7	0.5	932
page 306 Chicken with Garlic, Thyme, and Olives	276	33.9	6.2	11.6	2.8	0.7	396
page 307 Chicken Breasts with Mexican Flavors	275	36.0	20.8	5.3	0.9	4.9	893
page 309 Celebration Guinea Hen Cooked with Black Truffles	278	30.7	0.4	15.9	5.2	0.2	334
page 311 Revisionist Confit of Duck Legs	339	41.7	0.2	17.8	4.6	0.0	753
page 317 Szechwan Pepper–Crusted Steak Smothered with Onions	298	34.4	15.2	10.7	4.3	3.1	373
page 319 Cumin-Crusted Quail with Cilantro Gremolata	348	32.9	3.0	22.3	5.7	0.9	721
page 320 Seared Lamb with Moroccan Spices and Tomato Jam	287	33.5	11.6	12.0	3.3	2.2	234
page 323 Milanese-Style Scaloppine with Peppery Greens	303	32.7	15.9	11.5	2.9	0.9	487
page 326 Spice-Rubbed Duck Steaks with Port Wine Sauce	303	32.1	27.3	6.5	1.1	0.0	435
page 327 Hash (Guide: rough average)	328	27.8	35.1	8.5	3.0	6.3	288
page 329 Duck Breasts with Thyme-Infused Honey and Balsamic Pan Sauce	249	32.0	15.2	6.1	2.3	0.2	536
page 331 Scaloppine Marsala	288	37.9	17.7	5.7	0.9	2.6	368
page 336 Chicken in Red Wine with Mushrooms, Bacon, and Pearl Onions	359	35.3	24.9	11.0	3.5	2.9	463
page 338 Chicken with Sherry Vinegar Sauce	312	34.1	15.6	10.4	2.3	0.9	500

	CALORIES (kcal)	PROTEIN (gm)	CARBO-HYDRATES (gm)	TOTAL FAT (gm)	SATURATED FAT (gm)	FIBER (gm)	SODIUM (mg)	
Meat Loaf with Wild Mushrooms	344	31.0	18.3	15.8	5.8	2.8	566	page 340
Country Terrine with Pistachios	258	28.5	11.2	7.7	2.2	0.8	579	page 342
Chicken Liver Pâté with Golden Raisins	116	7.9	10.8	4.1	1.4	0.5	216	page 345
Homemade Sausages	222	25.6	7.3	9.3	3.1	0.6	286	page 347
Turkey Burgers with Apples, Onions, and Sage	200	27.3	11.4	4.5	1.8	1.2	336	page 348

QUICK BREADS FROM PIZZA TO PANCAKES

	CALORIES (kcal)	PROTEIN (gm)	CARBO-HYDRATES (gm)	TOTAL FAT (gm)	SATURATED FAT (gm)	FIBER (gm)	SODIUM (mg)	
Basic Pizza Dough (per ounce uncooked dough)	76	2.2	14.0	1.1	0.1	0.1	109	page 355
Thick-Crust Pizza (Guide: rough average, without toppings)	399	17.9	43.2	16.8	7.6	0.1	624	page 358
Thin-Crust Pizza (Guide: rough average, without toppings)	273	10.0	30.0	13.0	5.0	0.0	324	page 360
Rosemary, Lemon, and Pepper Focaccia	237	6.7	40.5	5.4	0.8	0.7	308	page 366
Pissaladière (Provençal Onion Tart)	243	7.5	38.0	6.9	0.9	2.4	563	page 367
Rustic Garlic Toasts	108	2.5	14.8	4.2	0.6	0.9	318	page 368
Parmesan Crisps	139	12.0	3.2	8.5	5.4	0.1	527	page 370
Savory Rosemary Biscotti (per biscotto)	36	1.4	4.3	1.5	0.3	0.1	68	page 371
Rosemary Buttermilk Biscuits (per biscuit)	104	2.6	15.8	3.3	1.9	0.5	210	page 374
Coriander-and-Orange-Scented Scones	249	5.1	42.0	6.7	3.9	0.9	314	page 375
Oat Bran Muffins with Dried Pears	216	7.1	44.0	5.2	0.6	4.3	296	page 376
Irish Brown Bread	136	4.9	23.5	3.2	1.7	2.6	234	page 377
Corn Blini	175	5.5	24.9	6.2	3.2	1.7	286	page 379
French Toast	179	7.0	18.3	8.2	4.0	0.9	295	page 380

SOUPS

		CALORIES (kcal)	PROTEIN (gm)	CARBO-HYDRATES (gm)	TOTAL FAT (gm)	SATURATED FAT (gm)	FIBER (gm)	SODIUM (mg)
page 386	Leek, Potato, and Sometimes Sorrel or Watercress Soup	145	5.6	17.0	7.0	3.8	1.6	299
page 387	Root Vegetable Crema	100	4.2	14.0	3.7	2.0	1.8	273
page 388	Garlic Soup with Pasta and Ham	290	18.0	40.1	7.0	3.5	1.8	700
page 390	Corn Soup with Chiles, Lime, and Cilantro Cream	428	15.3	72.0	14.0	6.0	8.1	543
page 392	Spicy Coconut Milk Soup	276	20.0	12.7	17.0	14.0	1.7	1,210
page 393	Roasted Pumpkin and Garlic Soup	79	4.2	14.0	1.8	0.7	1.1	296
page 394	Roasted Tomato Soup with Herb Cream	190	6.2	18.0	12.0	5.0	3.2	412
page 398	Soothing Japanese Noodle Soup	268	16.0	54.0	0.5	0.1	3.0	1,270
page 400	Beans and Wild Mushrooms in Fennel Broth	230	10.7	32.8	7.0	3.3	7.5	695
page 401	Simple Summer Soup with Pesto	293	8.4	27.4	19.0	3.1	10.3	750
page 402	French Winter Vegetable Soup	204	3.6	34.0	7.3	1.0	6.7	485
page 403	Basic Bean Soup (Guide: rough average, without embellishments)	257	16.0	40.0	4.3	1.4	12.3	587
page 406	Chicken and Vegetable Stew with Cilantro, Cumin, and Saffron	594	44.0	79.0	13.2	5.0	8.0	583

	CALORIES (kcal)	PROTEIN (gm)	CARBO- HYDRATES (gm)	TOTAL FAT (gm)	SATURATED FAT (gm)	FIBER (gm)	SODIUM (mg)	
Herb Salad	63	2.0	4.0	5.0	0.7	2.4	65	page 415
Peppery or Bitter Greens with Seasonal Fruits and Roasted Nuts (Guide: rough average)	106	3.3	8.7	7.3	0.8	2.2	58	page 417
Belgian Endive with Apples, Walnuts, and Blue Cheese	178	4.0	12.3	14.0	2.3	6.0	147	page 418
Salads with Shaved Parmesan	152	7.0	7.3	11.3	4.0	2.7	343	page 419
Classic Coleslaw	50	1.8	6.4	2.5	1.4	1.7	136	page 423
Celery Root "Rémoulade"	99	3.0	14.0	4.2	2.2	1.7	188	page 424
Cucumbers with Curry Cream	60	2.3	7.0	3.0	1.7	1.3	210	page 425
Moroccan "Gazpacho" Salad	87	2.4	13.0	4.0	0.5	3.2	212	page 426
Chopped Salad from the '21' Club	97	4.0	10.0	5.0	3.0	3.0	343	page 427
Southeast Asian Slaw	116	4.5	14.1	8.8	0.8	4.7	182	page 429
French Beans with Tarragon Cream Dressing and Hazelnuts	85	3.0	9.0	5.1	2.0	4.0	94	page 432
Chayote Squash Salad with Peanuts and Lime	139	4.2	18.0	7.2	1.3	2.2	99	page 433
Carrots in Chermoula	142	2.6	24.0	5.1	0.7	6.7	110	page 434
Beet Salad	90	2.3	10.7	4.8	0.7	2.7	252	page 436
Grilled Corn, Poblano, and Tomato Salad	202	6.2	34.0	7.0	1.0	5.2	69	page 437
Warm Potato Salad with Olives, Lemon Zest, and Thyme	217	3.8	36.0	5.7	0.8	3.2	241	page 438
Warm Bean Salad with Fresh Herbs and Olives	254	13.8	36.3	7.0	1.0	9.2	459	page 443
Warm Bean Salad with Balsamic-Bacon Vinaigrette	249	14.0	41.0	3.0	1.0	8.0	386	page 444
Farro Salad with Green Apple, Toasted Spices, and Pine Nuts	276	8.5	38.0	12.0	1.8	7.1	154	page 445
Quinoa Salad with Lemon-grass, Cilantro, and Mint	237	8.0	34.0	8.7	3.1	4.3	94	page 446
Pan-Seared Quail over Greens	422	37.0	4.0	28.0	7.0	1.8	391	page 450
Warm Goat Cheese Salad	216	12.0	4.0	17.0	9.0	1.5	309	page 451
Warm Wild Mushroom Salad	184	6.3	22.0	9.0	1.2	4.2	327	page 452
Warm Frisée Salad with Bacon and Croutons	204	7.0	14.0	14.0	5.0	4.0	388	page 454

	CALORIES (kcal)	PROTEIN (gm)	CARBO-HYDRATES (gm)	TOTAL FAT (gm)	SATURATED FAT (gm)	FIBER (gm)	SODIUM (mg)
page 465 Frozen Lychees (per lychee)	6	0.0	1.6	0.0	0.0	0.1	0.0
page 465 Tropical Fruits with Passion Fruit Sauce (per fruit)	17	0.0	4.2	0.1	0.0	1.8	5.0
page 466 White Peaches with Crushed Raspberry Sauce	78	1.1	19.7	0.3	0.0	4.0	0.0
page 467 Basic Vanilla Bean Syrup	39	0.0	9.0	0.0	0.0	0.0	0.1
page 468 Alain Senderens's Syrup for Tropical Fruits	36	0.0	9.3	0.0	0.0	0.0	0.0
page 469 Berry Elixir	46	0.1	11.9	0.0	0.0	0.3	0.0
page 472 Warm Spilling Fruit (Guide: rough average)	78	0.8	19.8	0.4	0.0	5.7	0.0
page 473 Prunes in Armagnac (per prune, with syrup)	30	0.2	5.9	0.0	0.0	0.6	0.0
page 474 Warm Sautéed Fresh Figs with Raspberry Coulis and Cream	164	1.0	26.5	7.2	4.3	4.5	4.0
page 476 Caramelized Roasted Pears	141	0.6	30.8	2.3	1.3	2.4	3.0
page 478 Apricots Roasted with Cardamom	213	2.8	55.2	0.4	0.0	0.0	7.0
page 479 Strawberry-Rhubarb Crumble	258	3.8	40.1	10.1	4.1	3.2	35.0
page 486 Rustic Rosemary-Apple Tart	277	3.4	43.7	10.6	6.3	1.8	116.0
page 487 Upside-Down Red Wine–Pear Tart	306	3.7	44.7	11.2	6.7	2.0	120.0
page 488 Lemon Curd Tart	212	4.0	26.4	10.4	6.1	0.1	106.0
page 490 Foolproof Flaky Butter Pastry (per ounce dough)	126	2.1	106.0	7.2	4.4	0.0	84.0
page 495 Individual Phyllo Disks	97	1.4	11.2	5.2	2.8	0.4	92.0
page 496 Thin Phyllo Wafers	81	1.0	10.5	3.9	2.1	0.3	69.0
page 498 Chocolate Chestnut Truffles (per truffle)	39	0.6	6.0	1.5	0.9	0.6	8.0
page 500 Chocolate Mousse Cake	180	3.3	27.1	7.5	4.4	1.6	42.0
page 502 Chocolate Angel Food Cake	167	5.9	36.5	0.4	0.2	1.0	99.0
page 504 Chocolate Malted Pudding	204	7.4	31.9	6.7	3.9	2.0	157.0
page 506 Fresh Lemon Cake	271	4.0	52.4	5.6	3.1	0.8	230.0
page 508 Gingerbread	269	4.3	45.8	7.8	4.4	0.7	277.0
page 509 Applesauce Cake	278	5.1	46.6	8.7	2.6	1.9	190.0
page 511 Nut Cake (Guide: rough average)	232	5.7	22.0	14.4	1.9	1.3	91.0
page 514 Pistachio and Almond Cake	227	6.8	26.0	11.1	1.7	2.3	109.0
page 516 Earl Grey Tea Wafers	22	0.3	2.9	1.1	0.6	0.0	5.5
page 518 Anne's Spicy Ginger Cookies	63	0.9	10.8	2.0	1.2	0.1	17.0

	CALORIES (kcal)	PROTEIN (gm)	CARBO-HYDRATES (gm)	TOTAL FAT (gm)	SATURATED FAT (gm)	FIBER (gm)	SODIUM (mg)	
Fruit Chips (per chip)								page 519
Apple	5	0.3	1.1	0.6	0.0	0.2	0.0	
Pear	4	0.0	1.1	0.0	0.0	0.2	0.0	
Banana	7	0.0	1.8	0.0	0.0	0.2	0.1	
Mango	3	0.0	0.9	0.0	0.0	0.1	0.1	
Real "Jell-O"	81	1.5	19.0	0.0	0.0	0.0	6.0	page 521
Risotto Rice Pudding	263	8.0	51.0	2.0	1.0	1.0	194.0	page 522
Pears, Peaches, or Quinces in Fragrant Red Wine Sauce	251	1.2	54.9	0.3	0.0	2.4	16.0	page 523
Quick Sorbets and Faux Ice Cream (Guide: rough average)	112	1.6	28.7	0.4	0.0	5.1	0.9	page 525
Banana and Coconut Milk Ice Cream	153	1.5	22.9	7.5	6.5	2.5	5.0	page 527
Fruit Coulis (per ¼ cup)	37	0.4	9.0	0.3	0.0	1.7	1.0	page 528
Strawberries in Beaujolais Sauce	84	0.8	18.2	0.3	0.0	2.2	5.0	page 529
Basic Vanilla Custard Sauce (per 2 tablespoons)	47	1.6	6.2	1.6	0.8	0.0	22.0	page 529
Tart, Ethereal Lemon Curd (per ¼ cup)	113	2.8	23.9	1.3	0.4	0.1	31.0	page 532
Real Whipped Cream or Crème Fraîche (per 3 tablespoons)	80	0.5	1.4	8.3	5.2	0.0	8.0	page 533
Rich Faux Cream (per tablespoon)	15	1.8	1.0	0.5	0.3	0.0	6.0	page 534
Yogurt Cream (per tablespoon)	29	1.6	2.2	1.5	1.0	0.0	22.0	page 535

	CALORIES (kcal)	PROTEIN (gm)	CARBO-HYDRATES (gm)	TOTAL FAT (gm)	SATURATED FAT (gm)	FIBER (gm)	SODIUM (mg)
SINCE MOST FLAVOR ESSENCES AND DRY RUBS ARE COMPOSED MAINLY OF SPICES AND HERBS, THEY YIELD LITTLE QUANTIFIABLE NUTRITIONAL DATA. DRY RUBS CAN CONTAIN UP TO 900 MG SODIUM (½ TEASPOON KOSHER SALT) PER SERVING, WITH THE FOLLOWING EXCEPTIONS:							
page 549 Tuscan Herb Salt (per teaspoon)	1.5	0.0	0.2	0.0	0.0	0.0	292
page 550 Szechwan Pepper Rub and Dipping Salt (per teaspoon)	3.5	0.0	0.9	0.0	0.0	0.2	55
UNLESS OTHERWISE NOTED, MARINADE VALUES REFLECT THE APPROXIMATE AMOUNT ABSORBED PER SERVING.							
page 554 Classic Greek Lemon and Olive Oil Marinade with Herbs	24	0.0	0.5	2.6	0.4	0.2	36
page 555 Rosemary and Orange Zest Marinade	32	0.0	0.4	3.4	0.5	0.0	36
page 556 Southeast Asian Marinade	16	0.8	2.7	3.3	0.0	0.0	336
page 557 Sesame-Ginger Marinade	37	0.2	3.7	2.4	0.3	0.1	101
page 558 Chipotle Adobo Marinade	9	0.6	1.0	0.2	0.1	0.0	66
page 558 Tandoori Marinade	9	0.4	1.1	0.3	0.2	0.3	59
page 559 Red Miso Glaze	36	1.2	5.9	0.8	0.0	0.4	485
page 560 Moroccan Spice Paste	39	0.4	1.7	3.7	0.5	0.5	74
page 561 Thai Green Curry Paste (per tablespoon)	17	0.3	1.3	1.3	1.0	0.3	50
page 562 Hoisin Barbecue Sauce	35	0.4	3.9	1.9	0.3	0.1	80
page 563 Jamaican Jerk Paste	22	0.2	3.0	1.2	0.2	0.4	112

BROTHS

	CALORIES (kcal)	PROTEIN (gm)	CARBO-HYDRATES (gm)	TOTAL FAT (gm)	SATURATED FAT (gm)	FIBER (gm)	SODIUM (mg)	
FIGURING THE NUTRIENT CONTENT OF BROTHS, WHICH ARE BASICALLY LIQUID INFUSIONS OF MEATS, POULTRY, VEGETABLES, AND HERBS, YIELDS, AT BEST, ROUGH ESTIMATES. THE FOLLOWING VALUES ARE FOR BASIC TYPES OF BROTHS YOU'LL FIND IN THE BROTHS CHAPTER. FOR INFUSED BROTHS, LOOK AT THE VALUES OF THE BASE BROTH USED IN THE RECIPE.								
Vegetable Broths: Fennel, Leek, Roasted Vegetable, and Basic Vegetable (rough average per ½ cup)	15	0.5	1.5	1.0	0.7	0.0	221	pages 568–571
Faux Veal Broth (per ½ cup)	78	0.4	8.0	4.5	2.5	0.0	205	page 572
Hearty Porcini-Miso Broth (per cup)	40	0.9	2.7	2.5	0.9	0.3	305	page 573
Classic Rich Poultry, Meat, or Game Broth (per cup, rough average)	34	5.2	0.8	0.0	0.0	0.0	200	page 574
Shortcut Poultry, Game, or Meat Broth (per cup, rough average)	60	7.0	2.2	3.0	1.0	0.0	300	page 576
White Wine Fish Broth (per cup)	40	4.3	0.6	1.5	0.5	0.0	45	page 577
Shortcut Seafood Broth (per cup)	9	1.0	0.2	0.0	0.0	0.0	295	page 578
Parmesan Broth (per cup)	50	6.0	2.0	2.0	2.0	0.0	300	page 580
Ginger-Sake Broth	61	4.0	5.4	2.8	1.5	0.0	141	page 582

FLAVORED OILS

	CALORIES (kcal)	PROTEIN (gm)	CARBO-HYDRATES (gm)	TOTAL FAT (gm)	SATURATED FAT (gm)	FIBER (gm)	SODIUM (mg)	
THE FLAVORING ELEMENTS OF FLAVORED OILS—HERBS, SPICES, AND AROMATICS—HAVE LITTLE QUANTIFIABLE NUTRITIONAL DATA. THE FOLLOWING DATA FOR 1 TEASPOON WILL YIELD A REASONABLE ESTIMATE OF FATS AND CALORIES.								
Flavored Oil (1 teaspoon)	40	0.0	0.0	4.5	0.6	0.0	0.0	pages 588–597

SAUCES

	CALORIES (kcal)	PROTEIN (gm)	CARBO-HYDRATES (gm)	TOTAL FAT (gm)	SATURATED FAT (gm)	FIBER (gm)	SODIUM (mg)
page 606	Everyday Vinaigrette (per teaspoon)	21	0.0	0.3	2.3	0.3	0.0	6
page 607	Lemon Vinaigrette with a Little Garlic (per teaspoon)	30	0.0	0.2	3.0	0.4	0.0	12
page 608	Classic Mustard Vinaigrette (per teaspoon)	23	0.0	0.0	3.0	0.3	0.0	5
page 609	Citrus Vinaigrette (per teaspoon)	11	0.0	0.2	1.1	0.2	0.0	10
page 610	Dieter's Balsamic Dressing (per tablespoon)	14	0.1	1.3	1.1	0.1	0.0	186
page 611	Roasted Sesame Seed Dressing (per tablespoon)	27	0.9	2.1	1.6	0.2	0.5	219
page 612	Impromptu Warm Herb Vinaigrette (Guide: rough average per tablespoon)	61	0.0	0.9	6.4	0.9	0.0	20
page 613	Warm Sesame, Ginger, and Scallion Vinaigrette (per tablespoon)	44	0.6	2.4	4.0	0.4	0.3	154
page 614	Warm Anchovy and Olive Oil Sauce (per tablespoon)	67	1.0	0.4	7.0	1.0	0.1	95
page 615	Warm Curry Vinaigrette (per tablespoon)	31	0.2	2.0	2.0	0.4	0.3	23
page 616	Warm Vermouth and Shallot Dressing (per tablespoon)	29	0.1	1.0	2.0	0.3	0.0	75
page 617	Fruit Juice Vinaigrette (per 1½ tablespoons)	77	0.6	9.0	5.0	0.6	0.2	1
page 618	Roasted Garlic Aïoli (per 2 tablespoons)	94	2.0	9.0	6.0	1.0	1.0	79
page 620	Romesco (per 2 tablespoons)	108	2.0	10.0	7.0	1.0	2.0	69
page 622	Mortar-Made Pesto Sauce (per 2 tablespoons)	180	3.7	2.2	18.0	3.0	1.1	147
page 623	Greek Garlic Sauce (per ⅓ cup)	147	1.4	16.0	9.0	1.2	1.4	120
page 624	Everyday Mayonnaise (per tablespoon)	28	0.5	0.4	2.8	0.4	0.0	19
page 625	Herb Cream (per 2⅔ tablespoon)	35	1.0	2.0	2.7	1.7	0.0	57
page 629	Apple, Cucumber or Green Mango Raita (per ¼ cup)	38	1.5	5.2	1.4	1.0	0.5	69

	CALORIES (kcal)	PROTEIN (gm)	CARBO-HYDRATES (gm)	TOTAL FAT (gm)	SATURATED FAT (gm)	FIBER (gm)	SODIUM (mg)	
Yogurt Sauce with Toasted Spices, Lime Zest, and Basil (per ¼ cup)	41	2.2	3.4	2.0	1.3	0.2	64	page 630
Russian Dressing (per tablespoon)	16	0.4	1.4	1.0	0.7	0.2	69	page 631
Roquefort or Maytag Blue Cheese Dressing (per tablespoon)	27	1.0	1.0	2.0	1.0	0.0	94	page 632
Rice Cream (per ¼ cup)	53	2.5	6.0	2.3	1.4	0.1	34	page 633
Leek and Saffron Cream (per 3 tablespoons)	60	2.0	5.0	4.0	2.3	0.2	89	page 634
Balsamic Syrup (per teaspoon)	14	0.0	3.0	0.0	0.0	0.0	0	page 636
Port Wine Sauce (per 2 tablespoons)	113	1.0	27.0	0.3	0.1	0.0	25	page 637
Brown Butter and Balsamic Sauce (per tablespoon)	60	0.2	1.0	6.0	4.0	0.0	40	page 638
Red Wine Essence (per tablespoon)	57	1.0	8.0	1.0	0.1	0.0	17	page 639
Shallot-and-Vinegar Butter Sauce (per 2⅔ tablespoons)	100	0.5	3.0	8.4	5.2	0.0	104	page 643
Port Wine Butter Sauce (per 2⅔ tablespoons)	128	1.6	11.0	9.0	5.4	0.0	99	page 644
Spicy Carrot Juice Sauce (per ½ cup)	110	1.3	13.0	6.3	3.8	1.1	111	page 648
Red Pepper–Juice Sauce (per ½ cup)	157	2.0	22.0	7.0	1.0	0.3	87	page 649
Warm Beet Juice Vinaigrette (per 2 tablespoons)	83	1.0	9.0	5.0	0.4	0.0	93	page 650
Tomato Sauce (per ½ cup)	69	2.0	11.0	3.0	0.4	1.0	162	page 652
Uncooked Fresh Tomato Sauce (per ½ cup)	68	1.3	8.5	4.0	0.5	1.0	84	page 654
Warm Olivada (Warm Crushed Olives) (per tablespoon)	11	0.1	0.4	1.0	0.1	0.2	155	page 655
Revisionist Mole (Ancho Chile Sauce) (per ¼ cup)	58	3.3	10.0	1.6	0.4	3.0	152	page 656
Pumpkin Seed Sauce (per ¼ cup)	61	2.4	4.9	4.0	0.7	1.3	115	page 658

	CALORIES (kcal)	PROTEIN (gm)	CARBO-HYDRATES (gm)	TOTAL FAT (gm)	SATURATED FAT (gm)	FIBER (gm)	SODIUM (mg)
page 660	Salsa (per ¼ cup) (Guide: rough average)	14	1.0	3.0	0.2	0.0	0.7	78
page 661	Roasted Tomatillo Salsa (per ¼ cup)	26	1.0	5.0	1.0	0.1	1.5	148
page 662	Charred Onion Salsa (per ¼ cup)	52	1.0	7.5	2.4	0.3	1.4	152
page 664	Warm Mango Chutney (per ¼ cup)	36	0.4	9.0	0.4	0.1	1.0	3
page 665	Cilantro and Coconut Chutney (per ¼ cup)	90	1.4	4.5	8.2	7.0	2.0	199
page 666	Balsamic-Cooked Peppers (per ¼ cup)	30	0.3	3.4	2.0	0.2	0.7	37
page 667	Onion Marmalade with Sherry Vinegar (per tablespoon)	18	0.4	3.0	0.6	0.3	0.6	37
page 668	Pears in Fragrant Wine (per ¼ cup)	39	0.2	9.0	0.1	0.0	1.0	2
page 668	Eleanor's Applesauce (per ¼ cup)	55	0.2	15.0	0.2	0.0	1.5	2
page 669	Red Wine–Cranberry Sauce (per ¼ cup)	101	0.3	25.0	0.1	0.0	2.0	2
page 670	Cranberry-Walnut Conserve (per 2 tablespoons)	46	1.0	8.0	2.0	0.2	1.0	1
page 671	"Wild" Plum Sauce (per ¼ cup)	40	0.4	9.0	0.2	0.2	1.0	1

MENUS AND DISHES FOR EVERY OCCASION. Great meals are all about context: the settings in which the food is served, the people gathered together, the balance of dishes that complement and play off each other to create a memorable harmony. The following menus are some of my favorite combinations, drawn from meals I have enjoyed while traveling or as the guest at someone's table, or that I found particularly successful when I planned parties. I've also included listings of recipes that are appropriate for specific occasions, such as Make-Ahead Main Dishes, to help make entertaining easy and fun.

ULTRA-EASY/QUICK MAIN DISHES

Spaghetti with Spicy Anchovies
and Parsley 124

Fresh Soybeans with Extra-Virgin Olive
Oil and Shaved Cheese 114

Mozzarella Rice 181

Polenta with Fragrant Herb Oil and
Caramelized Garlic 200

Salt-Roasted Shrimp 223

Slow-Roasted Salmon with Chive Oil
224, 590

Miso-Sake–Glazed Fish Fillets and
Steaks 236

Curry-Crusted Shrimp 242

Sesame-Crusted Swordfish with Cilantro
and Coconut Chutney 243

Shellfish Cooked in an Iron Skillet 250

Classic Moules Marinière 256

Mussels in Curry Broth 256

Clams Steamed in Sake 256

Pan-Smoked Salmon 268

Butterflied Roast Chicken 292

"Wood-Smoked" Steak Smothered with
Onions 318

Cumin-Crusted Quail with Cilantro
Gremolata 319

Warm Goat Cheese Salad 451

PICNIC

Country Terrine with Pistachios, with country
bread, grainy mustard, cornichons 342

Warm Potato Salad with Olives, Lemon Zest,
and Thyme 438

Celery Root "Rémoulade" or Classic
Coleslaw 424, 423

Fresh Lemon Cake or Individual Chocolate
Angel Food Cakelets 506, 503

Strawberries

KIDS' FAVORITES

Macaroni and Cheese 153

Pork chops and "Fried" Onions, with
Eleanor's Applesauce 315, 62, 668

Meat Loaf with Wild Mushrooms 340

French Toast 380

Pizzas 355–362

Turkey Burgers with Apples, Onions,
and Sage 348

Foolproof Roast Chicken with Its Own
Pan Sauce 291

Foolproof Rice 178

Mozzarella Rice 181

Brown Butter Orzo "Risotto" 126

Cold Spicy Sesame Noodles 127

Hummus (Chickpea Puree) 101

Buttermilk Mashed Potatoes 77

Potato Chips 47

Crispy Twice-Roasted Potatoes 46

Real "Jell-O" 521

Chocolate Malted Pudding 504

Chocolate Angel Food Cake 502

Applesauce Cake 509

LIGHT LUNCHEON MENUS

Rosemary, Lemon, and Pepper Focaccia 366

Crab with Louis Dressing 631

Mesclun salad

Peach-Blackberry Crumble 480

Rosemary, Lemon, and Pepper Focaccia 366

Pan-Smoked Salmon with Yogurt Sauce
with Toasted Spices, Lime Zest, and Basil
268, 630

Herb Salad 415

Warm Fresh Cherries with Kirsch 472

Watercress with Roasted Sesame Seed
Dressing 611

Miso-Sake–Glazed Fish fillets or steaks,
with Wasabi Mashed Potatoes 236, 79

Lemon Curd Tart 488

MENUS FOR DINNER PARTIES

Chicken or Duck Liver Pâté with Golden
  Raisins 345

Leg of Lamb Roasted on a Bed of Herbs
  with Red Wine Essence and Celery Root
  and Apple Puree 296, 639, 81

Herb Salad, with a selection of cheeses 415

Lemon Curd Tart 488

"Fried" Artichokes with Crispy Garlic
  and Sage 66

Boneless Leg of Lamb Stuffed with Crushed
  Olives and New Potatoes Roasted with
  Lemon and Saffron or Crispy Saffron
  Noodle Gratin 297, 49, 155

Mesclun salad

Quinces in White Wine and Honey with
  Real Whipped Crème Fraîche 525, 533

Fennel Salad with Parmigiano-Reggiano and
  Peppers Roasted with Garlic and
  Anchovies 419, 42

Herb-Scented Tuscan Pork Roast and
  Polenta "Gnocchi" Gratin or Mashed
  Potatoes Seasoned with Fragrant Oil
  293, 203, 78

Warm Sautéed Fresh Figs with Raspberry
  Coulis and Cream or Caramelized
  Roasted Pears with vanilla ice cream and
  artisan balsamic vinegar 474, 476, 640

Rosemary, Lemon, and Pepper Focaccia 366

Pan-Smoked Salmon with Yogurt Sauce
  with Toasted Spices, Lime Zest, and Basil
  268, 630

Herb Salad, with goat cheese 415

Roasted peaches and blackberry Warm
  Spilling Fruit, with Real Whipped Crème
  Fraîche and Individual Phyllo Disks
  475, 472, 533, 495

"Fried" Artichokes with Crispy Garlic
  and Sage 66

Baked Penne with Wild Mushroom Ragù
  and Ricotta Salata 150

Arugula salad with pears and roasted
  pine nuts 417

Hazelnut Cake 513

Mushrooms with Sake and Lemon 60

Miso-Sake–Glazed Fish fillets or steaks,
  with Wasabi Mashed Potatoes and
  Sautéed baby bok choy 236, 79, 74

Tropical fruits in Alain Senderens's Syrup 468

Ginger and "Yuzu" Wafers 517

AMERICAN DINER SUPPER

Classic Green Salad with Russian
  Dressing 416

Meat Loaf with Wild Mushrooms and
  Ancho Chile Ketchup 340

Buttermilk Mashed Potatoes 77

Chocolate Malted Pudding 504

SUNDAY SUPPER

Chopped Salad from the '21' Club 427

Foolproof Roast Chicken with Its Own Pan
  Sauce and Roasted Garlic Mashed
  Potatoes 291, 78

Apple Crumble 480

STEAK DINNER

Classic Green Salad with Blue Cheese
  Dressing 416

Szechwan Pepper–Crusted Steak
  Smothered with Onions and Mashed
  Potato Cake or Parsnip Fries 317, 54, 46

Rustic Rosemary-Apple Tart 486

AMERICAN SHORE SUPPER

The Best Tomato Salad 426

Classic Maryland Shore Crab Cakes and
  Classic Coleslaw 270, 423

Peach Blackberry Crumble or Inside
  a Blueberry Pie with vanilla ice cream
  480, 473

PROVENÇAL DINNER

Black Olive and Herb Focaccia or Rustic
Chickpea-Flour Pancakes 365, 113

Fennel-Roasted Fish with Citrus and
Olive Oil Sauce for Roasted or Grilled Fish
and crushed roasted fingerling potatoes
219, 34

Warm Sautéed Fresh Figs with Raspberry
Coulis and Cream 474

White Peaches with Crushed Raspberry
Sauce or white peaches and figs in
Rosemary and Lavender Syrup 466, 468

VINEYARD DINNER

Salad of peppery greens, figs, and roasted
hazelnuts 417

Chicken with Sherry Vinegar Sauce, with
Brown Butter Orzo "Risotto" 338, 126

Pears in Spiced Wine Syrup or Caramelized
Roasted Pears with Saffron-Scented
Custard Sauce 524, 476, 530

SOUTHWESTERN FRANCE DINNER

Duck Liver Pâté with Golden Raisins 345

Revisionist Confit of Duck Legs, crisped
in a pan with Roasted Root Vegetables
and Pears in Fragrant Wine 311, 34, 668

Frisée salad with roasted pecans and
Nut Oil Vinaigrette 417, 607

Prune Croustade 474

ITALIAN SUPPER

Peppers Roasted with Garlic and Anchovies
or fava beans with shaved Parmesan
42, 419

"Fried" Artichokes with Crispy Garlic
and Sage 66

Baked Penne with Wild Mushroom Ragù
and Ricotta Salata 150

Hazelnut Cake 512

GREEK SUPPER

Cooked beets with Greek Garlic Sauce
683, 623

Leg of Lamb Roasted on a Bed of Herbs,
with Greek-Style Potatoes with Lemon and
Thyme 296, 49

Quinces in White Wine and Honey or
Apricots Roasted with Cardamom,
Yogurt Cream, and Thin Phyllo Wafers
or Risotto Rice Pudding 525, 478, 535,
496, 522

MIDDLE EASTERN DINNER

Moroccan "Gazpacho" Salad with Carrots
in Chermoula 426, 434

Seared Lamb with Moroccan Spices and
Tomato Jam, with couscous 320, 197

Herb Salad 415

Apricots Roasted with Cardamom 478

ASIAN FLAVORS

Lacquered Baby Back Ribs 304

Cold Spicy Sesame Noodles 127

Southeast Asian Slaw 429

Frozen Lychees 465

CRISPY ROAST DUCK DINNER

The Ultimate Roast Duck, with
Pears in Fragrant Red Wine Syrup,
braise-sautéed root vegetables, and
Cabbage Braised with Smoky Ham
and Riesling 300, 523, 64, 70

Frisée salad with roasted walnuts and
Nut Oil Vinaigrette 417, 607

Honeydew melon and blackberries in
Rose Water Syrup 467

COCKTAIL PARTY
(HORS D'OEUVRES BUFFET)

Pissaladière (Provençal Onion Tart) 367

Warm Olivada (Warm Crushed Olives) 655

Parmesan Crisps 370

Savory Rosemary Biscotti 371

Potato Chips 47

Rosemary, Lemon, and Pepper Foccacia 366

Peperonata 63

Peppers Roasted with Garlic and
  Anchovies 42

Chicken Liver Pâté with Golden
  Raisins 345

Country Terrine with Pistachios 342

Home-Cured Salmon 276

Bruschetta 369

DESSERT BUFFET

Mocha Pecan Cake 513

Chocolate Mousse Cake 500

Filled Lemon Cake 507

Anne's Spicy Ginger Cookies,
  served warm off the cookie sheet
  with Real Whipped Cream 518, 533

Risotto Rice Pudding 522

Chocolate Chestnut Truffles 498

Earl Grey Tea Wafers 516

Lemon Curd Tart 488

Apricot Tart 484

Fresh berries in Berry Elixir 469

GREAT BREAKFASTS

Yogurt Cream with fresh fruits 535

Blueberry Cornmeal Cakes with Warm
  Spilling Fruit or Chive French Toast with
  Home-Cured Salmon and sour cream
  380, 472, 381, 276

Polenta or basic cooked kernel grains
  porridge with milk and maple syrup 198, 174

Coriander-and-Orange-Scented Scones 375

Homemade Sausages and Rosemary
  Buttermilk Biscuits 347, 374

Oat Bran Muffins with Dried Pears 376

Home-Cured Salmon with Yogurt Cream on
  bagels 276, 535

AFTERNOON TEA

Coriander-and-Orange-Scented Scones 375

Yogurt Cream 535

Earl Grey Tea Wafers 516

Anne's Spicy Ginger Cookies 518

Pistachio and Almond Cake 514

Country Terrine with Pistachios, thinly sliced
  on baguette toasts 342

Rosemary Buttermilk Biscuits, filled with
  sliced country ham or chicken 374

Home-Cured Salmon, on thin slices of lightly
  buttered black bread 276

GREAT FOOD GIFTS

Savory Rosemary Biscotti with a split
  of Champagne and fine flutes 371

Parmesan Crisps 370

Prunes in Armagnac 473

Gingerbread 508

Earl Grey Tea Wafers 516

Anne's Spicy Ginger Cookies 518

Pear Chips 519

Cranberry-Walnut Conserve 670

SOURCES.

INGREDIENTS.

EXOTIC RICES, GRAINS,
BEANS, SPICES, NUTS, AND
DRIED FRUITS FROM THE
MEDITERRANEAN, MIDDLE
EAST, AND INDIA

Kalustyan
212-685-3451
www.kalustyan.com

GOURMET, ETHNIC, AND
EXOTIC INGREDIENTS

ChefShop
877-337-2491
www.chefsshop.com

Dean & DeLuca
877-826-9243
www.deananddeluca.com

www.ethnicgrocer.com

www.tavolo.com

SELECTED TREASURES:
OLIVE OILS, VINEGARS, DRIED
PASTAS, HONEYS, AND TEAS

Williams-Sonoma
800-541-1262
www.williams-sonoma.com

Zingerman's
888-636-8162
www.zingermans.com

BEANS (DRIED)

Indian Harvest
800-346-7032
www.indianharvest.com

CHEESES

www.fromages.com
French cheeses, many raw
milk, imported directly

Murray's Cheese
888-692-4339 or
212-243-3289
www.murrayscheese.com

**Vermont Butter and
Cheese Company**
800-884-6287
www.vtbutterandcheeseco.com
Fresh cheeses, such as
crème fraîche and quark

CHESTNUT PUREE

Dean & DeLuca
877-826-9243
www.deananddeluca.com

www.ethnicgrocer.com

CHESTNUTS (PEELED, WHOLE)

ChefShop
877-337-2491
www.chefshop.com

DEMI-GLACE

Dean & DeLuca
877-826-9243
www.deananddeluca.com

More Than Gourmet
800-860-9392
www.morethangourmet.com

GARLIC (FRESH)

Filaree Farm
509-422-6940
sells about 100 varieties

GRAINS, GRAIN PRODUCTS,
AND SPECIALTY FLOURS

**Bob's Red Mill Natural
Foods**
800-349-2173
www.bobsredmill.com

**Gold Mine Natural Food
Company**
800-475-3663

ITALIAN FOOD PRODUCTS
(PROSCIUTTO, CHEESES,
OLIVE OILS, ETC.)

Esperya
877-907-2525
www.esperya.com/usa

Todaro Brothers
877-472-2767
www.todarobros-specialty-
foods.com

JAPANESE PRODUCTS

Katagiri
212-755-3566
www.katagiri.com

MISO

Great Eastern Sun
www.great-eastern-sun.com

Katagiri
212-755-3566
www.katagiri.com

South River Miso Company
www.southrivermiso.com

RICES FOR RISOTTO

ChefShop
877-337-2491
www.chefshop.com

ROASTED NUT OILS

**Rosenthal Wine Merchants,
Ltd.**
212-249-6650
www.madrose.com/home2.
html

SPICES AND HERBS, VANILLA
BEANS, CHILES AND DRY RUBS

Adriana's Caravan
800-316-0820
www.adrianascaravan.com

Penzey's Spice House
800-741-7787
www.penzeys.com

TEAS

In Pursuit of Tea
866-878-3832
www.inpursuitoftea.com

Upton Tea Imports
800-234-8327
www.uptontea.com

TRUFFLES (FROZEN
AND FRESH—IN SEASON)

Urbani Truffles
800-281-2330
www.urbani.com

WILDFLOWER HONEY

Plan Bee Honey Company
518-854-9239
212-627-0046
www.planbeehoney.com

WILD MUSHROOMS
(FRESH AND DRIED)

Marché aux Delices
888-547-5471
www.auxdelices.com

WILD RICE (NATIVE,
HAND-HARVESTED)

**Leech Lake Brand
of Ojibwe Wild Rice**
877-246-0620

BONELESS PEKIN
DUCK BREASTS

Culver Duck Farms
800-825-9225

FREE-RANGE LAMB

Jamison Farm
800-237-5262
www.jamisonfarm.com

GAME, FREE-RANGE
CHICKENS, DUCK BREASTS,
FOIE GRAS, AND GOOSE FAT

D'Artagnan
800-327-8246
www.dartagnan.com

NATURALLY RAISED BEEF,
PORK, AND LAMB

Niman Ranch
510-808-0340
www.nimanranch.com

NATURALLY RAISED BUFFALO

Eichten's Hidden Acres
800-657-6752 or
651-257-6286
eichtencheeseandbison@msn
.com

New West Foods
800-289-2833

ORGANIC MEATS AND POULTRY

Organic Valley
888-444-6455
www.organicvalley.com

For an extensive listing of
mail-order Web sites, visit:

**dmoz.org/Shopping/Food/
Meat/Natural_and_Organic**

PANCETTA, PROSCIUTTO,
AND OTHER CURED MEATS

Todaro Brothers
877-472-2767
www.todarobros-specialty-
foods.com

SEAFOOD: LUMP CRAB,
LIVE SCALLOPS, LOBSTERS,
AND SALMON

Farm2Market
800-663-4326
www.farm-2-market.com

EQUIPMENT
AND SERVICES.

BENRINER VEGETABLE SLICERS

Katagiri
212-755-3566
www.katagiri.com

COOKBOOKS
(NEW AND OUT OF PRINT)

Around the Kitchen
203-438-2338
www.aroundthekitchen.com

Jessica's Biscuit
800-878-4264
www.jessicasbiscuit.com

Kitchen Arts and Letters
212-876-5550

COPPER POT RETINNING

**Retinning & Copper
Repair, Inc.**
212-244-4896
www.retinning.com

KITCHEN EQUIPMENT

Bridge Kitchenware
212-688-4220
www.bridgekitchenware.com

Broadway Panhandler
866-266-5273
www.broadwaypanhandler.com

Chef's Catalog
800-338-3232
www.chefscatalog.com

Sur La Table
800-243-0852
www.surlatable.com

Tavolo
www.tavolo.com

SILPAT NONSTICK BAKING
MATS AND OTHER BAKING
EQUIPMENT AND INGREDIENTS

The Baker's Catalogue
800-827-6836
www.bakerscatalogue.com

WOOD CHIPS FOR SMOKING

Broadway Panhandler
212-966-3434
www.broadwaypanhandler.com

BOOKS AND WEB SITES.

GENERAL REFERENCE BOOKS.

Child, Julia. **The Way to Cook.** NEW YORK: KNOPF, 1989.

Davidson, Alan. **The Oxford Companion to Food.** OXFORD: OXFORD UNIVERSITY PRESS, 1999.

Herbst, Sharon Tyler. **The New Food Lover's Companion.** HAUPPAUGE, NY: BARRON'S EDUCATIONAL SERIES, 1995.

McGee, Harold. **On Food and Cooking.** NEW YORK: CHARLES SCRIBNER'S SONS, 1984.

Peterson, James. **The Essentials of Cooking.** NEW YORK: ARTISAN, 1999.

Toussaint-Samat, Meguelonne. **History of Food.** CAMBRIDGE, MA: BLACKWELL REFERENCE, 1992.

SEMINAL SINGLE-SUBJECT BOOKS.

Bayless, Rick, with Deann Groen Bayless. **Authentic Mexican.** NEW YORK: WILLIAM MORROW, 1987.

Beranbaum, Rose Levy. **The Cake Bible.** NEW YORK: WILLIAM MORROW, 1988.

del Conte, Anna. **The Gastonomy of Italy.** NEW YORK: PRENTICE HALL, 1987.

Field, Carol. **The Italian Baker.** NEW YORK: HARPER & ROW, 1985.

Hazan, Marcella. **The Classic Italian Cookbook.** NEW YORK: KNOPF, 1990.

Jenkins, Steve. **Cheese Primer.** NEW YORK: WORKMAN, 1996.

Kasper, Lynn Rosetto. **The Italian Country Table.** NEW YORK: SCRIBNER'S, 1999.

——. **The Splendid Table.** NEW YORK: WILLIAM MORROW, 1992.

Kremezi, Aglia. **The Foods of the Greek Islands.** BOSTON: HOUGHTON MIFFLIN, 2000.

Olney, Richard. **Lulu's Provençal Table.** NEW YORK: HARPERCOLLINS, 1994.

Peterson, James. **Fish and Shellfish.** NEW YORK: WILLIAM MORROW, 1996.

——. **Sauces.** NEW YORK: VAN NOSTRAND REINHOLD, 1991.

Robinson, Jancis, ed. **The Oxford Companion to Wine.** OXFORD: OXFORD UNIVERSITY PRESS, 1994.

Sahni, Julie. **Classic Indian Cooking.** NEW YORK: WILLIAM MORROW, 1980.

Traunfeld, Jerry. **The Herb Farm Cookbook.** NEW YORK: SCRIBNER'S, 2000.

Tropp, Barbara. **The Modern Art of Chinese Cooking.** NEW YORK: WILLIAM MORROW, 1982.

Tsuji, Shizua. **Japanese Cooking.** TOKYO: KODANSHA INTERNATIONAL, 1980.

Von Welanetz, Diana, and Paul Von Welanetz. **The Von Welanetz Guide to Ethnic Ingredients.** LOS ANGELES: WARNER BOOKS, 1982.

Waters, Alice. **Chez Panisse Vegetables.** NEW YORK: HARPERCOLLINS, 1996.

Wolfert, Paula. **The Cooking of South-West France.** GARDEN CITY, NY: DIAL/DOUBLEDAY, 1983.

——. **The Cooking of the Eastern Mediterranean.** NEW YORK: HARPERCOLLINS, 1994.

Young, Grace. **The Wisdom of the Chinese Kitchen.** NEW YORK: SIMON AND SCHUSTER, 1999.

NUTRITION AND WELL-BEING.

Kiple, Kenneth F., and Kriemhild Conee Ornelas, eds. **The Cambridge World History of Food.** 2 VOLS. CAMBRIDGE: CAMBRIDGE UNIVERSITY PRESS, 2000.

Steingarten, Jeffrey. **The Man Who Ate Everything.** NEW YORK: KNOPF, 1997.

INSPIRATION.

Ackerman, Diane. **A Natural History of the Senses.** NEW YORK: VINTAGE, 1991.

Bras, Michel, Alain Boudier, and Christian Millau. **Le Livre de Michel Bras.** RODEZ, FR: ÉDITIONS DU ROUERGUE, 1991.

David, Elizabeth. **A Book of Mediterranean Food.** LONDON: LEHMAN, 1950.

———. **French Country Cooking.** LONDON: LEHMAN, 1951.

———. **Summer Cooking.** LONDON: MUSEUM PRESS, 1961.

Fisher, M.F.K. **The Art of Eating.** INDIANAPOLIS: HUNGRY MINDS, INC., 1990.

Gray, Patience. **Honey from a Weed.** NEW YORK: HARPER & ROW, 1987.

Keller, Thomas. **The French Laundry Cookbook.** NEW YORK: ARTISAN, 1999.

Liebling, A. J. **Between Meals.** SAN FRANCISCO: NORTH POINT, 1986.

Olney, Richard. **Simple French Food.** INDIANAPOLIS: HUNGRY MINDS, INC., 1992.

WEB SITES.

www.google.com This search engine is easy to use and very effective.

www.recipelinks.netfirms.com This is a well-categorized collection of useful food links.

www.theatlantic.com/food/food.htm *Atlantic* senior editor Corby Kummer's insightful columns and articles can be found here.

www.splendidtable.org This is the companion Web site to *The Splendid Table*, the informative, entertaining radio show hosted by Lynne Rosetto Kasper, author of *The Splendid Table*.

www.outlawcook.com John and Matt Thorne's electronic companion to their renowned newsletter, *Simple Cooking*, is wonderfully written, opinionated, and no-nonsense.

www.cooksillustrated.com This companion Web site to *Cook's Illustrated* magazine is a great resource of techniques, recipes, and product ratings.

www.blonz.com The Blonz Guide is one of the best resources I've found in the fields of nutrition, foods, food science, health, and wellness.

www.nal.usda.gov/fnic/cgi-bin/nut_search.pl You can use the U.S. Department of Agriculture's nutrient database to calculate the nutritional values of specific foods.

www.nlm.nih.gov/medlineplus The National Library of Medicine's easy-to-use Web page of consumer health information has references to more than 11 million articles from 4,300 biomedical journals.

www.cspinet.org The Center for Science in the Public Interest, an independent organization dedicated to educating the public and policy makers about the importance of nutrition and food safety, offers information about nutrition and diet issues.

www.oldwayspt.org Oldways Preservation and Exchange Trust is a food issues think tank that promotes healthy eating, sustainable food choices, and traditional foodways.

www.slowfood.com Slow Food is an international movement to counter the fast-food trend and promulgate pleasure in and protection of traditional foods and heritage.

www.eco-labels.org Consumers Union evaluations of "eco" claims.

www.foodsubs.com The Cook's Thesaurus is a cooking encyclopedia that covers thousands of ingredients and kitchen tools.

ACKNOWLEDGMENTS.

When I look at *A New Way to Cook* sitting on my table, I think of the extraordinary people who helped me over the ten years it took to bring it to fruition—ten years of wild and unpredictable life. It is built out of their love, talent, and generosity.

Three people worked intensely on *A New Way to Cook* for several years and are truly at its very heart. Maria Robledo, whose photographs grace this book, taught me more about art, vision, and friendship than just about anybody. Suzanne Shaker, an inspired stylist and artist with a superb and unerring eye, helped *A New Way to Cook* come alive in Maria's photographs and brought so much joy to the process. Sally Jo O'Brien assisted me in more ways than I can count, and always went way beyond the call of duty.

My editor at Artisan, Ann Bramson, has been called "visionary" with very good reason. She has been a lesson to me in working organically and pushing limits. Thank you, Peter Workman and Bruce Harris, with your incisive publishing savvy, for seeing *A New Way to Cook*'s potential and making it happen. Burgin Streetman, Nancy Murray, Rachel Godfrey, and the superb staff at Artisan produced a big, complex book in way too short a time, with exceptional grace and generosity. Special thanks to Deborah Weiss Geline, who accomplished the very difficult job of coordinating the vast amount of input from various editors, author, and designer, with extraordinary equanimity and precision. Her insight and good sense were invaluable.

A New Way to Cook's thirteen pounds of information and ideas would have been daunting had it not been for the help of several astute and tenacious souls. Judith Sutton honed the book by her careful reading and thoughtful questions. Beth Crossman helped hammer out the many thorny organizational issues the book presented.

Stephen Doyle of Doyle Partners created an inspired and highly innovative design that perfectly expressed the book's essence in a way I never imagined. Vivian Ghazarian patiently fit the pieces together and solved the endless design problems to make it an elegant accessible whole that is a pleasure to use.

In addition, Toni Smith painstakingly analyzed the nutrition of the recipes. Sandy Gluck was a great help in the early recipe development. Paula Frazier came to my rescue several times, and especially at the very end, Josh Titus, Genie Arnot, and Sabine Tucker were the "support system" for the photo shoots.

Legendary editor Maria Guarnaschelli first encouraged me to write *A New Way to Cook* ten years ago and gave an insightful early critique of the manuscript. Elise and Arnold Goodman helped start it on its long road to being published. Special thanks to my lawyer, Alan Kaufman, who steered the book through some very rough waters. And to Fern Berman and Robin Insley of Fern Berman Communications for introducing it to the world in such a lovely way.

Deep appreciation to Dana Cowin, editor in chief of *Food & Wine*, who invited me to write a column based on my book in progress, and to Tina Ujlaki, Stephen Scoble, and the *Food & Wine* staff for helping to hone it into a beautiful monthly column.

Special thanks to Oldways Preservation and Exchange Trust, especially to K. Dun Gifford and Sara Baer-Sinnott, whose illuminating symposia in the Mediterranean provided me with information, inspiration, and valuable resources. And to La Fondacion de L'Art de la Napoule for viewing food as an artform and providing me with time and a clear space in which to work.

I will always feel incredibly lucky for having answered an ad in *The New York Times* and finding Lee Haiken, the editor of *Weight Watchers Magazine*. She helped me make the leap, many years ago, from cheffing to writing about food and well-being.

My greatest blessing has been my friends, who fed me when I was tired, talked me off ledges, cut me slack, bolstered me, and reminded me of what I really knew when I forgot it; their love was my fuel. My sincere thanks to Betty Alfenito, Francis Boswell, Beatrice da Costa and Edouard Prulhiere, Anne Disrude, Christopher Eldredge, Tom Fallon, Gyo Fujikawa, Isabel Galián and José Ramo, Dana Gallagher, Pi Gardiner, Gail Gilbert, Stanley Harper and Michael Eurey, Irene Hartford and Mary Hicks, Becky and Stephen Lewis, Miranda Magagnini and Matthew Pilkington, Peggy Markel, Megan Moore, Lisa Morphew, Holton Rower, Mary and Howard Rower, Sandy Rower, Elena Prentice Rulon-Miller, Lisa Ryan, Felicia Sachs, Albert Sanders, Susy Schneider, and Margot Wellington.

And to my open-hearted friends in the food, publishing, and art worlds who shared their insights and passion: Christopher Hirschheimer, Coleman Andrews, and Dorothy Kalins; Mario Batali, Ed Blonz, Sondra Davidson, Barry Estabrook, Stephen Frailey, Mindy Heiferling, Ann Herold, Pam Hunter and Carl Doumani, Nancy Harmon Jenkins, Lynne Rosetto Kasper, Corby Kummer, Deborah Madison, Rux Martin, James Peterson, Cara de Silva, and Alan Tardi and Karen Bussen. Miriam Cooper, Naja Cory, Martha Gallahue, Marcia Kilgore, William Levin, Isis Medina, Jack Porter, and Wendy Schantzer lent their specialized and much appreciated expertise to make this work, and my life, go smoothly. Carmen Garcia was always there to impose order when things got wild. David Saltman helped make the ending an illuminating beginning.

Very special thanks to Tom Booth, Speed and Martha Carroll, Mary Ehni, Joshua Eisen and Ellen Silverman, Vicki Beth Lynn, Eleanor Mailloux, Rogers McAvoy, and Patrick Rulon-Miller, who showed their faith and support in ways I will never forget. And to my mother, Nelly Schneider, who really came through.

There are many more people to thank—a lifetime's worth—who shared their tables and recipes with me as I traveled around America, Latin America, and Europe. Each has taught me, in very different ways, what it means to be really fed.

INDEX.

honey:
and balsamic pan sauce, thyme-infused, duck breasts with, 329–30
-cured pork loin with peppery juniper and fennel seed rub, 294–95
-mustard vinaigrette, 608
quinces in white wine and, 515

hors d'oeuvres and side breads, 363–72
bruschetta, 369
Parmesan crisps, 370–71
pissaladière (Provençal Onion Tart), 367
rustic garlic toasts, 368
savory rosemary biscotti, 371–72
see also focaccia

horseradish mashed potatoes, 79

hummus (chickpea puree), 101

ice cream(s):
banana and coconut milk, 527
faux, and quick sorbets, 525–26
infused broths, 578–80
infused oils, 588–89
ingredients:
additive-free, 7
high-quality, 3, 7
locally grown, 7
organic, 6
sources for, 7, 711
strategic, 6–15
weighing and measuring, 4
inside a blueberry pie, 473
Irish brown bread, 377–78

jam, tomato, 321
Jamaican jerk paste, 563
Japanese noodle soup, soothing, 398–99
Japonica rice, 172
jasmine white rice, 171
"Jell-O," real, 521–22
Jerusalem artichokes with smoky bacon, 60
Job's tears, 170
juicer, electric vegetable, 27
julienned raw vegetable salads, 421
juniper:
and fennel seed rub, honey-cured pork loin with, 294–95
rabbit roasted with fennel and, 300

rub, wild, 550–51
salmon cured with aquavit and, 277
steam-roasted fennel with pancetta and, 58–59

kamut, 170
kasha, 173
kernel grains, 168–94
basic cooked, 174–77
cooking of, 169–73
leftover, 175
see also rice; risotto
kernel grains, dressing with:
brown butter, nut-flavored oils, or bacon fat, 177
with cheese, 176–77
with nuts, seeds, and dried fruit, 176
kirsch:
apricots roasted with, 479
syrup, 467
warm fresh cherries with, 472–73
knife sharpeners, 23
knives, 23
kosher salt, 10

lamb:
burgers, 348
seared, with Moroccan spices and tomato jam, 320–21
six simple ways to season, 322
lamb, leg of:
boneless, stuffed with crushed olives, 297–98
roasted on a bed of herbs, 296–97
lasagna noodles with pesto and summer vegetables, 129
lavender and rosemary syrup, 468
leafy greens, sautéed, 73
leafy salads. See salads, leafy
leek(s), 14
pasta with pepper, aged goat cheese and, 140–41
and potato soup, with sorrel or watercress, 386
and saffron cream, 634–35
vinaigrette, steam-roasted, 58
wild rice with wild mushrooms and, 182
leek broth, 569–70
quick, for beurre blanc–style butter sauces, 642

legumes:
basic cooking time for, 93
dry, 89–103
see also specific legumes
lemon(s), 14
and clove wafers, 517
-garlic dressing, 419
Greek-style potatoes with thyme and, 49
mushrooms with sake and, 60–61
olive oil, 590
and olive oil marinade with herbs, classic Greek, 554–55
potatoes roasted with saffron and, 49
rosemary, and pepper focaccia, 366
vinaigrette with a little garlic, 607
lemon cake:
filled, 507
fresh, 506–7
lemon curd (sauce):
Meyer, 533
tart, ethereal, 532
lemon curd tart, 488–89
with berries or mangoes, 489
lemongrass:
essence, 546
mussels or clams with ginger, chiles, and, 257
quinoa salad, with cilantro, mint and, 446–47
rub, 546
lemongrass dressing, 274, 429–30
Thai seafood salad with, 274–75
lemon zest:
slivered, celery root, fennel, and apple salad with hazelnuts and, 422
warm potato salad with olives, thyme and, 438–39
lentil(s), 12, 89
basic cooked, 92–93
basics of, 88–91
bed of, 244
combining with grains, 91
lentilles du Puy, 12
soaking and salting of, 90–91
soup with ginger, 405
warm, crispy salmon with balsamic essence and, 244–45
see also beans, peas and lentils, embellished cooked

SALLY SCHNEIDER is an award-winning food writer and stylist whose work has appeared in *Vogue*, *Elle*, *Saveur*, *Self*, *Working Woman*, and *Health* magazines, as well as the *Los Angeles Times* and *The New York Times*. A professional chef for six years, she was a contributing editor to *Food & Wine* and the author of the monthly "Well-Being" column. She is currently a regular contributor to NPR's *A Splendid Table* and lives in New York City.